# CALENDAR OF SUSSEX COUNTY DELAWARE PROBATE RECORDS 1680-1800

Compiled by
Leon deValinger, Jr.
State Archivist

A Facsimile Reprint

Published 1993 by
HERITAGE BOOKS, INC.
1540-E Pointer Ridge Place,
Bowie, Maryland 20716
(301) 390-7709

ISBN 1-55613-819-9

A Complete Catalog Listing Hundreds of Titles
on Genealogy, History, and Americana
Available Free on Request

Copy 2
Cataloged

# PREFACE

This volume is a companion to the *Calendar Of Kent County Probate Records, 1680-1800*, published by this Commission in 1944. Long ago our Commissioners realized that the information contained in the probate records and on the file cards in the Hall of Records would be of much greater value if it could be published and made available in book form. This *Calendar* is the culmination of years of careful and exacting work of classifying, collating and calendarizing the probate records of Sussex County.

The probate records of Delaware provide the richest source of information for those seeking genealogical data or material for social or economic history in the early years. This volume begins with 1680, rather than an earlier date of the Swedish (1638-1655), Dutch (1655-1664), or Duke of York (1664-1682) regimes because of the legal procedures of the countries making those settlements. In those periods of colonization here, wills could be made orally or in writing before a notary public or a similar public judicial officer. As public recording of the wills was not required, the notaries retained among their own papers the few wills that were made, with the result that these records have since become scattered or lost. With the acquisition of the Delaware territory by the Duke of York the system did not change noticeably because the laws governing this territory were not published until 1676. Even then the justices of the Whorekill Court were slow or remiss in following the new procedures, as few records prior to 1680 have survived. With the establishment of St. Jones County (Kent) in 1680 and the change of name from Whorekill to Deale on December 25th of the same year, the Lower Counties began recording in an orderly manner. The County was renamed Sussex in 1683 by William Penn.

It should be borne in mind that the volume is a calendar and does not attempt to give a complete abstract of the wills and administration accounts. The calendar was selected as the form for publishing this material as it serves as a guide to the records available and supplies most of the information generally requested. It is recognized that a complete abstract would have enhanced the value of this work but it would also have curtailed considerably the period of years that could have been included within the scope of this volume.

All of the original probate records in the Hall of Records have been compared with the recorded copies in the Sussex County Court House in an effort to obtain as complete and accurate a record as possible. When both the original record and the recorded copy are extant the Register of Wills liber and folio are cited as well as the Archives volume and page on which the original document is mounted.

Researchers should note that the recorded wills in the Sussex County Court House at Georgetown, begin with liber A-1 in 1682; whereas the Account Books on estates begin with A-1 in 1863 and the Letters of Administration, volume 1, begin in 1906. There are, however, individual papers for some intestate estates which have been preserved in the State Archives at Dover. In addition to the original probate records in the Hall of Records at Dover and the recorded copies in the Sussex County Court House, we transcribed and calendarized the probate records which are recorded in Sussex County Records, volume AM. 2013 in the Historical Society of Pennsylvania, 1300 Locust Street, Philadelphia, and in the manuscript volume of Sussex County Court Records, 1680-1699 in the Delaware State Archives at Dover.

The probate records are arranged in chronological order by the probate date of the wills and by the date of granting letters of administration in the case of intestate estates. By this means a fairly accurate estimate may be obtained of the death date of each decedent. In the absence of the date of probate or granting letters of administration, the date when the will was made or the settlement date of the administration account is used.

Only in proper names has the orthography been preserved. When more than one spelling of a name occurs, as it frequently does, or when an interpretation has been supplied the alternate spelling and the added information appears in brackets.

It should be remembered that the Gregorian Calendar was not adopted in Delaware and the other English colonies in America until 1752. Under the old Augustine Calendar the year began on March 25th and December was the tenth, rather than the twelfth month. Thus a date appearing in the text as 1682/83 will indicate that the year 1682 is nearly terminated and that 1683 is approaching. Furthermore, the difference between the Augustine and Gregorian Calendars will explain why some probate records would appear to be probated before they were made. Dates recorded in the Quaker method of dating have been transposed to conform with either the Augustine or the Gregorian Calendars. For example, 12th of 10th month 1682 has been changed to December 12, 1682, according to the Augustine or Old Style Calendar.

Even more confusing to research workers than the calendar changes are the relationships contained in some of these early probate records. Frequently, step-father or step-mother is intended when the record states father-in-law or mother-in-law. In other instances the step-parents will be designated as father or mother. There are also instances when the word cousin is used instead of nephew and niece. The compiler has not attempted to interpret such inconsistencies, but has presented them as they appear in the document.

The word "copy" in parentheses following the word "Will" indicates that the document in the files at the Hall of Records is not the original record. The original document being missing the hiatus has been filled with a contemporary manuscript, typed or photostat copy. Unless thus indicated the probate record in the custody of the Public Archives Commission is the original document.

. There are some wills in which the foreign or out-of-state residence of the testator causes the reader to wonder why such a probate record was included with those of Sussex County. These foreign wills were recorded in this county to show what disposition was made of the non-resident's property within the county, or because he may have made a death-bed will while visiting here, or because of the indefinite delineation of the boundaries. A number of the wills show that the testator was from Worcester, Somerset or Caroline County in Maryland. This is explained by the long boundary dispute which continued in the English courts for nearly a century between the Proprietors of Pennsylvania and Maryland. The dispute was finally settled and ratified by them in 1775, but meanwhile citizens living in the border counties were uncertain of the boundaries and did not know where to record their documents. This was especially true of the southern and southwestern parts of Sussex County, which had previously been considered as belonging to Maryland.

In the compilation of this text with its multiplicity of details every effort has been made to achieve accuracy. To this end much time has been spent in checking and rechecking. Despite these precautions there are undoubtedly some discrepancies that have been overlooked. We can only ask our readers to be understanding if such errors do occur.

Finally it should be acknowledged that this volume could not have been produced if it had not been for the wholehearted support of the Public Archives Commissioners, the Delaware Legislature which appropriated the funds for printing and the careful work of Mrs. Herbert E. Abbott, Mrs. John M. Bounds and Miss Virginia E. Shaw in the preparation of the text and index.

Dover, Delaware
1964

Leon deValinger, Jr.
State Archivist

# ABBREVIATIONS

| | |
|---|---|
| acct. | account |
| Admin. | Administration |
| Adm'r | Administrator |
| Adm'rx | Administratrix |
| Arch. | Archives |
| bro. | brother |
| c. | circa |
| C. T. A. | Con Testamento Annexo (with the will attached) |
| dau. | daughter |
| D. B. N. | De Bonis Non (of the goods or property not yet administered upon) |
| dec'd | deceased |
| Exec'r | Executor |
| Exec'rx | Executrix |
| Hd. | Hundred |
| Hist. Soc. Penna. | Historical Society of Pennsylvania |
| Jr. | Junior |
| Md. | Maryland |
| n. d. | no date |
| nunc. | nuncupative |
| Phila. | Philadelphia |
| prob. | probate |
| Reg. of Wills | Register of Wills |
| sic. | indicates a literal quotation |
| Sr. | Senior |
| vol. | volume |
| Wits. | Witnesses |

## CALENDAR OF SUSSEX COUNTY, DELAWARE, PROBATE RECORDS 1680-1800

**Booth, Edward.** Will (copy). Made Dec. 7, 1682. Deal County. Heirs: John (son of John) and Martha Kiphaven; John and Jacob (son of John) Depree; John and Elizabeth Whitman; William Emmatt, Jr.; Mathiaas Everson; Norton Claypoole; and Mr. Avery. [No exec'r]. Wits., Jeffrey Summerford, Steven Witman, William Emmatt. Trustee, Andrew Depree. [No prob.]. Arch. vol. A60, page 17. Reg. of Wills, Liber A, folios 1-2.

**Leudritt, Elizabeth.** Will (nunc.). Heirs: son, Richard Bracey; Richard Bundock. Admr. C. T. A. Richard Bundock. Wits., Jeffrey Sumerford, Elizabeth Johnson, and wits. to codicil, Richard Gill. Prob. Aug. 14, 1683. Penna. Hist. Soc. Papers, vol. AM. 2013, pages 7-8

**Lotton, James.** Admin. of, to Robert Hart, Sr. Granted Sept. 12, [c. 1683]. Penna. Hist. Soc. Papers, vol. AM 2013, page 2.

**Stocker, Andrew.** Admin. of, to William Douvall, of Kent County. Granted Sept. 18, 1683. Penna. Hist. Soc. Papers, vol. AM, 2013, page 5.

**Shoulter, Richard.** Will (copy). Made Jan. 28, 1682. Heirs: Capt. Nathaniel Walker; Richard Bundock. Exec'rs, Capt. Nathaniel Walker, Richard Bundock. Wits., John Barker, William Emmatt. Prob. Sept. 30, 1683. Penna. Hist. Soc. Papers, vol. AM, 2013, pages 6-7.

**Verhoofe, Cornelius.** Will (copy). Made Dec. 23, 1683. Heirs: sister Eve Verhoofe (in Holland); bro-in-law Jan Lebenoint (in Holland); Barbara Parling, dau. of Elizabeth; Simon Parling; Richard Bundock and wife (alias Jones); Thomas Gollidge; servant Richard Pye; John Vines; John Betts. Admr. C. T. A. Peter Groundick and Halmainus Wiltbanck. Wits., Randle Shand, William Emmatt. Prob. Jan. 9, 1683/4. Penna. Hist. Soc. Papers, vol. AM, 2013, pages 11-13.

**Richards, Robert.** Admin. of, to Elloner Richards, widow. Granted Jan. 11, 1684. Penna. Hist. Soc. Papers, vol. AM, 2013, page 26.

**Depree, John.** Will (copy). Made Jan. 5, 1684. Heirs: wife unnamed; sons John and Jacob Depree; other children unnamed. Exec'rs, sons Andrew Depree and John Crew. Wits., William Emmatt, William Footcher. Prob. Jan. 13, 1684. Penna. Hist. Soc. Papers, vol. AM 2013 2013, pages 27-28.

**Endrson, Matthias.** Admin. of, to John Cullison and wife Barbrey. Granted Jan. 21, 1684. Penna. Hist. Soc. Papers, vol. AM, 2013, page 31.

**Cornelison, Harmon.** Admin. of, to Thomas Hodgkings. Granted Jan. 24, 1684. Penna. Hist. Soc. Papers, vol. AM, 2013, page 34.

**Shaltham, Jacob.** Admin. of, to Thomas Hodgskings. Granted Jan. 24, 1684. Penna. Hist. Soc. Papers, vol. AM 2013, page 33.

**Southrin, Edward.** Admin. of, to Mary Southrin, widow. Granted Jan. 24, 1684. Penna. Hist. Soc. Papers, vol. AM. 2013, page 32.

**Marsh, Paul.** Admin. of, to George Truitt of Somerset Co., Md. Granted Feb. 23, 1684. Penna. Hist. Soc. Papers, vol. AM 2013, page 37.

**Trayle, Robert.** Lewes. Will (copy). Made May 31, 1684. Heirs: Alexander Moulliston; William Hambleton; Edward Southrin; Henrick Mouliston. Admr. C. T. A. Alexander Moulston. Wits., John Kiphaven, Mathias Vanderhagen, Albertus Jacobs. Prob. Jan. 21, 1684/5. Penna. Hist. Soc. Papers, vol. AM. 2013, pages 29-30.

**Fisher, John.** Will (copy). Made Feb. 6, 1685/6. Heirs: wife Margrett Fisher; sons (eldest) Thomas, John and James Fisher; daus. Rachell, Sarah and Allis (youngest) Fisher, and Annie Adkins (wife of Samuel) ; Thomas Scott. Exec'rs, wife Margrett Fisher, eldest son Thomas Fisher. Wits., W[illia]m Emmatt, Richard Coore, Ann Dougdull. Prob. April 30, 1685. Penna. Hist. Soc. Papers, vol. AM, 2013, pages 63-65.

**Hart, Robert.** Admin. of, to son Robert Hart, Jr. Granted June 10, 1685. Penna. Hist. Soc. Papers, vol. AM. 2013, page 157b.

**Walker, Nathaniel, Capt.** Admin. of, to Admr. C. T. A. Major William Dyer. Granted July 20, 1685. Penna. Hist. Soc. Papers, vol. AM. 2013, page 74. [Note:—Decedent described as "formerly of New England, late of Northampton County in the Province of Virginia."].

**Avery, John, Capt.** Admin. of, to Robert Clifton. Granted Oct. 6, 1685. Sussex County Court Record 1680-1699, pages 39, 299, 436, 468 and 469.

**Godsell, Robert.** "Late of the Kingdom of Ireland". Will (nunc.), Made Nov. 10, 1685. Heirs: wife Sarah Godsell; son Peter Godsell; Edward Barrey; James Welsh. Exec'rx, wife Sharah [Sarah] Godsell. Wits., Charles Spooner, Edward Barrey, John White, Apalina Taylor. Overseer: William Clark, of Lewes. Prob. Nov. 23, 1685. Penna. Hist. Soc. Papers, vol. AM, 2013, pages 54-55.

**Hart, Robert.** Cedar Creek. Will (copy). Made Oct. 7, 1685. Heirs: wife Margret Hart; son Robert Hart; dau. Margret Hart. Exec'rx, wife Margret Hart. Wits., Jonathan Fox, Ann Jenings, Symon Charles. Prob. Dec. 10, 1685. Penna. Hist. Soc. Papers, vol. AM. 2013, pages 56-58.

**Getto, Henry.** Will (copy). Made March 6, 1687. Heirs: wife Dorothy Getto; son Henry Smith; grandchild Peter Godssell (son of Sarah Smith). Exec'r, son Henry Smith. Wits., Edward Berry, Henry Bowman. Prob. May 4, 1687. Penna. Hist. Soc. Papers, vol. AM. 2013, pages 78-80.

**Pearce, John.** Admin. of, to Alexander Draper. Granted Oct. 31, 1687. Penna. Hist. Soc. Papers, vol. AM. 2013, page 82.

**Roads [Roades], John.** Will (copy). Made Sept. 17, 1687. Heirs: wife Comfort Roads; son John Roads; daus. Elizabeth and Patience Roads; mother unnamed; bro. Richard Tull; Grace White (sister of Wrixam White); Nehemiah Field; Sarah Stretcher (wife of Henry); John How. Adm'rx, C. T. A. Comfort Roads, widow. Wits., John Millington, Nehemiah Field. Prob. Dec. 6-8, 1687. Penna. Hist. Soc. Papers, vol. AM. 2013, pages 85-86. Arch. vol. A96, page 73. Reg. of Wills, Liber A, folios 10-12.

**Harte, Joane.** Will (copy). Made Jan. 20, 1686/7. Heirs: son John Richards; Sarah Richards (dau. of son John). Exec'r, son John Richards. Wits., Alexander Draper, William Emmatt. Prob. Nov. 1, 1687. Penna. Hist. Soc. Papers, vol. AM. 2013, page 83.

**Sykes, James.** Will (nunc.). Undated. Heirs: son unnamed; dau. unnamed. Admr., C. T. A. Nathaniel Sykes, "heir apparent". Wits. Alexander Draper, Th[omas] Price. Prob. Dec. 8, 1687. Penna. Hist. Soc. Papers, vol. AM. 2013, pages 87-88. [Note:—Will mentions two other children in England, both unnamed.].

**Badger, John.** Will (nunc.). Undated. Heirs: Antony Inloyce. [No exec'r]. Wits., Robert Tomlinson, James Hughs. Prob. March 6, 1687/8. Penna. Hist. Soc. Papers, vol. AM. 2013, page 88.

**Riggs, George.** Will (copy). Made Aug. 6, 1687. Heirs: wife Ann Riggs. Exec'rx, wife Ann Riggs, William Clark and Thomas Wynne. Wits., Barrents Gerris, Daniel Ithell, Thomas Besent. Prob. March 7, 26, 1688. Penna. Hist. Soc. Papers, vol. AM, 2013, pages 90-91.

**Spencer, William, Sr., Major.** Will (copy). Dated Nov. 29, 1687. Heirs: wife Frances Spencer; son William Spencer; dau. Margarett Spencer; other children unnamed; negro servant "Black Will". Exec'r, son William Spencer. Wits., Johnson VanKerk, Robert Twilley, William Emmatt. Prob. May 2, 1688. Penna. Host. Soc. Papers, vol. AM. 2013, pages 94, 107.

**Dyre, William, Major.** Will (copy). Made Feb. 20, 1687/88. Heirs: wife Mary Dyre; eldest son William Dyre, of Boston; youngest son Edmund Dyer, son James Dyre; dau. (eldest) Sarah Dyer, (youngest) Mary Dyer. Exec'rs, wife Mary Dyer, son William Dyre, John Hill and Samuel Gray (friends). Trustee for New England property, Sir Edmund Andross. Wits., Charles Sanders, Will Rodeney. Prob. June 5, 1688. Penna. Hist. Soc. Papers, vol. AM 2013, pagees 95-97. Arch. vol. A70, page 27. Reg. of Wills, Liber A, folios 85-88. [Note:—Arch. vol. A70, page 27 mentions dec'd father William].

**Claypoole, Norton.** Admin. of, to Rachel Claypoole, widow. Granted [c. Aug. 1688]. Sussex County Court 1680-1699, page 239.

**Young, Mary,** wife of George. Will (copy). Made [c. Sept. 1688]. Heirs: Mrs. Daniel Hilliard; John Hilliard (son of Daniel). Sussex County Court, 1680-1699, pages 263, 264, and 299.

**Mouleston, Thomas.** Admin. of, to John Richards, husband of decedent's widow. Granted Oct. 3, 1688. Penna. Hist. Soc. Papers, vol. AM. 2013, page 98.

**Footcher, William.** Admin. of, to Mary Footcher, widow. Granted Feb. 23, 1689. Penna. Hist. Soc. Papers, vol. AM. 2013, page 111.

**Hignet, James.** Admin. of. Sussex County Court 1680-1699, page 398. [Note:—Page 398 shows a petition for letters of administration to father Robert Hignet was refused at March Term 1689/90.].

**Simons, John.** Admin. of, to Jane Simons, widow. Granted Sept. 9, 1689. Penna. Hist. Soc. Papers, vol. AM. 2013, page 103.

**Millington, John.** Admin. of, to Morris Edwards. Granted Oct. 6, 1689. Penna. Hist. Soc. Papers, vol. AM. 2013, page 104.

13

**Vines, John.** Admin. of, to Admr. C. T. A. William Emmatt. Granted Dec. 4, 1689. Penna. Hist. Soc. Papers, vol. AM. 2013, page 109.

**Depray, Andrew.** Will (copy). Made Jan. 9, [...]. Heirs: wife Bridgett; sons Thomas and Andrew Depray; daus. Margaret and Elizabeth Depray. Exec'rx, wife Bridgett Depray. Wits., Luke Wattson, Roger Corbett, John Crew. Prob. Jan. 25, [1680/90]. Arch. vol. A68, page 219. Reg. of Wills, Liber A, folios 12-13.

**Vines, John.** Will (copy). Made Jan. . . ., 1684. Heirs: Honour Clark (wife of William Clark); William Clark, Jr., (son of William Clark); Edward Stretcher (son of Henry); Sarah Stretcher (wife of Henry); William Emmatt, Jr.; William Emmatt, Sr.; son of dau. Ann Crosly, unnamed. Exec'r, William Emmatt, Sr. Wits., Benjamin Kirll, George Dodd. Prob. 3rd day of 10th month, 1689. Arch. vol. A103, page 143. Reg. of Wills, Liber A, folios 9-10.

**Spencer, William, Jr.** Admin. of, to Thomas May and wife Mary, sister of the decedent. Granted May 1, 1690. Penna. Hist. Soc. Papers, vol. AM. 2013, page 113.

**Smith, Henry.** Admin. of, to Sarah Smith, widow. Granted Sept. 15, 1690. Penna. Hist. Soc. Papers, vol. AM. 2013, page 126.

**Davids, George.** Admin. of, to Samuel Preston. Granted Sept. 20, 1690. Penna. Hist. Soc. Papers, vol. AM. 2013, page 127.

**Bellamy, John.** Admin. of, to Luke Wattson, Sr., Thomas Price, Sr., Luke Wattson, Jr. Granted Dec. 10, 1690. Penna. Hist. Soc. Papers, vol. AM. 2013, page 131.

**Draper, Alexander.** Admin. of, to Rebecca Draper, Henry Mollston, [C. T. A.]. Granted March 23, 1690/91. Penna. Hist. Soc. Papers, vol. AM. 2013, page 133.

**Cornwell, Francis.** Admin. of, to Mary Cornwell, widow. Granted Nov. 12, 1691. Penna. Hist. Soc. Papers, vol. AM. 2013, page 135.

**Bonde [Bowde, Barode], Isaac.** Lewes. Admin. of, to Jane Scott, former wife. Granted Sept. 6, 1692. Penna. Hist. Soc. Papers, vol. AM. 2013, page 136.

**Haward [Howard], Knights.** Will (copy). Made Jan. 2, 1693. Heirs: Luke Wattson, Jr.; Elizabeth Wattson (sister of Luke, Jr.), Capt. Thomas Pemberton. Exec'r, Luke Wattson, Jr. Wits., Nathaniel Starr, John Pey, William Emmatt. Prob. Jan. 18, 1693. Penna. Hist. Soc. Papers, vol. AM. 2013, pages 151-152. Arch. vol. A78, page 142. Reg. of Wills, Liber A, folios 17-18.

**Morgan, Edward.** Will (copy). Made March 11, 1693. Heirs: child unnamed in Maryland; Mary Wattson; Thomas Price, Jr.; William Stapleton; . . . Wattson; [Mrs.] Bowman. Exec'r, Luke Wattson, Jr. Wits., Charles Haynes, Susannah Davids. Prob. Sept. . . ., 1963. Penna. Hist. Soc. Papers, vol. AM. 2013, pages 141-142.

**Sweatman, William.** Will (copy). Made Sept. 16, 1693. Heir: wife Jean Sweatman. Admrx. C. T. A. widow Jean Sweatman. Wits., Edward Gould, Henry Stretcher, James Peterkin. Prob. Oct. 23, 1693. Penna. Hist. Soc. Papers, vol. AM. 2013, pages 143-144. Arch. vol. A101, page 88. Reg. of Wills, Liber A, folios 13-14.

**Patte, Richard.** Will (copy). Made May 17, 1693. Heirs: wife unnamed; son John Patte; daus. Lidey [Patte], Ann [Patte], dau. unnamed. Admr. C. T. A. son John Patte. Wits., John Tuxbury, Ellenor Tuxbury (his wife). Prob. Nov. 11, 1693. Penna. Hist. Soc. Papers, vol. AM. 2013, page 145.

**Branscomb, Thomas.** Will (copy). Made June 30, 1693. Heirs: wife Mary Branscomb; dau. Sarah Branscomb; sons-in-law William, Richard and John Footcher. Admrx. C. T. A. Mary Branscomb, widow. Wits., Charles Johnson, Robert Walker, Thomas Besent. Prob. Dec. 9, 1693. Penna. Hist. Soc. Papers, vol. AM. 2013, pages 138, 139, 146 and 147. Arch. vol. A60, page 128. Reg. of Wills, Liber A, folios 14-15.

**Wiltbanck, Halmanius [Hermanis].** Admin. of, to Jane Wiltbanck, widow. Settled Dec. . . ., 1693. Penna. Hist. Soc. Papers, vol. AM. 2013, page 14. [Note:—Settlement 1693 shows widow Jane had married . . . Hoskins; and names sons Cornelius, Abraham and Isaac Wiltbank; unnamed dau. the wife of John Williams; mentions John Hill, guardian of son Isaac].

**Hodgkins, Jane.** Will (copy). Made Dec. 23, 1692. Heirs: sons Cornelius, Abraham and Isaac Wiltbanck; dau. Rebeckah Williams. Exec'r, friend, John Hill. Wits., John Pye, Nath[anie]l Starr, Nehemiah Field. [No prob.]. Penna. Hist. Soc. Papers, vol. AM. 2013, page 148. [Note:—Will mentions deceased's former husband, Hermanus Wiltbanck.]

**Newcomb, Baptis.** Will (copy). Made Sept. 13, Nov. 8, 1693. Heirs: wife unnamed; sons William, Baptis and Daniel

Newcomb; John Register. Exec'rs, wife Ann Newcomb, John Hill, William Piles. Wits., Barnes Gerritt, Mark Mitchell. Prob. Jan. 22, 1693/4. Penna. Hist. Soc. Papers, vol. AM. 2013, pages 153-154 and Sussex County Court 1680-1699, page 664.

**Paynter, Richard.** Admin. of, to Sarah Paynter, widow. Granted March 4, 1694. Penna. Hist. Soc. Papers, vol. AM. 2013, page 166.

**Roades, Elizabeth,** widow. Will (copy). Made Feb. 26, 1693 94. Heirs: daus. Martha Tull and Mary Morgan; grandsons John Tull, John Wells; granddaus. Rachel Fasit (wife of Charles), Elizabeth and Patience Roades; Sarah Branscomb (dau. of Thomas and Elizabeth, both dec'd). Admr. C. T. A. Robert Clifton, Joseph Allif. Wits., Tho[mas] Midghey, Sarah Clifton, Tho[mas] Besent. Prob. May 9, 1694. Penna. Hist. Soc. Papers, vol. AM. 2013, pages 155-156.

**Bracey, Robert, Sr.** Will (nunc.). Made June, 1694. Heirs: son Robert Bracey; daus. Mary and Elizabeth Bracey. [No exec'r]. Wits., Nehemiah Field. [No prob.]. Sussex County Court 1680-1699, pages 662, 695, 696. [Note:—Petition for probate at June Term, 1695 by son Robert, with counter claim for a prior will by widow unnamed].

**Godwin, Cesar.** Will (copy). Undated. [No heirs]. Exec'rx, widow unnamed. Wits., Albertus Jacobs, Johannis Kiphaven. Prob. June Term, 1694. Sussex County Court 1680-1699, pages 665, 676.

**Coudrey [Cowthry], William.** Admin. of, to bro.-in-law Joseph Booth, D. B. N. Granted July 11, 1694. Penna. Hist. Soc. Papers, vol. AM. 2013, pages 1 and 157; also Sussex County Court Record, 1680-1699, page 663. [Note:—Sussex County Court Record, page 663, records J. Booth's application dated June 6, 1694, for letters of administration, mentioning the decedent's son, Joshua Cowthry, and the previous administrator, Henry Bowman, dec'd].

**Bembrick, Edward.** Admin. of, to Jane Bembrick, widow. Granted July 17, 1694. Penna. Hist. Soc. Papers, vol. AM. 2013, page 158.

**Gray, Samuel.** Will (copy). Made Oct. 23, 1692. Heirs: wife Susannah Gray; sons Isaac, Jonathan (eldest), David, Thomas, Samuel and John Gray; daus. Elizabeth, Rebeckah and Sarah Gray. Exec'rx, wife Susannah Gray. Wits., Sam[uel] Preston, Mary Lloyd, Michael Chambers, John Chambers, Elias Herington. Overseers: friends, Samuel

Preston, Luke Watson, Jr. Prob. Dec. 5, 1694. Penna. Hist. Soc. Papers, vol. AM. 2013, pages 159-161. Arch. vol. A73, page 26. Reg. of Wills, Liber A, folios 15-17.

**Spooner, Charles.** Will (nunc.). Undated. Heir: wife Susan Spooner. Adm'rx C. T. A., Susan Spooner, widow. Wits., Barnes Garrett, Anthony Haverley. Prob. Dec. 5, 1694. Penna. Hist. Soc. Papers, vol. AM. 2013, page 168.

**Fretwell, Roger.** Barbadoes. Merchant. Admin. of, to John Edmondson of Talbot Co., Md., att'y for Dorothea Fretwell, widow of Ralph and mother of decedent. Granted Dec. 28, 1694. Penna. Hist. Soc. Papers, vol. AM 2013, pages 163-164. [Note:—Page 164 shows that decedent died before April, 1689].

**Moalston, Thomas.** Will (nunc.). Undated. Heirs: William Davies; William Richards (son of John); Sarah Clark; John Richards; Barnes Garrett; Anthony Haverly, Jr. Admr'x C. T. A. Mary Richards, widow of John, who was decedent's father-in-law. Wits., Briant Rowles, Thomas Coverdale. Prob. March 5, 1694/5. Penna. Hist. Soc. Papers, vol. AM. 2013, pages 172-173.

**Richards, John.** Admin. of, to Mary Richards. Granted March 9, 1694/5. Penna. Hist. Soc. Papers, vol. AM. 2013, page 170; Sussex County Court 1680-1699, pages 684-685. [Note—Pages 684-685 show that a will was refused probate at Dec. Term, 1694, and mentions a son William by a former wife.]

**Price, Thomas. Sr.** Planter. Slaughter Neck. Will (copy). Made March 14, 1694/5. Heirs: wife Catharine Price; son Thomas Price; grandson William Price; granddaus. Catharine, Jane and Rachel Price. Exec'r, son Thomas Price. Wits., Thomas Phelmon, Jeremiah Barthelmy, William Fisher. Prob. March 25, 1695. Arch. vo. A94, page 140. Reg. of Wills, Liber A, folios 19-20. Penna. Hist. Soc. Papers, vol. AM. 2013, pages 177 and 177a.

**Jones, John.** Admin. of, to Jane Jones, widow. Granted May 4, 1695. Penna. Hist. Soc. Papers, vol. AM. 2013, page [175].

**Goit, Peter.** Merchant. Will (copy). Made July 10, 1695. Heirs: Peter and Mary Williams (children of Ruth Williams); Mary Duke; Robert Duke (son of Mary); John Richards. Exec'rs, friends Dr. Luke Wattson, Joseph Booth and William Freeman. Wits., Ann Granger, Joseph Hickman, Thomas Manley. Prob. July 15, 1695. Arch. vol. A72, page 172. Reg. of Wills, Liber A, folios 20-22.

**Davis [Davies], Thomas, Sr.** Will (copy). Made Jan. 13, 1698. Heirs: sons Thomas, Richard, Robert, John, Samuel and Benjamin Davis. Exec'r, friend John [Joseph] Nutter and John [Joseph] Hill. Wits., Thomas Tilton, Thomas Price, William Stapleton. Prob. Feb. 1697/98. Arch. vol. A68, page 131. Reg. of Wills, Liber A, folios 26-27. Sussex County Court 1680-1699, pages 715, 721. [Note:—Page 715 shows J. Hill resigned the administration to Samuel Watson, husband of decedent's eldest dau.; page 721 mentions a son Robert Davies.]

**Croutch, John.** Will. Undated. No heirs. Exec'r, Capt. Thomas Pemberton. Wits., Nehemiah Field, Henry Stretcher, Edward Gould. Prob. Feb. Term 1697/98. Sussex County Court 1680-1699, page 715.

**Williams, Patrick.** Admin. of, to Martha Jacobs. Granted March Term, 1697/98. Sussex County Court 1680-1699, page 721.

**Massey, William.** Admin. of. Sussex County Court 1680-1699, page 746. [Note:—Petition to Sept. Term, 1698, by minor son George Massey for letters of administration, with Thomas Fenwick and Nehemiah Field as guardians.]

**Williams, Richard.** Will (copy). Made Sept. 8, 1698. Heirs: wife Anne Williams; son Richard Williams; dau. Elizabeth Williams. Exec'rx, wife Anne Williams. Wits., Henry Stretcher, Thomas May, Roger Corbett. Guardian, friend Thomas May. Prob. Sept. 14, 1698. Arch. vol. A108, page 33. Reg. of Wills, Liber A, folios 24-26.

**Aleefe, Joseph.** Angola Neck. Will (copy). Made Nov. 13, 1700. Heirs: wife Bridgett; son William; dau. Bridgett; wife's son Ebenezer Jones; and child unnamed. Exec'rx, wife Bridgett. Wits., Thomas Carey, Ledah C. Carey, Roger Corbett, Elizabeth Simmons. Prob. Jan. 20, 1700. Arch. vol. A57, page 114. Reg. of Wills, Liber A, folios 30-32.

**Kipshaven, John.** Will (copy). Made Jan. 14, 1700. Heirs: dau. Martha Johnson( now wife of Adam); grandsons John and Albert Jacobs (sons of Alburtus Jacobs by dau. Martha); granddau. Bredah Jacobs (sister of John and Albert Jacobs); bro. Dirrick Kipshaven; children of bro. Dirrick Kipshaven; Cornelius Pluckhoy (Blindman); Simon Pauling; Peter Clause. Eec'rs, John Hill, Samuel Preston, Jacob Kollock. Wits., Ja. Sangster, Henry Hill, Nehemiah Field. Prob. Jan. 25, 1700. Arch. vol. A82, page 161. Reg. of Wills, Liber A, folios 33-35.

**Nutter, John. Yeoman.** Will (copy). Made Nov. 29, 1702. Heirs: wife Elizabeth Nutter; sons John and Christopher Nutter; dau. Mary Nutter; Joseph Hickman; Elizabeth Richardson. Exec'rx, wife Elizabeth Nutter. Wits., Joseph Hickman, James Tyer, John Areskin. Overseer, bro. Charles Nutter. Prob. Jan. 15, 1701 [sic]. Arch. vol. A91, page 128. Reg. of Wills, Liber A, folios 36-39.

**Asueress [Asuerus, Asuersee], Hendrick.** Will (copy). Made Nov. . . ., 1694. Heir: Art Johnson Vankirk. [No exec'r]. Wits., John Manlove, Jr., Henry Moliston. Prob. Feb. 4, 1701. Arch. vol. A57, page 196. Reg. of Wills, Liber A, folios 18-19.

**Piles, William. Husbandman.** Will (copy). Made March 7, 1700. Heirs: sons John, Joseph, Isaac and William Piles; daus. Rebeckah, Lucie and Comfort Piles, Elizabeth Carwithin (wife of Caleb); sons-in-law Caleb Carwithin and James Carpenter. Exec'rs, friend Samuel Preston and John Miers (a Hatter of Lewes). Wits., John Lighty, W[illia]m Warring, W[illia]m Richards. Prob. March 25, 1701. Arch. vol. A93, page 87. Reg. of Wills, Liber A, folios 28-30.

**Heaverly, Antoney. Planter.** Will (copy). Made Nov. 8, 1700. Heirs: unnamed wife; sons Antoney, Jr., John, William, Andrew, Daniel, and James Heaverly. Exec'r, son Antoney, Jr. Wits., Elizabeth Hill, Nehemiah Field. Prob. May 31, 1701. Arch. vol. A76, page 15. Reg. of Wills, Liber A, folios 32-33.

**Anderson, Cornelus. Planter.** Will (copy). Made Nov. 8, 1701. Heirs: friends William Millinnor and Thomas Wilson. Exec'r, Thomas Wilson. Wits., Joseph Hickman, Joshua Hickman, John Abbott. Prob. Nov. 19, 1701. Arch. vol. A57, page 134. Reg. of Wills, Liber A, folios 35-36.

**West, George. Planter.** Will (copy). Made Jan. 11, [1702]. Heirs: sons Thomas, John, Robert and George West; daus. Jane West, Susanna West, Alice Williams and Elizabeth Barker, widow; grandson John Numparsons. Exec'rs, sons Thomas and John West. Wits., James Walker, Roger Corbett. Prob. Feb. 2, [1702]. Arch. vol. A106, page 121. Reg. of Wills, Liber A, folios 39-40.

**Abbott, Robert. Planter.** Will (copy). Made Jan. 25, 1702/3. Heirs: wife Elizabeth; son (nephew of John Abbott); daus. Comfort, Susanna, Elizabeth (niece of Ralph Justis), and Mary (niece of William Abbott); sons-in-law Richard and Robert Hill (sons of Robert Hill, dec'd). Exec'rx, wife Elizabeth. Wits., Joseph Hickman, William Hedger, Gabriel Henry. Prob. March 3, 1702. Arch. vol. A57, page 20. Reg. of Wills, Liber A, folios 40-43.

**Inlows, Anthony.** Will (copy). Made Feb. 27, 1702/3. Heirs: wife Frances Inlows; sons Peter, Abharkin and Thomas Inlows; dau. Elizabeth Inlows; Robert Hill. Exec'rs, Samuel Davis and James Simson. Wits., Thomas Smith, John Johnson, John Stuart. Prob. April 10, 1703. Arch. vol. A79, page 178. Reg. of Wills, Liber A, folios 43-44.

**Futcher, William.** Yeoman. Will (copy). Made March 26, 1703. Heirs: wife Elizabeth Futcher, dau. Mary Futcher; bros. John and Richard Futcher. Exec'rx, wife Elizabeth Futcher. Wits., Richard Paynter, Thomas Stockley, Roger Corbett. Prob. April 17, 1703. Arch. vol. A72, page 97. Reg. of Wills, Liber A, folios 44-45.

**Brown, James.** Will (copy). Made Oct. 29, 1703. Heir: Joseph Booth. Exec'r, Joseph Booth. Wits., Henry Spencer, Abigail Vankirk. Prob. Feb. 15, 1703/4. Arch. vol. A60, page 196. Reg. of Wills, Liber A, folios 46-47.

**Perry, Rowlin.** Planter. Will (copy). Made Jan. 22, 1703/4. Heir: wife Ester Perry. Exec'rx, wife Ester Perry. [No wits.]. Prob. March 14, 1703/4. Arch. vol. A92, page 183. Reg. of Wills, Liber A, folios 45-46.

**Richards, John, Sr.** Cooper. Will (copy). Made March 7, 1703/4. Heirs: wife Grace Richards; son John Richards; daus. Mary, Elsie, Grace and Elizabeth Richards, Sarah Fleming and Isanna Tyer; son-in-law Thomas Tyer. Exec'rs, wife Grace Richards and son John Richards. Wits., Joseph Hickman, John Mullinex, Thomas Tyer, Jr. Prob. April 24, 1704. Arch. vol. A95, page 84. Reg. of Wills, Liber A, folies 47-50.

**Potter, Jane.** Will (copy). Made Sept, 16, 1703. Heirs: son unnamed; William Farmer; Frances Gum; John Davis (son of John). Exec'r, friend Richard Dobson. Wits., Nathan Starr, William Farmer, John Smith. Prob. Aug. . . ., 1704. Arch. vol. A94, page 16. Reg. of Wills, Liber A, folios 48-49.

**Harmenson, John.** Will (copy). Made Aug. 12, 1704. Heirs: wife Hellenar Harmenson; sons Hendrick and John Harmenson; daus. Susanna and Deborah Harmanson. Exec'rs, friends Joseph Booth and John Dinavan. Wits., John Wheelor, John Hepburn. [No prob.]. Arch. vol. A74, page 99. Reg. of Wills, Liber A, folios 49-50.

**Clarke, William.** Gentleman. Lewes. Will (copy). Made April 24, 1705. Heirs: wife Honnour; son William; dau.-in-law Rebeckah Clarke; son-in-law Thomas Pemberton; and granddaus. Mary Pemberton and Elizabeth Brown (wife of Daniel). Exec'rx, wife Honnour. Wits., Jos[eph] Booth, Robert R. Burton, Jonas Greenwood. Overseers, bro-in-law Walton Huling and friend Thomas Fisher. Prob. July 24, 1705. Arch. vol. A64, page 198. Reg. of Wills, Liber A, folios 2-3.

**Huling, Walton.** Lewes. Will (copy). Made Sept. 10, 1705. Heirs: wife Martha Huling; daus. Elizabeth and Esther Huling. Exec'rx, wife Martha Huling. Wits., Samuel Davis, Jonathan Bailey, Rebecca Clark. Prob. Aug. 3, 17 . . . Arch. vol. A79, page 93. Reg. of Wills, Liber A, folios 54-55.

**Sangster, James.** Town of Lewes. Will (copy). Made May 25, 1705. Heirs: wife Mary Sangster; sons James, John and William Sangster; dau. Margori Sangster. Exec'rx, wife Mary Sangster. Wits., Phillip Russell, Joseph Russell. Prob. Nov. 6, 1705. Arch. vol. A98, page 9. Reg. of Wills, Liber A, folio 55.

**Wattson, Luke, Sr., Esq.** Lewes. Will (copy). Made Sept. 6, 1705. Heirs: wife Sarah Wattson; sons Luke, John, Samuel and Isaac Wattson; daus. Mary Wattson (by former wife Margery, dau. of Capt. Henry Smith), and Elizabeth Morris wife of Antoney Morris, Sr., of Phila.). Exec'rx, wife Sarah Wattson. Wits., Phillip Russell, Sarah Russell, Dorothy Givens, Anna Corbett, Roger Corbett. Overseers: son-in-law Richard Paynter, Justice Phillip Russell. Prob. Nov. 6, 1705. Arch. vol. A106, page 27. Reg. of Wills, Liber A, folios 52-54.

**Lillingston, Elizabeth.** Widow. Will (copy). Made Dec. 1, 1705. Heirs: dau. Mary Lillingston; mother Mary Watson; father Luke Watson. Exec'r, father Luke Watson. Wits., John Hill, John Watson, Sam[ue]l Watson. Prob. Dec. 8, 1705. Arch. vol. A84, page 76. Reg. of Wills, Liber A, folios 439-440.

**Stewart [Stuart], John.** Will (copy). Made Sept. 1, 1704. Heirs: wife Elizabeth Stewart; sons Samuel, David, John and William Stewart; daus. Elizabeth, Johannah and Mary Stewart. Exec'rs, Alexander Innis, Lewis Marrice. Wits., James Simson, Samuel Knowles, Roger Corbett. Prob. Jan. 13, 1705/6. Arch. vol. A100, page 184. Reg. of Wills, Liber A, folios 50-52.

**Depray, John.** Yeoman. Will (copy). Made Aug. 30, 1706. Heirs: wife Mary Depray; sons John and William Depray. Exec'rx, wife Mary Depray. Wits., John Crew, John Futcher, Roger Corbett. Prob. Oct. [. . .], 1706. Arch. vol. A68, pages 220-221. Reg. of Wills, Liber A, folios 55-57.

**Walton, John.** Will (copy). Made Nov. 19, 1706. Heirs: wife Percey Walton; sons John, George and William Walton; daus. Mary and Alice Walton and Ann Draper; granddau. Elizabeth Draper; son-in-law Alexander Draper. Exec'rx, wife Percey Walton. Wits., Joseph Hickman, Thomas Manley, Mark Manley. Trustees: son-in-law Alexander Draper and friend Nicholas Granger. Prob. Jan. 1, 1706/7. Arch. vol. A104, page 138. Reg. of Wills, Liber A, folios 209-213.

**Burton, John.** Will (copy). Made Feb. 10, 17[0]8/9. Heirs: Samuel, Benjamin, Thomas, Joseph, Stratton, Jacob, Woolsey and William Burton, Sr.; Ann Bagwell; Frances Kaning; and Aminadal Hangar. Exec'r, bro. William. Wits., William Bagwell, Thomas Gear, Mary Oakey. Prob. . . . 1708. Arch. vol. A61, page 183. Reg. of Wills, Liber A, folios 443-444.

**Harmonson, Christian.** Will (copy). Made Feb. 10, 1708/9. Heirs: sons Harmon and John Harmonson; dau. Mary Harmonson; sons-in-law William Butcher and Robert Butcher; sister-in-law Mary Crague; friend Alexander Moleston; Mary Cupman; John Dreadin (uncle of son John Harmonson). Exec'rs, William Shankland, Edward Crague, Alexander Molliston. Wits., Nathaniel Scarborough, Samuel Hopkins, Sr., Jennett Hopkins, John Hall. Prob. Feb. 14, 1708. Arch. vol.A74, page 97. Reg. of Wills, Liber A, folios 71-75.

**Clifton, Thomas.** Yeoman. Will (copy). Made March 27, 1707/8. Heirs: wife Darans; sons Robert, Michael and George; and dau. Tabith[a]. Exec'rs, wife Darans and son Robert. Wits., James Simson, Margaret Simson, John Hepburn. [No prob.]. Arch. vol. A65, page 48. Reg. of Wills, Liber A, folios 64-65.

**Newcomb, William.** Will (copy). Made April 3, 1708. Heirs: wife Elizabeth Newcomb; child unnamed; bro. Daniel Newcomb; sister Ann Brabon (wife of Joseph); Daniel Brabon (son of Ann and Joseph); William Light. Exec'r, bro.-in-law Richard Dobson. Wits., Tho[mas] Fisher, Frances Dunaven, William Lighty [sic.]. [No prob.]. Arch. vol. A91, page 82. Reg. of Wills, Liber A, folios 68-69. [Note:— Arch. vol. A91, page 82 mentions dec'd father, Baptis Newcomb].

**Mason, William.** Lewes. Will (copy). Made April 1, 1708. Heirs: son-in-law Richard Whety; Torlah Senew; Toney Johnson. Exec'rs, Torlah Senew, Toney Johnson. Wits., James Holonds, William Butter, John Meulah. Prob. April 14, 1708. Arch. vol. A87, page 44. Reg. of Wills, Liber A, folios 66-67.

**Senew, Torlah.** Will (copy). Made April 20, 1708. Heirs: wife May Senew; dau. unnamed. Eec'rs, wife May Senew, John Crew. Wits., Christean Harmonson, John Mucloh, Anabalow Crew. [No prob.]. Arch. vol. A98, page 44. Reg. of Wills, Liber A, folios 442-443.

**Wiltbank, Isaac.** Yeoman. Will (copy). Made March 19, 1707/8. Heirs: wife Elizabeth Wiltbank; sons Samuel, Isaac and Cornelius Wiltbank; Mary Gray; father-in-law Samuel Gray. Exec'rs, wife Elizabeth Wiltbank, Cornelius Wiltbank, Captain John Hill. Wits., John Reece, Susanna Pettion, John Hepburn. Prob. April 20, 1708. Arch. vol. A108, page 151. Reg. of Wills, Liber A, folios 59-60.

**Watson, Luke.** Yeoman. Will (copy). Made Oct. 10, 1707. Heirs: wife unnamed; bros. Isaac and Samuel Watson; granddau. Mary Lillington. Exec'rx, wife unnamed. Wits., Hannah Crosswell, Richard Davis, Samuel Watson. Trustee: bro. Samuel Watson. Prob. April 26, 1708. Arch. vol. A106, page 28. Reg. of Wills, Liber A, folios 440-441. [Note:—Reg. of Wills, Liber A, folio 440 mentions heirs of son Luke].

**Macknab, Joseph.** Carpenter. Will (copy). Made April 4, 1708. Heirs: George Davis; friend Richard Paynter. Exec'r, friend Richard Paynter. Wits., Richard Hinman, Thomas Bowman, John Futcher. Prob. May 4, 1708. Arch. vol. A86, page 19. Reg. of Wills, Liber A, folios 63,64 and 66.

**Stapleton, William, Sr.** Will (copy). Made Aug. 12, 1708. Heirs: wife Ann Stapleton; sons James, William and Avery Stapleton; daus Ann, Elenor, Elizabeth and Mary Stapleton. Exec'rx, wife Ann Stapleton. Wits., Charles Haynes, Jane F. Haynes, Richard Hill. [No prob.]. Arch. vol. A100, page 111. Reg. of Wills, Liber A, folios 60-61.

**Page, Edward.** Planter. Will (copy). Made 20th of 5th month . . . Heirs: dau. Elizabeth Page. Exec'r, John Miers. Wits., Phillip Russel, Joseph Russel, Mary M. Miers. Prob 7 [Septem]ber 14, 1708. Arch. vol. A92, page 37. Reg. of Wills, Liber A, folios 65-66.

**Haynes, Charles, Sr.** Will (copy). Made Nov. 18, 1708. Heirs: wife Jeanne Haynes; sons Charles and John Haynes; dau. Margret Haynes. Exec'rx, wife Jeanne [Jane] Haynes.

Wits., John Bywater, Ann Stappillton, Joseph Hickman. [No prob.]. Arch. vol. A74, page 247. Reg. of Wills, Liber A, folios 61-63.

**Hill, John.** Gentleman. Lewes. Will (copy). Made March 1, 1696/7. Heirs: wife Elizabeth Hill; cousin Richard Hill (son of bro. Richard of London, England); Antoney Haverly; Nehemiah Field. Exec'rx, wife Elizabeth Hill. Wits., Luke Wattson, Jr., Henry Moliston, Nehemiah Fields. [Codicil. Wits., Thomas Grove, Edward Carey, Abraham Parsley]. Prob. Dec. 29, 1708. Arch. vol. A76, page 127. Reg. of Wills, Liber A, folios 23-24.

**Granger, Nicholas.** Yeoman. Will (copy). Made March 19, 1710. Heirs: wife Ann Granger; son Nicholas Granger; daus. Hannah, Mary, Abigail, Sarah and Ann Granger. Exec'r, son Nicholas Granger. Wits., Henry Spencer, Philip Grindy, Abigail Varkirk. [No prob.]. Arch. vol. A72, page 249. Reg. of Wills, Liber A, folios 76-77.

**Coggeshall, Isaac.** Lewes. Will (copy). Made Jan. 19, 1707/8. Heirs: wife Sarah; bro. [Preserved]; and father-in-law Thomas Harford. Exec'rx, wife Sarah. Wits., Phillip Russell, Wrixham White. Trustees: friends John Coe and Isaac Wiltbank. Prob. April 15, 1710. Arch. vol. A65, page 99. Reg. of Wills, Liber A, folios 58-59.

**Manlove, Thomas.** Will (copy). Made Jan. 26, 1709. Heirs: wife Mary Manlove; dau. Sarah Manlove; a child unnamed. Exec'rx, wife Mary Manlove. Wits., Richard Manlove, John Clandene, Philip Grende. Prob. Sept. 24, 1710. Arch. vol. A86, page 44. Reg. of Wills, Liber A, folios 75-76.

**Crew, John.** Will (copy). Made Aug. 21, 1712. Heirs: wife Anabelle; dau. Elizabeth Walls; grandson John Walls (son of Elizabeth); and son-in-law Richard Harvey. Exec'rx, wife Anabelle. Wits., Edward Bran, Edward Parker, Robert Bocher. Prob. May 27, 1713. Arch. vol. A67, page 188. Reg. of Wills, Liber A, folios 118-119.

**Fisher, Thomas.** Will (copy). Made Nov. 17, 1713. Heirs: wife Margery; sons Joshua and James Fisher; daus. Margaret, Margery and Elizabeth Fisher. Exec'rx, wife Margery Fisher. Wits., Cornelius Wiltbank, Richard Williams, John Lupecuea. [No prob.]. Arch. vol. A71, page 157. Reg. of Wills, Liber A, folios 81-83.

**Johnson, Adam.** Yeoman. Will (copy). Made Dec. 16, 1713. Heirs: wife Martha Johnson; sons James, Isaac and John Kipshaven Johnson; dau. Elizabeth Johnson. Exec'rx, wife

Martha Johnson. Wits., John Coe, James Langster, Roger Corbett. Prob. Dec. 27, 1713. Arch. vol. A81, page 8. Reg. of Wills, Liber A, folios 77-79.

**Pennington, Henry.** Will (copy). Made Dec. 30, 1713. Heirs: wife Deborah Pennington; dau. Mary Nuel; Elizabeth Wattson, Jr., (dau. of Isaac and Elizabeth Wattson). Exec'rx, wife Deborah Pennington. Wits., Caleb Cirwithin, Elizabeth Cirwithin, John Nutter. Prob. May 24, 1714. Arch. vol. A92, page 148. Reg. of Wills, Liber A, folios 79-81.

**Gibb, John.** Lewes. Will (copy). Made Nov. 5, 1714. Heir: wife Anne Gibb. Exec'rx, wife Anne Gibb. Wits., Nathaniel Hall, John Shankland, Edward Stretcher, James White. Prob. Nov. 12, 1714. Arch. vol. A72, page 106. Reg. of Wills, Liber A, folios 83-84.

**Gibb, Anne.** Widow. Will (copy). Made Jan. 29, 1716. Heirs: sons William and James Stapleton; daus. Anne Cary (wife of Edward), Mary Heverloe (wife of Antoney), Elizabeth Parker and Elinor Bywater; John Price. Exec'r, son William Stapleton. Wits., Tho[mas] Gear, Phil[lip] Russel, Jr., Marg. Hepburn. Prob. Feb. 2, 1716. Arch. vol. A72, page 103. Reg. of Wills, Liber A, folios 91-92.

**Godden, Michael.** Will (copy). Made . . . 1715/16. Heirs: wife Mary; sons Michall, Cesar, William and Thomas Godden; dau. Mary Godden. Exec'rs, wife Mary Godden and bro. William Godden. Wits., Alexander Herring, Thomas Gordon, James White. Prob. Feb. 10, 1716. Arch. vol. A72, page 167. Reg. of Wills, Liber A, folios 84-85.

**Wolfe, Riss.** Yeoman. Will (copy). Made Feb. 18, 1715/16. Heirs: sons Mathew, William and Risi Wolfe. Exec'rs, sons Mathew, William and Risi Wolfe. Wits., Edward Craig, Humphrey Smith. [No prob.]. Arch. vol. A109, page 35. Reg. of Wills, Liber A, folios 88-89.

**Hemmons, Thomas.** Yeoman. Cedar Creek Hd. Will (copy). Made March 31, 1716. Arch. vol. A76, page 40. [No other information].

**Spencer, Henry.** Yeoman. Will (copy). Made Feb. 28, 1715/16. Heirs: wife Mary Spencer; sons William, Jehu and Henry Spencer; daus. Frances and Mary Spencer; child unnamed; bro. Samuel Spencer. Exec'rs, wife Mary Spencer and son William Spencer. Wits., Ja[me]s Booth, John May, Samuel Spencer. Prob. April 5, 1716. Arch. vol. A100, page 54. Reg. of Wills, Liber A, folios 89-91.

**Harford, Thomas.** Will (copy). Made Aug. 25, 1709. Heirs: wife Rebekah Harford; son-in-law Preserved Coggeshall. Exec'rs, wife Rebakah Harford and son-in-law Preserved Coggeshall. Wits., Philip Russell, Joseph Russell, John Miers. Prob. [Dec. 4, 1716]. Arch. vol. A74, page 73. Reg. of Wills, Liber A, folios 3-4.

**Stevens, Mathew.** Yeoman. Will (copy). Made Sept. 15, 1716. Heirs: wife Mary Stevens; Mathew and William Woolfe (sons of Rice and Mary Woolfe); Mary Wastcoat. Exec'rx, wife Mary Stevens. Wits., Henry Runnells, Elizabeth Hicraft, Preserved Coggeshall. Prob. Dec. 4, 1716. Arch. vol. A100, page 171. Reg. of Wills, Liber A, folios 96-98.

**Hammond, Elizabeth** (formerly widow of James Duncan). Will (copy). Made Nov. 30, 1716. Heirs: friend Rev. Samuel Davis, Sr. Exec'r, Rev. Samuel Davis, Sr. Wits., Samuel Davis, Jr., Robert Shankland, Margt. Simson. Prob. Dec. 22, 1716. Arch. vol. A74, page 30. Reg. of Wills, Liber A, folios 92-94.

**Burton, Jacob.** Will (copy). Made Nov. 14, 1716. Heirs: bros. Joseph, Stratton, Woolsey and Benjamin; niece Ann (dau. of Benjamin); and nephews William (son of Joseph) and John (son of Woolsey). Exec'r, bro. Woolsey. Wits., Samuel Davis, Jr., Thomas Stockley, W. White. Prob. Jan. 20, 1716/17. Arch. vol. A61, page 156. Reg. of Wills, Liber A, folios 94-95.

**Seattown [Sealtown], James.** Yeoman. Will (copy). Made Jan. 21, 1717. Heirs: wife Elizabeth Seattown; Elias Baily; Sarah Baily (wife of Elias); Seattown Baily (son of Sarah); Jane Wiltbanck (wife of Cornelius, Esq.). Exec'rs, wife Elizabeth Seattown, wife's uncle Cornelius Wiltbanck. Wits., Nath[ani]el Starr, Nicholas Green, John Murphey. Prob. Feb. 4, 1717. Reg. of Wills, Liber A, folios 122-124.

**Craig, Edward.** Yeoman. Will (copy). Made Sept. 10, 1717. Heirs: sons William and Robert; dau. Mary; Elizabeth Craig (dau. of Robert); Jean Diall; and Alexander Macullah. Exec'rs, sons William and Robert Craig. Wits., Daniel Hosman, Elizabeth Gray, David, Gray. Prob. Jan. 8, 17 . . . Arch. vol. A67, page 130. Reg. of Wills, Liber A, folios 120-121.

**Bedwell, Thomas.** Will (copy). Made Nov. 18, 1716. Heirs: daus. Mary Anne and Elenor Bedwell, Anna Hall and Mellicent Hill; grandson John Hill (son of Mellicent Hill). Exec'rs, daus. Mary Anne and Elenor, and son-in-law John Hall.

Wits., James Clayton, Michal Donohoe, Mary Donohoe. Prob. Nov. 6, 1717. Arch. vol. A59, page 26. Reg. of Wills, Liber A, folios 95-96.

**Manlove, Mark.** Yeoman. Cedar Creek Hd. Will (copy). Made March 5, 1717/18. Heirs: wife Anne Manlove; son Thomas Manlove; dau. Mary Manlove; servants George and Hugh Perkins. Exec'rx, wife Anne Manlove. Wits., Art Vankirke, Sr., George Walton, Thomas May, Jr. [No prob.]. Arch. vol. A86, page 41. [No Reg. of Wills Liber].

**Drummond, Robert.** Will (copy). Made March 9, 1717/18. Heirs: wife Elizabeth Drummond; son John Drummond. Exec'rx, wife Elizabeth Drummond. Wits., Robert West, Katherine Davis, Thomas Cale. Prob. May 22, 1718. Arch. vol. A69, page 234. Reg. of Wills, Liber A, folio 444. [Note:—Arch. vol. A69, page 234 mentions friends William Godwin and John Roades to assist said Exec'rx].

**Thomson, Andrew.** Will (copy). Made April 8, 1718. Heirs: wife unnamed; children unnamed; bro. John Thomson. Exec'r, bro. John Thomson. Wits., John Allan, Esther Thomson, Joseph Shankland. Prob. June 14, 1718. Arch. vol. A101, page 148. Reg. of Wills, Liber A, folios 446-447.

**Hill, Richard.** Yeoman. Cedar Creek Hd. Will (copy). Made Feb. 19, 1718/19. Heirs: wife Mary Hill; sons Robert and Johnson Hill; daus. Ruth, Mary, Elizabeth and Sarah Hill. Exec'rx, wife Mary Hill. Wits., Mary Hirons, Thomas May, Jr., Sarah Clendinen. Prob. March 31, 1719. Arch. vol. A76, page 148. Reg. of Wills, Liber A, folios 113-114.

**Starr, Nathaniel.** Will (copy). Made April 8, 1719. Heirs: wife Mary Starr; sons Richard and Nathaniel Starr; daus. Ann and Sarah Starr; child unnamed. Exec'rx, wife Mary Starr. Wits., Elizabeth Darack, Walter Reed, W[illia]m Darter. Prob. April 6, 1719. Arch. vol. A100, page 122. Reg. of Wills, Liber A, folios 114-16.

**Ponder, John.** Yeoman. Will (copy). Made March 4, 1718/19. Heirs: wife Mary Ponder; sons John, James and Daniel Ponder; daus. Sarah, Mary, Margaret and Rosannah Ponder. Exec'rx, wife Mary Ponder. Wits., Mary Cartell, John Heaveloe, William Burkett. Prob. April 15, 1719. Arch. vol. A93, page 180. Reg. of Wills, Liber A, folios 107-109.

**Parker, Mathew.** Yeoman. Lewes. Will (copy). Made July 14, 1718. Heirs: wife Elizabeth Parker; dau. Naomy Parker. Exec'rx, wife Elizabeth Parker. Wits., W. White, Anderson Parker, John Bywater. Prob. May 5, 1719. Arch. vol. A92,

page 77. Reg. of Wills, Liber A, folios 111-113. [Note:—
Arch. vol. A92, page 77 mentions John Roades and Wrixam
White as Trustees or assistants to wife and dau.].

**Smith, Thomas.** Will (copy). Made April 25, 1719. Heirs: son
Thomas Smith; dau. Rebeckah Smith. Exec'rs, dau. Re-
beckah Smith, friends Robert Lodge and Joseph Eldridge.
Wits., Mary Baldrey, Thomas Bate. Prob. May 30, 1719.
Arch. vol. A100, page 8. Reg. of Wills, Liber A, folios 109-
111.

**Ayliff, William.** Yeoman. Will (copy). Made April 11, 1719.
Heirs: wife Margret; bro. Joseph and Ebenezer Jones.
Exec'r, Ebenezer Jones. Wits., George Dodd, John W. Cat-
hall, Thomas Bate. Prob. June 6, 1719. Arch. vol. A58,
page 30. Reg. of Wills, Liber A, folios 108-109.

**Prettyman, Thomas, Sr.** Yeoman. Will (copy). Made May 17,
1719. Heirs: wife Comfort Prettyman; sons Thomas and
Robert Prettyman; dau. Elizabeth Prettyman; bros. William, Robert and John Prettyman. Exec'rx, wife Comfort
Prettyman. Wits., Hugh Verdin, Elizabeth Walker, Anderson Parker. Prob. July 17, 1719. Arch. vol. A94, page 114.
Reg. of Wills, Liber A, folios 213-214.

**White, Wrixam.** Will (copy). Made Dec. 24, 1719. Heirs: wife
Hannah White; children unnamed. Exec'rx, wife Hannah
White. Wits., Jacob Kollock, Jacob Kollock, Jr., James
White. Prob. Feb. 2, 1719/20. Arch. vol. A107, page 96.
Reg. of Wills, Liber A, folios 127-128.

**Burton, Joseph.** Will (copy). Made Nov. 19, 1719. Heirs: wife
Elizabeth; sons William, Cornelius and Jacob; and dau. Ann
Catherine. Exec'rs, wife Elizabeth and bro. Woolsey. Wits.,
Phil[ip] Askie, Paul Waples, Frances Ragnell. Prob. Feb.
25, 1719/20. Arch. vol. A61, page 202. Reg. of Wills, Liber
A, folios 124-126.

**Gray, David.** Yeoman. Will (copy). Made Jan. 10, 1719/20.
Heirs: wife Elizabeth Gray; son Samuel Gray; bro. Thomas
Gray; Alexander Maccullah. Exec'rx, wife Elizabeth Gray.
Wits., Robert Craige, Ruth Craige, James White. Prob.
Feb. 19, 1719-20. Arch. vol. A73, page 3. Reg. of Wills,
Liber A, folios 128-129.

**Williams, Francis, Sr.** Will (copy). Made Feb. 16, 1716/17.
Heirs: wife Elizabeth Williams; sons John, Henry, Francis
and Nicholas Williams; daus. Mary and Comfort Williams.

Exec'rx, wife Elizabeth Williams. Wits., Elizabeth Ainsworth, Thomas Bate. Prob. March 28, 1720. Arch. vol. A107, page 173. Reg. of Wills, Liber A, folios 134-135.

**Sanderson, Jane.** Will (copy). Made March 7, 1919/20. Heirs: son John Sanderson; daus. Margaret and Anne Sanderson, Jane Okeley. Exec'r, son John Sanderson. Wits., Sarah Curtis, Jacob Chaple, Tho[mas] Tomison. Prob. April . . ., 1720. Arch. vol. A98, page 7. Reg. of Wills, Liber A, folios 129-130.

**Clifton, Robert.** Yeoman. Lewes. Will (copy). Made May 10, 1720| Heirs: wife Anne; dau. Sarah; and sons Thomas and Benjamin. Exec'rx, wife Anne. Wits., James Simson, Edward Naws, James White. Prob. May 16, 1720. Arch. vol. A65, page 44. Reg. of Wills, Liber A, folios 136-138.

**Cirwithin, Caleb.** Prime Hook Neck. Will (copy). Made Jan. 1, 1719. Heirs: wife Elizabeth; son Caleb; and daus. Grace, Elizabeth, Abigail, Mary, Martha, Febe, Rebecka and Hannah. Exec'rs, [Joseph Peplo and Axell Corbett]. Wits., William Thompson, Axell Corbett, Joseph Peplo. Prob. Aug. 20, 1720. Arch. vol. A64, page 157. Reg. of Wills, Liber A, folios 126-127.

**Eyre, Daniel.** Will (copy). Made Sept. 14, 1720. Heirs: wife Elizabeth Eyre; sisters Sarah Nock (wife of Thomas Nock of Kent County), Mary Mifflin (wife of Edward Mifflin of Northampton County, Virginia) and Margaret Booth (wife of Joseph Booth, Jr., of Kent County). Exec'rx, wife Elizabeth Eyre. Wits., Henry Hall, Thomas Turner, John Murphy, William Rodney. Prob. Oct. 24, 1720. Arch. vol. A71, page 54. Reg. of Wills, Liber A, folios 138-139. [Note:— Arch. vol. A71, page 54 mentions his deceased mother Anne Eyre].

**Eyre, Elizabeth.** Will (copy). Made Dec. 17, 1720. Heirs: bros. James, Joshua and Jabesh Maud Fisher; sisters Margery Fisher, Margret Booth; cousin Sarah Smith; Mary Miers. Exec'r, Joseph Booth, Jr. Wits., John Murphey, Sarah Murphey, John May. Prob. Jan. 6, 1720/21. Arch. vol. A71, page 55. Reg. of Wills, Liber A, folios 142-143.

**Murphy, John.** Will (copy). Made Dec. 30, 1720. Heirs: bro. Thomas Murphy; Martha Tinley; Mary, Bridget, Thamer and Nehemiah Tinley (children of Martha). Exec'rx, Martha Tinley. Wits., Tho[ma]s May, Jr., John May, William Donily, Thomas Hemmons. Prob. Jan. 31, 1720/21. Arch. vol. A90, page 194. Reg. of Wills, Liber A, folios 135-136.

**Gordon, Thomas, Sr.** Farmer. Will (copy). Made Jan. 10, 1720/21. Heirs: wife Mary Gordon; sons Thomas and John Gordon; daus. Mary, Sarah and Marion Gordon; grandsons Thomas Cole (son of dau. Jeanne), Thomas Cole (son of Thomas Cole and dau. Margaret). Exec'rs, wife Mary Gordon and son Thomas Gordon. Wits., Robert Perrie, Henry Chambers, John Chambers, George Fleming. Prob. March 9, 1720/21. Arch. vol. A72, page 184. Reg. of Wills, Liber A, folios 146-148.

**Kollock, Jacob.** Merchant. Lewes. Will (copy). Made Dec. 30, 1720. Heirs: wife Mary Kollock; sons Jacob, Simon and Cornelus Kollock; daus. Magdalane, Hannah and Hester Kollock, Jane Irons (wife of William). Exec'rs, wife Mary Kollock and his 7 children. Wits., Sam[ue]l Davis, Jr., Preserved Coggeshall, Timothy Coe. Prob. March 14, 1720/21. Arch. vol. A83, page 3. Reg. of Wills, Liber A, folios 130-134.

**Bagwell, Francis.** Yeoman. Will (copy). Made March 12, 1720. Heirs: son Thomas; and Ann Drake. Exec'rs, friends Jno. Russell and Job Barker. Wits., Woolsey Burton, Thomas Gear, George Mariner. Prob. March 23, 1720/21. Arch. vol. A58, page 50. Reg. of Wills, Liber A, folios 145-146.

**Lucas, Peter.** Will (copy). Made March 7, 1720/21. Heir: sister Sarah Lucas. Exec'rx, sister Sarah Lucas. Wits., Samuel Stewart, William Stuart, William Darter. Prob. March 27, 1721. Arch. vol. A85, page 169. Reg. of Wills, Liber A, folio 148.

**Williams, Richard.** Will (copy). Made March 22, 1720. Heirs: cousins John Killingworth, Stephen Simons, John and Adam, Jr., Fisher (sons of Adam Fisher); Henry Skidmore; John Smith; Tabush Fisher, Ann, Rachel and Thomas Newcom (children of Baptist Newcom); Abigail and Ann Bravin (daus. of Joseph Bravin, dec'd). [No exec'r]. Wits., William Craige, William Anderson Parker, Anderson Parker. Prob. March 31, 1721. Arch. vol. A108, page 34. Reg. of Wills, Liber A, folios 143-145.

**Miers, John.** Lewes. Will (copy). Made March 26, 1721. Heirs: wife Mary Miers; sons John and James Miers; daus. Mary and Sarah Miers. Exec'rx, wife Mary Miers. Wits., Alexander Molston, James Simson, Edward Miers. Prob. April 11, 1721. Arch. vol. A88, page 153. Reg. of Wills, Liber A, folios 148-150.

**Coe, Timothy.** Will (copy). Made Jan. 30, 1720. Heirs: wife unnamed; sons Daniel and Timothy; dau. Mary; son-in-law John Morgan. Exec'rx, wife unnamed. Wits., W. Rolins, Levin Gale, Thomas Dixon. Prob. April 22, 1721. Arch. vol. A65, page 72. Reg. of Wills, Liber A, folios 139-140.

**Futcher, John.** Yeoman. Will (copy). Made Feb. 3, 1720. Heirs: wife Mary; son William Futcher; cousins Mary Whitehead, Elizabeth Foster, James Asken; Tabitha and Sarah Walker (daus. of John Walker). Exec'rs, wife Mary Futcher and father-in-law John Prettyman. Wits., Richard Paynter, Margaret Paynter, Phil[ip] Russel. Prob. May 1, 1721. Arch. vol. A72, page 91. Reg. of Wills, Liber A, folios 141-142.

**May, Thomas, Jr.** Will (copy). Made Jan. 27, 1720/21. Heirs: wife Anna May; son Jonathan May; daus.-in-law Elizabeth and Mary May; Lucilla May. Exec'rx, wife Anna May. Wits., Samuel Kellso, Art Vankirk, Elizabeth May. Prob. May 11, 1721. Arch. vol. A87, page 100. Reg. of Wills, Liber A, folios 155-157.

**May, John.** Will (copy). Made May 7, 17 . . . Heirs: wife Elizabeth May; daus. Margret, Rosin, Sarah and Elizabeth May. Exec'rs, wife Elizabeth May, friend Abraham Wynkoop. Wits., William Sethredge, Cornelius Wiltbank, John Wynkoop. Prob. May 17, 1721. Arch. vol. A87, page 98. Reg. of Wills, Liber A, folios 308-309.

**Morris [Morrice], John.** Will (copy). Made April 10, 1721. Heirs: wife Mary Morris; Archabald Smith. Exec'rx, wife Mary Morris. Wits., W[illia]m Dauter, James Simson, Edward Parker, Patrick Delaney. Prob. May 20, 1721. Arch. vol. A90, page 74. Reg. of Wills, Liber A, folios 116-117 and Liber A, folios 150-151.

**Pettyjohn, Thomas.** Will (copy). Made April 9, 1721. Heirs: wife unnamed; dau. Isabell Pettyjohn; bro. Richard Pettyjohn. Exec'r, father John Pettyjohn. Wits., John Pettyjohn, Jr., W[illia]m Darter. Prob. July 24, 1721. Arch. vol. A93, page 14. Reg. of Wills, Liber A, folios 152-153.

**Prettyman, Robert.** Will (copy). Made July 13, 1720/21. Heirs: wife Sarah Prettyman; son William Prettyman; daus. Sarah, Catharine and Ann Prettyman; son-in-law Robert Lassey; dau.-in-law Elizabeth Lassey. Exec'rx, wife Sarah Prettyman. Wits., Woolsey Burton, Francis Pope, William Waples. Prob. Aug. 1, 1721. Arch. vol. A94, page 99, Reg. of Wills, Liber A, folios 154-155.

**Askey, James.** Yeoman. Will (copy). Made May 15, 1721. Heirs: James Walker, Esq.; Elizabeth Foster (wife of Thomas). Exec'r, James Walker, Esq. Wits., John Hill, John Price, Abraham Inloss, Cord Hazzard. Prob. Aug. 4, 1721. Arch. vol. A57, page 194. Reg. of Wills, Liber A, folios 153-154.

**Hall, Nathaniel, Sr.** Lewes. Will (copy). Made Jan. 8, 1713/14. Heirs: wife Jane Hall; nephew Nathaniel (son of bro. John Hall); Mary Prat. Exec'rx, wife Jane [also called Inna] Hall. Wits., Roger Train, Nathaniel Garner, Alexander Moleston. Prob. Sept. 8, 1721. Arch. vol. A73, page 236. Reg. of Wills, Liber A, folios 119-120.

**Piles, John.** Yeoman. Will (copy). Made Jan. 15, 1721/22. Heirs: wife Sarah Piles; son James Piles; Benjamin Carpenter. Exec'rx, wife Sarah Piles. Wits., Arthur Johnson, And[re]w White, William Craig. Prob. Jan. 31, 1721/22. Arch. vol. A93, page 86. Reg. of Wills, Liber A, folios 216-217.

**Davis, John.** Yeoman. Will (copy). Made March 10, 1721/22. Heirs: son John Davis; daus. Sarah, Mary and Cicely Davis. Exec'r, bro. John Smith. Wits., Thomas Grove, John Coursey, James White. Prob. March 22, 1721/22. Arch. vol. A68, page 77. Reg. of Wills, Liber A, folio 158.

**Williams, John.** Will (copy). Made April 12, 1722. Heirs: wife Alice Williams; son John Williams; dau. Elizabeth Williams. Exec'rx, wife Alice Williams. Wits., Humphry Turner, Harmon Harmonson, R[ichar]d Newcombe. Prob. April 21, 1722. Arch. vol. A107, page 186. Reg. of Wills, Liber A, folios 165-166.

**Smith, John.** Will (copy). Made April 23, 1722. Heirs: wife Mary Smith; daus. Hester, Ann, Patience and Feeby Smith; father-in-law John Hall; Joseph Colter; Martha Wilson; Elenor M. Cartney. Exec'rx, wife Mary Smith. Wits., William King, Rob Smith. Prob. June 3, 1722. Arch. vol. A99, page 165. Reg. of Wills, Liber A, folios 166-167.

**Hemmons, John.** Will (copy). Made Oct. 22, 1721. Heirs: wife Mary Hemmons; sons John and Thomas Hemmons; daus. Margaret and Mary Hemmons. Exec'rx, wife Mary Hemmons. Wits., William Daniley, Mapp Daniley. Prob. Aug. 23, 1722. Arch. vol. A76, page 35. Reg. of Wills, Liber A, folios 151-152.

**Fling, Daniel.** Will (copy). Made Aug. 7, 1722. Heirs: wife Esther and son Daniel Fling. [No exec'r]. Wits., James Holland, Charity Westly, Richard Westly. Prob. Sept. 4, 1722. Arch. vol. A71, page 207. Reg. of Wills, Liber A, folios 163-165.

**Paynter, Richard.** Yeoman. Will (copy). Made Nov. 21, 1722. Heirs: wife Marg[are]t Paynter; sons Richard, John and Doegood Paynter. Exec'rs, wife Marg[are]t Paynter and son Richard Paynter. Wits., Henry Courtman, Nicholas McLander, Phil[ip] Russel. Prob. Dec. 1, 1722. Arch. vol. A92, page 132. Reg. of Wills, Liber A, folios 162-163.

**Cary, John.** Will (copy). Made Sept. 15, 1723. Heirs: wife Bridget; sons Samuel, Thomas and William; and dau. Mary. Exec'rx, wife Bridget. Wits., Ebenezer Jones, Abraham Inloss, Phil[ip] Askie. Prob. Nov. 18, 1723. Arch. vol. A64, page 51. Reg. of Wills, Liber A, folios 169-170.

**Granger, Nicholas.** Planter. Will (copy). Made Feb. 1, 1723/24. Heir: wife Frances Granger. Exec'rx, wife Frances Granger. [No Wits.]. [No prob.]. Arch. vol. A72, page 250. Reg. of Wills, Liber A, folios 178-179.

**Codd, Berkeley.** Gentleman. Will (copy). Made Sept. 29, 1723. Heirs: wife Mary; bro. St. Legar; sister Mary Paterson (wife of Thomas Paterson of Dorset County, Maryland); and Rev. William Becket. Exec'rs, wife Mary and bro. St. Legar. Wits., William Becket, John Barr, Preserved Coggeshall. Overseers: William Shankland, Esq., and Jonathan Bailey. Prob. March 12, 1723/24. Arch. vol. A65, page 71. Reg. of Wills, Liber A, folios 167-169.

**Prettyman, John, Sr.** Will (copy). Made March 24, 1724. Heirs: sons John and William Prettyman; dau. Mary Day; grandsons John and James Prettyman (sons of William); granddau. Ann West. Exec'rs, sons John and James Prettyman, and dau. Mary Day. Wits., John West, Ann Handzor, Anderson Parker. Prob. March 31, 1724. Arch. vol. A94, page 71. Reg. of Wills, Liber A, folios 177-178.

**Wiltbanck, Cornelius.** Gentleman. Will (copy). Made March 10, 1723/24. Heirs: wife Hannah Wiltbanck; son Isaac Wiltbanck; bro. Abraham Wiltbanck; cousins Abraham, Jacob, Cornelius Wiltbanck; sons-in-law Ambrose and Jacob White; daus.-in-law Mary and Comfort White; Marg[are]t Simson. Exec'rs, friends William Beckett and Jacob Kollock. Wits.,

William Fisher, John Yorke, Jane Chamber. Prob. April 1, 1724. Arch. vol. A108, page 145. Reg. of Wills, Liber A, folios 174-177.

**White, William, Sr.** Carpenter. Will (copy). Made June 13, 1723. Heirs: wife Elizabeth White; sons Benjamin, John and William White; daus. Elizabeth Pettyjohn, Mary Little and Tabitha Virden; son-in-law John Simon. Exec'rx, wife Elizabeth White. Wits., Elias Bailey, Hannah Comings, Enoch Comings. Prob. May 9, 1724. Arch. vol. A107, page 90. Reg. of Wills, Liber A, folios 172-174.

**Burton, Robert, Jr.** Yeoman. Will (copy). Made April 25, 1724. Heirs: wife Catharine; sons William, Samuel, Robert and Joseph; daus. Catharine, Elizabeth, Comfort and Sarah. Exec'rs, wife Catharine and son William. Wits., Samuel Davis, William Burton, Danet Penoyre. Prob. May 28, 1724. Arch vol. A61, page 243. Reg. of Wills, Liber A, folios 184-186.

**McCulley, Alexander.** Will (copy). Made Aug. 28, 1724. Heirs: bro. John McKollah; sisters Elizabeth Gray and Ruth Craig; bro.-in-law Robert Craig; cousins Elizabeth, Mary, Hambleton, Robert Craig (children of Robert), Samuel Gray (son of David), Alexander McKollah (son of bro. John); friend David Cawhoun. Exec'r, bro. John McKollah. Wits., Samuel Davis, Hugh Hart, Adson Parker. Prob. Oct. 1, 1724. Arch. vol. A87, page 143. Reg. of Wills, Liber A, folios 182-184.

**Williams, Henry.** Yeoman. Will (copy). Made Sept. 18, 1723. Heirs: wife Marg[a]ret Williams; sons Jacob, Floid and Henry Williams; daus. Thamer and Rachel Williams. Exec'rx, wife Marg[a]ret Williams. Wits., William Cookson, Marg[a]ret Cookson, John May. Prob. Nov. 10, 1724. Arch. vol. A107, page 174. Reg. of Wills, Liber A, folios 170-171.

**Hinman, John.** Yeoman. Will (copy). Made Augu. 27, 1724. Heirs: wife Mary Hinman; sons John and Richard Hinman; dau. Elizabeth Hinman; bro. Richard Hinman (guardian of dau. Elizabeth). Exec'rs, sons John and Richard Hinman and wife Mary Hinman. Wits., John Hall, Samuel Black, Jennet F. Black. Prob. Jan. 1, 1724/25. Arch. vol. A76, page 178. Reg. of Wills, Liber A, folios 217-219.

**Wattson, Samuel.** Cedar Creek Hd. Will (copy). Made Dec. 21, 1724. Heirs: wife unnamed; sons John, Luke and Samuel Wattson; daus. Mary, Susanna, Elizabeth and Sarah Wattson. Exec'rs, unnamed wife and son Luke Wattson. Wits., William Till, Thomas Davis, Andrew Haverlo. Prob. Jan. 27, 1724/25. Arch. vol. A106, page 41. Reg. of Wills, Liber A, folios 179-181.

**May, Thomas.** Gentleman. Cedar Neck Hd. Will. Made Jan. 30, 1725. Heirs: wife Elizabeth May; son John May; dau. Lucilla Saltridge; grandson Jonathan May; granddaus. Elizabeth Saltridge, Margret, Rosen and Sarah May; Rev. William Beckett; Daniel Macdaniel. Exec'r, son John May. Wits., George Walton, E. Simson, John Russel. Prob. Feb. 19, 1725. Arch. vol. A87, page 101. Reg. of Wills, Liber A, folios 200-202.

**Smith, John.** Yeoman. Cedar Creek Hd. Will (copy). Made Feb. 19, 1724. Heirs: Wife unnamed; son Henry Smith; daus. Mary, Sarah and Elizabeth Smith. Exec'rx, unnamed wife. Wits., William Till, Mary Till, William Haverloe. Prob. May 5, 1725. Arch. vol. A99, page 166. Reg. of Wills, Liber A, folios 181-182.

**Clifton, Robert.** Yeoman. Will (copy). Made Feb. 20, 1824/25. Heirs: wife Mary; sons John, Robert, Ephraim, Absolam and William; dau. Mary. Exec'rx, wife Mary. Wits., Joseph Booth, John Richards, John May. Prob. May 7, 1725. Arch. vol. A65, page 45. Reg. of Wills, Liber A, folios 190-192.

**Johnson, Isaac.** Yeoman. Will (copy). Made Feb. 9, 1720/21. Heirs: bros. John and Alburtis Jacobs, John Kiphaven Johnson; sister Elizabeth Johnson. Exec'r, bro. John Jacobs. Wits., Samuel Black, Sam[uel] Davis, Jr., James White. Prob. May 7, 1725. Arch. vol. A81, page 40. Reg. of Wills, Liber A, folios 157-158.

**Nutter, John.** Yeoman. Will (copy). Made April 14, 1725. Heirs: wife Mary Nutter; sons John, Thomas and Purnell Nutter; daus. Betty and Mary Nutter. Exec'rx, wife Mary Nutter. Wits., Thomas Davis, Thomas Davis, Jr., Ja[me]s White. Prob. May 7, 1725. Arch. vol. A91, page 129. Reg. of Wills, Liber A, folios 202-204.

**Cole, Thomas.** Will (copy). Made Aug. 18, 1725. Heirs: wife Jane; sons John and William; daus. Sarah, Jane and Patience; son-in-law John Lewis. Exec'rx, wife Jane. Wits., John Gordon, John Roades, Elizabeth Gray. Prob. Aug. 28, 1725. Arch. vol. A65, page 117. Reg. of Wills, Liber A, folios 195-197.

**Burton, Robert.** Yeoman. Will (copy). Made Sept. 16, 1724. Heirs: wife Comfort; son William; daus. Sarah, Anne and Patience Burton, Elizabeth Prettyman (wife of William Prettyman), and Comfort Walker; grandchildren Robert, Joseph, Samuel, Catherine, Elizabeth, Comfort and Sarah children of Robert Burton, dec'd), Joseph and William (sons of Joseph Burton), Thomas Bagwell (son of Frances), Robert Prettyman (son of Robert Prettyman), Catherine, Cornelius, Jacob and Joseph (children of dau. Elizabeth Prettyman by her former husband Joseph Burton), nine children [unnamed] of dau. Mary Waples, dec'd (wife of William Waples), two children [unnamed] of dau. Comfort Walker by her first husband Thomas Prettyman; Elenor Letherberry. Exec'rs, wife Comfort and daus. Anne Burton, Sarah Prettyman and Patience Burton. Wits.: Thomas Leatherbury, Job Barker, Oliver Stockley. Overseers: John Rhodes and Richard Henman. Prob. Oct. 16, 1725. Arch. vol. A61, pages 241-242. Reg. of Wills, Liber A, folios 187-190.

**Williams, Morgan.** Will (copy). Made Oct. 21, 1725. Heirs: wife Sarah Williams; sons William, Joseph, Morgan and Aaron Williams; dau. Mary Williams. [No exec'r]. Wits., Henry Draper, Ann Watson, David Smith. Prob. Nov. 24, 1725. Arch. vol. A108, page 18. Reg. of Wills, Liber A, folios 193-195.

**Fisher, William, Esq.** Will (copy). Made Dec. 10, 1725. Heirs: wife Rebecca; son Elias Fisher; dau. Rebecca Conwell; grandsons William and John Conwell; granddaus. Hannah Conwell and Mary Grove; cousins Henry Fisher and Elias Conwell. Exec'rs, son Elias Fisher and friend Philip Russell. Wits., Jonathan Baily, Marg[a]ret Stretcher, John Hinman. Prob. Dec. 22, 1725. Arch. vol. A71, page 159. Reg. of Wills, Liber A, folios 197-199.

**Marsh, Peter.** Will (copy). Made Nov. 27, 1725. Heirs: sons Peter, Joseph and James Marsh; dau. Elizabeth Marsh. Exec'r, friend Richard Hinman. Wits., Alexander Richie, Hugh Richie, John Roades. Prob. Jan. 1, 1725/26. Arch. vol. A86, page 116. Reg. of Wills, Liber A, folios 199-200.

**Hill, John.** Yeoman. Will (copy). Made Jan. 28, 1725/26. Heirs: wife Sarah Hill; sons John, Absalom and Robert Hill; dau. Elizabeth Hill. Exec'rs, wife Sarah Hill, son John Hill, and friend Philip Askne. Wits., James Walker, Tho[mas] Cokayne, Abraham Inloss. Prob. Feb. 18, 1725/26. Arch. vol. A76, page 128. Reg. of Wills, Liber A, folios 204-206.

**Henry, Gabriel.** Cooper. Will (copy). Made April 27, 1725. Heir: wife Catharine Henry. Exec'rx, wife Catharine Henry. Wits., James H. Hevorly, Cano Hevorly, John Bennett. Prob. May 11, 1726. Arch. vol. A76, page 50. Reg. of Wills, Liber A, folios 192-193.

**McIlvaine [Muckelvaine, McCalvaine], Andrew.** Yeoman. Will (copy). Made Oct. 4, 1726. Heirs: sons John, James, George and Andrew McCalvaine; dau. Martha McCalvaine; Andrew McKee; William McKee; Alexander Mucklewaine. Exec'r, son James McCalvaine. Wits., Daniel Micker, Tho[mas] Cokayne, . . . Mackelvaine. Prob. Oct. 28, 1726. Arch. vol. A87, page 170. Reg. of Wills, Liber A, folios 206-207.

**Dod, George.** Will (copy). Made Dec. 5, 1726. Heirs: wife Naomy Dod; son George Dod; other children unnamed; John Pettyjohn, grandfather of my son; William Pettyjohn, uncle of my son. Exec'rs, Thomas Dod and John Pettyjohn. Wits., William Pettyjohn, Rob[ert] Smith. Prob. Dec. 12, 1726. Arch. vol. A69, page 98. Reg. of Wills, Liber A, folios 207-208.

**Bennett, John, Jr.** Yeoman. Will (copy). made Jan. 4, 1726/27. Heirs: wife Grace and son John. Exec'rx, wife Grace. Wits., Dormand Lofland, James White, Margaret Henry. Prob. Jan. 27, 1726/27. Arch. vol. A59, page 81. Reg. of Wills, Liber A, folios 208-209.

**Warrington, Stephen.** Cooper. Will (copy). Made Feb. 4, 1722/23. Heirs: wife Mary Warrington; son Stephen Warrington; daus. Catharine, Mary, Elizabeth and Tabitha Warrington, and Sarah Hill. Exec'rx, wife Mary Warrington and daus. Catharine, Mary, Elizabeth and Tabitha Warrington. Wits., Dennis McCarty, Sarah Parsons, Cord Hazzard. Prob. April 1, 1727. Arch. vol. A105, page 167. Reg. of Wills, Liber A, folios 159-162.

**Racliff, Nathaniel.** Will (copy). Made March 11, 1726. Heirs: wife unnamed; son Nathaniel Racliff; daus. Mary, Elizabeth and Hannah Racliff. Exec'rx, wife [Mary Racliff]. Wits., Woodman Stockley, Jno. Thomson, John Thomson. Prob. April 15, 1727. Arch. vol. A94, page 187. Reg. of Wills, Liber A, folios 221-223.

**Godwin, William.** Will (nunc. copy). Made June 13, 1727. Heirs: wife unnamed; son William Godwin; daus. Anne and Hannah Godwin. Exec'r, unnamed. Wits., Henry Fisher, Joseph Godwin. Joseph Turner. Prob. June 14, 1727. Arch. vol. A72, page 169. Reg. of Wills, Liber A, folios 229-230.

**Rowland, Samuel, Esq.** Will (copy). Made Jan. 22, 1725. Heirs: wife Jennet Rowland; sons William and Samuel Rowland; dau. Mary Eldridge (wife of Joseph); grandsons Thomas and John Rowland; granddau. Sarah Rowland; son-in-law Joseph Eldridge. Exec'rs, son William Rowland, son-in-law Joseph Eldridge. Wits., Simon Kollock, Sam[ue]l Davis, Phil[lip] Russel. Prob. Dec. 20, 1727. Arch. vol. A97, page 115. Reg. of Wills, Liber A, folios 219-221.

**Green, Nicholas.** Will (copy). Made Dec. 31, 1724. Heir: wife Jemima Green. Exec'rx, wife Jemima Green. Wits., William Godwin, Marg[a]ret Simson, John Rhoads. Prob. Jan. 15, 1728. Arch. vol. A73, page 67. Reg. of Wills, Liber A, folios 186-187.

**Cornwallice, William.** Will (copy). Made March 24, 1727/8. Heirs: wife Rebecca; dau.-in-law Hannah Conwell; and sons-in-law John and William Conwell. Exec'rs, wife Rebecca and John May. Wits., William Fisher, John Fisher, David Mackain. Prob. April 9, 1728. Arch. vol. A66, page 227. Reg. of Wills, Liber A, folios 225-227. [Note:—Arch. vol. A66, page 227 mentions Yeats Conwell, wife's former husband].

**Seymour, Ebenezer.** Somerset County, Md. Will (copy). Made May 3, 1728. Heirs: wife unnamed; Edmond Cropper; friend John Dagworthy. Exec'rs, friends John Dagworthy and Samuel Davis. Wits., John Hullack, John Mixon. Prob. Aug. 7, 1728. Arch. vol. A98, page 46. Reg. of Wills, Liber A, folios 305-306.

**Palmer, Daniel.** Yeoman. Will (copy). Made 12th day, 11th mo. [January], 1727. Heirs: wife Mary Palmer; son Joseph Palmer; dau. Sarah Palmer. Exec'rx, wife Mary Palmer. Wits., John May, Thomas Gray, Judith Rickets. Prob. Sept. 6, 1728. Arch. vol. A92, page 39. Reg. of Wills, Liber A, folios 230-231.

**King, Hugh.** Will (copy). Made Oct. 23, 1728. Heirs: wife unnamed; son James King; dau. Prisilla King; son-in-law Newcomb Braben; bro. Philip King; sister Sarah Ralph. Exec'rs, wife and bro. Philip King. Wits., Ann Bravan, Jean Craige, William Craige. Prob. Nov. 29, 1728. Arch. vol. A82, page 102. Reg. of Wills, Liber A, folios 304-305.

**Mullinex, Penelope.** Will (copy). Made Dec. 26, 1720. Heirs: sons William and John Mullinex; daus. Mary Mullinex and Penelope O'Brian. Exec'rx, dau. Mary Mullinex. Wits.,

William Dainley, Joseph Lane, John May. Prob. Jan. 17, 1729. Arch. vol. A90, page 172. Reg. of Wills, Liber A, folios 214-215.

**Jackson, John.** Yeoman. Will (copy). Made Jan. 4, 1729. Heirs: wife Sarah Jackson; son Joseph Bains Jackson. Exec'rx, wife Sarah Jackson. Wits., Henry Fisher, John Lech, James White. Prob. Jan. 21, 1729. Arch. vol. A80, page 22. Reg. of Wills, Liber A, folios 239-240.

**Pepperlo, Joseph.** Cedar Creek Hd. Will (copy). Made Jan. 17, 1729. Heirs: Thomas Lay; Thomas Davis, Sr.; Elizabeth Davis, (wife of Thomas); wife of William Heaverloe. Exec'r, friend Thomas Davis, Sr. Wits., Luke Wattson, Thomas Davis, Jr., Nehemiah Davis. Prob. Jan. 28, 1729. Arch. vol. A92, page 169. Reg. of Wills, Liber A, folios 491-493.

**Walton, George.** Gentleman. Will (copy). Made Feb. 6, 1729. Heirs: wife; sons John, George, Huling and Joseph Walton. Exec'r, bro. John Walton. Wits., Abraham Wynkoop, Ja[me]s McMillin, Patience Twilley. Prob. Feb. 24, 1729. Arch. vol. A104, page 196. [No Reg. of Wills Liber].

**Wattson, John.** Yeoman. Will (copy). Made Jan. 3, 1729. Heirs: wife Sarah Wattson; sons James, Luke and Hezekith Wattson; daus. Mary Wattson and Elizabeth Townsend (wife of Stephen). Exec'rx, wife Sarah Wattson. Wits., Chris Philipson, Elizabeth Cirwithin, Ja[me]s White. Prob. Feb. 27, 1729. Arch. vol. A106, page 18. Reg. of Wills, Liber A, folios 237-239.

**Miers, Mary.** Widow. Lewes. Will (copy). Made Aug. 27, 1707. Heirs: sons John and James Miers; Daniel Palmer, Jonathan Ozburn; daus. Sarah Ozburn, Mary Palmer; grand-daus. Sarah Palmer, Sarah Rowland, Elizabeth and Sarah Miers; grandsons Joseph Palmer, Samuel Rowland, John Rowland and John Miers. [No exec'r]. Wits., William Burton, Edward Rickets, Judith Rickets. Prob. May 7, 1729. Arch. vol. A88, page 156. Reg. of Wills, Liber A, folios 235-236.

**Waltham, John.** Laborer. Will (copy). Made Sept. 25, 1729. Heirs: bro. Stephen Waltham; uncle Phillip Askue. Exec'r, uncle Phillip Askue. Wits., Jos[eph] Carter, Samuel Davis, John Day. Prob. Oct. 1, 1729. Arch. vol. A102, page 127. Reg. of Wills, Liber A, folios 236-237.

**Smith, Archibald.** Merchant. Lewes. Will (copy). Made Nov. 27, 1729. Heirs: wife Isabella Smith; sisters Mary Simonton (wife of Toplielus [Theopolus] Simonton) and Rachel

Curry (in Ireland); cousins Ann Edmonton, James and Jennett Smith (children of Robert), Adam and James Smith (of Ireland); Anne, Mary and Magdalen (daus of bro. Robert Smith, in Ireland); Jane Thomson (dau. of Rev. John Thomson). Exec'r, cousin James Smith. Wits., John Shankland, W[illia]m Molleston, Phil[ip] Russel. Prob. Dec. 4, 1729. Arch. vol. A99, page 115. Reg. of Wills, Liber A, folios 240-243. [Note:—Arch. vol. A99, page 115 mentions dec'd uncle, Robert Perrie].

**Wiltbanck, Abraham.** Yeoman. Will. Made Jan. 1, 1729/30. Heirs: wife Ann Wiltbanck; sons Abraham and Jacob Wiltbanck. Exec'rs, wife Ann Wiltbanck and sons Abraham and Jacob Wiltbanck. Wits., John Parker, Susannah Parker, Tho[mas] Cokayne. Prob. Feb. 11, 1730. Arch. vol. A108, page 143. Reg. of Wills, Liber A, folios 245-246.

**Simson, James.** Yeoman. Lewes. Will. Made Jan. 27, 1730. Heirs: wife Margaret Simson; daus. Elizabeth and Margaret Simson, and Mary Ponter. Exec'rx, wife Margaret Simson. Wits., John Shankland, R. Shankland, John Asson. Prob. Feb. 19, 1730. Arch. vol. A99, page 68. Reg. of Wills, Liber A, folios 246-248.

**Burton, Woolsey.** Will (copy). Made April 9, 1728. Heirs: wife Anne; sons John, Woolsey and Benjamin; and daus. Anne, Agnes, Comfort and Patience. Exec'rx, wife Anne. Wits., [...] Cummings, Esq., Thomas Gear, Phil[ip] Russel. Prob. July 18, 1730. Arch. vol. A62, pages 46-47. Reg. of Wills, Liber A, folios 231-234. [Note:—Arch. vol. A62, page 46 mentions dec'd father-in-law Robert Burton].

**Rackliff, Mary.** Widow of Nathaniel. Will (copy). Made Nov. 19, 1730. Heirs: son Nathaniel Rackliff; daus. Hannah, Pathenia, Mary and Elizabeth Rackliff. Exec'r, Woodman Stockley. Wits., Alex[ande]r Cambell, C. Fowler, John Russell. Guardan, Edmond Crapper. Prob. Nov. 24, [1730]. Arch. vol. A94, page 186. Reg. of Wills, Liber A, folios 248-250.

**Shankland, William W., Sr.** Gentleman. Will (copy). Made Sept. 14, 1730. Heirs: sons William, Robert, John and Joseph Shankland; grandchildren Sarah, Esther and John (children of son John Shankland), Robert, William and Elizabeth (children of son Robert Shankland), Andrew, Margaret, Elizabeth and 3 other granddaus. unnamed (children of dau. Elizabeth Thomson, dec'd). Exec'r, son Joseph Shankland.

Wits., Tho[ma]s Gear, Mary Gear, Joshua Fisher. Prob. Feb. 7, 1730/31. Arch. vol. A98, page 62. Reg. of Wills, Liber A, 250-253.

**Cary, Edward.** Yeoman. Will (copy). Made Jan. 25, 1731. Heirs: wife Anne; sons Thomas, Edward and William; daus. Mary, Bette and Rohade [Rhoda]. Exec'rx, wife Anne. Wits., David Lane, Elizabeth Cowden, John May. Prob. Feb. 27, 173[1]. Arch. vol. A64, page 33. Reg. of Wills, Liber A, folios 243-245.

**Walker, Thomas.** Will (copy). Made Sept. 22, 1731. Heirs: wife Comfort Walker; sons Jacob, James and George Walker; dau. Comfort Walker. Exec'rx, wife Comfort Walker. Wits., William Prettyman, Thomas Prettyman. Prob. Oct. 11, 1731. Arch. vol. A104, page 37. Reg. of Wills, Liber A, folios 253-255.

**Finwick, Thomas.** Will (copy). Made March 22, 1708. Heirs: son James Finwick; daus. Anne Clifton and Margaret Stretcher (wife of Edward); grandson Thomas Clifton; granddau. Sarah Clifton; son-in-law Edward Stretcher; Robert Clifton; Marg[a]ret Hepbourn and Jacob Kollock. Exec'rs, Samuel Davis and John Hepburn. Wits., Phillip Russell, John Hepburn, John Coe. Codicil, March 28, 1708. Prob. Jan. 13, 1732. Arch. vol. A71, page 77. Reg. of Wills, Liber A, folios 262-263.

**Lewis, Wrixam.** Will (copy). Made April 26, 1732. Heirs: wife Esther [Hester] Lewis; son Wrixham Lewis; daus. Elizabeth and Sarah Lewis. Exec'rs, wife Esther Lewis and friend Jacob Kollock. Wits., John Lewis, William Cole, Elizabeth Russell. Prob. May 10, 1732. Arch. vol. A84, page 71. Reg. of Wills, Liber A, folios 258-260.

**Paynter, John, Sr.** Blacksmith. Will (copy). Made Aug. 5, 1732. Heirs: wife Mary; sons John, Samuel, William, Richard and James Paynter. Exec'rx, wife Mary Paynter. Wits., Jacob Kollock, Jacob Phillips, Richard Wilson. Prob. Oct. 4, 1732. Arch. vol. A92, page 121. Reg. of Wills, Liber A, folios 260-261.

**Willson, Thomas.** Will (copy). Made March 8, 1727/8. Heirs: wife Mary Wilson; sons Daniel and William Wilson; daus. Sarah, Jemimah, Rebecah and Mary Wilson, Elizabeth White, Mercy Lay and Anne Lee. Exec'rs, wife Mary Wilson and son David Wilson. Wits., John May, Elizabeth Wilson, Jr., William Boutton. Prob. Oct. 17, 1732. Arch. vol. A108, page 122. Reg. of Wills, Liber A, folios 227-229.

**Finwick, James.** Will (copy). Made Dec. 21, 1732. Heirs: wife Sidney; sons Thomas, William and James; daus. Mary and Sidney Finwick. Exec'rx, wife Sidney. Wits., David Macklain, Henry Martin, Jabiz Maud Fisher. Prob. Jan. 13, 1732/33. Arch. vol. A71, page 75. Reg. of Wills, Liber A, folios 262-263.

**Miller, Robert.** Weaver. Will (copy). Made Jan. 16, 1732/33. Heirs: sons John, Robert and William Miller; daus. Mary, Anne and Elizabeth Miller; James Andrew. Exec'rs, son John Miller and James Andrew. Wits., Josh[ua] Hickman, Elizabeth Davis, James White. Overseers, Thomas Davis, Thomas Price. Prob. Jan. 27, 1732/33. Arch. vol. A89, page 1. Reg. of Wills, Liber A, folios 256-258.

**Manlove, Sarah.** Will (copy). Made Jan. 27, 1732/33. Heirs: bro. Henry Spencer; sister Hannah Spencer; cousins Mary and Elizabeth Manlove; Nottingham Jacobs. Exec'r, bro. Henry Spencer. Wits., John Way, William Spencer, Margaret VanKirk. Prob. Feb. 8, 1732/33. Arch. vol. A86, page 43. Reg. of Wills, Liber A, folios 255-256.

**Roades, John.** Gentleman. Will (copy). Made March 23, 1732. Heirs: wife Alice Roades; sons William and John Roades; daus. Alice, Patience and Agnes Roades, Elizabeth Wiltbanck (wife of Jacob), and Comfort Wiltbanck (wife of Cornelius); sons-in-law John and William Walker; daus.-in-law Elizabeth Walker and Mary Coe; grandchildren Jacob and Abraham Wiltbanck (children of Jacob), John and Elizabeth Wiltbanck (children of Cornelius); Presbyterian Meeting House. Exec'rs, wife Alice and son John Roades. Wits., Richard Hinman, Jonathan Henry, Robert Shankland. Prob. April 2, 1733. Arch. vol. A96, page 74. Reg. of Wills, Liber A, folios 415-418.

**Dogin, Cornelius.** Will (copy). Made May 3, 1733. Heir: Elizabeth Ann Carady. Exec'rx, Elizabeth Ann Carady. Wits., John Chapman, Richard Jefferson, Gilbert Mariner. Prob. May 12, 1733. Arch. vol. A69, page 114. Reg. of Wills, Liber A, folio 265.

**Loughten, John.** Yeoman. Will (copy). Made Feb. 15, 1732/33. Heirs: wife Persilla Loughten; sons William, Cornelius, Gabriel, Dormond and John Loughten; daus. Elizabeth and Rosanna Loughten, and Persilla Letton. Exec'rx, wife Persilla Loughten. Wits., Robert Turk, Jonas Webb, Cornelius Loughlen. Prob. June 8, 1733. Arch. vol. A85, page 54. Reg. of Wills, Liber A, folios 265-267.

**Pettyjohn, John.** Yeoman. Will (copy). Made Oct. 26, 1733. Heirs: sons Richard, William, John and James Pettyjohn; grandson George Dodd; granddaus. Isabell Pettyjohn and Rachel Reed. Exec'rs, sons William and Richard Pettyjohn. Wits., Sam[ue]l Blundell, John Russell, John Nixon. Prob. Nov. 5, 1733. Arch. vol. A93, page 7. Reg. of Wills, Liber A, folios 263-265.

**Pemberton, Joseph.** Yeoman. Lewes. Will (copy). Made April 8, 1734. Heirs: wife Susanna Pemberton; children unnamed. Exec'rx, wife Susanna Pemberton. Wits., Simon Kollock, Henry Fisher, William Beckett. Prob. April 13, 1734. Arch. vol. A92, page 146. Reg. of Wills, Liber A, folies 273-274.

**Parsons, John.** Carpenter. Will (copy). Made April 11, 1734. Heirs: wife Sarah Parsons; sons Jno., Thomas and Isaac Parsons; daus. Neomy Parsons, Esther Butler (wife of William), Mary Knawood. Exec'rx, wife Sarah Parsons. Wits., John Hill, Wiilliam Hazzard, Joseph Burton. Prob. April 30, 1734. Arch. vol. A92, page 99. Reg. of Wills, Liber A, folios 274-275.

**Jacobs, Richard.** Yeoman. Will (copy). Made April 22, 1734. Heirs: wife Hannah Jacobs; sons Jonathan and Nottingham Jacobs; daus. Rachel Jacobs, Elizabeth Kirk; child unnamed; cousin Leah Nawse. Exec'rs, wife Hannah Jacobs and friend Abraham Parsley. Wits., Peter Hendrickson, Jno. Reading, Elizabeth Jacobs. Prob. May 11, 1734. Arch. vol. A80, page 73. Reg. of Wills, Liber A, folios 267-270.

**Chant, William.** Yeoman. Will (copy). Made Oct. 5, 1732. Heirs: wife Mary; son Spencer; and daus. Mary Anne and Avis. Exec'rx, wife Mary. Wits., William Daniley, Lewis Davis, John May. Prob. June 9, 1734. Arch. vol. A64, page 129. Reg. of Wills, Liber A, folios 275-277.

**Hall, Nathaniel.** Mariner. Lewes. Will (copy). Made Jan. 1, 1734/35. Heirs: wife Jane Hall; sons David and Peter Hall; daus. Bersheba and Lydia Hall; children of daughter Mary. Exec'rs, sons David and Peter Hall. Wits., William Powell, Mary Bassnett, Ralph Bassnett. Prob. Feb. 7, 1734/35. Arch. vol. A73, page 237. Reg. of Wills, Liber A, folios 277-279.

**Holland, James.** Yeoman. Will (copy). Made Feb. 19, 1734/35. Heirs: wife Mary Holland; sons William, James and John Holland, daus. Esther, Elizabeth and Mary Holland; granddau. Esther Woodward. Exec'rs, wife Mary Holland and son

William Holland. Wits., William Stockley, William Becket. Prob. March 6, 1734/35. Arch. vol. A77, page 86. Reg. of Wills, Liber A, folios 270-271.

**Draper, Alexander.** Merchant. Will. Made March 1, 1727/28. Heirs: wife Anne Draper; sons Alexander, William, John, Samuel, Joseph and Nehemiah Draper; daus. Anne and Mary Draper. Exec'rx, wife Anne Draper. Wits., Anthony Woodward, Isaac Warner, James White. Prob. March 12, 1734/35. Arch. vol. A69, page 181. Reg. of Wills, Liber A, folio 223.

**Hickman, Joshua.** Yeoman. Will (copy). Made March 13, 1734/35. Heirs: wife Rebecca Hickman; sons Joshua, Joseph, Isaac and Jacob Hickman; daus. Naomy, Elizabeth, Sarah and Rebecca Hickman. Exec'rs, wife Rebecca Hickman and son Joseph Hickman. Wits., John May, Joshua Madock, Joseph Williams. Prob. March 19, 1734/35. Arch. vol. A76, page 72. Reg. of Wills, Liber A, folios 271-273.

**May, Anne.** Widow. Will (copy). Made Sept. 20, 1736. Heirs: son Jonathan May; daus. Mary Davis (wife of Nehemiah), Elizabeth Manlove. Exec'rs, son Jonathan May and son-in-law Nehemiah Davis. Wits., John Davis, Frances Parsley, Ja[me]s White. Prob. Oct. 4, 1736. Arch. vol. A87, page 89. Reg. of Wills, Liber A, folios 279-281.

**Sharp, Richard.** Surgeon. Late of the Parish of Saint Dunstans in the West of the City of London, now of Lewes. Will (copy). Made Sept. 28, 1735. Heirs: wife Anna Maria Sharp. Exec'rx, wife Anna Maria Sharp. Wits., Simon Kollock, W[illia]m Becket, Daniel Munez. Prob. Oct. 18, 1736. Arch. vol. A98, page 94. Reg. of Wills, Liber A, folios 283-284.

**Russell, Joseph.** Will (copy). Made Oct. 10, 1736. Heirs: wife Sarah Russell; sons Joseph, Jacob, Thomas, Samuel, Ephraim and Phillip Russell; dau. Sarah Russell. Exec'rx, wife Sarah Russell. Wits., Robert Weare, Edward Lay, Enoch Cummings. Prob. Dec. 4, 1736. Arch. vol. A97, page 141. Reg. of Wills, Liber A, folios 285-288.

**Townsend, William.** Yeoman. Will (copy). Made Jan. 4, 1728/29. Heirs: wife Elizabeth Townsend; sons Stephen, Costin, Solomon and Charles Townsend; daus. Abigail Townsend and Elizabeth Deputy; son-in-law Silvester Deputy. Exec'r, son Costin Townsend. Wits., Simon Beply, Philip Dernie, John May. Prob. Jan. 17, 1736/37. Arch. vol. A102, page 83. Reg. of Wills, liber A, folios 284-285.

**Herring, Alexander.** Will (copy). Made Sept. 19, 1735. Heirs: wife Margaret Herring; son Alexander Herring; daus. Cady Herring; Esther Wood and Sarah Prettyman. Exec'r, son Alexander Herring. Wits., John Mariner, Elizabeth Mariner, John Russell, Sr. Prob. March 22, 1736/37. Arch. vol. A76, page 59. Reg. of Wills, Liber A, folios 288-290.

**Draper, Henry.** Yeoman. Will (copy). Made Feb. 22, 1736/37. Heirs: wife Sarah Draper; sons Henry, Isaac and Avery; daus. Elizabeth Draper, Sarah Davis (wife of Thomas); dau.-in-law Rebeckah Cirwithin. Exec'rx, wife Sarah Draper. Wits., Hanes Birestrim, John Aston, Joseph White. Prob. March 23, 1736/37. Arch. vol. A69, page 190. Reg. of Wills, Liber A, folios 281-282.

**Williams, John.** Will (copy). Made April 14, 1737. Heirs: wife Mary Williams. Exec'rx, wife Mary Williams. Wits., Comfort Moleston, Mary McIntosh, Joseph Carter. Prob. May 24, 1737. Arch. vol. A107, page 187. Reg. of Wills, Liber A, folio 295.

**Baily, Jonathan, Sr.** Will (copy). Made Aug. 1, 1737. Heirs: sons James and Jonathan; daus. Sarah Baily, Mary Naws and Hannah and Abigail Jacobs; seven grandchildren unnamed (children of son Elias, dec'd). Exec'rs, sons James and Jonathan and daus. Sarah Baily; Mary Naws, Hannah and Abigail Jacobs. Wits., Nehemiah Field, Luke Shield, Phil[lip] Russel. Prob. Sept. 13, 1737. Arch. vol. A58, page 76. Reg. of Wills, Liber A, folios 293-295.

**Price, Thomas.** Yeoman. Will (copy). Made Oct. 22, 1737. Heirs: son Thomas Price; cousins John Langden, Rachel Willson, William Airy, Marg[a]ret Airy. Exec'rs, son Thomas Price and Nepthali Carpenter. Wits., Nehemiah Davis, Mary Davis, Ja[me]s White. Prob. Oct. 22, 1737. Arch. vol. A94, page 141. Reg. of Wills, Liber A, folios 311-313.

**Onorton, John.** Will (copy). Made Dec. 20, 1737. Heirs: wife Isabella Onorton; daus. Morton [Norton] Onorton and Elizabeth Briedel; grandson John Smith (son of William and Mary Smith); friend Charles Powell. Exec'rs, wife Isabella Onorton and dau. Morton [Norton] Onorton. Wits., William Laughinhouse, John Russell, Charles Powell. Prob. Feb. 8, 1737/38. Arch. vol. A91, page 164. Reg. of Wills, Liber A, folios 290-293.

**Ozburn, Mathew.** Yeoman. Will (copy). Made Dec. 10, 1733. Heirs: wife Mary Ozburn; sons Mathew, Thomas and Henry

Ozburn; dau. Mary Hand; grandsons Jonathan Ozburn, Samuel Ozburn (son of son Mathew); granddau. Mary Ozburn. Exec'rs, sons Thomas and Henry Ozburn. Wits., John Brice, Benjamin May, Frances Dunnarant. Prob. April 2, 1738. Arch. vol. A92, page 32. Reg. of Wills, Liber A, folios 295-297.

**Cord, Joseph.** Planter. Broadkill Hd. Will (copy). Made April 3, 1738. Heirs: wife Ann; sons John, Hezekiah and Joseph; and daus. Ann, Esther and Elizabeth. Exec'rs, wife Ann and son John. Wits., John Wright, Ann Hill, William Becket. Prob. May 5, 1738. Arch. vol. A66, pages 185-186. Reg. of Wills, Liber A, folios 298-301.

**Johnson, Agness.** Will (copy). Made June 19, 1738. Heirs: sons John and Samuel Johnson. Exec'rs, Hugh Thomson, Robert Crevens. Wits., Robert McCarrell, Anne McCarrell. Prob. Aug. 10, 1738. Arch. vol. A81, page 9. Reg. of Wills, Liber A, folios 297-298.

**Carpenter, James.** Yeoman. Will. Made . . . 1734. Heirs: sons William, James, Laban, Benjamin and Nepthali; and daus. Affiance and Elizabeth Carpenter, Bathsheba Davis. Exec'r, son Nepthali. Wits., Thomas Davis, Nehemiah Davis, James White. Prob. Oct. 18, 1738. Arch. vol. A63, page 229. Reg. of Wills, Liber A, folios 302-304.

**Newcomb, Baptis.** Will (copy). Made April 12, 1739. Heirs: wife Rachel Newcomb; sons Baptis and Thomas Newcomb; dau. Rachel Dod; children of Ann Lay and children of Thomas Newcomb. Exec'rx, wife Rachel Newcomb. Wits., Newcomb Braven, Anne King. Prob. May 10, 1739. Arch. vol. A91, page 76. Reg. of Wills, Liber A, folios 306-308.

**Carpenter, Affiance.** Widow of James Carpenter. Will (copy). Made Nov. 20, 1739. Heirs: sons William, James, Laben, Benjamin and Nepthali; daus. Elizabeth Carpenter and Affiiance Wattson; granddau. Betty Davis; grandson Piles Carpenter (son of William). Exec'rx, dau. Elizabeth. Wits., John Langen, Margaret Langen, David Smith. Prob. Jan. 8, 1740. Arch. vol. A63, page 214. Reg. of Wills, Liber A, folios 320-321. [Note:—Arch. vol. A63, page 214 mentions father William Piles].

**Goldsmith, Thomas.** Yeoman. Will (copy). Made March 2, 1739/40. Heirs: son Thomas Goldsmith; daus. Jemima, Comfort, Mary, Naomy Goldsmith and Patience Williams (wife of Joseph). Exec'rs, son Thomas Goldsmith and son-in-law Joseph Williams. Wits., Thomas Wattson, John Reading, Jonathan May. Prob. March 25, 1739/40. Arch. vol. A72, page 170. Reg. of Wills, Liber A, folios 309-311. [Note:—Arch. vol. A72, page 170 mentions a bequest to servant man Peter Riggs].

**Shankland, John.** Lewes. Will (copy). Made April 10, 1740. Heirs: wife Mary Shankland; sons David and John Shankland; daus. Sarah and Esther Shankland; child unnamed; Jane Hall (grandmother of dau. Sarah). Exec'rs, bro. Joseph Shankland, cousin William Shankland. Guardians: Rev. James Martin, bro. Peter Hall. Prob. April 20, 1740. Arch. vol. A98, page 51. Reg. of Wills, Liber A, folios 313-319. [Note:—Arch. vol. A98, page 51 mentions dec'd father William Shankland, and late bro. Robert Shankland].

**Nutter, John.** Will (copy). Made May 1, 1740. Heirs: sister Betty Smith; cousin David and Mary Smith (children of sister Betty), Mary Nutter (dau. of Christopher Nutter; uncle Christopher Nutter; bro.-in-law John Smith; Isaac Wattson; Bethuel Wattson. Exec'r, bro.-in-law John Smith. Wits., David Smith, W[illia]m Smith, Rebeckah Hickman. Prob. May 28, 1740. Arch. vol. A91, page 130. Reg. of Wills, Liber A, folios 319-320.

**Williams, Mary.** Will (copy). Made Feb. 22, 1738. Heirs: bro. Samuel Johnson; grandson John Lewis; granddaus. Mary and Nanny Lewis. Exec'r, son-in-law William Lewis. Wits., Tabitha Green, Joseph Carter, Comfort Moleston. Prob. Dec. 10, 1740. Arch. vol. A108, page 15. Reg. of Wills, Liber A, folios 301-302.

**Wiltbanck, Cornelius.** Will (copy). Made Feb. 7, 1741. Heirs: wife Comfort Wiltbanck; son John Wiltbanck; daus. Elizabeth and Mary Wiltbanck; Hinman and John Rhoads (sons of John Rhoads, dec'd) ; grandfather Harmanus Wiltbanck. Exec'rs, wife Comfort Wiltbanck, Joshua Fisher. Wits., Henry Fisher, Sarah Palmer, William Shankland. Prob. March 23, 1741. Arch. vol. A108, page 146. Reg. of Wills, Liber A, folios 321-323.

**Hopkins, Samuel, Sr.** Yeoman. Will (copy). Made March 6, 1741. Heirs: wife Tenat Hopkins; sons William and Samuel Hopkins; daus. Marg[a]ret, Ann and Jean Hopkins. Exec'rs, friends Archabald Hopkins and Robert Neill. Wits., William Hopkins, Richard Loucom. Prob. April 15, 1741. Arch. vol. A78, page 20. Reg. of Wills, Liber A, folios 328-329.

**Reed, William.** Yeoman. Will (copy). Made Nov. 1, 1739. Heirs: wife Jane Reed; sons John and William Reed; friend John

Bowdan. [No exec'r]. Wits., Woodman Stockley, Daniel
Hoseman, Martha Cary. Prob. May 9, 1741. Arch. vol. A95,
page 41. Reg. of Wills, Liber A, folios 324-325.

**Day, William.** Will (copy). Made Nov. 24, 1741. Heirs: sons
Prettyman and George Day; daus. Marg[a]ret Hill and
Mary West. Exec'r, son Prettyman Day. Wits., William
Boucher, Hugh Verdin, John White. Prob. Dec. 2, 1741.
Arch. vol. A68, pages 185-186. Reg. of Wills, Liber A, folios
326-327.

**Bracy, Richard.** Yeoman. Will (copy). Made March 28, 1741.
Heirs: daus. Sarah Christopher (wife of Wr[i]xham) and
Bridget Pratt; and sons-in-law Wr[i]xham Christopher and
Charles Pratt. Exec'rs, Charles and Bridget Pratt. Wits.,
Robert Homes, Thomas Gragg. Prob. Dec. 12, 1741. Arch.
vol. A69, page 78. Reg. of Wills, Liber A, folios 329-330.

**Salthredge, William.** Bricklayer. Will (copy). Made Dec. 26,
1741. Heirs: son William Salthredge; daus. Elizabeth
Agnes, Mary and Rosen May Salthredge. Exec'rs, friends
Jacob Kollock, Abraham Wynkoop. Wits., Elizabeth May,
Rob[ert] Jameson, James Fisher. Prob. March 1, 1741/42.
Arch. vol. A98, page 4. Reg. of Wills, Liber A, folios 323-
324.

**Littleton, Jonathan.** Elizabeth Town, County of Essex, East
New Jersey. Will (copy). Made Feb. 26, 1738. Heirs: dau.
Constant Comfort Littleton; bro. Robert Littleton; nep-
hews John and James Littleton (sons of bro. John), Joseph
Littleton (son of bro. Robert) and Abraham Littleton (son
of bro. Anthony). Exec'r, bro. Robert Littleton. Wits.,
Thomas Tyre, William Sheltman, Enoch Cummings. Prob.
March 27, 1742. Arch. vol. A84, page 178. Reg. of Wills,
Liber A, folios 341-342.

**Collet, James.** Will (copy). Made July 6, 1742. Heirs: wife
Betty and children unnamed. Exec'rx, wife Betty. Wits.,
Humphry Turner, Richard Tompkins, Peter Henderickson.
Prob. July 13, 1742. Arch. vol. A65, page 122. Reg. of
Wills, Liber A, folios 330-331.

**Hinman, Richard.** Will (copy). Made Jan. 30, 1741. Heirs: dau.
Naomy Roades (widow of John Roades); grandsons Hin-
man and John Roades (sons of dau. Naomy). Exec'rs, dau.
Naomy Roades and friend Cornelius Wiltbank. Wits., John
Bicknall, John Lewis, John Moleston. Prob. Aug. 13, 1742.
Arch. vol. A76, page 179. Reg. of Wills, Liber A, folios
342-344.

**Smith, Robert.** Merchant. Will (copy). Made June 13, 1742. Heirs: wife Jean Smith; sons Samuel, Robert, Walter and James Smith; daus. Jennet, Mary and Jean Smith. Exec'rs, wife Jean Smith, friend Ryves Holt, Esq., John Neill. Wits., James Hood, Robert Frame, James Campbell. Prob. Sept. 16, 1742. Arch. vol. A99, page 194. Reg. of Wills, Liber A, folios 385-386.

**Potter, Abraham.** Kembels Neck. Will (copy). Made March 27, 1742. Heirs: wife Mary Potter; sons Abraham, John and Joshua Potter; dau. Jane Russel. Exec'rx, wife Mary Potter. Wits., John Stuart, Enoch Cummings. Prob. Nov. 23, 1742. Arch. vol. A94, page 11, Reg. of Wills, Liber A, folios 331-333.

**West, Robert.** Will (copy). Made March 8, 1736/37. Heirs: wife Elizabeth West; sons William, John Wrixham, Robert, Lewis and Peter West. Exec'rx, wife Elizabeth West. Wits., John Russel, Jr., John Russel, Esther Wood. Prob. Nov. 24, 1742. Arch. vol. A106, page 172. Reg. of Wills, Liber A, folios 333-335.

**Goldsmith, Thomas.** Yeoman. Will (copy). Made Dec. 14, 1741. Heirs: sisters Comfort, Jemima, Patience, Mary and Neomi Goldsmith. Exec'rs, friends Abraham Parsley and Emanuel Manlove. Wits., William Burroughs, Patience Williams, Ralph Bassnet. Prob. Dec. 2, 1742. Arch. vol. A72, page 171. Reg. of Wills, Liber A, folios 335-336.

**Fisher, Jabez Maud.** Will (copy). Made Sept. 13, 1742. Heirs: wife Sarah; sons Joshua, Edward and Finwick Fisher; daus. Margaret, Elizabeth and Sarah Fisher. Exec'rs, wife Sarah and bro. Joshua Fisher. Wits., Margery Miers, Ralph Brock, Robert Hauckshaw. Codicil, Sept. 30, 1742. Wits., Enoch Cummings, Finwick Stretcher, Margery Miers. Prob. Dec. 8, 1742. Arch. vol. A71, page 122. Reg. of Wills, Liber A, folios 336-338.

**Naws, Edward.** Will (copy). Made Sept. 4, 1742. Heirs: wife Mary Naws; dau. Hannah Naws; grandchild (child of Mary Naws, widow of Nathaniel); three sons unnamed living in Maryland. Exec'rx, wife Mary Naws. Wits., Jeremiah Claypoole, Mary Claypoole, John Pinder. Prob. Feb. 3, 1742/43. Arch. vol. A91, page 24. Reg. of Wills, Liber A, folios 339-341.

**Martin, James.** Clerk. Will (copy). Made April 2, 1743. Heirs: cousins Josias Martin, James Martin and James Martin (son of Josias); a servant Timothy. Exec'rs, Jacob Kollock, Esq.,

Harmon Harmonson. Wits., James Jackson, John Nieill, Neall McNeill. Prob. April 7, 1743. Arch. vol. A86, page 145. Reg. of Wills, Liber A, folios 388-389.

**Becket, William, Rev.** Missionary. Will (copy). Made [Aug.] 17, 1743. Heirs: daus. Elizabeth and Susannah; son-in-law William Furcher and wife; friends Ryves Holt, Esq. and Capt. Cord Hazzard. Exec'rs, daus. Elizabeth and Susannah. Wits., Jno. Plaskett, Ann Plaskett, Cornelius Burton. Prob. [Aug.] 29, 1743. Arch. vol. A59, page 24. Reg. of Wills, Liber A, folios 350-352. [Note:—Arch. vol. A59, page 24 mentions two wives].

**Draper, Sarah.** Widow. Will (copy). Made Aug. 29, 1743. Heirs: sons Henry, Isaac and Avery Draper; daus. Sarah Davis (wife of Thomas), Betty May (wife of Jonathan May) and Bebeckah Cirwithin (widow of Caleb); son-in-law Thomas Davis; grandsons John (son of Henry), Henry (son of Isaac), Henry (son of Avery), Isaac and Henry Davis (sons of Sarah and Thomas), John May (son of Betty May); granddau. Malley Draper (dau. of Isaac); and the seven unnamed children of dau. Rebeckah Cirwithin. Exec'rs, sons Henry, Isaac, Avery Draper, Thomas Davis and Jonathan May. Wits., James White, Susanna Tennant, David Moor. Prob. Sept. 15, 1743. Arch. vol. A69, page 223. Reg. of Wills, Liber A, folios 348-350.

**Truitt, Joseph.** Will (copy). Made Aug. 26, 1743. Heirs: wife Ruth Truitt; son Jesse Truitt; dau. Rachel Truitt; bro.in-law John Brown. Exec'rs, wife Ruth Truitt and John Brown. Wits., Benjamin Truitt, Samuel Truitt, Joseph Truitt, Jr. Prob. Sept. 23, 1743. Arch. vol. A102, page 142. Reg. of Wills, Liber A, folio 347.

**Vankirk [Venkirk], Art.** Yeoman. Will (copy). Made Nov. 20, 1742. Heirs: wife Ann Vankirk; son George Vankirk; daus. Dorothy Vankirk, Marg[a]ret Clendaniel, Grace Loffly. Exec'rx, wife Ann Vankirk. Wits., John Clendaniel, John Hart, John Reading. Prob. Sept. 30, 1743. Arch. vol. A103, page 48. Reg. of Wills, Liber A, folios 344-345.

**Manlove, Manuel.** Cordwinder. Will (copy). Made Oct. 19, 1743. Heirs: wife unnamed; sons Jonathan, Manuel and Boaz Manlove. Exec'rx, unnamed wife. Wits., William Burroughs, Edward Burroughs, Geo[rge] Grier. Prob. Nov. 25, 1743. Arch. vol. A86, page 39. Reg. of Wills, Liber A, folios 345-347.

**Draper, Samuel.** Yeoman. Will (copy). Made Oct. 31, 1743. Heirs: wife Elizabeth Draper; dau. Sarah Draper. Exec'rs, wife Elizabeth Draper and bro. Joseph Draper. Wits., James White, Mary Smith, Mary Heverlow. Prob. Jan. 14, 1743/44. Arch. vol. A69, page 218. Reg. of Wills, Liber A, folios 352-353.

**Price, Elizabeth.** Widow. Lewes. Will (copy). Made Dec. 22, 1742. Heirs: sons Avery and John Price; daus. Mary Price and Magdelan Tull (wife of William). Exec'rs, bro. Avery Morgan and son-in-law William Tull. Wits., Marg[a]ret Simeon, Jacob Phillips, Jacob Kollock. Prob. Jan. 18, 1743/44. Arch. vol. A94, page 135. Reg. of Wills, Liber A, folios 338-339.

**Sangster, James.** Yeoman. Will (copy). Made Dec. 29, 1743. Heirs: wife Elizabeth Sangster; dau. Mary Biwens (wife of Cornelius); Thomas Peterkin (wife's grandson); Mary Willbore (wife's granddau.). Exec'rx, wife Elizabeth Sangster. Wits., Ja[me]s White; David Peterkin, Thomas Dickason. Prob. Feb. 19, 1744. Arch. vol. A98, page 10, Reg. of Wills, Liber A, folios 361-363.

**Day, George.** Will (copy). Made Feb. 27, 1744. Heirs: sister Margaret Bronenton; cousins George Hill and John Hill. Exec'r, bro. Prettyman Day. Wits, John Holmes, Betty Prettyman. Prob. March 11, 1744. Arch. vol. A68, page 180. Reg. of Wills, Liber A, folio 361.

**Carey, William.** Will (copy). Made Feb. 4, 1744. Heirs: mother Ann Molton; bros. Thomas and Edward; sisters Mary and Rhody; and Clifton Carey. Exec'r, father-in-law Matthew Molton. Wits., Hezekiah Truitt, Jonathan Martin, James Fisher. Prob. March 12, 1744. Arch. vol. A64, page 109. Reg. of Wills, Liber A, folios 369-370.

**McCarrell, Robert.** Will (copy). Made April 22, 1743. Heirs: wife Anne McCarrell; son James McCarrell; daus. Anne McCarrell and Jean Groome. Exec'r, son James McCarrell. Wits., John Brice, Mary Godwin, Jane Russell. Prob. May 1, 1744. Arch. vol. A87, page 113. Reg. of Wills, Liber A, folios 357-359.

**Danely, William.** Turner. Will (copy). Made Nov. 10, 1744. Heirs: wife Mapp; and daus. Mapp, Mary, Jemina and Keria. [No exec'r]. Wits., William Smith, Rachel Smith, Cornelius Lofland. Prob. Dec. 1, 1744. Arch. vol. A68, page 11. Reg. of Wills, Liber A, folios 327-328.

**Woodward, Anthony.** Tailor. Will (copy). Made June 24, 1740. Heirs: wife Katharine Woodward; sons John and Joseph Woodward; dau. Sarah Draper (wife of Isaac). Exec'rs, wife Katharine Woodward and son-in-law Isaac Draper. Wits., Ja[me]s White, Jno. Bennet, David Peterkin. Prob. Dec. 15, 1744. Arch. vol. A109, page 50. Reg. of Wills, Liber A, folios 367-369.

**Clendaniel, William.** Farmer. Will (copy). Made Dec. 31, 1744. Heirs: wife Marg[a]ret; son John; daus. Betty, Rachel and Abigail. Exec'rx, wife Marg[a]ret. Wits., Joseph Spencer, Donovan Spencer, John Clendaniel. Prob. Jan. 25, 1744/45. Arch. vol. A65, page 1. Reg. of Wills, Liber A, folios 356-357.

**Fasset, William.** Will (copy). Made Dec. 14, 1744. Heirs: wife Naomi; sons William, David and Levin Fasset; dau. Sophia Fasset; bro. Rous Fasset; Hinman Rhoads; John Rhoads. Exec'rs, wife Naomi and bro. Rous Fasset. Wits., William Shankland, Joseph Hemblin, John Lewis. Prob. Jan. 26, 1744/45. Arch. vol. A71, page 57. Reg. of Wills, Liber A, folios 370-372. [Note:—Arch. vol. A71, page 56 mentions an unborn child and also mentions Rous Fasset as Guardian of all his children].

**Davidson, James.** Farmer. Will (copy). Made Feb. 5, 1744/45. Heirs: wife Mary Davidson; son William Davidson; dau. Ann Davidson. Exec'r, son William Davidson. Wits., William McKelvy, Alex[ander] Reed, Thomas Hally. Prob. Feb. 5, 1744/45. Arch. vol. A68, page 53. Reg. of Wills, Liber A, folios 359-361.

**Stockley, Oliver.** Will (copy). Made Feb. 11, 1744/45. Heirs: wife Margaret Stockley; sons Alexander, John, Oliver and Prettyman Stockley; daus. Elizabeth, Jane and Sarah Stockley. Exec'rx, wife Margaret Stockley. Wits., Tho[ma]s Warrington, Thomas Prettyman, Benjamin Stockly. Trustee: bro. Benj[amin] Stockley. Prob. March 5, 1744/45. Arch. vol. A101, page 29. Reg. of Wills, Liber A, folios 366-367.

**Price, Thomas.** Yeoman. Will (copy). Made Feb. 21, 1744/45. Heirs: cousins John Langan, Rachel Willson, Marg[a]ret White; uncles Napthali, Labon, William, James and Benjamin Carpenter; Affiance Wattson; Elizabeth Hill. Exec'r, uncle Napthali Carpenter. Wits., Henry Draper, Isaac Draper, Avery Draper. Prob. March 23, 1744/45. Arch. vol. A94, page 142. Reg. of Wills, Liber A, folios 363-364.

**Prettyman, John.** Yeoman. Indian River Hd. Will (copy). Made April 21, 1745. Heirs: wife Elizabeth Prettyman; son Thomas Prettyman; daus. Marg[a]ret and Elizabeth Prettyman. Exec'r, son Thomas Prettyman. Wits., John Hall, Alex[ander] Reed, Sarah Dobson. [no prob.]. Arch. vol. A94, page 72. [No Reg. of Wills Liber].

**Piles, James.** Yeoman. Will (copy). Made Feb. 21, 1743/44 [signed March 6, 1744]. Heirs: Benjamin Carpenter. Exec'r, Benjamin Carpenter. Wits., Laben Carpenter, John Smith, Anthony Woodward. Prob. May 2, 1745. Arch. vol. A93, page 85. Reg. of Wills, Liber A, folios 373-374.

**Bailey, James.** Pilot. Will (copy). Made April 29, 1745. Heirs: sons James and Steward; daus. Hannah and Ann. Exec'rs, Jonathan Bailey and Jacob Phillips. Wits., Richard Metcalfe, Albertus Jacobs, Francis Richardson. Prob. May 8, 1745. Arch. vol. A58, page 69. Reg. of Wills, Liber A, folios 392-393.

**Claypoole, Jeremiah.** Will (copy). Made Dec. 10, 1744. Heirs: wife Mary; sons George, Jehu, Joseph and John; daus. Elizabeth Claypoole, Comfort and Rachel Conwell, Mary Fowler and Sarah Gum; and child unnamed. Exec'rs, wife Mary, assisted by friends John Conwell and John Clewes. Wits., Jno. Clewes, Anthony Haverlo. Prob. May 9, 1745. Arch. vol. A64, page 231. Reg. of Wills, Liber A, folios 374-375.

**Walton, John.** Will (copy). Made Jan. 14, 1744. Heirs: wife Anne Walton; sons John, Luke, Ezekiel and William Walton; daus. Betty and Pearcy Walton. Exec'rx, wife Anne Walton. Wits., Solomon Truett, Sr., John Brown. Prob. May 20, 1745. Arch. vol. A104, page 139. Reg. of Wills, Liber A, folios 365-366.

**Carpenter, Benjamin.** Farmer. Will (copy). Made Sept. 9, 1745. Heirs: sons Benjamin and Samuel; nephew John (son of bro. James). Exec'r, Napthali Carpenter. Wits., Caleb Cirwithian, Mary Cirwithian, William Hickman. Prob. Sept. 16, 1745. Arch. vol. A63, page 219. Reg. of Wills, Liber A, folios 376-377. [Note:—Arch. vol. A63, page 219 mentions uncle,John Piles, dec'd].

**Townsend, Elisabeth.** Widow. Will (copy). Made Sept. 21, 1745. Heirs: sons Steven, Costin, Solomon and Charles Townsend; daus. Elisabeth Deputy and Abigail Clendaniel; grandsons William Townsend (son of Steven), Costin and Charles Townsend; granddaus. Betty, Sarah and Mary Deputy,

Sarah Townsend (dau. of Steven), Betty Townsend (dau. of Solomon), Elisabeth Townsend (dau. of Steven); Mary Clendaniel. Exec'r, loving son. Wits., Tho[ma]s David, Thomas Lay, Rebecca Lay. Prob. Nov. 2, 1745. Arch. vol. A102, page 51. Reg. of Wills, Liber A, folios 490-491.

**Fisher, Henry.** Will (copy). Made Aug. 28, 1746. Heirs: wife Dinah; sons Wood and Henry Fisher; daus. Elizabeth Fisher and Cornelia England. Exec'rx, wife Dinah. Wits., Susanna Pemberton, Elizabeth Neill, John Neill. Prob. Jan. 19, 1746. Arch. vol. A71, page 114. Reg. of Wills, Liber A, folios 380-381.

**Paynter, Richard.** Will (copy). Made Jan. 9, 1745/46. Heirs: wife Mary Paynter; son Richard Paynter; other children unnamed; bro. Dogood Paynter. Exec'rs, wife Mary Paynter and bro.-in-law (and overseer) John Allen. Wits., Dogood Paynter, John Allen, Jr., John Allen, Sr. Prob. Feb. 14, 1745/46. Arch. vol. A92, page 133. Reg. of Wills, Liber A, folios 372-373.

**Waples, William.** Will. Made Oct. 2, 1744. Heirs: wife Margaret Waples; sons Peter, Paul, Thomas, Burton and William Waples; daus. Elizabeth Carey and Mary Dirixson. Exec'rs, wife Margaret Waples, sons Peter, Paul, Thomas and Burton Waples, dau. Mary Dirixson. Wits., William Evans, Joseph Carter, Bevan Morris. Prob. March 16, 1746. Arch. vol. A105, page 62. Reg. of Wills, Liber A, folios 381-383.

**Aliff, Joseph.** Will (copy). Made Feb. 13, 1745/46. Heirs: wife Amy; sons John and Parker; dau. Mary. Exec'rx, wife Amy. Wits., John Lovine, Joseph Morgan, Gilbert Parker. Prob. March 29, 1746. Arch. vol. A58, page 29. Reg. of Wills, Liber A, folios 377-378.

**Atkins, John.** Yeoman. Will (copy). Made Jan. 4, 1745. Heirs: son William; daus. Anne and Betty Atkins and Jane Foster; son-in-law Thomas Foster. Exec'r, son William. Wits., Elizabeth Davis, Charles Pratt Russel. Prob. July 15, 1746. Arch. vol. A57, page 208. Reg. of Wills, Liber A, folios 378-380.

**Fisher, James.** Will (copy). Made Feb. 22, 1747. Heirs: dau. Esther Fisher; cousins Thomas Wynkoop and Mary Miers; Mary Heaverlo (dau. of Mary Davis). Exec'rs, friends Luke Wattson, Abraham Wynkoop. Wits., John Crapper, Margery Miers; John Hudson, Jr. Prob. March 3, 1747. Arch. vol. A71, page 126. Reg. of Wills, Liber A, folios 384-385.

**Cornwallis, Rebekah.** Will (copy). Made Oct. 7, 1745. Heirs: sons John and Elias; dau. Hannah Gum; grandsons Thomas and Yeates Conwell. Exec'rs, sons John and Elias. Wits., Deodt Woodbridge, Anthony Heaverlo, Mary Kollock, Sheppard Kollock. Prob. April 20, 1747. Arch. vol. A66, page 226. Reg. of Wills, Liber A, folios 386-387. [Note:—Arch. vol. A66, page 226 mentions dec'd father William Fisher].

**Dunaven, Randel.** Lewes. Will (copy). Made March 26, 1747. Heirs: wife Mary Dunaven. Exec'rx, wife Mary Dunaven. Wits., John Rodney, Naomy Wiltbank, Mary Caddy. Prob. April 11, 1748. Arch. vol. A70, page 6. Reg. of Wills, Liber A, folios 391-392.

**Stockley, Woodman, Esq.** Will (copy). Made Aug. 19, 1748. Heirs: wife Mary Stockley; sons Cornelius, Woodman and Joseph Stockley; daus. Comfort Waples, Elizabeth Stockley, Mary Stockley; bros. Benjamin and Joshua Stockley; Colston Bains. Exec'rx, wife Mary Stockley. Wits., Benj[amin] Stockley, Deodt Woodbridge, Alex[ander] Learmouth. Prob. Sept. 6, 1748. Arch. vol. A101, page 38 Reg. of Wills, Liber A, folios 395-397.

**Baily, Jonathan.** Lewes. Will (copy). Made March 9, 1746. Heirs: wife Bethiah; sons John and Joseph; daus. Mary and Esther. Exec'rs, wife Bethiah and friend Joseph Turner. Wits., John Maull, Shephard Kollock, William Rowland. Prob. Sept. 8, 1748. Arch. vol. A58, page 75. Reg. of Wills, Liber A, folios 394-395.

**Mariner, Thomas, Jr.** Yeoman. Will (copy). Made Sept. 21, 1748. Heirs: wife Marg[a]ret Mariner; sons Constant and Moses Mariner; daus. Sarah, Naomy and Jemina Mariner. Exec'rx, wife Marg[a]ret Mariner. Wits., William Mariner, John Himmons, Benjamin Stockley. Prob. Oct. 5, 1748. Arch. vol. A86, page 84. Reg. of Wills, Liber A, folios 398-399.

**Prettyman, William.** Will (copy). Made Feb. 20, 1743/44. Heirs: sons Isaac, Thomas, Robert, John, Joseph and Jacob Prettyman; daus. Betty, Ann, Comfort and Temperance Prettyman. Exec'rs, sons Isaac, Thomas and Robert Prettyman. Wits., Daniel Hosman, Darby Byrn, Joseph Carter. Prob. Nov. 25, 1748. Arch. vol. A94, page 122. Reg. of Wills, Liber A, folios 400-402.

**Marriner, Thomas.** Will (copy). Made Aug. 4, 1748. Heirs: sons Henry, Thomas, William, John, Bowman and Jacob Marriner; daus. Comfort Marriner and Elizabeth Jesups.

Exec'r, son Thomas Marriner. Wits., Henry Brereton, John Hemmons, John Russel. Prob. Jan. 22, 1749. Arch. vol. A86, page 83. Reg. of Wills, Liber A, folios 410-411.

**Dickenson, Thomas.** Will (copy). Made Dec. 10, 1748. Heirs: wife Annah Dickenson; dau. Leah Dickenson. Exec'rs, wife Annah Dickenson and Samuel Spencer, Jr. Wits., Robert Davis, Thomas Stapleford, Joseph Williams. Prob. Jan. 27, 1748/49. Arch. vol. A69, page 75. Reg. of Wills, Liber A, folios 389-390.

**Webb, Jonas.** Will (copy). Made July 19, 1748. Heirs: wife Ann Webb; sons Benjamin, John, Jonas and Liddelton Webb. Exec'rs, wife Ann Webb and son Benjamin Webb. Wits., Agnes Wills, Comfort Johnson, Samuel Johnson. Prob. Jan. 28, 1748/49. Arch. vol. A106, page 65. Reg. of Wills, Liber A, folios 399-400.

**Pettyjohn, William.** Yeoman. Will (copy). Made Jan. 15, 1749. Heirs: son William Pettyjohn; daus. Levina, Sarah Pettyjohn, Mary Donavon, Agathey Light; grandchildren Mary, Betty and William Light (children of Agathey); grandson William Pettyjohn; granddaus. Betty and Esther Prettyman; Absolam Little and wife Esther Little. Exec'r, son William Pettyjohn. Wits., John White, John Neill, Mary McIlvain. Prob. Feb. 2, 1749. Arch. vol. A93, page 19. Reg. of Wills, Liber A, folios 403-405.

**Collins, Thomas.** Yeoman. Will (copy). Made Dec. 5, 1748. Heirs: wife Mary and bro. Leven. Exec'rx, wife Mary. Wits., Neh[emiah] Draper, Neomy Davis, Luke Davis. Prob. Feb. 7, 1748/49. Arch. vol. A66, page 25. Reg. of Wills, Liber A, folios 390-391.

**Stockly, Joseph.** Yeoman. Will (copy). Made Feb. 14, 1749. Heirs: wife Sarah Stockly; son Woodman Stockly; daus. Betty and Sarah Stockly; bro. Woodman Stockly. Exec'rx, wife Sarah Stockly. Wits., Tho[ma]s Warrington, Joseph Morgan, Henry Blackwood. Prob. Feb. 24, 1749. Arch. vol. A101, page 20. Reg. of Wills, Liber A, folios 414-415.

**Barker, Job.** Yeoman. Will (copy). Made Feb. 26, 1749. Heirs: wife Anne; sons Perry, William, Leatherbury, John and Job; daus. Anne, Temperance and Elizabeth. Exec'rx, wife Anne. Wits., Job Barker, John Barker, Thomas Gray. Prob. March 20, 1749. Arch. vol. A58, page 184. Reg. of Wills, Liber A, folios 402-403.

**Tull, William.** Will (copy). Made July 8, 1749. Heirs: wife Magdaline Tull; sons John, Thomas and William Tull; dau. Elizabeth Tull. Exec'rs, wife Magdaline Tull and friend John Neill. Wits., Jacob Phillips, Mary Woodbridge, Daniel Munez, Jr. Prob. July 31, 1749. Arch. vol. A102, page 186. Reg. of Wills, Liber A, folios 411-412.

**Houston, Joseph.** Will (copy). Made Nov. 18, 1749. Heirs: wife Comfort Houston; sons William and Micajah Houston; daus. Sophia and Elizabeth Houston. Exec'rs, bro. James Houston and Robert Burton. Wits., William Marriner, Sarah Burton, Deodt Woodbridge. Prob. Dec. 14, 1749. Arch. vol. A78, page 95. Reg. of Wills, Liber A, folio 412.

**Lofland, Dorman.** Will (copy). Made Dec. 25, 1749. Heirs: wife Jemime Lofland; sons Dorman, Danielly and Branson Lofland; daus. Sarah, Elenor, Priscilla and Easter Lofland. Exec'rs, wife Jemime Lofland, bro. John Lofland. Wits., John Hudson, William Loughland, Samuel Johnson. Prob. Jan. 5, 1749/50. Arch. vol. A85, page 16. Reg. of Wills, Liber A, folios 407-408.

**Haverlo, Anthony.** Yeoman. Will (copy). Made Jan. 21, 1749/50. Heirs: wife Mary Haverlo; sons Andrew, James, Samuel, Anthony and William Haverlo; daus. Elizabeth and Barsheba Haverlo, Neomy Spencer. Exec'rs, wife Mary Haverlo, son Anthony Haverlo. Wits., Jno. Clowes, Jno. Cord, Jno. Dogherdy [Dougherty]. Prob. Jan. 29, 1749/50. Arch. vol. A74, page 243. Reg. of Wills, Liber A, folios 405-407.

**Burton, John.** Will (copy). Made Jan. 18, 1750. Heirs: sons Joshua, John and William; dau. Sarah. Exec'r, bro. Joshua. Wits., Job Ingram, William Burton, John Russel Burton. Guardian, bro. Joshua. Prob. Feb. 27, 1750. Arch. vol. A61, pages 177-178. Reg. of Wills, Liber A, folios 428-429.

**Miers, John.** Mariner. Will (copy). Made Nov. 31, 1749. Heirs: wife Ann Miers; dau. Jane Cord; Jane Rowland (dau. of Samuel and Tabitha); Samuel Rowland (son of Thomas and Sarah); Mary Palmer (dau. of Joseph and Mary); Joseph Palmer (son of Daniel and Mary). Exec'rx, wife Ann Miers. Wits., Tho[mas] Ozburn, Samuel Robinett, Ann Stuart. Prob. Feb. 28, 1749/50. Arch. vol. A88, page 154. Reg. of Wills, Liber A, folios 408-410.

**Andrews, Robinson.** Will (copy). Made Jan. 22, 1750. Heirs: wife Sarah; son Thomas; dau. Elizabeth; and William Beavens. Exec'rx, wife Sarah. Wits., Sarah Nixon, John Neill, John Stockley. Prob. March 5, 1750. Arch. vol. A57, page 149. Reg. of Wills, Liber A, folios 435-436.

57

**Cirwithian, Caleb.** Yeoman. Will (copy). Made Feb. 4, 1750. Heirs: wife Mary; sons John, Caleb and George; daus. Sarah, Jemina, Pheby, Mary, Ann and Lydia. Exec'rs, wife Mary and son John. Wits., John Conwell, Andrew Higgons, Richard Loncom. Prob. March 19, 1750. Arch. vol. A64, page 158. Reg. of Wills, Liber A, folios 421-423.

**White, Benjamin.** Yeoman. Will (copy). Made March 16, 1749. Heirs: wife Sarah White; son Wrixham White; daus. Betty and Comfort White. Exec'rx, wife Sarah White. Wits., John Orr, Elizabeth Campbell. Prob. April 6, 1750. Arch. vol. A107, page 50. Reg. of Wills, Liber A, folios 423-424.

**Hart, John.** Planter. Will (copy). Made March 14, 1753. Heirs: wife Mary Hart; bro. Robert Hart. Exec'rx, wife Mary Hart. Wits., Samuel Spencer, Thomas Hemmans. Prob. April 16, 1750. Arch. vol. A74, page 162. Reg. of Wills, Liber A, folios 50-52.

**Stretcher, Fenwick.** Lewes. Will (copy). Made April 4, 1750. Heirs: sons Edward and Fenwick Shepard Stretcher; dau. Mary Stretcher. Exec'rs, David Hall, Shepard Kollock. Wits., Comfort Kollock, Robert Gill, Deodt Woodbridge. Prob. May 6, 1750. Arch. vol. A101, page 49. Reg. of Wills, Liber A, folios 434-435.

**Hazzard, Joseph.** Yeoman. Will (copy). Made May 12, 1750. Heirs: wife Sarah Hazzard; sons David, Arthur and Joseph Hazzard; daus. Sarah, Nancy and Comfort Hazzard, Esther Dodd (wife of Jacob Dodd), Elizabeth Stockly (wife of Paynter Stockly). Exec'rx, wife Sarah Hazzard. Wits., Benjamin Stockly, Cord Hazzard, Rachel Hazzard. Prob. July 25, 1750. Arch. vol. A75, page 91. Reg. of Wills, Liber A, folios 424-427.

**Godwin, Elizabeth.** Widow. Will (copy). Made July 6, 1750. Heirs: dau. Charity Sanders (wife of Bartholemew); grand-daus. Elizabeth and Elishaba Sanders (daus. of Charity and Bartholemew Sanders). Exec'r, friend Jacob Kollock, Esq. Wits., Robert Gill, John Hall, Jacob Wiltbank, Jr. Prob. Oct. 17, 1750. Arch. vol. A72, page 162. Reg. of Wills, Liber A, folios 427-428.

**Clendan[i]el, John.** Will (copy). Made Dec. 30, 1750. Heirs: wife Prudence; son George; daus. Sarah and Elizabeth. Exec'rx, wife Prudence. Wits., Samuel Spencer, Jr., Jonathan Jacobs, Jonathan Clark. Prob. Feb. 6, 1750/51. Arch. vol. A64, page 243. Reg. of Wills, Liber A, folios 419-421.

**Turner, Joseph.** Will (copy). Made Aug. 23, 1750. Heirs: wife Sarah Turner; daus. Martha, Elizabeth, Priscilla and Sarah Turner; bros. Humphry and Cornelius Turner; 3 children of bro. Humphry's former wife Ann; William Henry; James Smith. Exec'rs, wife Sarah Turner and bro. Cornelius Turner. Wits., James Gordon, Thomas Gordon, John Lewis. Prob. Feb. 6, 1750/51. Arch. vol. A103, page 19. Reg. of Wills, Liber A, folios 431-432.

**Pettyjohn, Richard.** Will (copy). Made March 14, 1751. Heirs: wife Hannah Pettyjohn; son John Pettyjohn; daus. Marg[a]ret], Isabell, Elizabeth and Ann Pettyjohn, Sarah Firman (wife of David); grandsons Richard and David Firman( sons of David and Sarah Firman). Exec'rs, wife Hannah Pettyjohn and James Pettyjohn, Jr. Wits., John Ennes, L[udwig] Warren, John Phipps. Prob. March 23, 1750/51. Arch. vol. A93, page 10. Reg. of Wills, Liber A, folios 429-431.

**Warrington, Thomas.** Yeoman. Will (copy). Made Feb. 13, 1750. Heirs: wife Elizabeth Warrington; sons Jacob, Joseph and John Warrington; dau. Mary Warrington; William Hazzard. Exec'rx, wife Elizabeth Warrington. Wits., Gilbert Mariner, Peter Johnson, Henry Blackwood. Overseers: friends Woodman Stockley and Thomas Carey. Prob. April 8, 1751. Arch. vol. A105, page 171. Reg. of Wills, Liber B, folios 14-17.

**Staton, Thomas.** Yeoman. Will (copy). Made April 11, 1751. Heirs: wife unnamed; sons Hill and Thomas Staton; daus. Sabre, Hester, Anna, Tabitha and Elizabeth Staton. Exec'rs, sons Hill and Thomas Staton. Wits., Jno. Clewes, Sam[uel] Coulter, Thomas Cale. Prob. April 23, 1751. Arch. vol. A100, page 128. Reg. of Wills, Liber B, folios 9-11.

**West, Elizabeth.** Widow. Will (copy). Made Jan. 30, 1746. Heirs: sons Wrixam, Robert, Joseph, John, Levin, Peter and Lewis West; grandson William West; sister Sarah White. Exec'rs, son John West and bro. Benjamin White. Wits., Benj[ami]n Stockley, Job Barker, Jean Barker. Prob. May 3, 1751. Arch. vol. A106, page 115. Reg. of Wills, Liber B, folios 11-14.

**Burton, Woolsey.** Will (copy). Made . . . [1751]. Heirs: wife Elizabeth; sons Woolsey and William; dau. Elizabeth; and child unnamed. Exec'rx, wife Elizabeth. Wits., Peter Waples, Burton Waples, Jacob Burton, Henry Blackwood. Prob. [May 8], 1751. Arch. vol. A62, page 48. Reg. of Wills, Liber B, folios 1-4.

**Simonton, John.** Cordwinder. Will (copy). Made May 29, 1751. Heirs: wife Margaret Simonton; son John Simonton; daus. Jean, Mary, Comfort, Sarah and Elizabeth Simonton. Exec'rx, wife Margaret Simonton. Wits., Alex[ander] Learmouth, William Piles, Thomas Inkins. Prob. June 22, 1751. Arch. vol. A99, page 41. Reg. of Wills, Liber A, folios 437-439.

**Spencer, Samuel.** Will (copy). Made Jan. 26, 1750. Heirs: wife Honour Spencer; sons Samuel, Ebenezer and Nathan Spencer; daus. Hannah and Sarah Spencer; grandsons Evan Spencer, Abner Clark (son of Jane Clark); granddau. Honour Spencer; Jane Clark. Exec'rx, wife Honour Spencer. Wits., Ann Wynkoop, Tho[ma]s Wynkoop, Mary Cantwell. Prob. July 8, 1751. Arch. vol. A100, page 64. Reg. of Wills, Liber B, folios 6-7. [Note:—Arch. vol. A100, page 64 mentions dec'd son Isaiah Spencer].

**Walton, John.** Will (copy). Made July 18, 1751. Heirs: wife Naomy Walton; sons George and Samuel Walton; unnamed child. Exec'rs, wife Naomy Walton and father-in-law Samuel Spencer. [No wits.]. Prob. Aug. 9, 1751. Arch. vol. A104, page 140. Reg. of Wills, Liber A, folios 436-437.

**Draper, Isaac.** Will (copy). Made Sept. 12, 1751. Heirs: wife Sarah Draper; son Isaac Draper; daus. Mary and Sarah Draper. Exec'rs, wife Sarah Draper and bro. Henry Draper. Wits., Thomas Davis, Robert Davis, Ann Draper. Prob. Oct. 1, 1751. Arch. vol. A69, page 192. Reg. of Wills, Liber B, folio 18. [Note:—Arch. vol. A69, page 192 shows that Sarah Draper later married John Spencer and upon his decease married Lawrence Riley who joined her in settling the estate. It also mentions Avery Draper].

**Mills, Edward.** Will (copy). Made . . ., 1750. Heirs: sons Bowman, Nathan, L[ittle]ton and Luke Mills; daus. Susannah and Agnes Mills, Ann Webb. Exec'r, son-in-law William Rickards. Wits., Elizabeth Only, Comfort Johnson. Prob. Oct. 14, 1751. Arch. vol. A89, page 17. Reg. of Wills, Liber B, folios 4-5.

**Cord, John.** Admin. of, Hannah Heaveloc (late Hannah Cord). Granted [c. 1751]. Arch. vol. A66, page 183. [Note:— Arch. vol. A66, page 183 mentions a dau. Mary Cord whose husband is Henry Smith].

**Scudder, David.** Yeoman. Will (copy). Made April 1, 1749. Heirs: wife Mary Scudder; son Jonathan Scudder; daus. Mar[ga]ret McAfee, Phebe Starr (wife of Richard Starr);

grandson Moses Scudder (son of Moses, dec'd). Exec'rs, wife Mary Scudder, son Jonathan Scudder. Wits., Jno. Clowes, Thomas Staton, Jno. Barber. Prob. Nov. 27, 1751. Arch. vol. A98, page 39. Reg. of Wills, Liber A, folios 432-434.

**Pettyjohn, James, Sr.** Yeoman. Will (copy). Made Nov. 11, 1748. Heirs: wife Hannah Pettyjohn; sons James, Jr., Samuel, Thomas, Jacob and Abraham Pettyjohn; daus. Naomi, Major and Lydia Pettyjohn, Sarah Nixon, Elizabeth Abel, Abigail Bignal and Mary Oglesbey. Exec'rx, wife Hannah Pettyjohn. Wits., Jno. Clowes, John Wright, John Pettyjohn, Jr. Prob. Jan. 4, 1752. Arch. vol. A93, page 4. Reg. of Wills, Liber B, folios 23-27.

**Mariner, William.** Yeoman. Will (copy). Made Aug. 6, 1751. Heirs: wife Mary Mariner; sons John, Thomas and William Mariner; daus. Abigail, Peggy and Sarah Mariner. Exec'rx, wife Mary Mariner. Wits., John Hemmons, John Mariner, Thomas Gray. Prob. March 2, 1752. Arch. vol. A86, page 87. Reg. of Wills, Liber B, folios 32-34.

**Inkins, Thomas.** Taylor. Lewes. Will (copy). Made Feb. 15, 1752. Heirs: wife Hester [Esther] Inkins; daus. Hester and Lydia Inkins. Exec'rs, wife Hester [Esther] Inkins and friend Shepard Kollock. Wits., Robert Gill, John Shield, Alex[ander] Learmouth. Prob. March 4, 1752. Arch. vol. A79, page 177. Reg. of Wills, Liber B, folios 36-37.

**Little, Amos.** Will (copy). Made Feb. 29, 1752. Heirs: wife Levina Little; bro. Adonijah Little. Exec'rs, bro. Adonijah Little and bro.-in-law William Pettyjohn. Wits., Robert Campbell, Marnix Virden, Robert Samples. Prob. April 1, 1752. Arch. vol. A84, page 162. Reg. of Wills, Liber B, folios 27-28.

**Crapper [Cropper], John.** Yeoman. Will (copy). Made March 15, 1752. Heirs: wife Elizabeth; sons Leven, Zadock and John Chambers Crapper; daus. Levinah, Mary, Rachel and Betty. Exec'rx, wife Elizabeth. Wits., Jno. Clowes, Joseph Easman, William Salmon. Prob. April 9, 1752. Arch. vol. A67, page 161. Reg. of Wills, Liber B, folio 37.

**Askie, Grace.** Widow. Will (copy). Made March 26, 1751. Heir: friend William Blizzard. Exec'r, friend William Blizzard. Wits., William Hazzard, Rackliff Orr, Robert Gill. Prob. April 13, 1752. Arch. vol. A57, page 195. Reg. of Wills, Liber B, folios 40-41.

**Dobson, Elenor.** Will. Made April 22, 1752. Heirs: daus. Rachel Macklin and Jane Kimmery; grandsons Aaron Kimmery, Alexander Parrimore, John Parrimore; granddaus. Mary West, Rachel and Sarah Macklin. [No exec'r]. Wits., John Short, Elizabeth Killey, Elisabeth Handworth. Prob. May 15, 1752. Arch. vol. A69, page 90. Reg. of Wills, Liber B, folio 34.

**Wright, John.** Will (copy). Made Aug. 1, 1752. Heirs: wife Ann Wright; sons Edward and Solomon Wright. Exec'rx, wife Ann Wright. Wits., James Pettyjohn, James Parrmor, Sam[ue]l Tamm. Overseer, John Clowes, Esq. Prob. Aug. 16, 1752. Arch. vol. A109, page 88. Reg. of Wills, Liber B, folios 41-43.

**Ingram, Jacob, Sr.** Planter. Will (copy). Made Aug. 7, 1752. Heirs: wife Charity Ingram; son Job Ingram; daus. Betty, Unice, Caana and Shilly Ingram, Patience Messick. [No exec'r]. Wits., Isaac Ingram, Philip Huggins, John Phipps. Prob. Aug. 20, 1752. Arch. vol. A79, page 143. Reg. of Wills, Liber B, folios 28-31.

**Bennett, Stephen.** Will (copy). Made Aug. 23, 1751. Heirs: wife Marg[a]ret; sons William, John and Jehu; daus. Mary and Sarah Bennett, Jemima Ponder and Rhoday Warrin. Exec'rx, wife Marg[a]ret. Wits., John Johnson, Magdalene Webb, Benjamin Webb. Prob. Jan. 19, 1753. Arch. vol. A59, page 116. Reg. of Wills, Liber B, folios 43-45.

**Burton, Richard.** Will (copy). Made Jan. 19, 1753. Heirs: sons William, Ebenezer, John and Robert; daus. Sarah, Frances, Ann and Tabitha Burton, and Elizabeth Hall (wife of Thomas Hall); and negro woman Kate. Exec'rs, wife Elizabeth, and bro.-in-law Job Ingram. Wits., Anderson Parker, Solomon Nock, John Fisher, Samuel Tiffinney. Prob. Feb. 3, 175[3]. Arch. vol. A61, page 240. Reg. of Wills, Liber B, folios 48 49.

**Miers, Margery.** Widow. Will (copy). Made Oct. 13, 1752. Heirs: daus. Hester and Mary Miers, Sarah Williams and Elizabeth Manloves. Exec'rx, dau. Mary Miers. Wits., Jno. Clowes, Andrew Heaverlo, Sarah Heaverlo. Prob. Feb. 8, 1752/3. Arch. vol. A88, page 155. Reg. of Wills, Liber B, folios 57-59.

**Ricords, Samuel.** Indian River Hd. Will (copy). Made Jan. 19, 1753. Heirs: son John Ricords; daus. Ann, Sarah Ricords and Mary Green. Exec'r, son John Ricords. Wits., Bowman

Mariner, Arthur Whitside, Thomas Prettyman. Prob. Feb. 9, 1753. Arch. vol. A95, page 183. Reg. of Wills, Liber B, folios 46-47.

**Lacey, Robert.** Farmer. Will (copy). Made March 13, 1753. Heirs: wife Bridget Lacey; sons John, Parker, Robert and William Baggs Lacey; daus. Amey, Ann, Sarah, Bridget and Jemima Lacey, and Betty Morris. Exec'rs, wife Bridget Lacey and son John Lacey. Wits., Henry Draper, Thomas Sirmane, Rachel Sirmane. Prob. June 15, 1753. Arch. vol. A83, page 21. Reg. of Wills, Liber B, folios 59-61.

**Simpson, Margaret.** Widow. Will (copy). Made June 28, 1753. Heirs: daus. Elizabeth Simpson, Margaret Martin and Mary Paynter. Exec'rx, dau. Elizabeth Simpson. Wits., Ruth Manlove, Ruth Rodney, J. Rodney. Prob. Nov. 25 ,1753. Arch. vol. A99, page 63. Reg. of Wills, Liber B, folios.52-54.

**Smith, David, Esq.** Will (copy). Made April 26, 1753. Heirs: wife Sarah Smith; sons John and William Smith; dau. Elizabeth Wattson; grandsons John and David Smith (sons of son William). Exec'rs, son William Smith and son-in-law Bethuel Wattson. Wits., Ja[me]s White, Isaac Wattson, Morgan Williams. Prob. Dec. 6, 1753. Arch. vol. A99, page 123. Reg. of Wills, Liber B, folios 54-57.

**Wynkoop, Abraham.** Will. Made Nov. 15, 1753. Heirs: wife Mary Wynkoop; sons Thomas, Benjamin, Abraham and James Wynkoop; daus. Phebe, Esther and Mary Wynkoop. Exec'rs, wife Mary Wynkoop, sons Thomas and Benjamin Wynkoop, and dau. Phebe Wynkoop. Wits., W[illia]m Bowness, Elizabeth May, Peter Clowes. Prob. Jan. 3, 1754. Arch. vol. A109, pages 125-126. Reg. of Wills, Liber B, folios 20-22. [Note:—Arch. vol. A109, page 126 shows the estate was settled May 10, 1783 by Benjamin Wynkoop, acting exec'r.].

**Leatherbury, Thomas.** Will (copy). Made Jan. 27, 1754. Heirs: wife unnamed; sons Thomas and William Perry Leatherbury; children unnamed. [No exec'r]. Wits., Thomas Bagwell, Jacob Heaton. Prob. Feb. 15, 1754. Arch. vol. A84, page 20. Reg. of Wills, Liber B, folio 67.

**McNeill, Neill.** Yeoman. Will (copy). Made Jan. 26, 1754. Heirs: son John McNeill; daus. Margaret McNeill, Mary Turner, Ruth Templen and Sarah Tamm; John Lear; grandson Benjamin Lear. Exec'rs, son John McNeill and Samuel Tamm. Wits., Tho[ma]s Ozburn, Robert Neill, Josias Martin. Prob. Feb. 20, 1754. Arch. vol. A88, page 14. Reg. of Wills, Liber B, folios 69-71.

**Prettyman, John.** Yeoman. Will (copy). Made Feb. 23, 1754. Heirs: sons William, John and Perry Prettyman; daus. Ann, Sarah, Elinor and Elizabeth Prettyman. Exec'rs, sons John, Perry and William Prettyman. Wits., Robert Burton, John Russel, Sam[ue]l Russel. Prob. March 12, 1754. Arch. vol. A94, page 73. Reg. of Wills, Liber B, folios 71-73. [Note:— Arch. vol. A94, page 73 mentions his father William Prettyman and his dec'd grandfather John Prettyman].

**Draper, Ann.** Widow of Alexander. Will (copy). Made Sept. 5, 1743. Heirs: sons John, William, Nehemiah, Joseph, Samuel and Alexander Draper; daus. Mary Smith and Ann Brinckle; granddau. May Brinckle (dau. of Ann). Exec'rs, sons Joseph and Samuel Draper. Wits., John Walton, Costin Townsend, Thomas Lay. Prob. March 20, 1753. Arch. vol. A69, page 187. Reg. of Wills, Liber A, folios 354-356.

**Futcher, William.** Will (copy). Made April 1, 1754. Heirs: wife Mary Futcher; son John Futcher; uncle Thomas Prettyman; cousin Oliver Stockley; Prettyman Stockley. Exec'r, uncle Thomas Prettyman. Wits., John Newbold, Comfort Paynter, James Foster, Sarah Hazzard. Prob. April 15, 1754. Arch. vol. A72, page 98. Reg. of Wills, Liber B, folios 74-75.

**Holms [Holmes], Robert.** Yeoman. Will. Made April 25, 1754. Heirs: wife Jennet Holms; son John Holms; dau. Isabel Coulter; son-in-law Charles Coulter; granddau. Elizabeth Campbell. Exec'r, Josias Martin. Wits., Charles Prat, Joseph Allen, Robert Butcher. Prob. May 9, 1754. Arch. vol. A77, page 156. Reg. of Wills, Liber B, folios 80-81.

**McIlvain, James.** Will (copy). Made April 8, 1754. Heirs: wife Frances McIlvaine; sons David, Robert, Andrew, James and John McIlvaine; daus. Mary and Frances McIlvaine, Prudence Wiltbank (wife of Jacob); Mills, Andrew, James, Lydia and Winifred McIlvaine (children of son Robert); bro. George. Exec'rx, wife Frances McIlvain. Wits., George West, Rebeckah Camell, Henry Blackwood. Prob. May 15, 1754. Arch. vol. A87, page 190. Reg. of Wills, Liber B, folios 82-86.

**Hall, John.** Yeoman. Will (copy). Made Aug. 17, 1745. Heir: wife Hannah Hall. Exec'rx, wife Hannah. Wits., Charles Huggins, Josias Rattun, Charles Perry. Prob. May 17, 1754. Arch. vol. A73, page 214. Reg. of Wills, Liber B, folios 61-63.

**Ferguson, Dugood.** Will. Made [no date]. Heirs: John, Mary, Dugood and Catharine Ferguson. Exec'rs, Samuel Paynter and John Hall. Wits., Samuel Liffiney, Alex[ande]r Learmouth Liffiney. Prob. May 27, 1754. [No Arch. vol.]. Reg. of Wills, Liber B, folios 67-68.

**Starr, Richard.** Yeoman. Will (copy). Made Sept. 17, 1753. Heirs: wife Phebe Starr; sons Nathaniel, Jonathan and James; daus. Margaret, Bethiah and [Jemima] Starr and Sarah Hopkings. Exec'rs, wife Phebe Starr and son Nathaniel Starr. Wits., Thomas Ozburn, James Barr, Ann Barr. Prob. Oct. 22, 1754. Arch. vol. A100, page 125. Reg. of Wills, Liber B, folios 63-66.

**Craig, William.** Yeoman. Will (copy). Made Dec. 20, 1752. Heirs: son William; Elenor Craig Prettyman (wife of Robert Prettyman); and Jane Craig McIlvaine (wife of James McIlvaine, Jr.). Exec'r, son William. Wits., Joseph Easman, Parker Robinson, Hugh King. Prob. Feb. 5, 1755. Arch. vol. A67, page 159. Reg. of Wills, Liber B, folios 110-111.

**Davis, Thomas.** Will (copy). Made Jan. 1, 1754. Heirs: wife Sarah Davis; sons Isaac and Henry Davis; dau. Betty Davis; bro. Nehemiah Davis. Exec'rs, wife Sarah Davis and son Isaac Davis. Wits., William Arnell, Isabella Brader, Henry Draper. Prob. Feb. 18, 1755. Arch. vol. A68, pages 132-133. Reg. of Wills, Liber B, folios 76-79. [Note:—Arch. vol. A68, page 133 mentions friend Avery Draper, sole guardian of his three children until they reach 20 years of age].

**Brereton, Henry, Sr.** Will (copy). Made March 12, 1755. Heirs: wife Marg[a]ret; sons William and Henry; daus. Mary Brereton, Sarah Brooksby and Hannah Hazzard; granddau. Patience Bagwell; and sons-in-law Thomas Hemmons and Benjamin Burton. Exec'rs, wife Marg[a]ret and son William. Wits., Sarah Hill, Thomas Gray, Thomas Whitesides. Prob. April 2, 1755. Arch. vol. A60, page 143. Reg. of Wills, Liber B, folios 93-95.

**Coulter, Charles.** Yeoman. Will (copy). Made Feb. 21, 1755. Heirs: wife Isabel C.; sons Joseph, Robert and James; dau. Sarah; and dau.-in-law Elizabeth Camble. Exec'rs, wife Isabel C. and cousin John Coulter, Jr. Wits., Elizabeth Coulter, John Homes, Richard Lancom. Prob. April 3, 1755. Arch. vol. A67, page 36. Reg. of Wills, Liber B, folios 91-93.

**Lofland, Cornelius.** Will. Made April 2, 1755. Heirs: wife Mary Lofland; sons John, Cornelius and Ebenezer Lofland; daus. Rhoda, Mary, Betty, Roseanna, Jemima and Sarah Lofland. Exec'r, son John Lofland. Wits., John Johnson, John Laughland, Gabriel Loflee. Prob. April 16, 1755. Arch. vol. A85, page 15. Reg. of Wills, Liber B, folios 89-90.

**Neill, Robert.** Weaver. Will (copy). Made Jan. 29, 1755. Heirs: wife Elizabeth Holland Neill; son John Neill; daus. Elizabeth Neill, Mary Hall (wife of James), Ruth Staton (wife of Hill Staton). Exec'rs, wife Elizabeth Holland Neill and friend Josiah Martin. Wits., Jno. Clowes, W[illia]m Boroness, Thomas Skidmore. Codicil: Mentions wife's sons and dau. by previous marriage, to wit: Isaac, James and William Holland, and dau. Elizabeth Foster. Prob. May 15, 1755. Arch. vol. A91, page 62. Reg. of Wills, Liber B, folios 106-110.

**Warrington, William.** Yeoman. Will (copy). Made Jan. 20, 1755. Heirs: wife Mary Warrington; sons William, John, Joseph, Benjamin and Thomas Warrington; daus. Anne and Vallance Warrington, and Susannah Virdin; grandsons William and Lewis Davidson (sons of dau. Comfort), William Warrington (son of John), William Warrington (son of Benjamin); granddau. Tilney Warrington; 3 children of dau. Tilney, dec'd; friend Robert Hopkins. Exec'rx, wife Mary Warrington. Wits., William Day, Jacob Wroughten, Benj[amin] Stockly. Prob. June 27, 1755. Arch. vol. A105, page 174. Reg. of Wills, Liber B, folios 103-106.

**Gray, Samuel.** Yeoman. Will. Made May 6, 1755. Heirs: wife Esther Gray; son David Gray; dau. Elizabeth Gray. Exec'rs, wife Esther Gray and David Hall, Esq. Wits., Alex[ander] Bruce, Richard Mariner, Sarah Clark. Prob. July 10, 1755. Arch. vol. A73, page 27. Reg. of Wills, Liber B, folios 100-102. [Note:—Arch. vol. A73, page 27, mentions Elizabeth Gray dec'd, grandmother of David].

**Bicknall [Bignall], John.** Will (copy). Made July 12, 1755. Heirs: wife Abigail; sons William and John; daus. Naomi, Sarah, Esther, Lydia, Ruth and Mary; grandson Joseph Darby. Exec'rx, wife Abigail. Wits., Gilbert Parker, John Lewis, Cornelius Turner. Prob. Aug. 6, 175[5]. Arch. vol. A59, page 175. Reg. of Wills, Liber B, folios 86-89.

**Bowman, John.** Yeoman. Cedar Creek. Will (copy). Made Sept. 15, 1755. Heirs: wife Mary; sons Henry and John; and dau. Mary. Exec'rx, wife Mary. Wits., Daniel Wilson, Spencer Chance, James White. Prob. Oct. 10, 1755. Arch. vol. A60, page 35. Reg. of Wills, Liber B, folios 98-100.

**Massey, Thomas.** Yeoman. Will (copy). Made Nov. 14, 1755. Heirs: wife Naomi Massey; son Thomas Massey; daus. Naomi Massey, Lurani Evans; grandson Owen Evans. Exec'r, son-in-law Thomas Evans. Wits., Joseph Massey, Harvey Massey, Joseph Shankland, Jr. Prob. Nov. 20, 1755. Arch. vol. A87, page 65. Reg. of Wills, Liber B, folios 96-97.

**Wynkoop, Thomas.** Will (copy). Made Aug. 6, 1755. Heirs: bro. Benjamin Wynkoop; sisters Esther Wynkoop and Phebe Vining; step-bros. James and Abraham Wynkoop; step-sister Mary Wynkoop. Exec'r, bro. Benjamin Wynkoop. Wits., John Crapper, James Metten, Elias Samples. Prob. Dec. 18, 1755. Arch. vol. A109, page 127. Reg. of Wills, Liber B, folios 114-116.

**Wilson, Daniel.** Yeoman. Will (copy). Made Dec. 10, 1755. Heirs: sons William and Daniel Wilson; daus. Rachel and Mercy Wilson; William Wattson; Isaac Wattson; Joshua Wattson. Exec'r, son-in-law Isaac Wattson. Wits., Ja[me]s White, Thomas Hinds, Mark Davis. Prob. Dec. 23, 1755. Arch. vol. A108, page 68. Reg. of Wills, Liber B, folios 112-114.

**Little, Jean.** Will (copy). Made Feb. 18, 1756. Heirs: bros. David and John Rankin; mother unnamed. Exec'rs, uncle John Mustard and unnamed mother. Wits., Ann White, Margaret Cannon. Prob. Feb. 21, 1756. Arch. vol. A84, page 163. Reg. of Wills, Liber B, folios 116-117.

**Walker, James.** Yeoman. Will (copy). Made March 3, 1756. Heirs: wife Ann Walker; son John Walker; dau. Catherine Walker Exec'rx, wife Ann Walker. Wits., Jacob Walker, Sarah Woodward, James Gordon. Prob. March 29, 1756. Arch. vol. A104, page 19. Reg. of Wills, Liber B, folios 117-119.

**Carey, Thomas.** Will (copy). Made April 28, 1756. Heirs: wife Frances; Woodman Stockley; Ezekiel Reed Fowler; children of Thomas and Bridget West; and mother unnamed. Exec'rs, wife Frances and Woodman Stockley. Wits., William Hazzard, Jacob Hazzard, Richard Little. Prob. June 1, 1756. Arch. vol. A64, page 101. Reg. of Wills, Liber B, folios 119-123.

**Carey, Samuel.** Will (copy). Made Jan. 21, 1754. Heirs: sons William, Joseph, Samuel and Eli; dau. Ann. Exec'r, son William. Wits., Joseph Carter, Sr., Benjamin Carter, Joseph Carter. Prob. Nov. 8, 1756. Arch. vol. A64, page 93. Reg. of Wills, Liber B, folios 128-131.

**Stuart, John.** Yeoman. Will (copy). Made Oct. 1, 1755. Heirs: wife Mary Stuart; son John Stuart; daus. Levinah and Elizabeth Stuart; grandson William Stuart; granddau. Mary Stuart. Exec'rs, wife Mary Stuart, son John Stuart, son-in-law William Stevenson. Wits., Thomas Ozburn, Hannah Evans, William Stevenson. Codicil. Dated Oct. 31, 1756. Wits., Thomas Ozburn, Jenet Stevenson, Margaret Colter, Sr. Prob. Nov. 23, 1756. Arch. vol. A101, page 53. Reg. of Wills, Liber B, folios 124-128.

**Waples, Marg[a]ret.** Will (copy). Made March 10, 1755. Heirs: sons William Waples and William Newbold; daus. Frances, Marg[a]ret and Anne [Waples]; children of son John Homes. Exec'r, son William Waples. Wits., John Waples, William Waples, Tho[ma]s Gray. Prob. Feb. 2, 1757. Arch. vol. A105, page 11. Reg. of Wills, Liber B, folios 158-160.

**Coulter, John.** Yeoman. Will (copy). Made July 15, 1754. Heirs: son John; daus. Mary Coulter, Elizabeth Harmonson (widow of John), Susannah Oliver (wife of George), Sarah Stockley (wife of John), Esther Orr (wife of John); grandson Moses Allen (son of Andrew Allen, dec'd, and wife Dorcas, dec'd); grandchildren Robert, Joseph, James Samuel and Susannah (children of Joseph Shankland and wife Frances). Exec'r, son John. Wits., Bowman Mariner, Mary Mariner, Henry Blackwood. Prob. Feb. 8, 1757. Arch. vol. A67, page 47. Reg. of Wills, Liber B, folios 150-153.

**Campbell, George.** Cooper. Will (copy). Made March 18, 1756. Heirs: wife Sarah; sons Robert and Joseph; daus. Isabella Frame and Esther Fleming; granddaus. Margaret, Elizabeth, Ann, Dorothy and Mary Campbell, and Jean Fleming; grandson Nathan Campbell. Exec'rs, wife Sarah and son Robert. Wits., William Martin, Jean Hopkins, Robert Hood. Prob. March 22, 1757. Arch. vol. A62, page 193. Reg. of Wills, Liber B, folios 156-158.

**Lingo, John.** Yeoman. Will (copy). Made March 18, 1757. Heirs: wife Elizabeth Lingo; sons Patrick, James, Michael and William Lingo; daus. Isabel, Mary, Elizabeth and Sarah Lingo; father-in-law Thomas Lay. Exec'rx, wife Elizabeth Lingo. Wits., James White; Isaac Lay; James Haverloe. Prob. April 27, 1757. Arch. vol. A84, page 135. Reg. of Wills, Liber B, folios 153-155.

**Truitt, Samuel.** Planter. Will. Made Dec. 9, 1756. Heirs: wife Mary Truitt; son Samuel Truitt. Exec'rx, wife Mary Truitt.

Wits., Bethuel Wattson, Jno. Rodney, Thomas Cary. Prob. May 3, 1757. Arch. vol. A102, page 157. Reg. of Wills, Liber B, folios 140-143.

**Chipman, James.** Fuller. Will (copy). Made Dec. 17, 1753. Heirs: wife Elizabeth; bros. Benjamin and Stephen. Exec'rs, wife Elizabeth, bro. Benjamin. Wits., Jno. Clowes, John Heavelo, Hannah Heavelo. Prob. May 5, 1757. Arch. vol. A64, page 141. Reg. of Wills, Liber B, folios 143-145.

**Williams, Nicholas.** Will (copy). Made May 19, 1757. Heirs: wife Mary Williams; dau. Naomi Little. Exec'rx, wife Mary Williams. Wits., Isaac Fleming, John Hopkins, Joseph Warrington, Henry Blackwood. Prob. June 16, 1757. Arch. vol. A108, page 26. Reg. of Wills, Liber B, folios 146-148.

**Newcomb, Hester.** Widow of Thomas. Will (copy). made Aug. 20, 1754. Heirs: sons Baptist and Thomas Newcomb; daus. Hester Rickard and Anna Russel. Exec'rs, son Baptist Newcomb, Benjamin Rickards. Wits., Jno. Clowes, William Clowes, Ruth Prentice. Prob. Sept. 2, 1757. Arch. vol. A91, page 78. Reg. of Wills, Liber B, folios 148-150.

**Woolf, William.** Weaver. Will (copy). Made Sept. 16, 1759. Heirs: mother Sarah Brooks; bros. Rice, John and Jonathan Woolf; sister Naomi Darby (wife of Sanders Darby); bro.-in-law Sanders Darby. Exec'r, bro. Rice Woolf. Wits., J. Rodney, Simon Darby, John Prettyman. Prob. Sept. 29, 1757. Arch. vol. A109, page 40. Reg. of Wills, Liber B, folios 194-196.

**Reed, James.** Will (copy). Made Sept. 4, 1757. Heirs: sons John, Thomas, James, Joseph and Jesse Reed; daus. Isabella and Sarah Reed; Joshua and James Riggs (sons of Mark Riggs); John Edgin (son of Benjamin). Exec'r, son John Reed. Wits., John Chadburn, Joshua J. Ready, Susannah E. Onley. Prob. Oct. 10, 1757. Arch. vol. A95, page 27. Reg. of Wills, Liber B, folios 138-140.

**Burton, Joseph.** Will (copy). Made Dec. 9, 1756. Heir: wife Patience. Exec'rx, wife Patience. Wits., Henry Draper, Benjamin Burton, James Hathaway. Prob. Dec. 20, 1757. Arch. vol. A61, page 203. Reg. of Wills, Liber B, folios 131-133.

**Waples, Paul.** Will (copy). Made Jan. 8, 1757. Heirs: wife Temperance Waples; sons Dirickson, Nathaniel, Samuel and Paul Waples; daus. Patience and Catharine Waples and Betty Vaughan. Exec'rx, wife Temperance Waples. Wits.,

Benjamin Carter, Elizabeth Carter, Joyce Carter. Prob. Dec. 27, 1757. Arch. vol. A105, page 32. Reg. of Wills, Liber B, folios 133-135.

**Draper, Isaac.** Admin. of, to Lawrence Riley and Sarah, his wife, (late Sarah Spencer). Granted [c. 1758]. Arch. vol. A69, page 193.

**Pike, John.** Doctor. Warwick. Will (copy). [Undated]. Heirs: wife Ann Pike. Exec'rx, wife Ann Pike. Wits., Thomas Clifton, James Hutchinson, Peter Waples. Prob. Jan. 3, 1758. Arch. vol. A93, page 84. Reg. of Wills, Liber B, folios 160-161.

**Williams, John.** Will (copy). Made Jan. 30, 1758. Heirs: wife Mary Williams; sons John, Richard and Jesse Williams; daus. Esther and Elizabeth Williams. Exec'rx, wife Mary Williams. Wits., John Lecy, William Cary, Henry Blackwood. Prob. Feb. 15, 1758. Arch. vol. A107, pages 188-189. Reg. of Wills, Liber B, folios 164-166. [Note:—Arch. vol. A107, page 189 shows the estate was settled Nov. 2, 1776 by Abraham Smith and wife Mary (late Mary Williams)].

**Harmonson, Wallace.** Yeoman. Will. Made March 2, 1758. Heirs: son Benjamin Harmonson; dau. Betty Harmonson. Exec'r, bro. John Harmonson. Wits., Thomas Green, Sarah Shankland, Jno. Russell. Prob. March 14, 1758. Arch. vol. A74, pages 106-107. Reg. of Wills, Liber B, folios 161-164. [Note:—Arch. vol. A74, page 107 shows the estate was settled by Peter Harmonson on Dec. 4, 1788].

**Adams, Peter.** Will (copy). Made May 15, 1758. Heirs: wife Mary; sons Levin, Peter and William; daus. Mary and Sarah; two unnamed children of dau. Elizabeth. Exec'rx, wife Mary. Wits., John Davis, John Homes. Prob. June 20, 1758. Arch. vol. A57, page 83. Reg. of Wills, Liber B, folios 169-171.

**Cary, Ester.** Widow. Will (copy). Made April 6, 1758. Heirs: sons William, Joseph, Samuel and Eli; dau. Ann. Exec'r, friend Burton Waples. Wits., Cornelius Kollock, Thomas Cary, William Cary. Prob. July 15, 1758. Arch. vol. A64, page 48. Reg. of Wills, Liber B, folios 166-169.

**Kollock, Shepard.** Yeoman. Lewes. Will (copy). Made June 24, 1756. Heirs: wife Mary Kollock; sons George, Simon, Hercules and Shepard Kollock; daus. Elizabeth and Alice Kollock, Comfort Prettyman. Exec'rx, wife Mary Kollock.

Wits., Gilbert Marriner, George Claypoole, Jr., Nathaniel Wright. Prob. Aug. 8, 1758. Arch. vol. A83, page 14. Reg. of Wills, Liber B, folio 171.

**Smith, John.** Yeoman. Will (copy). Made Nov. 5, . . . . Heirs: wife Betty Smith; sons David, Nutter, Thomas and John Smith; daus. Comfort and Mager Smith, and Mary Davis (wife of Mark); grandson John Hickman. Exec'rs, wife Betty Smith and son David Smith. Wits., Isaac Wattson, Ja[me]s White, John Bass. Prob. Dec. 12, 1758. Arch. vol. A99, page 167. Reg. of Wills, Liber B, folios 184-187.

**Rowland, William.** Lewes. Will (copy). Made March 13, 1758. Heirs: wife Elizabeth Rowland; sons David and Jonathan Rowland; dau. Esther Rowland. Exec'rs, wife Elizabeth Rowland, Edward Fisher. Wits., Jno. Rodney, Joseph Baily, Samuel Davis. Prob. Jan. 13, 1759. Arch. vol. A97, page 124. Reg. of Wills, Liber B, folios 178-180.

**Skidmore, Henry.** Yeoman. Will (copy). Made March 19, 1759. Heirs: wife Elizabeth Skidmore; sons Thomas, Henry and Elijah Skidmore; dau. Sarah Pettyjohn; children of son Thomas Skidmore; children of dau. Sarah Pettyjohn. Exec'r, son Thomas Skidmore. Wits., Thomas Ozburn, Thomas Brian, John Fisher. Prob. April 9, 1759. Arch. vol. A99, page 98. Reg. of Wills, Liber B, folios 188-190.

**Smith, Betty [Bette].** Widow. Will (copy). Made April 28, 1759. Heirs: sons Nutter, John, Thomas and David Smith; daus. Comfort, Major and Betsey Smith, and Mary Davis; grandson John Hickman (son of Betsey). Exec'r, son-in-law William Hickman. Wits., Charles Rawlins, Luke Watson, John Bass. Guardian, uncle Isaac Wattson. Prob. June 25, 1759. Arch. vol. A99, page 116. Reg. of Wills, Liber B, folios 180-184.

**Molliston, Mary.** Will (copy). Made April 29, 1759. Heirs: son William Molliston; sister Elizabeth Molliston; Jonathan and Martha Molliston (children of sister Elizabeth). [No exec'r]. Wits., Mark Jacobs, Nathaniel Baily, Albartus Jacobs. Prob. July 20, 1759. Arch. vol. A89, page 87. Reg. of Wills, Liber B, folios 176-177.

**Townsend, Stephen.** Yeoman. Will (copy). Made Jan. 10, 1759. Heirs: sons William, Stephen, Littleton, Jesse, Noe and Jehu Townsend; daus. Abigail Townsend and Betty Spencer; grandsons Stephen, Oliver and Elijah Cobb (sons of dau. Sarah); granddau. Leah Townsend (dau. of son William); Sam[uel] Coston Townsend. Exec'r, son Stephen

Townsend. Wits., Ja[me]s White, Christ[topher] Nutter, Jemima Townsend. Prob. Sept. 6, 1759. Arch. vol. A102, page 78. Reg. of Wills, Liber B, folios 190-194.

**Metcalfe, Richard.** Lewes. Will (copy). Made Aug. 1, 1759. Heirs: housekeeper Sarah Sims; Henrietta Sims (dau. of Sarah); dau. Elizabeth Metcalfe (now or late of London); friend Thomas Parke (of Freeman Court in Cornhill, London). Exec'rs, [nephews] William Plumsted, Samuel Neave. Wits., Samuel Liffinsey, Sam[ue]l Paynter, Mathias Harris. Prob. Sept. 11, 1759. Arch. vol. A88, page 141. Reg. of Wills, Liber B, folios 173-176.

**Love, James.** Will (copy). Made Nov. 19, 1759. Heirs: sister Mary Mariner; Robert Mariner (son of sister Mary); Mary, James and Robert Colter (children of John Colter). Exec'r, bro.-in-law John Colter. Wits., Dean Grover, Thomas Howell, William Pugh. Prob. Dec. 27, 1759. Arch. vol. A85, page 144. Reg. of Wills, Liber B, folios 197-198.

**Perry, Charles.** Will (copy). Made Nov. 28, 1757. Heirs: wife Ellinor Perry; daus. Winifred and Catharine Perry, Margaret Cole. Exec'rs, wife Ellinor and dau. Winifred Perry. Wits., Farn Lewis, Mary Kenne, Mark Smith. Prob. Jan. 5, 1760. Arch. vol. A92, page 178. Reg. of Wills, Liber B, folios 198-200.

**Lofly, Gabriel.** Will (copy). Made Jan. 14, 1760. Heirs: wife Elizabeth Lofly; son Joshua Lofly; daus. Betty, Mary and Meriam Lofly. Exec'rx, wife Elizabeth Lofly. Wits., Charles Rawlins, James Rawlins, Nathan Young. Prob. Feb. 6, 1760. Arch. vol. A85, page 14. Reg. of Wills, Liber B, folios 201-203.

**Mustard, John.** Will (copy). Made Aug. 13, 1759. Heirs: wife Jane (Jean) Mustard; sons John, James and David Mustard; dau. Elizabeth Mustard. Exec'rx, wife Jane Mustard. Wits., Tho[ma]s Gray, Jos[eph] Martin, Francis McIlvain. Prob. Feb. 16, 1760. Arch. vol. A91, page 21. Reg. of Wills, Liber B, folios 203-207.

**Parker, Anderson.** Will (copy). Made May 9, 1759. Heirs: sons Anderson and Peter Parker; dau. Sarah Fisher; granddaus. Elizabeth and Sarah Fisher, Comfort and Sarah Bradford; grandson Nathaniel Bradford; grandchildren Anderson, Thomas and Elizabeth Parker (children of dec'd son Thomas), John, William, Thomas and Betty Parker (children of dec'd son William). Exec'rs, sons Anderson and

Peter Parker, son-in-law John Fisher. Wits., Hester Harris, Mathias Harris, John Baily. Prob. March 25, 1760. Arch. vol. A92, page 52. Reg. of Wills, Liber B, folios 211-214.

**Maxwell, John.** Yeoman. Rehoboth Hd. Will (copy). Made June 1, 1760. Heirs: wife Elizabeth Maxwell; John Henry (son of William Henry, my wife's bro.). Exec'rx, wife Elizabeth Maxwell. Wits., Robert Shankland, James Shankland, Rice Woolfe, Jr. Prob. July 7, 1760. Arch. vol. A87, page 87. Reg. of Wills, Liber B, folios 214-216.

**Mariner, John.** Will (copy). Made Feb. 23, 1760. Heirs: wife Elizabeth Mariner; sons Joshua, Jacob, John and Henry Mariner; dau. Rachel Mariner. Exec'rx, wife Elizabeth Mariner. Wits., Thomas Waples, Lewis West, Thomas Prettyman. Prob. Nov. 5, 1760. Arch. vol. A86, page 57. Reg. of Wills, Liber B, folios 216-218.

**Hand, Mary.** Spinster. Will (copy). Made Sept. 27, 1760. Heirs: sons Samuel, William and John Hand; dau. Mary Hand. Exec'r, son William Hand. Wits., Thomas Ozburn, Thomas Brian, John Neill. Prob. Nov. 25, 1760. Arch. vol. A74, page 34. Reg. of Wills, Liber B, folios 219-221.

**West, Robert.** Will (copy). Made Dec. 10, 1760. Heirs: bros. Joseph, John, Wrixam, Lewis and Peter West; nephews Joseph, Benjamin, John and William West; nieces Elizabeth and Comfort West (daus. of bro. John West), and Mary West (dau. of bro. Wrixam West). Exec'r, bro. Joseph West. Wits., Sanders Darby, John Lewis, John Harmonson. Prob. Jan. 2, 1761. Arch. vol. A106, page 173. Reg. of Wills, Liber B, folios 221-222.

**Cary, Ann.** Admin. of, to Thomas Cary. Granted [c. March 3, 1761]. Arch. vol. A64, page 24. [Note:—Arch. vol. A64, page 24 mentions heirs: Samuel and Joseph Cary; bros. William and Eli].

**Gordon, Thomas.** Yeoman. Will (copy). Made March 9, 1761. Heirs: wife Catherine Gordon; sons James, Thomas, John and Nathaniel Gordon; daus. Esther, Leah and Anna Gordon. Exec'rx, wife Catherine Gordon. Wits., William Lingo, John Rowland, J. Russel. Prob. May 5, 1761. Arch. vol. A72, page 185. Reg. of Wills, Liber D, folio 94.

**Robinson, William.** Will (copy). Made Oct. 17, 1757. Heirs: wife Ann Robinson; sons Thomas and Parker Robinson; grandchildren Mary and William Steward (children of dec'd dau. Ann Steward and John Steward). Exec'rs, wife Ann

Robinson and son Thomas Robinson. Wits., Parker Alif, Tho[ma]s Gray, Daniel Stewart. Prob. May 5, 1761. Arch. vol. A96, page 190. Reg. of Wills, Liber B, folios 223-226.

**Coulter, John.** Planter. Will (copy). Made April 17, 1761. Heirs: wife Jenet; sons James, Robert and Josiah; dau. Mary; sister Esther Orr. Exec'rs, wife Jenet and father-in-law Josiah Martin. Wits., William Hazzard, Jno. Barbour, Mary Harmonson. Prob. June 22, 1761. Arch. vol. A67, page 48. Reg. of Wills, Liber B, folios 231-233.

**Wiltbanck, Abraham.** Lewes. Will (copy). Made June 2, 1761. Heirs: wife Naomi Wiltbanck; nephews Isaac and Abraham Wiltbanck. Exec'rs, wife Naomi Wiltbanck and John Wiltbanck. Wits., Mathias Harris, Daniel Nunez, William Green. Prob. June 25, 1761. Arch. vol. A108, page 144. Reg. of Wills, Liber B, folios 234-237.

**Sherman, Thomas.** Will (copy). Made May 31, 1761. Heirs: wife unnamed; sons George, John and Charles Sherman; dau. Susannah Rider; George Rider. Exec'r, son John Sherman. Wits., Robert Lacey, Bridget Lacey, Ralph Boardman. Prob. June 29, 1761. Arch. vol. A98, page 117. Reg. of Wills, Liber B, folios 229-231.

**Draper, William.** Will (copy). Made Sept. 26, 1761. Heirs: unnamed wife; sons William, Alexander, John and Samuel Draper. Exec'rs, unnamed wife and son William Draper. Wits., Stephen Townsend, Jonathan Clark, Richard Melony. Prob. Nov. 18, 1761. Arch. vol. A69, page 229. Reg. of Wills, Liber B, folios 237-239.

**Russel, John.** Yeoman. Will (copy). Made Nov. 15, 1761. Heirs: wife Mary Russel; son John Russel; dau. Sarah Atkins; grandsons David and Jesse Atkins; son-in-law William Atkins; John Mariner. Exec'rs, wife Mary Russel, son John Russel. Wits., Ephraim Darby, W[illia]m Stockley, Jr., Richard Paynter. Prob. Nov. 26, 1761. Arch. vol. A97, page 135. Reg. of Wills, Liber B, folios 239-241.

**Mullinex, William.** Will (copy). Made Jan. 10, 1762. Heirs: wife Jean Mullinex; sons Richard, William, John and Israel Mullinex; daus. Alice, Mary, Jean and Rosanna Mullinex. Exec'rs, wife Jean Mullinex. Wits., Jno. Johnson, Warren Burrougs, Samuel Davis. [No prob.]. Arch. vol. A90, page 173. Reg. of Wills, Liber B, folio 250.

**Prettyman, Thomas.** Will (copy). Made Nov. 10, 1761. Heirs: wife Comfort Prettyman; sons William and Benjamin Prettyman; daus. Jean and Elizabeth Prettyman. Exec'rx, wife Comfort Prettyman. Wits., John West, Thomas Waples, Arbuckle Rodgers. Prob. Jan. 22, 1762. Arch. vol. A94, page 115. Reg. of Wills, Liber B, folios 242-244.

**Darby, Ephraim.** Yeoman. Will. Made July 23, 1759. Heirs: wife Elizabeth; sons Sanders, Ephraim, John, Simon, Samuel and William Darby; dau. Elizabeth Gordin [Gordon]; grandson Joseph Darby. Exec'rx, wife Elizabeth Darby. Wits., Thomas Gordon, Cornelius Potter, John Craige. Prob. Feb. 13, 1762. Arch. vol. A68, pages 17-18. Reg. of Wills, Liber B, folios 245-247. [Note:— Arch. vol. A68, page 17 mentions Hanbleton Craige, Cornelius Turner, Gilbelsher Parker and John Harmonson as friends of the dec'd; also shows Joseph Darby, D. B. N., settled the estate in lieu of Elizabeth Darby, widow, on Sept. 7, 1785].

**Riley, Benjamin.** Will (copy). Made Feb. 14, 1762. Heirs: sons Thomas, George, Griffin, Lawrence, Benjamin, John and William Riley; daus. Mary, Ann, Elizabeth and Sarah Riley. Exec'rs, sons Thomas and George Riley. Wits., Charles Rawlins, Edward Carry, Elizabeth Clark. Prob. March 8, 1762. Arch. vol. A96, page 35. Reg. of Wills, Liber B, folios 247-250.

**Warrington, Mary.** Will (copy). Made July 26, 1759. Heirs: sons Joseph, Thomas and Benjamin Warrington; daus. Naney Warrington, Susannah Verdin and Valance Day; William, John and Ann Warrington (children of John Warrington). Exec'r, son Thomas Warrington. Wits., James McIlvaine, Jean J. McIlvaine. Prob. March 12, 1762. Arch. vol. A105, page 162. Reg. of Wills, Liber B, folios 252-254.

**Phillips, Jacob.** Will (copy). Made March 27, 1760. Heirs: wife Hester Phillips; nephew Phillip Kollock (son of Jacob); niece Hannah Nunez (wife of Daniel). Exec'r, Jacob Kollock, the elder. Wits., Sam[ue]l Paynter, John Paynter, Matthew Willson. Prob. April 19, 176[2]. Arch. vol. A93, page 36. Reg. of Wills, Liber B, folios 207-211.

**Humphrey, Mary.** Will. Made April 21, 1769. Heirs: sister Naomi Godwin; grandson William Russell (son of Thomas Russell); Thomas and Purnal Johnson (sons of Purnal Johnson). Exec'r, William Fowler. Wits., John Clowes, Jr., Nelley Virden, Manley Virden. Prob. May 5, 1762. Arch. vol. A79, page 94. Reg. of Wills, Liber B, folios 340-341.

**Bartlett, William.** Will (copy). Made April 26, 1762. Heirs: wife Marg[a]ret; sons Solomon and Nicholas Bartlett; daus. Leah and Marg[a]ret Bartlett. Exec'rx, wife Marg[a]ret Bartlett. Wits., Burton Waples, Thomas Hardy, Bechamp Harper. Prob. May 10, 1762. Arch. vol. A58, page 222. Reg. of Wills, Liber B, folios 254-257.

**Eldridge, Joseph.** Will (copy). Made March 10, 1762. Heirs: wife Mary Eldridge; daus. Mary Eldridge, Ruth Eldridge, Rebeckah Stokes and Martha Wood; grandsons Thomas Evans, Thomas Moore, Obediah Eldridge, Thomas Harmonson and Joshua Fisher; granddau. Phebe Lippincott. Exec'rs, wife Mary Eldridge and son-in-law Jabez Fisher. Wits., Richard Mariner and Isaac Wiltbank. Prob. May 13, 1762. Arch. vol. A70, page 41. Reg. of Wills, Liber B, folios 257-260.

**Craig, Robert.** Will (copy). Made Jan. 10, 1763. Heirs: sons John and Hamilton Craig; daus. Mary White (wife of Jacob White) and Ruth Robinson (wife of Parker Robinson); dau.-in-law Hannah Craig; grandsons Robert Craig (son of Alexander Craig, dec'd), Isaac and Robert White (sons of Jacob and Mary White); granddau. Ann Robinson (dau. of Parker and Ruth Robinson). Exec'rs, sons John and Hamilton Craig. Wits., Priscilla Craig, William Craig, William Shankland. Prob. Jan. 22, 1763. Arch. vol. A67, pages 154-155. Reg. of Wills, Liber B, folios 263-267.

**Stephenson, James.** Will (copy). Made Dec. 30, 1762. Heirs: wife Jennet Stephenson; daus. Elizabeth and Jane Stephenson, and Martha Maniel. Exec'rx, wife Jennet Stephenson. Wits., John Clowes, Jr., Hugh Stephenson, Mary Stephenson. Prob. Jan. 24, 1763. Arch. vol. A100, page 157. Reg. of Wills, Liber B, folios 261-263.

**Butcher, Robert.** Will (copy). Made Feb. 4, 1763. Heirs: sons William and Robert Butcher. Exec'r, bro. William Butcher. Wits., William Hazard, Jr., William Prettyman. Guardian, bro. William Butcher. Prob. Feb. 7, 1763. Arch. vol. A62, page 74. Reg. of Wills, Liber B, folios 268-270.

**Hall, John.** Cordwinder. Will (copy). Made Dec. 24, 1759. Heirs: wife Elinor Hall; sons James, John and Hugh Hall; daus. Jean Shelsman, Elinor Welch, Mary Wes[tcott]; heirs of Joshua Hall. Exec'rs, wife Elinor and son James Hall. Wits., George G. Laws, Margaret Coulter, James Stephenson. Prob. Aug. 22, 1763. Arch. vol. A73, page 215. Reg. of Wills, Liber B, folios 270-272.

**Claypoole, George.** Yeoman. Admin. of, to George Conwell, Fisher Conwell and Elias Conwell, D. B. N., all in right of Elias Conwell, Yeoman, dec'd. Granted Sept. 3, 1763. Arch. vol. A64, page 226.

**White, James.** Yeoman. Will (copy). Made Sept. 16, 1763. Heirs: wife Margaret White; daus. Sophia and Isabella White, Mary Dyden (widow), Sarah White; grandson Isaac White (son of eldest son Thomas White); granddaus. Elizabeth and Hester White (daus. of eldest son Thomas White), Sarah Williams (dau. of eldest dau. Elizabeth White); children of son William White. Exec'rx, wife Margaret White. Wits., Jacob Hickman, Ann Hickman, John Langen. Prob. Oct. 13, 1763. Arch. vol. A107, page 68. Reg. of Wills, Liber B, folios 272-275.

**Adderson, Jacob.** Admin. of, to Matthew Wilson. Granted [c. 1764]. Arch. vol. A57, page 107.

**Coverdale, John, Sr.** Will (copy). Made Jan. 27, 1764. Heirs: wife Mary; sons Nathaniel, Charles and Richard Coverdale; dau. Sarah Coverdale. Exec'rx, wife Mary. Wits., Hezekiah Truett, Jehu Truett, John Webb, Sr. Prob. March 3, 1764. Arch. vol. A67, page 80. Reg. of Wills, Liber B, folios 276-278.

**Clark, John.** Carpenter. Admin. of, to Mary Clark who intermarried with Andrew Collings. Settled [c. Jan. 16, 1765]. Arch. vol. A64, page 184. [Note:—Arch. vol. A64, page 184 mentions heirs: Miers and John Clark; also shows that Mary Clark was Mary Williams before she married John Clark and had a son Reynear Williams, Jr.].

**Prettyman, Thomas, Esq.** Will (copy). Made . . ., 1762. Heirs: wife Comfort Prettyman; Sarah Dobson; Mary Russel, John Futcher (son of William). Exec'rx, wife Comfort Prettyman. Wits., Andrew McIlvaine, John Warrington, Leatherbury Barker. Prob. Jan. 22, 1765. Arch. vol. A94, page 116. Reg. of Wills, Liber B, folios 278-280.

**Ozburn, Thomas.** Will (copy). Made Dec. 15, 1764. Heirs: son Thomas Ozburn; dau. Elizabeth Ozburn. Exec'r, son Thomas Ozburn. Wits., John Spencer, Baptis Lay, William Hand. Prob. Feb. 6, 1765. Arch. vol. A92, page 34. Reg. of Wills, Liber B, folios 280-282.

**Frame, Robert.** Admin. of, to Nathan Frame. Granted [c. Feb. 19, 1765]. Arch. vol. A72, pages 46-47. [Note:—Arch. vol. A72, page 46 mentions Smith, George, Mary and William

Frame; page 47 mentions widow Isabella Frame, also mentions Smith Frame a grandson of Dorothy Frame and son of Robert Frame].

**Veghte, Nicholas.** Will (copy). Made Feb. 13, 1765. Heirs: wife Elenor Veghte; sons John, Abraham, Dennis, Isaac and Nicholas Veghte. Exec'rs, son John Veghte, Andrew McDowel, Levin Crapper. Wits., John Vankirk, Joseph Truitt, Jehu Truitt. Prob. March 9, 1765. Arch. vol. A103, page 98. Reg. of Wills, Liber B, folios 288-291. [Note:—Arch. vol. A103, page 98 shows son John Veghte renounced his right as exec'r].

**Davis, Henry.** Gentleman. Will (copy). Made May 9, 1765. Heirs: wife Susannah Davis; son Thomas Davis; cousin Thomas (son of uncle Samuel Davis); sister Betty Stretcher, (wife of Edward Stretcher of Phila.); children of sister Betty Stretcher. Exec'rx, wife Susannah Davis. Wits., Jno. Cirwithin, Thomas Heaverlo. Prob. Aug. 7, 1765. Arch. vol. A68, page 72. Reg. of Wills, Liber B, folio 283.

**Salmon, Benjamin.** Worcester Co., Md. Made July 1, 1765. Heirs: wife Agnes Salmon; sons William, Benjamin, Josiah, Robert, Aydelott and Solomon Salmon; daus. Mary, Patience and Agnes Salmon. Exec'rx, wife Agnes Salmon. Wits., W[illia]m Tunnell, Solomon Willes, James Salmon. Codicil, Oct. 26, 1765. [No prob.]. Arch. vol. A97, page 177. [Note: —Arch. vol. A97, page 177 shows the estate was settled Sept. 7, 1785 by Benjamin Salmon who was exec'r of Agnes Salmon, dec'd].

**Bagswell, John, Sr.** Will (copy). Made Feb. 4, 1766. Heirs: sons William and Thomas Bagwell; daus. Elizabeth and Sarah Bagwell, Leah Semare and Rachel Walton; grandson Bagwell Walton; housekeeper Mary Bailey. Exec'r, Nehemiah Davis, Sr. Wits., Levi Spencer, Joshua Spencer. Prob. Feb. 12, 1766. Arch. vol. A58, page 51. Reg. of Wills, Liber B, folios 286-288.

**Willson, William.** Yeoman. Will (copy). Made March 10, 1766. Heirs: wife Temperance Wilson; sons Thomas, William, John, Reubin and Joshua Wilson; dau. Naney Wilson; grandsons Thomas Wilson (son of Thomas), Richard Pettyjohn (son of John), John Parimore (son of John), William Parimore (son of Richard). Exec'r, son Thomas Wilson. Wits., John Clowes, Jr., Solomon Dodd, Thomas Dodd. Prob. March 11, 1766. Arch. vol. A108, page 132. Reg. of Wills, Liber B, folios 291-293. [Note:—Arch. vol. A108, page 132 shows the estate was settled by Thomas Wilson on June 9, 1785].

**Depray, John.** Will (copy). Made May 29, 1765. Heirs: wife Mary Depray; son John Depray; daus. Esther West, (wife of Gabriel West), Mary Staton, (wife of Jehu Staton), Elizabeth Collings, (wife of Elisha Collings), Comfort Ricords, (wife of John Ricords); dau.-in-law Rachel Ricords; Silby and William Records, (sons of Rachel). Exec'rx, wife Mary Depray. Wits., William Hazzard, Jr., Benjamin Young Truitt, George Truitt. Prob. May 8, 1766. Arch. vol. A68, pages 228-229. Reg. of Wills, Liber B, folios 293-295.

**Rowland, Samuel, Jr.** Will (copy). Made Dec. 15, 1765. Heirs: wife Elizabeth Rowland; sons John, James, Samuel and Wrixam Rowland; daus. Elizabeth and Comfort Rowland. Exec'rs, wife Elizabeth Rowland, bro. Wrixam Lewis. Wits., William Craig, Baptis Lay, John Maull, Samuel Hand, William Dellaney. Prob. May 10, 1766. Arch. vol. A97, page 116. Reg. of Wills, Liber B, folios 296-298.

**Stockly, Benjamin.** Will (copy). Made Nov. 30, 1762. Heirs: son Benjamin Stockly, Jr.; daus. Jean Stockly, Temperance Little, Comfort West, Ann West (wife of Wrixam), Esther West (wife of Lewis), Elizabeth Horsman (wife of Daniel), and Abigail Waples (wife of William); sons-in-law Wrixam West, Lewis West, Daniel Horsman and William Waples; granddau. Patience Barker. Exec'r, son-in-law Daniel Horsman. Wits., Naomi Stockly, Edward Records, Joe Shankland, Jr. Prob. June 24, 1766. Arch. vol. A100, page 192. Reg. of Wills, Liber B, folios 299-300.

**Morris, Bevins.** Will (copy). Made June 12, 1766. Heirs: wife Mary Morris; sons William, Bevins, Noah and Isaac; dau. Mary Morris. Exec'rs, wife Mary Morris and son William Morris. Wits., Dennis Morris, Jacob Morris, John Spencer. Prob. July 2, 1766. Arch. vol. A90, page 17. Reg. of Wills, Liber B, folios 302-304.

**Finwick, Sidney.** Will (copy). Made April 3, 1766. Heirs: son William; dau. Mary Skidmore; granddaus. Jean and Mary Skidmore. Exec'rx, dau. Mary Skidmore. Wits., Elisha Knox, Thomas Noutton. Prob. July 5, 1766. Arch. vol. A71, page 76. Reg. of Wills, Liber B, folios 304-305.

**Eldridge, Mary.** Widow. Will (copy). Made July 8, 1766. Heirs: daus. Mary and Martha Eldridge; grandsons Obadiah Eldridge, Thomas Moor, Thomas Harmonson, Joshua Fisher, Obadiah Dingee and Jacob Dingee. Exec'r, son-in-law Fretwell Wright. Wits., John Rodney, Peter Fretwell Wright, John Brittan. Prob. Aug. 11, 1766. Arch. vol. A70, page 42. Reg. of Wills, Liber B, folios 306-308.

**Adams, Roger.** Gentleman. Dorchester Co., Md. Admin. of, to Roger Adams, Yeoman, C. T. A. Granted [(c. Sept. 9, 1766]. Arch. vol. A57, page 91. [Note:—Arch. vol. A57, page 91 mentions heirs: daus. Mary Clarkson (wife of William), Nicey Turner (wife of Jehu), Sterling Cannon (wife of Constantine) and Major Fountain (wife of William); son Charles Nutter Adams; cousins Ezekiel, Boaz and Mary Adams; heirs of Isaac Adams, Daniel, Jeremiah, John, Rebecca and Elijah; James Adams (son of Isaac) and . . . Smith (wife of Thomas), dau of Isaac].

**Prettyman, William.** Will (copy). Made April 5, 1757. Heirs: wife Sarah Prettyman; son Burton Prettyman; daus. Sarah and Magdalene Prettyman, Naomi Boyce and Margaret Houston. Exec'rs, wife Sarah Prettyman and bro. Robert Prettyman. Wits., John Waples, Lewis West, John Woods. Prob. Sept. 13, 1766. Arch. vol. A94, page 123. Reg. of Wills, Liber B, folios 308-311.

**Finney, Samuel Latham.** Doctor. Will. Made Jan. 3, 1759. Heir: wife Martha Finney. Exec'rx, wife Martha Finney. Wits., Micader Hazzard, Charles Staton, Mathias Harris. Prob. Oct. 2, 1766. Arch. vol. A71, page 74. Reg. of Wills, Liber B, folios 341-342.

**Razer, Peter.** Lewes. Collector of Customs. Will (copy). Made Feb. 5, 1766. Heirs: Elizabeth Chipman; Peter Hall (son of David Hall); James West, Esq. Exec'r, David Hall, Esq. Wits., Mary Hall, Jean Hall, David Gray. Prob. Nov. 18, 1766. Arch. vol. A95, page 2. Reg. of Wills, Liber B, folios 311-312.

**Spencer, John, Esq.** Admin. of, to Sarah Spencer. Settled Dec. 18, 1766. Arch. vol. A100, page 56.

**Ricords, Ann.** Will (copy). Made Dec. 13, 1766. Heirs: sons Levin, Thomas Ricords, John Coulter; dau. Elizabeth Ricords; grandson Calvin Coulter. Exec'r, son Thomas Ricords. Wits., Gilb[ert] Parker, Isaac Hollan, Comfort Ricords. Prob. Dec. 20, 1766. Arch. vol. A95, page 156. Reg. of Wills, Liber B, folios 312-314.

**Jacobs, Hannah.** Will (copy). Made Dec. 16, 1766. Heirs: bro. Nathaniel Jacobs; sister Abigail Peters; nephews Albertus Jacobs (son of James), Benjamin and Isaac Smith (sons of Mark and Sarah); nieces Lydia Jacobs, Elizabeth Smith (dau. of Mark and Sarah), Hannah Jacobs (dau. of Nathaniel), Elizabeth Peters. Exec'rx, sister Abigail Peters. Wits.,

Ephraim Darby, Elizabeth Smith, James Gordon. Prob. Jan. 23, 1767. Arch. vol. A80, page 54. Reg. of Wills, Liber B, folios 314-317.

**Draper, Nehemiah.** Will (copy). Made Dec. 10, 1766. Heirs: wife Sarah Draper; sons Alexander, Nehemiah and James Draper; dau. Elizabeth Draper. Exec'rs, wife Sarah Draper and son Alexander Draper. Wits., Bethuel Watson, Charles Draper, Esther Draper. Prob. March 5, 1767. Arch. vol. A69, page 214. Reg. of Wills, Liber B, folios 317-319.

**Whiteside, Arthur.** Yeoman. Will. Made March 3, 1767. Heirs: wife Nancy Whiteside; dau. Fanny Whiteside; bros. Thomas and William Whiteside. Exec'rs, wife Nancy Whiteside and bro. Thomas Whiteside. Wits., John Woods, Zachariah Bold, Margaret Whiteside. Prob. April 2, 1767. Arch. vol. A107, page 101. Reg. of Wills, Liber B, folio 343.

**Prettyman, Isaac.** Will (copy). Made March 23, 1767. Heirs: wife Sarah Prettyman; son Joseph Prettyman. Exec'rx, wife Sarah Prettyman. Wits., Burton Waples, Thomas Leatherbury, Sarah Rogers. Prob. May 6, 1767. Arch. vol. A94, page 64. Reg. of Wills, Liber B, folios 319-321.

**Cord, Hezekiah.** Will (copy). Made April 16, 1767. Heirs: bro. Joseph Cord; sisters Elizabeth and Hester Burton, and Ann Bagwell; children of three sisters; cousins Mary and Lydia Burton (daus. of Elizabeth and Esther Burton); Mary Smith (wife of Henry). Exec'rs, friends Benjamin Burton and Daniel Nunez, Jr. Wits., Joseph Burton, Mary Steward. Prob. June 4, 1767. Arch. vol. A66, pages 179-180. Reg. of Wills, Liber B, folios 321-323. [Note:—Arch. vol. A66, page 179 mentions dec'd father Joseph Cord and dec'd bro. John; page 180 shows William Burton as husband of Elizabeth, Thomas Bagwell as husband of Ann and Benjamin Burton as husband of Hester].

**Allen, John.** Will (copy). Made Feb. 21, 1767. Heirs: son Joseph; grandsons William and Moses Allen, and Allen Reed; granddau. Jean Allen; children of daus. Mary Paynter and Elizabeth White. Exec'rs, James Thompson, son Joseph Allen and Moses Allen. Wits., Richard Little, William Little, Joseph E. Atkins. Prob. June 17, 1767. Arch. vol. A57, page 117. Reg. of Wills, Liber B, folios 324-326.

**Cary, Thomas, Sr.** Planter. Will (copy). Made May 24, 1766. Heirs: wife Elizabeth; sons William, Ebenezer, Thomas, Jno. and Samuel; daus. Bridget, Elizabeth and Catherine Cary, and Mary Collins; grandson Thomas (son of William).

Exec'rx, wife Elizabeth Cary. Wits., Cornelius Kollock, William Stephenson, Simon Kollock. Prob. July 22, 1767. Arch. vol. A64, pages 102-103. Reg. of Wills, Liber B, folios 326-329.

**Paynter, Samuel,** the elder. Will (copy). Made Oct. 16, 1767. Heirs: sons Samuel and John Paynter; daus. Hannah and Elizabeth Paynter, Mary Adams (wife of Peter). Exec'r, son Samuel Paynter. Wits., Daniel Nunez, Jr., Reece Woolf, Jr., Thomas Martin. Prob. Nov. 6, 1767. Arch. vol. A92, page 136. Reg. of Wills, Liber B, folios 329-331.

**Day, Prettyman.** Will (copy). Made Feb. 10, 1766. Heirs: wife Abigail; sons John and William Day; daus. Marg[a]ret and Mary Day and Nelly Virdan; granddaus. Abigail and Mary Virdan. Exec'rs, sons John and William Day. Wits., William Lay, Samuel Tam. Prob. Feb. 4, 1768. Arch. vol. A68, pages 182-183. Reg. of Wills, Liber B, folio 332.

**Harper, James.** Will (copy). Made June 10, 1765. Heirs: wife Rebeckah Harper; son William Harper; daus. Priscilla, Rebeckah and Sarah Harper. Exec'rx, wife Rebeckah Harper. Wits., Peter Adams, Isaac Clark, Mitchell Black. Prob. March 8, 1768. Arch. vol. A74, page 112. Reg. of Wills, Liber B, folios 334-336.

**Boyd, John.** Yeoman. Will. Made March 9, 1761. Heirs: bros. Jacob and Robert Morgan; sister Hannah Morgan; uncle Albertus Jacobs; cousins William Moliston and Magdalene Price; aunt Elizabeth Smith and children Jonathan, Martha and Nice. Exec'rs, friend Nathaniel Gordon and Rice Woolf, Jr. Wits., Es[the]r Darby, Catherine Gordon, Jane Skidmore. Prob. May 5, 1768. Arch. vol. A60, page 71. Reg. of Wills, Liber B, folios 343-344.

**Hinds, Thomas.** Will. Made April 27, 1768. Heirs: wife Barbara Hinds; sons Thomas, William, Charles and Benjamin Hinds; daus. Sarah and Mary Hinds. Exec'rx, wife Barbara Hinds. Wits., John Hasley, Dorman Lofland, Ann Lay. Prob. May 13, 1768. Arch. vol. A76, pages 175-176. Reg. of Wills, Liber B, folios 336-338. [Note:—Arch. vol. A76, page 176 shows the estate was settled June 24, 1775 by Branson Lofland and wife Barbara (late Barbara Hinds)].

**Stephenson [Stepenson], Jeames [James].** Will. Made June 1, 1768. Heirs: wife Martha Stepenson; son William Stepenson; bro. Robert Stepenson; sister Isabella Annit. Exec'rx, wife Martha Stepenson. Wits., William Godwin, Clark Nottingham, Janet Nottingham. Prob. June 14, 1768. Arch. vol. A100, page 158. Reg. of Wills, Liber B, folios 345-346.

**Salmon, William.** Worcester Co., Md. Admin. (copy) of, to Agnes Salmon. Settled July 3, 1768. Arch. vol. A98, page 1.

**West, Joseph.** Will. Made May 6, 1768. Heirs: bros. Wrixham, Lewis and Peter West; nephew William West; Joseph, John, Elizabeth and Comfort West (children of dec'd bro. John West); niece Ruth West (dau. of bro. Peter West); children of bro. Wrixham West; children of bro. Lewis West. Exec'r, bro. Lewis West. Wits., Daniel Hosman, Temperance Little, Richard Little. Prob. Aug. 4, 1768. Arch. vol. A106, page 151. Reg. of Wills, Liber B, folios 348-350.

**Mariner, Richard.** Will. Made Nov. 16, 1768. Heirs: wife Betty Mariner; sons John, Gilbert and Stockly Mariner; dau. Elizabeth Mariner; bros. William and Gilbert Mariner; cousins Richard and Mary Mariner. Exec'rs, wife Betty Mariner and bro. William Mariner. Wits., William Parker, John Gumly, James Ricords. Prob. Nov. 23, 1768. Arch. vol. A86, page 70. Reg. of Wills, Liber B, folios 352-354.

**May, Jonathan.** Gentleman. Admin. of, to Rhoads Shankland (surviving adm'r). Inventory dated Nov. 30, 1768. Arch. vol. A87, page 94.

**Coulter, Samuel.** Yeoman. Will. Made May 18, 1767. Heirs: wife Anna; sons Charles and William Coulter. Exec'r, son Charles Coulter. Wits., Thomas Staton, Moses Scudder, Samuel Stevenson. Prob. Dec. 3, 1768. Arch. vol. A67, page 66. Reg. of Wills, Liber B, folios 338-339.

**Russel, Joseph.** Yeoman. Will. Made Dec. 3, 1768. Heirs: bro. Samuel Russel; sister Sarah Thomas (wife of Jacob); cousins Lida, Sarah and Ephraim Russel (children of dec'd bro. Ephraim Russel). Exec'r, Parker Robinson, Esq. Wits., Jno. Clowes, Jos[eph] Cord, Esther Little. Prob. Dec. 27, 1768. Arch. vol. A97, page 142. Reg. of Wills, Liber B, folios 346-348.

**Wood, Martha.** Bordentown, Burlington Co., New Jersey. Will (copy). Made Jan. 28, 1769. Heirs: nephew Thomas Moore (son of sister Mary); niece Martha Moore (dau. of sister Mary); Obediah Eldridge (son of Obediah); Friends Monthly Meeting at Duck Creek, Kent County, Delaware. Exec'rx, niece Martha Moore. Wits., Thomas Watson, Jno. Biggins, Edward Wheatcraft. [No prob.]. Arch. vol. A109, page 47. Reg. of Wills, Liber B, folios 354-356.

**Roades, John.** Will. Made Nov. 24, 1768. Heirs: wife Elon Roades; son Hinman Roades; bros. James, Layfield, Francis and William Newbold; sisters Naomi Warrington and Mary

Thompson; uncle William Roades; aunts Comfort Stuart, Agnes Marsh, Elsey Parker; children of aunts Elizabeth Wiltbanks and Patience Shankland. [No exec'r]. Wits., William Dodd, William Little, Richard Little. Prob. Feb. 11, 1769. Arch. vol. A96, page 75. Reg. of Wills, Liber B, folios 373-375.

**Homes [Holmes], Jannet.** Will. Made Oct. 11, 1768. Heirs: John Homes; Robert Homes (son of John and Ann Homes); Sarah Homes (dau. of John and Ann Homes); Robert, Joseph, James and Sarah (children of Charles and Isabel Coulter); John Black (son of James). Exec'r, friend James Black. Wits., Mills McIlvain, Andrew McIlvaine. Prob. Feb. 25, 1769. Arch. vol. A77, pages 154-155. [No Reg. of Wills Liber]. [Note:—Arch. vol. A77, page 155 shows the estate was settled March 25, 1775 by Elizabeth Black, exec'rx of James Black].

**Nunez, Daniel.** Innholder. Lewes. Will. Made Dec. 7, 1764. Heirs: wife Dina Nunez; son Daniel Nunez; dau. Sarah Bailley; Esther Nunez Fisher (dau. of Henry Fisher). Exec'rx, wife Diana Nunez. Wits., Penelope Holt Coward, Alex[ande]r Shankland, Elias Hugg. Prob. March 4, 1769. Arch. vol. A91, page 119. Reg. of Wills, Liber B, folios 358-360.

**Hall, Thomas.** Will. Made Oct. 25, 1768. Heirs: wife Mary Hall; sons John, William, Thomas and Samuel Hall; daus. Sarah and Ann Hall. Exec'rs, wife Mary and son John. Wits., Rachel Bennum, William Burton, James Gordon. Prob. March 13, 1769. Arch. vol. A74, page 6. Reg. of Wills, Liber B, folios 360-362.

**Jones, James.** Yeoman. Will (copy). Made March 9, 1768. Heirs: wife Anna Jones; sons Jacob and Joshua Jones; daus. Elizabeth Garva, Mary Davis, Rebecca Glover. Exec'rx, wife Anna Jones. Wits., John Killingsworth, Sarah Cirwithin, Caleb Cirwithin. Prob. March 25, 1769. Arch. vol. A81, page 164. Reg. of Wills, Liber B, folios 362-364.

**Prettyman, Robert.** Will. Made March 22, 1769. Heirs: sons Thomas, William and Robert Prettyman; daus. Magdalen and Elizabeth Prettyman and Mary Burton. Exec'r, friend Burton Waples. Wits., Peter West, William Burton, William Prettyman. Prob. May 20, 1769. Arch. vol. A94, page 100. Reg. of Wills, Liber B, folios 364-366.

**Clowes, John, Esq.** Will. Made April 8, 1761. Heirs: wife Mary; sons William, Gerhardus, David and John, Jr., daus. Catherine, Lidia and Mary Clowes. Exec'r, son John, Jr. Wits., Cord Hazzard, Joseph Hazzard, Hugh King. Prob. June 21, 1769. Arch. vol. A65, pages 54-55. Reg. of Wills, Liber B, folios 368-374. [Note:—Arch. vol. A65, page 54 mentions dec'd father Samuel].

**Turner, Charity.** Will. Made March 26, 1769. Heirs: sons Nathan, William, Westly, Ephraim and John Turner; daus. Mary Turner, Elizabeth Ponder, Ann Jeffreys. Exec'r, son Ephraim Turner. Wits., Wrixam White, Catherine White, Bethsheba Westly. Prob. July 6, 1769. Arch. vol. A103 page 10. Reg. of Wills, Liber B, folios 371-373.

**Marsh, Peter.** Will. Made July 6, 1769. Heirs: wife Agnes Marsh; sons Peter, John, Phillip, Thomas, Purnal Marsh; daus. Hester and Sarah Marsh, Mary Maull. Exec'rs, wife Agnes Marsh and son Peter Marsh. Wits., William Shankland, Rhoads Shankland, William Little. Prob. Aug. 19, 1769. Arch. vol. A86, pages 117-118. Reg. of Wills, Liber B, folios 375-379. [Note:—Arch. vol. A86, page 117 mentions Peter Marsh, dec'd, grandfather of son Peter].

**Arnall, Samuel.** Pilot. Lewes. Will. Made Jan. 15, 1770. Heirs: sons John and Samuel Arnall; two daus. unnamed. Exec'rs, Joseph Baily and William Arnall. Wits., Luke Shield, Jr., Daniel Murphy, Samuel Edwards. Prob. Feb. 12, 1770. Arch. vol. A57, page 187. Reg. of Wills, Liber B, folios 382-383. [Note:—Arch. vol. A57, page 187 shows Joseph Baily, surviving adm'r settled the estate March 8, 1786].

**Fisher, John.** Yeoman. Will. Made Feb. 8, 1770. Heirs: sons Thomas, James and Jabez Fisher; daus. Sarah Wiltbank (wife of Isaac), Elizabeth Wr[ight] (wife of Peter), and Hannah Fisher; grandsons Joshua and Thomas (sons of Jabez Fisher); granddau. Tabitha Brock. Exec'rs, son James Fisher, dau. Hannah Fisher, sons-in-law Isaac Wiltbank and Peter Wr[ight]. Wits., Parker Robinson, Thomas Redman, Stephen Wood. Prob. Feb. 15, 1770. Arch. vol. A71, page 132. Reg. of Wills, Liber B, folios 379-381.

**Sims, Henrietta.** (Copy). Admin. of, to Daniel Nunez. Dated March 24, 1770. Arch. vol. A99, page 196. [Note:—Order by John Penn to escheat the property of the decedent to the Governor, to be applied to the use of Christ Church, Lewes].

85

**Leatherberry, William Perry.** Will. Made March 15, 1770. Heirs: wife Elizabeth Leatherberry; sister Sarah Prettyman; cousins Leah, Elizabeth, Nancy, Phebe, Comfort, Sheppard and Joseph Prettyman. Exec'rx, wife Elizabeth Leatherberry. Wits., Burton Waples, Robert Burton, Jr., Woolsey Burton. Prob. April 21, 1770. Arch. vol. A84, pages 22-23. Reg. of Wills, Liber B, folios 383-385. [Note:—Arch. vol. A84, page 23 shows the estate was settled March 9, 1784 by Woodman Stockley and Elizabeth, his wife, late Elizabeth Leatherberry].

**Russel, William.** Will. Made April 19, 1770. Heirs: sons Emanuel and Levi Russel; daus. Elizabeth, Mary, Ruth and Tabitha Russel. Exec'rs, sons Emanuel and Levi Russel. Wits., Marnix Virden, Charles Johnson, George Hill. Prob. May 8, 1770. Arch. vol. A97, page 154. Reg. of Wills, Liber B, folios 385-386.

**Inkins, Comfort.** Will (copy). Made July 1, 1769. Heirs: bro. John Lewis; William, Wrixam and Mary Lewis (children of bro. John and Fern Lewis); Elizabeth Rowland; Elizabeth Rowland, Jr. and Comfort Rowland (daus. of Elizabeth Rowland); Lydia Cuningham; Esther Inkins. Exec'rs, David Hall, Esq., and Mary Lewis. Wits., John Wiltbank, John Harmonson, Richard Little. Prob. May 10, 1770. Arch. vol. A79, page 176. Reg. of Wills, Liber B, folios 426-428.

**Lingo, William.** Will. Undated. Heirs: wife Betty Lingo; sons William, Samuel and Henry Lingo; dau. Sarah Lingo. Exec'rx, wife Betty Lingo. Wits., Elizabeth Gordon, James Gordon, Sarah Stockley. Prob. May 19 & 21, 1770. Arch. vol. A84, pages 156-157. Reg. of Wills, Liber B, folios 387-388. [Note:—Arch. vol. A84, page 157 shows that the estate was settled June 3, 1788 by William Davidson and Betty, his wife, late Betty Burns who was Betty Lingo].

**Carpenter, William.** Yeoman. Will. Made Oct. 27, 1760. Heirs: wife Comfort; sons William, George and Jacob; daus. Barshebah, Affiance and Rachel. Exec'rx, wife Comfort. Wits., William Lofland, Robert Warren, Lawrence Wills. Prob. May 22, 1770. Arch. vol. A64, pages 10-11. Reg. of Wills, Liber B, folios 366-367.

**Clowes, David.** Shipcarpenter. Will. Made April 13, 1770. Heirs: wife Sophia; dau. Hannah; bro. John; sisters Catherine and Mary. Exec'r, bro. John Clowes. Wits., Jeremiah Conwell, William Hazzard, Solomon Wright. Guardian, bro. John Clowes. Prob. May 29, 1770. Arch. vol. A65, pages 52-53. Reg. of Wills, Liber B, folios 389-391.

**West, Peter.** Will. Made March 24, 1767. Heirs: wife Comfort West; dau. Ruth West. Exec'rx, wife Comfort West. Wits., Wrixam West, Joseph West, Betty Prettyman. Prob. June 8, 1770. Arch. vol. A106, page 163. Reg. of Wills, Liber B, folios 391-392.

**Lindell, Thomas.** Will. Made April 25, 1770. Heirs: wife Comfort Lindell; bros. Joseph, Zadock and Peter Lindell; niece Comfort Warker (dau. of sister Sary Warker). Exec'rs, wife Comfort Lindell and bro. Joseph Lindell. Wits., John Lofland, Jr., Eli Parker, John Jones (schoolmaster). Prob. June 18, 1770. Arch. vol. A84, page 111. Reg. of Wills, Liber B, folios 392-394.

**Spencer, Levi.** Will. Made April 30, 1770. Heirs: wife Percy Spencer; sons Levi and Luke Spencer; daus. Betty, Nancy and Percy Spencer; child unnamed. Exec'rx, wife Percy Spencer. Wits., Ann Oldson, Joshua Spencer. Prob. June 23, 1770. Arch. vol. A100, page 61. Reg. of Wills, Liber B, folios 394-396. [Note:—Arch. vol. A100, page 61 shows the estate was settled May 4, 1784 by Joseph Crouch and wife Percy, late Percy Collings and who was Percy Spencer].

**Bagwell, Thomas.** Will. Made May 30, 1770. Heirs: wife Ann; sons John, Thomas and William; daus. Elizabeth, Catherine and Lydia Bagwell, and Ann McMain. Exec'rs, wife Ann and sons John and William. Wits., William Burton, Jr., Woolsey Burton, Jr.; Benjamin Burton. Prob. Aug. 3, 1770. Arch. vol. A58, page 59. Reg. of Wills, Liber B, folios 396-398.

**Art, Jacob.** Pilot. Admin. of, to Hannah Art, widow. Granted [c. Sept. 1770]. Arch. vol. A57, pages 192-193. [Note:—Arch. vol. A57, page 192 mentions minors: James, Jacob, Hannah and Baily Art; also shows that Hannah Art later married Robert Massey].

**Rodney, William.** Planter. Worcester Co., Md. Will (copy). Made Dec. 3, 1767. Heirs: wife Mary Rodney; son William Rodney; daus. Lydia Rodney, Leah Simpler, Susannah Marvill, Comfort Marvill and Mary Magdaline Jones; son-in-law Thomas Prettyman. Exec'rx, wife Mary Rodney. Wits., W[illia]m Kollock, Simon Kollock, Joshua Morris. Prob. Oct. 19, 1770. Arch. vol. A97, page 28. [Not recorded in Sussex County, Delaware].

**Manlove, Magdalene.** Will. Made March 21, 1770. Heirs: sons Jonathan, Boas and Manuel Manlove; daus. Elizabeth Manlove, Ann Burroughs; grandson James Owens; granddaus. Eunice Waller, Sarah and Betty Manlove (daus. of George). [No exec'r]. Wits., Charles Polk, Sr., Charles Polk, Jr., George Polk. Prob. Nov. 22, 1770. Arch. vol. A86, page 38. Reg. of Wills, Liber B, folios 406-407.

**Cornish, Ezer.** Ditcher. Will. Made Dec. 7, 1770. Heirs: wife Mary; sons Samuel and Amos Cornish; daus. Sarah and Elener Cornish. Exec'rs, wife Mary and son Samuel. Wits., Jesse Townsend, Sarah Townsend, Mitchell Jackson. Prob. Dec. 31, 1770. Arch. vol. A66, page 223. Reg. of Wills, Liber B, folios 408-409.

**Craige, John.** Admin. of, to Molly Craige. Settled [c. Dec. 31, 1770]. Arch. vol. A67, page 151.

**Bicknell, Sarah.** Will. Made Dec. 8, 1770. Heirs: William Bicknell; sisters Mary Bicknell, Ruth Woolf and Lidia Jackson; niece Alice Bicknell (dau. of sister Esther Bicknell, dec'd) ; John Bicknell; Joseph and John Thompson Hepburn. Exec'r, Jonathan Woolf. Wits., Ephraim Turner, Jean Chambers, Mary Peck. Prob. Jan. 11, 1771. Arch. vol. A59, page 176. Reg. of Wills, Liber B, folios 409-411.

**Hazzard, Cord.** Yeoman. Will. Made Jan. 31, 1766. Heirs: wife Rachel Hazzard; sons Joseph and David Hazzard; daus. Hannah and Arcada Robinson, Rhoda Fowler, Rachel Burton, Mary King; granddaus. Mary Hazzard (dau. of son William, dec'd), Elizabeth Hazzard (dau. of son Cord, dec'd). Exec'rs, wife Rachel and son Joseph Hazzard. Wits., Hamilton Craige, Mary Craige, Cornelius Stockley. Prob. Jan. 11, 1771. Arch. vol. A75, page 39. Reg. of Wills, Liber B, folio 411.

**Turner, Nathan.** Will. Made Dec. 29, 1770. Heirs: wife Leticia Turner; son Cornelius Turner; child unnamed; bro. William Westly Turner; sister Mary Turner. Exec'r, William Stockly, Jr. Wits., Ephraim Turner, William Roach, John Westly. Prob. Jan. 18, 1771. Arch. vol. A103, page 23. Reg. of Wills, Liber B, folios 417-419.

**Wiltbanck, Naomy.** Will. Made Sept. 22, 1770. Heirs: Naomy and John Shankland (children of John, dec'd) ; Ann Craper (wife of Leavin Craper) ; Comfort W[right] (wife of Edward W[right]. Exec'r, friend Edward W[right]. Wits., John Heavelo, Jeremiah Conwell, Lidia Conwell. Prob. Feb. 2, 1771. Arch. vol. A108, page 160. Reg. of Wills, Liber B, folios 419-420.

**Coverdell [Coverdale], Richard.** Yeoman. Will. Made Feb. 10, 1770. Heirs: wife Elizabeth; sons John, Richard, Israel and Matthew Coverdell; daus. Mary, Sarah, Jean [Jane], Rosannah and Elizabeth. Exec'rs, wife Elizabeth and son Israel. Wits., Warren Burrough, David Passwaters, Charles Polk, Jr. Prob. Feb. 6, 1771. Arch. vol. A67, pages 94-95. Reg. of Wills, Liber B, folios 421-422. [Note:—Arch. vol. A67, page 95 shows the estate was settled June 8, 1785 by Israel Coverdale, surviving exec'r].

**West, Wrixam.** Will. Made May 17, 1768. Heirs: wife Betty West; sons Benjamin and John West; daus. Ann and Mary West. Exec'r, bro. Lewis West. Wits., Naomy Shankland, Jos[eph] Shankland, John Allen. Prob. April 6, 1771. Arch. vol. A106, page 193. Reg. of Wills, Liber B, folios 422-426. [Note:—Arch. vol. A106, page 193 shows the estate was settled June 4, 1775 by Benjamin B. West, who was adm'r of Lewis West].

**Simonton, Margaret.** Widow. Will. Made March 21, 1771. Heirs: daus. Jane Baily, Sarah Shankland, Mary Davison and Elizabeth Lewis. Exec'r, John Rodney. Wits., Matthew Wilson, Prettyman Stockley, Mary Skidmore. Prob. April 17, 1771. Arch. vol. A99, page 42. Reg. of Wills, Liber B, folios 435-437.

**Stockley, John.** Weaver. Angola Neck. Will. Made April 7, 1771. Heirs: wife Mary Stockley; children unnamed. Exec'rx, wife Mary Stockley. Wits., John Harmonson, Oliver Stockley, Jacob Stockley. Prob. April 31, 1771. Arch. vol. A101, page 16. Reg. of Wills, Liber B, folios 424-426.

**Riley, Thomas.** Will. Made April 15, 1771. Heirs: wife Jacamen Riley; sons George and Thomas Riley. Exec'rx, wife Jacamen Riley. Wits., David Wattson, Rachel Townsend, David Thornton. Prob. May . . ., 1771. Arch. vol. A96, pages 54-55. Reg. of Wills, Liber B, folios 428-430. [Note: —Arch. vol. A96, page 55 shows the estate was settled April 9, 1775 by Isaac Townsend and wife Jacamen, late Jacamen Riley].

**Turner, William Westley.** Will. Made Feb. . . ., 1771. Heirs: sisters Mary Turner, Ann Jeffris; bros. Ephraim and John Turner; nieces Elisabeth and Unice Turner, Ruth and Ann Jeffris, Esther, Sarah and Elsie Ponder. Exec'rx, sister Mary Turner. Wits., Simon Darby, John Ponder, Elisabeth Ponder. Prob. June 5, 1771. Arch. vol. A103, page 27. Reg. of Wills, Liber B, folios 430-431.

89

**Roades, John.** Admin. of, to David Hazzard. Settled Nov. 8, 1771. Arch. vol. A96, page 76.

**Riggs, John.** Cedar Creek. Admin. of, to Levi Riggs. Settled Nov. 20, 1771. Arch. vol. A96, page 28.

**Scudder, Jonathan.** Will. Made Oct. 28, 1771. Heirs: wife Cloe Scudder; dau. Rachel Scudder. Exec'rs, wife Cloe Scudder and James Martin. Wits., Ruth Black, William Perry, James Tamplin. Prob. Nov. 23, 1771. Arch. vol. A98, page 41. Reg. of Wills, Liber B, folios 431-433.

**Downey, Martha.** Will. Made Oct. 28, 1771. Heirs: mother Mary Turner; cousins Benjamin Lear, John Tam, Joseph Tam, Martha Stevenson, Rhody Stevenson, Isaac Templain, Mary Templain and Richard Templain; father-in-law Samuel Turner; aunt Sarah Tam. Exec'rs, aunt Sarah Tam and cousin Benjamin Lear. Wits., Samuel Hand, Mary Vent, Thomas Hall. Prob. Dec. 2, 1771. Arch. vol. A69, page 170. Reg. of Wills, Liber B, folios 433-435.

**Prettyman, William.** Will (nunc.). Made July 20, 1766. Heirs: wife Elizabeth Prettyman; sons Burton and Robert Prettyman; dau. Magdalene Prettyman. [No exec'r]. Wits., Robert Prettyman. Prob. (recorded) Jan. 3, 1772. Arch. vol. A94, page 124. Reg. of Wills, Liber B, folio 350.

**Prettyman, Comfort.** Widow. Will. Made Jan. 5, 1765. Heirs: bro. Charles Smith; Margaret Hill, John Futcher; Sarah Dobson; Robert Burton (son of Robert Burton, Jr.). Exec'rs, John Futcher and Sarah Dobson. Wits., Solomon Stockly, Elizabeth Titus, Lemuel Coleson Paynter. Prob. Jan. 4, 1772. Arch. vol. A94, page 54. Reg. of Wills, Liber B, folios 351-352.

**Little [Littel], William.** Will. Made Jan. 2, 1772. Heirs: wife and dau. unnamed; bro. John Little. Exec'rs, bro. John Little and unnamed wife. Wits., Richard Little, Thomas Gordon, Thomas West. Prob. Jan. 13, 1772. Arch. vol. A84, pages 171-172. Reg. of Wills, Liber B, folios 440-441.

**Truitt, Solomon.** Will. Made Oct. 12, 1770. Heirs: wife Mary Truitt; sons Benjamin, Joseph, John, Solomon and Hezekiah Truitt; daus. Mary Alcock and Sarah Hilford; grandchildren William, Frederick and Persis Halden, Sarah Hunter (children of dec'd dau. Elizabeth, wife of Robert Hunter). Exec'r, son John Truitt. Wits., Elijah Truitt, Edward Cary, Susanna Cary. Trustees: Samuel and Joshua Spencer. Prob. Feb. 4, 1772. Arch. vol. A102, page 159. Reg. of Wills, Liber B, folios 441-445.

**Marriner, William.** Admin. of, to Woodman Stockley, in right of Sarah Marriner, widow. Adm'rs bond dated Feb. 6, 1772. Arch. vol. A66, pages 88-89.

**Pettit, Laban.** Yeoman. Will. Made Feb. 7, 1772. Heirs: wife Joanna Pettit; son Jacob Pettit. Exec'rx, wife Joanna Pettit. Wits., John Black, Thomas May, George Walton. Prob. Feb. 15, 1772. Arch. vol. A92, pages 191-192. Reg. of Wills, Liber B, folios 455-457. [Note:—Arch. vol. A92, page 192 shows the estate was settled June 7, 1790 by William Bell and Joanna Bell, his wife (late Joanna Pettit)].

**Willson, Moses.** Will. Made Jan. 31, 1772. Heirs: wife Ann Willson; sons Aaron, Isaac, Jesse, John and Moses Willson; daus. Sarah Willson and Mary Hazzard (wife of Powell Hazzard). Exec'r, son Isaac Willson. Wits., William Peery, Rhoda Hatfield, Whitlay Hatfield. Prob. Feb. 19, 1772. Arch. vol. A108, page 102. Reg. of Wills, Liber B, folios 457-459.

**Kollock, Jacob, Esq.** Lewes. Will. Made Feb. 17, 1767. Heirs: wife Margaret Kollock; sons Phillip and Jacob, Jr.; daus. Hester and Mary Kollock, Catherine Wiltbank (wife of Abraham), Hannah Nunez, and Magdelan Swift; granddau. Mary Swift; children of dec'd dau. Jane Lewis. Exec'rx, wife Margaret Kollock. Wits., Samuel Paynter, John Rodney, Henry Neill. Codicil. June 14, 1771. Wits., John Woods. Mentions dau. Mary Field (wife of Nehemiah). Prob. Feb. 21, 1772. Arch. vol. A83, page 4. Reg. of Wills, Liber B, folios 445-455.

**Steel, Daniel.** Will. Made Nov. 1, 1771. Heirs: wife Elizabeth Steel; sons Nathaniel, Daniel, Benjamin, James and William Steel; daus. Rachel and Barsheba Steel; grandson Valentine Pride; granddau. Ann Pride. Exec'rs, wife Elizabeth Steel and son Nathaniel Steel. Wits., Prisgrave Steel, William Wilson, Abr[aha]m Farrill. Prob. Feb. 22, 1772. Arch. vol. A100, page 135. Reg. of Wills, Liber B, folios 459-460.

**Collings, Ezekiel.** Admin. of, to Bucor Johnson. Granted Feb. 24, 1772. Arch. vol. A65, page 161. [Note:—Arch. vol. A65, page 161 mentions sons William and John, and dec'd wife].

**Spencer, Ebenezer.** Admin. of, to John Metcalf and wife Betty. Settled c. March 3, 1772. Arch. vol. A100, page 52.

**Chance, Spencer.** Yeoman. Admin. of, to John Chance. Granted [ante March 17, 1772]. Arch. vol. A64, page 128.

**Poor, Mary.** Will. Made March 10, 1772. Heirs: sons Major, Luke, Nehemiah and Joshua Poor; daus. Margaret, Naomi, Phebe, Lorana, Jemima and Mary Poor. Exec'r, son Major Poor. Wits., William Hudson, Ellis Hudson, Joseph Truitt. Prob. April 9, 1772. Arch. vol. A94, page 6. Reg. of Wills, Liber B, folios 460-462. [Note:—Arch. vol. A94, page 6 shows Robert Warren, a friend, and Richard Shockley, a bro.-in-law, were appointed Guardians].

**Spencer, Samuel.** Will. Made Dec. 30, 1771. Heirs: wife Catharine Spencer; sons Jesse, Luke and Joshua Spencer; daus. Phebe Spencer, Anne Draper (wife of William), Naomi Maccay (wife of Alexander); grandsons John Spencer (son of son John, dec'd), Samuel Spencer (son of son Joshua); grandchildren Samuel, John and Catharine Spencer (children of son Joseph, dec'd), Walton, Samuel, Luke, Levi, Percy, Nancy and Elizabeth Spencer (children of dec'd son Levi); granddau. Nice Wallter (wife of John); son-in-law William Draper. Exec'rs, sons Jesse and Luke Spencer and son-in-law William Draper. Wits., David Wattson, Mary Hazel, Edward Stapleford. Prob. May 6, 1772. Arch. vol. A100, page 65. Reg. of Wills, Liber B, folios 462-467.

**Hudson, Ananias.** Will. Made Feb. 6, 1772. Heirs: wife Sophia Hudson; daus. Loranah and Ruth Hudson. Exec'rs, wife Sophia Hudson and father-in-law William Poynter. Wits., Joseph Truitt, William Poynter, William Haldon. Prob. May 8, 1772. Arch. vol. A78, pages 168-169. Reg. of Wills, Liber B, folios 471-472. [Note:—Arch. vol. A78, page 169 shows that the estate was settled by Coverdale Cole and Sophia, his wife, late Sophia Hudson].

**Stockley, William, Jr.** Yeoman. Will. Made May 14, 1771. Heirs: wife Elizabeth Stockley; sons Jacob, William and Paynter Stockley; daus. Letetia Turner and Sarah Roach. Exec'rs, wife Elizabeth Stockley and son Jacob Stockley. Wits., Rhoads Shankland, William Virden, John Russel. Prob. June 10, 1772. Arch. vol. A101, page 36. Reg. of Wills, Liber B, folios 437-439. [Note:—Arch. vol. A101, page 36 shows the estate was settled March 6, 1788 by Jacob Stockley, the surviving exec'r; also mentions Letitia Newman].

**Hugg, Elias.** Lewes. Will. Made March 17, 1772. Heirs: wife Mary Hugg; uncle Alexander Shankland; aunts Mary

Shankland, Ann Molleston; William Molleston; John Neill; Henry Neill; Robert Shankland (son of Mrs. Sarah Shankland); David Hall, Trustee for Presbyterian Meeting House. Exec'rs, wife Mary Hugg and Henry Neill. Wits., Hannah Price, Jacob Moore, John Mackemy. Prob. June 12, 1772. Arch. vol. A79, pages 80-81. Reg. of Wills, Liber B, folios 467-468.

**Ricords, Joseph.** Will. Made June 7, 1772. Heirs: wife Sarah Ricords; bro. James Ricords. Exec'r, friend John Harmonson. Wits., Samuel Darby, William Bicknel, Thomas Walker. Prob. June 12, 1772. Arch. vol. A95, page 173. Reg. of Wills, Liber B, folios 509-510.

**Frame, Nathan.** Worcester Co., Md. Will (copy). Made Oct. 11, 1770. Heirs: bro. Smith Frame. Exec'r, Smith Frame. Wits., John Moriss, Gobiz Townsend, Thomas Wingate. Prob. June 29, 1772. Arch. vol. A72, page 40. Reg. of Wills, Liber B, folio 405.

**Spencer, John, Esq.** Admin. of, to Lawrence Riley and wife Sarah. Settled July 4, 1772. Arch. vol. A100, pages 57-58. [Note:—Arch. vol. A100, page 58 mentions two children, John Spencer, Jno. Waller and wife Uncey].

**Cowing, Alexander.** Will. Made April 8, 1772. Heirs: wife Betty; son George Cowing; daus. Nanney and Esther Cowing, and Betty Conner (wife of Bundik Conner). Exec'rs, wife Betty and son George Cowing. Wits., William Hazzard, Benjamin Truitt, Solomon Truitt. Prob. July 9, 1772. Arch. vol. A67, page 117. Reg. of Wills, Liber B, folios 469-470.

**Prettyman, William.** Admin. of, to Perry Prettyman, in right of Comfort Prettyman, dec'd. Settled July 27, 1772. Arch. vol. A94, page 125.

**Coverdale, Susannah.** Admin. of, to John Coverdale, surviving adm'r. Date of admin. bond Dec. 2, 1772. Arch. vol. A67, page 103.

**Bagwell, William.** Admin. of, to Thomas Laws. Granted [c. 1773]. Arch. vol. A58, page 61.

**Benson, James.** Worcester County, Md. Admin. of, to Elihu Jackson and wife Elizabeth (late Elizabeth Benson), C. T. A. Granted [c. 1773]. Arch. vol. A59, page 133.

**Conwell, George.** Admin. of, to Eunice Conwell. Granted [c. 1773]. Arch. vol. A66, page 108.

**Manlove, Manuel.** Dorchester County, Md. Admin. of, to Sydenham Thorn and wife Betty (late Betty Manlove). Granted [c. 1773]. Arch. vol. A86, page 40. [Note:—This admin. also shown with the will in Arch. vol. A39, page 536. Arch. vol. A86, page 40 shows that Betty Manlove married Levin Crapper and then later married Sydenham Thorn].

**Conwell, Jeremiah.** Yeoman. Admin. of, to Lydia Conwell. Granted [c. Jan. 1773]. Arch. vol. A66, pages 114-115. [Note:—Arch. vol. A66, page 115 mentions minor children: Shepard, Gerhardus and John Conwell; also shows that Lydia Conwell later married Lott Clark].

**Campbell, Nathan.** Admin. of, to Esther Campbell. Granted [c. Feb. 13, 1773]. Arch. vol. A62, page 204.

**Russel, John.** Will. Made Jan. 29, 1773. Heir: wife Sara Russel. Exec'r, Josias Martin. Wits., Jonathan Martin, Sacker Wyatt, John Veasy. Prob. Feb. 15, 1773. Arch. vol. A97, page 136. Reg. of Wills, Liber B, folios 510-511.

**Mariner, Sarah.** Widow of William Mariner. Admin. of, to Woodman Stockley. Admr's bond dated Feb. 19, 1773. Arch. vol. A86, pages 76-77.

**Collins, William.** Admin. of, to Sarah Johnson, D. B. N., in right of Baker Johnson. Granted [c. Feb. 24, 1773]. Arch. vol. A66, page 44.

**Stuart, John.** Will. Made March 11, 1773. Heirs: wife Elizabeth Stuart; sons John, Thomas, David and William Stuart; daus. Ann, Ruth, Elizabeth and Sarah Stuart, and Mary Stapleford (wife of Edward). Exec'rx, wife Elizabeth Stuart. Wits., William Peery, James Coulter, Sarah Beesy. Prob. . . ., 1773. Arch. vol. A101, page 54. Reg. of Wills, Liber B, folios 472-474.

**Stephenson, Hannah.** Will. Made March 8, 1773. Heirs: son John West; bro. John Stockly; son-in-law Joseph West; dau.-in-law Comfort West. Exec'r, bro. John Stockly. Wits., Mary Stockly, Patience Stockly, Tho[ma]s Gray. Prob. March 19, 1773. Arch. vol. A100, page 156. Reg. of Wills, Liber B, folios 511-513.

**Lofland [Loughland], John, Sr.** Will. Made Sept. 14, 1770. Heirs: wife Rachel Loughland; sons John and Zadock Loughland; daus. Mary, Comfort, Elizabeth, Rachel, Suzannah, Sarah and Abigail Loughland. Exec'rs, wife Rachel and son John Loughland. Wits., John Clowes, Ahab Clendaniel, Avery Clendaniel. Prob. March 24, 1773. Arch. vol. A85, page 56. Reg. of Wills, Liber B, folios 478-481.

**Townsend, Solomon, Jr.** Will. Made March 2, 1773. Heirs: wife Elizabeth Townsend; bros. Jacob, Luke and William Townsend; sister Phebe Morris; nephews John Townsend (son of bro. Luke), Solomon Townsend (son of William); niece Nancy Townsend (dau. of bro. Luke); Selah Watson; Richard Coverdale; John Lofland, Jr. Exec'rs, wife Elizabeth Townsend and bro.-in-law John Lofland. Wits., Wrixsom Warren, Benjamin Webb, Sealah Robison. Prob. March 24, 1773. Arch. vol. A102, page 77. Reg. of Wills, Liber B, folios 481-482.

**Wattson, Isaac.** Will. Made Jan. 27, 1773. Heirs: wife Mary Wattson; sons Joseph and Isaac Wattson; dau. Elizabeth Draper; grandson Isaac Riley; granddau. Mary Riley. Exec'rs, wife Mary Wattson, son Isaac Wattson. Wits., Elijah Truitt, Alice Wattson, Reynear Williams. Prob. March 24, 1773. Arch. vol. A106, pages 5-6. Reg. of Wills, Liber B, folios 476-478. [Note:—Arch. vol. A106, page 6 mentions John Draper as the husband of Elizabeth Draper].

**Joice, Samuel.** Will (copy). Made May 9, 1772. Heirs: wife Mary Joice; son Samuel Joice; dau. Sarah Cropper (wife of John). Exec'rs, wife Mary Joice and friend Donovan Spencer. Wits., William Hazzard, Thomas May, Ann May. Prob. March 29, 1773. Arch. vol. A81, page 130. Reg. of Wills, Liber B, folios 482-483.

**Hudson, John.** Will. Made Jan. 30, 1769. Heirs: sons John, William, Joshua, Major, Henry and Ananias Hudson; daus. Mary Hays (wife of Richard, Jr.), Elizabeth Willey, Rachel Davis (wife of Thomas). Exec'r, son Henry Hudson. Wits., Joseph Truitt, Sr., John Truitt, Margaret Fisher. Prob. April 12, 1773. Arch. vol. A79, pages 13-14. Reg. of Wills, Liber B, folios 485-487. [Note:—Arch. vol. A79, page 14 mentions Luranah Hudson].

**Truitt, Benjamin.** Yeoman. Will. Made March 15, 1773. Heirs: wife Edy Truitt; sons John, Joseph, Benjamin, Elijah and George Truitt; daus. Rachel, Edy and Elizabeth Truitt. Exec'rs, sons John, Joseph and Benjamin Truitt. Wits., W[illia]m Hazzard, Thomas Cary, Leah Depray. Prob. April 12, 1773. Arch. vol. A102, page 98. Reg. of Wills, Liber B, folios 484-485.

**Woolf, Rees.** Innholder. Lewes. Will. Made March 1, 1772. Heirs: dau. Mary Paynter; grandsons Rees, Richard and Samuel Paynter. Exec'rx, dau. Mary Paynter. Wits., Reece

Woolf, Jr., Ann Reed, John McCullah. Prob. April 21, 1773. Arch. vol. A109, page 36. Reg. of Wills, Liber B, folios 491-492.

**Williams, Reynear.** Will. Made April 1, 1773. Heirs: wife Ann Williams; bro. James Draper; sisters Elizabeth, Sarah and Phebe Draper; friend Littleton Townsend; Elizabeth Robertson. Exec'rs, wife Ann Williams, friend Littleton Townsend. Wits., Thomas Evans, Jr., Joseph Draper, Sally Hays. Prob. May 5, 1773. Arch. vol. A108, pages 30-31. Reg. of Wills, Liber C, folios 83-85. [Note:—Arch. vol. A108, pages 30 and 31 show the estate was settled by Littleton Townsend (surviving partner in trade) as well as surviving exec'r].

**Spencer, Joseph.** Admin. of, to Edward Stapleford and wife Mary, late Mary Spencer. Settled May 9, 1773. Arch. vol. A100, page 60. [Note:—Arch. vol. A100, page 60 mentions Catharine Spencer, John Spencer, Samuel Spencer, Mary Spencer].

**Collings, Andrew.** Yeoman. Worcester County, Md. Will. Made May 15, 1773. Heirs: sons Andrew and John Collings; daus. Elizabeth Bradley and Mary Truitt; grandsons Collings and John (son of Samuel) Truitt; granddau. Elizabeth Truitt (dau. of Samuel). Exec'rs, sons Andrew and John Collings. Wits., Samuel Hand, Salathiel Collins, Phillip Truitt, John Clowes. Prob. June 18, 1773. Arch. vol. A65, pages 125-128. Reg. of Wills, Liber D, folio 125. [Note:—Arch. vol. A65, page 128 shows the estate was settled Sept. 7, 1786 by John Collings, surviving exec'r].

**Waller, John.** Shipwright. Will. Made June 17, 1773. Heirs: wife Eunice Waller; son George Waller; dau. Mary Waller. Exec'rx, wife Eunice Waller. Wits., Boaz Manlove, Charles Waller, David Train. Prob. July 19, 1773. Arch. vol. A104, pages 65-66. Reg. of Wills, Liber B, folios 492-494. [Note:—Arch. vol. A104, page 66 shows the estate was settled June 7, 1784 by George Conwell and wife Eunice (late Eunice Waller)].

**Riley, John.** Admin. of, to Isaac Wattson and wife Mary, late Mary Riley. Admr's bond dated Aug. 25, 1773. Arch. vol. A96, page 41.

**Lay, Thomas.** Admin. of, to Isaac Lay. Granted [c. Aug. 28, 1773]. Arch. vol. A83, page 168.

**Campbell, John.** Worcester County, Md. Will (copy). Made July 19, 1773. Heirs: wife Esther Campbell; son John Simpson Campbell; dau. Mary Positt; Esther Draper (wife's dau.); and wife's other children unnamed. Exec'r, son John Simpson Campbell. Wits., Jno. Dato, Anne Postly, John Postly. Prob. Sept. 7, 1773. Arch. vol. A62, page 197. Reg. of Wills, Liber C, folios 31-32.

**Neall [Neill], Elisabeth.** Will. Made Aug. 10, 1771. Heirs: sons James, William and Isaac Holland; grandsons Peter Adams, Peter Foster; granddaus. Comfort and Naomi Foster; grandchildren, children of Isaac Holland, children of James Holland and 2 children of son William Holland. Exec'rs, sons James and William Holland. Wits., Richard Little, John Ponder, Abraham Mackimme. Prob. Sept. 24, 1773. Arch. vol. A91, page 27. Reg. of Wills, Liber B, folios 494-496.

**Jones, Isaac.** Yeoman. Admin. of, to Abigail Jones. Admr's bond dated Nov. 6, 1773. Arch. vol. A81, page 152.

**Anderson, Sarah.** Widow. Will. Made Nov. 8, 1773. Heirs: friends Woodman Stockley and wife Elizabeth. Exec'r, Woodman Stockley. Wits., Robert Prettyman, Allenar Prettyman, Agnes Tull. Prob. Nov. 13, 1773. Arch. vol. A57, pages 146-147. Reg. of Wills, Liber B, folios 513-514.

**Virden, Hugh.** Will. Made Oct. 20, 1772. Heirs: son William Virden; other children unnamed. Exec'r, son William Virden. Wits., David Stevenson, Samuel Hudson, Aaron Dodd. Prob. Dec. 11, 1773. Arch. vol. A103, page 175. Reg. of Wills, Liber B, folios 496-497.

**Fowler, Ari [Arthur], Sr.** Worcester Co., Md. Will (copy). Made Oct. 19, 1772. Heirs: wife Mary Fowler; sons Jonathan, Arthur, Jesse, John and George Fowler; daus. Phebe Sanders, Esther Owens, Keziah Staton, Mary Royal and Sarah Hurt. Exec'rs, wife Mary and son Jonathan Fowler. Wits., Joseph Vaughn, John Chance, William Owens. Prob. Sept. [Dec.] 14, 1773. Arch. vol. A72, pages 1-2. Reg. of Wills, Liber A, folios 494-495. [Note:—Arch. vol. A72, page 2 shows the estate was settled March 6, 1778 by Jonathan Fowler, but does not mention the other exec'r, wife Mary Fowler].

**Warren [Warring], Lodwick.** Admin. of, to Easter Warring. Granted Dec. 14, 1773. Arch. vol. A105, page 112.

**Campbell, Samuel.** Admin. of, to William Ironshire and wife Sarah (late Sarah Campbell). Granted [c. 1774]. Arch. vol. A62, page 212.

**Clarkson, William.** Admin. of, to James Brown, Jr., exec'r of Abraham Clarkson, dec'd, who in turn was exec'r of Richard Clarkson, Jr., dec'd, adm'r of this estate. Granted [c. 1774]. Arch. vol. A64, page 222.

**Lofland, Mary.** Will. Made Oct. 5, 1773. Heirs: son Cornelius Lofland; daus. Sarah, Betty and Mary Lofland, Jemima Veach (wife of William); grandsons Watman, Purnal and Isaac Lofland (sons of son John); Art Vankirk; granddau. Avis . . .; grandchildren, children of Joseph Lindal and children of son Ebenezer Lofland; son-in-law Joseph Lindal; dau.-in-law Elizabeth Lofland (widow of Ebenezer). Exec'r, son-in-law William Veach. Wits., Joseph Truitt, Benjamin Webb, Elias Veach. Prob. Jan. 29, 1774. Arch. vol. A85, pages 71-72. Reg. of Wills, Liber B, folios 474-476. [Note: —Arch. vol. A85, page 72 mentions Mary Vankirk].

**Mitten, James.** Admin. of, to Elizabeth Mitten. Granted Feb. . . ., 1774. Arch. vol. A89, page 84.

**Riley, Laurence, Sr.** Yeoman. Will. Made Jan. 21, 1774. Heirs: wife Sarah Riley; sons Laurence, John and Benjamin Riley; daus. Mary and Elizabeth Riley, Sarah Torbert, Susannah Heaverloe. Exec'rs, sons Laurence and John Riley. Wits., Samuel Hand, Joseph Darby, David Train. Prob. Feb. 2, 1774. Arch. vol. A96, pages 44-45. Reg. of Wills, Liber B, folios 497-499.

**Waples, William.** Will. Made Nov. 12, 1773. Heirs: wife Abigail Waples; Thomas Marriner (sòn of John); Presbyterian Churches of Sussex County. Exec'rx, wife Abigail Waples. Wits., Burton Waples, Sr., Thomas Bartlet, Elizabeth Newton. Prob. Feb. 17, 1774. Arch. vol. A105, page 63. Reg. of Wills, Liber B, folios 500-501. [Note:—Arch. vol. A105, page 63 shows the estate was settled Nov. 25, 1775 by Burton Waples, Jr., admr. of Abigail Waples, dec'd].

**Darby, Elizabeth.** Widow. Admin. of, to Joseph Darby, D. B. N., in lieu of Samuel Darby, yeoman. Date of inventory Feb. 26, 1774. Arch. vol. A68, page 16. [Note:—Arch. vol. A68, page 16 mentions Ephraim Darby, grandfather of Joseph Darby].

**Draper, Alexander.** Will. Made Feb. 6, 1774. Heirs: wife Esther Draper; daus. Mary and Sally Draper. Exec'rx, wife Esther Draper. Wits., David Thornton, Thomas Evans, Joseph Morgan. Prob. Feb. 28, 1774. Arch. vol. A69, pages 182-183. Reg. of Wills, Liber B, folio 501. [Note:—Arch. vol. A69, page 183 shows that Esther Draper later married Nathaniel Young].

**Stuart, Daniel.** Will. Made Feb. 21, 1774. Heirs: sons John and William Stuart; daus. Sarah, Ann and Martha Stuart, and Comfort Lingo. Exec'rx, dau. Sarah Stuart. Wits., Joshua Richards, Lewis West, Benjamin West. Prob. March 7, 1774. Arch. vol. A101, page 51. Reg. of Wills, Liber B, folios 502-503.

**West, Comfort.** Widow. Will. Made Feb. 21, 1774. Heirs: sons William and Benjamin Prettyman; daus. Jeanne Prettyman, Ruth West and Betty Waples; son-in-law Burton Waples; grandson Woolsey Waples; granddau. Nancy Waples. Exec'rs, son William Prettyman and son-in-law Burton Waples. Wits., Thomas Waples, Burton Waples, Sr., Elisabeth Prettyman. Prob. March 9, 1774. Arch. vol. A106, page 107. Reg. of Wills, Liber B, folios 504-505.

**Williams, Bethuel.** Will. Made Jan. 27, 1774. Heir: bro. Lemuel Williams. Exec'r, bro. Lemuel Williams. Wits., William Thorpe, William Mitten, Elizabeth Ponder. Prob. March 22, 1774. Arch. vol. A107, page 154. Reg. of Wills, Liber B, folios 505-506.

**Hall, Mary** (wife of Joshua Hall). Worcester Co., Md. Will, Made March 29, 1774. Heir: bro. Smith Frame. [No exec'r]. Wits., Simon Kollock, James Cooper, William Butcher. Codicil, mentions husband Joshua. [No prob.]. Arch. vol. A73, page 230. Reg. of Wills, Liber C, folios 87-88. [Note:—Arch. vol. A73, page 230 mentions dec'd father Robert Frame].

**White, Jacob.** Lewes. Will. Made Dec. 11, 1769. Heirs: wife Mary White; sons Wrixam, Philip, Isaac and Robert White; daus. Hester White, Sarah Lamb (wife of Abner Lamb), Mary Allen (wife of William Allen); grandson Jacob White (son of Wrixam). Exec'rs, sons Isaac and Robert White. Wits., Jno. Rodney, Samuel Paynter, John Neill. Prob. March 31, 1774. Arch. vol. A107, page 62. Reg. of Wills, Liber B, folios 515-520. [Note:—Arch. vol. A107, page 62 shows the estate was settled by Robert White, surviving exec'r].

**Leatherbury, Diana.** Widow. Will. Made Oct. 8, 1773. Heirs: daus. Elizabeth Stockley (formerly wife of William Leathbury), Elizabeth Hemmons (wife of John Hemmons), Comfort Salmons (wife of William Salmons), Barshaba Waples (wife of Paul Waples), Sarah Barns (wife of George Barns); grandsons Joseph and Shepard Prettyman; granddaus. Elizabeth, Ann, Phebe and Comfort Prettyman. Exec'rx, dau. Elizabeth Hemmons. Wits., Comfort West, Burton Waples,

Sr., William Prettyman. Prob. April 16, 1774. Arch. vol. A84, pages 18-19. Reg. of Wills, Liber B, folios 506-509.

**Jones, William.** Yeoman. Will (copy). Made Dec. 28, 1773. Heirs: wife Mary Jones; sons White, Ebenezer, William, James and John Jones; dau. Mary Jones. Exec'rx, wife Mary Jones. Wits., Burton Prettyman, Jesse Townsend, Mitchell Jackson. Prob. April 20, 1774. Arch. vol. A81, pages 195-196. Reg. of Wills, Liber B, folios 520-521. [Note:—Arch. vol. A81, page 196 mentions Endless Morris and wife].

**Day, William.** Admin. of, to John Day. Granted [c. June . . ., 1774]. Arch. vol. A68, page 187.

**Craige, John.** Admin. of, to Mary Smith, D. B. N., the exec'rx of Isaac Smith, Esq., who was adm'r in right of his wife Mary (late Mary Craige). Granted before June 1, 1774. Arch. vol. A67, page 150. [Note:—Arch. vol. A67, page 150 mentions heirs: Ruth and John Craige].

**Hugg, Mary.** Widow of Elias Hugg. Will. Made May 14, 1773. Heirs: mother Cornelia Adams (wife of John Adams); sisters Cornelia King (wife of James), Rebeckah Westly (wife of John Westly); uncle Henry Fisher. Exec'rxs, sisters Cornelia King and Rebeckah Westly. Wits., William Davis, Daniel Nunez, George Wiltbank. Prob. July 1, 1774. Arch. vol. A79, page 82. Reg. of Wills, Liber B, folios 522-523.

**Staton, Elisabeth.** Will. Made June 28, 1774. Heirs: daus. Tabitha Starr, Esther Coulter and Betty Price; grandsons John Price and Eli Staton; granddaus. Nanny Price, Comfort and Sarah Staton; Ruth Staton (widow of Hill Staton). Exec'r, William Price. Wits., Phillis Hardy, George West, James Gordon. Prob. Aug. 3, 1774. Arch. vol. A100, page 127. Reg. of Wills, Liber B, folios 524-525.

**Gordon, James.** Yeoman. Admin. of, to Thomas Gordon. Granted Aug. 6, 1774. Arch. vol. A72, page 178. [Note:—Arch. vol. A72, page 178 mentions heirs Thomas, Catharine, Ephraim and Anne Gordon, minor children of James].

**Green, Stephen.** Ship Wright. Will. Made Dec. 29, 1763. Heirs: wife Naomi Green; sons William, Richard, Stephen, John and Ambrose Green; daus. Elinor and Marth[a] Green, Sarah Tindel; granddau. Jean Green (dau. of William). Exec'rs, wife Naomi Green, David Hall, Esq. Wits., Cornelius Turner, Joseph Shankland, Jr., John Westly. Prob. Aug. 16, 1774. Arch. vol. A73, pages 73-74. Reg. of Wills, Liber B, folios 525-529.

**Leatherbury, Thomas.** Admin. of, to John Hemmons and Elizabeth Hemmons. Admr's bond dated Nov. 2, 1774. Arch. vol. A84, page 21.

**Cord, John.** Worcester County, Md. Admin. of, to William Evans, D. B. N. for Rhoda Cord, dec'd. Granted [c. Nov. 4, 1774]. Arch. vol. A66, page 184.

**Carey, John.** Admin. of, to Eunice Carey. Granted [c. Nov. 26, 1774]. Arch. vol. A64, page 52.

**Collings, William.** Yeoman. Will. Made Nov. 11, 1774. Heirs: wife Jane; sons William, Frederick, Thomas and Levi; dau. Rachel; grandson Charles. Exec'rs, wife Jane and son Levi Collings. Wits., Nathan Spencer, Seagoe Potter. Prob. Nov. 26, 1774. Arch. vol. A66, pages 39-40. Reg. of Wills, Liber B, folios 530-532.

**Postles, Thomas.** Yeoman. Will. Made Aug. 23, 1774. Heirs: son John Postles; dau. Sarah Daniels; grandsons Thomas Postles and William Daniels; granddau. Mary Daniels and unnamed granddaus. Exec'rs, son John Postles and son-in-law William Daniels. Wits., Joseph Truitt, John Webb, William Lofland. Prob. Dec. 5, 1774. Arch. vol. A94, page 8. Reg. of Wills, Liber B, folios 532-534.

**Allen, Joseph.** Will. Made Jan. 9, 1768. Heir: friend Moses Allen. Exec'r, Moses Allen. Wits., William West, John Little, Richard Little. Prob. Dec. 15, 1774. Arch. vol. A57, pages 120-121. Reg. of Wills, Liber C, folios 85-86. [Note: —Arch. vol. A57, page 120 mentions dec'd father John].

**Russel, Katherine.** Admin. of, to Joseph Hall and wife Lydia, late Lydia Russel. Admr's bond dated Dec. 21, 1774. Arch. vol. A97, page 144.

**Bryan, Thomas.** Admin. of, to Jean Bryan. Granted [c. 1775]. Arch. vol. A61, page 10. [Note:—Arch. vol. A61, page 10 shows the estate was settled by George West, bondsman for Jean Bryan, dec'd].

**Nunez, Daniel.** Will. Made May 9, 1772. Heirs: wife Hannah Nunez; Henry Fisher; niece Hester Nunez Fisher (dau. of Henry and Margaret Fisher); Mary Kollock (dau. of Jacob Kollock, Esq.); Sarah Prettyman (dau. of William and Comfort Prettyman, dec'd); children of Jacob Kollock, Esq.; children of John and Magdalan Swift; Wardens of St. Peters Church of Lewes. Exec'rx, wife Hannah Nunez. Wits., Elizabeth Paynter, Hannah Woods, John Woods.

Prob. . . ., 1775. Arch. vol. A91, pages 120-122. Reg. of Wills, Liber C, folios 1-2. [Note:—Arch. vol. A91, page 122 mentions Mary Train].

**Gray, David.** Broadkiln Hd. Will. Made July 29, 1774. Heirs: wife Jean Gray; David Hall, Sr. Exec'rx, wife Jean Gray. Wits., David Hall, Jr., Joseph Hall. Prob. Jan. 5, 1775. Arch. vol. A73, page 4. Reg. of Wills, Liber B, folios 534-535.

**Black, James.** Admin. of, to Elizabeth Black. Granted [c. Feb. 1775]. Arch. vol. A59, page 190.

**Black, Sarah.** Will. Made Jan. 29, 1775. Heirs: sons William and George; daus. Jane and Nancy; bros. John and William Smith; Sophia Smith. Exec'r, uncle Bethuel Watson. Wits., John Haslet, Benton Smith, John Smith. Prob. Feb. 18, 1775. Arch. vol. A59, page 201. Reg. of Wills, Liber B, folios 536-537.

**Tharp [Thorp], Nathan.** Admin. of, to W[illia]m Hazzard. Granted [c. March 25, 1775]. Arch. vol. A101, page 143.

**Waples, Abigail.** Will. Made Feb. 25, 1775. Heirs: Lydy, Hesse and Robert West (children of Lewis West); Elizabeth Newton; Mary Stratten; Magdalen Jackson (wife of Stephen Jackson); Esther Stephens (wife of William Stephens); Betty Waples (wife of Burton Waples, Jr.); Thomas Marner (son of John Marner, dec'd); cousin Wrixam Lewis West (son of Lewis West); cousins Woolsey, Nancy and Nealey Waples (children of Burton Waples, Jr.). Exec'r, friend Burton Waples, Jr. Wits., Burton Waples, Sr., Thomas Prettyman, Mary Prettyman. Prob. March 1, 1775. Arch. vol. A104, pages 165-166. Reg. of Wills, Liber B, folios 538-540.

**Vaughan, William.** Joiner. Will. Made Feb. 28, 1775. Heirs: wife Betty Vaughan; sons Nathaniel, William and Ephraim Vaughan; daus. Mary and Betty Vaughan. Exec'rx, wife Betty Vaughan. Wits., Burton Waples, Sr., Mitchell Jackson, Jonathan Jackson. Prob. March 15, 1775. Arch. vol. A103, pages 82-83. Reg. of Wills, Liber B, folios 543-545. [Note:—Arch. vol. A103, page 83 shows the estate was settled March 9, 1782 by Jesse King and wife Betty, late Betty Vaughan].

**Collings, William.** Will (copy). Made March 3, 1775. Heirs: wife Sarah; sons John, William and Mathias Collings; daus. Sarah Collings, Ann West (wife of John), Hannah Carey (wife of Ebenezer), Mary Wharton (wife of Francis) and Rhoda Darby (wife of Samuel); grandson John Collings (son of William). Exec'rs, son Mathias Collings and dau. Sarah Collings. Wits., Burton Waples, Sr., Thomas Carey, Nehemiah Coffin. Prob. March 15, 1775. Arch. vol. A66, pages 41-43. Reg. of Wills, Liber B, folios 553-556.

**Waples, Dirickson.** Will. Made Feb. 23, 1775. Heirs: mother Temperance Waples; bros. Samuel and Nathaniel Waples; sisters Betty Vaughan, Catherine White and Patience Fisher; Mary Vaughan (dau. of William); Nathaniel Vaughan (son of William); Betty Vaughan (wife of Levin); Eli White (son of Wrixam White); Nanny Miller (wife of Joh[n]; Three Meeting Houses (one at Head of Indian River, one at Coolspring and one at Lewes). Exec'r, William Vaughan. Wits., Burton Waples, Sr., Cornelius Waples, Mary Dirickson. Prob. March 15, 1775. Arch. vol. A104, page 182. Reg. of Wills, Liber B, folios 541-543.

**Stockley, Oliver.** Admin. of, to Thomas Turner and wife Mary (late Mary Stockley). Admr's bond dated March 21, 1775. Arch. vol. A101, page 30.

**Waples, Stockley.** Admin. of, to Thomas Waples and wife Mary (late Mary Waples). Admr's bond dated March 21, 1775. Arch. vol. A105, page 52.

**Richards, Joshua.** Will. Made Feb. 28, 1775. Heirs: wife Temperance Richards; sons Isaac, David, Jacob and Benjamin Richards; daus. Patience and Jean Prettyman Richards. Exec'rx, wife Temperance Richards. Wits., Burton Waples, Sr., Stratton Burton, William Prettyman. Prob. April 14, 1775. Arch. vol. A95, page 92. Reg. of Wills, Liber B, folios 550-553.

**Crapper, Levin.** Will. Made April 10, 1775. Heirs: wife Betty; sons Milton and Levin; daus. Amelia Crapper, Leah Parker (wife of John), Sarah Rench (wife of James). Exec'rs, wife Betty and son Milton Crapper. Wits., Matthew Brown, Thomas F. Eccleston, William Polk, John Laws, Jr., Francis Stevens. Prob. April 23, 1775. Arch. vol. A67, pages 169-176. Reg. of Wills, Liber C, folios 80-83. [Note:—Arch. vol. A67, page 173 shows the estate was settled Feb. 12, 1791 by Sydenham Thorne and Betty, his wife, (late Betty Crapper) who survived Milton Crapper].

**Yaw, Thomas.** Admin. of, to Susannah Yaw. Settled July 10, 1775. Arch. vol. A109, page 128.

**Marvel, Robert.** Planter. Worcester County, Md. Will. Made March 27, 1772. Heirs: wife Rachel Marvel; sons Thomas, Joseph, Robert and Phillip Marvel; daus. Rachel, Patience and Betty Marvel, Ann Smith (wife of Charlton), Chloe Scudder (wife of Jonathan). Exec'rx, wife Rachel Marvel. Wits., Levin Connaway, John Willis, Joseph Piper, Simon Kollock. Prob. July 25, 1775. Arch. vol. A87, pages 18-19. Reg. of Wills, Liber C, folios 3-4.

**Truitt, James.** Worcester County, Md. Made Oct. 17, 1770. Heirs: son Peter Truitt; daus. Mary Brittingham, Casa Jerman, Tabitha Crippin (wife of John), Rachel Dunaho (wife of Thomas); grandsons James, Riley and Purnal Truitt (sons of Riley Truitt); granddaus. Elizabeth and Lovey Kelly (daus. of James Kelly); Elizabeth Sharp (wife of William Sharp). Exec'rs, son Peter Truitt and grandson James Truitt (son of Riley). Wits., John Collings, John Lynch, Philip Huggins. Prob. July 25, 1775. Arch. vol. A102, page 124. Reg. of Wills, Liber B, folios 556-558.

**Craig, Robert.** (Minor son of Alexander Craig, Yeoman). Admin. of, to Hamilton Craig. Settled Aug. 11, 1775. Arch. vol. A67, page 156.

**Otwell, Francis.** Worcester County, Md. Will. Made Sept. 10, 1774. Heirs: wife Lurany Otwell. Exec'rx, wife Lurany Otwell. Wits., Jacob Roton, Nehemiah Roton, Robert Hopkins, Sr. Prob. Aug. 11, 1775. Arch. vol. A91, page 176. Reg. of Wills, Liber B, folios 559-560.

**West, John.** Yeoman. Indian River Hd. Admin. of, to Benjamin West. Settled Aug. 26, 1775. Arch. vol. A106, page 142. [Note:—Arch. vol. A106, page 142 mentions dec'd father Wrixam West; Robert West, dec'd; Lewis West; Straten Burton and wife Mary (late Mary West)].

**Windsor, Phillip.** Yeoman. Worcester County, Md. Made April 13, 1775. Heirs: sons Jesse, Phillips, Thomas Windsor; daus. Leah, Elisabeth, Alice and Nelly Windsor, Rebecca Messick, Mary Sharp; son-in-law John Messick; grandsons George and Leonard Messick (sons of Rebecca and John Messick), Thomas Windsor; granddau. Elisabeth Windsor; Ann Windsor (mother of Thomas and Elisabeth Windsor). Exec'r, son Jesse Windsor. Wits., Elzey Spicer, Phillip Conway, Bersheba Conway. Prob. Sept. 18, 1775. Arch. vol. A108, page 171. Reg. of Wills, Liber C, folios 13-15.

**Laws, William.** Yeoman. Admin. of, to James Laws. Admr's bond dated Sept. 19, 1775. Arch. vol. A83, page 153.

**Owens, David, Sr.** Planter. Worcester County, Md. Will. Made Feb. 23, 1775. Heirs: sons David and Paris Owens; daus. Sarah, Betty and Ann Owens, Sophia Gaskens. Exec'rx, dau. Sarah Owens. Wits., William Owens, Elizabeth Owens, Rachel Nicolls. Prob. Oct. 2, 1775. Arch. vol. A91, page 193. Reg. of Wills, Liber C, folios 4-6. [Note:—Arch. vol. A91, page 193 shows Sarah Owens later married James Stafford].

**Hudson, Amy Parker.** Admin. of, to George Hill. Granted Oct. 4, 1775. Arch. vol. A78, page 170. [Note:—Arch. vol. A78, page 170 mentions Samuel, Walter, Mary, and Anderson Hudson; Hannah Dodd; Rhoda Black; Ann Hill; Sarah Hiller and Margaret Hill].

**Martin, Josias.** Will. Made Sept. 9, 1775. Heirs: wife Elizabeth Martin; sons James and Josias Martin; grandsons Josias and William Martin (sons of William, dec'd), John, William, Josias, Robert and James Martin (sons of Jonathan); grand-dau. Elizabeth Stephenson (dau. of Jonathan); nephew Josias Hopkins, cousin Ruth Fleming; James Wilson (son of Rev. Matthew Wilson). Exec'r, son James Martin. Wits., William Peery, Hugh Virden, Marnix Virden. Prob. Oct. 4, 1775. Arch. vol. A86, pages 166-167. Reg. of Wills, Liber C, folios 6-8.

**Callaway, Joshua.** Admin. of, to Elsie Callaway and William McBride. Granted [c. Oct. 27, 1775]. Arch. vol. A62, page 162.

**Waples, Temperance.** Widow. Will. Made March 15, 1775. Heirs: sons Nathaniel and Samuel Waples; daus. Betty Vaughan (wife of William), Catherine White (wife of Wrixam), Patience Fisher (wife of William); granddau. Polly Vaughan. Exec'rs, sons Nathaniel and Samuel Waples. Wits., Burton Waples, Sr., Cornelius Waples, Joseph Waples. Prob. Nov. 6, 1775. Arch. vol. A105, page 53. Reg. of Wills, Liber C, folios 9-10.

**Bainum, Eleanor.** Will. Made Sept. 1, 1771. Heirs: daus. Rachel and Eleanor Bainum, Elizabeth Butler; sons Levi, Bartholomew and William Bainum; John Bainum; grandson William Beavens Bainum; granddau. Nina Steal (dau. of dau. Eleanor); Mary Warren. Exec'r, son William Bainum. Wits., Robert Watson Maccally, John Day. Prob. Nov. 8, 1775. Arch. vol. A58, page 101. Reg. of Wills, Liber C, folios 11-12.

**McCracken, David, Jr.** Yeoman. Will. Made Dec. 1, 1775. Heirs: son Elihu McCracken. Exec'r, James Heavelo. Wits., Richardson Cade, John Neill, Boaz Manlove. Prob. Dec. 15, 1775. Arch. vol. A87, pages 133-134. Reg. of Wills, Liber C, folios 12-13.

**Clarkson, Richard.** Planter. Caroline County, Md. Will. Made June 28, 1775. Heirs: son Abraham Clarkson; daus. Sarah, Elizabeth and Lucretia Brown, Priscilla Cannon; granddaus. Diana and Lucretia Cannon; grandsons Richard Clarkson Cannon, Clarkson Cannon and Richard Clarkson (son of William). Exec'r, son Abraham Clarkson. Wits., James Cannon, Sr., Ezekiel Brown, Jonathan Shahan. Codicil, Sept. 29, 1775. Wits., Ezekiel Brown, Hayward Cannon. Prob. Dec. 17, 1775. Arch. vol. A64, page 214. Reg. of Wills, Liber C, folios 16-18. [Note:—Arch. vol. A64, page 214 mentions James Brown, White Brown and James Cannon].

**Black, William.** Cordwinder. Admin. of, to John Stephenson and wife Rhoda (late Rhoda Black). Granted [c. 1776]. Arch. vol. A59, page 203.

**Holland, William.** Will. Made Dec. 27, 1775. Heirs: wife Elizabeth Holland; sons Israel, Benjamin, William, Marmaduke, John and Lemuel Holland; daus. Elizabeth Holland and Rhoda Godwin; Perry Robinson. Exec'rs, son Benjamin Holland and Thomas Godwin. Wits., John Guttre, Caty Massey, John Wise. Prob. Jan. 22, 1776. Arch. vol. A77, pages 127-132. Reg. of Wills, Liber C, folios 21-24.

**Abbott, William, Sr...** Will. Made Oct. 8, 1773. Heirs: wife Susannah Abbott; sons Nicholas, John and William Abbott; dau. Temperance Abbott; grandsons William and Mason (sons of Nicholas), William, Stephen and George (sons of John), James Read (son of Ezckiel Read), William and John Blockson (sons of William Blockson); grandchildren Littleton, John, Arcada, Tabitha, Susannah and Elizabeth Read (children of John Read, dec'd). Exec'rs, son William Abbott and dau. Temperance Abbott. Wits., Hugh Baker, John Clowes, William Carpenter. Prob. Jan. 31, 1776. Arch. vol. A67, page 25. Reg. of Wills, Liber C, folios 24-26.

**Turpin, Solomon.** Will. Made Feb. 10, 1776. Heirs: son Joseph Turpin; daus. Rebeckah and Elisabeth Turpin, Love Moore, Sarah Mastin, Mary Clarkson. Exec'rs, daus. Rebeckah and Elisabeth Turpin. Wits., Jesse Cannon, William Cannon. [No prob.]. Arch. vol. A103, page 35. Reg. of Wills, Liber C, folios 89-90.

**Coffin, John, Jr.** Yeoman. Admin. of, to Peleg Walter. Granted [ante Feb. 12, 1776]. Arch. vol. A65, page 82.

**Warren, Robert.** Yeoman. Will. Made Jan. 7, 1774. Heirs: wife Mary Warren; sons Wrixam, Levi, Absolam and David Warren; grandson Robert Warren. Exec'rs, wife Mary Warren and son David Warren. Wits., Elijah Truitt, Richard Coverdall, Mary Lain. Prob. Feb. 13, 1776. Arch. vol. A105, page 123. Reg. of Wills, Liber C, folios 26-27. [Note:—Arch. vol. A105, page 123 shows the estate was settled Dec. 28, 1782 by David Warren, acting exec'r].

**Townsend, Costen.** Admin. of, to Littleton Townsend, in right of Julia Townsend, widow. Admr's bond dated Feb. 13, 1776. Arch. vol. A102, page 48.

**Annett, Isabella.** Admin. of, to Mary Annett. Granted [c. Feb. 14, 1776]. Arch. vol. A57, page 153.

**Layton, Thomas.** Caroline County, Md. Will. Made March 16, 1775. Heirs: wife Ann Layton; sons William, Thomas, David and Spencer Layton; daus. Sarah, Mary and Nancy Layton. Exec'rx, wife Ann Layton. Wits., David Nutter, Thomas Hickman, Jonathan Hatfield. Prob. Feb. 14, 1776. Arch. vol. A84, page 7. Reg. of Wills, Liber C, folios 27-28.

**Mecottor, William.** [Joiner]. Will. Made Feb. 8, 1776. Heirs: friend Jacob Gumm; Joseph Flemon; Samuel Wiltbank. Exec'r, friend Jacob Gumm. Wits., Thomas May, Joseph Fleming, George Black. Prob. Feb. 17, 1776. Arch. vol. A90, page 185. Reg. of Wills, Liber C, folios 28-29.

**Waples, Dirickson.** Admin. of, to Nathaniel Waples, D. B. N., for Temperance Waples. Granted [c. Feb. 24, 1776]. Arch. vol. A104, page 183. [Note:—Arch. vol. A104, page 183 mentions heirs Betty Vaughan; Nathaniel Vaughan; Wrixam White; Eli White; wife of William Fisher; Mary Vaughan; Nathaniel Waples; Samuel Waples; William Fisher; Betty King].

**Stephenson, Jannett.** Widow. Will. Made April 29, 1773. Heirs: dau. Martha Stephenson; grandsons James Nottingham, James McNeal, Thomas Dutton, James Dutton (son of John); granddaus. Jannett McNeal, Jannett Nottingham. Exec'rx, dau. Martha Stephenson. Wits., John Clowes, John Rowland, Jane Rowland. Prob. Feb. 27, 1776. Arch. vol. A100, page 160. Reg. of Wills, Liber C, folios 30-31.

**Davis, Samuel.** Admin. of, to Draper May, D. B. N. Granted [c. March 2, 1776]. Arch. vol. A68, page 128. [Note:—

Arch. vol. A68, page 128 mentions Draper May, Adm'r of Mary May, Exec'rx of Thomas May who was Adm'r of Samuel Davis].

**Donoho, Thomas.** Yeoman. Admin. of, to James Brooks and Rachel, his wife. Granted [c. March 4, 1776]. Arch. vol. A69, page 134. [Note:—Arch. vol. A69, page 134 shows Rachel Donoho later married James Brooks].

**Waller, William, Sr.** Somerset County, Md. Will. Made Feb. 20, 1770. Heirs: wife Rachel Waller; sons Joshua, Thomas, Ephraim, William and James Waller. Exec'rx, wife Rachel Waller. Wits., Nathaniel Waller, William Green, Isaac Macdowell. Prob. March 7, 1776. Arch. vol. A104, page 84. Reg. of Wills, Liber C, folios 33-34. [Note:—Arch. vol. A104, page 84 shows the estate was settled Feb. 4, 1783 by James Waller, adm'r of Rachel Waller, dec'd].

**Truitt, Micajah.** Yeoman. Will. Made Feb. 27, 1776. Heirs: wife Sarah Truitt; sons Peter and Bradford Truitt; daus. Naomi and Mary Truitt; nephew Parker Truitt. Exec'rx, wife Sarah Truitt. Wits., Jehu Claypoole, John Ingram, William Bowness. Prob. March 9, 1776. Arch. vol. A102, page 152. Reg. of Wills, Liber C, folios 35-37.

**Dodd, Joseph.** Broadkiln Hd. Will. Made Dec. 14, 1773. Heirs: bro. Emanuel Dodd; half sister Ruth Dodd; nephew Joseph Dodd (son of Emanuel). Exec'rx, half sister Ruth Dodd. Wits., Samuel Tingley, J[acob] Moore. Prob. April 5, 1776. Arch. vol. A69, page 103. Reg. of Wills, Liber C, folios 38-39. [Note:—Arch. vol. A69, page 103 mentions dec'd father Joseph Dodd].

**West, George.** Yeoman. Admin. of, to Joshua Morgan and wife Levina (late Levina West). Admr's bond dated April 5, 1776. Arch. vol. A106, page 122.

**Poynter, William.** Will. Made Dec. 14, 1775. Heirs: son William Poynter; dau. Castelia Poynter. Exec'r, bro. Ratcliff Poynter. Wits., W[illia]m Hazzard, Richard Clifton, Jemimah Simpson. Prob. April 11, 1776. Arch. vol. A94, page 43. Reg. of Wills, Liber B, folios 546-547.

**Gordon, Catharine.** Will. Made May 19, 1774. Heirs: sons Thomas, Nathaniel and James Gordon; daus. Ann Jones (wife of Robert), Leah Walker (wife of Jacob), Esther Walker (wife of George); grandsons Thomas Walker (son of Jacob and Leah Walker), John Walker (son of James), James Walker (son of George), James Gordon (son of Nathaniel), Thomas Gordon (son of James); granddaus.

Catherine Walker (dau. of George and Esther), Catherine Stewart (wife of William), Catherine Gordon (dau. of James) and Catherine Gordon (dau. of Thomas). Exec'r, son James Gordon. Wits., William Peery, William Hall, Jean Hopkins. Prob. April 15, 1776. Arch. vol. A72, pages 173-174. Reg. of Wills, Liber C, folios 39-41.

**Ozburn, Richard.** Tailor. Admin. of, to Thomas Gray and wife Miriam, (late Miriam Ozburn). Granted [c. April 18, 1776]. Arch. vol. A92, page 33.

**Harmon, John.** Will. Made April 6, 1776. Heirs: wife Saborah Harmon; dau. Saborah Harmon. Exec'rx, wife Saborah Harmon. Wits., Hester Samuels, Elizabeth Harmon( dau. of Angel Harmon). Prob. April 24, 1776. Arch. vol. A74, page 95. Reg. of Wills, Liber C, folio 41.

**Ricords, John.** Prime Hook Neck. Made April 6, 1776. Heirs: wife Neoma Ricords; son Peter Ricords; dau. Mary Watson. Exec'rx, wife Neoma Ricords. Wits., John Cirwithen, Thomas Heavelo, Richard Anslo. Prob. April 27, 1776. Arch. vol. A95, page 172. Reg. of Wills, Liber C, folios 58-59. [Note:—Arch. vol. A95, page 172 shows the estate was settled by Thomas Jones and wife Neomi, (late Neoma Ricords), on December 28, 1782].

**Starr, Phebe.** Will. Made . . ., 1775. Heirs: sons Nathaniel and James Starr; daus. Sarah Hopkins, Jemima Dean and Bethiah Neal. Exec'r, son James Starr. Wits., James Gordon, Joseph Robnet, Thomas Reynolds. Prob. (Registered) May . . ., 1776. Arch. vol. A100, page 117. Reg. of Wills, Liber B, folios 547-548.

**West, Joseph.** Admin. of, to Benjamin West. Admr's bond dated May 9, 1776. Arch. vol. A106, page 152. [Note:—Arch. vol. A106, page 152 mentions Joseph West (son of John); John, Ann and Ruth West.

**Smith, Henry.** Yeoman. Will. Made Feb. 1, 1776. Heirs: sons John, Henry and Jonathan Smith; dau. Sarah Smith. Exec'rs, friends William Conwell and Caleb Cirwithen. Wits., Rachel Longeon, Purnel Bennet, John Cirwithen, Isaac Watson (son of Elias). Prob. May 10, 1776. Arch. vol. A99, pages 145-146. Reg. of Wills, Liber C, folios 42-43.

**Stuart, William.** Planter. Will. Made May 7, 1776. Heirs: wife unnamed; dau. Nancy Stuart; child or children unnamed. Exec'rx, unnamed wife. Wits., Lawrence Riley, Phillips Russel, Jonathan Stevenson. Prob. May 16, 1776. Arch. vol. A101, page 70. Reg. of Wills, Liber C, folios 43-44.

[Note:—Arch. vol. A101, page 70 shows the estate was settled June 12, 1795 by Archibald Fleming and wife Catharine, (late Catharine Stewart)].

**Tunnell, William.** Yeoman. Will. Made Dec. 8, 1775. Heirs: wife Elizabeth Tunnell; sons Scarborough, Nehemiah, Isaac, William, John and Washburn Tunnell; dau. Elizabeth Dirickson. Exec'rs, wife Elizabeth Tunnell, George Howard, Isaac Evans. Wits., Uriah Brookfield, Elizabeth Howard, William Holland. Prob. May 24, 1776. Arch. vol. A103, page 8. Reg. of Wills, Liber C, folios 37-38. [Note:—Arch. vol. A103, page 8 shows the estate was settled June 10, 1783 by George Howard and Isaac Evans].

**Schoolfield, Benjamin, Sr.** Worcester County, Md. Will. Made May 1, 1774. Heirs: wife Bridgett Schoolfield; sons Joseph, Benjamin, William, John and Henry Schoolfield; daus. Mary, Diligance and Bridgett Schoolfield, Sarah Wharton and Rhoda Powell. Exec'rs, wife Bridgett Schoolfield and son Joseph Schoolfield. Wits., W[illia]m Tingle, Beavins Morris, Jerusha Morris. Prob. May 29, 1776. Arch. vol. A98, page 30. Reg. of Wills, Liber C, folios 44-45. [Note:—Arch. vol. A98, page 30 shows the estate was settled Sept. 15, 1778 by Angelitta Schoolfield, admr'x of Joseph Schoolfield, one of the exec'rs].

**Shelpman, Jacob.** Will. Made April 26, 1773. Heirs: son Isaac Shelpman; daus. Alice, Sarah and Mary Shelpman; grandsons Cornelius and William Shelpman; granddaus. Alice and Magdelin Shelpman. Exec'r, son Isaac Shelpman. Wits., William Peery, James Hall, John Hall. Prob. May 29, 1776. Arch. vol. A98, page 108. Reg. of Wills, Liber C, folios 34-35. [Note:—Arch. vol. A98, page 108 shows the estate was settled March 10, 1779 by Alice Shelpman, Joseph Dodd and wife Sarah, late Sarah Shelpman, who were exec'rs of Isaac Shelpman, dec'd].

**Kollock, George.** Will. Made April 27, 1776. Heirs: wife Elizabeth Kollock; children unnamed. Exec'rx, wife Elizabeth Kollock. Wits., Thomas Gray, Hercules Kollock. Prob. June 5, 1776. Arch. vol. A83, page 1. Reg. of Wills, Liber C, folios 45-46.

**Wharton, William.** Yeoman. Worcester County, Md. Will. Made March 10, 1774. Heirs: wife Elizabeth Wharton; dau. Patience Jesups; grandson Wrixam Wharton. Exec'r, friend Simon Kollock, merchant. Wits., Tho[ma]s Hutson, William Vezey, Simon Kollock. Prob. June 22, 1776. Arch. vol. A107, page 35. Reg. of Wills, Liber C, folios 46-48.

**Rogers, Solomon.** Worcester County, Md. Will. Made Sept. 6, 1774. Heirs: sons Jacob, America, Parker, Matthew, Joshua and Solomon Rogers; daus. Tabitha and Elizabeth Rogers. Exec'r, son Parker Rogers. Wits., Adam Bravard, Isaac Evans, Mary Evans. Prob. June 28, 1776. Arch. vol. A97, page 53. Reg. of Wills, Liber C, folios 48-49.

**Rogers, Solomon.** Admin. of, to Jacob Rogers. Admr's bond dated June 28, 1776. Arch. vol. A97, page 54. [Note:—Arch. vol. A97, page 54 mentions Agnes, Joshua, America and Elizabeth Rogers].

**West, Lewis.** Admin. of, to Benjamin West. Granted [c. June 29, 1776]. Arch. vol. A106, page 156. [Note:—Arch. vol. A106, page 156 mentions heirs Joseph West (son of John); John West, dec'd; Ruth West; Robert West, dec'd; Mary, Benjamin, Ann, John and Lewis West (children of Wrixam West)].

**Schofield (Schoolfield), Bridget.** Will (copy). Made July 8, 1776. Heirs: sons Joseph, Benjamin, William, John and Henry Schofield; daus. Diligence and Bridget Schofield, Rhoda Powell, Sarah Wharton and Mary Smith. Exec'r, son Benjamin Schcfield. Wits., W[illia]m Tingle, W[illia]m Evans, Zipporaw Crapper. [No prob.]. Arch. vol. A98, page 32. [Note:—Arch. vol. A98, page 32 shows the estate was settled by William Tingle, adm'r of Benjamin Schofield; also mentions Francis Wharton and wife, and Rebecca Schofield].

**Stafford, Henry.** Planter. Will. Made May 21, 1776. Heirs: wife Elizabeth Stafford; sons Henry, Levi, Nathan, Zarobabel, Zadoc and Robertson Stafford; daus. Elizabeth, Rachel, Lovey and Delight Stafford, and Mary Pegg. Exec'rx, wife Elizabeth Stafford. Wits., Robert Clarkson, James Cooper, Valentine Hager. Prob. July 11, 1776. Arch. vol. A100, page 99. Reg. of Wills, Liber C, folios 49-50.

**Williams, David.** Will. Made June 19, 1776. Heirs: wife Mary Williams; sons Elijah, Morgan, William, John, David and Curtis Williams; daus. Lucretia, Mary, Peggy and Nelly Smith Williams, Rebeckah Carlisle; Robert Ross. Exec'rs, wife Mary Williams and son William Williams. Wits., Samuel Barnet, John Hudson, Luke Davis, Thomas Davis. Prob. July 24, 1776. Arch. vol. A107, page 158. Reg. of Wills, Liber C, folios 50-52.

**Carpenter, Luke.** Will. Made July 24, 1776. Heirs: son James; dau. Sarah; Moses Argo. Exec'rx, friend Joshua Burton.

Wits., Hap Hazzard, Priscilla Hazzard, Phebe Hickman. Prob.
Aug. 17, 1776. Arch. vol. A63, pages 241-244. Reg. of Wills,
Liber C, folios 52-53.

**Kendrick, James.** Will. Made Feb. 10 [15], 1773. Heirs: son
William Kendrick; Sarah Dodd. Exec'r, friend Jacob Hick-
man. Wits., David Wattson, John Young, James Young.
Prob. Sept. 6, 1776. Arch. vol. A82, pages 50-51. Reg. of
Wills, Liber B, folios 549-550 and Liber C, folios 18-19.

**Hosman, Jane.** Mantelmaker. Lewes. Made Nov. 12, 1773.
Heirs: John Russel; Jane Russel (wife of John); John and
Elisabeth Russel (children of John and Jane Russel); Elisabeth Mariner (wife of Gilbert); Sarah Shelmont; Magdalen
Shelmont (dau. of Sarah). Exec'r, John Russel. Wits.,
Thomas Gray, Jane Russel, Mary Friend. Codicil, Feb. 10,
1774. Wits., Thomas Gray, Sophia Gray. Prob. Sept. 7,
1776. Arch. vol. A78, page 76. Reg. of Wills, Liber C,
folios 19-21.

**Otwell, Urania.** Admin. of, to Simon Kollock. Admr's bond dated
Sept. 24, 1776. Arch. vol. A91, page 180. [Note:—Arch.
vol. A91, page 180 mentions husband Francis Otwell].

**Tindel, Charles.** Yeoman. Admin. of, to Letitia Tindel and Rees
Woolf. Admr's bond dated Sept. 27, 1776. Arch. vol. A102,
page 9.

**Jacobs, Albertus.** Yeoman. Will (copy). Made Aug. 21, 1776.
Heirs: wife Sarah Jacobs; sons Albertus and John Jacobs;
daus. Comfort and Sarah Jacobs, and Esther Bruce (wife of
Alexander). Exec'rs, wife Sarah Jacobs and son John Jacobs. Wits., Jonathan Bryan, William Bailey, Stephen
Green. Prob. Sept. 28, 1776. Arch. vol. A80, pages 41-42.
Reg. of Wills, Liber C, folios 54-56. [Note:—Arch. vol. A80,
page 42 mentions Hannah Newbold; also shows the estate
was settled by Sarah Burton, late Sarah Jacobs, as the surviving exec'r].

**Ingram, Isaac, Sr.** Yeoman. Will (copy). Made Feb. 26, 1776.
Heirs: wife Rachel Ingram; son Isaac Ingram; dau. Aberilla Collins (wife of Elijah); son-in-law Elijah Collins;
grandson Shepherd Collins (son of Aberilla and Elijah Collins); John Clowes. Exec'r, son Isaac Ingram. Wits., John
Jones, Job Smith, Mary Smith. Prob. Oct. 5, 1776. Arch.
vol. A79, page 141. Reg. of Wills, Liber C, folios 53-54.

**Coffan, John.** Yeoman. Will (copy). Made Sept. 7, 1776. Heirs:
wife Comfort; sons Cornelius, Abner, William and Thomas;
dau. Mary Chester; grandsons Aydlott and Richard Hudson.

Exec'rx, wife Comfort. Wits., Andrew Williams, William Woodcraft, John Mideap. Prob. Oct. 14, 1776. Arch. vol. A65, pages 79-81. Reg. of Wills, Liber C, folio 57.

**Griffith, William.** Yeoman. Admin. of, to Thomas Cary and wife Phebe, late Phebe Griffith. Granted Oct. 16, 1776. Arch. vol. A73, page 150.

**Collings, George.** Yeoman. Admin. of, to Abraham Smith and wife Mary (late Mary Collings). Granted [c. Nov. 2, 1776]. Arch. vol. A65, page 164. [Note:—Arch. vol. A65, page 164 mentions a son George Collings].

**Walls, William.** Will. Made Jan. 1, 1776. Heirs: wife Elizabeth Walls; sons Joshua and William Walls; daus. Comfort and Eleanor Walls, Temperance Wilson; Esther Massey; grandsons Avery Atkins, Joshua Wilson; granddau. Esther Atkins. Exec'r, son Joshua Walls. Prob. Nov. 18, 1776. Arch. vol. A104, page 112. Reg. of Wills, Liber C, folios 59-60.

**Waller, Nathaniel, Sr.** Somerset County, Md. Will. Made April 21, 1775. Heirs: daus. Marg[ar]et Mays and Mary Bell; grandsons Nathan and Elijah Waller. Exec'rs, dau.-in-law Jane Waller and grandson Nathan Waller. Wits., James English, Betty Brown, Joshua Kinny. Prob. Dec. 5, 1776. Arch. vol. A104, page 73. Reg. of Wills, Liber C, folios 15-16.

**Collins, John.** Will. Made June 25, 1775. Heirs: wife Edy; sons John, Hancock and Andrew; daus. Elizabeth Collins, Edy Townsend (wife of Elias), Rachel Wattson (wife of Jesse) and Mary Tatman (wife of Mitchell); grandson John Tatman (son of Mitchell). Exec'rs, wife Edy and son John Collins. Wits., William Hazzard, Jonathan Millman, Michael Millman. Prob. Dec. 29, 1776. Arch. vol. A65, pages 182-183. Reg. of Wills, Liber C, folios 60-62. [Note:—Arch. vol. A65, page 183 shows the estate was settled by John and Ada Collins; also mentions legacies to David Smith].

**Clarke, Isaac.** Yeoman. Admin. of, to Nancy Clarke. Granted [c. 1777]. Arch. vol. A64, pages 180-181. [Note:—Arch. vol. A64, page 180 shows that Nancy Clarke later married Jesse Lewis; also shows a dau. Nancy Clarke].

**Gray, Bridget.** Will. Made March 21, 1776. Heirs: sons James and William Gray; granddau. Hannah Gray (dau. of James). [No exec'r]. Wits., John Gibbons, Sr., Sarah Green, Priscilla Highway. Prob. . . ., 1777. Arch. vol. A73, page 2. Reg. of Wills, Liber C, folio 66.

**Fisher, George.** Will. Made April 22, 1775. Heirs: wife Elizabeth; sons James, Isaac, John, Curtis and George Hardy Fisher; daus. Bette, Sophia, Letitia Fisher and Mary White; grandson, John Fisher (son of George Hardy Fisher). Exec'rs, wife Elizabeth and son Isaac Fisher. Wits., Samuel Shankland, James Williams, David Casey. Prob. Jan. 1, 1777. Arch. vol. A71, page 111. Reg. of Wills, Liber C, folios 62-64.

**Jacobs, Albertus, Jr.** Admin. of, to Sarah Jacobs, widow. Admr's bond dated Jan. 22, 1777. Arch. vol. A80, page 43.

**Carpenter, Laben [Laban].** Yeoman. Will (nunc.). Made Feb. 17, 1777. Heirs: wife Comfort; William Carpenter; William Ward. Exec'rs, wife Comfort and William Carpenter. Wits., David Thornton, Joshua Bennett. Prob. March 7, 1777. Arch. vol. A63, pages 236-237. Reg. of Wills, Liber C, folios 64-65. [Note:—Arch. vol. A63, page 237 shows Samuel Heavelo and wife Comfort (late Comfort Carpenter, widow) presented an account on the estate which was recorded March 12, 1783].

**Lingo, Leven.** Yeoman. Admin. of, to Aaron Clifton. Admr's bond dated March 8, 1777. Arch. vol. A84, page 137.

**Truitt, Benjamin.** Will. Made Feb. 23, 1777. Heirs: wife Rachel Truitt; son Solomon Truitt; dau. Esther Boroughs (wife of Jonathan); grandson Benjamin Boroughs. Exec'rs, wife Rachel Truitt and son Solomon Truitt. Wits., John Truitt, Thomas Evans, Jesse Hudson. Prob. March 11, 1777. Arch. vol. A102, pages 99-100. Reg. of Wills, Liber C, folio 65. [Note:—Arch. vol. A102, page 100 shows the estate was settled Feb. 23, 1796 by George Walton D. B. N.].

**Shelpman, Isaac.** Yeoman. Will. Made Feb. 22, 1777. Heirs: sisters Alice and Sarah Shelpman. Exec'rxs, sisters Alice and Sarah Shelpman. Wits., Edward Stevenson, James Hall, William Peery. Prob. March 17, 1777. Arch. vol. A98, page 107. Reg. of Wills, Liber C, folios 66-67. [Note:—Arch. vol. A98, page 107 shows the estate was settled March 10, 1779 by Alice Shelpmans, Joseph Dodd and Sarah, his wife, nee Sarah Shelpman].

**Smith, David.** Shipcarpenter. Admin. of, to Elizabeth Smith. Granted March 18, 1777. Arch. vol. A99, page 124.

**Draper, Avery.** Yeoman. Will. Made Feb. 26, 1777. Heirs: sons Henry, Samuel and Avery Draper; daus. Betty Draper and Sarah Cirwithin (wife of Caleb). Exec'rs, sons Henry and Samuel Draper and son-in-law Caleb Cirwithin. Wits., Mark

Davis, Naphtali Carpenter, Bethuel Watson, Jr. Prob. March 24, 1777. Arch. vol. A69, pages 188-189. Reg. of Wills, Liber C, folios 69-71.

**Jacobs, John.** Will (copy). Made March 15, 1777. Heirs: mother unnamed; sisters Comfort, Sarah, Esther and Hannah Jacobs. Exec'rx, unnamed mother. Wits., Samuel Paynter, Sr., Hannah Holland, Richard Little. Prob. March 24, 1777. Arch. vol. A80, page 57. Reg. of Wills, Liber C, folios 68-69. [Note:—Arch. vol. A80, page 57 shows the estate was settled by Sarah Jacobs].

**Hudson, John.** Will. Made March 4, 1777. Heirs: wife Sarah Hudson; sons John, Henry, William and Richard Hudson; daus. Betty, Sarah, Mary and Ellie Hudson, and Rhoda Fearies; granddau. Gesefie Hudson. Exec'rs, wife Sarah Hudson and son Richard Hudson. Wits., Joseph Truitt, Jehu Clifton, John Mills. Prob. March 25, 1777. Arch. vol. A79, page 15. Reg. of Wills, Liber C, folios 71-73.

**Newbold, Francis.** Will. Made March 16, 1777. Heirs: wife Mary Newbold; sons John and Thomas Newbold; dau.-in-law Sarah Newbold. Exec'rs, sons John and Thomas Newbold. Wits., George Wallace, Jesse Griffith, David Carey. Prob. March 29, 1777. Arch. vol. A91, page 63. Reg. of Wills, Liber C, folios 74-75.

**Reynolds, Richard.** Admin. of, to Thomas Reynolds. Granted March 29, 1777. Arch. vol. A95, page 53.

**Turner, Lazarus.** Admin. of, to Hugh Baker and wife Mary (late Mary Turner). Admr's bond dated March 31, 1777. Arch. vol. A103, page 20.

**Robinson, Perry.** Port Penn, St. Georges Hd. Will. Made Feb. 8, 1777. Heirs: cousins Parker Robinson, Daniel Robinson, Hannah Robinson (dau. of uncle Cornelius Robinson). Exec'r, cousin Simon Kollock. Wits., John Stewart, Martha Porter, William Hall. Prob. April 2, 1777. Arch. vol. A96, page 167. Reg. of Wills, Liber C, folios 88-89.

**Carrel, Joseph.** Yeoman. Will. Made March 7, 1777. Heirs: wife Margar[et]; daus. Elizabeth and Sarah Carrel; bro. Jacob Carrel. Exec'rs, wife Margar[et] and friend John Plowman. Wits., William Hazzard, Jesse Bradley, Samuel Morris. Prob. April 4, 1777. Arch. vol. A64, pages 15-16. Reg. of Wills, Liber C, folios 75-76. [Note:—Arch. vol. A64, page 16 shows that Margaret Carrel later married William Ward, who settled the estate in 1778].

**Dorman, Major.** Worcester County, Md. Will. Made April 14, 1771. Heirs: wife Juda Dorman; son Charles Dorman; dau. Rachel Vinson. [No exec'r]. Wits., Isaac Jones, Collings Parker, Benjamin Evans. Prob. April 4, 1777. Arch. vol. A69, page 161. Reg. of Wills, Liber C., folios 73-74. [Note: —Arch. vol. A69, page 161 shows that Mary Dorman and Isaac Jones settled the estate in right of Charles Dorman, dec'd].

**May, Thomas.** Will (copy). Made March 6, 1777. Heirs: wife Mary May; son Jonathan May; daus. Ann and Betsy May. Exec'rx, wife Mary May. Wits., W[illia]m Hazzard, George Black, James Mutton. Prob. April 4, 1777. Arch. vol. A87, pages 102-105. Reg. of Wills, Liber C, folios 78-80. [Note: —Arch. vol. A87, page 103 shows Draper May entered an account as adm'r of Mary May on March 1, 1782; pages 104 and 105 show that Andrew Fountain, adm'r D. B. N. of Thomas May, made a final account on the estate Sept. 7, 1785].

**Prettyman, Elizabeth.** Will. Made Feb. 4, 1777. Heirs: sons John Stratton Burton, William Burton and Robert Prettyman; dau. Ann Bagwell. Exec'rs, sons John Stratton Burton and William Burton, dau. Ann Bagwell. Wits., Mary Hathaway, Eli Burton, Benjamin Burton. Prob. April 4, 1777. Arch. vol. A94, page 57. Reg. of Wills, Liber C, folios 76-78. [Note:—Arch. vol. A94, page 57 shows Ann Bagwell, wife of William Bagwell].

**Bennett, John.** Yeoman. Will. Made March 25, 1777. Heirs: sons Purnell and Lemuel Bennett; daus. Sally and Margaret Bennett, Rosannah Crippen. Exec'rs, sons Purnell and Lemuel Bennett. Wits., [Wrixam] Warren. Prob. April 12, 1777. Arch. vol. A59, page 82. Reg. of Wills, Liber C, folios 93-94.

**Houston, John.** Planter. Will. Made June 29, 1775. Heirs: wife Mary Houston; sons John, Leonard and Littleton Houston. Exec'rs, wife Mary Houston, bro. Robert Houston, John Collins, John Mitchell. Wits., Robert Houston, John Collins, James Edger, John Holt. Codicil, April 10, 1777, mentions son James Houston. Wits., Peter Dolbee, Jarred Hitchens. Prob. April 25, 1777. Arch. vol. A78, pages 82-85. Reg. of Wills, Liber C, folios 91-93. [Note:—Arch. vol. A78, page 85 shows the estate was settled by Mary Houston and Robert Houston on Aug. 3, 1794].

**Wootton [Wooten], John, Jr.** Yeoman. Admin. of, to William Duskey and wife Leah. Adm'rs bond dated April 25, 1777. Arch. vol. A109, page 58.

**Cirwithen, John.** Prime Hook Neck. Will. Made March 15, 1777. Heirs: wife Nancy; daus. Sarah, Mary, Rebecca, Betty and Martha Cirwithen. Exec'rs, wife Nancy Cirwithen and bro. Caleb Cirwithen. Wits., Chris[topher] Nutter, John Nutter, Thomas Collings. Prob. May 15, 1777. Arch. vol. A64, page 170. Reg. of Wills, Liber C, folios 96-98.

**Clifton, Levin.** Will (copy). Made April 3, 1773. Heirs: wife Ursley Clifton; sons Aaron and Phillip Clifton; daus. Elizabeth Clifton and Mary Turner. Exec'rx, wife Ursley Clifton. Wits., Peter Dagman, Richard Austins, John Killingsworth. Prob. May 15, 1777. Arch. vol. A65, page 19. Reg. of Wills, Liber C, folios 94-96.

**Burton, William.** Will. Made May 28, 1772. Heirs: wife Elizabeth Burton; sons Joseph, William and Peter Burton; dau. Ann Cord Burton. Exec'rs, wife Elizabeth and son William Burton. Wits., Ann Burton, Woolsey Burton, Jr., Benjamin Burton. Prob. May 19, 1777. Arch. vol. A62, page 22. Reg. of Wills, Liber C, folios 98-100.

**Hill, Robert.** Will. Made Feb. 23, 1777. Heirs: wife Penelope Hill; sons William and Robert Hill; daus. Esther Covington (wife of Jacob) and Elizabeth Lofland (wife of George); grandson Robert Hill (son of William). Exec'r, son William Hill. Wits., William Hazzard, Edward Stapleford, William Strong. Prob. May 26, 1777. Arch. vol. A76, pages 149-150. Reg. of Wills, Liber C, folios 100-102. [Note:—Arch. vol. A76, page 150 shows the estate was settled Feb. 5, 1783 by Nehemiah Davis and Sarah, his wife (late Sarah Hill), who was exec'rx of the estate of William Hill].

**Dorman, Charles.** Will. Made May 19, 1777. Heirs: wife Mary Dorman; sons William and Joshua Dorman. Exec'rs, wife Mary Dorman and Isaac Jones., Jr. Wits., Isaac Jones, William Holt, Nancy Evans. Prob. May 31, 1777. Arch. vol. A69, pages 154-155. Reg. of Wills, Liber D, folio 56. [Note:—Arch. vol. A69, page 155 mentions John and Polly Dorman, children of the dec'd; also shows that Mary Dorman later married Isaac Whaley].

**Newbold, William.** Province of Pennsylvania. Will. Made April 28, 1777. Heirs: wife Margaret Newbold; son William Newbold. Exec'rs, wife Margaret Newbold and son William Newbold. Wits., William Kollock, George Messick, W[illia]m Salmons. Prob. June 6, 1777. Arch. vol. A91, page 71. Reg. of Wills, Liber C, folios 104-105.

**West, Benjamin.** Yeoman. Admin. of, to John Burton, Jr., and wife Mary (late Mary West, widow). Admr's bond dated June 10, 1777. Arch. vol. A106, page 103. [Note:—Arch. vol. A106, page 103 mentions Lydia and Hester West, minors; Robert West, minor son of Lewis West; Wrixam Lewis West; Phillips Russel and wife Ruth; Thomas Brereton and wife Ann [Nancy] (late Nancy West)].

**Carpenter, James.** Tailor. Admin. of, to Rachel Atkinson Carpenter. Granted [c. June 11, 1777]. Arch. vol. A63, page 230.

**Evans, Thomas.** Will. Made June 12, 1777. Heirs: sons Jehu, Owen, Elisha, Thomas, John and Hance Evans. Exec'r, son Jehu Evans. Wits., Thomas Willin, James Brooks. Prob. [c. 1777]. Arch. vol. A71, pages 26-27. Reg. of Wills, Liber D, folios 56-57.

**Coston, Benton.** Yeoman. Broadkill Hd. Will. Made June 10, 1777. Heirs: wife Elizabeth; sons Benton, Stephen, Somerset, Matthias, Joshua and Ezekiel Coston; daus. Comfort, Director and Euphama. Exec'rx, wife Elizabeth Coston. Wits., Somerset Dickerson, Peter Dickerson, Sarah Dickerson. Prob. June 28, 1777. Arch. vol. A67, pages 7-10. Reg. of Wills, Liber C, folios 105-108. [Note:—Arch. vol. A67, page 8 shows that Elizabeth Coston later married Thomas Skidmore].

**Green, John.** (Minor). Admin. of, to Richard Green, bro. Granted [c. July 25, 1777]. Arch. vol. A73, page 64.

**Shockley, John.** Admin. of, to Littleton Townsend. Admr's bond dated Aug. 16, 1777. Arch. vol. A98, page 138.

**West, Thomas, Sr.** Gentleman. Worcester County, Md. Will. Made April 27, 1771. Heirs: wife Bridget West; sons Robert, Jehu and Thomas West; daus. Bridget, Ann and Mary West. Exec'r, son Thomas West. Wits., Job Ingram, William Ingram, John Evans. Prob. Aug. 24, 1777. Arch. vol. A106, pages 178-179. Reg. of Wills, Liber C, folios 108-110. [Note:—Arch. vol. A106, page 179 shows the estate was settled March 7, 1792 by son Thomas West].

**Cannon, Constantine.** Yeoman. Admin. of, to William Causey and wife Starling (late Starling Cannon). Granted [c. Sept. 22, 1777]. Arch. vol. A62, pages 243-244.

**Hudson, Major.** Admin. of, to James Hatfield and wife Piercy (late Piercy Hudson). Granted Sept. 27, 1777. Arch. vol. A79, page 36.

**Turner, Nicholas.** Will. Made Feb. 3, 1776. Heirs: wife Rachel Turner; sons Nicholas, Levi, John and Turner Turner; daus. Mary, Betty, Rachel and Hannah Turner; 3 children of son Edward Turner, dec'd. Exec'rx, wife Rachel Turner. Wits., David Watson, Jonathan Williams, William Coffin. Prob. Sept. 29, 1777. Arch. vol. A103, page 24. Reg. of Wills, Liber C, folios 110-112.

**Barnes, Daniel.** Will. Made Oct. 6, 1777. Heirs: wife Mary Barnes; sons Robert, Thomas and Simeon Barnes; daus. Anna and Mary Barnes. Exec'rs, wife Mary Barnes and son Robert Barnes. Wits., Andrew Williams, William Robinson, Elisabeth Benton. Prob. . . . [1777]. Arch. vol. A58, page 201. Reg. of Wills, Liber C, folios 132-133. [Note:— Arch. vol. A58, page 201 shows Robert Barnes renounced his right as exec'r to Thomas Blades Wildgoss].

**Dirickson, Benjamin.** Worcester County, Md. Will. Made Sept. 15, 1777. Heirs: sons John, William, Benjamin, Andreas, George and Job D. Dirickson; dau. Susannah Rickards; grandson Caleb Dirickson. Exec'r, Benjamin Schoolfield. Wits., Joseph Dirickson, Jonathan Dazey, Joshua Evans. Prob. Oct. 18, 177[7]. Arch. vol. A69, page 22. Reg. of Wills, Liber C, folio 8.

**Handzer, Aminadab** (son of Aminadab and Rose Handzer). Will (copy). Made Oct. 26, 1777. Heirs: father Aminadab Handzer; mother Rose Handzer; bro. Samuel Handzer; sisters Ann and Mary Handzer. Exec'r, father Aminadab Handzer. Wits., Job Barker, Jno. Russell. [No prob.]. Arch. vol. A74, page 47. Reg. of Wills, Liber A, folio 122.

**Marriner, Thomas.** Will. Made Oct. 4, 1777. Heirs: wife Jean [Jane] Marriner; sons George and Thomas Marriner; daus. Mary, Sukey, and Unice Marriner; George and Robert Hardy (sons of Thomas). Exec'rx, wife Jane Marriner. Wits., William Johnson, William Bryan, Ann Bryan. Prob. Oct. 30, 1777. Arch. vol. A86, pages 85-86. Reg. of Wills, Liber C, folios 112-114. [Note:—Arch. vol. A86, page 86 shows an inventory was made of the estate by Warrington Owens and Jane, his wife (late Jane Marriner) on Aug. 4, 1785].

**Argo, Alexander.** Nanticoke Hd. Will. Made June 20, 1777. Heirs: wife Sarah Argo; sons Joseph, David, George and Alexander Argo; dau. Alice Simpson. Exec'rs, wife Sarah

Argo and son Joseph Argo. Wits., John Jones; Thomas Vinson, Sr., Levin Vinson. Prob. Nov. 3, 1777. Arch. vol. A57, pages 154-155. Reg. of Wills, Liber C, folios 115-118.

**Jessup, James.** Yeoman. Admin. of, to John Jessup. Granted Nov. 3, 1777. Arch. vol. A80, page 187.

**Crapper, Molton.** Merchant. Will. Made Sept. 24, 1777. Heirs: wife Esther; son Zadock; bro. Levin Crapper. Exec'rx, wife Esther Crapper. Wits., Sydenham Thorne, Amos Cary, James Cary, Frederick Loever. Prob. Nov. 4, 1777. Arch. vol. A67, pages 177-179. Reg. of Wills, Liber C, folios 114-115. [Note:—Arch. vol. A67, page 179 shows that Daniel Rogers and wife Esther (late Esther Crapper) settled the estate c. Oct. 12, 1779].

**Minors, Charles.** Admin. of, to Elizabeth Prior, widow of Charles Minors. Granted [c. Nov. 5, 1777]. Arch. vol. A89, page 24.

**Hill, John.** Angola Neck. Will (nunc.). Made Nov. 10, 1777. Heirs: dau. Molly Hill. Exec'r, Ezekiel West. Wits., Mary Day, Sarah Hazzard, Margaret West, William Blizzard. Prob. Nov. 13, 1777. Arch. vol. A76, pages 129-131. Reg. of Wills, Liber C, folios 119-120. [Note:—Arch. vol. A76, pages 130-131 mentions Nehemiah, Mary, John and Jehu Hill].

**Polk, Leah.** Admin. of, to James Polk. Admr's bond dated Nov. 26, 1777. Arch. vol. A93, page 139.

**Claypoole, Jehu.** Yeoman. Will. Made Nov. 28, 1777. Heirs: son George; daus. Sarah, Anna, Elizabeth and Rachel Claypoole. Exec'r, friend and nephew William Conwell. Wits., Letitia Fisher, William Claypoole, Jacob Gum. Guardian, friend and nephew William Conwell. Prob. Dec. 1, 1777. Arch. vol. A63, pages 228-230. Reg. of Wills, Liber C, folios 120-122.

**Aydelott, Joseph.** Tailor. Indian River Hd. Will. Made Nov. 13, 1777. Heirs: wife Frances Aydelott; nephews Cornelius and Elon Aydelott (children of bro. John). Exec'rs, wife Frances Aydelott and bro. Henry Aydelott. Wits., Thomas Gray, Eli Collins, Hannah Collins. Prob. Dec. 5, 1777. Arch. vol. A58, pages 9-13. Reg. of Wills, Liber C, folios 124-129. [Note:—Arch. vol. A58, page 11 shows that letters of administration were granted to Frances Stockley (late Frances Aydelott) and co-exec'r Henry Aydelott renounced Dec. 7, 1777 and that Woodman Stockley, Jr. settled the account Aug. 20, 1794].

**Ellegood, John.** Will. Made Jan. 27, 1776. Heirs: wife Sarah Ellegood; son William Ellegood; daus. Nancy and Sarah Ellegood; father William Ellegood. Exec'rx, wife Sarah Ellegood. Wits., Thomas Cockayne, William Huffington, Robert Ellegood. Prob. Dec. 5, 1777. Arch. vol. A70, page 43. Reg. of Wills, Liber C, folios 122-124.

**Lewis, Wrixam, Esq.** Admin. of, to Sarah Lewis. Granted Dec. 9, 1777. Arch. vol. A84, pages 72-74. [Note:—Arch. vol. A84, page 74 shows that Sarah Lewis later married . . . Harmonson; also mentions minors Susanna and Hester Lewis].

**Dazey, Thomas, Sr.** Will. Made Nov. 13, 1777. Heirs: wife Jemima Dazey; sons John and Moses Dazey; daus. Assenath, Martha, Anne, Elizabeth Dazey, Sarah Hodgson, Mary Powders and Rachel Latchem. Exec'rx, wife Jemima Dazey. Wits., Richard Barker, Thomas Aydelott, John Evans. Prob. Dec. 22, 1777. Arch. vol. A68, page 203. Reg. of Wills, Liber C, folios 129-132.

**Marsh, Agnes.** Widow. Admin. of, to son John Fields. Admr's bond dated Dec. 22, 1777. Arch. vol. A86, page 92. [Note: —Arch. vol. A86, page 92 mentions minors Hester and Sarah Marsh].

**Conwell, David.** Admin. of, to John and Mary Hazzard. Granted [c. 1778]. Arch. vol. A66, page 96.

**Hill, Solomon.** Will. Made Jan. 8, 1778. Heirs: wife Betty Hill; daus. Comfort Shaw and Nanny Brian. [No exec'r]. Wits., John Bradley, Samuel Cary, William Kollock. Prob. Jan. 20, 1778. Arch. vol. A76, page 155. Reg. of Wills, Liber C, folios 328-329.

**Phippen, Lott.** Yeoman. Admin. of, to Alexander Reed and wife Elizabeth (late Elizabeth Phippen). Admr's bond dated Jan. 23, 1778. Arch. vol. A93, page 65. [Note:—Arch. vol. A93, page 65 mentions a minor son and dau. John and Sarah Phippen].

**Johnson, Josephus.** Will. Made Dec. 20, 1777. Heir: wife Mary Johnson. Exec'rs, wife Mary Johnson and bro. William Johnson. Wits., William Johnson, James Rose James, David Lafeyette. Prob. Jan. 25, 1778. Arch. vol. A81, pages 64-66. Reg. of Wills, Liber C, folios 133-134. [Note:—Arch. vol. A81, page 66 shows the estate was settled by William Johnson, William James and wife Mary (late Mary Johnson)].

**Spencer, Donovan.** Yeoman. Will. Made Jan. 15, 1778. Heirs: sons Joseph, Nathan, Isiah and Donovan Spencer; daus. Sarah, Mary and Celia Spencer; Mary Joice (grandmother of sons). Exec'rs, sons Nathan and Donovan Spencer. Wits., W[illia]m Hazzard, Magdalena Owens, Daniel Dingee. Prob. Feb. 2, 1778. Arch. vol. A100, page 50. Reg. of Wills, Liber C, folios 134-137.

**Hill, William.** Yeoman. Will. Made Dec. 15, 1777. Heirs: wife Sarah Hill; sons Nathan and Robert Hill; daus. Sarah and Betty Hill. Exec'rx, wife Sarah Hill. Wits., William Hazzard, Simeon Lewis, John Crippen. Prob. Feb. 9, 1778. Arch. vol. A76, page 165. Reg. of Wills, Liber C, folios 138-140.

**May, Mary.** Widow. Admin. of, to Draper May. Admr's bond dated Feb. 9, 1778. Arch. vol. A87, page 99. [Note:—Arch. vol. A87, page 99 mentions children Ann, Betsey and Jonathan May, also Thomas May, dec'd].

**Smith, Mary.** Will. Made Sept. 29, 1777. Heirs: sons Jesse and Ezekiah Smith; daus. Betsey Smith and Christine Johnson. Exec'r, son Jesse Smith. Wits., Levin Connaway, Elisha Long, Elijah Morgan. Prob. Feb. 16, 1778. Arch. vol. A99, page 185. Reg. of Wills, Liber C, folios 137-139.

**Tatman, Lowder [Louder].** Yeoman. Admin. of, to Rachel Tatman. Admr's bond dated Feb. 19, 1779. Arch. vol. A101, page 106.

**Johnson, Peter.** Will. Made March 5, 1778. Heirs: wife Rachel Johnson; sons Isaac, Peter, John and Job Johnson; daus. Leah, Sarah and Mary Johnson, and Comfort Evans. Exec'rs, sons Isaac and Peter Johnson. Wits., Thomas Godwin, Aaron Irons, Jacob Irons. [No prob.]. Arch. vol. A81, pages 80-81. Reg. of Wills, Liber C, folios 337-339.

**Hayes, Thomas.** Admin. of, to Comfort Hayes. Admr's bond dated March 11, 1778. Arch. vol. A75, page 30. [Note:—Arch. vol. A75, page 30 mentions Thomas Hayes in behalf of his mother Comfort Hayes, admr'x].

**Millman, Jonathan.** Yeoman. Admin. of, to Mary Millman. Admr's bond dated March 11, 1778. Arch. vol. A89, page 5. [Note:—Arch. vol. A89, page 5 mentions bros. and sisters Thomas, Peter, Ephraim, Judah, Nanney, Mary and Elizabeth Millman].

**Smith, George.** Planter. Will. Made Feb. 3, 1777. Heirs: wife Alice Smith; sons Curtis, George, Allen and Henry Smith; daus. Lydia, Alice and Charlotte Smith, Molly Brown (wife of Ezekiel). Exec'rs, sons Curtis, George and Allen Smith. Wits., John Tennent, Constantine Jacobs, David Cavender. Prob. March 31, 1778. Arch. vol. A99, page 135. Reg. of Wills, Liber C, folios 140-142.

**Spencer, Catharine.** Admin. of, to Joshua Spencer. Granted April 1, 1778. Arch. vol. A100, page 49.

**Shaver, Isaac.** Yeoman. Admin. of, to Ann Shaver. Admr's bond dated April 7, 1778. Arch. vol. A98, page 101.

**Salmon, James.** Will. Made Oct. 6, 1777. Heirs: sons Joseph and James Salmon; daus. Lydia and Annabel Salmon; bro. William Salmon. Exec'r, Solomon Willey. Wits., Benjamin Phillips, Benjamin Salmon, Sanders Kimmey. Prob. April 13, 1778. Arch. vol. A97, pages 185-186. Reg. of Wills, Liber C, folios 152-154.

**Aydelott, Henry.** Will. Made March 13, 1778. Heirs: father John Aydelott; bros. Mathias and Howard Aydelott; sister Levinah White; niece Betsey (dau. of Howard Aydelott); nephews Oliver and Selac Hazzard (sons of Uriah). Exec'r, father John Aydelott. Wits., Joseph Roberts, Jasper Aydelott, Joseph Dirickson. Prob. April 23, 1778. Arch. vol. A57, pages 237-238. Reg. of Wills, Liber C, folios 143-144. [Note: —Arch. vol. A57, page 238 shows that the estate was settled May 23, 1799 by Mary Aydelott and Thomas Hazzard].

**Goslin [Gauslin], Daniel.** Will. Made June 17, 1777. Heirs: wife Betty Gauslin; sons Thomas, Joshua, George, Richard, Daniel, Louder and John Gauslin; daus. Ann and Betty Gauslin. Exec'rx, wife Betty Gauslin. Wits., James English, Sr., Levin English. Prob. April 24, 1778. Arch. vol. A72, page 102. Reg. of Wills, Liber C, folios 144-146.

**Cowing, Elizabeth.** Widow. Will. Made March 26, 1773. Heirs: son George Cowing; daus. Esther and Nanney Cowing, Elizabeth Conner (wife of Bundick Conner), and Sarah Fisher (wife of Jonathan Fisher); grandson William Poynter; granddau. Castilla Poynter. Exec'r, son George Cowing. Wits., William Hazzard, Thomas Cary, Edward Cary. Prob. April 30, 1778. Arch. vol. A67, pages 118-119. Reg. of Wills, Liber C, folios 157-159.

**Wharton, Hinman, Sr.,** Will. Made Dec. 19, 1775. Heirs: wife Mary Wharton; sons David, Watson and Hinman Wharton; daus. Mary Barker, Elizabeth Smith, Cathrine Evans, Rhoda

Aydelott. Exec'rs, sons David, Watson and Hinman Wharton and daus. Elizabeth Smith, Cathrine Evans and Rhoda Aydelott. Wits., William Tunnell, Elizabeth Tunnell, John Evans. Prob. May 4, 1778. Arch. vol. A107, page 18. Reg. of Wills, Liber C, folios 146-148. [Note:—Arch. vol. A107, page 18 shows the estate was settled March 8, 1786 by Watson Wharton, acting exec'r].

**Waples, Cornelius.** Yeoman. Admin. of, to William Hall and wife Elizabeth (late Elizabeth Waples). Granted May 5, 1778. Arch. vol. A104, pages 178-179. [Note:—Arch. vol. A104, page 179 mentions heirs Wallace and Cornelius B. Waples, sons; page 178 mentions Jane Wilkins White and Isaac White, children of Isaac White].

**Adams, Richard.** Yeoman. Will. Made June 1, 1777. Heirs: sons Roger, James, Absalom, Richard, Moses and William Adams; daus. Ann Nash, Mar[gar]et Smith and Betty Taylor; heirs of dau. Sarah Carsey, dec'd. Exec'r, son Roger. Wits., William Owens, Isaac Minshall, Curtis Otwell. Prob. May 6, 1778. Arch. vol. A57, pages 89-90. Reg. of Wills, Liber C, folios 148-150.

**Boyce, Joseph.** Yeoman. Will. Made Feb. 15, 1778. Heirs: wife Magdalene; sons Joshua and Eleze Boyce; daus. Leah, Comfort and Writtie Boyce. Exec'rs, wife Magdalene Boyce and bro. Jonathan Boyce. Wits., Peter Dolbee; Joseph Boyce, Jr., John Crockett. Prob. May 6, 1778. Arch. vol. A60, pages 52-53. Reg. of Wills, Liber C, folios 150-152.

**Flowers, Elizabeth.** Widow. Will. Made Feb. 20, 1778. Heirs: sons John, Charles and Bartholomew Flowers; grandsons Edmund Ellis, Tilghman, John, Lamlock and Thomas Flowers; granddau. Elizabeth Flowers; dau.-in-law Priscilla Flowers; Mary Flowers. Exec'r, John Flowers. Wits., Levin Cannon, Jesse Cannon. Prob. May 18, 1778. Arch. vol. A71, pages 210-211. Reg. of Wills, Liber C, folios 154-156.

**Hazzard, David.** Will. Made April 5, 1778. Heirs: wife Sarah Hazzard; sons John and Ebenezer Hazzard; dau. Arcada Hazzard. Exec'r, bro. John Hazzard. Wits., John Hazzard, John Rickards, William Robinson. Prob. May 22, 1778. Arch. vol. A75, pages 42-44. Reg. of Wills, Liber C, folios 156-157.

**Robinson, William.** Will. Made April 26, 1778. Heirs: wife unnamed; daus. Nanny, Mary and Betty Robinson. Exec'rs, unnamed wife and bro. Cornelius Robinson. Wits., Littleton Townsend, Adam Hall, William Hall. Prob. June 4, 1778.

Arch. vol. A96, page 191. Reg. of Wills, Liber C, folios
346-347. [Note:—Arch. vol. A96, page 191 shows the
adm'rx as Elizabeth Robinson].

**Collings, Thomas.** Yeoman. Admin. of, to Percey Collings.
Granted June 8, 1778. Arch. vol. A66, pages 30-31. [Note:
—Arch. vol. A66, page 31 shows that Percey Collings later
married Joseph Couch].

**Lindall, Peter.** Admin. of, to William Voss and wife Jane, late
Jane Lindall. Adm'rs bond dated June 10, 1778. Arch. vol.
A84, page 109.

**Dingle, Richard.** Will. Made May 6, 1778. Heir: mother El[iza-
beth] Gibbens. Exec'r, father-in-law John Gibbens. Wits.,
Benjamin Phillips, Peter Sharpe. Prob. June 16, 1778. Arch.
vol. A69, page 84. Reg. of Wills, Liber C, folio 161. [Note:
—Arch. vol. A69, page 84 mentions the exec'r as his father-
in-law and also mentions his deceased father, Edward
Dingle].

**Woodgate, John.** Yeoman. Will. Made May 28, 1778. Heirs:
son Jonathan Woodgate; wife unnamed. Exec'rs, wife unnamed and Thomas Laws. Wits., Geo[rge] Wallace,
Tho[ma]s Laws, Edw[ar]d Vaughan. Prob. June 16, 1778.
Arch. vol. A109, page 49. Reg. of Wills, Liber C, folios 159-
160. [Note:—Arch. vol. A109, page 49 shows the estate
was settled Feb. 11, 1785 by William Polk, Esq. and wife
Mary (late Mary Woodgate) and Thomas Laws].

**Salmons, Agnes.** Will. Made June 9, 1778. Heirs: sons Benjamin, William, Solomon and [Aydelott] Salmons; daus.
Agnes Salmons, Mary Tamplin and Patience Homes; granddau. Agnes Homes. Exec'r, son Benjamin Salmons. Wits.,
Jacob Burton, Tho[ma]s Cade. Prob. June 19, 1778. Arch.
vol. A97, pages 174-175. Reg. of Wills, Liber C, folios 329-
330.

**Little, John.** Lewes & Rehoboth Hd. Will. Made June 9, 1778.
Heirs: wife Naomi Little; son Nicholas Little; daus. Naomi
Little, Hester Williams (wife of Jesse); grandson Robert
Burton; granddau. Betty Burton (children of John Burton).
Exec'r, son Nicholas Little. Wits., William Stephenson, G.
Parker, Jacob Moore. Prob. June 22, 1778. Arch. vol. A84,
page 164. Reg. of Wills, Liber C, folios 164-169.

**White, Wrixam.** Will. Made Feb. 13, 1777. Heirs: wife Catherine White; sons Paul, William, Eli and James White; child
unnamed. Exec'rx, wife Catherine White. Wits., Comfort
Waples, John White, Benjamin West. Prob. June 26, 1778.

Arch. vol. A107, pages 97-98. Reg. of Wills, Liber C, folios 162-164. [Note:—Arch. vol. A107, page 98 mentions Nancy White].

**Johnson, William.** Mulatto. Admin. of, to John Rowland. Admr's bond dated July 25, 1778. Arch. vol. A81, page 121.

**Aydelott, Thomas.** Will. Made May 12, 1778. Heirs: sons Joseph and Thomas Aydelott; Li[da] Evans. [No exec'r]. Wits., John Evans, [Elizabeth] Dazey, Moses Dazey. Prob. Aug. 3, 1778. Arch. vol. A58, page 19. Reg. of Wills, Liber C, folios 169-170.

**Hemmons, Thomas.** Yeoman. Admin. of, to Dorothy Hemmons and John Hemmons. Granted Aug. 3, 1778. Arch. vol. A76, page 41.

**Miller, Peter.** Admin. of, to Lucilla Miller. Admr's bond dated Aug. 4, 1778. Arch. vol. A88, page 199.

**Craige, Hamilton.** Farmer. Will. Made March 20, 1777. Heirs: sons John, Edward and Robert Craige; daus. Mary, Ruth and Esther Craige, Elizabeth Prettyman (wife of William Prettyman). Exec'rs, sons John and Edward Craige. Wits., [Gilbert] Parker, David Shankland, John Shankland. Prob. Aug. 19, 1778. Arch. vol. A67, pages 137-146. Reg. of Wills, Liber C, folios 170-175. [Note:—Arch. vol. A67, page 137 shows dec'd wife was the dau. of Harmon Harmonson].

**Holeagor [Holleger], Ephraim.** Yeoman. Will. Made Aug. 21, 1778. Heirs: wife Rachel Holeagor; sons Thomas and John Holeagor; daus. Sarah and Elizabeth Holeagor; bro. Andrew Holeagor; sister Martha Holeagor. Exec'rs, wife Rachel and bro. Andrew Holeagor. Wits., David Watson, Philip Holeagor, Nancy Wall. Prob. Aug. 26, 1778. Arch. vol. A77, page 50. Reg. of Wills, Liber C, folios 175-177.

**Jones, David.** Admin. of, to John Jones. Admr's bond dated Sept. 8, 1778. Arch. vol. A81, page 139.

**Wright, Solomon.** Yeoman. Admin. of, to John Cade, Jr., and wife Hannah (late Hannah Wright). Admr's bond dated Oct. 9, 1778. Arch. vol. A109, page 101.

**Warrington, Joseph.** Will. Made Oct. 20, 1778. Heirs: wife unnamed; sons Robert, Joseph and Alex[ander] Warrington; daus. Rachel and Tenely Warrington, Esther Stockly. Exec'rs, Rhodes Shankland and Allick [Alexander] Warrington. Wits., Evan Morgan, Allen Reid, Ann C. Holmes. Prob. Oct. 26, 1778. Arch. vol. A105, page 154. Reg. of

Wills, Liber C, folios 177-179. [Note:—Arch. vol. A105, page 154 mentions widow Sarah Warrington; also shows the estate was settled March 8, 1787 by Rhodes Shankland, surviving exec'r].

**Masten, John.** Will. Made Oct. 14, 1778. Heirs: wife Sarah Masten; sons John and Gilbert Masten; dau. Rebecca Masten; Ann Black; Burton and Rachel Forkner. Exec'rx, wife Sarah Masten. Wits., Hezekiah Morris, Daniel Morris, Jr., Daniel Morris, Sr. Prob. Nov. 5, 1778. Arch. vol. A87, pages 66-67. Reg. of Wills, Liber C, folios 179-180. [Note:— Arch. vol. A87, page 67 shows the estate was settled March 2, 1795 by Isaac Jones, Jr., and Sarah, his wife (late Sarah Masten)].

**Wilson, William, Sr.** Will. Made Oct. 22, 1778. Heirs: wife Hannah Wilson; sons Thomas and John Wilson; dau. Mary Shockley (wife of Levin Shockley). Exec'rs, wife Hannah Wilson and son John Wilson. Wits., David Watson, Collins Truitt, William Shockley. Prob. Nov. 11, 1778. Arch. vol. A108, page 133. Reg. of Wills, Liber C, folios 182-183.

**Sirman, Job.** Planter. Somerset County, Md. Will. Made Dec. 18, 1772. Heirs: wife Abigail Sirman; sons Louder, William and Job Sirman; dau. Nancy Sirman; grandson Job Sirman (son of William); granddau. Nancy Sirman. Exec'r, son Louder Sirman. Wits., Elisha Cordry, Josiah Cordry, Shadrach Hall. Prob. Nov. 16, 1778. Arch. vol. A99, page 77. Reg. of Wills, Liber C, folios 180-181. [Note:—Arch. vol. A99, page 77 mentions Mary Sirman].

**Thoroughgood, Paul.** Will. Made Nov. 21, 1778. Heirs: wife Elisabeth Thoroughgood; sons Miller, William, Elisha, Paul, Elihu and John Thoroughgood; daus. Anna and Elisabeth Thoroughgood. Exec'rs, sons Miller and William Thoroughgood. Wits., Benjamin Phillips, Solomon Willey, Annabel Salmon. [No prob. date]. Arch. vol. A101, page 185. Reg. of Wills, Liber C, folios 183-185.

**Holt, Catherine.** Widow. Will. Made Nov. 9, 1774. Heir: granddau. Penelope Holt Jones. Exec'rx, granddau. Penelope Holt Jones. Wits., John Rodney, Hannah Woods, Elizabeth White. Prob. . . ., 1779. Arch. vol. A77, page 157. Reg. of Wills, Liber C, folios 219-220.

**Jacobs, Patience.** Widow. Admin. of, to William Jacobs. Admr's bond dated Jan. 13, 1779. Arch. vol. A80, page 72. [Note:— Arch. vol. A80, page 72 mentions Hannah Jacobs, dau. of Nathaniel].

**Burton, John Stratton.** Will. Made Jan. 21, 1779. Heirs: wife Sarah Burton; sons John, Woolsey, Isaiah and Eli Burton; dau. Lydia. Exec'rs, wife Sarah Burton and Woolsey Hathaway. Wits., Robert Burton, Jr., Benjamin Burton, Ann Bagwell. [No prob. date]. Arch. vol. A61, pages 179-180. Reg. of Wills, Liber C, folios 188-191.

**Connaway, William.** Admin. of, to John Truitt and wife Ruth (late Ruth Connaway). Granted [c. Feb. 4, 1779]. Arch. vol. A66, page 76.

**Cannon, Thomas.** Admin. of, to White Brown (attorney for Charles Brown) and wife Sarah (late Sarah Cannon). Granted [ante Feb. 4, 1779]. Arch. vol. A63, pages 139-140. [Note:—Arch. vol. A63, page 139 mentions heirs: Leah, Clarkson, Richard, Diana, Lucretia and Sarah Cannon].

**Green, Elinor.** Spinster. Admin. of, to Richard Green, bro. Granted Feb. 23, 1779. Arch. vol. A73, page 50.

**Clarkson, Abraham.** Planter. Will. Made Feb. 16, 1779. Heirs: Richard, Sterling and Elizabeth Clarkson (children of William); sisters Sarah Brown (wife of Charles), Elizabeth Brown (wife of James), Lucretia Brown (wife of White), Priscilla Cannon (wife of James); Peggy Nutter Brown (dau. of James, Jr.); and Abraham Cannon. Exec'r, James Brown, Jr. Wits., Robert Clarkson, James Andrew, William Neal, John Neal. Prob. March 4, 1779. Arch. vol. A64, pages 206-207. Reg. of Wills, Liber D, folios 3-4.

**Watson, John.** Cordwainer. Admin. of, to Isaac Watson. Admr's bond dated April 5, 1779. Arch. vol. A106, page 19.

**Say, Mary.** Will. Made June 29, 1774. Heirs: daus. Elizabeth and Ann Say, and Sarah Argo. Exec'rx, dau. Sarah Argo. Wits., Alex[ande]r Argo, Jr., Charles Macklin, Elizabeth Macklin. Prob. April 26, 1779. Arch. vol. A98, page 28. Reg. of Wills, Liber C, folios 185-186.

**Messick, Isaac.** Planter. Will. Made March 31, 1779. Heirs: wife Ann Messick; sons Covington, John, Luke, George, Nehemiah, Joseph and Isaac Messick; daus. Bethany Messick, Sarah Easom, Alice Beavins, Ann Owens, Constant Dolbee and Priscilla Mooney. Exec'r, son Covington Messick. Wits., Levin Connaway, Reuben James, Spencer Benson. Prob. April 28, 1779. Arch. vol. A88, pages 108-109. Reg. of Wills, Liber C, folios 331-332.

**Green, Naomi.** Widow of Stephen Green. Admin. of, to Richard Green. Granted May 3, 1779. Arch. vol. A73, page 66.

**Milby, Elizabeth.** Will. Made April 12, 1779. Heirs: bro. John Milby; sister Polly Milby; Sarah Milby (dau. of Levin); Patience Milby (dau. of Nathaniel); Elizabeth Burton (dau. of John); Peter Bagwell. Exec'r, John Burton. Wits., Stratton Burton, Mary Caddy. Prob. May 7, 1779. Arch. vol. A88, pages 159-160. Reg. of Wills, Liber C, folios 187-188. [Note:—Arch. vol. A88, page 160 also mentions Levin, Nathaniel, William, Zadoc, John and Mary Milby].

**Vaughan, Jethro.** Will. Made Feb. 4, 1779. Heirs: wife Mary Vaughan; sons William and Charles Vaughan; daus. Eunice and Mary Vaughan, Betty Collins, Prudence Kellum. Exec'r, son William Vaughan. Wits., Jno. Polk, Davis Bacon, Levin Bacon. Prob. May 7, 1779. Arch. vol. A103, page 65. Reg. of Wills, Liber C, folios 186-187.

**Darby, Samuel.** Yeoman. Will. Made April 7, 1779. Heirs: sons Joseph, Saunders and Oliver Darby; daus. Elizabeth and Mary Darby (adopted children). Exec'r, Joseph Darby. Wits., John Harmonson, Susannah Virden, Matthew Wilson. Prob. May 29, 1779. Arch. vol. A68, pages 27-29. Reg. of Wills, Liber D, folios 4-5.

**Forster, Sarah.** Lewes and Rehoboth Hd. Will. Made April 13, 1779. Heirs: nieces Comfort Forster (dau. of bro. William) and Sally Forster (dau. of bro. Thomas). [No exec'r]. Wits., Isaac Smith, Jacob Moore, Esq. Prob. May 24, 1779. Arch. vol. A71, page 224. Reg. of Wills, Liber C, folios 191-192.

**Hays, Richard.** Will. Made March 31, 1773. Heirs: son Nathaniel and Richard Hays; daus. Rachel and Elizabeth Hays; grandson Curtis Hays (son of Richard). Exec'r, son Richard Hays. Wits., Ephraim Polk, Manuel Polk, Mary Polk. Prob. May 31, 1779. Arch. vol. A75, page 26. Reg. of Wills, Liber C, folios 102-104.

**Otwell, Curtis.** Will. Made April 13, 1779. Heirs: wife Trufener Otwell; children unnamed; sister Mary Otwell. Exec'rx, wife Trufener Otwell. Wits., Joseph Godwin, Leaven Jump, Roger Adams. Prob. May 31, 1779. Arch. vol. A91, page 175. Reg. of Wills, Liber B, folios 192-201.

**Fowler, John, Sr.** Will (copy). Made May 26, 1779. Heirs: wife Rachel Fowler; sons William, Thomas, John and Archibald Fowler; daus. Sarah Currier, Molly Dodd, Nanny Dodd and Ruth Pettyjohn; granddau. Charlotte Pettyjohn (dau of

Ruth); children of daus. Sarah Currier, Molly Dodd and
Nancy Dodd. Exec'rs, wife Rachel Fowler and son Thomas
Fowler. Wits., Robert Watson McColley, William Cary,
Elizabeth Pettyjohn. Prob. June 7, 1779. Arch. vol. A72,
pages 13-14. Reg. of Wills, Liber C, folios 201-203. [Note:
—Arch. vol. A72, page 13 mentions Levinia Reynolds].

**Hopkins, Robert, Sr.** Planter. Will. Made April 27, 1779. Heirs:
wife Hannah Hopkins; sons George, Robert and Levin;
daus. Leah and Betty Hopkins, Sarah Collins, Jane [Jean]
Mears, Comfort Parsons, Rachel Patton, Ann Nebbs.
Exec'rs, wife Hannah Hopkins and son Robert Hopkins.
Wits., Levin Connaway, James Otwell, Luke Fleetwood.
Prob. Aug. . . ., 1799. Arch. vol. A78, pages 10-11. Reg. of
Wills, Liber C, folios 332-334.

**Bounds, Jacob.** Will. Made May 20, 1779. Heirs: wife Mary
Bounds; sons John and Jesse Bounds; dau. Jenny Bounds.
Exec'rx, wife Mary Bounds. Wits., Jesse Bounds, Jo[s]hua
Gibbons, Samuel Gibbons. Prob. Aug. 1, 1779. Arch. vol.
A60, pages 27-28. Reg. of Wills, Liber C, folios 204-205.
[Note:—Arch. vol. A60, page 28 shows that Mary (Polly)
Bounds later married Edward Blades].

**Milles, Levin.** Yeoman. Admin. of, to Henry Warren. Granted
Aug. 4, 1779. Arch. vol. A89, page 4.

**Paremore, Matthew.** Yeoman. Admin. of, to Mary Paremore.
Granted Aug. 4, 1779. Arch. vol. A92, page 89.

**Roach, William.** Admin. of, to Sarah Warrington (late Sarah
Roach). Granted Aug. 5, 1779. Arch. vol. A96, page 68.

**Polk [Pollock], John.** Will. Made Feb. 9, 1779. Heirs: son John
Polk; daus. Elinor and Jenny Polk, Nanny Maxwell and
Mary Williams. Exec'r, son John Polk [Pollock]. Wits.,
John Polk, John Pollock, James Pollock. Prob. Aug. 9, 1779.
Arch. vol. A93, page 173. Reg. of Wills, Liber C, folios
205-209.

**Brown, Mary.** Widow. Dorchester County, Md. Will. Made Sept.
18, 1770. Heirs: daus. Betty, Mary and Sarah Brown. [No
exec'r]. Wits., Daniel Sullivan, Susanna Sullivan, Daniel
Sullivan, Jr. Codicil, Feb. 16, 1777 mentions granddau.
Mary (dau. of son Charles Brown). Prob. Oct. 12, 1779.
Arch. vol. A60, page 220. Reg. of Wills, Liber C, folio 209.

**West, Margaret.** Widow. Admin. of, to George Hill. Admr's
bond dated Oct. 14, 1779. Arch. vol. A106, page 157.

**Penton, Philip.** Yeoman. Admin. of, to Esther Penton. Admr's bond dated Oct. 26, 1779. Arch. vol. A92, page 158.

**Arnold, William.** Pilot. Admin. of, to Isabella Arnold. Granted Nov. 3, 1779. Arch. vol. A57, page 189.

**Davidson, William.** Admin. of, to Mary Davidson. Granted Nov. 3, 1779. Arch. vol. A68, page 65.

**Leatherbury, Arthur.** Admin. of, to Hudson Miles. Admr's bond dated Nov. 3, 1779. Arch. vol. A84, page 17.

**Halbert, Sarah.** Widow. Admin. of, to Isaac Watson. Granted Nov. 4, 1779. Arch. vol. A73, pages 176-177. [Note:— Arch. vol. A73, page 177 mentions Sally, Polly, Becky and Betsy Cirwithin, minor children of Sarah Cirwithin who was a daughter of Samuel Halbert].

**Hepburn, Abigail.** Widow. Admin. of, to G[ilbert] Parker. Granted Nov. 5, 1779. Arch. vol. A76, page 57. [Note:— Arch. vol. A76, page 57 mentions Joseph and John Thompson Hepburn].

**Massey, Daniel.** Will. Made July 13, 1779. Heirs: wife Sarah Massey; sons Ezekiel, Joseph, Kendal and Mitchell Massey; dau. [Harriet] Massey; a child unnamed; cousin John Roberts. Exec'rx, wife Sarah Massey. Wits., John Onions, Sanders Roberts, William Morris. Prob. Nov. 22, 1779. Arch. vol. A87, pages 46-47. Reg. of Wills, Liber C, folios 211-213. [Note:—Arch. vol. A87, page 47 mentions Susanna Massey].

**Hart, Robert.** Yeoman. Cedar Creek Hundred. Will. Made Nov. 18, 1779. Heirs: wife Mary Hart; Robert Hart (son of Absalom Hart); Benjamin Hart (son of Absalom Hart); Robert Hart (son of Robert Hart); sister Susannah Davis (wife of Robert Davis); nephew Mathias Davis (son of Susannah Davis); Curtis Clifton. Exec'rs, Robert and Benjamin Hart. Wits., James Rench, Robert Bell, William Bell, Jr. Prob. Nov. 23, 1779. Arch. vol. A74, pages 168-169. Reg. of Wills, Liber C, folio 213.

**Dodd, Moses.** Will. Made Nov. 19, 1779. Heirs: sons Joseph and Samuel Dodd; daus. [Althea], Ada and Cady Dodd, Mary Vent (wife of James) and Prudence Rawlinson (wife of Richard); granddau. Betsy Rawlinson. Exec'rs, sons Joseph and Samuel Dodd, son-in-law James Vent. Wits., Hugh Stephenscn, John Coulter, William Peery. Prob. Nov. 27, 1779. Arch. vol. A69, page 106. Reg. of Wills, Liber C, folios 334-336.

**Watson, Luke.** Yeoman. Admin. of, to Rebecca Watson and Isaac Watson. Admr's bond dated Nov. 27, 1779. Arch. vol. A106, page 29.

**Polk [Pollock], David, Sr.** Yeoman. Admin. of, to Alexander Laws, John Collins. Granted c. Dec. 1, 1779. Arch. vol. A93, page 172. [Note:—Arch. vol. A93, page 172 mentions heirs: Francis Roberts and wife; William Juitt and wife; Alexander Laws and wife].

**Andrews, Thomas.** Carpenter. Will. Made Nov. 24, 1779. Heirs: friend Martha Davidson; bro.-in-law William Waltham; children of William Frame. Exec'r, William Walthan. Wits., John Abbott Warrington, Arthur Hazzard, William Harrison. Prob. Dec. 11, 1779. Arch. vol. A57, pages 150-151. Reg. of Wills, Liber C, folios 215-217.

**Steel, William.** Will. Made Sept. 20, 1779. Heirs: wife Betty Steel; son Prisgrave Steel; dau. Elizabeth Pettyjohn; grandsons Zachariah Pettyjohn, James and Ishmal Steel (sons of James); Coana Williams. Exec'rs, wife Betty Steel and son Prisgrave Steel. Wits., Robert W. McColley, Rowland

Beavens, Joshua Pepper. Prob. Dec. 14, 1779. Arch. vol. A100, page 147. Reg. of Wills, Liber C, folios 217-219.

**Chase, Isaac.** Admin. of, to Sarah Chase. Granted [c. 1780]. Arch. vol. A64, page 130. [Note:—Arch. vol. A64, page 130 mentions minor children: Peggy, Jacob and Polly].

**Conwell, Elizabeth.** Will. Made Dec. 24, 1779. Heir: John Spencer Conwell. [No exec'r]. Wits., William King, Sarah King, Sarah Heavelo. Prob. . . ., 1780. Arch. vol. A66, page 102. Reg. of Wills, Liber C, folios 220-221.

**Jefferson, Richard.** Will (copy). Made Jan. 2, 1780. Heirs: wife Mary Jefferson; sons Elihu, John, Richard, Joshua, Job and Warring Jefferson; daus. Elizabeth and Ede Jefferson, and Rhoda Ennis. Exec'r, son Warring [Warren] Jefferson. Wits., Ezekiel Green, Mary Green, William Johnson. Prob. . . ., 1780. Arch. vol. A80, pages 165-167. Reg. of Wills, Liber C, folios 237-240.

**Lord, John.** Planter. Worcester County, Md. Will. Made Aug. 23, 1774. Heirs: wife Sarah Lord; sons John, Adam and William Lord; dau. Anna Crock; Wootten Lord; Unice Lord; Isaac Lord; Betsy Lord; Thomas Lord. Exec'rx, wife Sarah Lord. Wits., Isaac Jones, Moses Elliott, Zephenias Maddox. Prob. . . ., 1780. Arch. vol. A85, page 138. Reg. of Wills, Liber C, folios 233-234.

**Nicolls, Zachariah.** Yeoman. Admin. of, to Joseph Godwin. Admr's bond dated Jan. 11, 1780. Arch. vol. A91, pages 103-104.

**Walter, Peleg.** Will. Made April 30, 1779. Heirs: wife Eleanor Walter; sons Mitchell and Ebey Walter; daus. Sally and Polly Walter. Exec'rx, wife Eleanor Walter. Wits., Jacob Rogers, John Wyatt, John Perkins. Prob. Feb. 1, 1780. Arch. vol. A104, page 125. Reg. of Wills, Liber C, folio 231. [Note:—Arch. vol. A104, page 125 mentions Ebenzer Walter; also shows that the estate was settled Sept. 6, 1786 by Stephen Styer and wife Eleanor (late Eleanor Walter)].

**Poynter, Nathaniel.** Yeoman. Will. Made Jan. 3, 1771. Heirs: wife Mary Poynter; sons Racklif [Radcliff], Nathaniel, Thomas and William Poynter; daus. Peninah Poynter, Edy Parks (wife of William), Elizabeth Mullinex (wife of Richard) and Mary Parmore (wife of Alexander). Exec'rs, wife Mary Poynter and son Nathaniel Poynter. Wits., W[illia]m Hazzard, John Bell, J[ame]s Rench. Prob. March 3, 1780. Arch. vol. A94, page 38. Reg. of Wills, Liber C, folios 221-223.

**Hall, Adam.** Will. Made Nov. 16, 1778. Heirs: son William Hall; dau. Mary Hall; grandsons John Buckley, Alexander and Adam Roberts. Exec'r, son William Hall. Wits., William Jordan Hall, Mary Cord, Tabitha Cord. Prob. March 6, 1780. Arch. vol. A73, pages 181-182. Reg. of Wills, Liber C, folios 224-225.

**Melson, Joseph.** Will. Made Nov. 28, 1775. Heirs: wife Ann Mary Melson; daus. Susannah Hopkins, Sarah Derickson, Ann Mary Johnson and Bette Aydelott; grandson Isaac Aydelott. Exec'r, son-in-law Samuel Aydelott. Wits., William Tingle, Jacob Rogers, Tabitha Rogers. Prob. March 8, 1780. Arch. vol. A88, page 54. Reg. of Wills, Liber C, folios 225-226.

**Westley, John.** Admin. of, to William Brereton and wife Rebecca (late Rebecca Westley). Admr's bond dated April 7, 1780. Arch. vol. A107, page 2.

**Williams, Aaron.** Admin. of, to Mary Williams. Admr's bond dated April 15, 1780. Arch. vol. A107, pages 140-142. [Note:—Arch. vol. A107, page 141 shows the estate was settled by Peter Millman and wife Mary Ann (late Mary Williams)].

**Prettyman, William.** Yeoman. Admin. of, to Robert Prettyman. Admr's bond dated April 17, 1780. Arch. vol. A94, page 126.

**Griffith, Samuel.** Yeoman. Admin. of, to John Stuart. Granted [c. May 3, 1780]. Arch. vol. A73, page 136.

**Hinds, Sarah.** Spinster. Admin. of, to Nehemiah Davis, Jr. Granted [c. May 3, 1780]. Arch. vol. A76, page 173.

**Johnson, Major.** Will. Made March 23, 1780. Heirs: wife Abigail Johnson; sons William, Henry and George Johnson; daus. Elizabeth, Hannah and Nancy Johnson; cousin Leonard Johnson. Exec'rs, wife Abigail Johnson and son William Johnson. Wits., Thomas Godwin, Noah Collins, Cornelius Robinson. Prob. May 3, 1780. Arch. vol. A81, pages 78-79. Reg. of Wills, Liber C, folios 340-341.

**McElvain, James, Jr.** Yeoman. Admin. of, to Sophia McElvain. Granted [c. May 3, 1780]. Arch. vol. A87, page 191.

**Walker, Jacob.** Admin. of, to Thomas Walker, in right of Leah Walker, widow, dec'd. Granted [c. May 3, 1789]. Arch. vol. A104, page 16.

**Walker, Leah** (the younger). Admin. of, to Thomas Walker, in right of Leah Walker, widow, dec'd. Granted [c. May 3, 1780]. Arch. vol. A104, page 31.

**Whitesett, Thomas.** Admin. of, to Moses Marriner and wife Margaret (late Margaret Whitesett). Granted [c. May 3, 1780]. Arch. vol. A107, page 100.

**Rowland, Elizabeth.** Widow. Admin. of, to Jacob Hazzard. Granted [c. May 4, 1780]. Arch. vol. A97, page 107. [Note: —Arch. vol. A97, page 107 mentions heirs: James, Samuel, Comfort Rowland, and wife of Jacob Hazzard].

**Jones, Zachariah.** Will (copy). Made May 19, 1780. Heirs: sons Wingate, Zachariah, Ephraim and Isaac Jones; daus. Hannah and Leah Jones, and Sally Connaway; bro. Thomas Jones. Exec'r, son Wingate Jones. Wits., William Powell, William Newbold, Simon Kollock. [No prob.]. Arch. vol. A82, pages 1-3. Reg. of Wills, Liber C, folios 240-244. [Note:—Arch. vol. A82, page 3 mentions Hannah Mears and Mary West].

**Hazzard, Sarah.** Will (copy). Made May 25, 1780. Heirs: son Arthur Hazzard; daus. Elizabeth Stockley, Hester Robinson, Sarah West, Ann Milby, Comfort Craige; grandsons David

Craige, Thomas Hazzard; granddaus. Ann and Sarah Hazzard (daus. of Arthur), Sarah Hazzard (dau. of Joseph). Exec'r, son Arthur Hazzard. Wits., Anderson Parker, Isaac Smith, Sarah Crippin. [No prob.]. Arch. vol. A75, page 117. Reg. of Wills, Liber C, folios 235-236.

**Gray, Thomas.** Yeoman. Will. Made May 10, 1780. Heirs: son Hezekiah Gray; dau. Elizabeth Thomson (wife of Andrew). Exec'r, son-in-law Andrew Thomson. Wits., Shepard Prettyman, Isaac Smith, Mary Warrington. Prob. May 29, 1780. Arch. vol. A73, page 29. Reg. of Wills, Liber D, folios 5-6.

**Merick, Sarah.** Admin. of, to Rickards Mills. Admr's bond dated May 29, 1780. Arch. vol. A88, page 71.

**Whorton, Charles, Sr.** Will. Made May 8, 1780. Heirs: wife Amy Whorton; sons Charles and Eli Whorton. Exec'rs, wife Amy Whorton and son Eli Whorton. Wits., Thomas Godwin, John West, Avery Morgan. Prob. June 6, 1780. Arch. vol. A107, page 10. Reg. of Wills, Liber C, folios 342-343.

**Roberts, Alexander.** Will. Made July 19, 1780. Heirs: wife Elizabeth Roberts; sons William, Joseph, Sanders and John Roberts; daus. Elizabeth, Tabitha, Mary and Sarah Roberts, and Marga[r]et Dirickson. Exec'rs, wife Elizabeth Roberts and son John Roberts. Wits., John Onions, Pearson Onions, William Rickards. [No prob.]. Arch. vol. A96, page 82. Reg. of Wills, Liber C, folios 229-230.

**Owens, Robert.** Will. Made July 31, 1780. Heirs: wife Sarah Owens; son William Owens; daus. Aseneth, Polly and Nancy Owens; dau.-in-law Sarah Williams; son-in-law Robert Williams. Exec'rs, wife Sarah Owens and son-in-law Robert Williams. Wits., W[illia]m Stayton, John Norton, William Arnett. [No prob.]. Arch. vol. A92, page 18. Reg. of Wills, Liber C, folios 226-229.

**Stokely, Mary.** Admin. of, to John Hill. Granted [c. Aug. 9, 1780]. Arch. vol. A101, page 22.

**Hammond, Bowden.** Worcester County, Md. Will. Made June 23, 1777. Heirs: wife Rachel Hammond; cousin Charles Hammond (son of Benjamin). Exec'rx, wife Rachel Hammond. Wits., Nathaniel Rackliffe [Radcliff], Elijah Fossitt, William Stevenson. Prob. Aug. 23, 1780. Arch. vol. A74, pages 24-25. Reg. of Wills, Liber C, folios 343-344. [Note: —Arch. vol. A72, page 25 shows estate was settled Nov. 9, 1785 by Rachel Irons (late Rachel Hammond)].

**Green, Stephen.** Mariner. Lewes & Rehoboth Hd. Will. Made Aug. 24, 1780. Heirs: bros. Ambrose and Richard Green. Exec'r, Dr. Joseph Hall. Wits., John Orr, Joshua Ball. Prob. Aug. 28, 1780. Arch. vol. A73, page 75. Reg. of Wills, Liber C, folio 345. [Note:—Arch. vol. A73, page 75 mentions father Stephen].

**Swiggett, James.** Yeoman. Will. Made July 22, 1780. Heirs: wife Elizabeth Swiggett; son Henry Swiggett; daus. Mary Swiggett and Elizabeth Smith. Exec'r, son Henry Swiggett. Wits., Benjamin Whittington, Rhoda Whittington, Preston Godwin. Prob. Aug. 28, 1780. Arch. vol. A101, page 92. Reg. of Wills, Liber C, folios 344-345.

**Jones, Jonas.** Will (copy). Made Jan. 7, 1780. Heirs: wife Elizabeth Jones; dau. Mahala Jones; Clement Custevens. [No exec'r]. Wits., James Douglass, William Hambury. Prob. Sept. 8, 1780. Arch. vol. A81, page 173. Reg. of Wills, Liber C, folios 236-237.

**Palmer, Joseph.** Shopkeeper. Little Creek Hd. Will. Made May 27, 1780. Heirs: son John Palmer; dau. Mary Fleetwood (wife of John). Exec'r, son John Palmer. Wits., Andrew Heaverlo, Daniel Heaverlo, Ephraim Turner. Prob. Oct. 4, 1780. Arch. vol. A92, page 42. Reg. of Wills, Liber C, folio 234.

**Sharp, Elizabeth.** Will. Made Sept. 6, 1780. Heirs: sons Joshua, Thomas, James, William and Peter Sharp; daus. Ann and Comfort Sharp and Mary Messick. Exec'r, son Thomas Sharp. Wits., Benjamin Phillips, Paul Thoroughgood. Prob. Oct. 12, 1780. Arch. vol. A98, page 73. Reg. of Wills, Liber C, folios 244-246.

**Cannon, Jacob.** Yeoman. Will. Made July 9, 1780. Heirs: wife Betty Cannon; son Isaac Cannon; daus. Anne, Zillah, Sarah and Lurane Cannon; a child unnamed. Exec'rx, wife Betty Cannon. Wits., John Flowers, John Turpin, Levin Farrington, Peter Hubbert. Prob. Oct. 27, 1780. Arch. vol. A63, pages 44-45. Reg. of Wills, Liber C, folios 246-248. [Note: —Arch. vol. A63, page 45 mentions a son Jacob].

**Miller, Joseph.** Will. Made Oct. 2, 1777. Heirs: wife Bathsheba Miller; son Nathaniel Miller; daus. Mary Bounds, Elizabeth Tingle; grandsons David, Joseph and John Miller (sons of son John); granddau. Nancy Miller (dau. of son John); children of John Miller; children of dau. Mary Bounds; children of dau. Elizabeth Tingle. Exec'rs, wife Bathsheba Miller and son Nathaniel Miller. Wits., Samuel Dirickson,

Elisabeth Dirickson, John Wise. Codicil, April 14, 1779 mentions grandchildren Burton, Mary and Comfort Miller (children of dec'd son Nathaniel). Wits., Samuel Dirickson, Elisabeth Dirickson, Joseph Freeman. Prob. Nov. 4, 1780. Arch. vol. A88, pages 194-195. Reg. of Wills, Liber C, folios 323-327.

**Simpler, Philip.** Yeoman. Admin. of, to Susannah Simpler. Granted [c. Nov. 8, 1780]. Arch. vol. A99, page 58.

**Clarkson, Richard, Jr.** Admin. of, to James Brown, Jr., D. B. N., in right of Abraham Clarkson, gentleman, dec'd. Granted ante Nov. 9, 1780. Arch. vol. A64, pages 215-217. [Note:— Arch. vol. A64, page 217 mentions heirs: White, Charles and James Brown, Jr.; and James Cannon].

**Holleger [Holeagor], Nathaniel.** Admin. of, to Rachel Holeagor, widow. Admr's bond dated Dec. 4, 1780. Arch. vol. A77, page 51.

**Mitchell, Randal.** Yeoman. Admin. of, to Stephen Mitchell. Admr's bond dated Dec. 29, 1780. Arch. vol. A89, page 64.

**Vaughan, Betty.** Minor dau. of William Vaughan. Admin. of, to John Burton, Jr. Granted c. 1781. Arch. vol. A103, page 60.

**Crockett, John.** Will. Made June 24, 1780. Heirs: wife Mary; dau. Elizabeth Crockett. Exec'rx, wife Mary Crockett. Wits., Levin Connaway, Isaac Connaway, Joseph Boyce. Prob. Jan. 2, 1781. Arch. vol. A67, pages 191-192. Reg. of Wills, Liber C, folios 249-250. [Note:—Arch. vol. A67, page 192 shows that Mary Crockett later married Gabriel Willey].

**Smith, Isaac.** Will. Made Nov. 21, 1779. Heirs: wife Mary Smith; sons Jacob and William Smith; daus. Elizabeth and Sarah Smith; child unnamed; bro. Jacob Smith. Exec'rx, wife Mary Smith. Wits., John Wiltbank, Jacob Moore. Guardian of Sarah: Catharine Dingee. Prob. Jan. 15, 1781. Arch. vol. A99, page 155. Reg. of Wills, Liber C, folios 259-262.

**Truitt, Elijah.** Yeoman. Admin. of, to Joseph Truitt. Admr's bond dated Jan. 25, 1781. Arch. vol. A102, page 107.

**Messick, George.** Will. Made May 14, 1777. Heirs: wife Patience Messick; sons Minus, George and Job Messick; daus. Meley, Rachel Messick, Nicey Rackliff (wife of William), Love Johnson (wife of Isiah), Mary Hemmons (wife of Jonathan) and Sarah Patter (wife of Seco) ; grandson George Crafford. Exec'rs, wife Patience Messick and George Messick. Wits.,

Thomas Macklin, Rhoads Shankland. Prob. Jan. 29, 1781. Arch. vol. A88, pages 92-93. Reg. of Wills, Liber C, folios 250-253.

**Moore, William.** Planter. Will. Made Sept. 28, 1779. Heirs: nephew John Williams; niece Elizabeth Williams. Exec'r, nephew John Williams. Wits., John Worrilaw, William Vaughan, Eunice Vaughan. Prob. Feb. 3, 1781. Arch. vol. A89, pages 151-152. Reg. of Wills, Liber C, folios 253-254.

**Kimmey, Jean.** Widow. Admin. of, to Aaron Kimmey. Granted Feb. 6, 1781. Arch. vol. A82, page 79.

**King, Hugh.** Will. Made Jan. 13, 1777. Heirs: wife Mary King; sons David, John, William and James King. Exec'rx, wife Mary King. Wits., William Peery, Caleb Cirwithen, John Young. Prob. March 10, 1781. Arch. vol. A82, pages 103-104. Reg. of Wills, Liber C, folios 254-255. [Note:—Arch. vol. A82, page 104 shows the estate was settled by Hap Hazzard and Mary, his wife (late Mary King), on May 7, 1786].

**Vaughan, Ephraim.** Minor son of William Vaughan. Admin. of, to John Burton. Admr's bond dated March 15, 1781. Arch. vol. A103, page 63.

**Dickerson, Peter.** Admin. of, to William Luke and wife Catherine, late Catherine Dickerson. Granted [c. March 26, 1781]. Arch. vol. A69, page 69.

**Young, John.** Admin. of, to John Clowes. Granted March 26, 1781. Arch. vol. A109, page 130.

**Wood, James.** Yeoman. Will. Made Oct. 16, 1779. Heirs: wife Esther Wood; dau.-in-law Esther Warring; Presbyterian Church at Cool Spring. Exec'rx, wife Esther Wood. Wits., John Clowes, James McNeill, Elias Mason. Prob. March 26, 1781. Arch. vol. A109, pages 43-44. Reg. of Wills, Liber C, folio 256. [Note:—Arch. vol. A109, page 44 mentions Hester [Hessey] Warren and Lodowick Warren [Warring]; also shows the estate was settled by Cassa Hall and Esther, his wife (late Esther Wood), on June 7, 1787].

**Poynter, William.** Yeoman. Will. Made March 3, 1781. Heirs: wife Ruth Poynter; sons William, John, Levin and Nathaniel Poynter; daus. Esther and Eunice Poynter, Sophia Cool (wife of Coverdale); child unnamed; granddau. Luranah Hudson (dau. of Sophia Cool). Exec'r, son Nathaniel Poynter. Wits., W[illia]m Hazzard, Radcliff Poynter, Shadrack Sturgis. Prob. April 21, 1781. Arch. vol. A94, pages 44-45. Reg. of Wills, Liber C, folios 256-259.

**Rickards, Michael.** Yeoman. Will. Made March 27, 1781. Heirs: wife Elizabeth Rickards; child unnamed; bros. Jehu and William Rickards; sisters Elizabeth and Margaret Rickards, and Esther Foster. Exec'rs, wife Elizabeth Rickards, bro. William Rickards, Dr. Stephen Hill. Wits., Woolsey Hathaway, James Hathaway, John Massey, Sr. Prob. April 23, 1781. Arch. vol. A95, page 142. Reg. of Wills, Liber C, folios 262-263.

**Neill, John.** Will. Made May 27, 1781. Heirs: wife Bethia Neill; sons Robert and John Neill; daus. Margaret, Mary, Elizabeth and Bethia Neill. Exec'rx, wife Bethia Neill. Wits., William Peery, James Coulter, William Delaney. Prob. June 25, 1781. Arch. vol. A91, pages 59-60. Reg. of Wills, Liber C, folios 263-265. [Note:—Arch. vol. A91, page 60 shows the estate was settled by Robert Neill, exec'r of Bethia Neill, on March 4, 1789].

**Paynter, John.** Will. Made July 5, 1781. Heirs: bros. Reese, Richard and Samuel Paynter; half-bros. Joseph and Arthur Hazzard; half-sister Comfort Hazzard. Exec'r, bro. Reese Paynter. Wits., Richard Little, Arthur Hazzard, Marg[a]ret Brian. Prob. July 13, 1781. Arch. vol. A92, page 122. Reg. of Wills, Liber C, folios 265-266.

**Wharton [Worten], Baker.** Will. Made April 23, 1781. Heirs: wife Betty Worten; sons George, Burton and Baker Worten; dau. Elisabeth Worten. Exec'rs, wife Betty Worten and son George Worten. Wits., Benj[amin] Phillips, Hinman Wharton, William Omford. Prob. July 23, 1781. Arch. vol. A107, page 7. Reg. of Wills, Liber C, folios 267-269. [Note :—Arch. vol. A107, page 7 shows the estate was settled by George Worten, surviving exec'r].

**Lockwood, Elisha.** Will (copy). Made July 12, 1781. Heirs: bros. Armwell, Benjamin, Samuel and William Lockwood; sisters Anne, Elizabeth and Mary Lockwood, and Sebarah Rachel Lear. Exec'r, father [Samuel Lockwood]. Wits., Francis Sellers, Israel Holland, Stephen Hill. Prob. Aug. 20, 1781. Arch. vol. A84, page 194. Reg. of Wills, Liber A, folios 493-494.

**Hill, John.** Admin. of, to Ann Hill. Admr's bond dated Aug. 27, 1781. Arch. vol. A76, page 132.

**Richards, Isaac.** Will. Made Nov. 22, 1779. Heir: friend Stokely Hossman (carpenter of Phila.). Exec'r, Stokely Hossman. Wits., Jno. Ord, W[illia]m Webb. Prob. Aug. 31, 1781. Arch. vol. A95, page 79. Reg. of Wills, Liber D, folio 62.

**Chipman, Paris.** Blacksmith. Will. Made Aug. 5, 1780. Heirs: wife Judah; sons Draper and Paris Chipman; daus. Sarah, Betsey, Kezia, Lovey, Milley and Memory Chipman. Exec'rs, wife Judah and son Paris. Wits., Robert Clarkson, Thomas Nutter Adams, Constantine Jacobs, Brown Twiford. Prob. Sept. 14, 1781. Arch. vol. A64, page 152. Reg. of Wills, Liber C, folios 269-270.

**Coulbourn, Solomon, Sr.** Farmer. Will. Made May 2, 1781. Heirs: wife Jean; sons Solomon, Stephen and William Coulbourn; dau. Mary Coulbourn. Exec'rs, sons William and Solomon Coulbourn. Wits., John Tennent, John Handy, Stephen Corbin. Prob. Oct. 12, 1781. Arch. vol. A65, page 106. Reg. of Wills, Liber C, folios 270-272.

**Wallace, Robert.** Will. Made Feb. 21, 1781. Heirs: sons Benjamin and John Wallace; daus. Elinor, Elizabeth, Mary and Alice Wallace. [No exec'r]. Wits., Geo[rge] Wallace, David Cavender, Abraham Downes. Prob. Oct. 17, 1781. Arch. vol. A104, page 53. Reg. of Wills, Liber C, folios 272-274. [Note:—Arch. vol. A104, page 53 shows the estate was settled by Benjamin Wallace].

**Tilghman, Elijah.** Admin. of, to John Mitchell. Admr's bond dated Nov. 3, 1781. Arch. vol. A101, page 188.

**Conwell, Samuel.** Cordwainer. Admin. of, to Francis Conwell. Granted [c. Nov. 8, 1781]. Arch. vol. A66, page 136.

**Wingate, Laurana.** Admin. of, to Lovey Wingate. Granted [c. Nov. 9, 1781]. Arch. vol. A108, page 192.

**Simpler, Susannah.** Widow. Will. Made Feb. 20, 1779. Heirs: sons Aaron, Thomas, William and Jacob Simpler. Exec'r, son Aaron Simpler. Wits., Levin Walls, John Rust, William Johnson. Prob. Nov. 10, 1781. Arch. vol. A99, page 60. Reg. of Wills, Liber C, folios 274-275.

**McCullah, John.** Will. Made Oct. 26, 1781. Heirs: Ann Reed (dau. of Alexander); nephew Alexander Reed (son of Alexander); friend Mary Walker (dau. of George). Exec'r, friend James Walker. Wits., William Burton, William Wyatt, Hap Hazzard. Prob. Nov. 26, 1781. Arch. vol. A87, pages 144-145. Reg. of Wills, Liber C, folios 317-318.

[Note:—Arch. vol. A87, page 145 shows the estate was settled Dec. 7, 1784 by Charles Connolly and wife Winifred (late Winifred Walker) who was adm'rx of James Walker].

**Beavens, William, Sr.** Will. Made July 5, 1781. Heirs: wife Mary Beavens; sons William, John, James and Shadrach Beavens; daus. Mary Ann Cahoon, Levina Ward and Allafare Wootten; Constant Beavens; son-in-law Elijah Wootten. Exec'rs, wife Mary and son William Beavens. Wits., Isaac Jones, William Driscoll, Elijah Hall. Prob. Dec. 10, 1781. Arch. vol. A59, page 22. Reg. of Wills, Liber C, folios 277-278. [Note:—Arch. vol. A59, page 22 mentions Joseph Ward and wife].

**Hudson, John** (son of David). Will. Made Feb. 9, 1781. Heirs: mother Esther Smith; bro. Parker Hudson; cousin Nancy Hudson (dau. of Elijah Hudson). Exec'rx, mother Esther Smith. Wits., John Tull, John Dyer, Jacob Esham. Prob. Dec. 10, 1781. Arch. vol. A79, page 16. Reg. of Wills, Liber C, folios 275-277.

**Rogers, Parker.** Will. Made Dec. 3, 1781. Heirs: wife Agnes Rogers; sons America and Isaac Rogers; daus. Elizabeth, Mary, Sarah, Esther and Nancy Rogers. Exec'rx, wife Agnes Rogers. Wits., John Coe, Arthur Williams, Tabitha Williams. Prob. Dec. 10, 1781. Arch. vol. A97, page 47. Reg. of Wills, Liber C, folios 279-281. [Note:—Arch. vol. A97, page 47 shows the estate was settled Nov. 2, 1796 by Ezekiel Williams, who was exec'r of Agnes Rogers].

**Plowman, John.** Will. Made Aug. 24, 1781. Heirs: wife Ann Plowman; sons William, John, Josiah, Joseph and James Plowman; dau. Polly Plowman. Exec'r, son James Plowman. Wits., W[illia]m Hazzard, Jacob Lynch, Sarah Lynch. Prob. Dec. 14, 1781. Arch. vol. A93, pages 94-95. Reg. of Wills, Liber C, folios 281-283. [Note:—Arch. vol. A93, page 95 shows the estate was settled Sept. 6, 1787 by James Johnson and Ann, his wife (late Ann Plowman)].

**King, Betty [Elizabeth].** Will. Made May 15, 1779. Heirs: sons William and Nathaniel Vaughan; dau. Mary Burton; granddau. Betty West (dau. of Mary Burton). Exec'r, son John Burton. Wits., William Grice, Betty Grice. Prob. Dec. 17, 1781. Arch. vol. A82, pages 89-90. Reg. of Wills, Liber C, folios 285-286.

**Wattson, William.** Will. Made Nov. 16, 1781. Heirs: wife Nanny [Ann] Wattson; sons William, Luke, John, Thomas, Israel, Bethuel and Samuel Wattson; daus. Sally, Sukky, Molly and

Naomi Wattson. Exec'rx, wife Nanny [Ann] Wattson. Wits., Nath[anie]l Young, Luke Wattson, John Wilcox. Prob. Dec. 17, 1781. Arch. vol. A106, page 48. Reg. of Wills, Liber C, folios 283-285.

**Davis, George.** Yeoman. Admin. of, to Esther Davis. Granted [c. 1782]. Arch. vol. A68, page 71.

**Butcher, William.** Planter. Will. Made Sept. 23, 1772. Heirs: wife Frances Butcher; sons William and Robert Butcher; daus. Mary and Naomi Butcher. Exec'r, son William Butcher. Wits., James Riggin, John Collings, Simon Kollock. Prob. Jan. 3, 1782. Arch. vol. A62, page 76. Reg. of Wills, Liber C, folios 286-288.

**Parker, Gil[bert].** Miller. Will. Made Oct. 18, 1779. Heirs: son-in-law David Shankland; grandsons John, David and Joseph Shankland; granddau. Elizabeth Shankland. Exec'r, son-in-law David Shankland. Wits., Edward Craige, Mary Aliff, Sarah Higgons. Prob. Jan. 14, 1782. Arch. vol. A92, page 67. Reg. of Wills, Liber C, folios 291-292. [Note:— Arch. vol. A92, page 67 shows the estate was settled by Joseph Shankland, acting exec'r of David Shankland].

**Hudson, Sarah.** Admin. of, to Purnal Bennett. Granted [c. Feb. 7, 1782]. Arch. vol. A79, page 51.

**Pettyjohn, John.** Yeoman. Admin. of, to Hannah Pettyjohn. Admr's bond dated Feb. 7, 1782. Arch. vol. A93, page 8.

**Vaughan, Edward.** Will. Made Jan. 10, 1782. Heirs: bro. Joseph Vaughan; sister Mary Polk; bro.-in-law William Polk; nephew Jonathan Vaughan Woodgate. Exec'r, bro.-in-law William Polk. Wits., Sam[ue]l Laverty, Abraham Short, Caleb Nutter. Prob. Feb. 8, 1782. Arch. vol. A103, page 62. Reg. of Wills, Liber C, folios 292-293. [Note:—Arch. vol. A103, page 62 shows the estate was settled Nov. 10, 1791 by Trusten Laws Polk, exec'r of William Polk].

**Abbott, Susannah.** Will. Made Feb. 27, 1780. Heirs: sons John and William Abbott; dau. Temperance Abbott; grandson Nickles, Jr., and granddau. Temperance (children of Nickles Abbott); granddaus. Susannah Reed, Caty Pearson and Elizabeth Collings. Exec'rs, John and William Abott. Wits., Rickson Warren, Ashab Clendaniel. Prob. Feb. 14, 1782. Arch. vol. A57, pages 21-22. Reg. of Wills, Liber C, folios 294-295. [Note:—Arch. vol. A57, page 22 shows John Parsons as husband of Caty Parsons [Pearson]].

**Black, Mitchell.** Yeoman. Admin. of, to George Black. Granted [c. Feb. 28, 1782]. Arch. vol. A58, page 198.

**Millman, Michael.** Yeoman. Admin. of, to Rickards Mills and wife Margaret, late Margaret Millman. Admr's bond dated Feb. 28, 1782. Arch. vol. A89, page 9.

**Conwell, William, Esq.** Will. Made Feb. 20, 1782. Heirs: wife Sarah Conwell; sons Abraham, George and William Conwell; daus. Deborah, Rebeckah and Anna Conwell, and Comfort Hazzard (wife of Cord). Exec'rs, sons Abraham and William Conwell. Wits., John Clowes, Thomas Grove, John Conwell, Jr. Prob. March 1, 1782. Arch. vol. A66, pages 140-145. Reg. of Wills, Liber C, folios 295-297. [Note:— Arch. vol. A66, page 141 shows William Conwell, surviving exec'r, settled the estate May 8, 1811].

**May, Ann.** Minor dau. of Thomas May. Admin. of, to Draper May. Granted [c. March 1, 1782]. Arch. vol. A87, page 90.

**May, Jonathan.** Minor son of Thomas May. Admin. of, to Draper May. Granted [c. March 1, 1782]. Arch. vol. A87, page 95. [Note:—Arch. vol. A87, page 95 mentions dec'd mother, Mary May].

**Callaway, John, [Sr.].** Yeoman. Will. Made Dec. 17, 1775. Heirs: dau. Given Hall; grandson John King; Mary King and Betty Gunby (daus. of son Peter Callaway and Maron Trussom). [No exec'r]. Wits., John Beavins, Isaac Jones, Henry Figgs. Prob. March 11, 1782. Arch. vol. A62, pages 155-156. Reg. of Wills, Liber C, folio 297. [Note:—Arch. vol. A62, page 156 shows John King, adm'r C. T. A., settled the estate May 6, 1784].

**Ralph, Mitchell.** Yeoman. Admin. of, to Elizabeth Ralph. Admr's bond dated April 13, 1782. Arch. vol. A94, page 182.

**Holland, James.** Yeoman. Admin. of, to Hannah Holland. Granted [c. May 7, 1782]. Arch. vol. A77, page 87.

**Pettyjohn, Thomas, Sr.** Will. Made April 3, 1782. Heirs: wife Jane Pettyjohn; sons Aaron, Thomas and John Pettyjohn; daus. Comfort and Sarah Pettyjohn. Exec'r, son Aaron Pettyjohn and friend Solomon Dodd. Wits., Rob[er]t M. McColley, James Lawless, Prisgrave Steel. Prob. May 8, 1782. Arch. vol. A93, page 15. Reg. of Wills, Liber C, folios 299-300.

**Collins, Isaac.** Yeoman. Will. Made Feb. 5, 1782. Heirs: sons Levin and Isaac Collins; dau. Esther Collins; wife unnamed. Exec'rs, unnamed wife and Isaac Cooper. Wits., William

**Moore, Anthony Bounds,** Aaron Floyd. Prob. May 9, 1782. Arch. vol. A65, pages 174-176. Reg. of Wills, Liber C, folios 298-299. [Note:—Arch. vol. A65, page 175 shows the estate was settled after Oct. 2, 1783 by Isaac Cooper, Jonathan Cathel and wife Betty, late Betty Collins].

**Stephenson, Robert.** Blacksmith. Admin. of, to Nathaniel Young. Granted [c. May 9, 1782]. Arch. vol. A100, page 164

**Bailey, Nathaniel.** Yeoman. Lewes and Rehoboth Hd. Will. Made May 28, 1782. Heirs: wife Jennet; sons William, Jonathan and Nathaniel Bailey; daus. Peggy and Comfort Bailey and Sarah Coulter (wife of William). Exec'rx, wife Jennet Bailey. Wits., Jno. Russel, Jean Russel, Elizabeth Russel. [No prob.]. Arch. vol. A58, pages 85-86. Reg. of Wills, Liber C, folio 310. [Note:—Arch. vol. A58, page 86 shows that Jennet Bailey later married William Dodd].

**Brown, Tilghman.** Yeoman. Admin. of, to James Brown, Jr. Granted [c. June 18, 1782]. Arch. vol. A60, pages 228-229. [Note:—Arch. vol. A60, page 228 mentions Charles, Curtis and John Brown, and John Jessup; also shows that Abner Dill married Elinor Montgomery].

**Clarkson, Richard, Sr.** Admin. of, to James Brown, Jr., D. B. N., in right of Abraham Clarkson, gentleman, dec'd. Granted [c. June 18, 1782]. Arch. vol. A64, page 216. [Note:—Arch. vol. A64, page 216 mentions heirs: Sarah, Elizabeth and Lucretia Brown; Abraham Clarkson; Priscilla and Richard Clarkson Cannon].

**Stephenson, Samuel.** Admin. of, to William Stephenson. Granted July 1, 1782. Arch. vol. A100, page 165b.

**Conwell, John.** Will. Made April 24, 1782. Heirs: wife Susanna Conwell; son John Conwell; dau. Leddy Coulter (wife of Thomas); grandsons Abraham (son of William Conwell, dec'd), John (son of John Conwell) and Jacob (son of Joseph Conwell, dec'd); granddaus. Hannah, Rachel, Rebeckah and Alice (daus. of Joseph Conwell). Exec'rs, wife Susanna and grandson Abraham Conwell. Wits., William Hazzard, Miers Clark, William Conwell. Prob. July 22, 1782. Arch. vol. A66, page 116. Reg. of Wills, Liber C, folios 304-306. [Note:—Arch. vol. A66, page 116 mentions bro. Elias].

**Collins, Hancock.** Admin. of, to Naomi Collins, widow. Granted (ante Aug. 6, 1782]. Arch. vol. A65, pages 166-167. [Note:—Arch. vol. A65, page 166 mentions Sally and Polly Collins; page 167 shows that Naomi Collins later married William Harrington].

144

**Chance, Mary.** Widow. Admin. of, to John Chance. Granted [ante Aug. 7, 1782]. Arch. vol. A64, page 126.

**Adams, Nannie.** Will. Made Feb. 10, 1780. Heirs: son Jacob Adams; dau. Sarah Adams. Exec'rx, dau. Sarah Adams. Wits., William Anderson, Abraham Adams. Prob. Aug. 7, 1782. Arch. vol. A57, page 76. Reg. of Wills, Liber C, folios 288-289.

**Williams, Samuel.** Yeoman. Admin. of, to William Walker and wife, late Susannah Williams. Granted [c. Aug. 9, 1782]. Arch. vol. A108, page 39.

**Croney, John.** Planter. Worcester County, Md. Will. Made Jan. 30, 1763. Heir: friend Bennona Barnard. Exec'r, friend Bennona Barnard. Wits., Joseph Collins, Charles Moore, Jonathan Bell. Prob. Aug. 11, 1782. Arch. vol. A67, page 201. Reg. of Wills, Liber C, folios 307-308. [Note:—Arch. vol. A67, page 201 mentions dec'd father James Croney].

**Conwell, Elias.** Will. Made Dec. 22, 1781. Heirs: sons George, Fisher, Elias and David Conwell; dau. Sarah King; William King (husband of Sarah); grandsons Shepard, Claudius and John (sons of son Jeremiah Conwell, dec'd); John (son of son George Conwell). Exec'rs, sons George, Fisher and Elias Conwell. Wits., William Conwell, Nathaniel Bradford, John Fleetwood. Prob. Aug. 14, 1782. Arch. vol. A663, page 97. Reg. of Wills, Liber C, folios 308-310.

**Irons, Aaron.** Worcester County, Md. Will (copy). Made Oct. 4, 1774. Heirs: sons Jacob, Lemuel, Aaron and David Irons; daus. Naomi and Jane Irons. Exec'rs, son Jacob Irons and Thomas Godwin. Wits., Jabez Fretwell, William Kollock, Leah Kollock. Prob. Sept. 11, 1782. Arch. vol. A79, pages 189-191. Reg. of Wills, Liber C, folios 312-313. [Note:—Arch. vol. A79, page 191 mentions John Massey and wife Naomi; also shows the estate was settled Sept. 5, 1786 by Rachel Irons, D. B. N., adm'rx of Jacob Irons, dec'd].

**Massey, Joseph, Sr.** Will. Made March 8, 1779. Heirs: sons Job, Isaac, Samuel and Moses Massey; dau. Ann Massey. Exec'rs, sons Isaac and Job Massey. Wits., Robert W. McCalley, Anthaliner McCalley, Eli McCalley. Prob. Oct. 29, 1782. Arch. vol. A87, pages 60-61. Reg. of Wills, Liber C, folios 314-315.

**Vankirk [Vinkirk], Barnard.** Will. Made Nov. 3, 1782. Heirs: wife Mary Vinkirk; sons John, Barnard and William Vinkirk; daus. Polly Vinkirk, Rachel Heaverlo; granddau. Mary

Vinkirk. Exec'rx, wife Mary Vinkirk. Wits., Eli Parker, William Lofland, Charles Williams. Prob. Nov. 14, 1782. Arch. vol. A103, pages 49-50. Reg. of Wills, Liber C, folios 315-317.

**Schoolfield, Benjamin.** Will. Made Oct. 27, 1782. Heirs: wife Ann Schoolfield; son William Schoolfield; child unnamed. Exec'r, William Lockwood. Wits., William Evans, Jno. Nicholson, William Howell. Prob. Dec. 10, 1782. Arch. vol. A98, page 31. Reg. of Wills, Liber C, folios 318-319.

**Polk, Roger Tasker.** Yeoman. Admin. of, to William Polk, Thomas Pollitt and wife Nancy, late Nancy Polk. Granted [c. Dec. 12, 1782]. Arch. vol. A93, page 150. [Note:—Arch. vol. A93, page 150 mentions Edward Roberts, minor son of Francis Roberts].

**Pollock [Polk], Priscilla.** Gentlewoman. Dorchester County, Md. Admin. of, to William and Nancy Polk, D. B. N. of Roger T. Polk. Granted [c. Dec. 12, 1782]. Arch. vol. A93, page 178. [Note:—Arch. vol. A93, page 178 mentions William Polk, minor son of David Polk; Esther Polk, minor dau. of David Polk; Roger Tasker Polk, dec'd].

**Roberts, Francis.** Yeoman. Admin. of, to William Polk and Nancy Polk. Granted [c. Dec. 12, 1782]. Arch. vol. A96, page 83. [Note:—Arch. vol. A96, page 83 shows that Nancy Polk later married Thomas Pollitt].

**Stockley, Cornelius.** Blacksmith. Admin. of, to Joseph Aydelott and wife Frances, late Frances Stockley. Granted [c. Dec. 12, 1782]. Arch. vol. A100, pages 195-196. [Note:—Arch. vol. A100, page 195 mentions daus. Frances Stockley, Mary Black and sons Woodman and Cornelius Stockley].

**Morris, Daniel.** Planter. Dorchester County, Md. Will. Made Nov. 30, 1772. Heirs: sons Hezekiah, Daniel, Nathaniel, John and Masten Morris; daus. Comfort, Hannah, Susannah, Sarah and Lydia Morris, Mary Clifton; grandson Curtis Morris (son of Daniel). Exec'rs, sons Nathaniel and John Morris. Wits., Jonathan Bready, Robert Owens, William Owens, Phebe Bready. Prob. Dec. 18, 1782. Arch. vol. A90, page 32. Reg. of Wills, Liber C, folios 321-323.

**Downom [Downham], John.** Yeoman. Admin. of, to Eleanor Downom. Granted [c. Dec. 26, 1782]. Arch. vol. A69, page 173.

**Jacobs, Hannah.** Admin. of, to Sarah Jacobs, widow, D. B. N., of Albertis Jacobs. Granted [c. Dec. 26, 1782]. Arch. vol. A80, page 55.

**Debety [Deputy], Solomon.** Admin. of, to Mary Debety and Silvester Debety. Granted [c. Dec. 30, 1782]. Arch. vol. A68, page 214.

**Collins, John** (of Thomas). Yeoman. Admin. of, to Elizabeth Collins. Granted [c. Dec. 30, 1782]. Arch. vol. A65, page 184.

**Culver, George.** Will. Made Feb. 28, 1782. Heirs: sons John, Jesse, Nathan, Isaac, Salathiel, William and George Culver; daus. Esther and Milley. Exec'r, son George Culver. Wits., Isaac Horsey, William Waller, Robert Low. Prob. Dec. 30, 1782. Arch. vol. A67, pages 215-216. Reg. of Wills, Liber C, folios 319-321.

**Hudson, Joshua.** Admin. of, to Silvester Debety [Deputy] and wife Esther, late Esther Hudson. Granted [c. Dec. 30, 1782]. Arch. vol. A79, page 29.

**Pullet, William.** Admin. of, to Nathaniel Young. Granted [c. Dec. 30, 1782]. Arch. vol. A94, page 161.

**Paynter, Lemuel Collison.** Yeoman. Admin. of, to Margaret Stephenson. Granted [c. Dec. 31, 1782]. Arch. vol. A92, page 128.

**Bevins, James.** Admin. of, to Mary Coverdale, late Mary Bevins, wife of Thomas Coverdale. Granted [c. 1783]. Arch. vol. A59, page 158. [Note:—Arch. vol. A59, page 158 mentions heirs: son Thomas and dau. Polly Bevins].

**Chambers, James.** Admin. of, to John Chambers. Granted [c. 1783]. Arch. vol. A64, page 122.

**Callaway, James.** Yeoman. Admin. of, to Ebenezer Callaway. Granted [c. 1783]. Arch. vol. A62, pages 152-153. [Note:— Arch. vol. A62, page 152 mentions widow, Rachel, and John Callaway].

**Adkins, Daniel.** Yeoman. Admin. of, to Ada Boyd. Granted [post Jan. 1, 1783]. Arch. vol. A57, page 199.

**Gibbins, George.** Worcester County, Md. Admin. of, to Joshua Gibbins. Granted [c. Jan. 1, 1783]. Arch. vol. A72, page 114. [Note:—Arch. vol. A72, page 114 mentions Sarah Gibbins].

**Moore, James.** Mariner. Admin. of, to William Smith and wife Nancy, late Nancy Moore. Granted [c. Jan. 3, 1783]. Arch. vol. A89, page 119.

**Moor[e], Joshua, Sr.** Will. Made Dec. 29, 1782. Heirs: wife Temperance Moor; sons Isaac, Joshua, William, Elisha and Robert Moor; dau. Patient Slantford; granddau. Emealea Slantford. [No exec'r]. Wits., Charles Moraim, John Cordry, Shiles Moor. Prob. Jan. 6, 1783. Arch. vol. A89, page 125. Reg. of Wills, Liber C, folios 289-291.

**Smith, John.** Broadkiln. Admin. of, to Mary Smith. Granted [c. Feb. . . ., 1783]. Arch. vol. A99, page 168.

**Cade, John.** Admin. of, to Mary Cade. Granted Feb. 7, 1783. Arch. vol. A62, page 93.

**Carpenter, Benjamin.** Cordwainer. Admin. of, to Richard Howard and wife Comfort, late Comfort Carpenter. Granted [c. Feb. 7, 1783]. Arch. vol. A63, page 220.

**Aydelott, Jesper.** Will. Made Jan. 23, 1783. Heirs: wife Mary Aydelott; bro. Cornelius Aydelott; sister Ellen Aydelott; and friend Mitchell Dirickson. Exec'r, Joseph Roberts. Wits., Ginnethan Harney, Joseph Roberts, William Bettsworth. Prob. Feb. 7, 1783. Arch. vol. A57, pages 242-243. Reg. of Wills, Liber D, folio 7.

**Skidmore, Thomas.** Will. Made Oct. 15, 1777. Heirs: sons Henry and Thomas Skidmore; daus. Elizabeth, Sarah and Lydia Skidmore. Exec'r, son Henry Skidmore. Wits., James Coulter, William Hand, George Conwell. Prob. Feb. 19, 1783. Arch. vol. A99, page 100. Reg. of Wills, Liber D, folios 8-9.

**Cordry, John.** Planter. Will. Made Feb. 6, 1783. Heirs: wife Rachel Cordry; son John Cordry; grandson Josiah Cordry (son of Elisha); Betty Cordry (widow of Elisha); William Polk; John Rhodes; Elisabeth Vaughan; and John Williams, Jr. Exec'r, son John Cordry. Wits., William Polk, John Williams, Robert King, Jr., Levi King. Prob. March 17, 1783. Arch. vol. A66, pages 203-205. Reg. of Wills, Liber D, folio 9. [Note:—Arch. vol. A66, page 204 mentions Nancy and Sarah Cordry and shows the estate was settled Sept. 30, 1812].

**Lynn, Moses.** Formerly of Fairfields, Conn. Will. Made June 8, 1781. Heirs: son Richard Wri[ght]; dau. Magdelan Lynn; Sarah Wri[ght]; William Wri[ght] bro of Sarah. Exec'r, Caleb Balding. Wits., Sarah Balding, Maddox Turner, Thomas Cox. Prob. March 24, 1783. Arch. vol. A86, pages

3-4. Reg. of Wills, Liber D, folios 10-11. [Note:—Arch. vol. A86, page 4 shows the estate was settled March 7, 1792 by Sarah Balding, exec'rx of Caleb Balding, dec'd].

**Johnson, John.** Will. Made Feb. 26, 1782. Heirs: Sarah Johnson Morgan (dau. of Rebeckah); nephews James Johnson (son of bro. James, dec'd), William Johnson (son of bro. Samuel), and Samuel Johnson (son of bro. William). Exec'rx, Sarah Johnson Morgan. Wits., Elijah Morgan, Joshua Tatman, Charles Polk, Jr. Prob. March 25, 1783. Arch. vol. A81, page 55. Reg. of Wills, Liber D, folio 11.

**Handy, Elizabeth.** Caroline County, Md. Will. Made May 3, 1774. Heirs: sons Samuel and John Handy; daus. Sarah, Mary, Grace and Nancy Handy and Jane Jones. Exec'r, son-in-law, Eben Jones. Wits., John Flower, Jesse Cannon, Curtis Smith. Prob. March 31, 1783. Arch. vol. A74, page 42. Reg. of Wills, Liber D, folios 11-12.

**Kenney, Isaac.** Planter. Will. Made Jan. 10, 1783. Heirs: sons Elijah, Josiah, Isaac and William Kenney; daus. Tabitha Kenney, Betty Greer, Lovey Benston. Exec'rs, son Elijah Kenney, Samuel Kellam. Wits., Samuel Kellam, Anthony Collins, Elizabeth Grear. Prob. April 16, 1783. Arch. vol. A82, pages 58-59. Reg. of Wills, Liber D, folios 12-13. [Note:—Arch. vol. A82, page 59 shows the estate was settled by Elijah Kenney, surviving exec'r on September 6, 1796].

**Baker, William.** Yeoman. Admin. of, to James Murray and wife Mary, late Mary Baker. Granted [c. May 6, 1783]. Arch. vol. A58, page 142. [Note:—Arch. vol. A58, page 142 mentions a dau. Mary Baker].

**Jewett, William.** Yeoman. Admin. of, to Mary Jewett. Granted May 6, 1783. Arch. vol. A81, pages 6-7. [Note:—Arch. vol. A81, pages 6-7 shows that Mary Jewett later married Jesse Griffith; also mentions William Polk, minor son of David Polk].

**Lacey, William Baggs.** Admin. of, to Stephen Mitchell and wife Elizabeth (Betty), late Elizabeth Lacey. Granted [c. May 6, 1783]. Arch. vol. A83, page 29.

**Rose, Truman.** Yeoman. Will. Made April 2, 1783. Heirs: wife Dorothy Rose; children unnamed. Exec'rs, wife Dorothy Rose, Luke Huffington. Wits., Tho[ma]s Cockayne, Agnes Dixon. Prob. May 6, 1783. Arch. vol. A97, page 59. Reg.

of Wills, Liber D, folios 13-14. [Note:—Arch. vol. A97, page 59 shows the estate was settled Aug. 5, 1784 by Dolly Rose].

**Hinds, John Tilton.** Sadler. Admin. of, to John Hinds. Granted [c. May 7, 1783]. Arch. vol. A76, page 172.

**Polk, Sarah.** Admin. of, to John Polk. Granted [c. May 7, 1783]. Arch. vol. A93, page 151.

**Windsor, James.** Yeoman. Admin. of, to Lydia Windsor. Granted [c. May 7, 1783]. Arch. vol. A108, page 166.

**McNeill, William.** Yeoman. Admin. of, to Sarah McNeill. Granted [c. May 8, 1783]. Arch. vol. A88, page 15.

**Potter, John.** Planter. Will. Made June 12, 1783. Heirs: wife Comfort Potter; son John Potter. Exec'rx, wife Comfort Potter. Wits., Thomas Robinson, Benjamin Robinson, Mary Robinson. [No prob.]. Arch. vol. A94, page 17.

**Collins, George.** Will. Made April 30, 1781. Heirs: bro. John; nephew George Scrogin; mother unnamed. [No exec'r]. Wits., William Hardy, Samuel Wootten, Polly Collins. Prob. July 19, 1783. Arch. vol. A65, page 163. Reg. of Wills, Liber D, folio 14.

**Black, Ann.** Will. Made June 18, 1783. Heirs: sons Adam, David, John, Benjamin and George Black; daus. Sarah Black, Elizabeth Campbell and Jean Walton (wife of George Walton); granddaus. Ann Walton, Jean and Ann Black (daus. of Mitchell Black), Betty May, Elizabeth and Magdalen Black and Mary Perry (children of son James Black, dec'd); grandsons William and Joseph Black; son-in-law William Hazzard (hus. of dau. Ann). Exec'rs, John and Benjamin Black. Wits., Thomas Evans, Isaac Beauchamp, Joseph Fleming. Prob. Aug. 5, 1783. Arch. vol. A59, page 183. Reg. of Wills, Liber D, folios 14-16.

**Whealer [Wheeler], William.** Will. Made June 1, 1783. Heirs: wife Miriam Whealer; sons John and William Whealer; daus. Sarah, Miriam, Rachel, Lydia, Selea and Betty Whealer; Mary Richardson, Susannah Whealer; grandson Noah Whealer; Sarah Welch. Exec'r, son John Whealer. Wits., Sylvester Webb, Levi Townsend, John Richards. Prob. Aug. 5, 1783. Arch. vol. A107, pages 44-45. Reg. of Wills, Liber D, folios 16-17.

**Cannon, Henry.** Will. Made July 1, 1782. Heirs: wife Frances; sons Charles, Newton, Willis, Wateman and Clement; daus. Ellenor Adams, Nancy Flower, Frances Coulburn and

150

[Euphamia] Charles. Exec'r, son-in-law Edward Adams. Wits., John Tennent; John Cannon, Sr., John Cannon, Jr. Prob. Aug. 6, 1783. Arch. vol. A63, page 27. Reg. of Wills, Liber C, folio 307.

**Hill, Penelope.** Widow. Will. Made April 23, 1779. Heir: dau. Sarah Fagan. Exec'rx, dau. Sarah Fagan. Wits., Nathaniel Young, Esther Young, Rachel Cary. Prob. Aug. 7, 1783. Arch. vol. A76, pages 146-147. Reg. of Wills, Liber D, folios 17-18. [Note:—Arch. vol. A76, page 147 mentions dec'd husband Robert Hill].

**Stevens, William.** Yeoman. Indian River Hd. Admin. of, to Esther Stevens, widow. Granted [c. Aug. 8, 1783]. Arch. vol. A100, page 172.

**Cannon, William.** Planter. Will. Made Aug. 17, 1780. Heirs: wife Mary Cannon; sons William Nutter, Daniel and Hughett Cannon; daus. Pris[cilla], Esther and Levinia Cannon, Sarah Nichols and Mary Jacobs; Jesse Clarkson (son of dau. Major Clarkson). Exec'r, son William Nutter Cannon. Wits., Levin Cannon, William Jacobs, John Marine. Prob. Aug. 15, 1783. Arch. vol. A63, pages 142-143. Reg. of Wills, Liber D, folios 18-19. [Note:—Arch. vol. A63, page 143 mentions Sarah Jacobs].

**Warrington, William.** Will. Made June 19, 1782. Heirs: wife Sarah Warrington; sons Luke, Levi and William Warrington; grandson Benjamin Warrington. Exec'r, son Levi Warrington. Wits., Robert Prettyman, William Prettyman, Micajah Houston. Prob. Aug. 30, 1783. Arch. vol. A105, page 175. Reg. of Wills, Liber C, folios 310-312.

**Clayton, Elizabeth.** Late of Trenton, N. J. Will. Made July 15, 1783. Heirs: nieces Abigail Bell and Elizabeth Harmeson; nephews George, Nathaniel and William Clayton Mitchell; William Clayton (son of Parnel Clayton, dec'd). Exec'rs, nephew George Mitchell and Levin Derrickson. Wits., Jonathan Nottingham, William Cottinghan, John Evans. Prob. Sept. 18, 1783. Arch. vol. A64, page 232. Reg. of Wills, Liber D, folios 19-20.

**White, Anne.** Widow. Lewes & Rehoboth Hd. Will. Made Sept. 12, 1783. Heirs: sons John, William, Jacob and Job White; dau. Hester White. Exec'r, son William White. Wits., Betty Hall, Mary White, William Hall. Prob. Oct. 1, 1783. Arch. vol. A107, page 46. Reg. of Wills, Liber D, folios 20-21.

**Gibson, Robert.** Admin. of, to Sarah Gibson. Granted [c. Oct. 2, 1783]. Arch. vol. A72, page 136.

**Bloxom [Bloxsom, Blocksom], William.** Farmer. Will. Made Sept. 17, 1783. Heirs: wife Eunice; sons William, John, Richard, Moses, Aaron and Thomas Bloxom; daus. Eunice, Sally and Polly Bloxom. Exec'rx, wife Eunice Bloxom. Wits., Eli Parker, John Lane. Prob. Oct. 14, 1783. Arch. vol. A60, pages 2-3. Reg. of Wills, Liber D, folios 21-22.

**Reavell [Revel], Stephen.** Will. Made June 29, 1783. Heirs: sons William and David Reavell; dau. Sarah Reavell. Exec'r, friend John Sheldon Dorman. Wits., Benjamin White, Samuel Glover, Windsor Rawlins. Prob. Oct. 18, 1783. Arch. vol. A95, page 45. Reg. of Wills, Liber D, folio 22.

**Morris, Jeremiah.** Planter. Will. Made Sept. 9, 1783. Heirs: wife Grace Morris; son Obediah Morris; dau. Elinor Morris; grandson Jeremiah Morris; granddaus. Nelly and Nancy Sirman. Exec'r, son Obediah Morris. Wits., John Williams, Benjamin Parker, Joseph Elliot. Prob. Oct. 24, 1783. Arch. vol. A90, pages 70-71. Reg. of Wills, Liber D, folios 22-24.

**Hitchens, Ezekiel.** Will. Made Oct. 22, 1783. Heirs: wife Sarah Hitchens; daus. Comfort and Alet[ica] Hitchens. Exec'rs, wife Sarah Hitchens and friend Hap Hazzard. Wits., Mary Wyatt, Sarah Hamilton. Prob. Nov. 3, 1783. Arch. vol. A77, pages 21-22. Reg. of Wills, Liber D, folios 23-24.

**Burton, Benjamin.** Will. Made Dec. 15, 1781. Heirs: wife Hester Burton; sons Woolsey, Benjamin, John, William, Daniel and Joseph Burton; daus. Hester and Comfort Burton; children unnamed; grandchildren Benjamin and William Robinson. Exec'rs, wife Hester and sons Woolsey and Benjamin Burton. Wits., John Roberts, Benjamin Benston, Joshua Burton. Prob. Nov. 10, 1783. Arch. vol. A61, pages 76-79. Reg. of Wills, Liber D, folios 24-26. [Note:—Arch. vol. A61, page 76 mentions bro. John; page 77 mentions Albertus Jacobs and Eliza, his wife, Abigail Peters, Lydia Burton (wife of Robert), Leah Burton (wife of William), Hester Hopkins (wife of David); page 78 shows the estate was settled April 3, 1798 by Woolsey Burton, surviving exec'r; also mentions Robert Burton, merchant; page 79 mentions William Burton of Benjamin].

**Hatfield, Cottingham.** Admin. of, to Wheatly Hatfield. Admr's bond dated Nov. 17, 1783. Arch. vol. A74, page 231.

**Lacey, Robert.** Yeoman. Admin. of, to Mary Lacey. Granted [c. Nov. 25, 1783]. Arch. vol. A83, page 22. [Note:—Arch. vol. A83, page 22 shows that Mary Lacey later married Claypoole Davidson].

**Parker, Alice.** Will. Made Nov. 14, 1783. Heirs: sons John and Peter Parker; daus. Naomi and Patience Parker; grandsons David and Peter Hazzard. Exec'rs, son John Parker and son-in-law Samuel Rowland. Wits., John Morgan, Anderson Parker, Sarah Hall. Prob. Nov. 25, 1783. Arch. vol. A92, pages 50-51. Reg. of Wills, Liber D, folios 28-29. [Note:— Arch. vol. A92, page 50 mentions daus. Alice Rowland (wife of Samuel) and Elizabeth Hazzard (wife of Jacob); Arch. vol. A92, page 51 shows the estate was settled June 12, 1790 by son John Parker].

**Hinds, Benjamin** (minor son of Thomas). Admin. of, to William Hinds. Granted [c. Nov. 27, 1783]. Arch. vol. A76, page 169. [Note:—Arch. vol. A76, page 169 mentions heirs William, Sarah, Mary and Charles Hinds].

**Hinds, Charles** (minor son of Thomas). Admin. of, to William Hinds. Granted [c. Nov. 27, 1783]. Arch. vol. A76, page 170. [Note:—Arch. vol. A76, page 170 mentions heirs, William, Sarah, Mary Hinds and William Lofland (son of Branson Lofland)].

**Hinds, Sarah** (minor dau. of Thomas). Admin. of, to Nehemiah *N.Q.* Davis [tailor]. Granted [c. Nov. 27, 1783]. Arch. vol. A76, page 174.

**Callaway, Benjamin.** Will. Made Oct. 25, 1783. Heirs: wife Ann Callaway; sons Nehemiah and Ebenezer Callaway; daus. Sealeah [Celia] and Ann Callaway, Mary Moore and Filis [Phillis] Lecat. Exec'r, son Ebenezer Callaway. Wits., Joshua Eliis, Stephen Ellis, Ebenezer Callaway. Prob. Dec. 2, 1783. Arch. vol. A62, pages 125-126. Reg. of Wills, Liber D, folios 30-31.

**Moore, William.** Will. Made Nov. 15, 1783. Heirs: dau. Elizabeth Shepard; grandsons Edward, William, John and Samuel Shepard. Exec'rs, dau. Elizabeth Shepard and friend John Pollock (of Joseph). Wits., Jehu Clifton, Mary Clifton, Aaror Williams. Prob. Dec. 2, 1783. Arch. vol. A89, pages 153-154. Reg. of Wills, Liber D, folios 32-33. [Note: —Arch. vol. A89, page 154 shows the estate was settled by Joseph Holston and Betty, his wife, late Elizabeth Shepard].

**Rider, George.** Farmer. Will. Made Nov. 18, 1780. Heirs: wife Elizabeth Rider; sons John and Wilson Rider; other child unnamed. Exec'rs, sons John and Wilson Rider. Wits., David Green, William Johnson, Thomas Burbage. Prob. Dec. 2, 1783. Arch. voi. A96, pages 4-5. Reg. of Wills, Liber D, folios 29-30. [Note:—Arch. vol. A96, page 5 mentions a son Charles Rider].

**Robinson, William.** Will. Made Sept. 10, 1783. Heirs: wife Mary Robinson; son Thomas Robinson; dau. Elizabeth Robinson. Exec'rs, wife Mary Robinson, W[illia]m Rickards. Wits., W[illia]m Rickards, Thomas Wildgoos, Elizabeth Robinson. Prob. Dec. 15, 1783. Arch. vol. A96, page 192. Reg. of Wills, Liber D, folios 31-32. [Note:—Arch. vol. A96, page 192 shows that Mary Robinson later married William Evans].

**Parremore, Mathew.** Will. Made Nov. 29, 1783. Heirs: sons Thomas, Ezekiel and Patrick Parremore. Exec'r, son Thomas Parremore. Wits., Arthur Hosea, John Goddard, Elizabeth Parremore. Prob. Dec. 16, 1783. Arch. vol. A92, page 90. Reg. of Wills, Liber C, folios 33-34.

**Lee, Wilson, Sr.** Will. Made Nov. 22, 1783. Heirs: wife Rachel Lee; sons Wilson, Richard, Robert and Thomas Lee; daus. Nancy and Nicey Lee and Rachel Brumley; grandson Wilson Brumley. Exec'r, son Wilson Lee. Wits., Richard Blocksom, William Monk, George Conwell. Prob. Dec. 18, 1783. Arch. vol. A84, page 53. Reg. of Wills, Liber D, folios 34-35.

**Cannon, Newton.** Shipwright. Admin. of, to George Cannon. Granted [c. 1784]. Arch. vol. A63, pages 118-119.

**Guttery, John.** Admin. of, to Solomon Davis, tailor. Granted [c. 1784]. Arch. vol. A73, page 173.

**Bell, Stephen.** Admin. of, to Ann Bell. Granted [c. 1784]. Arch. vol. A59, page 62.

**Bruce, Magdaline.** Widow. Admin. of, to John Field and wife Mary, late Mary Hazzard. Granted [c. 1784]. Arch. vol. A60, page 241. [Note:—Arch. vol. A60, page 241 shows William Hazzard as father of Mary].

**Sirman, John.** Yeoman. Admin. of, to David Green and wife Anne, late Anne Sirman. Granted [c. 1784]. Arch. vol. A99, page 81. [Note:—Arch. vol. A99, page 81 mentions daus. Elizabeth and Sarah Sirman].

**Smith, Mary.** Widow. Will. Made Sept. 15, 1781. Heirs: sons Peremore, John and Bartholomew Smith; daus. Mary and Charity Smith. Exec'rx, dau. Mary Smith. Wits., Abraham Harris, James Wilkens, Rob[er]t Wattson MacCalley. Prob. Jan. 13, 1784. Arch. vol. A99, page 186. Reg. of Wills, Liber D, folios 35-36.

**Stockley, Jacob.** Admin. of, to Newcomb White and wife Patience, late Patience Stockley. Admr's bond dated Jan. 18, 1784. Arch. vol. A101, page 9.

**Burton, Robert.** Admin. of, to Anne and Joshua Burton. Granted [c. Jan. 25, 1784]. Arch. vol. A61, pages 246-247. [Note: —Arch. vol. A61, page 247 shows Joshua Burton was the surviving exec'r in 1796].

**McCay, Alexander.** Will. Made Aug. 6, 1783. Heirs: sons Spencer and Alexander McCay; daus. Cath[a]rine, Naomi, Phebe McCay, Sarah and Ann Semmons. Exec'rs, dau. Catharine McCay and bro.-in-law Luke Spencer. Wits., George Walton, Jr., William McCay, Joshua Spencer. Prob. Jan. 26, 1784. Arch. vol. A87, pages 128-130. Reg. of Wills, Liber D, folios 36-37. [Note:— Arch. vol. A87, page 130 shows the estate was settled June 8, 1787 by Luke Spencer, surviving exec'r].

**Heaveloe, John.** Admin. of, to Hannah Heaveloe. Granted [c. Feb. 5, 1784]. Arch. vol. A75, page 224.

**Russom, James.** Gentleman. Admin. of, to William Polk and wife Christiana, late Christiana Russom. Granted [c. Feb. 7, 1784]. Arch. vol. A97, page 156.

**Hathaway, Agnes.** Will. Made Oct. 10, 1783. Heirs: sons Woolsey, Burton and James Hathaway; dau. Patience Burton; grandson John Hathaway (son of Woolsey); granddau. Anne Warrington. Exec'r, son Woolsey Hathaway. Wits., Joseph Houston, Agnes Waples, Comfort Waples, the elder. Prob. Feb. 9, 1784. Arch. vol. A74, page 240. Reg. of Wills, Liber D, folios 37-38.

**Shockley, Levin.** Admin. of, to Mary Shockley. Admr's bond dated Feb. 14, 1784. Arch. vol. A98, page 141.

**Truitt, John.** Admin. of, to Margaret Truitt. Admr's bond dated Feb. 14, 1784. Arch. vol. A102, pages 134-135.

**McIlvain, James.** Will (copy, nunc.). Made Jan. 12, 1784. Heirs: William McIlvain (son of David); William Water (son of Nelson); James Brereton (son of John). Exec'r, Robert

Prettyman. Wits., Robert Prettyman, Sarah Prettyman. Prob. Feb. 18, 1784. Arch. vol. A87, page 192. Reg. of Wills, Liber D, folio 38.

**Joseph, Jeremiah.** Yeoman. Admin. of, to Nathan Joseph. Granted [c. March 8, 1784]. Arch. vol. A82, page 10.

**Westley, Richard.** Pilot. Lewes. Admin. of, to Ann Westley. Granted [c. March 9, 1784]. Arch. vol. A107, page 3. [Note: Arch. vol. A107, page 3 mentions minor children, Mary, George and Richard Westley].

**Polk, William** (Minor of David). Admin. of, to John Nelms. Admr's bond dated March 18, 1784. Arch. vol. A93, page 155.

**Taylor, Travour.** Will. Made Dec. 13, 1783. Heirs: wife unnamed; sons Thomas, Tandy and Andrew Taylor; son-in-law Robert Wildgoos. Exec'rx, unnamed wife. Wits., Partheny Tingle, Elizabeth Tingle, John Evans. Prob. March 19, 1784. Arch. vol. A101, page 131. Reg. of Wills, Liber D, folios 38-39.

**West, Robert.** Will. Made March 2, 1784. Heirs: wife Sarah West; sons Nathaniel and Isaac West; daus. Hannah, Mary, Tabitha and Elon West. Exec'rs, sons Nathaniel and Isaac West. Wits., Littleton Townsend, William West, Caleb West. Prob. March 23, 1784. Arch. vol. A106, page 174. Reg. of Wills, Liber D, folios 40-41.

**Harney, Ginnethon.** Will. Made Feb. 7, 1784. Heirs: wife Isabel Harney; sons William, Eli, Selby, George Washington and Adam Harney; daus. Naney and Oliv[e] Harney. Exec'rx, wife Isabel Harney. Wits., Thomas Harney, Mills Harney, Thomas Harney, Jr. Prob. March 30, 1784. Arch. vol. A74, pages 108-110. Reg. of Wills, Liber D, folio 41.

**Draper, Henry.** Yeoman. Admin. of, to Samuel Draper. Granted [c. April 1, 1784]. Arch. vol. A69, page 191.

**Dolbee, Jonathan.** Farmer. Will. Made Nov. 22, 1783. Heirs: wife Constant Dolbee; sons Jonathan Dolbee and Upsherd Messick (alias Dolbee); daus. Polly Dolbee, Leah Dolbee, Nancy Robinson, Peggy Windsor; granddau. Sally Windsor (dau. of Peggy Windsor). Exec'rx, Constant Dolbee. Wits., Leven Connaway, Elijah Freeny. Prob. April 5, 1784. Arch. vol. A69, pages 127-128. Reg. of Wills, Liber D, folios 41-43. [Note:—Arch. vol. A69, page 128 shows that Constant Dolbee later married Hales Spicer].

**Bacon, Dodson.** Turner. Will. Made Oct. 3, 1783. Heirs: wife Elisabeth Bacon; sons Levin, John and George Bacon; daus. Mary, Sarah, Betty, Eunice and Nancy Bacon. Exec'r, son Levin. Wits., John Williams, Michael Linch, James Windsor. Prob. April 9, 1784. Arch. vol. A58, page 32. Reg. of Wills, Liber D, folios 45-46.

**Turpin, Elizabeth.** Will. Made Jan. 8, 1784. Heirs: bros. J[eremiah], James and Isaac Adams; sister Sarah Wright; cousins Nancy and Priscilla Turpin; friend Millie Oaks. Exec'r, friend Joshua Wright. Wits., John Turpin, Francis Turpin, William Adams. Prob. April 9, 1784. Arch. vol. A103, page 29. Reg. of Wills, Liber D, folios 43-44.

**Turpin, James.** Admin. of, to Joshua Wright. Admr's bond dated April 9, 1784. Arch. vol. A103, page 30.

**Turpin, Mary.** Will. Made Dec. 17, 1783. Heirs: sons John and Francis Turpin; daus. Nancy and Prissy Turpin; granddau. Polly Darby. Exec'r, son John Turpin. Wits., Jeremiah Cannon. Tho[ma]s Hubbert, Andrew Wingate. Prob. April 9, 1784. Arch. vol. A103, page 34. Reg. of Wills, Liber D, folios 44-45. [Note:—Arch. vol. A103, page 34 mentions Mary and Benjamin Darby].

**Shield, Luke.** Admin. of, to Mary Shield, Luke Shield, Margaret Fisher. Granted April 19, 1784. Arch. vol. A98, page 113.

**Starr, Nathaniel.** Will. Made March 22, 1784. Heirs: wife Tabitha Starr; sons David, James and Richard Starr; daus. Ann and Margaret Starr, and Unice Coulter (wife of John). Exec'rx, wife Tabitha Starr. Wits., William Peery, Dorinda Knox, Clark Nottingham. Codicil:—March 26, 1784. Wits., Parker Robinson, Lavin Lank, Richard Bloxsom. Prob. April 21, 1784. Arch. vol. A100, page 123. Reg. of Wills, Liber D, folios 46-47. [Note:—Arch. vol. A100, page 123 shows that Tabitha Starr later married Solomon Parramore].

**Moore, Jacob.** Lewes. Will (nunc.). Made April . . ., 1784. Heir: wife Hester Moore. Exec'rx, wife Hester Moore. Wits., Richard Bassett, Edward Tilghman, Esq. Prob. April 26, 1784. Arch. vol. A89, page 118. Reg. of Wills, Liber D, folios 48-50.

**Coleburn, William.** Yeoman. Admin. of, to Catharine Coleburn. Granted ante April 30, 1784. Arch. vol. A65, page 114.

**157**

**Couch, Joseph.** Admin. of, to Percy Couch. Granted [c. May 1784]. Arch. vol. A67, pages 32-33. [Note:—Arch. vol. A67, page 33 mentions Levi Spencer, an heir of his sister Betsy's estate].

**Hall, Moses.** Admin. of, to Lott Clark and wife Esther. Granted [c. May 4, 1784]. Arch. vol. A73, page 232.

**Robinson, Joshua.** Will. Made March 30, 1783. Heirs: wife Elizabeth Robinson; sons Michael and Joshua Robinson; daus. Mary and Elizabeth Robinson; William Rickards; Hannah Evans. Exec'rx, wife Elizabeth Robinson. Wits., William Rickards, Jones Rickards, Mary Rickards. Prob. May 4, 1784. Arch. vol. A96, pages 150-151. Reg. of Wills, Liber D, folios 108-109. [Note:—Arch. vol. A96, page 151 shows the estate was settled June 8, 1785 by David Tubbs and wife Elizabeth, late Elizabeth Robinson; also mentions Michael Robinson, dec'd, wife's bro.].

**Robinson, Michael.** Yeoman. Admin. of, to Mary Robinson. Granted [c. May 5, 1784]. Arch. vol. A96, page 161.

**Hodgson, Jacob.** Admin. of, to Isaac Killo, Jr., and wife Sarah, late Sarah Hodgson. Granted [c. May 5, 1784]. Arch. vol. A77, page 45.

**Richards, James.** Gentleman. Admin. of, to William Richards. Granted [c. May 5, 1784]. Arch. vol. A95, pages 82-83.

**Spencer, John, Dr.** Admin. of, to John Clowes. Granted [c. May 5, 1784]. Arch. vol. A100, page 59.

**Stephenson, Samuel.** Admin. of, to James Stephenson. Granted [c. May 5, 1784]. Arch. vol. A100, page 165a.

**Vaughan, William.** Will. Made Jan. 22, 1776. Heirs: bros. Levin and Isaac Vaughan; mother Betty Vaughan. Exec'rs, mother Betty Vaughan and bro. Levin Vaughan. Wits., Matthew Creighton, John Boadley. Prob. May 5, 1784. Arch. vol. A103, page 84. Reg. of Wills, Liber D, folios 51-52. [Note:—Arch. vol. A103, page 84 mentions grandfather William Vaughan].

**Wooten, Benjamin.** Yeoman. Admin. of, to James Trusham and wife Meron, late Meron Wootten. Granted [c. May 6, 1784]. Arch. vol. A109, page 51.

**Parker, Peter.** Yeoman. Admin. of, to John Parker, in right of Alice Parker, dec'd. Granted [c. May 7, 1784]. Arch. vol. A92, page 78.

**Polk, John.** Dorchester County, Md. Admin. of, to bro. William
Polk of Northwest Ford Hd., Sussex County. Granted [c.
May 7, 1784]. Arch. vol. A93, page 124. [Note:—Arch. vol.
A93, page 124 mentions heirs: William Polk, Esther Ann
Standfield, Betty Thorn, Daniel Polk, John Laws and wife
Anna; heirs of Christopher Nutter and wife Sarah, late
Sarah Polk].

**Rust, Jonathan.** Yeoman. Admin. of, to William Welch and
wife Rachel, late Rachel Rust. Granted [c. May 7, 1784].
Arch. vol. A97, page 165. [Note:—Arch. vol. A97, page
165 mentions two children, George and Lydia Rust.

**Prettyman, Phebe.** Admin. of, to William Prettyman. Granted
May 8, 1784. Arch. vol. A94, page 98.

**Collins, Andrew.** Yeoman. Will (nunc.). Made May 15, 1784.
Heirs: dau. Betsy Collins and Polly Jackson. [No exec'r].
Wits., James Brooks, Elijah Collins. Prob. May 17, 1784.
Arch. vol. A65, page 129. [No Reg. of Wills Liber].

**Barr, William.** Admin. of, to Archibald Fleming and wife Catharine, late Catharine Barr. Granted May 19, 1784. Arch.
vol. A58, page 215.

**Dagworthy, John, Esq.** Will. Made June 18, 1781. Heirs: wife
Martha Dagworthy; sisters Mary Dagworthy, Sarah De-
hart and Elizabeth Clayton; nephews James, Nathaniel,
George and William Clayton Mitchell; niece Abigail Bell;
Elizabeth Dagworthy Aydelott (minor); James Mitchell,
Sr. Exec'rs, wife Martha Dagworthy, George Mitchell, Lam-
bert Cadwallader and Levin Derickson. Wits., Stephen Hill,
Levin Hill, Adam Black. Codicil, July 27, 1782. Wits., Nan-
cy Scudder, Peggy Stevens, Downing Howell Hendren. Prob.
May 24, 1784. Arch. vol. A68, pages 1-3. Reg. of Wills,
Liber D, folios 52-54.

**Marriner, Richard.** Yeoman. Admin. of, to Thomas Warrington.
Granted [c. June 5, 1784]. Arch. vol. A86, page 71.

**Prettyman, Perry.** Blacksmith. Admin. of, to Jabez Fisher and
wife Prudence, late Prudence Prettyman, widow. Granted
[c. June 9, 1784]. Arch. vol. A94, page 93.

**Coston, Director.** Will (nunc. copy). Made July 3, 1784. Heirs:
son Elisha Coston and bro. Somerset Coston. Exec'r, Somerset Dickinson [Dickerson]. Wits., Elizabeth Scidmer,
[Euphamy] Coston. Prob. July 20, 1784. Arch. vol. A67,
pages 11-12. Reg. of Wills, Liber D, folio 55. [Note:—

Arch. vol. A67, page 11 mentions mother unnamed; page 12 shows that Sarah Dickerson settled the estate May 6, 1788 in right of Somerset Dickerson].

**Houston, Micajah.** Admin. of, to Magdalen Houston. Admr's bond dated July 22, 1784. Arch. vol. A78, pages 112-113. [Note:—Arch. vol. A78, page 113 shows the estate was finally settled by Robert Prettyman, adm'r of Magdalen Houston's estate].

**Vinyard, Rachel.** Widow. Admin. of, to Israel Brown. Granted [c. Aug. 3, 1784]. Arch. vol. A93, page 88.

**Draper, James.** Minor son of Nehemiah Draper. Admin. of, to Thomas Bowman. Granted Aug. 4, 1784. Arch. vol. A69, page 196.

**Draper, Nehemiah.** Minor son of Nehemiah Draper. Admin. of, to Thomas Bowman, D. B. N. Granted [c. Aug. 4, 1784]. Arch. vol. A69, page 215.

**Black, John.** [Tailor]. Admin. of, to Aaron Perry. Granted [c. Aug. 6, 1784]. Arch. vol. A59, page 191.

**Williams, Elijah.** Yeoman. Admin. of, to John Hudson. Granted [c. Aug. 7, 1784]. Arch. vol. A107, page 164. [Note:— Arch. vol. A107, page 164 mentions Mary Williams, widow of David].

**Turpin, John.** Will. Made Nov. 17, 1783. Heirs: sisters Sarah Wright, Elizabeth Turpin. Exec'r, friend Jeremiah Cannon. Wits., Julius Aug[us]t Jackson, John Twyford, William Adams. Prob. Aug. 9, 1784. Arch. vol. A103, pages 31-32. Reg. of Wills, Liber D, folio 43.

**Polk, Clement.** Will. Made March 17, 1784. Heirs: unnamed mother; unnamed aunts and uncles; grandfather Joseph Polk. Exec'rx, unnamed mother. Wits., Trusten L. Polk, William Polk, Jr., Joseph Vaughan, Nancy Russum. Prob. Aug. 21, 1784. Arch. vol. A93, page 110. Reg. of Wills, Liber D, folios 57-58. [Note:—Arch. vol. A93, page 110 shows the estate was settled Sept. 2, 1794 by Betty Thorn and Peter Caverly, exec'rs of Sydenham Thorn, dec'd, who was adm'r of Betty Polk, of the goods and chattels of Clement Polk].

**Price, Mary.** Widow. Admin. of, to William Price. Granted [c. Aug. 23, 1784]. Arch. vol. A94, page 139.

**Polk, Charles.** Planter. Will. Made July 21, 1781. Heirs: sons Charles and George Polk; daus. Priscilla, Ann and Mary Polk. Exec'rs, son Charles Polk and bro. Ephraim Polk. Wits., John Polk, James Polk, Ann Polk, Avery Polk. Prob. Sept. 8, 1784. Arch. vol. A93, page 106. Reg. of Wills, Liber D, folio 62.

**Waller, Richard.** Will. Made June 6, 1784. Heirs: wife Isabel Waller; sons Ebenezer, Thomas, George and Jonathan Waller; daus. Rachel Dow and Nancy Cooper; grandsons, Esme Marshall Waller, Benjamin and Richard Waller, William Waller (son of Richard); granddau. Mary Gum. Exec'rs, sons Ebenezer and Jonathan Waller. Wits., William Low, Thomas Goslee, W[illia]m Ralph. Prob. Sept. 13, 1784. Arch. vol. A104, pages 76-77. Reg. of Wills, Liber D, folios 62-63.

**Robinson, Parker.** Gentleman. Will. Made Sept. 5, 1784. Heirs: wife Alethia Robinson; son Jehu Robinson; grandsons Robinson and David Manlove; granddaus. Sarah Manlove and Lydia Hall (dau. of Joseph). Exec'rs, wife Alethia Robinson and cousin Peter Robinson. Wits., Nancy Hazzard, Nancy Brice, William Harrison. Prob. Sept. 25, 1784. Arch. vol. A96, pages 163-164. Reg. of Wills, Liber D, folios 63-65. [Note:—Arch. vol. A96, page 164 shows the estate was settled June 21, 1796 by John Abbott Warrington and wife Alethia, late Alethia Robinson].

**Flower, John.** Will. Made Nov. 18, 1783. Heirs: sons Thomas, Julius Augustus, Henry, John, Jeremiah and Bartholomew Flower; daus. Elizabeth, Frances, Ann, Esther and Euphamey Flower; Charles McKeel Flower. Exec'r, son Henry Flower. Wits., William Cannon, James Tull, Joseph Turpin. Prob. Sept. 30, 1784. Arch. vol. A71, pages 212-213. Reg. of Wills, Liber D, folios 27-28.

**Ready, John.** Yeoman. Admin. of, to John Goddard. Granted Sept. 30, 1784. Arch. vol. A95, pages 8-9.

**Stephenson, Eli.** Admin. of, to John Holland. Granted [c. Sept. 30, 1784]. Arch. vol. A100, page 154.

**Stephenson, Jonathan.** Admin. of, to John Holland. Granted [c. Sept. 30, 1784]. Arch. vol. A100, page 161.

**Polk, John.** Admin. of, to John Polk. Granted [c. Oct. 1, 1784]. Arch. vol. A93, page 125.

**Elliott, Margaret.** Will. Made July 5, 1784. Heirs: sons William and Jehu Bennett; daus. Jemimah, Mary, Sarah, Rhoda Warren; grandsons Parker, Asa and Robert Warren; grand-daus. Sarah and Margaret Warren. Exec'rs, sons-in-law Levi Warren and Absolom Warren. Wits., Alex[ande]r Argo, Sr., Thomas Crouch, Howard Wall. Prob. Oct. 26, 1784. Arch. vol. A70, pages 89-90. Reg. of Wills, Liber D, folio 65.

**Hart, John.** Yeoman. Lewes Hd. Will. Made Oct. 12, 1784. Heirs: wife Sarah Hart; sons Thomas and John Hart. Exec'rs, wife Sarah Hart and son Thomas Hart. Wits., Jennet Bailey, Sarah Edenfield, Jno. Russel. Prob. Oct. 26, 1784. Arch. vol. A74, pages 163-164. Reg. of Wills, Liber D, folios 65-66.

**Callaway, Levin.** Admin. of, to Mary Callaway. Granted ante Nov. 2, 1784. Arch. vol. A62, pages 166-167.

**Parker, John.** Admin. of, to Mary Parker. Granted [c. Nov. 2, 1784]. Arch. vol. A92, page 71.

**Riggins, James.** Admin. of, to Euphama Riggin. Granted [c. Nov. 2, 1784]. Arch. vol. A96, page 25.

**Bradley, William.** Planter. Will. Made April 18, 1792. Heirs: sons William, Isaac and Joseph Bradley; daus. Mary Ban-nister and Betty Freeney; son-in-law Charles Brown (son of Joseph); grandsons William Brown and William Bradley (son of Joseph); granddau. Polly-Bradley (dau. of Isaac). Exec'r, son Isaac Bradley. Wits., Edward Williams, Thomas Duncan, William Owens. Prob. Nov. 4, 1784. Arch. vol. A60, page 113. Reg. of Wills, Liber D, folios 66-67.

**Riggin, Joshua.** Admin. of, to Isabella Riggin, widow. Granted [c. Nov. 4, 1784]. Arch. vol. A96, page 26.

**Bell, Jonathan, Esq.** Admin. of, to Robert Houston. Granted ante Nov. 5, 1784. Arch. vol. A59, pages 56-58.

**Cole, Matthias.** Admin. of, to Leah Cole. Granted [c. Nov. 5, 1784]. Arch. vol. A65, page 116.

**Mariner, Nathaniel Bowman.** Yeoman. Admin. of, to son Robert Mariner. Granted [c. Nov. 5, 1784]. Arch. vol. A86, page 63.

**Dolbee, Peter.** Will. Made Dec. 23, 1780. Heirs: wife Hannah Dolbee; sons Benjamin and Peter Dolbee; daus. Betsey Melson, Sarah, Selah and Tabitha Dolbee. Exec'rs, wife Hannah Dolbee and son Peter Dolbee. Wits., Teague Matthews, Matthew Parremore, Smith Hitchens, William Duzey. Prob. Nov. 5, 1784. Arch. vol. A69, pages 129-130. Reg. of Wills, Liber D, folios 6-7.

**Waples, Patience.** Widow. Will. Made Nov. 13, 1784. Heirs: sons William and Peter Waples; daus. Lida Waples and Sarah Prettyman. Exec'r, friend Joseph Waples. Wits., Mary Stratten, Ann Stratten, Edward Johnson, N. Waples. Prob. Dec. 1, 1784. Arch. vol. A105, page 31. Reg. of Wills, Liber D, folios 67-68.

**McIlvain, Mills.** Yeoman. Admin. of, to Archibald Hopkins and wife Prudence, late Prudence McIlvain. Granted [c. Dec. 6, 1784]. Arch. vol. A88, pages 1-2. [Note:—Arch. vol. A88, page 2 mentions a minor son David Mills McIlvain; minors Arcada and Cornelia McIlvaine].

**Silevan [Sullivan], William.** Yeoman. Will. Made Sept. 29, 1784. Heirs: wife Esther Silevan; dau. Elizabeth Silevan. Exec'rx, Esther Silevan. Wits., Luke Townsend, Schofield Lindell. Prob. Dec. 6, 1784. Arch. vol. A101, page 77. Reg. of Wills, Liber D, folios 68-69.

**Truitt, Micage [Micajah].** Admin. of, to Peter and James Truitt. Admr's bond dated Dec. 6, 1784. Arch. vol. A102, page 151.

**Truitt, Sarah.** Admin. of, to Peter Truitt. Admr's bond dated Dec. 6, 1784. Arch. vol. A102, page 158. [Note:—Arch. vol. A102, page 158 mentions decedent's children Naomi, Bradford and Micajah Truitt].

**Enis, Jesse.** Admin. of, to Thomas Reynolds. Granted [c. Dec. 8, 1784]. Arch. vol. A70, page 139.

**Handzer, David, Jr.** Admin. of, to David Handzer. Granted [c. Dec. 8, 1784]. Arch. vol. A74, page 48.

**Bicknell, William.** Admin. of, to John Chambers and wife Bathsheba, late Bathsheba Bicknell. Granted [c. 1785]. Arch. vol. A59, pages 177-178. [Note:—Arch. vol. A59, page 178 mentions Hester and Penelope Bicknell].

**Bruce, Alexander.** Admin. of, to Richard Green. Granted [c. 1785]. Arch. vol. A60, page 237.

**Burton, Robert, Jr.** Late of Nova Scotia. Admin. of, to Joshua Burton. Granted [c. 1785]. Arch. vol. A62, page 4.

**Clarke, William.** Admin. of, to Charles Macklin. Granted [c. 1785]. Arch. vol. A64, pages 199-200.

**Collins, Andrew.** Admin. of, to Clement Jackson, D. B. N. Granted [c. 1785]. Arch. vol. A65, pages 131-133. [Note:— Arch. vol. A65, page 131 shows Mary Collins as original adm'rx; page 132 mentions Clement Jackson and wife Polly, and Peter Jackson and wife Elizabeth; page 133 shows the estate was finally settled by Miers Clark, D. B. N.].

**Coulter, James.** Admin. of, to Thomas and William Coulter. Granted [c. 1785]. Arch. vol. A67, page 43.

**Waples, John.** Admin. of, to Patience Waples. Granted [c. 1785]. Arch. vol. A105, page 3. [Note:—Arch. vol. A105, page 3 shows final settlement made by Joseph Waples].

**Warrington, Benjamin.** Yeoman. Admin. of, to Samuel Johnson and wife Sarah, late Sarah Warrington. Granted [c. Jan. 4, 1785]. Arch. vol. A105, page 145. [Note:—Arch. vol. A105, page 145 mentions a dau. Mary Warrington].

**Lockwood, Mary.** Will. Made Aug, 1, 1783. Heirs: daus. Leah Weldredge, Elizabeth Williams, Tabitha Williams, Mary D. Taylor and Ann Ake; Elizabeth Ake; Milley Harney; William Taylor (son of Thomas). Exec'r, Arthur Williams. Wits., John Evans, George Hill. Prob. Jan. 13, 1785. Arch. vol. A84, pages 196-197. Reg. of Wills, Liber D, folio 69.

**Waples, Marg[a]ret.** Will. Made Jan. 1, 1785. Heirs: son Peter Waples; daus. Jenney and Elizabeth Waples and Marg[a]ret Oliver. Exec'r, son-in-law Thomas Waples. Wits., Burton Waples, Leah Parker, Frances Harmonson. Prob. Jan. 15, 1785. Arch. vol. A105, page 12. Reg. of Wills, Liber D, folio 70.

**Cannon, Sarah.** Will. Made Sept. 16, 1779. Heirs: sons James, William, Joseph, Elijah, Matthew, Jacob and Jeremiah Cannon; daus. Elizabeth Cannon, Sarah Derickson, Margery Bayly, Keziah Wright, Constant Adams and Mary Turpin; Elizabeth and Sarah Turpin (daus. of Constant); granddau. Elizabeth Wingate; grandson Jeremiah Cannon (son of Isaac). Exec'r, son Jeremiah Cannon. Wits., John Flower, Peter Hubbert, Henry Hooper, Jr. Prob. Jan. 18, 1785. Arch. vol. A63, page 133. Reg. of Wills, Liber D, folios 70-71.

**Hickman, Joshua.** Will. Made Dec. 27, 1784. Heirs: wife Priscilla Hickman; sons John and Robert Hickman; daus. Leah, Sarah, Nelly and Peggy Hickman. Exec'rx, wife Priscilla Hickman. Wits., Thomas Layton, John Smith, Levin Clifton. Prob. Jan. 19, 1785. Arch. vol. A76, pages 73-74. Reg. of Wills, Liber D, folios 71-72.

**Hazzard, William.** Merchant. Will. Made March 7, 1782. Heirs: wife Mary Hazzard; sons George, Jacob, and William Hazzard; daus. Rachel, Rebeckah, Arcada and Nancy Hazzard. Exec'rs, wife Mary and bros. Hap and Jacob Hazzard. Wits.,

George Black, Benj[amin] Burrows, William Burrows. Prob. Jan. 29, 1785. Arch. vol. A75, pages 136-137. Reg. of Wills, Liber D, folios 72-73. [Note:—Arch. vol. A75, page 137 shows that Hap Hazzard and Jacob Hazzard, adm'r D. B. N., settled the estate April 30, 1799].

**Jones, Burrell.** Will (copy). Made Dec. 24, 1784. Heirs: unnamed wife; bro. Thomas Jones; grandson Jones Ellingsworth. [No exec'r]. Wits., William Dulaney, Nathaniel Steel, Peggy Stephens. Prob. Feb. 8, 1785. Arch. vol. A81, page 137. Reg. of Wills, Liber D, folios 73-74.

**Hutson, Thomas.** Will. Made Dec. 28, 1784: Heir: wife Naoma Hutson. Exec'rx, wife Naoma Hutson. Wits., Benjamin Phillips, Paul Waples. Prob. Feb. 9, 1785. Arch. vol. A79, page 135. Reg. of Wills, Liber D, folio 74.

**Lecount, Philemon.** Will. Made Oct. 23, 1784. Heirs: wife unnamed; dau. Sarah Lecount. Exec'rx, wife unnamed. Wits., Stephen Wright, William Moss. Prob. Feb. 10, 1785. Arch. vol. A84, pages 38-40. Reg. of Wills, Liber D, folio 75. [Note:—Arch. vol. A84, page 40 shows the estate was settled Sept. 8, 1789 by Elizabeth Lecount].

**Hamblen, Joseph.** Worcester County, Md. Will (copy). Made Sept. 9, 1783. Heirs: son Solomon Hamblen; daus. Mary and Ziporah Hamblen. Exec'rx, dau. Mary Hamblen. Wits., Charles Taylor, John Smith, James Conner. Prob. March 4, 1785. Arch. vol. A74, page 23. Reg. of Wills, Liber D, folios 75-76.

**Butcher, Robert.** Yeoman. Admin. of, to William Butcher. Granted [c. March 7, 1785]. Arch. vol. A62, page 75.

**Woodcraft, William, Jr.** Admin. of, to Arthur Williams, in right of Mary Lockwood, dec'd. Granted [c. March 7, 1785]. Arch. vol. A109, page 48.

**Manlove, Jonathan.** Admin. of, to Charles Mason. Granted March 8, 1785. Arch. vol. A86, pages 34-36.

**Caulk, Lambeth.** Yeoman. Admin. of, to John Walker and wife. Granted [c. March 9, 1785]. Arch. vol. A64, page 116.

**Taylor, John.** Tailor. Admin. of, to Tabitha Taylor. Granted [c. March 9, 1785]. Arch. vol. A101, page 119.

**Burroughs, Charles.** Admin. of, to Boaz Burroughs. Granted [c. March 10, 1785]. Arch. vol. A61, page 56.

**Burroughs, Mary.** Widow. Admin. of, to Boaz Burroughs. Granted [c. March 10, 1785]. Arch. vol. A61, page 57.

**Spencer, Betsy.** Admin. of, to Joseph Couch. Granted [c. March 10, 1785]. Arch. vol. A100, page 48. [Note:—Arch. vol. A100, page 48 mentions dec'd father Levi Spencer and also shows that Thomas Collings married the widow of Levi Spencer].

**Reed, John.** Will. Made Feb. 16, 1785. Heirs: wife [Martha] Reed; dau. Mary Warrington; grandson James Reed Warrington. Exec'rx, wife [Martha] Reed. Wits., Allen Reed, Jean McIlvain, John Holmes. Prob. March 19, 1785. Arch. vol. A95, pages 30-31. Reg. of Wills, Liber D, folio 76. [Note:—Arch. vol. A95, page 31 shows the estate was settled March 2, 1790 by George Prettyman and wife Martha, late Martha Reed].

**Veasey, Charles.** Will. Made Nov. 15, 1784. Heirs: wife Tabitha Ve[a]sey; sons Zadock, Gideon, Hezekiah and Gilb[ert] Ve[a]sey; daus. Patience and Levicey Ve[a]sey; child unnamed. Exec'rx, wife Tabitha Ve[a]sey. Wits., Jebediah Hall, Elihu Waples. Prob. March 24, 1785. Arch. vol. A103, page 89. Reg. of Wills, Liber D, folios 76-77.

**Starr, Catherin[e].** Will. Made June 4, 1782. Heirs: mother Ann Barr [Starr]; Michael Lank. Exec'r, Michael Lank. Wits., Parker Robinson, James Starr, Elisabeth Starr. Prob. March 26, 1785. Arch. vol. A100, page 114. Reg. of Wills, Liber D, folios 77-78.

**Cord, Rhoda.** Widow. Will. Made Dec. 30, 1784. Heirs: sons William, Shibna, John Robins and Samuel Cord; daus. Ann Cord, Elizabeth Deal, Mary Whorton and Sarah Evans. Exec'r, son-in-law William Evans. Wits., Solomon Evans, John Buckley, William Hall. Guardian: Campbell Deal. Prob. March 29, 1785. Arch. vol. A66, pages 187-188. Reg. of Wills, Liber D, folios 78-79.

**Tilney, Stringer.** Will. Made March 30, 1785. Heirs: wife Betty Tilney; sons Jacob Stringer, John and Jonathan Tilney; daus. Sarah Tilney, Mary Tilney, El[si]e Laws, Betty Melson (widow), Rachel Atkinson Davis; son-in-law Nehemiah Davis. Exec'rx, wife Betty Tilney. Wits., Caleb Cirwithin, Lot Clark, El[isha] Shankland. Prob. April 25, 1785. Arch. vol. A101, page 191. Reg. of Wills, Liber D, folios 79-80.

**Harmonson, John.** Will (copy). Made April 17, 1784. Heirs: wife Sarah Harmonson; sons Peter and Wallace Harmonson; daus. Lydia, Mary and Elizabeth Harmonson. Exec'r, son Peter Harmonson. Wit., John Clowes, Edward Craig, David Shankland. Prob. May 5, 1785. Arch. vol. A74, pages 100-101. Reg. of Wills, Liber D, folios 81-82.

**Williams, Ann.** Widow. Admin. of, to Joshua Williams. Granted [c. May 5, 1785]. Arch. vol. A107, page 145.

**Turner, Ephraim.** Admin. of, to Levi Russell. Admr's bond dated May 31, 1785. Arch. vol. A103, page 13.

**Joyce, Samuel.** Admin. of, to Joseph Fle[ming]. Yeoman. Granted [c. June 7, 1785]. Arch. vol. A81, page 131.

**Melson, John.** Admin. of, to Daniel Melson, Jr. Granted [c. June 7, 1785]. Arch. vol. A88, page 45.

**Abdell, Littleton.** Admin. of, to Alice Abdell, widow. Granted [c. June 8, 1785]. Arch. vol. A57, page 31.

**Cahoon, Sampson.** Cordwainer. Admin. of, to Isaac Wattson (son of Isaac). Granted [c. June 8, 1785]. Arch. vol. A62, page 116.

**Stuart, David.** Admin. of, to Sophia Stuart. Granted [c. June 8, 1785]. Arch. vol. A101, page 52. [Note:—Arch. vol. A101, page 52 mentions a minor dau. Sarah Stuart].

**Coulter, Esther.** Admin. of, to Tabitha Starr, D. B. N., for Nathaniel Starr, yeoman. Granted [c. June 9, 1785]. Arch. vol. A67, page 40.

**Draper, Samuel.** Admin. of, to John Draper. Granted [c. June 9, 1785]. Arch. vol. A69, page 219. [Note:—Arch. vol. A69, page 219 shows that the account was settled by John Walter and wife Elizabeth, late Elizabeth Draper widow of John Draper, the adm'r].

**Mason, Elias.** Admin. of, to Sarah Mason. Granted June 9, 1785. Arch. vol. A87, pages 37-39. [Note:—Arch. vol. A87, page 38 mentions children: Kaziah, Isaac and Mary Mason].

**Evans, Joshua.** Will. Made May 3, 1785. Heirs: wife Elizabeth Evans; son William Evans; daus. Sabrina Evans, Beckey Stinson, Hannah Wilkins, Polly Derrickson and Elizabeth Ellis; son-in-law William Ellis. Exec'r, son-in-law William Ellis. Wits., Mary Hughes, Margaret Evans, John Evans. Prob. June 10, 1785. Arch. vol. A70, pages 239-241. Reg. of Wills, Liber D, folios 82-83. [Note:—Arch. vol. A70, page 241 mentions John Derrickson and Rebecca Stephenson].

**Knox, John.** Admin. of, to Margery Knox and Charles Knox. Granted [c. June 10, 1785]. Arch. vol. A82, page 197.

**McIlvain, William.** Yeoman. Admin. of, to David McIlvain. Granted [c. June 10, 1785]. Arch. vol. A88, page 6.

**Warrington, Joseph.** Admin. of, to Elias West and wife Sarah, late Sarah Warrington. Granted [c. June 10, 1785]. Arch. vol. A105, page 155.

**Wolfe, Francis.** Cordwainer. Will. Made May 8, 1785. Heirs: bros. George, Henry, David, Benjamin, Daniel, William and Reece Wolfe; sisters Esther and Sarah Wolfe, and Comfort Orr (wife of John Orr). Exec'r, father Reece Wolfe. Wits., William Harrison, John Wolfe, John Caddy, Evan McHam. Codicil: Heir, Nancy Fisher (dau. of Jabez Fisher), friend. Prob. June 17, 1785. Arch. vol. A109, page 22. Reg. of Wills, Liber D, folios 84-85.

**Morris, Bevins.** Admin. of, to John Tharp and wife Leah, late Leah Morris. Granted [c. July 28, 1785]. Arch. vol. A90, page 18.

**Houston, Littleton.** Will. Made April 29, 1785. Heirs: wife Sally Minors Houston; bros. John and Leonard Houston. [No exec'r]. Wits., Robert Houston, Hughfort Taylor, Henry Edger. Prob. Aug. 3, 1785. Arch. vol. A78, page 103. Reg. of Wills, Liber D, folios 84-85.

**Roberts, Joseph.** Will. Made June 1, 1784. Heirs: wife Mary Roberts; sons John and James Roberts; children of bros. William, Sanders and John Roberts. Exec'rs, wife Mary Roberts and bro. Sanders Roberts. Wits., Mathias Aydelott, Mary Aydelott, Levin Derickson. Prob. Aug. 3, 1785. Arch. vol. A96, page 88. Reg. of Wills, Liber D, folio 84. [Note:—Arch. vol. A96, page 88 shows the estate was settled Jan. 11, 1788 by Sanders Roberts, surviving exec'r].

**Jessups, Aaron.** Admin. of, to Patience Jessups. Granted Aug. 13, 1785. Arch. vol. A80, page 186.

**Waples, Elizabeth.** Widow. Will. Made April 9, 1783. Heirs: sons Paul and Peter Waples; daus. Mary Lockwood, Sarah Morrison, Cath[erine] Hance and Ann Waglen; grandsons John Smith Waples (son of Paul Waples), Elihu Waples and John Waples; granddau. Priscilla Waples. Exec'r, son Peter Waples. Wits., Burton Waples, William Waples, William Tingle, Jr. Prob. Aug. 17, 1785. Arch. vol. A104, page 186. Reg. of Wills, Liber D, folios 85-86. [Note:— Arch. vol. A104, page 186 shows the estate was settled June 14, 1791 by Sarah Waples, adm'rx of Peter Waples, dec'd].

**Collins, Mary.** Widow. Will. Made Oct. 3, 1784. Heirs: sons Miers and John Clark; daus. Mary Jackson and Elizabeth Collins; granddau. Margery Fisher Jackson. Exec'r, son John Clark (of Broad Kiln Hd.). Wits., Eli Parker, Rachel Parker, Abigail Parker. Prob. Aug. 25, 1785. Arch. vol. A65, pages 223-224. Reg. of Wills, Liber D, folios 86-87.

**Draper, Sarah.** Admin. of, to Thomas Bowman and wife Elizabeth, late Elizabeth Draper. Granted Aug. 26, 1785. Arch. vol. A69, pages 224-226. [Note:—Arch. vol. A69, page 226 mentions Elizabeth (Draper) Bowman, Sarah, Phebe and James Draper, heirs of bro. Nehemiah Draper].

**Dirickson, Levin.** Will. Made May 13, 1785. Heirs: wife Sarah Dirickson; bros. Samuel and Joseph Dirickson; nephews Charles and Joseph Dirickson, Mitchell Kershaw; Sally Semmon Minors; Betty Wingate. Exec'rx, wife Sarah Dirickson. Wits., George Mitchell, Jonathan Nottingham, Jacob Burton. Prob. Aug. 31, 1785. Arch. vol. A69, page 37. Reg. of Wills, Liber D, folios 87-88.

**Lofland, Ebenezer.** Yeoman. Admin. of, to Elias Veach and wife Elizabeth, late Elizabeth Lofland. Granted Sept. 5, 1785. Arch. vol. A85, pages 19-20.

**Turpin, Solomon.** Admin. of, to Joshua Wright. Granted [c. Sept. 6, 1785]. Arch. vol. A103, page 36.

**Watson, Purnal.** Yeoman. Admin. of, to Isaac Beauchamp and wife Mary, late Mary Watson. Granted [c. Sept. 7, 1785]. Arch. vol. A106, page 34. [Note:—Arch. vol. A106, page 34 mentions children Thomas, Sarah, William, Mary and Ann Watson].

**Parker, Anderson, Jr.** Admin. of, to William Grice and wife Ruth, late Ruth Parker. Granted [c. Sept. 9, 1785]. Arch. vol. A92, page 53.

**Turpin, Joseph.** Will. Made Aug. 17, 1785. Heirs: sons Solomon, White, Thomas Baynard Turpin; dau. Peggy Turpin; Jeremiah Cannon; Betty Cannon, widow. Exec'rs, Henry Baynard, Thomas Baynard, Jr., and John Baynard. Wits., Charles Flower, Henry Flower, Zadock Jones. Prob. Oct. 1, 1785. Arch. vol. A103, page 33. Reg. of Wills, Liber D, folios 88-89. [Note:—Arch. vol. A103, page 33 shows the estate was settled Sept. 13, 1797 by John Baynard; Henry and Thomas Baynard, Jr., having renounced their right to act. Also mentions dec'd father Solomon Turpin].

**Milman, Mary.** Cedar Creek Hd. Widow. Will. Made Jan. 24, 1785. Heirs: cousins Alice Webb, Mary Laton, Peggy Tatman (dau. of Alexander Laton), William Tatman, Anne Lindal], Andrew Fist; Rachel Fist (wife of Andrew); Betty Fist (dau. of Andrew and Rachel); servants Isaac, Jacob, Adam, Major, Esther and Hannah. Exec'r, Andrew Fist. Wits., David Watson, Thomas Pollitt, George Ricards. Prob. Oct. 26, 1785. Arch. vol. A89, pages 6-7. Reg. of Wills, Liber D, folios 90-92.

**West, Joseph.** Will. Made Oct. 12, 1785. Heirs: wife Eleanor West; son Burton West; dau. Molly West. Exec'rx, wife Eleanor West. Wits., Robert West, Leah Ennis, James Sirman. Prob. Oct. 26, 1785. Arch. vol. A106, page 153. Reg. of Wills, Liber D, folio 90. [Note:—Arch. vol. A106, page 153 shows that Eleanor West later married John Morris].

**Waller, George.** Will. Made Nov. 7, 1785. Heirs: wife unnamed; nephew William Waller (son of bro. Charles). Exec'rx, wife [Ann]. Wits., William Cullen, William Burroughs, Hessey Burrows. Prob. Nov. 14, 1785. Arch. vol. A104, pages 60-61. Reg. of Wills, Liber D, folio 92. [Note:—Arch. vol. A104, page 61 shows the estate was settled March 12, 1790 by Ann Waller].

**Waples, Eli.** Admin. of, to Mary Jackson. Admr's bond dated Nov. 30, 1785. Arch. vol. A104, page 184.

**Salmons, Aydelott.** Admin. of, to William Salmons. Granted [c. Dec. 5, 1785]. Arch. vol. A97, page 176.

**Willey, Gabriel.** Admin. of, to Mary Willey. Admr's bond dated Dec. 5, 1785. Arch. vol. A107, page 125.

**O'Day, Henry.** Admin. of, to John O'Day. Granted [c. Dec. 6, 1785]. Arch. vol. A91, page 141.

**Fisher, Jonathan.** Admin. of, to Sarah Fisher. Granted [c. Dec. 7, 1785]. Arch. vol. A71, pages 141-142.

**Lank, Levin.** Admin. of, to Naomi Lank. Granted [c. Dec. 7, 1785]. Arch. vol. A83, page 78. [Note:—Arch. vol. A83, page 78 mentions minors Lydia, Polly, David and Cornelius Lank].

**Riggs, Peter.** Admin. of, to Ezekiel and Isaac Riggs. Granted [c. Dec. 7, 1785]. Arch. vol. A96, page 32.

**Wright, Jeremiah.** Admin. of, to Jesse Wright. Granted [c. Dec. 7, 1785]. Arch. vol. A109, page 84.

**Stockley, Painter [Paynter].** Will. Made June 29, 1784. Heirs: wife Elizabeth Stockley; Lida Paynter (dau. of Nancy Lynch); Rebeckah Lewis (dau. of Mary Tindle); Priscilla Turner (granddau. of bro. William Stockley); Cornelius Turner (grandson of bro. William Stockley). Exec'rx, wife Elizabeth Stockley. Wits., John Craige, Comfort Craige, Naomi Stockley. Prob. Dec. 8, 1785. Arch. vol. A101, page 31. Reg. of Wills, Liber D, folios 92-93. [Note:—Arch. vol. A101, page 31 shows the estate was settled by Cornelius Turner, exec'r of Elizabeth Stockley, dec'd].

**Walton, Samuel.** Tanner. Admin. of, to Luke Spencer, D. B. N. Granted [c. Dec. 9, 1785]. Arch. vol. A104, pages 163-164.

**Williams, John.** Admin. of, to William Williams. Granted [c. Dec. 9, 1785]. Arch. vol. A107, page 190.

**Macklen, Thomas.** Will. Made Dec. 13, 1785. Heirs: wife Rachel Macklen; son Job Macklen; daus. Hester Macklen, Sarah Messick, Annace Messick, Mary Deputy and Rachel Carpenter (wife of Jacob). Exec'r, son Job Macklen. Wits., Eli Parker, John Walton, Alice Dickenson. Prob. Dec. 16, 1785. Arch. vol. A86, pages 17-18. Reg. of Wills, Liber D, folios 93-94.

**Barr, James.** Admin. of, to Jacob Nottingham and wife Chloe, late Chloe Barr. Granted [c. Dec. 21, 1785]. Arch. vol. A58, pages 212-213.

**Connaway, Hannah.** Admin. of, to John Connaway. Granted ante Dec. 22, 1785. Arch. vol. A66, page 55.

**Barr, John.** Yeoman. Admin. of, to Ferraby Barr. Granted [c. 1786]. Arch. vol. A58, page 250.

**Brookfield, Eli.** Admin. of, to John Wattson and wife Sally (late Sally Brookfield). Granted [c. 1786]. Arch. vol. A60, page 157.

**Cannon, Levin.** Admin. of, to Edward Wheatly and Elizabeth, his wife, late Elizabeth Cannon. Granted [c. 1786]. Arch. vol. A63, pages 101-102.

**Wallace, John.** Admin. of, to Charles Rickards. Granted [. . ., 1786]. Arch. vol. A104, page 51. [Note:—Arch. vol. A104, page 51 mentions Henry Wallace].

**Bennett, Purnell.** Cedar Creek Hd. Will. Made April 1, 1782. Heirs: wife Miriam Bennett; sons John, Lofland and Purnell Bennett; daus. Betty, Patience, Mary and Miriam Bennett. Exec'rx, wife Miriam Bennett. Wits., David Wattson,

William Coffin, Joseph Bennett. Guardian, bro. Joshua Bennett. Prob. Jan. 6, 1786. Arch. vol. A59, pages 111-113. Reg. of Wills, Liber D, folios 94-95. [Note:—Arch. vol. A59, pages 112-113 show that Miriam Bennett later married Sylvester Webb, who with the widow settled the estate May 6, 1789].

**Simpler, Paul.** Will. Made March 2, 1785. Heirs: wife Margaret Simpler; sons William and Anderson Simpler; daus. Elisabeth Johnson and Mary Clark; grandsons William, Joseph and Paul Clark. Exec'rx, wife Margaret Simpler. Wits., Andrew Simpler, Meger Pool, Perry Pool. Prob. Jan. 12, 1786. Arch. vol. A99, page 57. Reg. of Wills, Liber D, folios 95-96.

**Frame, Smith.** Planter. Will. Made Jan. 20, 1786. Heirs: sons John, Nathan and Dugood Paynter Frame; dau. Jenny Frame. Exec'rs, William Peery, Robert Hood. Wits., Simon Kollock, George Frame, Paynter Frame. Prob. Jan. 24, 1786. Arch. vol. A72, pages 51-52. Reg. of Wills, Liber D, folios 96-97. [Note:—Arch. vol. A72, page 52 also mentions Jane Simonton Frame].

**Heaverlo, Andrew.** Yeoman. Broadkiln Hd. Will. Made Nov. 29, 1783. Heirs: wife Sarah Heaverlo; son Daniel Heaverlo; daus. Jane, Ruth and Naomi Heaverlo, Sarah Gordon. Exec'rs, wife Sarah Heaverlo and son Daniel Heaverlo. Wits., John Palmer, Lydia Palmer, Jonathan Heaverlo. Prob. Jan. 27, 1786. Arch. vol. A75, pages 205-206. Reg. of Wills, Liber D, folios 97-98. [Note:—Arch. vol. A75, page 206 shows the estate was settled March 3, 1790 by Sarah Heaverlo, surviving exec'r].

**Melony, Susanna.** Widow. Will. Made Aug. 29, 1785. Heirs: sons William and Manuel Melony. Exec'r Alexander Draper. Wits., David Wattson, John S. Campbell, Littleton Townsend. Prob. Jan. 28, 1786. Arch. vol. A88, pages 30-31. Reg. of Wills, Liber D, folio 99.

**Wattson, William.** Yeoman. Prime Hook. Will. Made Dec. 26, 1785. Heir: bro. Luke Wattson. Exec'r, bro. Luke Wattson. Wits., Isaac Wattson, Robert Wattson, John Wilcocks. Prob. Jan. 28, 1786. Arch. vol. A106, page 49. Reg. of Wills, Liber D, folio 98.

**Dingee, Daniel.** Will. Made Oct. 3, 1785. Heirs: sons Daniel and Charles Dingee; daus. Esther Dingee, Elizabeth Annesley and Mary Fountain (widow). Exec'rs, cousin Samuel Rowland Fisher and sister-in-law Ann Hazard. Wits.,

George Barn[e]s, Mary Fountain, James Couch, Miers Fisher. Prob. Feb. 8, 1786. Arch. vol. A69, page 79. Reg. of Wills, Liber D, folio 99. [Note:—Arch. vol. A69, page 79 mentions Samuel R. Fisher, guardian for sons Daniel and Charles Dingee; and Ann Hazard, guardian for dau. Esther Dingee].

**Macklin, Rachel.** Widow. Will. Made Feb. 6, 1786. Heirs: son Job Macklin; daus. Hester Macklin, Anna Messick, Sarah Messick, Rachel Carpenter, Mary Deputy. Exec'r, son Job Macklin. Wits., Eli Parker, Patience Parker, Elinor Lane [Lain]. Prob. Feb. 9, 1786. Arch. vol. A86, page 16. Reg. of Wills, Liber D, folio 100.

**Clarkson, Mary.** Will. Made Feb. 14, 1786. Heirs: sister Betsey Flowers; Rit[a] Flowers (dau. of Betsey Flowers); bro.-in-law Julius Augustus Flowers. Exec'r, Julius Augustus Flowers. Wits., Henry Flower, Lennard Outerbridge, Betsey Moor. [No prob.]. Arch. vol. A64, page 213.

**Sharp, James.** Yeoman. Will. Made Feb. 11, 1786. Heirs: wife Mary Sharp; son John Sharp; dau. Betsey Sharp. Exec'r, friend Woodman Stockly. Wits., Peter Robinson, Jesse Williams, John Stephenson. Prob. Feb. 18, 1786. Arch. vol. A98, page 76. Reg. of Wills, Liber D, folio 101.

**Shelpman, Alice.** Spinster. Broadkiln Hd. Will. Made Sept. 11, 1770. Heirs: sister Sarah Dodd; nephews Jacob Laws and William Shelpman; nieces Magdaline Shelpman (dau. of Jacob Shelpman, dec'd), and Alice Shelpman (dau of John Shelpman, dec'd); cousins Magdaline Shelpman, William Shelpman, Alice Shelpman and Jacob Laws. Exec'rx, niece Magdaline Shelpman. Wits., Jno. Russel, Jean Russel, Phillips Russel. Prob. Feb. 20, 1786. Arch. vol. A98, page 106. Reg. of Wills, Liber D, folio 102. [Note:—Arch. vol. A98, page 106 shows that Magdaline Shelpman later married Samuel Dodd and that the estate was settled Oct. 18, 1796].

**Hall, James.** Admin. of, to William Hall and John Hall. Granted [c. Feb. 23, 1786]. Arch. vol. A73, page 210.

**Townsend, Julian.** Admin. of, to Richard Hays, Esq., in right of Littleton Townsend. Admr's bond dated Feb. 25, 1786. Arch. vol. A102, page 62.

**Walker, Jacob.** Will. Made Feb. 7, 1786. Heirs: wife Martha Walker; nephew David Walker and niece Mary Walker (children of bro. Thomas Walker). Exec'rx, wife Martha Walker. Wits., Elizabeth Holland, Jos[eph] Hall, William Holland. Prob. Feb. 28, 1786. Arch. vol. A104, pages 17-18.

Reg. of Wills, liber D, folio 101. [Note:—Arch. vol. A104, page 18 shows that Martha Walker later married Joseph Burton].

**Brereton, John.** Admin. of, to Alexander Reed and wife Esther, late Esther Brereton). Granted [c. March 7, 1786]. Arch. vol. A60, page 145. [Note:—Arch. vol. A60, page 145 mentions a son James].

**Johnson, Purnal, Jr.** Admin. of, to Robert Hall and Mary, his wife, (late Mary Johnson). Granted [c. March 8, 1786]. Arch. vol. A81, page 88.

**Vaughan, Nathaniel.** Admin. of, to John Burton. Granted [c. March 8, 1786]. Arch. vol. A103, page 81. [Note:—Arch. vol. A103, page 81 mentions Ephraim and Betsy Vaughan].

**Wildgoose, Jesse.** Worcester Co., Md. Admin. of, to Thomas Wildgoose. Granted [c. March 8, 1786]. Arch. vol. A107, page 107. [Note:—Arch. vol. A107, page 107 mentions Elizabeth and Thomas Wildgoose].

**Chance, John.** Admin. of, to Daniel Clifton and wife Susannah (late Susannah Chance). Granted [ante March 9, 1786]. Arch. vol. A64, pages 124-125. [Note:—Arch. vol. A64, page 125 shows Susannah Clifton as surviving exec'rx in Sept. 1786; also shows the estate was settled by Isaac Beauchamp, security for Susannah Chance and Mathias Davis].

**Johnson, Hannah.** Widow. Admin. of, to Elias Shockley. Granted [c. March 9, 1786]. Arch. vol. A81, pages 38-39.

**Johnson, Samuel.** Yeoman. Admin. of, to Elias Shockley. Granted [c. March 9, 1786]. Arch. vol. A81, page 99. [Note:— Arch. vol. A81, page 99 shows that Elias Shockley was adm'r of Hannah Johnson, dec'd, who was adm'rx of Samuel Johnson].

**Veazey, William.** Admin. of, to Comfort Veazey. Granted [c. March 9, 1786]. Arch. vol. A103, page 94.

**Norwood, Nathan.** Admin. of, to Jemima Norwood. Granted [c. March 10, 1786]. Arch. vol. A91, page 116.

**Price, Magdalin.** Admin. of, to Sarah Jacobs, D. B. N., surviving exec'rx of Albertus Jacobs, yeoman, dec'd, who was adm'r. Granted [c. March 10, 1786]. Arch. vol. A94, page 138.

**Piper, John.** Will. Made Jan. 11, 1786. Heirs: wife Elizabeth Piper; sons Benjamin and William Piper; dau. Lovey Piper; child unnamed. Exec'rx, wife Elizabeth Piper. Wits., William Swain, Moses McDaniel, Mary Isaacs. Prob. March 14, 1786. Arch. vol. A93, page 90. Reg. of Wills, Liber D, folios 103-104. [Note:—Arch. vol. A93, page 90 mentions bro. Joseph Piper, as guardian of his children].

**Gill, William.** Will. Made April 20, 1775. Heirs: wife Margaret Gill; son William Gill; daus. Patience, Priscilla, Mary, Elizabeth, Sarah, Naomi and Margaret Gill. Exec'rs, wife Margaret Gill and son William Gill. Wits., John Rodney, John Field. Prob. March 28, 1786. Arch. vol. A72, pages 143-145. Reg. of Wills, Liber D, folios 104-105. [Note:—Arch. vol. A72, page 144 mentions William Mitten and wife Sarah (late Sarah Eldridge); also shows that the estate was settled by Margaret Gill on Sept. 1, 1788].

**Langrall, Asa.** Will. Made Jan. 17, 1786. Heirs: bros. William, Philemon, Charles, Levin and John Langrall; sisters Mary Elliott and Edie Brown; cousin Henry Smith. Exec'r, bro. John Langrall. Wits., Robert Clarkson, William Neal, Eccleston Brown, Charles Twyford. Prob. March 28, 1786. Arch. vol. A83, page 56. Reg. of Wills, Liber D, folio 104.

**Clifton, Daniel.** Planter. Will. Made March 16, 1786. Heirs: wife Susannah Clifton; sons Thomas, Robert, Mathias, Ezekiel, Nathan, Daniel and Brinkley Clifton; daus. Mahala and Mary Clifton. Exec'rs, sons Thomas and Robert Clifton. Wits., Noah Spencer, Levi Spencer, Betty Wheeler. Prob. March 31, 1786. Arch. vol. A65, pages 9-11. Reg. of Wills, Liber D, folios 107-108.

**Crapper, John, Sr.** Will. Made Feb. 27, 1786. Heirs: wife Mary Crapper; son John Crapper; daus. Elizabeth Laws and Es-[tella] Johnson. Exec'r, son John Crapper. Wits., David Walton, Samuel Ansley, George Black. Prob. March 31, 1786. Arch. vol. A67, pages 162-166. Reg. of Wills, Liber D, folio 105. [Note:—Arch. Vol. A67, pages 164-166 show John Mason, adm'r, D. B. N., C. T. A., settled the account April 22, 1794 in right of Susannah Crapper, D. B. N., who previously administered the account in right of John Crapper, Jr.].

**Hurley, Joshua.** Will. Made Sept. 21, 1785. Heirs: unnamed wife; sons Joshua, Pharah, Caleb, William, Adam, John and Simon Hurley; dau. Nancy Hurley. Exec'r, son William Hurley. Wits., Paris Owens, Robert Owens, William Owens. Prob. March 31, 1786. Arch. vol. A79, page 118. Reg. of Wills, Liber D, folio 106.

**White, Ansley.** Will. Made Jan. 14, 1785. Heirs: wife Sarah White; sons Ansley and John White; daus. Mel[ody] and Ann White. Exec'rx, wife Sarah White. Wits., Stephen Mitchell, Avery Draper, Charles Draper. Prob. April 1, 1786. Arch. vol. A107, page 48. Reg. of Wills, Liber D, folio 79.

**Savage, Robinson.** Yeoman. Will. Made April 1, 1786. Heirs: son Robinson Savage; daus. Nancy and Peggy Savage. Exec'rx, dau. Nancy Savage. Wits., Somerset Dickinson, Richard Abbott. Prob. April 7, 1786. Arch. vol. A98, pages 26-27. Reg. of Wills, Liber D, folios 106-107. [Note:— Arch. vol. A98, page 27 shows the estate was settled Nov. 27, 1793 by William Argo and wife Nancy, late Nancy Savage].

**Hosey, Arthur.** Admin. of, to James English and wife, late Nancy Hosey. Admr's bond dated April 14, 1786. Arch. vol. A78, page 75. [Note:—Arch. vol. A78, page 75 mentions children Martha, Sally and Thomas Hosey].

**Sirman, George.** Admin. of, to William Goslee, in right of Jennie Sirman, dec'd. Admr's bond dated April 25, 1786. Arch. vol. A99, page 76.

**Robinson, Joshua.** Will. Made March 17, 1783. Heirs: wife Martha Robinson; son Joseph Robinson; daus. Mary Waples and Priscilla Waples; grandson Joshua Robinson; granddau. Betty Long. Exec'rx, wife Martha Robinson. Wits., Benj[ami]n Phillips, Betty Phillips, William Sharp. Prob. April 26, 1786. Arch. vol. A96, page 152. Reg. of Wills, Liber D, folios 50-51.

**Wharton, Baker.** Yeoman. Admin. of, to Levin Anderson and wife Rhoda (late Rhoda Wharton). Admr's bond dated April 27, 1786. Arch. vol. A107, page 8.

**Smith, Mary.** Will. Made Jan. 25, 1786. Heirs: bros. Paremore, John and Bartholemew Smith; sister Charity Smith. Exec'rx, sister Charity Smith. Wits., Thomas Marvel, Samuel Warren, Pris[cill]a Marvel. Prob. May 2, 1786. Arch. vol. A99, page 187. Reg. of Wills, Liber D, folio 109.

**Hosea, Daniel.** Painter. Will. Made April 1, 1786. Heirs: wife Mary Hosea; bro.-in-law Thomas Bowlin. Exec'r, Stephen Lewis, Esq. Wits., William Bowness, James Darter, Daniel Polk. Prob. May 3, 1786. Arch. vol. A78, pages 64-65. Reg. of Wills, Liber D, folios 109-110. [Note:—Arch. vol. A78, page 65 shows that Stephen Lewis, Esq., renounced and asked that letters be granted to the widow Mary [Polly] Hosea, who later married Reuben Allen].

**Hearn, Ebenezer.** Admin. of, to Priscilla Hearn and Lowder Hearn. Granted [c. May 4, 1786]. Arch. vol. A75, page 146.

**Waller, Nathaniel, Sr.** Farmer. Will. Made Feb. 23, 1786. Heirs: son Nathaniel Waller; other children unnamed. Exec'r, son Nathaniel Waller. Wits., Tho[ma]s Gray, Elijah Lecat, Noah Morgan. Prob. May 4, 1786. Arch. vol. A104, page 74. Reg. of Wills, Liber D, folio 110.

**Tindall, John.** Will. Made April 4, 1786. Heirs: wife Betty Tindall; sons Samuel, John, Jesse, Isaac and Purnal Tindall; daus. Nancy, Lovey, Hannah Tindall and Sarah Jones. Exec'rs, wife Betty Tindall and son Samuel Tindall. Wits., John Thoroughgood, Phillip Short. Prob. May 9, 1786. Arch. vol. A102, page 12. Reg. of Wills, Liber D, folio 111.

**Short, Elizabeth.** Will. Made May 15, 1786. Heirs: sons Jacob, Shadrach, Phillip, Isaac and Edward Short; daus. Betty Tindal, Nancy Melson, Rachel Stockley, Comfort Benston and Patience Ellingsworth. Exec'r, son Phillip Short. Wits., Joseph Piper, Robert Hopkins. Prob. May 25, 1786. Arch. vol. A98, page 171. Reg. of Wills, Liber D, folios 111-112. [Note:—Arch. vol. A98, page 171 shows the estate was settled March 5, 1788; also mentions Spencer Benston in right of his wife, and Richard Ellingsworth in right of his wife].

**Parker, John.** Will. Made April 4, 1785. Heirs: wife Sarah Parker; daus. Milly, Sarah, Ann, Zipporah and Alice Parker. Exec'rx, wife Sarah Parker. Wits., John Worrilaw, William Lawson, John Spear. Prob. June 2, 1786. Arch. vol. A92, page 72. Reg. of Wills, Liber D, folio 112. [Note:—Arch. vol. A92, page 72 shows the estate was settled June 14, 1791 by Thomas Parremore, adm'r of the estate of Sarah Parker].

**Robinson, Alexander.** Admin. of, to Benjamin Warrington. Granted [c. June 6, 1786]. Arch. vol. A96, page 104.

**Tree, Daniel.** Yeoman. Admin. of, to Isaac Cooper. Granted [c. June 6, 1786]. Arch. vol. A102, page 95. [Note:—Arch. vol. A102, page 95 mentions widow Sarah Tree and minor dau. Sarah Tree and minor son Jethro Tree].

**Truitt, Joseph.** Admin. of, to Betty Truitt. Granted [c. June 6, 1786]. Arch. vol. A102, page 143. [Note:—Arch. vol. A102, page 143 mentions heirs Piercy, Mary, Amelia and Joseph Truitt].

**Wright, Comfort.** Admin. of, to Sinar Bradford. Granted [c. June 6, 1786]. Arch. vol. A109, page 77. [Note:—Arch. vol. A109, page 77 mentions son Nathaniel Wright].

**Gray, Thomas.** Admin. of, to James Martin, Esq., D. B. N. Granted [c. June 7, 1786]. Arch. vol. A73, page 30.

**Price, Elizabeth.** Widow. Admin. of, to Solomon Parremore and wife Tabitha, late Tabitha Starr. Admr's bond dated June 7, 1786. Arch. vol. A94, page 136.

**Thompson, George.** Admin. of, to Jarred Hitchens and wife Elizabeth, late Elizabeth Philby and late Elizabeth Thompson, widow of Jesse Thompson. Granted [c. June 8, 1786]. Arch. vol. A101, page 149. [Note:—Arch. vol. A101, page 149 mentions heirs George, Priscilla, Charles, John, James, Nathan and Elizabeth Thompson; Jenkins Parker and wife Mary; Aaron Jester and wife Ann; Sarah Jester].

**Mooney, Charles.** Admin. of, to Philip Spicer and wife Priscilla, late Priscilla Mooney. Admr's bond dated June 12, 1786. Arch. vol. A89, page 89.

**Coulter, John.** Yeoman. Will. Made April 27, 1786. Heirs: sons Cornelius and David Coulter; dau. Nicey Coulter; other children unnamed. [No exec'r]. Wits., George Dutton, Ebenezer Pettyjohn, Robert Neill. Prob. June 16, 1786. Arch. vol. A67, page 49. Reg. of Wills, Liber D, folios 257-258.

**Griffith, Samuel.** Will. Made May 10, 1786. Heirs: sons Robert, Jesse, Seth, Josiah and Isaac Griffith; dau. Nancy Ingram. Exec'r, son Robert Griffith. Wits., Charles Brown, Paris Griffith, Thomas Williams. Prob. June 17, 1786. Arch. vol. A73, page 137. Reg. of Wills, Liber D, folio 113.

**Mountford, Samuel.** Blacksmith. Will. Made Aug. 10, 1784. Heirs: wife Frances Mountford; daus. Mary and Elisabeth Mountford, and Marg[a]ret King; son-in-law John King. Exec'rx, wife Frances Mountford. Wits., John Heavelo, John Stewart. Prob. July 17, 1786. Arch. vol. A90, page 169. Reg. of Wills, Liber D, folios 113-114.

**Marriner, William.** Will. Made July 7, 1785. Heirs: wife Edah Marriner; son William Marriner; daus. Nancy and Selah Marriner. Exec'rx, wife Edah Marriner. Wits., Levin

Walls, William Blizzard, William Johnson. Prob. July 26, 1786. Arch. vol. A86, pages 90-91. Reg. of Wills, Liber D, folio 114. [Note:—Arch. vol. A86, page 91 shows the estate was settled c. December 19, 1797 by Spencer Atkins and wife Edah, late Edah Marriner].

**Townsend, Stephen.** Cedar Creek Hd. Will. Made June 29, 1786. Heirs: wife Betty Townsend; sons Stephen and John Townsend; daus. Betty and Mary Townsend. Exec'rx, wife Betty Townsend. Wits., Thomas Evans, Charles Draper, John Metcalf. Prob. July 29, 1786. Arch. vol. A102, page 79. Reg. of Wills, Liber D, folio 115. [Note:—Arch. vol. A102, page 79 shows friend, John Young, was appointed guardian; also shows the estate was settled June 4, 1788 by John Hayes and wife Elizabeth, late Elizabeth Townsend].

**Hardy, Betty Jones.** Admin. of, to Phillis Hardy. Admr's bond dated Aug. 8, 1786. Arch. vol. A74, page 64.

**Hardy, Joseph.** Will. Made March 2, 1786. Heirs: wife Phillis Hardy; son Joseph Hardy; daus. Rachel, Phillis, Allafair, Margaret Fillet and Betty Jones Hardy; son-in-law Henry Wilson; grandsons Joshua Jones Wilson and Samuel G. Wilson. Exec'rx, wife Phillis Hardy. Wits., Moses Culver, Aaron Culver, William Wilson. Prob. Aug. 8, 1786. Arch. vol. A74, pages 65-67. Reg. of Wills, Liber D, folio 116.

**Hardy, Margaret Fillet.** Admin. of, to Phillis Hardy. Admr's bond dated Aug. 8, 1786. Arch. vol. A74, page 68.

**Kellam, Samuel.** Admin. of, to Prudence Kellam. Granted [c. Aug. 11, 1786]. Arch. vol. A82, page 41.

**Moore, Elisha.** Will. Made April 10, 1786. Heirs: wife Ann Moore; son Isaac Moore. Exec'r, uncle George Moore. Wits., Daniel Wailes, Curtis Moore, William Moore. Prob. Aug. 9, 1786. Arch. vol. A89, page 98. Reg. of Wills, Liber D, folio 117.

**Russel, Phillip.** House Carpenter & Joiner. Lewes. Admin. of, to James Wakeman and wife Ruth, late Ruth Russel. Granted Aug. 11, 1786. Arch. vol. A97, page 148.

**Hazzard, Mary.** Cedar Creek Hd. Will (nunc.). Made July 11, 1786. Heirs: sons Charles and William Hazzard; dau. Ann Hazzard. Exec'r, son-in-law George Hazzard. Wits., Israel Brown, Susannah Cary, Ann Walter. Prob. Aug. 30, 1786. Arch. vol. A75, page 105. Reg. of Wills, Liber D, folios 117-118.

**Baley, Jonathan.** Will. Made June 9, 1779. Heirs: wife Mary Baley; sons Samuel Jackson and George Baley; dau. Mary Nickelson; grandsons Thomas, John and Stephen Baley. Exec'r, son Davis Baley. Wits., James English, Sr., Joshua Bennett, Jacob Gordy. Prob. Sept. 4, 1786. Arch. vol. A58, page 77. Reg. of Wills, Liber D, folios 118-119.

**Fisher, James.** Admin. of, to Chloe Fisher. Granted Sept. 5, 1786. Arch. vol. A71, page 127.

**Carpenter, George.** Blacksmith. Admin. of, to Jonathan Hemmons and wife Mary, late Mary Carpenter. Granted [c. Sept. 6, 1786]. Arch. vol. A63, page 223.

**Williams, Joseph.** Will. Made Sept. 27, 1786. Heirs: wife Elizabeth Williams; sons Manuel and Elias Williams; daus. Sarah and Nicey Williams, Rachel Hudson, Tashafie Wharton. [No exec'r]. Wits., Aaron Williams, James Johnson. Prob. Oct. 7, 1786. Arch. vol. A108, page 10. Reg. of Wills, Liber D, folios 130-131.

**Schofield, Joseph.** Yeoman. Admin. of, to Angeleta Schofield. Granted Nov. 3, 1779. Arch. vol. A98, page 33. [Note:— Arch. vol. A98, page 33 shows that Angeleta Schofield later married Watson Wharton].

**Layton, Robert.** Farmer. Will. Made Oct. 9, 1786. Heirs: wife Rose Layton; sons Purnel and Burton Layton; daus. Hessy Layton and Margaret Leddenham. Exec'rs, wife Rose Layton and son Purnel Layton. Wits., W[illia]m Layton, Thomas Layton, William Bowness. Prob. Nov. 9, 1786. Arch. vol. A83, pages 199-200. Reg. of Wills, Liber D, folios 119-120. [Note:—Arch. vol. A83, page 200 shows the estate was settled Aug. 9, 1797 by Thomas Leddenham and wife Rose, late Rose Layton, with Purnel Layton].

**Pierce, Jonathan.** Yeoman. Admin. of, to William Pierce. Granted [c. Nov. 9, 1786]. Arch. vol. A93, page 73.

**Adams, Roger, Jr.** Planter. Will. Made Sept. 7, 1786. Heirs: wife Esther Adams; son Daniel Cannon Adams; daus. Peggy and Priscilla Adams. Exec'rx, wife Esther Adams. Wits., Robert Clarkson, Roger Adams, Levina Cannon. Prob. Nov. 23, 1786. Arch. vol. A57, pages 92 and 95. Reg. of Wills, Liber D, folio 120.

**Collison, George.** Admin. of, to Edward Minner. Granted ante Nov. 23, 1786. Arch. vol. A66, page 47.

**Cahoon, Frances.** Lewes. Will. Made Oct. 14, 1786. Heirs: Elizabeth Sanders; James Thompson; and Deacons of Presbyterian Meeting House. Exec'r, friend James Thompson (of Lewes). Wits., Richard Little, Joseph Coulter, Jr., William Roach. Prob. Nov. 25, 1786. Arch. vol. A62, pages 112-113. Reg. of Wills, Liber D, folio 121. [Note:—Arch. vol. A62, page 113 shows that William Thompson, Elizabeth Sanders and Richard Little were adm'rs D. B. N., in right of James Thompson, dec'd, and settled the estate c. Jan. 30, 1787; also mentions widow . . . Sanders].

**Wallace, Benjamin.** Will. Made Sept. 28, 1786. Heirs: bro. John Wallace; sisters Mary and Alice Wallace; Sarah Hopkins Brown; Abel Hopkins Brown (son of Charles and Elinor Brown); Robert Wallace (son of Thomas Wallace); other children of Thomas Wallace. Exec'r, Charles Ricords. Wits., Joseph Ricords, Levin Ricords, Loxley Ricords. Prob. Nov. 25, 1786. Arch. vol. A104, page 45. Reg. of Wills, Liber D, folios 120-121.

**Barker, Perry.** Yeoman. Admin. of, to Leatherberry Barker. Granted Dec. 5, 1786. Arch. vol. A58, page 192. [Note:— Arch. vol. A58, page 192 mentions heirs: widow Ann Catherine Barker; sons Jno. Burton, Perry and Jehu Barker; daus. Sarah and Comfort Barker.

**Taylor, John.** Will. Made Oct. 22, 1786. Heirs: wife Comfort Taylor; sons William, Joshua and Elias Taylor; dau. Leah Taylor. Exec'rs, sons William and Joshua Taylor. Wits., William Rickards, Mary Rickards, Isaac Evans. Prob. Dec. 14, 1786. Arch. vol. A101, page 120. Reg. of Wills, Liber D, folios 122-123.

**Lofland, William, Sr.** Will. Made Dec. 15, 1785. Heirs: wife Grace Lofland; sons William, Littleton, Gabriel, George and Dorman Lofland; daus. Nancy, Rachel and Marga[re]t Lofland. Exec'rs, wife Grace Lofland and son Dorman Lofland. Wits., John Lofland, William Veach, John Clifton. Prob. Dec. 16, 1786. Arch. vol. A85, page 86-87. Reg. of Wills, Liber D, folios 122-123.

**Gordon, Thomas.** Will. Made Dec. 6, 1785. Heirs: son John Gordon; daus. Peggy and Catherine Gordon, and Ann Elliott. Exec'r, son John Gordon. Wits., Robert Jones, Ann Jones, Nathaniel Gordon. Prob. Dec. 20, 1786. Arch. vol. A72, pages 186-188. Reg. of Wills, Liber D, folio 94. [Note: —Arch. vol. A72, pages 187 and 188 shows the estate was settled on April 21, 1796 by John Elliott, adm'r of John John Gordon, D. B. N.].

**Marvel, Joseph.** Will. Made Dec. 6, 1786. Heirs: wife Rachel Marvel; bros. Thomas, Robert and Philip Marvel; wife's dau. Mary [Smith]. Exec'rs, wife Rachel Marvel and bro. Thomas Marvel. Wits., Leven Connaway, William Marvel. Prob. Dec. 28, 1786. Arch. vol. A86, pages 197-200. Reg. of Wills, Liber D, folios 123-124. [Note:—Arch. vol. A86, page 198 shows Thomas Marvel, John Mann and Rachel, his wife, late Rachel Marvel, exhibited an account on the estate March 4, 1789; page 199 shows Elizabeth Marvel and Philip Marvel exhibited an account August 11, 1795 as exec'rs of Thomas Marvel].

**Hill, George.** Will. Made Nov. 28, 1786. Heirs: wife Polly Hill; sons John, Virden, Levi, George and Mitchell Hill; daus. Sarah and Margaret Hill. Exec'rs, wife Polly Hill and son John Hill. Wits., William Blizzard, Ezekiel West, Mary Hill. Prob. Dec. 29, 1786. Arch. vol. A76, pages 120-123. Reg. of Wills, Liber D, folios 124-125. [Note:—Arch. vol. A76, pages 122-123 show that Polly Hill later married Annanias Hudson].

**Bagwell, William.** Admin. of, to William and Ann Burton, late Ann Bagwell. Granted [c. 1787]. Arch. vol. A58, pages 60 and 62.

**Barker, Ann.** Widow. Admin. of, to Leatherberry Barker, D. B. N. Granted [c. 1787]. Arch. vol. A58, page 191. [Note: —Arch. vol. A58, page 191 mentions Perry Barker, adm'r dec'd].

**Becket, Bede.** Admin. of, to Peter Becket. Granted [c. 1787]. Arch. vol. A59, page 23.

**Clifton, Aaron.** Admin. of, to Patience Clifton. Granted [c. 1787]. Arch. vol. A65, page 4.

**Cro[c]ket[t], Richa[r]d.** Will. Made Nov. 8, 1786. Heirs: wife Sarah Crockett; sons John Seers Crockett and Richard Venables Crockett; daus. Sally Venables Crockett and Nelly Winder Crockett. Exec'rx, wife Sarah Crockett. Wits., Thomas Willin, Melvin Duke, William Adams, Jr. Prob. Jan. 3, 1787. Arch. vol. A67, pages 199-200. Reg. of Wills, Liber D, folios 126-127. [Note:—Arch. vol. A67, page 200 shows that Pharoah Hurley and wife Sarah, late Sarah Crockett, settled the estate Sept. 7, 1789].

**Owens, Paris.** Will. Made Sept. 15, 1786. Heirs: bro. David Owens; sisters Ann Owens and Sarah Safford; Robert Gaskens; William Gaskens. Exec'r, bro. David Owens. Wits.,

William Owens, Robert Owens, Charles Knox. Prob. Jan. 3, 1787. Arch. vol. A92, page 16. Reg. of Wills, Liber D, folio 126.

**Bradley, Thomas.** Yeoman. Admin. of, to Hewitt Layton and wife Nancy [Ann], late Nancy [Ann] Bradley. Granted [c. Jan. 4, 1787]. Arch. vol. A60, pages 110-112.

**Gibbins, John.** Will. Made Nov. 3, 1786. Heirs: wife Mary Gibbins; sons Emory and George Gibbins; daus. Sarah Gibbins and Nelly Autwell; grandson John Autwell; sons-in-law Edward Carty Dingle and Greenberry Massey. Exec'rs, wife Mary Gibbins and bro. Joshua Gibbins. Wits., Thomas Brown, Martha Brown, Sarah Carpenter, Mary Berry, William Berry. Prob. Jan. 4, 1787. Arch. vol. A72, pages 116-117. Reg. of Wills, Liber D, folio 128. [Note:—Arch. vol. A72, page 117 shows the estate was settled by Joshua Gibbins surviving exec'r on May 27, 1794].

**Wallace, George.** Will. Made Dec. 16, 1786. Heirs: wife Esther Wallace; son William Wallace; daus. Amelia Bridgett and Molly Wallace, Nancy Brown (wife of Charles Brown), and Sarah Smith (wife of Allen Smith). Exec'rs, wife Esther Wallace and son-in-law Allen Smith. Wits., Maryann Williams, Robert Laws, Thomas Laws. Prob. Jan. 4, 1787. Arch. vol. A104, pages 46-47. Reg. of Wills, Liber D, folio 127. [Note:—Arch. vol. A104, page 47 shows the estate was settled March 3, 1786 by Allen Smith].

**Flowers, Charles McKeil.** Will. Made Sept. 14, 1786. Heirs: wife Priscilla Flowers; sons Lambert, Charles, John and Revel Flowers; daus. Rhoda and Nelly Flowers. Exec'rs, wife Priscilla Flowers and friend Jesse Cannon. Wits., Henry Flowers, Stoughton Tull, John Tull. Prob. Jan. 5, 1787. Arch. vol. A71, pages 208-209. Reg. of Wills, Liber D, folio 129.

**Hudson, Hezekiah.** Yeoman. Baltimore Hd. Will. Made Jan. 18, 1786. Heirs: wife Mary Hudson; sons John Aydelott, Benjamin and David Hudson; daus. Nancy and Sarah Hudson, Mary Campbell. Exec'rx, wife Mary Hudson. Wits., Obediah McCabe, Selby Hickman, Benjamin Long, John Walker. Prob. Jan. 8, 1787. Arch. vol. A79, page 2. Reg. of Wills, Liber D, folios 129-130.

**Cullen, George.** Will. Made Dec. 25, 1786. Heirs: wife Sarah; sons Charles, Jonathan and John Cullen; daus. Sarah and Percey [Piercy] Cullen. Exec'rs, wife Sarah and son John Cullen. Wits., John Wheeler, Sylvester Webb, Noah Wheeler. Prob. Jan. 20, 1787. Arch. vol. A67, pages 206-208. Reg. of Wills, Liber D, folio 131. [Note:—Arch. vol. A67, page 208 shows an account was exhibited on the estate by John Cullen, surviving exec'r, Sept. 9, 1789].

**Lewis, John.** Lewes. Will. Made March 24, 1786. Heirs: sons Noble and William Lewis. Exec'rs, sons Noble and William Lewis. Wits., Peter F. Wright, William Harrison. Prob. Jan. 22, 1787. Arch. vol. A84, pages 58-59. Reg. of Wills, Liber D, folios 131-132.

**Gray, James.** Admin. of, to George Hill and wife Polly, late Polly Gray. Granted [c. Feb. 1, 1787]. Arch. vol. A73, page 7.

**Miller, John.** Admin. of, to Baptist Lay, in right of Rachel Miller. Granted [c. Feb. 7, 1787]. Arch. vol. A88, page 192.

**Griffith, Joram.** Will. Made April 25, 1785. Heirs: wife Pearcy Griffith; sons Joram, Bartlet, Luke and Benjamin Griffith; daus. Jemima, Ann and Elizabeth Griffith. Exec'rs, wife Pearcy Griffith and son Joram Griffith. Wits., Joseph Truitt, Elizabeth Truitt, Jehu Clifton. Prob. Feb. 13, 1787. Arch. vol. A73, page 124. Reg. of Wills, Liber D, folio 132.

**Fisher, Jabez.** Will. Made Nov. 16, 1783. Heirs: sons Thomas, Joshua and John Fisher; daus. Esther, Elizabeth and Ann Fisher. Exec'r, son Thomas Fisher. Wits., Peter Fretwell Wright, John Wolf. Prob. Feb. 28, 1787. Arch. vol. A71, pages 123-125. Reg. of Wills, Liber D, folios 102-103.

**Craig[e], Esther.** Spinster. Will (copy). Made April 20, 1784. Heirs: bros. John, Edward and Robert Craige; sisters Elizabeth Prettyman, Mary Walton and Ruth Walker; William Craige (son of John). Exec'r, bro.-in-law George Walton. Wits., David Shankland, John Harmonson, Catherine Gordon. Prob. March 8, 1787. Arch. vol. A67, pages 135-136. Reg. of Wills, Liber D, folios 133-134.

**Davis, Nehemiah.** Will. Made Jan. 17, 1787. Heirs: wife Rachel Davis; son Mark Tilney Davis; daus. Elizabeth and Ann Davis. Exec'r, father Mark Davis. Wits., William Hinds, Manlove Davis, Nehemiah Davis, Jr. Prob. March 8, 1787. Arch. vol. A68, pages 110-112. Reg. of Wills, Liber D, folio 133. [Note:—Arch. vol. A68, page 110 mentions father Mark Davis, guardian for minor children; pages 111-112 shows the estate was settled by Mark Davis].

**Long, John.** Yeoman. Admin. of, to Mary Long. Granted [c. March 8, 1787]. Arch. vol. A85, page 128.

**Ozbun, Mary.** Admin. of, to Nimrod Maxwell. Granted [c. March 8, 1787]. Arch. vol. A92, page 31.

**Newbold, Francis, Jr.** Yeoman. Admin. of, to Sarah Stafford, late Sarah Newbold. Arch. vol. A91, page 64.

**Warrington, Sarah.** Admin. of, to John Rowland. Granted [c. March 9, 1787]. Arch. vol. A105, page 164.

**Truitt, James, Sr.** Planter. Will. Made Jan. 12, 1787. Heirs: wife unnamed; sons Thomas, John, Josiah and James Truitt; daus. Priscilla Truitt, Mary Matthews and Esther Short. Exec'rx, unnamed wife. Wits., Tho[ma]s Conner, Phillip Wingate, Stephen Pusey. Prob. March 30, 1787. Arch. vol. A102, page 125. Reg. of Wills, Liber D, folio 136. [Note:— Arch. vol. A102, page 125 shows the estate was settled March 1, 1790 by Priscilla Truitt [unnamed wife], as exec'rx].

**Gum, Jacob.** Will. Made April 7, 1787. Heirs: sons William Cottman, Roger, Abraham and John Gum; daus. Hannah Gum and Rachel Conwell. Exec'r, son William Cottman Gum. Wits., David C. Conwell, Alice Conwell, George Claypoole. [No prob.]. Arch. vol. A73, pages 162-164.

**Coulbourn, Stephen.** Planter. Will. Made Aug. 3, 1784. Heirs: wife Priscilla Coulbourn; son Josiah Coulbourn; dau. Peggy Coulbourn. Exec'rx, wife Priscilla Coulbourn. Wits., Robert Clarkson, John Handy, Ann Hensey. Prob. April 16, 1787. Arch. vol. A65, pages 107-108. Reg. of Wills, Liber D, folios 136-137. [Note:—Arch. vol. A65, page 107 mentions dec'd father, Solomon; page 108 shows the estate was settled by John Handy, adm'r D. B. N., C. T. A., June 20, 1792].

**Groves, Thomas.** Will. Made April 4, 1787. Heirs: nephew William Walton; nieces, Mary Dean (wife of John W.), and Sarah Conwell (wife of Abraham). Exec'r, nephew William Walton. Wits., Sarah Longcomb, William Hazzard, Amelia Hazzard. Prob. April 17, 1787. Arch. vol. A73, pages 159-160. Reg. of Wills, Liber D, folios 137-138. [Note:—Arch. vol. A73, page 159 mentions Susanna Conwell, dec'd, aunt of Mary Dean and Sarah Conwell].

**Townsend, Luke.** Will. Made March 17, 1787. Heirs: wife Rachel Townsend; sons Job, Jeremiah, John, William, Stephen and Charles Townsend; dau. Nancy Townsend. Exec'rs, wife Rachel Townsend and bro. Jacob Townsend. Wits., John Lofland, Bennett Warren, Wrixam Warren. Prob. May 5, 1787. Arch. vol. A102, pages 68-69. Reg. of Wills, Liber D, folios 138-139.

**Adams, Abraham.** Will. Made Dec. 11, 1782. Heirs: wife Sarah Adams; son Isaac Adams; dau. Leah Willen; grandson Isaac Adams Willen. Exec'r, son Isaac Adams. Wits., Robert McCalley, Eli McCalley, John Day. Prob. May 8, 1787. Arch. vol. A57, pages 32-33. Reg. of Wills, Liber D, folios 139-140.

**Bounds, Jesse** (Minor son of Jacob). Admin. of, to Edmund Blades. An account passed in court May 9, 1787. Arch. vol. A60, page 31. [Note:—Arch. vol. A60, page 31 mentions John and Jenny Bounds].

**Massey, Levin.** Will. Made April 18, 1787. Heirs: wife Sophia Massey; son Whittington Massey; dau. Milley Massey. Exec'rx, wife Sophia Massey. Wits., Jehu Evans, Betsey Evans, Moses McDaniel. Prob. May 9, 1787. Arch. vol. A87, page 62. Reg. of Wills, Liber D, folio 140.

**Owens, William.** Admin. of, to Solomon Layton. Adm'rs bond dated May 9, 1787. Arch. vol. A92, page 24.

**Lewis, John** (the younger). Admin. of, to Peter Fretwell Wright. Granted May 10, 1787. Arch. vol. A84, page 60.

**Clifton, Benjamin.** Will. Made March 30, 1787. Heirs: wife Mary Clifton; sons Thomas and Benjamin Clifton; daus. Nancy Brittel and Mary Fields. Exec'rx, wife Mary Clifton. Wits., James Hickman, George Hurt, Elijah Griffin. Prob. May 18, 1787. Arch. vol. A65, page 7. Reg. of Wills, Liber D, folios 134-135.

**Robinson, Ananias.** Will. Made May 24, 1787. Heirs: mother-in-law Mary Roberson; Solomon Perkins; James Dough Perkins (son of Solomon); William, Luke and Leah Tingle (children of Israel); aunt Pretheny Tingle; Rhoda Tingle; Nancy Tingle; Leah Walter; Elizabeth Tubbs; heirs of William and Michael Robinson (sons of uncle William Robinson). Exec'r, William Tingle. Wits., Ezekiel Williams, William Ellis, Thomas Gray. Prob. May 29, 1787. Arch. vol. A96, page 107. Reg. of Wills, Liber D, folios 141-142.

**White, Catherine.** Widow of Wrixam White. Will. Made July 24, 1786. Heirs: sons Eli, James, Paul and William White; dau. Nancy White. Exec'rs, son Paul White and friend John Burton. Wits., Noble Lewis, Levi Roach, Ephraim Gordon, N. Waples. Prob. May 31, 1787. Arch. vol. A107, pages 51-52. Reg. of Wills, Liber D, folios 143-144.

**Dickerson, Somerset.** Broadkiln Hd. Will. Made July 13, 1777. Heirs: wife Sarah Dickerson; bros. Edmond and Peter Dickerson; sisters Elizabeth Coston, Director Harris and Scarbor[ough] Smuling; niece Elizabeth Smuling. [No exec'r]. Wits., Bethiah Neill, Margaret Neill, Mary Neill. Prob. June 1, 1787. Arch. vol. A69, page 73. Reg. of Wills, Liber D, folios 144-145. [Note:—Arch. vol. A69, page 73 shows the estate was settled by Sarah Dickerson Sept. 2, 1788].

**Derrickson, Benjamin.** Admin. of, to Thomas Hazzard and wife Leah, late Leah Derrickson. Granted June 6, 1787. Arch. vol. A69, page 23.

**Mifflin, Benjamin.** Will. Made . . ., 1784. Heirs: wife Sarah Mifflin; son Benjamin Mifflin; daus. Hannah McCaskey (wife of Alexander), Elizabeth Draper (wife of Isaac), Susannah Caldwell (wife of Train) and Esther Irwin (wife of Matthew of Phila.); son-in-law Capt. John Ashmead. Exec'rx, wife Sarah Mifflin. Wits., John Clowes, Esq., John Wilson Dean. Prob. June 7, 1787. Arch. vol. A88, page 157. Reg. of Wills, Liber D, folio 145.

**Spencer, Jesse.** Admin. of, to Avery Draper, D. B. N. Granted [c. June 8, 1787]. Arch. vol. A100, page 55. [Note:—Arch. vol. A100, page 55 mentions Catharine and John Spencer].

**Warrington, Alexander.** Yeoman. Admin. of, to Jacob Stockley. Granted [c. June 8, 1787]. Arch. vol. A105, page 140.

**Collins, John.** Yeoman. Cedar Creek Hd. Will. Made June 1, 1787. Heirs: wife Mary Collins; son John Collins; daus. Eliza and Edith Collins. Exec'rx, wife Mary Collins. Wits., Nehemiah Cary, Benjamin Hudson, Richard Mills. Prob. June 16, 1787. Arch. vol. A65, pages 185-186. Reg. of Wills, Liber D, folios 145-147.

**Rowland, Alice.** Will. Made June 24, 1787. Heirs: dau. Elizabeth Rowland; son John Rowland; bro. Peter Parker; sisters Patience and Neomy Parker. Exec'r, friend John Rowland. Wits., Hap Hazzard, Corn[e]l[ius] Wiltbank, Reece Ricords. Prob. June 27, 1787. Arch. vol. A97, pages 104-105. Reg. of Wills, Liber D, folios 147-148.

**Goslee, William.** Will. Made Feb. 9, 1786. Heirs: wife Sarah Goslee; sons William and Job Goslee; daus. Elizabeth, Sarah and Hannah Goslee, Anna Collins. Exec'rs, wife Sarah Goslee and Simon Kollock. Wits., Joshua Sharp, Andrew Thompson, Simon Kollock. Prob. July 5, 1787. Arch. vol. A72, page 223. Reg. of Wills, Liber D, folios 148-149.

**Collins, John.** Will. Made April 22, 1787. Heirs: son Joseph Scroggin Collins; daus. Polly, Jenny and Margaret Collins; Samuel Scroggin; George Scroggin (son of Samuel); Sarah Anderson; Isaac Horsey; Shiles Moore; George Bacon. Exec'rs, [George Purvis and Thomas Scroggin]. Wits., Thomas Scroggin, George Purvis, Jude Oneill. Prob. July 7, 1787. Arch. vol. A65, page 187. Reg. of Wills, Liber D, folio 149.

**Neill, Bethia.** Will. Made June 4, 1787. Heirs: sons Robert and John Neill; daus. Bethia Neill, Mary Neill (wife of Taylor Neill), Elizabeth Coulter (wife of James Coulter), Margaret Polk (wife of Joseph Polk); granddau. Bethia Polk; bro. James Starr. Exec'rs, son Robert Neill and bro. James Starr. Wits., William Peery, Somerset Costen, Euphama Costen. Prob. July 11, 1787. Arch. vol. A91, pages 55-56. Reg. of Wills, Liber D, folios 150-151.

**Johnson, Bartholemew, Sr.** Farmer. Will. Made Oct. 14, 1786. Heirs: wife Sarah Johnson; sons John, Jacob, Benjamin, Jonathan and Bartholemew Johnson; dau. Lydia Spicer; Comfort Connaway; Betty Adams. Exec'r, son Bartholemew Johnson. Wits., Levin Connaway, Sr., Spencer Benson. Prob. July 19, 1787. Arch. vol. A81, page 16. Reg. of Wills, Liber D, folios 151-152.

**Ponder, John.** Yeoman. Broadkiln Hd. Will. Made Aug. 15, 1786. Heirs: wife Elisabeth Ponder; son James Ponder; daus. Kezia Allee, Levina Dogman, Alice Hand, Elisabeth Hand and Sarah Mitten; granddau. Alice Mitten. Exec'r, son James Ponder. Wits., John W. Dean, Rhoda Mason, Sarah Mason. Prob. July 20, 1787. Arch. vol. A93, page 181. Reg. of Wills, Liber D, folios 152-153.

**Cardiff, Christopher.** Yeoman. Will. Made June 24, 1787. Heirs: wife Margaret Cardiff; son Christopher Cardiff; daus. Betsey, Rachel, Sally, Nancy and Rebecca Cardiff. Exec'rx, wife Margaret Cardiff. Wits., Jeremiah Cannon, Peter Hubbert, Isaac Wingate. Prob. Aug. 7, 1787. Arch. vol. A63, pages 157-158. Reg. of Wills, Liber D, folio 154.

**Dean, Charles.** Admin. of, to Isaac Reed and wife Ibe, late Ibe Dean. Granted Aug. 7, 1787. Arch. vol. A68, page 212.

**King, Henry.** Planter. Will. Made Feb. 16, 1779. Heirs: wife Elizabeth King; sons Henry and Edward King; daus. Elizabeth and Mary King. Exec'rs, wife Elizabeth King and son Henry King. Wits., John Flower, Charles Dean, Ebe Dean. Prob. Aug. 7, 1787. Arch. vol. A82, pages 100-101. Reg. of Wills, Liber D, folio 153.

**Williams, John.** Planter. Will. Made Feb. 14, 1781. Heirs: son Samuel Williams. Exec'r, son Samuel Williams. Wits., James Hall, Peter Hall, Ezekiah Morris. Prob. Aug. 8, 1787. Arch. vol. A107, page 191. Reg. of Wills, Liber D, folios 154-155.

**Milby, Levin.** County of Camden, North Carolina. Will (copy). Made April 29, 1787. Heirs: wife Nanney Milby; sons Nathaniel, Levin, Zadock, Arthur, Joseph Hazard and John Milby; daus. Elizabeth, Nanney, Archady Milby, and Sarah Robertson. Exec'rs, bro. John Milby, wife Nanney Milby, son-in-law Benjamin Robertson. Wits., Leonard McIlwain, John Grandy, Mallachi Murden. Prob. Sept. . . ., 1787. Arch. vol. A88, pages 165-171. Reg. of Wills, Liber D, folio 155. [Note:—Arch. vol. A88, page 171 shows the estate was settled by Sarah Robertson and Arthur Milby, exec'rs of Nanney Milby and Benjamin Robertson].

**Martin, Josias, Jr.** Admin. of, to Mary Martin. Granted [c. Sept. 4, 1787]. Arch. vol. A86, page 168.

**Wingate, Rebecca.** Admin. of, to Smith Wingate. Granted [c. Sept. 4, 1787]. Arch. vol. A109, page 5.

**Cordrey, Jacob.** Admin. of, to Job Gozle and wife Edy. Granted [c. Sept. 5, 1787]. Arch. vol. A66, page 202.

**Draper, John.** Admin. of, to John Walton and Elizabeth, his wife, late Elizabeth Draper. Granted Sept. 5, 1787. Arch. vol. A69, pages 197-198. [Note:—Arch. vol. A69, page 198 shows that Elizabeth Walton later married John Robinson].

**Tatman, Mitchell.** Yeoman. Admin. of, to Mary Tatman. Granted [Sept. 5, 1787]. Arch. vol. A101, page 107.

**Riccords, Jehu.** Admin. of, to William Riccords. Granted [c. Sept. 5, 1787]. Arch. vol. A95, page 171.

**Manlove, George.** Admin. of, to Charles Cary and wife Sally, late Sally Manlove. Granted [c. Sept. 6, 1787]. Arch. vol. A86, page 33.

**Ralph, William.** Admin. of, to Mary Ralph. Granted Sept. 6, 1787. Arch. vol. A94, page 184.

**Callaway, Elisabeth.** Will. Made Sept. 9, 1787. Heirs: Betsey Joiles; William Joiles (bro. of Betsey); and children of William Joiles. Exec'r, schoolmaster John Evans. Wits., John Hazzard, Mary Hazzard, Sarah West. Prob. Oct. 18, 1787. Arch. vol. A62, pages 142-143. Reg. of Wills, Liber D, folio 156.

**Bryan, Bennett.** Cedar Creek Hd. Will. Made Oct. 28, 1787. Heirs: wife Rachel Bryan; sons James, Shepherd and Jonathan Bryan; daus. Charity, Mary, Rachel, Sarah, Rebeckah and Elizabeth Bryan, and Comfort Cordery. Exec'r, son Shepherd Bryan. Wits., John Jester, Daniel Sturgis, William Poynter. Prob. Nov. 5, 1787. Arch. vol. A60, pages 243-246. Reg. of Wills, Liber D, folios 156-157.

**Coverdall, John.** Will. Made Nov. 5, 1787. Heirs: wife [Jennifer] Coverdall; sons Samuel, William, Isaac, Richard and John Coverdall; daus. Susanna, Phebe and Hessie Coverdall; grandson Levi Coverdall. Exec'rs, sons Samuel and William Coverdall. Wits., Rebeckah Douce, Aaron Bloxam, John Lofland. Prob. Nov. 22, 1787. Arch. vol. A67, page 81. Reg. of Wills, Liber D, folios 158-159.

**Horsey, Nathaniel.** Will. Made Oct. 5, 1787. Heirs: wife Sally Horsey; sons Holsey, Nathaniel, Tomson and Revel Horsey; daus. Nancy and Sally Horsey, Sally Tull, Mary Smith; granddau. Betsy Coulbourn. Exec'rs, Levin Tull and John Neale. Wits., John Tennent, Riley Baker, William Baker. Prob. Nov. 26, 1787. Arch. vol. A78, pages 42-45. Reg. of Wills, Liber D, folios 159-160.

**Laws, William.** Will. Made Feb. 24, 1786. Heirs: wife Vilater Laws; son William Laws; daus. Polly Laws, Vilater Fisher, [Henrietta] Sourden and Sarah Anderson; grandsons Abel Killing and William Fisher; granddau. Polly Killing; son-in-law John Fisher; Society of the Church of England. Exec'r, son William Laws. Wits., David Owens, William Carlisle, Jr., John Laws, Jr., Elijah Layton. Prob. Nov. 26, 1787. Arch. vol. A83, pages 154-155. Reg. of Wills, Liber D, folios 161-162.

**Derickson, Sarah.** Widow. Admin. of, to Robert Minors. Granted [c. Dec. 4, 1787]. Arch. vol. A69, page 45. [Note:— Arch. vol. A69, page 45 mentions Betsy Wingate and Sally Minors].

**Craig, Robert.** Admin. of, to George Walton. Granted [c. 1788]. Arch. vol. A67, page 157.

**Hatfield, Elijah.** Admin. of, to Delilah Hatfield. Granted [c. Jan. 9, 1788]. Arch. vol. A74, page 232.

**Mitchell, John.** Will. Made Dec. 20, 1787. Heirs: son Tubman Mitchell; bro. William Mitchell; Anne Windsor; Polly Furbush; Sally Furbush. Exec'rs, John Mitchell, Jr., Cyrus Mitchell, James Brattan. Wits., John Marsh, James Pollock, Alex[ande]r Smith. Prob. Jan. 9, 1788. Arch. vol. A89, pages 47-50. Reg. of Wills, Liber D, folio 163. [Note:—Arch. vol. A89, page 50 shows the estate was settled June 22, 1792 by Cyrus Mitchell and James Brattan, surviving exec'rs].

**Townsend, Jesse.** Will. Made Sept. 21, 1786. Heirs: wife Sarah Townsend; sons William, Jesse and Levin Townsend; dau. Sarah Townsend. Exec'rs, wife Sarah Townsend and son William Townsend. Wits., Burton Prettyman, William Prettyman, Mary Jones. Prob. Jan. 31, 1788. Arch. vol. A102, page 59. Reg. of Wills, Liber D, folio 166.

**Clendaniel, Luke.** Will. Made Jan. 7, 1788. Heirs: wife Judea Clendaniel; sons William, Jeremiah and Luke Clendaniel; daus. Jemima and Elizabeth Clendaniel, and Mary Veach (wife of Purnal); child unnamed; granddau. Sarah Veach. Exec'rs, wife Judea and son William Clendaniel. Wits., John Morris, Ahab Clendaniel, George Messick. Prob. Feb. 5, 1788. Arch. vol. A64, pages 246-248. Reg. of Wills, Liber D, folios 166-168. [Note:—Arch. vol. A64, page 248 mentions Rachel Clendaniel, born after the death of her father; also shows Judith Clendaniel settled the estate, D. B. N., C. T. A., c. 1790].

**Steele, Prisgrave.** Admin. of, to Elizabeth Steele. Admr's bond dated Feb. 13, 1788. Arch. vol. A100, page 144.

**Wheeler, John.** Yeoman. Cedar Creek Neck. Will. Made Oct. 18, 1787. Heirs: mother Miriam Wheeler; sisters Rachel and Miriam Wheeler; nephew John Latcham (son of George). Exec'rx, mother Miriam Wheeler. Wits., Isaac Beauchamp, Jesse Smith, Noah Wheeler. Prob. Feb. 26, 1788. Arch. vol. A107, pages 39-40. Reg. of Wills, Liber D, folios 169-170.

**Houston, Robert.** Farmer. Will. Made Jan. 23, 1788. Heirs: wife Priscilla Houston; sons James, Clement, John, Robert, Joseph, Liston and Purnel Houston; daus. Nancy and Priscilla Houston, Mary Hazzard, Sally Collins and Liza Cary; granddaus. Priscilla Cary and Priscilla Collins. Exec'rx, wife Priscilla Houston. Wits., John G. Jones, Castill Truitt, Benjamin Riley. Prob. Feb. 25, 1788. Arch. vol. A78, pages 116-117. Reg. of Wills, Liber D, folios 168-169.

**Fisher, William.** Admin. of, to William Roach and wife Patience, late Patience Fisher. Granted [c. March 5, 1788]. Arch. vol. A71, pages 160-162. [Note:—Arch. vol. A71, page 160 mentions Derickson, Sally, Penelope and Hessie Fisher; also mentions Patience Roach was the widow of William Roach on March 5, 1788 when she filed an accounting on his estate].

**Starr, Bethia.** Admin. of, to John W. Dean. Granted [c. March 5, 1788]. Arch. vol. A100, page 113.

**Stockley, Elizabeth.** Widow. Admin. of, to Jacob Stockley. Granted [c. March 5, 1788]. Arch. vol. A101, page 2.

**Christopher, Benjamin.** Admin. of, to John Jacobs. Granted [c. March 6, 1788]. Arch. vol. A64, page 154. [Note:—Arch. vol. A64, page 154 mentions children: Michael, Rebecca, Isaac and William Christopher; also mentions Elizabeth Christopher].

**Long, Elisha.** Will. Made Aug. 15, 1787. Heirs: wife Mary Long; sons Daniel, Horatio and Elijah Long; daus. Rebecca Morgan, Lear Spear and Sarah Johnson; grandchildren Sally Long and Daniel Long Johnson (children of dau. Sarah), Elisha Long (son of Daniel), Polly Long, Sally, Nancy Wilson and Hetty Spear (daus. of dau. Lear Spear). Exec'rx, wife Mary Long. Wits., Rob[er]t W. McCalley, Stouten Smith, Jane Smith. Prob. March 6, 1788. Arch. vol. A85, page 110. Reg. of Wills, Liber D, folios 170-171.

**Draper, Samuel.** Admin. of, to Mark Davis, D. B. N., in right of Nehemiah Davis. Granted [c. March 7, 1788]. Arch. vol. A69, page 220-221.

**Irons, Jacob.** Admin. of, to Rachel Irons. Granted [c. March 7, 1788]. Arch. vol. A79, pages 195-196.

**Steel, Nathaniel.** Admin. of, to Sarah Steel. Granted March 20, 1788. Arch. vol. A100, page 143.

**Stayton, Nehemiah.** Will. Made Aug. 25, 1786. Heir: wife Sarah Stayton. Exec'rx, wife Sarah Stayton. Wits., Joshua Polk, John Polk, John Marsh. Prob. March 22, 1788. Arch. vol. A100, page 131. Reg. of Wills, Liber D, folio 172.

**Burton, John (son of John G. Burton).** Will. Made Jan. 6, 1788. Heirs: bro. Isaiah Burton; sister Leah Parker. Exec'r, bro. Isaiah Burton. Wits., William Burton, Sr., Benjamin Burton, Joshua Burton. Prob. March 28, 1788. Arch. vol. A61, pages 181-182. Reg. of Wills, Liber D, folios 172-173.

**Wharton, George.** Admin. of, to Burton Wharton. Granted April . . ., 1788. Arch. vol. A107, page 16.

**Jones, Isaac.** Planter. Will (copy). Made Dec. 11, 1784. Heirs: wife Elizabeth Jones; sons James and West Jones; daus. Anna, Phillis, Polly and Tempy Jones; Jonathan King (son of William). Exec'rs, wife Elizabeth Jones and son James

Jones. Wit., John Williams, John Hosea, John Carey. Prob.
April 11, 1788. Arch. vol. A81, pages 147-148. Reg. of
Wills, Liber A, folios 178-179.

**Messick, Obediah.** Admin. of, to Sarah Messick. Admr's bond
dated April 16, 1788. Arch. vol. A88, page 128.

**Walker, John.** Will. Made April 14, 1788. Heirs: mother un-
named; sister Catharine Fleming; nephew and nieces Mar-
garet Barr, John Barr, Ann Stewart, Mary Stewart (chil-
dren of sister Catharine Fleming); father-in-law Robert
Jones (son of James Jones); Archibald Fleming; Littleton
Beckett; cousin Ann Gordon (dau. of James Gordon).
Exec'rs, father-in-law Robert Jones and Archibald Fleming.
Wits., Joseph Hall, Thomas Stuart, Hap Hazzard. Prob.
April 22, 1788. Arch. vol. A104, pages 22-23. Reg. of Wills,
Liber D, folios 179-181.

**Rowland, Samuel.** Admin. of, to Alice Rowland, and Jacob Hazzard. Granted [c. May 1, 1788]. Arch. vol. A97, page 117.

**Johnson, Purnal, Sr.** Yeoman. Broadkill Hd. Will. Made Nov.
20, 1778. Heirs: wife Sarah Johnson; sons Burton, David
and Purnal Johnson; daus. Polly and Betsy Johnson, and
Nice Warrington (wife of John); grandson Purnal Warrington (son of John and Nice); children of son Purnal
Johnson. Exec'rs, wife Sarah Johnson and friend David
Train. Wits., Alexander Bruce, William Burton, Isabella
Bruce. Prob. [ante May 7, 1788]. Arch. vol. A81, pages
85-87. Reg. of Wills, Liber D, folios 1-2. [Note:—Arch.
vol. A81, page 86 shows Sarah Johnson, surviving exec'rx,
exhibited an account on the estate May 7, 1788].

**Callaway, William.** Admin. of, to John Evans, D. B. N., in lieu
of Elizabeth Callaway. Granted before May 9, 1788. Arch.
vol. A62, page 177.

**Short, Abraham.** Will. Made April 30, 1788. Heirs: wife Mar-
gate Short; sons Allen, John and James Short; daus. Elizabeth Piper, Hannah Lynch; grandson Jacob Short (son of
James); granddaus. Sally Short (dau. of Allen), Peggy and
Nancy Reynolds (daus. of Elizabeth Piper). Exec'rs, son
Allen Short and son-in-law John Lynch. Wits., John Short,
Betty Short, Robert Griffith. Prob. May 22, 1788. Arch.
vol. A98, pages 150-151. Reg. of Wills, Liber D, folios 182-
183. [Note:—Arch. vol. A98, page 151 shows the estate
was settled March 10, 1791 by John Lynch surviving exec'r].

**Carlisle, William, Sr.** Will. Made Feb. 21, 1788. Heirs: sons William, Zachariah and John Brown Carlisle; daus. Barsheba Roley, Polly Nock, Sine Griffith, and Elizabeth Carlisle; grandsons William Carlisle (son of John Brown Carlisle), and William Roley (son of William Roley). Exec'r, son William Carlisle. Wits., Richard Hays, Joshua Mitten, Nathaniel Randal. Prob. May 24, 1788. Arch. vol. A63, pages 185-186. Reg. of Wills, Liber D, folios 183-185.

**Laws, John, Jr.** Will. Made April 20, 1788. Heirs: wife un-unnamed; sons Alexander and John Laws; other children unnamed. Exec'rx, unnamed wife. Wits., John Fisher, Nobel Cordray, Betty Thorne. Prob. May 24, 1788. Arch. vol. A83, pages 135-137. Reg. of Wills, Liber D, folios 185-186. [Note:—Arch. vol. A83, page 137 shows the estate was settled by Anna Laws].

**Hossman, Stokely.** House Carpenter (now mate of the Schooner *Musquito* and bound for North Carolina). Will (copy). Made Oct. 2, 1776. Heirs: wife Hannah Hossman. Exec'rx, wife Hannah Hossman. Wits., John Ord, John Ord, Jr. Prob. May 27, 1788. Arch. vol. A78, pages 77-78. Reg. of Wills, Liber D, folios 187-188. [Note:—Arch. vol. A78, page 78 mentions heirs, James Henderson and Benjamin Stockley].

**Smith, Jonathan.** Pilot. Will. Made May 23, 1788. Heirs: wife Hester Smith; sister Eunice Smith. Exec'rx, wife Hester Smith. Wits., Elizabeth Saunders, Caleb Rodney, W. Harrison. Prob. May 30, 1788. Arch. vol. A99, page 182. Reg. of Wills, Liber D, folios 186-187. [Note:—Arch. vol. A99, page 182 shows the estate was settled June 2, 1789 by Joseph Dyer and wife Hester, late Hester Smith].

**Johnson, Job.** Yeoman. Admin. of, to Ann Mary Johnson. Granted [c. June 4, 1788]. Arch. vol. A81, page 52. [Note: —Arch. vol. A81, page 52 shows that Ann Mary Johnson later married Jones Riccords; also mentions a son Nathaniel Johnson].

**Kollock, William.** Admin. of, to Leah Kollock. Granted [c. June 5, 1788]. Arch. vol. A83, page 19.

**Porter, Mary.** Widow. Will. Made Sept. 26, 1784. Heirs: sons William and David Porter, Curtis and Morgan Williams; daus. Rebecca, Lucretia and Mary Porter, Nelly and Peggy Williams. Exec'rs, son Morgan Williams and bro.-in-law Morgan Williams. Wits., Joseph Truitt, Elizabeth Truitt,

Jesse Murphey. Prob. June 7, 1788. Arch. vol. A94, page 7. Reg. of Wills, Liber D, folio 188.

**Cannon, John, [Sr.].** Planter. Northwest Fork Hd. Will. Made May 13, 1788. Heirs: sons John, Hudson and Whit[ting]ton Cannon; daus. Nancy, Susannah, Lucretia and Sophia Cannon; grandchildren John, Allen, Prettyman and Betsey Cannon (children of dau. Nancy). Exec'rs, son John Cannon and son-in-law Curtis Smith. Wits., Ezekiel Brown, John Tennent, Noble Tull. Prob. June 10, 1788. Arch. vol. A63, pages 76-78. Reg. of Wills, Liber D, folios 188-191. [Note: —Arch. vol. A63, page 76 mentions son-in-law Elijah Cannon (father of four grandchildren named as heirs); page 77 mentions a legacy paid to George Smith; and page 78 mentions Susanna Smith].

**Bell, John.** Admin. of, to Watson Pepper, D. B. N., in lieu of William Bell, adm'r. Granted June 14, 1788. Arch. vol. A59, page 53.

**Harper, William.** Will. Made Nov. 3, 1786. Heirs: wife Elizabeth Harper; son John Harper; daus. Sarah, Nelly, Rita, Esther, and Rebecca Harper, Rachel West (wife of Edward), Priscilla Stubbs (wife of Henry), and Mary Currey (wife of Thomas). [No exec'r]. Wits., Solomon Causey, John Hubart, Roger Adams. Prob. July 29, 1788. Arch. vol. A74, page 115. Reg. of Wills, Liber D, folios 157-158.

**Coleburn, Priscilla.** Admin. of, to John Handy. Date of inventory Aug. 5, 1788. Arch. vol. A65, page 105. [Note:— Arch. vol. A65, page 105 mentions Stephen Coleburn].

**Edger, James.** Farmer. Broad Creek. Admin. of, to Marg[a]ret Edger. Granted Aug. 7, 1788. Arch. vol. A70, page 38.

**Robinson, Thomas.** Nova Scotia, formerly of Sussex County, Del. Will (copy). Made July 26, 1786. Heirs: sons Thomas and Peter Robinson; dau. Arcada Cannon; bros. Burton and Peter Robinson. Exec'rs, bros. Burton and Peter Robinson and son Thomas Robinson. Wits., Nancy Burton, James Humphreys, William Leonard. Prob. Aug. 9, 1788. Arch. vol. A96, pages 176-177. Reg. of Wills, Liber F, folios 82-86.

**Clarkson, Benniah.** Will. Made Dec. 28, 1787. Heirs: wife Marg-[are]t Clarkson; sons Willis and Thomas Clarkson; four daus. unnamed. Exec'rx, wife Marg[are]t Clarkson. Wits., Leven Cannon, Stephen Cannon, James Outerbridge. Prob. Aug. 14, 1788. Arch. vol. A64, pages 209-210. Reg. of Wills, Liber D, folios 176-177.

**Burton, Robert, [Sr.].** Angola Neck Hd. Will (copy). Made July 16, 1779. Heirs: wife Elizabeth Burton; sons John, William, Luke and Robert Burton; daus. Sarah Futcher and Elizabeth Watson. Exec'rs, sons Robert and John Burton. Wits., Peter Robinson, Burton Robinson, Richard Marriner. Prob. Aug. 28, 1788. Arch. vol. A61, pages 244-245. Reg. of Wills, Liber D, folios 191-192.

**Parker, Peter.** Admin. of, to John Wiltbank, Esq., D. B. N. Granted [c. Sept. 1, 1788]. Arch. vol. A92, page 79.

**Cavender, Arthur.** Will. Made Dec. 6, 1786. Heirs: wife Sinah Cavender; son John Cavender; bro. David Cavender. Exec'r, bro. David Cavender. Wits., John Owens, Robert Owens. Prob. Sept. 2, 1788. Arch. vol. A64, pages 118-120. Reg. of Wills, Liber D, folio 193.

**Coulter, John.** Admin. of, to Margaret Coulter. Granted [c. Sept. 2, 1788]. Arch. vol. A67, page 50.

**Driggass, Drake.** Admin. of, to John Wiltbank, Esq. Granted [c. Sept. 2, 1788]. Arch. vol. A69, page 232. [Note:—Arch. vol. A68, page 232 mentions a sister Rhoda Hodgskin].

**Darby, John.** Admin. of, to William Newbold and Mary Darby. Granted [c. Sept. 3, 1788]. Arch. vol. A68, page 22.

**Fountain, Samuel.** Admin. of, to Andrew Fountain, D. B. N. Granted [c. Sept. 3, 1788]. Arch. vol. A71, pages 235-236.

**Fountain, William.** Dorchester Co., Md. Admin. of, to Andrew Fountain, D. B. N., in lieu of Major Fountain. Granted [c. Sept. 3, 1788]. Arch. vol. A71, page 239. [Note:—Arch. vol. A71, page 239 shows that Samuel Fountain married Major Fountain who was adm'rx of William Fountain; also mentions a bro. Nathaniel Fountain].

**Hazzard, William** (the younger). Admin. of, to Hap Hazzard and Jacob Hazzard. Granted [c. Sept. 3, 1788]. Arch. vol. A75, page 138.

**McDaniel, Moses.** Will. Made Aug. 29, 1788. Heirs: wife Sarah McDaniel; sons James and Moses McDaniel; dau. Marg-[ar]et McDaniel; nephew Owen O'Day; dau.-in-law Alice Sheltman; Jonathan Dickason (grandfather of son James). Exec'rx, wife Sarah McDaniel. Wits., Jehu Evans, John Collings, Stephen Smith. Prob. Sept. 6, 1788. Arch. vol. A87, pages 147-149. Reg. of Wills, Liber D, folios 194-195. [Note:—Arch. vol. A87, pages 148-149 shows the estate was settled Nov. 10, 1792 by Dennis Callaghan and wife

Sarah, late Sarah McDaniel; also mentions Abraham Short
and Phillip O'Day].

**Evans, John.** Will (copy). Made Oct. 30, 1786. Heirs: wife
Catherine Evans; sons John, Job, Enoch, Elijah and Eli
Evans; daus. Elizabeth, Mary, Tabitha and Catherine Evans.
Exec'rx, wife Catherine Evans. Wits., William Cord, Bailey
Hickman, Daniel Handcock. Prob. Nov. 4, 1788. Arch. vol.
A70, pages 216-218. Reg. of Wills, Liber D, folios 195-196.
[Note:—Arch. vol. A70, page 217 mentions his father and
mother John and Catherine Evans].

**Polk, John.** Admin. of, to Leven Wales and wife Mary, late Mary
Polk. Granted [c. Nov. 6, 1788]. Arch. vol. A93, pages 127-
128.

**Dickerson, Sarah.** Widow of Somerset Dickerson. Will. Made
Nov. 16, 1788. Heirs: bro. Daniel Roach; [sisters] Mary,
Priscilla, Leah Roach; Sarah Roach (dau. of Daniel Roach);
John Roach (son of Daniel Roach); Edmond Dickerson;
Peter Dickerson (son of Edmond Dickerson). Exec'r, bro.
Daniel Roach. Wits., John W. Dean, James Wiley, Levin D.
Newton. Prob. Nov. 21, 1788. Arch. vol. A69, page 72.
Reg. of Wills, Liber D, folio 199.

**Brotherer, Joseph.** Planter. Will. Made Aug. 26, 1788. Heirs:
wife Eleanor Brotherer; daus. Tabby Ellingsworth and Sarah
Phillips (wife of John); grandsons Joseph, Shepperd and
Spencer Phillips; granddaus. Lavinia and Mary Phillips.
Exec'r, son-in-law John Phillips, Sr. Wits., George Hopkins,
Robert Hopkins, Simon Kollock. Prob. Dec. 2, 1788. Arch.
vol. A60, pages 161-163. Reg. of Wills, Liber D, folios 200-
201. [Note:—Arch. vol. A60, page 162 mentions Richard
and Tabby Ellingsworth; page 163 shows John and Spencer
Phillips exhibited an account on the estate Sept. 7, 1795
in right of John Phillips, dec'd].

**Tull, Noble.** Admin. of, to William Fraim and Elon, his wife,
late Elon Tull. Granted [c. Dec. 2, 1788]. Arch. vol. A102,
page 178.

**McNeill, James.** Admin. of, to Jane McNeill. Granted Dec. 3,
1788. Arch. vol. A88, page 13. [Note:—Arch. vol. A88,
page 13 shows that Jane McNeill later married Robert
Owens].

**May, Draper.** Yeoman. Admin. of, to Andrew Fountain and
wife, Ann, late Ann May. Granted [c. Dec. 4, 1788]. Arch.
vol. A87, pages 91-92.

**Pennington, Benedict.** Admin. of, to Thomas Reynolds, **Jr.** Granted [c. Dec. 5, 1788]. Arch. vol. A92, page 147.

**Pettyjohn, Hannah.** Will. Made Aug. 1, 1788. Heirs: daus. Patience, Sinderiah and Anzelah Pettyjohn; sons John, James and Richard Pettyjohn; grandson Job Pettyjohn; granddau. Leah Pettyjohn. Exec'r, Isaac Wilson. Wits., Isaac Wilson, Nancy Carey, Matthew Parremore. Prob. Dec. 12, 1788. Arch. vol. A93, page 3. Reg. of Wills, Liber D, folios 201-202. [Note:—Arch. vol. A93, page 3 shows Isaac Wilson refused to act as exec'r and Zachariah Read was appointed to settle the estate].

**Lofland, Dorman, Jr.** Will. Made Nov. 29, 1788. Heirs: mother Grace Lofland. Exec'rx, mother Grace Lofland. Wits., Samuel Owens, Sr., William Veach, John Lofland. Prob. Dec. 13, 1788. Arch. vol. A85, pages 17-18. Reg. of Wills, Liber D, folio 202.

**Davis, Mary.** Widow of Samuel Davis. Will. Made Nov. 17, 1788. Heirs: sons Isaac and William Davis; daus. [Nancy] and Elizabeth Davis. Exec'rx, dau. Elizabeth Davis. Wits., Ratcliff Poynter, David Williams, Shadrach Sturgis. Prob. Dec. 20, 1788. Arch. vol. A68, pages 98-99. Reg. of Wills, Liber D, folio 203.

**Vaughan, Jonathan.** Late of Worcester Co., Md. Admin. of, to James Douglass and John Smith, D. B. N. (unadministered by Ann Vaughan). Admr's bond dated Dec. 20, 1788. Arch. vol. A103, page 67.

**Craige, Edward.** Will. Made Jan. 4, 1788. Heirs: wife Sarah Craige; son Harmon Craige; dau. Peggy Craige. Exec'r, friend Rhoads Shankland. Wits., William Prettyman, Stephen Parramore, Polly Jessop. Guardian of son Harmon: Rhoads Shankland. Prob. Dec. 22, 1788. Arch. vol. A67, pages 131-132. Reg. of Wills, Liber D, folios 203-204.

**Barker, Annie [Ann].** Admin. of, to William Houston. Granted [c. 1789]. Arch. vol. A58, pages 174-175.

**Bryan, Jonathan.** Admin. of, to Comfort Bryan. Granted [c. 1789]. Arch. vol. A60, page 249. [Note:—Arch. vol. A60, page 249 mentions Betsy Craig, (minor of John Craig), John, Mary, Sarah, Lydia, David and William Craig].

**Coulter, Esther.** Admin. of, to Joseph Coulter. Granted [c. Jan. 4, 1789]. Arch. vol. A67, page 41.

**Robbins, Josiah.** Admin. of, to William Robbins. Granted [c. Jan. 6, 1789]. Arch. vol. A96, page 101.

**Laws, Alexander.** Will. Made May 25, 1785. Heirs: sons Saxo-
gotha and William Laws; daus. Sarah, Amelia and Mary
Laws; bro. John Laws; cousin Alexander Laws. Exec'rs,
bro. John Laws and John Collins (son of Andrew). Wits.,
Jesse Fowler, David Cavender, Daniel Morgan. Guardians,
bro.-in-law John Collins, bro. John Laws and friends Jesse
Griffith and Mary Griffith. Prob. Jan. 23, 1789. Arch. vol.
A83, pages 116-119. Reg. of Wills, Liber D, folios 254-255.

**Pettyjohn, John.** Admin. of, to Zachariah Read, D. B. N. Admr's
bond dated Jan. 23, 1789. Arch. vol. A93, page 9.

**Potter, Comfort.** Widow of John Potter. Will. Made Jan. 14,
1789. Heirs: son Joseph Houston; dau. Arcada White;
grandsons William, Joseph and Robert Houston; granddau.
Betsy Houston; daus.-in-law Comfort and Magdalen Houston. Exec'rs, son Joseph Houston and son-in-law William
White. Wits., John Burton, Jacob Warrington, Mary Hancock. Prob. Jan. 29, 1789. Arch. vol. A94, page 13. Reg.
of Wills, Liber D, folios 205-206.

**Reed, Mary, Jr.** Admin. of, to Mary Reed. Granted [c. Feb. 3,
1789]. Arch. vol. A95, page 35.

**Webb, John.** Admin. of, to Alice Webb. Granted [c. Feb. 3,
1789]. Arch. vol. A106, page 64. [Note:—Arch. vol. A106,
page 64 mentions heirs Jeremiah and William Webb, minor
children].

**Hudson, Parker.** Will. Made Aug. 14, 1787. Heirs: heirs of sister Winifred Hudson; Nancy and Lydia Hudson (daus. of
sister Winifred) ; cousin Richard Hudson (son of Eliah Hudson). Exec'r, Richard Hudson. Wits., Ezekiel Williams,
Clement Quillen, Sarah Rogers. Prob. Feb. 4, 1789. Arch.
vol. A79, page 42. Reg. of Wills, Liber D, folios 206-207.

**Brookfield, Uriah.** Gentleman. Will. Made Dec. 16, 1788. Heirs:
wife Ann Brookfield; grandsons Uriah and Azariah Brookfield, and Uriah Thomas; granddaus. Nancy, Elizabeth, Rebecca and Mary Thomas, Sarah Jump and Nancy Brookfield. Exec'rs, wife Ann Brookfield and Michael Thomas.
Wits., Simon Kollock, Miller Thoroughgood, Elihu Thoroughgood. Prob. Feb. 12, 1789. Arch. vol. A69, pages 158-
159. Reg. of Wills, Liber D, folios 207-209.

**Bell, Thomas.** Will (nunc.). Made Feb. 8, 1789. Heirs: sons
Thomas and Smith Bell; other children unnamed. [No
exec'r]. Wits., William Moor, Thomas Godwin, James Lecompt. Prob. Feb. 16, 1789. Arch. vol. A59, page 63. Reg.
of Wills, Liber D, folio 209.

**Clifton, Jonathan.** Will. Made March 18, 1788. Heirs: wife Leah Clifton; sons Nathan and Henry Clifton; daus. Sarah and Mary Clifton, Priscilla Thomas and Siney Middleton. Exec'r, son Nathan Clifton. Wits., Curtis Morris, John Griffith, Jr., Charles Griffith. Prob. Feb. 17, 1789. Arch. vol. A65, pages 16-17. Reg. of Wills, Liber D, folios 210-211. [Note:—Arch. vol. A65, page 16 shows that Mary Clifton settled the estate in right of Nathan Clifton, dec'd, c. May 6, 1789].

**Griffith, John.** Will. Made Dec. 14, 1788. Heirs: sons John and Charles Griffith; daus. Betsey and Rachel Griffith, Polly Willey and Barsheba Tatman; granddaus. Ann and Unice Griffith. Exec'r, son John Griffith. Wits., William Stayton, Jehu Stayton, Rachel Hurley. Prob. Feb. 17, 1789. Arch. vol. A73, page 120. Reg. of Wills, Liber D, folios 209-210.

**Hopkins, John.** Will. Made Feb. 25, 1787. Heirs: wife Sophia Hopkins; sons Josiah, David, Samuel, Cornelius, Lemuel, Archibald, John, William and Robert Hopkins; daus. Lydia Hopkins, Janet Hudson (wife of Samuel), Elizabeth Stephenson (wife of David). Exec'rs, sons Archibald and William Hopkins. Wits., William Peery, Mary Peery, Joseph Miller. Prob. March 3, 1789. Arch. vol. A77, pages 190-191. Reg. of Wills, Liber D, folio 212.

**Steen, Christopher.** Admin. of, to James Steen. Granted [c. March 3, 1789]. Arch. vol. A100, page 149. [Note:—Arch. vol. A100, page 149 mentions widow Mary Steen].

**Barns, George.** Admin. of, to Miriam Wheeler in lieu of John Wheeler, dec'd. Granted [c. March 4, 1789]. Arch. vol. A58, page 202.

**Cannon, James, Sr.** Yeoman. Will. Made Dec. 29, 1788. Heirs: wife Mary Cannon; son Jacob Cannon; daus. Nancy and Rebeckah Cannon, Sarah Messick and Mary Elliott. Exec'r, son Jacob Cannon. Wits., Constantine Jacobs, Jeremiah Cannon, Levi Cannon. Prob. March [7], 1789. Arch. vol. A63, pages 54-56. Reg. of Wills, Liber D, folios 214-215. [Note:—Arch. vol. A63, page 54 mentions bro. Jeremiah Cannon].

**Buchanan, James.** Merchant. Will. Made Feb. 22, 1789. Heirs: wife Sarah Buchanan; sons James and Thomas Buchanan; dau. Betsey Buchanan. Exec'rs, wife Sarah Buchanan and John Tennent. Wits., John Marsh, James Pollock, John Tennent. Prob. March 9, 1789. Arch. vol. A61, pages 13-16. Reg. of Wills, Liber D, folios 215-216. [Note:—Arch.

vol. A61, page 16 shows that Sarah Buchanan later married Jesse Green].

**Flower, Thomas.** Will. Made Nov. 18, 1788. Heirs: wife Clarret Flower; son Daniel Flower; dau. Elizabeth Flower. Exec'r, Daniel [Shehan], Jr. Wits., John Turpin, Daniel [Shehan], William Fletcher. Prob. March 9, 1789. Arch. vol. A71, pages 216-218. Reg. of Wills, Liber D, folios 213-214.

**Polk, Mary.** Widow. Will (nunc.). Made Feb. 19, 1789. Heirs: sons Jonathan Woodgate and Clement Polk; daus. Polly and Margaret Polk, other daus. unnamed. [No exec'r]. Wits., Margaret N. Polk, Elenor [Julian]. Prob. March 9, 1789. Arch. vol. A93, page 142. Reg. of Wills, Liber E, folio 45. [Note:—Arch. vol. A93, page 142 shows the estate was settled by Margaret Nutter Polk on Sept. 6, 1796].

**Craig[e], Sarah.** Widow. Will (copy). Made March 7, 1789. Heirs: dau. Margaret Craig; David Orr (son of cousin John Orr); Ann Roach (dau. of Levi Roach); Margaret Lewis (dau. of Noble Lewis); and Nathaniel Fisher Hall (son of Dr. Joseph Hall). Exec'r, friend Dr. Joseph Hall. Wits., John Orr, Elizabeth Jacobs, John Lewis. Prob. March 13, 1789. Arch. vol. A67, page 158. Reg. of Wills, Liber D, folio 217.

**Grice, Thomas.** Will. Made Sept. 24, 1784. Heirs: wife Easter Grice; sons William and Thomas Grice; daus. Polly Grice, Ann Collings (wife of John), Elizabeth Hudson (wife of Anderson), Sarah Andres (wife of Southey), Amy Cappell (wife of William) and Abigail Bell (wife of Robert). Exec'r, son William Grice. Wits., Robert Prettyman, Sarah Prettyman, Elizabeth Prettyman. Prob. March 18, 1789. Arch. vol. A73, page 88. Reg. of Wills, Liber D, folios 217-219.

**Bryan, Jonathan.** Will. Made Feb. 7, 1789. Heir: dau. Ann Bryan. [No exec'r]. Wits., Milby Simpler, William Matthews. Prob. March 23, 1789. Arch. vol. A60, page 248. Reg. of Wills, Liber D, folio 219.

**Young, Robert.** Prime Hook Neck, Cedar Creek Hd. Will (copy). Made Feb. 24, 1786. Heirs: wife Rhoda Young; daus. Sarah and Christian Young. Exec'rx, wife Rhoda Young. Wits., Nath[anie]l Young, J. A. Rench, Mary Clark. Prob. March 27, 1789. Arch. vol. A109, page 141. Reg. of Wills, Liber D, folios 135-136. [Note:—Arch. vol. A109, page 141 shows the estate was settled Oct. 10, 1798 by John Smith and Rhoda, his wife, late Rhoda Young].

**Davis, Nehemiah, Sr.** Will. Made Jan. 30, 1788. Heirs: wife Susannah Davis; sons Nehemiah, Mark and William Davis; dau. Elizabeth Draper; grandson Nehemiah (son of Nehemiah Davis); heirs of Eunice Draper (wife of Samuel Draper, dec'd); heirs of Sarah Draper (wife of Henry Draper, dec'd); heirs of Elizabeth Draper (widow of Joseph Draper, dec'd). Exec'r, William Davis. Wits., Thomas Davis, Rachel Atkinson Davis, Elias Townsend. Prob. April 13, 1789. Arch. vol. A68, pages 119-121. Reg. of Wills, Liber D, folios 220-222.

**Hickman, Joshua.** Admin. of, to Luke Hayes and wife Sinar, late Sinar Hickman. Admr's bond dated April 13, 1789. Arch. vol. A76, page 75.

**Spence, John.** Will. Made March 18, 1789. Heirs: wife Nancy Spence; sons Enoch and Nathan Spence; daus. Peggy, Lavina and Tamsey Spence. Exec'rx, wife Nancy Spence. Wits., Olive Jump, Jesse Jester, William Hollis. Prob. April 20, 1789. Arch. vol. A100, page 41. Reg. of Wills, Liber D, folios 222-223.

**Hazzard, Rachel.** Will. Made Sept. 2, 1778. Heirs: sons David and Joseph Hazzard; daus. Rhoda, Cada and Hannah Robinson, Rachel Burton, Mary King; granddaus. Elizabeth Stockly, Mary Field. Exec'r, son Joseph Hazzard. Wits., Sally Hall, Betty Mason, William Conwell. Prob. April 6, 1789. Arch. vol. A75, page 116. Reg. of Wills, Liber D, folio 219.

**Watson, John.** Admin. of, to Luke Watson, D. B. N. Granted [c. April 6, 1789]. Arch. vol. A106, page 21.

**Maddox, Lazarus.** Admin. of, to Mary Maddox. Admr's bond dated April 13, 1789. Arch. vol. A86, page 20.

**Carpenter, Sarah.** Admin. of, to Joshua Burton. Granted [c. May . . ., 1789]. Arch. vol. A64, page 9. [Note:—Arch. vol. A64, page 9 mentions Betsy and Hessy Carpenter].

**Robinson, John.** Will. Made March 26, 1789. Heirs: wife Jean Robinson; sons John and Joseph Robinson; daus. Sarah and Phillip Robinson. Exec'rx, wife Jean Robinson. Wits., Joseph Wil[gus], Betsy Gibbons, Jonathan Gibbons. Prob. May 4, 1789. Arch. vol. A96, pages 140-141. Reg. of Wills, Liber D, folios 224-225. [Note:—Arch. vol. A96, page 141 shows the estate was settled by Joseph Wil[gus] and Jane [Jean] his wife, late Jean Robinson on April 25, 1798].

**Turner, James.** Admin. of, to John Walton. Granted [c. May 6, 1789]. Arch. vol. A103, page 17.

**Williams, John.** Planter. Will. Made May 22, 1786. Heirs: wife Sarah Williams; daus. Elizabeth, Mary and Rhoda Williams. [No exec'r]. Wits., William Burcher, Esther Williams, Naomi Robinson. Prob. May 6, 1789. Arch. vol. A107, pages 192-193. Reg. of Wills, Liber D, folio 225. [Note:— Arch. vol. A107, page 193 shows Jesse Williams as adm'r].

**Newbold, Margaret.** Will (nunc.). Made May 4, 1789. Heirs: son William Newbold; daus. Esther Thorogood, Marg[ar]et Ingram, Mary Hood; son-in-law Robert Hood. [No exec'r]. Wits., Thomas Jones, Wingate Jones. Prob. May 7, 1789. Arch. vol. A91, page 69. Reg. of Wills, Liber D, folio 226.

**Polk, John.** Little Creek Hd. Will. Made April 29, 1782. Heirs: wife Sarah Polk; son William Polk; daus. Sarah Bacon, Elizabeth Sirman and Eunice Scroggin; grandsons William, John and Josiah Polk (children of dec'd son John). Exec'r, son William Polk. Wits., James Cooper, Samuel Windsor, William Brown. Prob. May 7, 1788. Arch. vol. A93, page 126. Reg. of Wills, Liber D, folios 181-182.

**Sirman, Louder.** Planter. Will. Made Nov. 14, 1783. Heirs: wife Elizabeth Sirman; sons Louder and Levin Sirman; daus. Nelly, Nancy and Betty Sirman. Exec'rx, wife Elizabeth Sirman. Wits., John Williams, Jr., John Moor, Hugh King. Prob. May 9, 1789. Arch. vol. A99, page 87. Reg. of Wills, Liber D, folio 141. [Note:—Arch. vol. A99, page 87 shows the estate was settled by John Bacon, exec'r of Elizabeth Sirman].

**Turlington, Sarah.** Spinster. Late of Virginia, last of Sussex County. Will (nunc.). Made March 31, 1789. Heirs: two sisters-in-law; Benjamin Warrington. [No exec'r]. Wits., Thomas Marvel, Philip Marvel. Prob. May 22, 1789. Arch. vol. A103, page 9. Reg. of Wills, Liber D, folio 226. [Note: —Arch. vol. A103, page 9 shows the estate was settled by Edmund Pettit and wife Rachel, late Rachel Warrington, and John Colony].

**Short, Phillip.** Will. Made April 24, 1789. Heirs: wife Betty Short; sons Edward, John, Purnal and Phillip Short; daus. Polly, Le[ah], Betsey and Millie Short. Exec'rs, wife Betty Short and son Edward Short. Wits., John Thoroughgood, Zachariah Jones. Prob. May 26, 1789. Arch. vol. A99, page 18. Reg. of Wills, Liber D, folios 227-228.

**Barns, Mary.** Admin. of, to Thomas Blades Wildgoose. Granted [c. June 3, 1789]. Arch. vol. A58, page 206. [Note:—Arch. vol. A58, page 206 mentions Simeon, Mary and Anna Barns].

**McIlvain, Shepherd.** Admin. of, to John Bready and wife Jenny, late Jenny McIlvain. Granted [c. June 4, 1789]. Arch. vol. A88, page 5. [Note:—Arch. vol. A88, page 5 mentions daus. Polly, Hessy and Ellen McIlvain].

**King, Hugh.** Will. Made May 12, 1789. Heirs: wife Elizabeth King; sons James, Isaac and Thomas King; dau. Tabitha King. Exec'r, bro. James King. Wits., Levi King, Samuel Hall, Daniel Melson. Prob. June 5, 1789. Arch. vol. A82, pages 105-106. Reg. of Wills, Liber D, folios 228-229. [Note:—Arch. vol. A82, page 106 shows the estate was settled March 22, 1796 by Joshua James and wife Betty, late Elizabeth King, exec'rx of Hugh King].

**Heavelo, Daniel.** Will. Made May 8, 1789. Heirs: mother Sarah Heavelo; sisters Naomi, Sarah and Ruth Heavelo, Jane Russell; half-bro. William Millard; Mary Millard (wife of William). Exec'rs, mother Sarah Heavelo, half-bro. William Millard. Wits., Samuel R. Fisher, Joshua Harlan, James Mease. Prob. June 6, 1789. Arch. vol. A75, page 215. Reg. of Wills, Liber D, folios 229-230. [Note:—Arch. vol. A75, page 215 shows William Millard settled the estate on Sept. 10, 1790 as the surviving exec'r].

**Simpler, Margaret.** Will (nunc.). Made June 7, 1789. Heirs: William Simpler; Andrew Simpler; heirs of William Simpler. [No exec'r]. Wits., Rebecca Stockley, William Handcock. Prob. June 20, 1789. Arch. vol. A99, page 52. Reg. of Wills, Liber D, folios 230-231.

**Barker, Leatherberry.** Will. Made Jan. 20, 1789. Heirs: wife Sarah Barker; sons Joseph and Bagwell Barker; dau. Nancy Barker. Exec'r, son Bagwell Barker. Wits., N[athaniel] Waples, Elisha Dickerson, Benjamin Burton. Prob. June 30, 1789. Arch. vol. A58, pages 187-190. Reg. of Wills, Liber D, folios 231-232.

**Moore, David, Jr.** Admin. of, to David Moore, Sr. Granted [c. July 28, 1789]. Arch. vol. A89, page 96.

**Connor, Ratcliff.** Admin. of, to Amy Connor. Granted [ante Aug. 4, 1789]. Arch. vol. A66, page 92.

**Brookfield, Azariah.** Admin. of, to Uriah Brookfield. Granted [c. Aug. 7, 1789]. to Thomas Dartor, adm'r D. B. N. in right of Uriah Brookfield, dec'd. Arch. vol. A60, page 155.

**Fowler, Jonathan.** Yeoman. Will. Made July 22, 1787. Heirs: wife Rachel Fowler; sons Jonathan, Levin and John Fowler. Exec'rs, wife Rachel Fowler and son Jonathan Fowler. Wits., Asa Fowler, Purnel Fowler, Unicy Crapper. Prob. Sept. 3, 1789. Arch. vol. A72, pages 16-17. Reg. of Wills, Liber D, folios 233-234. [Note:—Arch. vol. A72, page 17 shows the estate was settled June 9, 1790 by Solomon Layton, bondsman of Rachel Fowler, dec'd].

**Morris, Isaac.** Admin. of, to Bevins Morris. Adm'rs bond dated Sept. 3, 1789. Arch. vol. A90, page 55.

**Basnett, Samuel.** Will (copy). Made May 20, 1789. Heirs: wife Sarah Basnett; son Nehemiah Basnett. Exec'rs, wife Sarah Basnett and son Nehemiah Basnett. Wits., John Snodenhook, Moses B[ayard], Andrew Turk. Prob. Sept. 4, 1789. Arch. vol. A58, pages 231 and 233. Reg. of Wills, Liber D, folios 174-175.

**Callaway, Ebenezer.** Planter. Will. Made Dec. 15, 1788. Heirs: wife Leah Callaway; sons William, Ebenezer and Eli Callaway; dau. Leah Callaway. Exec'r, son Eli Callaway. Wits., John Williams, Elisha Callaway, Jehu Callaway. Prob. Sept. 7, 1789. Arch. vol. A62, pages 131-132. Reg. of Wills, Liber D, folios 234-235.

**Turpin, William.** Admin. of, to William Adams, in right of his wife, late Constant Turpin. Granted [c. Sept. 8, 1789]. Arch. vol. A103, page 37. [Note:—Arch. vol. A103, page 37 mentions heirs Elizabeth, Solomon, James, Charles Turpin and Sarah Wright (wife of Joshua)].

**Jessop, John.** Admin. of, to Eunice Jessop. Granted [c. Sept. 10, 1789]. Arch. vol. A80, page 188. [Note :—Arch. vol. A80, page 188 shows William Jessop, as guardian of Sarah Jessop].

**Nutter, Christopher.** Admin. of, to John Nutter. Granted [c. Sept. 10, 1789]. Arch. vol. A91, pages 126-127.

**McIlvain, Andrew.** Will. Made June 18, 1787. Heirs: wife Comfort McIlvaine; sons Alexander, Leonard, James Mills and Wrixam McIlvain; daus. Mary McIlvain (wife of Benjamin), Ellen Hazzard (wife of David), Bersheba Burton (wife of William) and Sarah White McIlvain; grandsons Andrew McIlvain, Thomas Waples McIlvain; granddau. Comfort

Waples McIlvain (dau. of Alexander); children of son Alexander; and children of son Leonard. Exec'rx, wife Comfort McIlvain. Wits., Joseph Waples, N. Waples, Joseph Vaughn. Prob. Sept. 21, 1789. Arch. vol. A87, pages 171-173. Reg. of Wills, Liber D, folios 235-237. [Note:—Arch. vol. A87, page 173 mentions deceased father James McIlvain and dec'd grandfather Andrew McIlvain].

**Godwin, Thomas.** Admin. of, to Nehemiah Howard and wife Rhoda, late Rhoda Godwin. Granted [c. Oct. 5, 1789]. Arch. vol. A72, page 168.

**West, John.** Will. Made Dec. 5, 1788. Heir: uncle John Stockley. Exec'r, uncle John Stockley. Wits., Nelson Waller, Mary Waller, James Coulter, Ann Stockley. Prob. Oct. 5, 1789. Arch. vol. A106, page 143. Reg. of Wills, Liber D, folios 237-238.

**Melony, Richard.** Admin. of, to Littleton Townsend. Granted [c. Oct. 7, 1789]. Arch. vol. A88, page 29.

**Fenwick, William.** Will. Made Oct. 15, 1789. Heirs: wife Agnes Fenwick; sons Gideon, David, William, Joseph and James Fenwick; daus. Sarah, Agnes and Ruth Fenwick. Exec'rx, wife Agnes Fenwick. Wits., James Dougherty, Baptist Lay, William Coffin. [No prob.]. Arch. vol. A71, page 78.

**Polk, William.** Will. Made Dec. 27, 1787. Heirs: wife unnamed; sons Trusten, William, Robert, Alexander and Clement Polk; daus. Anne, Nancy, Betsey, Polly and Kitty Polk, Sarah Nutter; son-in-law Nathaniel Russum; . . . Hooper. Exec'r, son Trusten Laws Polk. Wits., Daniel Polk, Thomas Laws, William Bowness, Loxley Ricards. Prob. Oct. 17, 1789. Arch. vol. A93, pages 158-161. Reg. of Wills, Liber D, folios 197-199. [Note:—Arch. vol. A93, page 159 mentions Esther Hooper; Mary Polk; Sarah Nutter dau. of Christopher Nutter. Page 161 shows the estate was settled by Robert Polk, D. B. N.].

**Boyce, Joseph, [Sr.].** Will. Made Nov. 3, 1788. Heirs: sons Joseph, Jr., John, William, Jehu and Stockley Boyce; daus. Sally Boyce, Tabitha Elliott and Nancy Swain. Exec'r, son Joseph Boyce, Jr. Wits., Robert Robinson, Jacob Adams, Henry Spear. Prob. Oct. 20, 1789. Arch. vol. A60, pages 55-56. Reg. of Wills, Liber D, folios 238-239. [Note:—Arch. vol. A60, page 56 shows the estate was settled Nov. 23, 1791 by John Boyce, D. B. N., C. T. A., in lieu of Joseph Boyce, Jr., dec'd].

**Kellam [Kellum], Edward.** Merchant. Will (nunc.). Made Oct. 3, 1789. Heirs: sons Samuel and James Kellum; dau. Sarah Solomon (wife of William). [No exec'r]. Wits., Woolsey Burton, Jacob Burton. Prob. Oct. 20, 1789. Arch. vol. A82, page 31. Reg. of Wills, Liber D, folio 239.

**Wharton, Wrixam.** Admin. of, to John Brown and wife Hannah, late Hannah Wharton. Adm'rs bond dated Oct. 21, 1789. Arch. vol. A107, page 38. [Note:—Arch. vol. A107, page 38 mentions Elisha and Wrixam Wharton].

**Rock, Charles.** Admin. of, to Zachariah Carlisle. Granted Nov. 1, 1789. Arch. vol. A97, page 7.

**Fleming, John.** Tailor. Will. Made Oct. 29, 1789. Heirs: son David Fleming. Exec'r, Archibald Hopkins. Wits., James Vent, Archibald Fleming, Elizabeth Fleming. Prob. Nov. 6, 1789. Arch. vol. A71, pages 204-206. Reg. of Wills, Liber D, folios 239-240.

**Hopkins, William.** Admin. of, to Cornelia Hopkins. Admr's bond dated Nov. 6, 1789. Arch. vol. A78, pages 26-27. [Note:—Arch. vol. A78, page 26 mentions minor children James and John].

**Clarkson, William.** Planter. Will. Made March 26, 1786. Heirs: dau. Easter and son Major Clarkson. Exec'r, friend Stephen Cannon. Wits., Robert Cannon, Edward Cannon, Thomas Coulbourn. Prob. Nov. 26, 1789. Arch. vol. A64, pages 223-225. Reg. of Wills, Liber D, folios 160-161.

**Turner, William.** Will. Made Oct. 30, 1789. Heirs: wife Sidney Turner; sons Clement, Bevins and William Turner; daus. Louisa, Lizzy and Amelia Turner, Anna Stayton, Nancy Boyce and Nelly Boyce. Exec'rs, wife Sidney Turner and son Clement Turner. Wits., John Martino, James Lowry, Sarah Huston. Prob. Nov. 26, 1789. Arch. vol. A103, pages 25-26. Reg. of Wills, Liber D, folios 240-241. [Note:— Arch. vol. A103, page 25 shows the estate was settled by Whittington Williams and wife Sidney, late Sidney Bownass (wife of William), late Sidney Turner].

**Polk, James.** Admin. of, to Alexander Smith and wife Lucilla, late Lucilla Polk. Granted [c. Dec. 1, 1789]. Arch. vol. A93, page 122.

**Short, Marg[a]ret.** Will. Made Nov. 13, 1789. Heirs: grandson Abram Short; granddau. Marg[a]ret Reynolds. Exec'r, son Eli Short. Wits., William Swain, Tilghman Short. Prob.

Dec. 1, 1789. Arch. vol. A99, page 11. Reg. of Wills, Liber D, folios 241-242.

**Windsor, Phillip.** Will. Made March 11, 1788. Heirs: wife Bersheba Windsor. Exec'rx, wife Bersheba Windsor. Wits., John Benson, Priscilla Moony. Prob. Dec. 5, 1789. Arch. vol. A108, pages 172-174. Reg. of Wills, Liber D, folios 242-243. [Note:—Arch. vol. A73, page 173 mentions Jesse Windsor's son, Jacky].

**Parremore, Patrick.** Yeoman. Admin. of, to Thomas Parremore. Appraiser's date Dec. 7, 1789. Arch. vol. A92, page 91.

**Wilkins, James.** Will. Made May 30, 1787. Heirs: wife Ruth Wilkins; sons John, Isaac and James Wilkins; daus. Mary, Betsy and Sally Wilkins. Exec'rx, wife Ruth Wilkins. Wits., Richard Durham, Betty Durham, Robert W. McCalley. Prob. Dec. 7, 1789. Arch. vol. A107, page 137. Reg. of Wills, Liber D, folio 243.

**Blizzard, William, Sr.** Planter. Will. Made Nov. 12, 1789. Heirs: wife unnamed; sons Thomas, William and Stephen Blizzard; daus. Jean and Alice Blizzard, Sarah Cornell, Mary Rawlins and Martha Parremore. Exec'rx, wife unnamed. Wits., Joseph Joseph, Robert Warrington, Elizabeth Oray. Prob. Dec. 8, 1789. Arch. vol. A59, pages 219-220. Reg. of Wills, Liber D, folios 246-247. [Note:—Arch. vol. A59, page 220 shows the estate was settled June 15, 1791 by Sarah Blizzard].

**Hall, Elijah.** Planter. Will. Made Oct. 6, 1786. Heirs: wife Givin Hall; son Jordon Hall; daus. Lewe and Betsey Hall. Exec'rx, wife Givin Hall. Wits., Samuel Hall, Shadrach Hall, John Williams. Prob. Dec. 8, 1789. Arch. vol. A73, page 202. Reg. of Wills, Liber D, folio 243.

**Hemmons [Hemons], John.** Will. Made July 28, 1788. Heirs: wife Elizabeth Hemmons; sons Thomas and William Leather Hemmons; daus. Mary Hemmons and Elizabeth Jacobs; granddau. Mary Jacobs. Exec'rs, wife Elizabeth Hemmons and son Thomas Hemmons. Wits., Charles Rawlins, Moses Marriner, Margaret Marriner. Prob. Dec. 8, 1789. Arch. vol. A76, pages 26-27. Reg. of Wills, Liber D, folios 247-248.

**Jessups, Patience.** Spinster. Will (copy). Made March 23, 1789. Heir: friend Levi Powell. Exec'r, Levi Powell. Wits., Mary Kimmey, Sanders Kimmey, Edward Dingle. Prob. Dec. 8, 1789. Arch. vol. A80, page 189. Reg. of Wills, Liber D, folios 249-250.

**Johnson, Elias.** Will. Made May 2, 1787. Heirs: wife Christen Johnson; sons Elisha and Simon Johnson; daus. Levinah Warren and Betsey Sharp. Exec'rs, wife Christen Johnson and son Simon Johnson. Wits., Robert W. McCalley, George Durham, Isaac Adams. Prob. Dec. 8, 1789. Arch. vol. A81, pages 32-33. Reg. of Wills, Liber D, folios 250-251.

**Lank, Naomi.** Will. Made Nov. 18, 1789. Heirs: sons Mitchell, John, James, Thomas, Levin, Cornelius, William and David Lank; daus. Lydia and Mary Lank. Exec'r, son James Lank. Wits., P[harao]h Barr, El[le]n Fowler. Prob. Dec. 8, 1789. Arch. vol. A83, pages 88-91. Reg. of Wills, Liber D, folios 244-245. [Note:—Arch. vol. A83, page 91 shows the estate was settled Aug. 9, 1796 by Ruth Lank, Adm'rx of James Lank, dec'd].

**Onions, Pearson.** Admin. of, to William Rickards. Granted [c. Dec. 9, 1789]. Arch. vol. A91, page 163.

**Draper, Samuel.** Admin. of, to Avery Draper. Granted [c. Dec. 9, 1789]. Arch. vol. A69, page 222. [Note:—Arch. vol. A69, page 222 mentions Nicey and Samuel Draper; Elizabeth Draper, dau. of Avery Draper].

**Layfield, Thomas.** Yeoman. Admin. of, to James Newbold. Granted [c. Dec. 9, 1789]. Arch. vol. A83, pages 169-170.

**Coulter, Marg[a]ret.** Will. Made Sept. 12, 1789. Heirs: sons James, John, William, [Eli], David and Cornelius Coulter; daus. Polly and [Eunice] Coulter. Exec'rs, sons James and David Coulter. Wits., William Virden, Agnes Todd, Tabitha L[orraine] Virden. Prob. Dec. 14, 1789. Arch. vol. A67, pages 58-60. Reg. of Wills, Liber D, folios 251-252.

**Hooper, Henry.** Planter. Will. Made July 25, 1789. Heirs: wife Sarah Hooper; sons John, Henry and Thomas Hooper; daus. Priscilla Hooper, Nancy Dal[gren], Molly Tennent, Mary Tennett; grandson Henry Wallace. Exec'rs, sons John and Henry Hooper. Wits., Joshua Obeir, Parry Obeir, Polly Small. Prob. Dec. 21, 1789. Arch. vol. A77, pages 171-173. Reg. of Wills, Liber C, folio 252. [Note:—Arch. vol A77, page 173 shows that John Hooper and John Tennent, adm'r D. B. N. of Henry Hooper, settled the estate April 4, 1799].

**Clifton, Levin.** Will. Made Oct. 22, 1789. Heirs: sons Levin, Noah, Edmond, David and John Clifton; daus. Nancy, Mary and Betsey Clifton. Exec'rs, wife Lydia Clifton and son Edmond Clifton. Wits., Thomas Layton, William Layton, Henry Manship. Prob. Dec. 30, 1789. Arch. vol. A65, pages 20-21. Reg. of Wills, Liber D, folio 256. [Note:—Arch.

vol. A65, page 21 shows the estate was settled by Francis Wright, surety for Lydia and Edmond Clifton].

**Bounds, Jesse.** Admin. of, to Charles King and wife Comfort, late Comfort Bounds. Granted [c. 1790]. Arch. vol. A60, pages 32-33.

**Burton, Anne.** Admin. of, to Joshua Burton, William Burton, Cornelius Wiltbank. Granted [c. 1790]. Arch. vol. A61, page 73. [Note:—Arch. vol. A61, page 73 mentions Polly Frame, late Polly Burton].

**Saunders, Silas.** Admin. of, to Mary Fisher, D. B. N. Admr's bond dated . . ., 10, 1790. Arch. vol. A98, page 20.

**Collins, John.** Will. Made Dec. 19, 1789. Heirs: wife Siner Collins; sons John and Darby Collins; daus. Jane and Elizabeth Collins; son-in-law Zachariah McDaniel. Exec'rx, wife Siner Collins. Wits., Robert W[attson] McCalley, Rachel Daughters, Elizabeth Smullen. Trustee, Abraham Harris, Jr. Prob. Jan. 1, 1790. Arch. vol. A65, pages 190-191. Reg. of Wills, Liber D, folios 268-269. [Note:—Arch. vol. A65, page 191 shows John Collins as son of Darby; also shows the estate was settled by Robert Wattson McCalley, security for Siner Collins].

**Massey, Isaac.** Will. Made Nov. 24, 1789. Heirs: wife Mary Massey; sons Elisha, Phillip and Job Massey; daus. Nancy, Bershaba and Elizabeth Massey. Exec'rs, wife Mary Massey, John Conway (son of Phillip). Wits., Robert W. McCalley, James Jones, Heziciah Beavens. Prob. Jan. 1, 1790. Arch. vol. A87, pages 50-51. Reg. of Wills, Liber D, folios 258-259.

**Parremore [Parmore], Solomon, Sr.** Will. Made July 24, 1789. Heirs: wife Tabitha Parmore; sons Stephen, Solomon, William and Levin Parmore; daus. Rachel, Tabitha and L[isa] Parmore, Mary Pettyjohn and Ann Lank. Exec'rs, Richard Abbott and Robert W. McCalley. Wits., Robert McCalley, John McCalley, Daniel McCalley. Prob. Jan. 1, 1790. Arch. vol. A92, page 94. Reg. of Wills, Liber D, folios 259-260. [Note:—Arch. vol. A92, page 94 shows the estate was settled by Nancy Abbott, exec'x of Richard Abbott, on June 20, 1792].

**White, Robert.** Will. Made Jan. 28, 1789. Heirs: wife Ann White; sons Jacob and Robert White; daus. Elizabeth and Esther White. Exec'rx, wife Ann White. Wits., William Peery, Cornelius Hopkins, Esther Campbell, Reece Woolf,

Paul White. Prob. Jan. 1, 1790. Arch. vol. A107, page 86. Reg. of Wills, Liber D, folios 267-268.

**Russel, John.** Carpenter. Admin. of, to Simon Marriner and wife, Sarah, late Sarah Russel. Granted Jan. 4, 1790. Arch. vol. A97, page 137. [Note:—Arch. vol. A97, page 137 mentions a daughter Jenny].

**Nicolls, Sarah.** Widow. Will. Made Dec. 15, 1789. Heirs: sons Levin, William and James Nicolls; daus. Stacey and Elizabeth Nicolls, Jewel Spence, Grace Cooper, Sally Stafford and Lovey Wright; grandson Daniel Nicolls (son of Nehemiah); granddau. Nancy Nicolls (dau. of Nehemiah); children of William Nicolls; children of Stacey Nicolls; children of Levin Nicolls. Exec'r, son Levin Nicolls. Wits., Isaac Bradley, James Spence, Esther Means. Prob. Jan. 12, 1790. Arch. vol. A91, page 98. Reg. of Wills, Liber D, folios 270-271.

**Pride, Anna.** Widow. Will. Made Dec. 20, 1789. Heirs: sons William, Luke, Oliver, Benjamin and Jacob Pride, Levi Hall; daus. Anna Williams, Sarah Sapp (wife of Joseph); grandson Joseph Hall (son of Levi); granddau. Mary Sapp (dau. of Joseph). Exec'r, son William Pride. Wits., Isaac Beauchamp, Daniel Godwin, Thomas Ozburn. Prob. Jan. 12, 1790. Arch. vol. A94, page 146. Reg. of Wills, Liber D, folios 269-270.

**Abbott, Richard.** Will. Made April 14, 1787. Heirs: wife Ann Abbott; sons Richard and John Abbott; daus. Elisabeth and Jean Abbott; child unnamed. Exec'rx, wife Ann Abbott. Wits., John Sullivan, [E]unice Sullivan, William Johnson. Prob. Jan. 15, 1790. Arch. vol. A57, pages 17-19. Reg. of Wills, Liber D, folios 271-272. [Note:—Arch. vol. A57, page 18 mentions daus. Sarah and Margaret Abbott; pages 18 and 19 show that Ann Abbott, widow, later married David Downing].

**Darter, Thomas.** Will. Made Jan. 10, 1790. Heirs: mother Sarah Darter; sisters Elizabeth and Jemima Darter. Exec'r, friend Isaac Cooper. Wits., Isaac Gray, Smothers Watson, Solomon Willey. Prob. Jan. 30, 1790. Arch. vol. A68, pages 48-49. Reg. of Wills, Liber D, folios 273-274.

**Ingram, Robert.** Will (copy). Made Jan. 7, 1790. Heirs: wife Ann Ingram; sons Job, Robert, Isaac, Jacob, Thomas and John Ingram; daus. Ellender, Jane, Sarah and Nancy Ingram. Exec'r, son Robert Ingram. Wits., Job Ingram, William Newbold. Prob. Jan. 30, 1790. Arch. vol. A79, page 173. Reg. of Wills, Liber D, folios 275-276.

**Sharp, William.** Will. Made Dec. 21, 1789. Heirs: wife Polly [also known as Mary] Sharp; son Joseph Melson Sharp; daus. Lovey, Nancy and Elisabeth Sharp. Exec'rx, wife Polly Sharp. Wits., Joseph Melson, Solomon Willey, John Phillips. Prob. Jan. 30, 1790. Arch. vol. A98, page 99. Reg. of Wills, Liber D, folios 274-275. [Note:—Arch. vol. A98, page 99 shows the estate was settled on April 15, 1794 by William Rodney and wife Mary, late Mary Sharp].

**Wingate, John.** Will. Made Jan. 11, 1790. Heirs: wife Ann Wingate; sons Ezekiah, John, Ephraim, Thomas, Henry, Phillip and Joshua Wingate; daus. Le[ah], Sally and Nancy Wingate. Exec'rs, wife Ann Wingate and son Henry Wingate. Wits., Benj[amin] Phillips, John Sharp, Solomon Willey. Prob. Jan. 30, 1790. Arch. vol. A108, pages 186-188. Reg. of Wills, Liber D, folios 272-273.

**Roach, William.** Will (nunc.). Made Jan. 23, 1790. Heirs: wife Patience Roach; son James Roach; dau. Catherine Roach; Hester and Penelope Fisher (wife's daus. by previous marriage). Exec'rx, wife Patience Roach. Wits., Nicholas Little, Hester Little, Mary White. Prob. Feb. 3, 1790. Arch. vol. A96, pages 69-70. Reg. of Wills, Liber D, folios 276-277. [Note:—Arch. vol. A96, page 70 shows the estate was settled by William Newman and wife Patience, late Patience Roach].

**Bacon, Levin.** Will. Made Jan. 28, 1790. Heirs: wife Jean Bacon; bro. Davis Bacon. Exec'rs, wife Jean Bacon and John Williams (son of John). Wits., Spencer Covington, Stephen Horsey, William Wright. Prob. Feb. 5, 1790. Arch. vol. A58, pages 46-48. Reg. of Wills, Liber D, folio 280.

**Sirman, Elizabeth.** Widow. Will. Made Dec. 7, 1789. Heirs: sons John, Loud[er] and Levin Sirman; dau. Betsey Sirman. Exec'r, John Bacon. Wits., John Williams, Elinor Carmean, Sophia Carmean. Prob. Feb. 5, 1790. Arch. vol. A99, pages 74-75. Reg. of Wills, Liber D, folios 280-281.

**McElvain, Andrew, Jr.** Admin. of, to Robert Marriner and wife Mary, late Mary McElvain. Granted [c. Feb. 6, 1790]. Arch. vol. A87, pages 174-175.

**Kollock, Margaret.** Widow. Will. Made Nov. 28, 1789. Heirs: son Phillips Kollock; daus. Hester Moore, Catharine Wiltbank, Mary Field; grandson Jacob Moore Kollock. Exec'rs, son Phillips Kollock, dau. Hester Moore. Wits., George Hazzard, W. Harrison. Prob. Feb. 8, 1790. Arch. vol. A83, page 8. Reg. of Wills, Liber D, folios 281-282.

**Read, Allen.** Admin. of, to Martha Read. Granted Feb. 10, 1790. Arch. vol. A95, page 3.

**Williams, Charles.** Will. Made Nov. 25, 1786. Heirs: wife Priscilla Williams; sons John, James, Charles, Henry and Edward Williams; daus. Jane, Polly, Sophia Williams; unnamed infant son. Exec'rs, son John Williams and friend Eli Parker. Wits., Eli Parker, John Carlisle, John Williams. Prob. Feb. 19, 1790. Arch. vol. A107, page 155. Reg. of Wills, Liber D, folios 282-283.

**Deputy, Joshua.** Admin. of, to James Crippin and Elinor, his wife, late Elinor Deputy. Granted March 3, 1790. Arch. vol. A68, page 237.

**Downs, Henry.** Will. Made Jan. 17, 1790. Heirs: wife Sarah Downs; sons Asa, Henry and William Downs. Exec'rs, wife Sarah Downs and son Asa Downs. Wits., David Nutter, Thomas Nutter, Robert Clifton. Prob. March 3, 1790. Arch. vol. A69, page 177. Reg. of Wills, Liber D, folio 283.

**Rickards, Jones.** Will. Made March 21, 1785. Heirs: wife Mary Rickards; sons Eli, Isaac, Dirickson and Job Rickards; Lucy and Rhoda Rickards (daus. of Susan Rickards); Nathaniel Johnson (wife's son). Exec'rs, wife Mary Rickards and son Eli Rickards. Wits., W[illia]m Rickards, James Miller, David Tubbs. Prob. March 3, 1790. Arch. vol. A95, pages 131-132. Reg. of Wills, Liber D, folios 261-263.

**Rider, Wilson.** Planter. Will. Made Oct. 17, 1785. Heirs: bros. John and Charles Rider. Exec'r, bro. John Rider. Wits., William Brittingham Ennis, Thomas Burbage, Robert Lacey. Prob. March 3, 1790. Arch. vol. A96, pages 16-17. Reg. of Wills, Liber D, folio 284. [Note:—Arch. vol. A96, page 17 shows the estate was settled by Thomas Hemmons, exec'r of John Rider].

**Draper, Joseph.** Yeoman. Admin. of, to Elizabeth Draper. Granted March 5, 1790. Arch. vol. A69, page 208. [Note: —Arch. vol. A69, page 208 shows that Elizabeth Draper later married Thomas Smith].

**Linch, Jacob.** Admin. of, to Phebe Linch. Granted [c. March 5, 1790. Arch. vol. A84, page 85.

**Booth, John.** Will. Made Nov. 17, 1789. Heirs: wife Sarah Booth and son Levin Booth. Exec'x, wife Sarah Booth.

Wits., Caleb Balding, William Wright, Joshua Megee. Prob. March 8, 1790. Arch. vol. A60, pages 18-19. Reg. of Wills, Liber D, folios 285-286.

**Horsey, Isaac.** Will. Made Feb. 10, 1790. Heirs: wife Mary Horsey; son Isaac Horsey; daus. Elizabeth, Martha and Elinor Horsey; bro. Nathaniel Horsey; William Moore; Francis Asbury for Methodist Conference. Exec'rs, wife Mary Horsey and friend William Moore. Wits., Campbel S. St.Clair, Isaac Cooper, Isaac Moore. Prob. March 8, 1790. Arch. vol. A78, pages 32-33. Reg. of Wills, Liber D, folios 286-288.

**Ludnum [Lednum], John.** Will. Made Jan. 4, 1790. Heirs: wife Lucy Ludnum; son Shadrach Ludnum; daus. Elizabeth, Selah, Sarah and Margaret Ludnum; granddau. Mary Ludnum (dau. of son John). Exec'rx, wife Lucy Ludnum. Wits., Olive Jump, James Spencer, John Masten Morris. Prob. March 8, 1790. Arch. vol. A84, pages 44-45. Reg. of Wills, Liber D, folios 284-285. [Note:—Arch. vol. A84, page 45 mentions Benjamin Nutter and wife].

**Clowes, John.** Will. Made Aug. 20, 1784. Heirs: wife Mary Clowes; sons Isaac and Peter Clowes; daus. Alletta and Sarah Clowes. Exec'rs, wife Mary Clowes and son Isaac Clowes. Wits., John Wilson Dean, John Tam, Benedict Pennington. Prob. March 15, 1790. Arch. vol. A65, pages 56-58. Reg. of Wills, Liber D, folios 288-289. [Note:—Arch. vol. A65, page 56 mentions bro. David Clowes, dec'd].

**Wattson, Isaac** (of Thomas). Carpenter. Will. Made June 24, 1788. Heirs: son Robert Wattson; daus. Sarah, Betsey and Susannah Albound Wattson. Exec'r, son Robert Wattson. Wits., Isaac Beauchamp, Mary Beauchamp, Thomas Wattson. Prob. March 15, 1790. Arch. vol. A106, pages 7-8. Reg. of Wills, Liber D, folios 260-261. [Note:—Arch. vol. A106, page 8 shows the estate was settled by Mary Wattson and Mark Davis, adm'rs of Robert Wattson, on April 11, 1797].

**Steward, Moses.** Will. Made March 8, 1790. Heirs: sons Moses, Annias and William Steward; daus. Betsey Steward and Sally Steen. Exec'r, James Steen. Wits., John Connaway, Levin Connaway, Sr., Barth[alomew] Windsor. Prob. March 16, 1790. Arch. vol. A100, page 187. Reg. of Wills, Liber D, folios 263-264.

**Ennis, William Brittingham.** Will (copy). Made March 1, 1790. Heirs: wife [Keziah] Ennis; sons William and Levin Ennis;

six unnamed daus. Exec'rs, wife [Keziah] Ennis and son William Ennis. Wits., William Blizzard, William Johnson, John Rider. Prob. March 30, 1790. Arch. vol. A70, pages 162-164. Reg. of Wills, Liber D, folio 265.

**Wilson, Matthew.** Will. Made March 29, 1790. Heirs: wife Elizabeth Wilson; scns James Patriot Wilson and Theodore Wilson; other unnamed children and unnamed grandchildren. Exec'rs, wife Elizabeth Wilson and son James Patriot Wilson. Wits., William Peery, Elizabeth Drain, Samuel Kerr. Prob. April 5, 1790. Arch. vol. A108, pages 100-101. Reg. of Wills, Liber D, folios 295-296.

**James, Reuben.** Will. Made March 23, 1790. Heirs: wife Mary James; sons Reuben and Noble James; daus. Sally and Patty James; dau.-in-law Nancy Hitchens. Exec'r, John Benston. Wits., John Messick, Elizabeth Short, Hannah Messick. Prob. April 6, 1790. Arch. vol. A80, pages 111-113. Reg. of Wills, Liber D, folios 289-291. [Note:—Arch. vol. A80, page 112 mentions Selah Boyce, Nancy Ellingsworth, Patty Spicer].

**Grice, William.** Admin. of, to Ruth Grice. Granted April 8, 1790. Arch. vol. A73, page 93.

**Robinson, Thomas.** Will. Made March 25, 1790. Heirs: wife Mary Robinson; sons Benjamin, William, Thomas, Parker, John and Peter Robinson. Exec'rs, wife Mary Robinson and son Benjamin Robinson. Wits., William Mathews, David Hazzard, George Hazzard. Prob. April 8, 1790. Arch. vol. A96, page 178-179. Reg. of Wills, Liber D, folios 291-292. [Note:—Arch. vol. A96, page 179 mentions Ann Robinson, grandmother of William Robinson].

**Stevenson, Robert.** Will. Made March 4, 1786. Heirs: sons Kend[all] and Robert Wilson Stevenson; daus. Mary, Sally, Nancy and Betty M[cKnight] Stevenson. Execr's, Thomas Deal and James Vent. Wits., Jesse Dean, Aaron Burton, John Carey. Prob. April 12, 1790. Arch. vol. A100, page 177. Reg. of Wills, Liber D, folios 293-294. [Note:—Arch. vol. A100, page 177 shows the estate was settled by Mary Vent, admr'x of James Vent].

**Morris, John.** Admin. of, to Dennis Morris. Admr's bond dated April 15, 1790. Arch. vol. A90, page 75.

**Burton, William** (of Benjamin). Lewes and Rehoboth Hd. Will. Made March 6, 1790. Heirs: wife Cornelia Burton; son Cord Burton; bros. Benjamin and Daniel Burton; sister

Hessy Burton; children of sister Lydia Burton; children of
sister Leah Burton (late wife of William Burton). Exec'rs,
wife Cornelia Burton and bro. Benjamin Burton. Wits.,
Reese Paynter, Nancy Hazzard, Daniel Rodney. Prob. April
16, 1790. Arch. vol. A62, page 23. Reg. of Wills, Liber D,
folios 294-295.

**Jones, Isaac Hardy.** Will (copy). Made March 22, 1790. Heirs:
wife Sarah Jones; sons Garrison and Asbury Jones; father
Mathias Jones; bros. William and James Jones; sister Fran-
ny Jones. Exec'r, bro. William Jones. Wits., Rob[er]t W.
McCalley, Isaac Connaway, David Ayres. Prob. April 20,
1790. Arch. vol. A81, pages 149-151. Reg. of Wills, Liber
D, folio 296.

**Matthews, Teague.** Planter. Will. Made March 23, 1790. Heirs:
wife Mary Matthews; sons Philip, David, James and Levi
Matthews; daus. Sally, Rebecca, Catharine, Priscilla Matthews and Betty Vinson. Exec'rs, wife Mary Matthews and
son Phillip Matthews. Wits., Thomas Conner, Rebecca Conner, Molly Roach. Prob. April 27, 1790. Arch. vol. A87,
pages 74-75. Reg. of Wills, Liber D, folios 297-298.

**Morris, Jacob.** Admin. of, to Joseph Morris. Granted [c. May
4, 1790]. Arch. vol. A90, pages 63-64.

**Barnes, Robert.** Will. Made March 18, 1790. Heirs: wife Betty
Barnes; bros. Simeon and Thomas Barnes; sisters Mary
and Annie Barnes. Exec'rs, wife Betty Barnes and bro.
Simeon Barnes. Wits., Andrew Williams, Arthur Williams,
John Evans. Prob. May 5, 1790. Arch. vol. A58, pages 207-
208. Reg. cf Wills, Liber D, folios 298-299.

**Hickman, William.** Admin. of, to Nutter Lofland and William
Rickards. Granted [c. May 5, 1790]. Arch. vol. A76, pages
96-97.

**Wilson, William.** Will. Made Jan. 2, 1789. Heirs: sons John,
Samuel, Thomas, William Bradley Wilson; daus. Arcada
and Mary Ann Wilson. Exec'r, son John Wilson. Wits., William Irving, Tilghman Layton, Joseph Gray. Prob. May 5,
1790. Arch. vol. A108, page 134. Reg. of Wills, Liber D,
folios 299-300.

**Moore, Robert.** Admin. of, to Jonathan Boyce, Henry Edger
and wife Polly, late Polly Moore. Granted [c. May 6, 1790].
Arch. vol. A89, page 138.

**Carey, Thomas.** Will. Made March 5, 1790. Heirs: wife Nelly
Carey; sons Thomas, Samuel and John Carey; daus. Eliza-

beth, Frances and Sarah Carey. Exec'rx, wife Nelly Carey. Wits., Eli Collins, Joseph Hall, Comfort Steel. Prob. May 7, 1790. Arch. vol. A64, page 104. Reg. of Wills, Liber D, folios 300-301.

**Smith, Mary.** Cedar Creek Hd. Will. Made May 1, 1790. Heirs: son John Young; daus. Sarah Davis, Rachel Mann, Betty Hays, Mary Millard and Phebe Lofland; dau.-in-law Anna Young; grandsons Nathan Young, Robert and Nathan Hill; granddaus. Betty Hill, Mary Townsend and Mary Young Marvel; Job Smith; and negro man Phillip. Exec'r, John Young. Wits., Joshua Bennett, Joshua Lofland, John Hickman. Prob. May 12, 1790. Arch. vol. A99, page 188. Reg. of Wills, Liber D, folios 301-302.

**Richards, John.** Yeoman. Will. Made Feb. 9, 1790. Heirs: sons William and David Richards; daus. Elizabeth Bradley and Jean Adams; grandchildren Elizabeth, Mary, Anna, Rebecca, Sarah and John Adams (children of dau. Jean Adams), John, Anna and Mary Bradley (children of Joseph Bradley), Sarah, Nancy and Margaret Richards (children of son Henry); children of daus. Nanny and Mary; son-in-law Elijah Adams. Exec'r, son David Richards. Wits., William Ross, John Wood, Levin Hickman. Prob. May 13, 1790. Arch. vol. A95, pages 85-86. Reg. of Wills, Liber D, folios 302-304.

**Douce, Levin, Sr.** Will. Made April 19, 1790. Heirs: wife Elizabeth Douce; dau. Sally. Young; grandson Benjamin Riley; nephew Levin Douce. Exec'rx, wife Elizabeth Douce. Wits., John Lofland, William Killingsworth, John Killingsworth. Prob. May 19, 1790. Arch. vol. A69, page 169. Reg. of Wills, Liber D, folio 304.

**Chase, William.** Will. Made Feb. 20, 1790. Heirs: mother Sarah Chase; bros. James, Isaac, John and Jacob Chase; sisters Sarah, Mary and Peggy Chase. Exec'r, bro. James Chase. Wits., William Young, James Dutton, Thomas Dutton. Prob. May 26, 1790. Arch. vol. A64, page 134. Reg. of Wills, Liber D, folio 305.

**Wattson, John.** Merchant. Admin. of, to Nanny Wattson, D. B. N. Granted [c. June 7, 1790]. Arch. vol. A106, page 20.

**Clendaniel, William.** Admin. of, to Judith Clendaniel. Granted [c. June 8, 1790]. Arch. vol. A65, page 2.

**Steele, James.** Yeoman. Admin. of, to Ann Pride, late Ann Steele, and Prisgrave Steele. Granted [c. June 8, 1790]. Arch. vol. A100, page 140.

**Tull, Joshua.** Yeoman. Will. Made March 15, 1789. Heirs: wife Esther Tull; sons John, Jesse, Stanton, William and Whittington Tull; dau. Elizabeth Tull; grandson Handy Tull; granddau. Milly Tull. Exec'r, son Jesse Tull. Wits., John Tennent, John Hooper, Julius A. Flower. Prob. June 8, 1790. Arch. vol. A102, page 175. Reg. of Wills, Liber D, folio 306.

**Bell, Thomas.** Admin. of, to Daniel Rogers and Sarah Bell, C. T. A. Granted [c. June 9, 1790]. Arch. vol. A59, pages 64-65. [Note:—Arch. vol. A59, page 65 also shows John Robinson and Sarah Robinson, late Sarah Conwell, and Daniel Rogers as admr's C. T. A.].

**Green, William.** Admin. of, to Nehemiah Green. [Granted June 9, 1790]. Arch vol. A73, page 76. [Note:—Arch. vol. A73, page 76 mentions Patty, Nelly and John Green, dec'd].

**Grice, Thomas.** Admin. of, to Ruth Grice, in lieu of William Grice, dec'd. Granted [c. June 9, 1790]. Arch. vol. A73, pages 89-90. [Note:—Arch. vol. A73, page 89 mentions Esther, Thomas and Polly Grice; page 90 mentions Nancy Collins, Betsy Hudson and Polly Grice].

**Heavelo, Sarah.** Admin. of, to William Millard. Admr's bond dated June 9, 1790. Arch. vol. A76, page 14. [Note:—Arch. vol. A76, page 14 mentions heirs: Sarah Gordon, wife of Joseph Russell].

**Pride, William.** Admin. of, to William Pride, [in lieu of Anna Pride, dec'd]. Granted [c. June 9, 1790]. Arch. vol. A94, page 152.

**Kimmy, Sanders.** Will. Made April 17, 1790. Heirs: wife Mary Kimmy; sons Sanders and Peterson Kimmy. Exec'rx, wife Mary Kimmy. Wits., Isaac Gray, Burton Wharton, Obe-[diah] Viggus. Prob. June 14, 1790. Arch. vol. A82, pages 82-83. Reg. of Wills, Liber D, folios 306-307.

**Jones, Penelope Holt.** Widow. of Jacob Jones. Lewes. Will (copy). Made June 27, 1786. Heirs: step-son Jacob Jones; unnamed bros. and sisters; friend Self Arnold; negro boy Charles. Exec'r, John Rodney, Esq. Wits., James Sykes, Agnes Sykes, Ann Sykes. Prob. June 24, 1790. Arch. vol. A81, pages 181-182. Reg. of Wills, Liber D, folios 307-308.

**Tharp, John.** Admin. of, to Mary Tharp. Admr's bond dated July 4, 1790. Arch. vol. A101, page 142.

**Hazzard, David.** Will. Made July 17, 1790. Heirs: wife Ellen Hazzard; sons Cord, David, James and John Hazzard.

Exec'rx, wife Ellen Hazzard. Wits., Joseph Hall, James Newbold, Levin Ennis. Prob. July 29, 1790. Arch. vol. A75, pages 45-46. Reg. of Wills, Liber D, folios 308-309.

**Chase, William.** Admin. of, to Mary Chase, in right of James Chase. Granted [c. Aug. 1790]. Arch. vol. A64, page 135.

**Griffin, Oliver.** Will. Made April 6, 1789. Heirs: sons Oliver and John Griffin; daus. Elizabeth Griffin and Rhoda Quill[en] (wife of Joseph); other children unnamed. Exec'r, son Oliver Griffin. Wits., William Munroe, John Gordy, Elinor Gordy. Prob. Aug. 6, 1790. Arch. vol. A73, page 94. Reg. of Wills, Liber D, folios 232-233.

**Truitt, Peter.** Will. Made Jan. 4, 1790. Heirs: wife Betty Truitt; sons William, Tatman, James and John Truitt; daus. Lottie, Lovey, Leah and Rachel Truitt, Sally Messick, Polly Coverdill and Betsey Kirk. Exec'rs, sons William and Tatman Truitt. Wits., Abraham Link, Joseph Lindell, William Tatman. Prob. Aug. 7, 1790. Arch. vol. A102, page 155. Reg. of Wills, Liber D, folio 309. [Note:—Arch. vol. A102, page 155 shows the estate was settled by William and Tatman Truitt, in right of Betty Truitt, on July 22, 1795].

**Wood, John.** Admin. of, to Stephen Wood. Admr's bond dated Aug. 12, 1790. Arch. vol. A109, page 45.

**Polk, Joshua.** Planter. Worcester Co., Md. Will. Made July 24, 1773. Heirs: wife Mary Polk. [No exec'r]. Wits., John Pollock, Charles Brown, Jr., W[illia]m Hunt. Prob. Aug. 30, 1790. Arch. vol. A93, page 136. Reg. of Wills, Liber D, folios 309-310.

**West, Ezekiel.** Will. Made Aug. 20, 1790. Heirs: Jehu and Mary Hill (children of John Hill, dec'd); Sarah Robinson (wife of William Robinson); Thomas West (son of John West). Exec'r, friend William Blizzard. Wits., Sacker Wyatt, Mary Brady, Joseph Warrenton. Prob. Sept. 3, 1790. Arch. vol. A106, pages 118-119. Reg. of Wills, Liber D, folios 310-311.

**Baker, Hugh.** Admin. of, to Mary Baker. Granted [c. Sept. 7, 1790]. Arch. vol. A58, page 117. [Note:—Arch. vol. A58, page 117 mentions the decedent's child, Sally Baker].

**Callaway, Ebenezer.** Admin. of, to Peter Callaway. Granted [c. Sept. 7, 1790]. Arch. vol. A62, page 133.

**Stockley, Prettyman.** Admin. of, to Ann Stockley. Granted [c. Sept. 7, 1790]. Arch. vol. A101, page 33. [Note:—Arch.

vol. A101, page 33 mentions Nancy, Betsy, Jacob, Pretty-man, David, Nathaniel, Comfort and Nehemiah Stockley].

**Vaughan, Ann.** Widow. Admin. of, to James Douglas and John Smith, in right of Edward Vaughan. Granted [c. Sept. 7, 1790]. Arch. vol. A103, page 59.

**Morris, George.** Admin. of, to Mary Morris. Granted [c. Sept. 8, 1790]. Arch. vol. A90, page 52.

**Welch, Henry.** Admin. of, Thomas Laws, D. B. N. Granted [c. Sept. 8, 1790]. Arch. vol. A106, page 85.

**Abbott, John.** Admin. of, to Ann Mary Abbott. Granted [c. Sept. 14, 1790]. Arch. vol. A57, pages 8-9. [Note:—Arch. vol. A57, page 9 shows that William Lofland settled the estate previously administered by George Abbott].

**Barton, William.** Will. Made Oct. 22, 1788. Heir: wife Elizabeth Barton. Exec'r, bro. Edward Barton. Wits., James Harris, Joshua Smith, James Safford. Prob. Oct. 1, 1790. Arch. vol. A58, pages 226-227. Reg. of Wills, Liber D, folios 311-312.

**Carpenter, James Cannon.** Will (copy). Made July 2, 1790. Heirs: cousins Mary Wilson and Stephen Cannon, Jr.; Elizabeth Cannon (dau. of Stephen). Exec'r, cousin Stephen Cannon, Jr. Wits., Clarkson Cannon, John Watts, Thomas Watts. Prob. Oct. 2, 1790. Arch. vol. A63, page 231. Reg. of Wills, Liber D, folio 312.

**Smith, John.** Will. Made Dec. 10, 1790. Heirs: wife Mary Smith; sons William, John and David Smith. Exec'rx, wife Mary Smith. Wits., Francis Wright, Edmond Clifton. Prob. Oct. 2, 1790. Arch. vol. A99, page 169. Reg. of Wills, Liber D, folios 312-313.

**Callaway, Matthew.** Will. Made Aug. 5, 1790. Heirs: wife Sarah Callaway; sons Hardy, John and Tubman Callaway; dau. Phillis Callaway. Exec'rs, wife Sarah Callaway and John Dashiell. Wits., Aaron Hastings, Moses Callaway. Prob. Oct. 8, 1790. Arch. vol. A62, pages 168-169. Reg. of Wills, Liber D, folio 313. [Note:—Arch. vol. A62, page 169 shows the estate was settled Oct. 14, 1796 by Samuel Kinny and wife Sarah, late Sarah Callaway and John Dashiell].

**Kinney, Joshua.** Will. Made July 17, 1790. Heirs: wife Annis Kinney; sons Samuel, John and Joshua Kinney; daus. Mary, Elizabeth, and Sarah Kinney, Anne Smith. Exec'rs, wife

Annis Kinney and son Samuel Kinney. Wits., Boaz Walston, Levin Walston, David Walston. Prob. Oct. 8, 1790. Arch. vol. A82, page 148. Reg. of Wills, Liber D, folios 313-314.

**Cannon, James.** Carpenter. Admin. of, to Stephen Cannon. Granted [Oct. 19, 1790]. Arch. vol. A63, page 63. [Note: —Arch. vol. A63, page 63 mentions heirs: Mary Wilson and Elizabeth Cannon].

**Prettyman, Thomas.** Planter. Will. Made Feb. 26, 1790. Heirs: wife Elizabeth Prettyman; sons William, George, Burton, Robert and Thomas Prettyman; daus. Hessy Prettyman, Comfort Rogers, Ann Morris, Tabitha Morris, Mary Ingram, Patience Noles, Sarah Marvel, Agnes Williams and [Isa]bell Pepper. Exec'rs, wife Elizabeth Prettyman and son William Prettyman. Wits., Samuel Green, Tabitha Walker, Kindall Warren. Prob. Oct. 26, 1790. Arch. vol. A94, pages 117-118. Reg. of Wills, Liber D, folios 314-316. [Note:—Arch. vol. A94, page 118 shows the estate was settled April 14, 1795 by Joseph Wharton and Elizabeth, his wife, late Elizabeth Prettyman].

**Irons, Jane.** Spinster. Admin. of, to Lemuel Irons. Granted Oct. 27, 1790. Arch. vol. A79, pages 197-198. [Note:— Arch. vol. A79, page 198 mentions heirs: Aaron and Lemuel Irons, heirs of Jacob Irons, and Naomi Massey].

**Basnett, Sarah.** Widow. Washington County, Md. Will (copy). Made Jan. 8, 1790. Heirs: sons Nehemiah, Boaz, Samuel and John Basnett. Exec'rs, son Nehemiah Basnett and William Willey, Sr. [No wits.]. Prob. Oct. 30, 1790. Arch. vol. A58, page 232. Reg. of Wills, Liber D, folios 175-176.

**Cannon, Jesse.** Yeoman. Will. Made Oct. 12, 1790. Heirs: sons Hugh[et]t, Levin, Matthew and Jesse Cannon; dau. Milly Cannon. Exec'rs, bro. William Cannon and bro.-in-law William Nutter Cannon. Wits., William Bowness, Daniel Jones, John Tennent. Prob. Nov. 3, 1790. Arch. vol. A63, pages 73-75. Reg. of Wills, Liber D, folios 316-317. [Note:— Arch. vol. A63, page 75 shows the estate was settled by William N. Cannon, surviving exec'r].

**Kollock, Jacob.** Gentleman. Will. Made July 20, 1790. Heirs: wife Mary Kollock; sons Cornelius, John Leech, Phillip and Jacob Kollock; daus. Rebecca Kollock, Mary Train, Alice Green (wife of John), Hester Hodgkinson (wife of Peter). Exec'rx, wife Mary Kollock. Wits., Hannah Nunez, Catharine Wiltbank, W. Harrison. Prob. Nov. 4, 1790. Arch. vol. A82, page 5. Reg. of Wills, Liber D, folio 317.

**Laws, John.** Will. Made March 2, 1790. Heirs: dau. Priscilla Houston; grandson Sax[eygotha] Laws; granddau. Mary Laws; heirs of son Alexander Laws, dec'd; heirs of son John Laws, dec'd; heirs of dau. Sarah Polk, dec'd; heirs of dau. Nancy Houston, dec'd; Christian Johnson; negroes Abner and wife Hannah. Exec'rs, grandsons John Laws and Trustin Laws Polk. Wits., William Owens, Joshua Polk, John Polk. Prob. Dec. 1, 1790. Arch. vol. A83, pages 138-139. Reg. of Wills, Liber D, folios 264-265.

**Kender, Jacob.** Planter. Will. Made Nov. 16, 1790. Heirs: wife Maria Kender; sons Jacob and Isaac Kender; dau. Nancy Kender. Exec'rx, wife Maria Kender. Wits., Rob[er]t Clarkson, Hugh[et]t Cannon, Joseph Stack. Prob. Dec. 2, 1790. Arch. vol. A82, page 48. Reg. of Wills, Liber D, folios 266-267.

**Pride, John.** Will. Made Dec. 4, 1789. Heirs: wife Betty Pride; sons Valentine, John, William and Henry Pride; daus. Nancy, Hannah, Rachel and Li[zzie] Pride. Exec'rx, wife Betty Pride. Wits., William Delaney, Luranah Delaney, M[arg]aret Stephens. Prob. Dec. 4, 1790. Arch. vol. A94, page 150. Reg. of Wills, Liber D, folio 318.

**Wilson, Mary.** Will. Made Nov. 23, 1789. Heirs: cousins Joseph Clarkson, Rebecca Clarkson, Al[ic]e Clarkson, Clarkson Bradley, Peggy Bradley, Cannon Bradley. Exec'r, David Nutter. Wits., Joseph Gray, William Wilson, Edward Wright. Prob. Dec. 8, 1790. Arch. vol. A108, pages 97-99. Reg. of Wills, Liber D, folios 248-249.

**Knock, Joseph.** Admin. of, to John Knock and Stephen Warrington, D. B. N., in right of Mary Knock, dec'd. Granted [c. Dec. 9, 1790]. Arch. vol. A82, page 167.

**Mitchell, James.** Will. Made June 11, 1790. Heirs: son Nathaniel Mitchell; dau. Abigail Bell. Exec'rs, son Nathaniel Mitchell and dau. Abigail Bell. Wits., John W. Batson, Geo[rge] Mitchell, Kendle Batson. Prob. Dec. 10, 1790. Arch. vol. A89, page 46. Reg. of Wills, Liber D, folios 318-319.

**Ozburn, Thomas.** Yeoman. Made Dec. 26, 1777. Heirs: wife Leah Ozburn; children of sister Elizabeth. Exec'rx, wife Leah Ozburn. Wits., W[illia]m Hazzard, Nathaniel Holleager, Phillip Holleager. Prob. Dec. 20, 1790. Arch. vol. A92, page 35. Reg. of Wills, Liber D, folios 319-320.

**Fisher, James.** Admin. of, to Patience Roach, D. B. N., in lieu of William Roach, dec'd. Granted [c. Dec. 24, 1790]. Arch. vol. A71, page 128.

**Hitchcock, Elinor.** Widow. Lewes. Will (copy). Made Nov. 2, 1790. Heirs: niece Sarah Norton; Jonathan Norton (son of Sarah); Jacob Kollock (son of Phillip). Exec'r, friend Phillip Kollock. Wits., Thomas Fisher, Hannah Turner, W. Harrison. Prob. Dec. 24, 1790. Arch. vol. A77, page 8. Reg. of Wills, Liber D, folio 320.

**Connor [Conwell], Benedict.** Admin. of, to George Cowan. Granted [c. Dec. 30, 1790]. Arch. vol. A66, pages 88-90.

**Aydelotte, Frances.** Admin. of, to Woodman Stockley. Granted [c. 1791]. Arch. vol. A57, pages 233-234.

**Bainum, Isaac.** Admin. of, to Samuel Fisher and wife Sarah, late Sarah Bainum. Granted [c. 1791]. Arch. vol. A58, pages 103-104.

**Bloxam, Elijah.** Admin. of, to John Collings and wife Leah, late Leah Bloxam. Granted [c. 1791]. Arch. vol. A59, pages 225-226. [Note:—Arch. vol. A59, page 226 mentions a son Elijah].

**Collins, Mathias.** Admin. of, to Walter Hudson, D. B. N., in right of Tabitha Collins. Granted [c. 1791]. Arch. vol. A66, pages 1-2.

**Chase, James.** Admin. of, to Mary Chase. Granted [c. 1791]. Arch. vol. A64, page 132. [Note:—Arch. vol. A64, page 132 mentions William and Sarah Chase].

**Short, Jacob.** Will. Made Nov. 29, 1790. Heirs: wife Nicey Short; sons Crawford, Job, Jacob, Elisha, Adam and Noah Short; dau. Lovey Short; Samuel Short; bro. Phillip Short. Exec'rs, sons Crawford and Job Short. Wits., Ben[amin] Phillips, Betty Tindel. Prob. Jan. 17, 1791. Arch. vol. A98, pages 184-185. Reg. of Wills, Liber D, folios 278-280.

**Ingram, Isaac.** Admin. of, to Abigail Ingram. Admr's bond dated Jan. 18, 1791. Arch. vol. A79, page 142.

**Hall, Shadrach.** Planter. Will. Made Dec. 16, 1790. Heirs: wife Abigail Hall; sons William and Shadrach Hall; daus. Temperance and Nelly Hall. Exec'rx, wife Abigail Hall. Wits., John Williams, Isaac Benson, Isaac Hall. Prob. Jan. 19, 1791. Arch. vol. A74, pages 3-4. Reg. of Wills, Liber D, folio 322.

**Thoroughgood, John.** Farmer. Will. Made Nov. 8, 1790. Heirs: wife Esther Thoroughgood; sons Newbold, William and John Thoroughgood; dau. Elisabeth Thoroughgood. Exec'rs, wife Esther Thoroughgood, Miller Thoroughgood, William Newbold. Wits., Edward Short, Joseph Wyatt, Levi Bainum. Prob. Jan. 19, 1791. Arch. vol. A101, page 177. Reg. of Wills, Liber D, folios 321-322.

**Vinson, Ebenezer.** Will. Made Dec. 11, 1790. Heirs: wife Rhoda Vinson; dau. Betsy Vinson. Exec'r, bro. Benjamin Vinson. Wits., Jesse Saunders, Nathan Saunders, Peter Dolbee. Prob. Jan. 19, 1791. Arch. vol. A103, page 147. Reg. of Wills, Liber D, folio 326.

**Thompson, James.** Town of Lewes. Will. Made Nov. 24, 1789. Heirs: son William Thompson; dau. Elizabeth Sanders; grandsons William Sanders, James and William Thompson; granddaus. Naomi West, Marg[a]ret Roades, Margaret Prettyman, Penelope Prettyman and Elizabeth Parker. Exec'rs, son William Thompson, dau. Elizabeth Sanders, Richard Little. Wits., Joseph Coulter, Eliz[abeth] Coulter, James Newbold. Prob. Jan. 26, 1791. Arch. vol. A101, page 151. Reg. of Wills, Liber D, folios 322-323.

**Bryan, Rachel.** Admin. of, to James Bryan. Granted Feb. 3, 1791. Arch. vol. A61, page 6.

**Hall, Casa.** Will. Made Jan. 23, 1791. Heirs: bro. Moses Hall; Lacey Virden (son of Levi Virden). Exec'rs, bro. Moses Hall and William Tull. Wits., James Wiley, John Vent, Martha Tull. Prob. Feb. 4, 1791. Arch. vol. A73, pages 187-188. Reg. of Wills, Liber D, folios 323-324.

**Polk, William.** Will. Made Nov. 20, 1786. Heirs: wife Leah Polk; son Robert Polk; daus. [Anny] Polk, Leah and Sally Andrews. Exec'rs, wife Leah Polk. Wits., John Williams, John Polk, John Elzey. Prob. Feb. 5, 1791. Arch. vol. A93, pages 156-157. Reg. of Wills, Liber D, folios 277-278.

**Whaley, Charles, Sr.** Will. Made April 10, 1790. Heirs: sons Charles and Nathaniel Whaley; grandson Josey [Joseph] Whaley; Rachel Booten; Polly Lingo. Exec'r, son Nathaniel Whaley. Wits., Daniel Evans, Robert Evans, John Evans. Prob. Feb. 7, 1791. Arch. vol. A107, page 4. Reg. of Wills, Liber D, folios 324-325.

**Scouvemont, Nicholas Joseph.** Formerly of York County, Virginia, but now of Sussex County, Del. Will. Made May 13, 1790. Heirs: son Ferdinand Scouvemont; dau. [Felix] Kervan (wife of Alexander Kervan). Exec'r, son Ferdinand

Scouvemont. Wits., Jeremiah Cannon, Isaac Cannon, Charles Littleton, Halsey Horsey. Prob. Feb. 9, 1791. Arch. vol. A98, page 38. Reg. of Wills, Liber D, folios 325-326.

**Smith, Samuel.** Admin. of, to John Outten. Granted [c. Feb. 9, 1791]. Arch. vol. A100, page 4.

**Coulter, John.** Will. Made Jan. 28, 1791. Heirs: bros. James, William, David, Cornelius and Eli Coulter; sisters Unice and Polly Coulter; father-in-law John Hall. Exec'r, father-in-law John Hall. Wits., Nancy Hall, Stephen Blizzard, William Johnson. Prob. Feb. 10, 1791. Arch. vol. A67, page 51. Reg. of Wills, Liber D, folios 326-327.

**Cirwithin, Caleb.** Cedar Creek Hd. Will. Made May 7, 1790. Heirs: sons Isaac and Samuel Cirwithin; daus. Sarah and [Cadea] Cirwithin. Exec'r, son Isaac Cirwithin. Wits., John Goodwin Jones, Thomas Watson, Jacob Stringer Tilney, Ann Tull. Prob. March 2, 1791. Arch. vol. A64, pages 159 and 163-165. Reg. of Wills, Liber D, folios 327-328. [Note:—Arch. vol. A64, page 163 shows Mary Cirwithin, admr'x of Isaac Cirwithin and page 165 shows Avery Draper, Adm'r D .B. N., C. T. A., settled the estate].

**Moore, Sarah.** Admin. of, to William Coffin. Adm'rs bond dated March 2, 1791. Arch. vol. A89, page 139.

**Townsend, Littleton.** Will. Made Feb. 15, 1791. Heirs: four children unnamed. Exec'r, Richard Hays, Esq. Wits., Ja[me]s Rench, Jonathan Williams, Johnson Messick. Prob. March 2, 1791. Arch. vol. A102, page 63. Reg. of Wills, Liber D, folio 327.

**Aydelott, John, Sr.** Yeoman. Will. Made May 15, 1789. Heirs: wife Mary Aydelott; sons George, Howard and Matthias Aydelott; daus. Nancy Aydelott, Sarah Hazzard (wife of Uriah) and Levina White (wife of Phillip); grandson [Felix] Hazzard. Exec'rs, wife Mary Aydelott and Thomas Hazzard. Wits., Samuel Black, James Collins, Leah Hazzard. Prob. March 5, 1791. Arch. vol. A57, pages 244 and 246. Reg. of Wills, Liber D, folio 330. [Note:—Arch. vol. A57, page 246 mentions heirs of Henry Aydelott: Oliver Hazzard, Selack Hazzard, Betsey Aydelott].

**Hitchens, Tamer.** Will. Made Feb. 15, 1791. Heirs: sons Isaac, Edward and William Hitchens; daus. Polly, Sally, Rebecca, Vina, [unnamed dau.] Hitchens. Exec'r, Thomas Hazzard. Wits., Joseph Dirickson, Jasper Tingle, Benjamin Long. Prob. March 5, 1791. Arch. vol. A77, page 38. Reg. of Wills, Liber D, folios 329-330.

**Knowles, Richard, Sr.** Planter. Will. Made Jan. 19, 1791. Heirs: sons Richard, Thomas, Zachariah, James, Edmond and Ephraim Knowles; daus. Prudence Knowles, Nancy Marvel, Patience Colling, Elizabeth Vinson, Sarah Hayward, Aseny Prettyman, Abigail Ellis (wife of Joshua Ellis); dau.-in-law Betty Knowles (widow of son Charles); grandsons Obediah Wills (son of dau. Eve Wills) and Charles Knowles; granddau. Agnes Knowles (dau. of Zachariah). Exec'rs, sons Thomas and Ephraim Knowles. Wits., Samuel Wilson, Peggy Wilson, Shiles Moore. Prob. March 5, 1791. Arch. vol. A82, pages 186-188. Reg. of Wills, Liber D, folios 331-332. [Note:—Arch. vol. A82, page 187 mentions Prudence Marvel].

**Rickards, William.** Will. Made Oct. 3, 1788. Heirs: wife Mary Rickards; sons John, William and Luke Rickards; daus. Hannah, Betty and Margaret Rickards; Jobe Derickson. Exec'rs, wife Mary Rickards and bro. John Rickards. Wits., David Tubbs, John Evans, Jones Rickards. Prob. March 5, 1791. Arch. vol. A95, pages 148-149. Reg. of Wills, Liber D, folios 332-333. [Note:—Arch. vol. A95, page 149 shows the estate was settled Oct. 11, 1797 by William Rickards and wife Betsy, adm'rs of John and Mary Rickards, dec'd].

**Wharton, Jonathan.** Will. Made Nov. 28, 1790. Heirs: wife Mary Wharton; sons David and John Cord Wharton; daus. Rhoda and Molly Wharton, and Hannah West; child unnamed. Exec'rx, wife Mary Wharton. Wits., Littleton Townsend, Tabitha Wharton, Samuel Cord. Prob. March 5, 1791. Arch. vol. A107, pages 29-30. Reg. of Wills, Liber D, folios 328-329. [Note:—Arch. vol. A107, page 30 mentions David Wharton, dec'd father; also shows the estate was settled Sept. 13, 1796 by Job Freeman and wife Mary, late Mary Wharton].

**Hemmons, Jonathan.** Admin. of, to Daniel Hinds. Granted [c. March 7, 1791]. Arch. vol. A76, page 34. [Note:—Arch. vol. A76, page 34 shows unnamed wife of Jonathan Hemmons later married Daniel Hinds].

**Ward, James.** Planter. Will. Made Aug. 7, 1790. Heirs: sons Joseph, Moses, John, Thomas and James Ward; daus. Betty, Mary and Nelly Ward. Exec'r, son Moses Ward. Wits., John Williams, Isaac Benson, Esther Benson. Prob. March 8, 1791. Arch. vol. A105, pages 78-79. Reg. of Wills, Liber D, folios 333-334.

**Hudson, John.** Yeoman. Cedar Creek Hd. Will. Made April 26, 1790. Heirs: wife Mary Hudson; sons Richard, Nunez and

Shadrach Hudson; dau. Helen Shockley (wife of Davis);
granddaus. Elizabeth Shockley (dau. of Davis and Helen),
Elisabeth Hudson (dau. of Richard), Elizabeth Hudson
(dau. of Shadrach). Exec'rs, wife Mary Hudson and sons
Shadrach and Nunez Hudson. Wits., William Daniel, Sally
Veach, Elias Shockley. Prob. March 9, 1791. Arch. vol.
A79, pages 17-19. Reg. of Wills, Liber D, folios 335-336.

**Lofland, Zadoc.** Yeoman. Admin. of, to Charles Lofland and
wife Temperance, late Temperance Lofland. Granted [c.
March 9, 1791]. Arch. vol. A85, page 93.

**Collings, John.** Planter. Will. Made Feb. 8, 1791. Heirs: wife
Nancy Collings; sons [Durustus], Julius [Augustus], Asa
and Horatio Collings; daus. S[ophia], Louisa and Patty
Collings. Exec'r, son Asa Collings. Wits., William Burcher,
James Lawson, Jehu Wyatt. Prob. March 10, 1791. Arch.
vol. A65, pages 192-194. Reg. of Wills, Liber D, folios 336-
338.

**Dodd, Hepburn.** Admin. of, to Wallace Harmonson, in lieu of
Lydia Dodd, dec'd. Granted [c. March 11, 1791]. Arch. vol.
A69, page 100.

**McCormick, John.** Admin. of, to William Hutcheson and wife
Sarah, late Sarah McCormick. Granted [c. March 12, 1791].
Arch. vol. A87, page 132.

**Megee, Samuel.** Admin. of, to John Megee, in right of Mary
Megee, dec'd. Granted [c. March 12, 1791]. Arch. vol.
A88, page 22.

**Roach, Levi.** Admin. of, to Peter Dawson and wife Martha, late
Martha Roach. Admr's bond dated March 15, 1791. Arch.
vol. A96, page 65.

**Balding, Caleb.** Will. Made Oct. 5, 1788. Heirs: wife Sarah
Balding; Eunice Balding Windsor; children of bro. Samuel
Balding. Exec'rx, wife Sarah Balding. Wits., Charles Moore,
Mage[e] Riggin, Joshua Magee. Prob. March 18, 1791.
Arch. vol. A58, pages 144-147. Reg. of Wills, Liber D,
folios 338-339. [Note:—Arch. vol. A58, pages 145 and 147
show that Joshua McGee [Magee] adm'r D. B. N., settled
the estate].

**King, John.** Farmer. Will. Made Feb. 7, 1791. Heirs: wife
Polly King; sons John Callaway and Joseph Windsor King;
dau. Polly King. Exec'rs, wife Polly King and Caldwell
Windsor. Wits., William Caldwell, Peggy King, John Benson. Prob. March 18, 1791. Arch. vol. A82, pages 112-113.

Reg. of Wills, Liber D, folio 338. [Note:—Arch. vol. A82, page 113 shows the estate was settled Aug. 17, 1796 by George Mitchell, Jr., and wife Polly, late Polly King].

**Hickman, Jacob.** Cedar Creek and Slaughter Neck. Will. Made Feb. 17, 1791. Heirs: wife Ann Hickman; sons William and Joseph Hickman; daus. Patience and Mary Hickman, Sarah Johnson, Elizabeth Smith (wife of William) and Nancy Riley (wife of Benjamin). Exec'rx, wife Ann Hickman. Wits., Nathaniel Young, John Young, Comfort Heavelow. Prob. March 22, 1791. Arch. vol. A76, pages 64-65. Reg. of Wills, Liber D, folios 340-342.

**Hudson, William.** Will. Made May 1, 1790. Heirs: wife Mary Hudson; sons John, Benjamin and Joseph Hudson; daus. Edith Veach, Mary Clifton, Nancy Clifton and Sally Pointer; granddau. . . . Hudson (dau. of William Hudson). Exec'rs, sons John and Joseph Hudson. Wits., Windsor Rawlins, Coverdill Cole, William Veach. Prob. March 22, 1791. Arch. vol. A79, pages 61-63. Reg. of Wills, Liber D, folio 342.

**Johnson, Bacor [Baker].** Cedar Creek and Slaughter Neck Hd. Will. Made Feb. 8, 1791. Heirs: wife Sarah Johnson; son William Bacor Johnson; daus. Patience, Elizabeth, Ann and Comfort Johnson and Mary Lofland (wife of Branson); granddaus. Betsey Johnson and Sarah Fisher (wife of John). Exec'rx, wife Sarah Johnson. Wits., Nathaniel Young, William Hickman, Thomas Smith, Daniel Carlisle. Prob. March 22, 1791. Arch. vol. A81, pages 14-15. Reg. of Wills, Liber D, folios 339-340. [Note:—Arch. vol. A81, page 15 shows the estate was settled June 17, 1799 by James Messick and Sarah, his wife, late Sarah Johnson; page 15 also mentions John Fisher, Nehemiah and Elizabeth Truitt].

**Polk, Ephraim.** Will. Made Jan. 5, 1789. Heirs: sons Emanuel, Ephraim, Joab and Joseph Polk; daus. Elizabeth and Mary Polk, Esther Owens; grandson William Polk (son of Joseph). Exec'rs, sons Emanuel and Ephraim Polk. Wits., John Polk, Sr., Edward Polk, Charles Polk, Robert Shankland. Prob. March 22, 1791. Arch. vol. A93, page 120. Reg. of Wills, Liber D, folios 343-344.

**Waller, Charles.** Admin. of, to John Tilney, in lieu of Elizabeth Waller, dec'd. Granted [c. March 23, 1791]. Arch. vol. A104, page 57.

**Davis, Mary Tilney** (Minor son of Nehemiah David, 3rd). Admin. of, to Peery Prettyman. Granted March 28, 1791. Arch. vol. A68, page 90.

**Laws, William.** Admin. of, to Saxagotha Laws. Admr's bond dated April 8, 1791. Arch. vol. A83, page 156.

**Wright, Peter Fretwell, Esq.** Will. Made March 7, 1791. Heirs: wife Elizabeth Wright; sons Peter, Fretwell, Samuel and Ellis Wright; daus. Elizabeth, Sally [Sarah] and Mary Wright. Exec'rs, wife Elizabeth Wright and son Fretwell Wright. Wits., Baptist Lay, Stephen Woods, Jos[eph] Hall. Prob. April 9, 1791. Arch. vol. A109, page 97. Reg. of Wills, Liber D, folios 344-345.

**West, Elijah.** Will. Made March 26, 1784. Heirs: wife Mary West sons Amos, Eli and Henry West; dau. Sally West. Exec'rs, wife Mary West. Wits., Thomas Godwin, Isaac West, William Johnson. Prob. April 10, 1791. Arch. vol. A106, pages 113-114. Reg. of Wills, Liber D, folios 177-178.

**Batson, Thomas.** Will. Made Sept. 17, 1783. Heirs: wife Tabitha Batson; sons Kindal, Thomas and John Wise Batson; daus. Elizabeth, Hannah and Sarah Batson. Exec'rs, wife Tabitha Batson and son John Wise Batson. Wits., Riley Evans, John Wyatt, Eleanor Wyatt. Prob. April 11, 1791. Arch. vol. A58, page 236. Reg. of Wills, Liber D, folios 345-346.

**Bayly, Clement Lee.** Will. Made Sept. 26, 1790. Heirs: wife Margery Bayly; sons John Lee, James Lee and Jeremiah Lee Bayly; daus. Betsey Lee and Nancy Lee Bayly; grand-daus. Sally, Nancy, Peggy and Betsey Bready; grandson Clement Bready. Exec'rs, wife Margery Bayly and son John Lee Bayly. Wits., Seth Griffith, Nathan Adams, Edward Brown. Prob. April 22, 1791. Arch. vol. A58, pages 66-67. Reg. of Wills, Liber D, folios 347-348. [Note:— Arch. vol. A58, page 67 shows that Frederick Travers, adm'r in lieu of John Lee Bayly, dec'd, exhibited the account for settlement Aug. 22, 1797].

**Smith, Curtis.** Planter. Will. Made Dec. 9, 1790. Heirs: wife Susannah Smith; sons Hudson, Constantine, John Cannon, Curtis and Trustan Smith; dau. Sally Hudson. Exec'rs, wife Susannah Smith and bro. Henry Smith. Wits., Ezekiel Brown, Robert J[ew]ett, Stephen Outerbridge. Prob. April 22, 1791. Arch. vol. A99, pages 121-122. Reg. of Wills, Liber D, folios 346-347. [Note:—Arch. vol. A99, page 122 shows the estate was settled by Joseph Coulbourn and wife Susannah, late Susannah Smith].

**Callaway, Ebenezer.** Broad Creek Hd. Will. Made May 15, 1784. Heirs: son Joshua Callaway; daus. Peggy and Sarah Callaway. Exec'r, friend William Owen, Jr. Wits., Isaac Jones, Ann Milston, Zachariah Barnett. Prob. May 4, 1791. Arch. vol. A62, page 134. Reg. of Wills, Liber D, folios 223-224.

**Huffington, Luke.** Admin. of, to Mary Huffington. Granted May 4, 1791. Arch. vol. A79, pages 68-70. [Note:—Arch. vol. A79, page 70 shows that Mary Huffington later married Isaac Wooten].

**Long, David, Sr.** Will. Made April 25, 1785. Heirs: wife Ann Long; sons David, Benjamin, John and Armwell Long; daus. Mary Hutson, Elizabeth Newport, Nancy Scudder, Rachel Holloway, M[iria]m Gray, Joyce Chamberlin. Exec'r, son Armwell Long. Wits., Joseph Dirickson, Isaac Collins, Benjamin Lockwood. Prob. May 4, 1791. Arch. vol. A85, page 103. Reg. of Wills, Liber D, folios 349-350.

**Stafford, James.** Admin. of, to Sarah Stafford. Granted [c. May 4, 1791]. Arch. vol. A100, page 100.

**Wharton, David.** Admin. of, to Elizabeth Wharton and Jonathan Wharton. Granted [c. May 4, 1791]. Arch. vol. A107, page 13.

**Rickets, Reece.** Admin. of, to Jonathan Stephenson and wife Ann, late Ann Rickets. Granted [c. May 6, 1791]. Arch. vol. A95, page 155.

**Wilson, William.** Admin. of, to William Wilson. Granted [c. May 7, 1791]. Arch. vol. A108, page 135. [Note:—Arch. vol. A108, page 135 mentions Arcada Wilson].

**Derickson, Job.** Admin. of, to Sophia Derickson. Granted [c. May 27, 1791]. Arch. vol. A69, page 29.

**Warrington, Benjamin.** Shipwright. Will. Made March 17, 1791. Heirs: wife Rachel Warrington; dau. Sally Warrington; sisters Mary Colony and Sar[ah] Wise; nephews George Wise (son of sister Sar[ah], Benjamin Colony (son of sister Mary). Exec'rs, wife Rachel Warrington, John Colony, Charles Rawlins. Wits., Andrew Thompson, William Okey, Sarah Okey. Prob. June 3, 1791. Arch. vol. A105, pages 146-147. Reg. of Wills, Liber D, folios 350-351. [Note:—Arch. vol. A105, page 147 shows the estate was settled July 21, 1795 by Edward Pettit and Rachel, his wife, late Rachel Warrington].

**Timmons, Aaron.** Will. Made March 10, 1791. Heirs: wife un-named; Samuel Brickham (son of Solomon); Joshua Ellis. [No exec'r]. Wits., Wingate Hall, Thomas Carter, William Collins. Prob. June 6, 1791. Arch. vol. A101, page 193. Reg. of Wills, Liber D, folio 351.

**Frame, Dagood Paynter.** Admin. of, to Robert Hood. Granted [c. June 14, 1791]. Arch. vol. A72, page 30. [Note:—Arch. vol. A72, page 30 mentions heirs: John B., Janet and Nathan Frame].

**Walker, Leah.** Widow. Admin. of, to Thomas Walker. Granted [c. June 14, 1791]. Arch. vol. A104, pages 32-33. [Note:— Arch. vol. A104, page 32 mentions George Walker; Jacob Walker, dec'd; and Leah Walker, Jr., dec'd].

**Bruce, Esther.** Admin. of, to Richard Green. Granted [c. June 16, 1791]. Arch. vol. A60, page 238.

**Collins, Tabitha.** Admin. of, to Walter Hudson. Granted June 16, 1791. Arch. vol. A66, page 24.

**McFarling, William.** Admin. of, to Elizabeth McFarling. Admr's bond dated June 27, 1791. Arch. vol. A87, page 164.

**Dirickson, Joseph.** Will. Made Nov. 19, 179[0]. Heirs: sons James and Levin Dirickson. Exec'r, son James Dirickson. Wits., William Lockwood, Thomas Hazzard, Sam[ue]l Dir-ickson. Prob. July 20, 179[1]. Arch. vol. A69, page 34. Reg. of Wills, Liber D, folio 352.

**McIlvain, James Mills.** Admin. of, to Comfort McIlvain. Admr's bond dated July 25, 1791. Arch. vol. A87, page 196.

**Burton, John.** Admin. of, to Robert Frame and wife Mary, late Mary Burton. Granted [c. Aug. 1791]. Arch. vol. A61, pages 164-165.

**Jacobs, Sarah.** Admin. of, to James Newbold. Granted [c. Aug. 2, 1791]. Arch. vol. A80, page 76.

**Owens, Sarah.** Admin. of, to David Owens. Granted [c. Aug. 2, 1791]. Arch. vol. A92, page 22.

**Edenfield, William.** Will (copy). Made May 7, 1791. Heirs: son John Edenfield; dau. Betsey Edenfield. [No execr]. Wits., Isaac Lord, Sarah Jacobs. Prob. Aug. 25, 1791. Arch. vol. A70, page 32. Reg. of Wills, Liber D, folios 352-353.

**Marvel, Rachel.** Will. Made Aug. 27, 1791. Heirs: sons Thomas, Robert, Philip and Joseph Marvel; daus. Ann Smith, Rachel

Robertson, Betsey McCalley, Cloe Nottingham and Patience
Brown (wife of William); granddaus. Nancy and Sally
Smith, and Betsey Barr; grandson Josiah Marvel. Exec'r,
son Phillip Marvel. Wits., John Harris, William Reynolds,
Temperance Huffman. Prob. Sept. 5, 1791. Arch. vol. A87,
pages 16-17. Reg. of Wills, Liber D, folios 353-354.

**Spence, James.** Will. Made Aug. 8, 1791. Heirs: wife Elizabeth
Spence; sons James Spence, Jr. and Abel Spence; dau.
Sena Spence; son-in-law Alexander Spence. Exec'r, son
James Spence, Jr. Wits., Olive Jump, William Ross, Wil-
liam Quinley. Prob. Sept. 5, 1791. Arch. vol. A100, page
38. Reg. of Wills, Liber D, folio 357. [Note:—Arch. vol.
A100, page 38 mentions Sena Nicolls].

**Gibb, Isabella.** Admin. of, to David Shankland and Thomas
Hudson, in right of his wife Betsey, late Betsey Gibb.
Granted Sept. 15, 1791. Arch. vol. A72, page 105.

**McGee, Mary.** Admin. of, to John McGee. Granted [c. Sept. 16,
1791]. Arch. vol. A87, page 167.

**Jones, John.** Will (copy). Made Jan. 13, 1791. Heirs: wife
Susannah Jones; son Gr[an]t Beery Jones; dau. Elizabeth
Jones; John Elliott. Exec'rs, wife Susannah Jones and
Peter Rust. Wits., Daniel Morris, Henry Clifton, Robert
R. S. Sta[ple]ford. Prob. Oct. 1, 1791. Arch. vol. A81,
page 168. Reg. of Wills, Liber D, folio 354.

**Lindale, Robert.** Admin. of, to Joseph Lindale and John Coverdill. Admr's bond dated Oct. 15, 1791. Arch. vol. A84,
page 110.

**Hasting, John.** Planter. Will. Made Feb. 3, 1791. Heirs: sons
Henry and Melvin Hasting; grandson Severn Hasting.
Exec'rs, sons Henry and Melvin Hasting. Wits., Edward
Creagh, Solomon Hasting. Prob. Nov. 8, 1791. Arch. vol.
A74, page 200. Reg. of Wills, Liber D, folios 354-355.

**Jones, Thomas.** Admin. of, to Joseph Hurst. Granted [c. Nov.
8, 1791]. Arch. vol. A81, page 188.

**Dukes, Isaac.** Yeoman. Will. Made Oct. 21, 1791. Heirs: sons
Andrew, Isaac, Jeremiah, Zebulon and Thomas Dukes; daus.
Frances, Mary, Rhoda and Nancy Dukes. Exec'r, son Jere-
miah Dukes. Wits., Robert Shankland, Jr., Edward Polk,
Rachel Robinson. Prob. Nov. 9, 1791. Arch. vol. A69, page
240. Reg. of Wills, Liber D, folios 357-358.

**Knox [Knock], Mary.** Admin. of, to John Knox and Stephen Warrington. Granted [c. Nov. 9, 1791]. Arch. vol. A82, page 168.

**Gordon, John.** Admin. of, to John Elliott. Granted [c. Nov. 22, 1791]. Arch. vol. A72, pages 179-180.

**Jefferson, Mar[ia].** Admin. of, to Joshua Jefferson. Granted [c. Nov. 22, 1791]. Arch. vol. A80, page 156.

**Coulter, Joseph.** Taylor. Admin. of, to Robert Coulter. Granted [c. Nov. 23, 1791]. Arch. vol. A67, pages 53-54.

**Shaver, Levin.** Yeoman. Admin. of, to Ruth Shaver. Granted [c. Nov. 23, 1791]. Arch. vol. A98, page 103.

**Welch, John.** Admin. of, to William Welch, D. B. N., in right of Mary Welch. Granted [c. Nov. 23, 1791]. Arch. vol. A106, page 86.

**Edger, Henry.** Admin. of, to William Hobbs. Granted Nov. 24, 1791. Arch. vol. A70, page 37.

**Morris, William.** Admin. of, to Tamer Morris. Granted [c. Nov. 24, 1791]. Arch. vol. A90, page 145.

**Reynolds, Richard.** Broadkill Hd. Will. Made Nov. 8, 1791. Heirs: wife Anne Reynolds; sons Zachariah, Benjamin, Bowen, Richard and James Reynolds; daus. Elizabeth and Hannah Reynolds, Agnes Addison (wife of Jonathan), and Eunice Pettit (wife of Jacob). Exec'rs, wife Anne Reynolds and son Zachariah Reynolds. Wits., Adoniah Stansborough, Jacob Pettit. Prob. Nov. 24, 1791. Arch. vol. A95, page 54. Reg. of Wills, Liber D, folios 355-356.

**Grice, Ruth.** Widow. Will. Made Nov. 1, 1791. Heirs: sons Peter and David Parker. Exec'r, friend Jacob Hazzard. Wits., Joseph Hall, Mary Brady, Sarah Coulter. Prob. Dec. 9, 1791. Arch. vol. A73, pages 86-87. Reg. of Wills, Liber D, folio 358.

**Bready, Solomon.** Admin. of, to Peggy Lee Bready. Granted [c. 1792]. Arch. vol. A60, page 135.

**Brookfield, Ann.** Admin. of, to Edward Dingle. Granted [c. 1792]. Arch. vol. A60, pages 153-154.

**Brown, Israel.** Admin. of, to Mary and Israel Brown. Granted [c. 1792]. Arch. vol. A60, page 195.

**Prettyman, Robert, Jr.** Admin. of, to Elizabeth Prettyman. Granted [c. 1792]. Arch. vol. A94, page 102.

**Layton, Burton.** Will. Made Nov. 14, 1791. Heir: sister Esther Layton. Exec'r, father-in-law Thomas Ludenum. Wits., Thomas Layton, Thomas Stafford. Prob. Feb. 8, 1792. Arch. vol. A83, pages 171-172. Reg. of Wills, Liber D, folios 359-360.

**Massey, John, Jr.** Will. Made March 5, 1791. Heirs: wife Naomi Massey; dau. Jane Massey; bro. William Massey; sister Nancy Massey. Exec'rs, wife Naomi Massey and bro. William Massey. Wits., Stephen Hill, Thomas Harney, John Roberts. Prob. Feb. 8, 1792. Arch. vol. A87, pages 52-53. Reg. of Wills, Liber D, folio 361.

**Rickards [Ricords], Charles.** Admin. of, to Whittington Williams. Admr's bond dated Feb. 8, 1792. Arch. vol. A95, page 106.

**Holder, John.** Will. Made Jan. 16, 1792. Heirs: wife Sophia Holder; dau. E[dna] Holder; father Joseph Holder; William Holder (relationship not mentioned); friend Mary Giles (of William). Exec'r, friend Smith Lingo. Wits., William Callaway, William Whaley, Samuel Hearn. Prob. Feb. 9, 1792. Arch. vol. A77, pages 46-49. Reg. of Wills, Liber D, folio 359.

**Polk, John.** Admin. of, to George Vinson and wife Mary, late Mary Polk. Granted [c. Feb. 9, 1792]. Arch. vol. A93, page 129.

**Douce [Dous], Elizabeth.** Widow of Levin Douce. Will. Made Dec. 13, 1791. Heirs: dau. Sarah Young; grandson Benjamin Riley; Levin Douce. Exec'r, Benjamin Riley, grandson. Wits., John Lofland, Samuel Farquhar, Mary Baker. Prob. Feb. 10, 1792. Arch. vol. A69, page 168. Reg. of Wills, Liber D, folio 360.

**Redden, Charles.** Admin. of, to James Lawless and wife Esther, late Esther Redden. Granted [c. Feb. 10, 1792]. Arch. vol. A95, page 10.

**Gill, Margaret.** Will. Made Nov. 8, 1786. Heirs. daus. Priscilla, Elizabeth, Sarah, Naomi and Margaret Gill. Exec'r, friend John Rodney. Wits., Reese Woolf, Sarah Woolf. Prob. Feb. 13, 1792. Arch. vol. A72, pages 141-142. Reg. of Wills, Liber D, folios 361-362.

**Cary, Amos.** Admin. of, to Donovan Spencer and wife Sarah, late Sarah Cary. Granted before March 2, 1792. Arch. vol. A64, pages 20-23. [Note:—Arch. vol. A64, page 20 mentions heirs: minors Rhoda, William and Sally Cary].

**Clifton, Jonathan.** Admin. of, to Henry Clifton, D. B. N., C. T. A. Granted [c. March 6, 1792]. Arch. vol. A65, page 18.

**Melson, William.** Admin. of, to Nancy Melson. Granted [c. March 6, 1792]. Arch. vol. A88, page 70.

**Newbold, Thomas.** Admin. of, to William Newbold. Granted [c. March 6, 1792]. Arch. vol. A91, page 70.

**White, George.** Admin. of, to Mary White. Granted [c. March 6, 1792]. Arch. vol. A107, page 59.

**Brown, Charles, Sr.** Admin. of, to William Bowness and wife Sidney, and Charles Brown, Jr. Granted March 7, 1792. Arch. vol. A60, pages 170-171. [Note:—Arch. vol. A60, page 170 mentions Sidney Bowness as late Sidney Brown; page 171 mentions Sidney Brown was formerly Sidney Turner].

**Polk, Nelly.** Admin. of, to Jane Owens, D. B. N., of William Owens. Granted [c. March 8, 1792]. Arch. vol. A93, page 149.

**Draper, Nelly.** Admin. of, to Mark Davis. Granted [c. March 9, 1792]. Arch. vol. A69, page 216.

**McIlvain, James.** Admin. of, to Robert Prettyman. Granted [c. March 26, 1792]. Arch. vol. A87, page 193. [Note:—Arch. vol. A87, page 193 mentions heir: James McIlvain].

**White, Isaac.** Admin. of, to William Hall. Granted [c. March 28, 1792]. Arch. vol. A107, page 61. [Note:—Arch. vol. A107, page 61 mentions heirs of Isaac White; Robert White; Peter White; Wrixam White].

**Prettyman, Robert, Sr.** Admin. of, to Elizabeth Prettyman, D. B. N., in right of William Prettyman. Granted [c. April 9, 1792]. Arch. vol. A94, page 101.

**Burton, John (of Benjamin).** Admin. of, to Woodman Stockley and wife Sarah, late Sarah Burton. Granted ante May, 1792. Arch. vol. A61, page 185.

**Price, William.** Will. Made Feb. 17, 1791. Heirs: cousins Abraham Callaway, Elizabeth Callaway and Thomas Callaway (son of Elizabeth). Exec'r, cousin Abraham Callaway. Wits., Charles Brown, William Wallace. Prob. May 1, 1792. Arch. vol. A94, pages 143-144. Reg. of Wills, Liber D, folios 348-349. [Note:—Arch. vol. A94, page 144 shows that a dau. Elizabeth Price married Langford Boyce].

**Rouse, John.** Mariner. Will. Made May 11, 1791. Heirs: wife Eunice Rouse; son James Rouse; daus. Bridget and L[aurie] Rouse; dau.-in-law Eunice Carey. Exec'rx, wife Eunice Rouse. Wits., James Pettyjohn, James P. Wilson, Joshua Coston. Prob. May 1, 1792. Arch. vol. A97, page 103. Reg. of Wills, Liber D, folio 362. [Note:—Arch. vol. A97, page 103 shows the estate was settled April 22, 1796 by Eli Coulter and wife Eunice, late Eunice Rouse].

**Lecompt, Ann.** Will. Made Feb. 5, 1783. Heirs: sons William, Samuel and Thomas Moore; grandson William Polk. Exec'r, son William Moore. Wits., Cha[rle]s Moore, George Wales, Obediah Marvel. Prob. May 9, 1792. Arch. vol. A84, page 38. Reg. of Wills, Liber D, folios 362-363.

**Willey, Absalom.** Admin. of, to Margaret Willey. Admr's bond dated May 9, 1792. Arch. vol. A107, page 121.

**Newbold, Thomas.** Admin. of, to William Newbold. Granted [c. June 20, 1792]. Arch. vol. A91, page 80.

**Young, William.** Admin. of, to Joseph Hazzard. Granted [c. June 21, 1792]. Arch. vol. A109, page 146.

**Welch, Pennington.** Admin. of, to Robert Jones. Granted [c. June 22, 1792]. Arch. vol. A106, page 90.

**Rowland, Samuel.** Pilot Town, Lewes & Rehoboth Hd. Will. Made April 16, 1790. Heirs: wife Hannah (late Turner) Rowland; son Isaiah Rowland; grandchildren Joshua, Nancy, Tabitha, Jane, Sarah and Elizabeth Rowland (children of son John, dec'd), Joseph, Sarah and Elizabeth Rowland (children of son Isaiah); Rachel Turner (wife of John Turner). Exec'r, son Isaiah Rowland. Wits., David Hall, Peter White. Prob. July 17, 1792. Arch. vol. A97, page 119. Reg. of Wills, Liber D, folios 363-365.

**Rider, Betty.** Widow. Will. Made Jan. 15, 1790. Heirs: sons Charles Rider, Woolsey Waples; daus. Comfort Burton Waples and Nela Waples. Exec'r, bro. Benjamin Prettyman. Wits., Jno. Anderson, Jane Brad[le]y, Celia Grear. Prob. July 27, 1792. Arch. vol. A96, pages 1-2. Reg. of Wills, Liber D, folios 365-366.

**Wiltbank, John, Esq.** Lewes. Will. Made March 21, 1791. Heirs: wife Mary Wiltbank; sons James, Cornelius and John Wiltbank; daus. Mary Shankland, Elizabeth Hall (wife of Adam); grandsons Woodman Hall (son of Adam and Elizabeth Hall), Thomas Emory (son of dau. Mary); granddaus. Comfort Wiltbank, Mary Wiltbank, Margaret Kollock, Matil[da] Emory (dau. of dau. Mary); children of dau. Elizabeth Hall; son-in-law Adam Hall. Exec'rs, wife Mary Wiltbank, son Cornelius Wiltbank. Wits., Jno. Russell, Joseph Russell, John Sharp. Codicil. Dated July 3, 1792, mentions grandson John Hall (son of dau. Mary). Wits., Jno. Russell, John Sharp, I. C. Wilson. Prob. July 30, 1792. Arch. vol. A108, pages 153-156. Reg. of Wills, Liber D, folios 366-371. [Note:—Arch. vol. A108, page 153 mentions dec'd father Cornelius Wiltbank; page 156 shows the estate was settled by Cornelius Wiltbank, surviving exec'r].

**Bratton, James.** Admin. of, to Mary Anderson, late Mary Bratton. Granted [c. August, 1792]. Arch. vol. A60, pages 133-134.

**Hatfield, William.** Planter. Will. Made March 27, 1792. Heirs: wife Marg[ar]et Hatfield; sons John, Whitely and Jonathan Hatfield. [No exec'r]. Wits., Riley Evans, Lemuel Evans, Elisha Rickards. Prob. Aug. 7, 1792. Arch. vol. A74, page 235. Reg. of Wills, Liber D, folio 371.

**Taylor, Hugh Porter.** Will. Made March 11, 1792. Heirs: sons Hugh, John and Elias Taylor; daus. Isabell, Mary, Esther and Nancy Taylor, and Sarah Callaway. Exec'rs, son Hugh Taylor and dau. Mary Taylor. Wits., Jonathan Boyce, Dickerson Beauchamp, William Knowles. Prob. Aug. 8, 1792. Arch. vol. A101, page 116. Reg. of Wills, Liber D, folis 372-373.

**Vinson, Daniel.** Planter. Will (copy). Made Dec. 27, 1783. Heirs: wife Elizabeth Vinson (widow of William Gullet); sons Charles and Newbold Vinson. Exec'rx, wife Elizabeth Vinson. Wits., Obediah Marvel, Shiles Moore, Jess . . . . Prob. Aug. 8, 1792. Arch. vol. A103, page 146. Reg. of Wills, Liber D, folio 373.

**Whorton, Daniel.** Will. Made June 22, 1785. Heirs: wife Esther Whorton; son Isaiah Whorton; daus. Tabitha, Comfort, Maris, Sarah, Nancy and Esther Whorton, Diligence Townsend, Betty Townsend, Rhoda Williams. Exec'rs, son Isaiah Whorton and dau. Tabitha Whorton. Wits., John Onions, John Evans, Sr., James Whorton. Prob. Aug. 8, 1792. Arch. vol. A107, page 12. Reg. of Wills, Liber D, folios 371-372.

**Short, Allen.** Admin. of, to Rachel Short. Granted [c. Sept. 4, 1792]. Arch. vol. A98, page 160.

**Polk, Avery.** Admin. of, to Alexander Smith and wife Lucilla, late Lucilla Polk. Granted [c. Sept. 6, 1792]. Arch. vol. A93, page 105.

**Wood, John.** Lewes. Admin. of, to George Parker and wife Hannah, late Hannah Wood. Granted [c. Sept. 6, 1792]. Arch. vol. A109, page 46.

**Cannon, Absalom.** Planter. Will. Made May 27, 1792. Heirs: wife Frances Cannon; sons Isaac, Edward and Joseph Cannon; daus. Sarah Cannon, Tamsey and Priscilla Vincent, Catharine Coleburn, Clara Jones and Frances Patchett. Exec'r, son Isaac Cannon. Wits., Robert Clarkson, Joseph Cannon, Levi Cannon. Prob. Oct. 2, 1792. Arch. vol. A62, page 216. Reg. of Wills, Liber D, folios 373-374.

**Miller, Bathsheba.** Will. Made June 23, 1790. Heirs: son Peter White; daus. Jenny Richards, Mary Perkins; grandsons David, John and Joseph Miller; granddaus. Polly Perkins (dau. of Mary), Nancy Hill and Bathsheba Richards. Exec'r, son Peter White. Wits., James Miller, Isaiah Dirickson, Solomon Dirickson. Prob. Oct. 9, 1792. Arch. vol. A88, page 185. Reg. of Wills, Liber D, folios 374-375.

**Rider, John.** Planter. Will. Made Oct. 18, 1791. Heirs: bro. Charles Rider; cousin John Rider; Thomas, William Leatherbury and Elizabeth Hemmons. Exec'r, Thomas Hemmons. Wits., John Goslee, Mary Goslee, William Clark. Prob. Oct. 9, 1792. Arch. vol. A96, page 6. Reg. of Wills, Liber D, folios 375-376. [Note:—Arch. vol. A96, page 6 mentions Comfort Waples, dau. of Burton Waples].

**Darby, Mary.** Will. Made Oct. 11, 1792. Heirs: sons William, Samuel and John Darby; dau. Hester Darby. Exec'r, Thomas Hazzard. Wits., Elihu Waples, Priscilla Waples, Elizabeth Christopher. Prob. Oct. 18, 1792. Arch. vol. A68, page 26. Reg. of Wills, Liber D, folio 376.

**Cavender, James, Sr.** Planter. Will. Made Oct. 16, 1788. Heirs: sons James, Thomas, Charles, Henry and David Cavender; dau. Mary Cannon. Exec'r, son David Cavender. Wits., George Cannon, Newton Cannon, Robert Juett. Prob. Oct. 24, 1792. Arch. vol. A64, page 121. Reg. of Wills, Liber D, folios 376-377.

**Coston, Somerset Dickerson.** Admin. of, to Elizabeth Coston and Stephen Reddin. Granted [c. Nov. 1792]. Arch. vol. A67, pages 14-17. [Note:—Arch. vol. A67, page 14 shows that Elizabeth Coston later married William Spicer].

**Newbold, John.** Yeoman. Admin. of, to Charles Rickards and wife Ann, late Ann Newbold. Granted [c. Nov. 9, 1792]. Arch. vol. A91, pages 67-68.

**Vent, James.** Admin. of, to Mary Vent. Admr's bond dated Nov. 10, 1792. Arch. vol. A103, page 100.

**Howard, George.** Will. Made May 2, 1789. Heirs: wife Elizabeth Howard; Nehemiah Howard; Scarborough Tunnell; Elizabeth Dirickson (wife of Samuel); M[il]ly Aydelott (wife of John who is a son of Samuel). Exec'r, Scarborough Tunnell. Wits., Joseph Dirickson, Sr., William Tingle, Jr., Thomas Hazzard. Prob. Nov. 13, 1792. Arch. vol. A78, pages 136-138. Reg. of Wills, Liber D, folios 377-378.

**Godwin, Mary.** Admin. of, to Thomas Wilkins. Granted Nov. 24, 1792. Arch. vol. A72, page 166.

**Conaway [Conway], Philip.** Will. Made Oct. 24, 1792. Heirs: wife Basheba Conaway; sons L[ud]wick, William and Philip Conaway; daus. Millie, Hester and Sarah Conaway. Exec'rx, wife Basheba Conaway. Wits., James Lawless, John Conway (son of Levin), Levin Conway (son of Levin). Prob. Nov. 27, 1792. Arch. vol. A66, pages 71-73. Reg. of Wills, Liber D, folios 378-380.

**Methvin, Mary.** Will. Made July 4, 1792. Heirs: sons James and Thomas Methvin; dau. Lizzy [Eliza] Hearn; granddau. Mary Methvin (dau. of Meshack Methvin). Exec'r, son Meshack Methvin. Wits., Joshua Lingo, Sally Lingo, William Langsdale. Prob. Nov. 27, 1792. Arch. vol. A88, page 145. Reg. of Wills, Liber D, folio 378.

**Lewis, Thomas, Sr.** Will. Made Aug. 14, 1792. Heirs: wife Leah Lewis; sons Thomas, Job, George, Sothey, William, Jacob and Stephen Lewis; daus. Nancy, Polly, Martha, Kessiah, Elizabeth, Peggy, Leah, Comfort and Sarah Lewis. Exec'rx, wife Leah Lewis. Wits., Jesse Saunders, John Wainright, John Jones. Prob. Dec. 4, 1792. Arch. vol. A84, page 69. Reg. of Wills, Liber D, folios 379-380.

**Bradford, Nathaniel.** Admin. of, to Sinar Bradford. Granted [c. Dec. 5, 1792]. Arch. vol. A60, page 127.

**Vinson, Newbold.** Planter. Will. Made 18, 1791. Heirs: wife Rachel Vinson; sons Newbold, Isaac, Purnal, Charles, Robertson, Elijah, George and Ebenezer Vinson; daus. Sally, Milly and Rachel Vinson. Exec'rx, wife Rachel Vinson. Wits., John Williams, William Caldwell, William Bell. Prob.

Dec. 5, 1792. Arch. vol. A103, page 162. Reg. of Wills, Liber D, folio 386.

**Atkins, John Hancock.** Admin. of, to Stephen Styer. Granted [c. 1793]. Arch. vol. A57, page 209.

**Chambers, John.** Admin. of, to Bersheba Chambers. Granted [c. 1793]. Arch. vol. A64, page 123.

**Watson, John.** Admin. of, to William Salmon. Granted [c. Jan. 7, 1793]. Arch. vol. A106, page 22.

**Rodney, John.** Will. Made May 14, 1791. Heirs: wife Ruth Rodney; sons Daniel, Caleb, John and Thomas Rodney; dau. Penelope Kollock; grandsons Jacob and John Kollock; granddaus. Myra, Hester and Hannah Kollock; Hannah and Mary Turner (daus. of Isaac Turner). Exec'rs, wife Ruth Rodney and sons Daniel, Caleb, John and Thomas Rodney. Wits., Robert Shankland, William Brereton, Simon Marriner. Prob. Jan. 14, 1793. Arch. vol. A97, page 13. Reg. of Wills, Liber D, folio 380. [Note:—Arch. vol. A97, page 13 mentions Phillip Kollock, husband of Penelope].

**Bell, William.** Will. Made April 7, 1792. Heirs: sons William, Robert and Tilney Bell; granddaus. Sarah and Susanna and grandsons John, Thomas and Smith Bell (children of Thomas Bell, dec'd); granddaus. Nancy and Susannah and grandsons Thomas and William Bell (children of John Bell, dec'd); granddaus. Sarah and Priscilla Bell (daus. of John Bell, dec'd, by his last wife). Exec'rs, sons Robert and Tilney Bell. Wits., Richard Hays, Manlove Hays, Elizabeth Hays. Prob. Jan. 29, 1793. Arch. vol. A59, pages 67-68. Reg. of Wills, Liber D, folios 380-381.

**Dazey, Thomas, Jr.** Admin. of, to Sarah Dazey. Granted [c. Feb. 5, 1793]. Arch. vol. A68, page 204.

**Ricords, Benjamin.** Broadkill Hd. Will. Made March 1, 1793. Heirs: wife Esther Ricords; sons John, James, Levin and Hap Ricords; daus. Priscilla Ricords and Ann Stevenson. Exec'rs, wife Esther Ricords and son John Ricords. Wits., Ab[raha]m Kimmey, Samuel Graham. Prob. March 1, 1793. Arch. vol. A95, page 157. Reg. of Wills, Liber D, folio 388. [Note:—Arch. vol. A95, page 157 shows the estate was settled by John Ricords the surviving exec'r].

**Fisher, James.** Admin. of, to Nathan Jefferson and wife Elizabeth, late Elizabeth Fisher. Granted [c. March 7, 1793]. Arch. vol. A71, pages 129-130.

**Horsey, Nathaniel.** Will. Made Feb. 9, 1793. Heirs: wife Nancy Horsey; mentions an unborn child; Betsey, Martha and George Wales Horsey (children of bro. William) ; Mary Horsey Moore, Kitturah Moore and William Moore (children of bro.-in-law William Moore and sister Nancy Moore) ; Dr. Thomas Robertson (son of sister Martha and bro.-in-law Dr. Thomas Robertson) ; Stephen Horsey. Exec'r, nephew Dr. Thomas Robertson. Wits., Thomas Moore, William Moore, John Cremeen. Prob. March 5, 1793. Arch. vol. A78, pages 46-49. Reg. of Wills, Liber D, folios 381-382.

**Durham, George.** Admin. of, to Richard Durham. Granted March 6, 1793. Arch. vol. A70, page 8.

**Lofland, Joshua.** Admin. of, to Thomas Riley and wife Smart. Granted [c. March 6, 1793]. Arch. vol. A85, page 61.

**Walton, Luke.** Admin. of, to John Walton, D. B. N., in right of Elizabeth Walton. Granted [c. March 6, 1793]. Arch. vol. A104, page 153.

**Stapleford, Thomas.** Admin. of, to Castilla Stapleford. Granted [c. March 7, 1793]. Arch. vol. A100, pages 108-109. [Note: —Arch. vol. A100, page 109 shows that Castilla Stapleford later married Joseph Truitt].

**Webb, Obediah.** Admin. of, to Sylvester Webb. Granted [c. March 7, 1793]. Arch. vol. A106, page 73.

**Donovan [Dunavan], Foster.** The Elder. Yeoman. Will. Made Feb. 9, 1793. Heirs: wife Naomi Donovan; sons Jacob, John, William, Job, Foster, Abraham, Azariah and James Donovan; daus. Rhoda Reed and Naomi Sharp. Exec'rs, wife Naomi Donovan and son Foster Donovan. Wits., Jno. Russell, William Robbins, Francis Cornwell. Prob. March 19, 1793. Arch. vol. A69, page 140. Reg. of Wills, Liber D, folios 382-383.

**Hall, William.** Blacksmith. Will. Made Oct. 20, 1792. Heirs: wife Betty Hall; daus. Nancy, Polly, Sally and Betty Hall; bro. Joshua Hall; son-in-law Wallace Waples. Exec'rx, wife Betty Hall. Wits., Joseph Hall, Robert Willis. Prob. March 28, 1793. Arch. vol. A74, pages 7-9. Reg. of Wills, Liber D, folios 384-385. [Note:—Arch. vol. A74, page 9 shows that Betty Hall later married Thomas Wilson].

**Moor[e], Thomas.** Will. Made Feb. 24, 1793. Heirs: wife Pris-[cilla] Moore; son Samuel Moore; daus. Esther, Mary and Patty Moore. Exec'rs, wife Pris[cilla] Moore and bro. John Moore. Wits., Eli Vinson, William Dodd, John Moore. Prob.

April 2, 1793. Arch. vol. A89, page 148. Reg. of Wills, Liber D, folios 386-387.

**Hazzard, Elon.** Will. Made Sept. 7, 1790. Heirs: sons James, John, Cord, David Hazzard and Hinman Rhoads; grandson John Rhoads; dau.-in-law Margaret Rhoads. Exec'r, son Cord Hazzard. Wits., James F. Baylis, Levin Ennis, Samuel Ennis. Prob. April 3, 1793. Arch. vol. A75, page 53. Reg. of Wills, Liber D, folio 387.

**Townsend, Solomon, Sr.** Will. Made Jan. 4, 1772. Heirs: sons Jacob, William, Solomon and Luke Townsend; daus. Abigail Carlisle (wife of John), Phebe Morris (wife of Joseph). Exec'r, son Jacob Townsend. Wits., John Clowes, Jesse Deputy, Joshua Deputy. Codicil. Dated March 23, 1773. Mentions grandson John Townsend (son of Luke); and widow of son Solomon Townsend. Wits., John Lofland, John Clowes. Prob. April 7, 1793. Arch. vol. A102, page 76. Reg. of Wills, Liber B, folios 487-491.

**Collins, John.** Admin. of, to Polly Collins. Granted [before April 24, 1793]. Arch. vol. A65, pages 188-189. [Note:— Arch. vol. A65, page 188 mentions Polly Edgar, an heir of William Venables].

**Parker, Anderson.** Gentleman. Will. Made March 21, 1793. Heirs: son John Parker; daus. Mary Parker, Ann Hazzard and Sarah Rowland; grandson John Thompson; son-in-law Jacob Hazzard; Trustees of Church of St. Georges in Indian River Hd.; Trustees of St. Peters Church at Lewes. Exec'rs, son John Parker, dau. Sarah Rowland and son-in-law Jacob Hazzard. Wits., Jno. Russell, Sarah Linch, Thomas Sanders. Prob. April 30, 1793. Arch. vol. A92, pages 54-55. Reg. of Wills, Liber D, folios 388-390. [Note: —Arch. vol. A92, page 54 mentions his late bro. Peter Parker, dec'd; also shows the estate was exhibited on Nov. 16, 1798 by one of the exec'rs Jacob Hazzard, and finally settled by Nancy Hazzard, exec'rx of Jacob Hazzard].

**Stockley, Nathaniel.** Admin. of, to Job Townsend and wife Elizabeth, late Elizabeth Stockley. Granted [c. May 9, 1793]. Arch. vol. A101, page 27.

**Rust, William.** Admin. of, to Jemima Rust. Granted [c. May 10, 1793. Arch. vol. A97, page 172.

**Prettyman, Robert.** Indian River Hd. Admin. of, to William Coleman, D. B. N. Granted [c. June 5, 1793]. Arch. vol. A94, page 103.

**Rickards, John.** Admin. of, to Elias Rickards. Granted June 5, 1793. Arch. vol. A95, page 124. [Note:—Arch. vol. A95, page 124 mentions an heir Esther Wharton].

**Sharp, Joshua.** Admin. of, to John Willers. Granted [c. June 6, 1793]. Arch. vol. A98, pages 89-90. [Note:—Arch. vol. A98, page 90 mentions an orphan, Sally Sharp].

**Evans, Ebenezer, Sr.** Will. Made March 1, 1793. Heirs: wife Sophia Evans; sons John and Samuel Evans; daus. Sarah Derickson, Molly Tracy, Rachel Bridell and Sophia Burton; son-in-law Elihu Bridell; grandson Isaac Burton; granddaus. Arcada Hazzard and Betty Rickards. Exec'rx, wife Sophia Evans. Wits., William Hall, Eli Evans, Littleton Townsend. Prob. July 1, 1793. Arch. vol. A70, pages 186-187. Reg. of Wills, Liber D, folios 390-391.

**Norman, John.** Will. Made June 12, 1793. Heirs: wife Ann Norman; son John Norman; daus. Major Coates, Selah Clifton, Nancy Hurst and Sarah Davis; son-in-law Hezekiah Downs. Exec'r, son-in-law Thomas Peachy Coates. Wits., David Nutter, Lydia Clifton, Joseph Nickols. Prob. July 23, 1793. Arch. vol. A91, page 111. Reg. of Wills, Liber D, folio 392.

**Reed, Matthew.** Will. Made May 2, 1793. Heirs: wife Patience Reed; sons John and Nathan Reed; daus. Margaret Gray and Elizabeth Kel[s]o; granddau. Sarah Kel[s]o. Exec'rs, wife Patience Reed and son John Reed. Wits., John Lofland, Isaac Lofiand, Sarah Douce. Prob. July 23, 1793. Arch. vol. A95, page 37. Reg. of Wills, Liber D, folios 392-393.

**Burton, Mary.** Admin. of, to David Burton. Granted [c. Aug. 1793]. Arch. vol. A61, page 223.

**Callaway, Elisha.** Planter. Will. Made June 6, 1793. Heirs: son Levin Callaway; daus. Nelly and Polly Callaway. Exec'rx, wife Rebecca Callaway. Wits., Isaac L[y]nch, Levin Callaway, John Humphries. Prob. Aug. 6, 1793. Arch. vol. A62, pages 139-140. Reg. of Wills, Liber D, folios 395-396.

**Callaway, William.** Planter. Will. Made March 22, 1791. Heirs: wife Sarah Callaway; sons Wingate, Winder, William and John Callaway; daus. Frankey, Polly, Betty, Sarah, Nancy, Hetty and Peggy. Exec'rx, wife Sarah Callaway. Wits., John Williams, Lewis Hall, John Cahoon. Prob. Aug. 6, 1793. Arch. vol. A62, pages 178-179. Reg. of Wills, Liber D, folios 393-395. [Note:—Arch. vol. A62, page 179 mentions Polly Ward; also shows that Sarah Callaway later married Marshall Smith].

**Hardyknight, John.** Will. Made June 15, 1793. Heirs: Moses Culver, Sr.; Lovey Culver, Roddy Rich. Exec'r, Moses Culver, Sr. Wits., Joseph Hardy, Ephraim Culver, James Culver. Prob. Aug. 6, 1793. Arch. vol. A82, page 166. Reg. of Wills, Liber D, folios 393-394.

**Lowe, Ralph.** Will. Made May 28, 1793. Heirs: wife Ann Lowe; sons Ralph and James Lowe; daus. Elinor Lowe, Ann Weatherly Waller (wife of James); grandsons James Lowe Waller (son of George); James Rencher Lowe; granddau. Mary Weatherly Waller (dau. of James Weatherly Waller); nephew William Lowe (son of bro. John); son-in-law William Elsy. Exec'rs, wife Ann Lowe and son James Lowe. Wits., Thomas English, Ezekiel Knowles, William Dodd. Prob. Aug. 6, 1793. Arch. vol. A85, pages 147-148. Reg. of Wills, Liber D, folios 394-395. [Note:—Arch. vol. A85, page 148 shows the estate was settled Oct. 8, 1794 by James Lowe surviving exec'r].

**Wells, Thomas.** Will. Made Sept. 20, 1791. Heirs: wife unnamed; son Jesse Wells; rest of children unnamed. [No exec'r]. Wits., Benja[min] Vinson, Jesse Kellam, Ebenezer Hearn. Prob. Aug. 6, 1793. Arch. vol. A106, page 93. Reg. of Wills, Liber D, folios 397-398.

**Simpson, Peter.** Joiner. Somerset Co., Md. Will. Made July 4, 1793. Heirs: sons John, William and Samuel Simpson; dau. Nancy Simpson. Exec'r, John Hooper. Wits., Nathan Adams, Sally Adams, William H. Travers. Guardian:—John Hooper. Prob. Aug. 7, 1793. Arch. vol. A99, page 64. Reg. of Wills, Liber D, folio 396.

**Smith, George.** Planter. Will. Made June 10, 1793. Heirs: wife Sophia Smith; sons George, Cannon, Thomas, Henry and Langran Smith. Exec'rs, wife Sophia Smith and bro. Henry Smith. Wits., John Handy, Allen Smith, Sally Smith. Prob. Aug. 7, 1793. Arch. vol. A99, page 136. Reg. of Wills, Liber D, folio 397. [Note:—Arch. vol. A99, page 136 shows that Sophia Smith later married Lowder Cannon].

**Dier, John.** Will. Made July 12, 1793. Heirs: wife Leah Dier; sons John, Charles, William and Potter Dier; daus. Mary and Sarah Dier. Exec'r, son John Dier. Wits., Ezekiel Williams, Benjamin Wharton, Henry Lawrence. Prob. Aug. 8, 1793. Arch. vol. A69, page 76. Reg. of Wills, Liber D, folio 398.

**Cary, Ebenezer.** Will. Made May 23, 1793. Heirs: wife Hannah Cary; sons Elijah, Purnel, Elisha, Zachariah and John Cary;

daus. Rhoda and Hannah Cary, and Nicey Thompson; Woolsey Cary (son of Rhoda Cary). Exec'r, son John Cary. Wits., Solomon Willey, Robert West. Prob. Aug. 9, 1793. Arch. vol. A64, pages 31-32. Reg. of Wills, Liber D, folios 398-399.

**Cannon, Wingate.** Admin. of, to Sally Cannon. Granted before Aug. 12, 1793. Arch. vol. A63, page 155.

**Kinneykin, Daniel.** Will. Made Feb. 12, 1792. Heirs: sons Waitman, Matthew and Daniel Kinneykin; daus. Sarah and Frances Kinneykin, Prudence Hasty, Sophia Stebins. Exec'r, son Waitman Kinneykin. Wits., William Sharp, Isaac Vinson, Stephen Wainright Thorns. Prob. Aug. 20, 1793. Arch. vol. A82, pages 135-136. Reg. of Wills, Liber D, folios 399-400.

**Luker, William.** Admin. of, to Thomas Quillen and wife Catharine, late Catharine Luker. Admr's bond dated Aug. 20, 1793. Arch. vol. A85, page 177.

**Paynter, John.** Admin. of, to Priscilla Paynter. Granted [c. Sept. 4, 1793]. Arch. vol. A92, page 123. [Note:—Arch. vol. A92, page 123 mentions minor sons Richard and Lemuel Paynter].

**Richardson, Sarah.** Admin. of, to Francis Anderton. Granted [c. Sept. 5, 1793]. Arch. vol. A95, page 103.

**Smith, Allen.** Admin. of, to James Wiley. Granted Sept. 5, 1793. Arch. vol. A99, pages 108-109.

**Pride, James.** Admin. of, to Sophia Pride. Granted [c. Sept. 6, 1793]. Arch. vol. A94, page 147.

**Oakey, Jeangull.** Lewes & Rehoboth Hd. Will. Made Sept. 29, 1792. Heir: son Jonathan Oakey. [No exec'r]. Wits., Elijah Cannon, Arcada Cannon, Leah Parremore. Prob. Sept. 7, 1793. Arch. vol. A91, page 134. Reg. of Wills, Liber D, folio 402.

**Hickman, Rachel.** Will. Made Nov. 5, 1790. Heirs: son Jacob Hickman; daus. Betty Ricords, Mary Lofland; Phebe Hickman (dau. of John Hickman). Exec'r, Jacob Hickman. Wits., John Young, Avery Draper, Henry Draper. Prob. Sept. 10, 1793. Reg. of Wills, Liber D, folios 402-403.

**Davis, Zerobabel.** Admin. of, to Nancy Davis. Granted [c. Sept. 14, 1793]. Arch. vol. A68, page 142.

**McDaniel, Elisabeth.** Widow. Will. Made Sept. 22, 1793. Heirs: Jehu Lawson; Betsey Lawson (dau. of James); Solbey Lawson (son of James). Exec'r, James Lawson. Wits., John Dazey, John Evans. [No prob.]. Arch. vol. A87, page 146.

**Lowry, James.** Will. Made Sept. 5, 1793. Heirs: son James Lowry; dau. Frances Lowry. Exec'rs, Henry Smith, Sidney Brown. Wits., L[udwig] Connaway, Samuel Massey, George Cannon. Prob. Oct. 1, 1793. Arch. vol. A85, pages 156-159. Reg. of Wills, Liber D, folios 400-401.

**Jones, Martha.** Spinster. Worcester Co., Md. Will (copy). Made Jan. 24, 1771. Heirs: bro. Thomas Jones; sisters Bridget Pettyjohn (wife of James) and Agnes Tindall (wife of Samuel). Exec'r, bro. Thomas Jones. Wits., Joseph Robinson, Thomas Marvel, Simon Kollock. Prob. Oct. 29, 1793. Arch. vol. A81, page 175. Reg. of Wills, Liber D, folios 401-402.

**Burbage, Thomas.** Will. Made Aug. 27, 1788. Heirs: son John Burbage; daus. Rachel, Nancy and Tabitha Burbage. Exec'r, son John Burbage. Wits., Robert Lacey, David McIlvain, Jno. Anderson. Prob. Nov. 5, 1793. Arch. vol. A61, pages 52-53. Reg. of Wills, Liber D, folios 403-404.

**Dolbee, Upsherd Messick.** Admin. of, to Hales Spicer. Granted Nov. 5, 1793. Arch. vol. A69, page 133.

**Burton, John [Sr.].** Admin. of, to Ann Catharine Burton. Granted [c. Nov. 6, 1793]. Arch. vol. A61, page 184.

**Morris, Tamer.** Widow of William. Will. Made July 22, 1793. Heirs: sons Stephen Morris and Jacob Hargis; dau. Hannah Morris. Exec'r, son Jacob Hargis. Wits., Leah Collings, Burton Waples. Prob. Nov. 8, 1793. Arch. vol. A90, pages 140-141. Reg. of Wills, Liber D, folios 404-405.

**Dodd, William.** Will. Made July 11, 1793. Heirs: wife Sarah Dodd; son William Dodd; grandchildren Jacob and Peggy Dodd. Exec'r, friend Peter Marsh. Wits., John Chambers, Barsheba Chambers, John Marsh. Prob. Nov. 9, 1793. Arch. vol. A69, page 112. Reg. of Wills, Liber D, folio 403.

**Irons, Jane.** Admin. of, to Lemuel Irons. Granted [c. Nov. 19, 1793]. Arch. vol. A79, page 197.

**Rickards, William.** Will. Made Oct. 25, 1793. Heirs: wife Agnes Rickards; sons William, Molton, Mills and Luke Rickards; dau. Zeporah Daniels; grandson Thomas Norman. Exec'r, son Luke Rickards. Wits., Elzey Richardson, John Tatman,

Ja[me]s Rench. Codicil: mentions granddau. Elizabeth Smith. Prob. Nov. 19, 1793. Arch. vol. A95, page 150. Reg. of Wills, Liber D, folios 405-406.

**Bloxam, Richard.** Admin. of, to Hannah Bloxam. Granted [c. Nov. 20, 1793]. Arch. vol. A59, page 238.

**Cannon, Stephen, Sr.** Will. Made Sept. 28, 1793. Heirs: son Stephen Cannon; dau. Elizabeth Wingate. Exec'r, son Stephen Cannon. Wits., Abraham Cannon, Levi Cannon, Thomas Watts. Prob. Nov. 20, 1793. Arch. vol. A63, pages 134 and 137. Reg. of Wills, Liber D, folio 406.

**Fentham, William Wyatt.** Admin. of, to William Hill Wells. Granted Nov. 20, 1793. Arch. vol. A71, page 58.

**Collins, Levi.** Admin. of, to Noah Collins. Granted Nov. 23, 1793. Arch. vol. A65, page 221.

**Fowler, William.** Admin. of, to Burton Robinson and wife Rhoda, late Rhoda Fowler. Granted [c. Nov. 26, 1793]. Arch. vol. A72, page 29. [Note:—Arch. vol. A72, page 29 mentions heirs: Sarah and John Conwell].

**Vinson, Elijah.** Admin. of, to Rachel Vinson. Granted [c. Nov. 28, 1793]. Arch. vol. A103, page 150.

**Warwick, Jeremiah.** Admin. of, to William Warwick. Granted [c. Nov. 28, 1793]. Arch. vol. A105, page 178.

**Morrison, Joseph.** Admin. of, to William Vaughan and wife Sarah, late Sarah Waples, who was adm'rx of Peter Waples, adm'r of this estate. Granted [c. Nov. 29, 1793]. Arch. vol. A90, pages 163-164.

**Wilson, Temperance.** Will (copy). Made Aug. 28, 1792. Heir: son Joshua Wilson. Exec'r, son Joshua Wilson. Wits., William Johnson, Staton Johnson, Lovey Johnson. Prob. Nov. 29, 1793. Arch. vol. A108, page 120. Reg. of Wills, Liber D, folio 406.

**Dean, John.** Admin. of, to Jesse Dean. Granted [c. Dec. 8, 1793]. Arch. vol. A68, page 217.

**Milman, Peter.** Farmer. Will. Made March 16, 1792. Heirs: sons Peter, Ephraim, Thomas, William, Jesse and Beniah Milman; dau. Mary Holston and other daughters unnamed. Exec'rs, sons Ephraim and Thomas Milman. Wits., Benjamin Hudson, Mary Hudson, Richard Blocksom. Prob. Dec. 10, 1793. Arch. vol. A89, page 10. Reg. of Wills, Liber D, folios 406-407. [Note:—Arch. vol. A89, page 10 shows the estate was settled Dec. 9, 1795 by Ephraim Milman, surviving exec'r].

**Willey, Ezekiel.** Admin. of, to Sarah Willey. Granted Dec. 17, 1793. Arch. vol. A107, page 123.

**Cirwithin, Isaac.** Admin. of, to Moses Hall and wife Mary, late Mary Lewes and also late Mary Cirwithin. Granted [c. 1794]. Arch. vol. A64, pages 166-167. [Note:—Arch. vol. A64, page 166 mentions son Caleb Cirwithin; also shows Roderick Lewes and wife Mary, late Mary Cirwithin, as exec'rs April 10, 1798].

**Coffin, William.** Admin. of, to James Starr. Granted ante Jan. 1794. Arch. vol. A65, pages 90-92.

**Dingle, William.** Will. Made Dec. 6, 1793. Heirs: nephews Edward and William Dingle. Exec'r, bro. Edward Dingle. Wits., William Hill Wells, Jno. Anderson, Joshua Harney. Prob. Jan. 7, 1794. Arch. vol. A69, page 85. Reg. of Wills, Liber D, folio 407.

**Pool, Major.** Will. Made Jan. 10, 1793. Heirs: son Andrew Pool; daus. Betsey and Sally Pool. Exec'r, Peter Robinson, Esq. Wits., William Johnson, Perry Pool, James F. Baylis. Prob. Jan. 21, 1794. Arch. vol. A93, pages 193-194. Reg. of Wills, Liber D, folio 408. [Note:—Arch. vol. A93, page 194 shows that Peter Robinson renounced his right to act as exec'r and the estate was settled by William Pool].

**Price, William.** Pilot. Admin. of, to Margaret Price, Daniel Rodney. Granted [c. Jan. 28, 1794]. Arch. vol. A94, page 145.

**Daughter, John.** Admin. of, to Robert McMichael. Granted [c. Feb. 5, 1794]. Arch. vol. A68, page 46.

**Stockley, Cornelius.** Admin. of, to Anderson Hudson and wife Elizabeth, late Elizabeth Stockley. Granted [c. Feb. 4, 1794]. Arch. vol. A101, page 1.

**Wiley [Willey], Andrew.** Merchant. Will. Made Sept. 23, 1793. Heirs: wife Ann Wiley, late Ann McNight; daus. Peggy and Ann Wiley. Exec'rx, [wife Ann Wiley]. Wits., Samuel Ratcliff, James Elliott, James McNaight. Guardians:—John Collins, Sr., John Ingram, Sr. Prob. Feb. 12, 1794. Arch. vol. A107, pages 114-115. Reg. of Wills, Liber D, folios 408-409. [Note:—Arch. vol. A107, page 115 shows the estate was settled by Samuel Paynter and Robert West, exec'rs of Ann Wiley].

**Montford [Mumford], William.** Admin. of, to John Montford. Granted [c. Feb. 18, 1794]. Arch. vol. A89, page 88.

**Carlisle, John.** Admin. of, to Elizabeth Carlisle. Granted [c. March 1974]. Arch. vol. A63, pages 162-163.

**Hosea, John.** Admin. of, to Levinah Hosea. Granted [c. March 4, 1794]. Arch. vol. A78, page 71.

**Richards, Joseph.** Admin. of, to John Richards. Granted [c. March 4, 1794]. Arch. vol. A95, page 89.

**Hearn, Jonathan.** Will (copy). Made Jan. 18, 1794. Heirs: sons Jonathan, Isaac, Elijah, William, Samuel, Ebenezer and George Hearn; dau. Sarah Hearn. Exec'rs, sons Isaac and Elijah Hearn. Wits., Joshua Hasting, Hezekiah Hasting, William Hasting. Prob. March 18, 1794. Arch. vol. A75, pages 158-160. Reg. of Wills, Liber D, folios 409-411.

**Polk, William.** Admin. of, to Nancy and Edward Polk. Granted [c. March 18, 1794]. Arch. vol. A93, page 162.

**Wallace, Alice.** Will. Made Dec. 21, 1793. Heirs: bro. Benjamin Wallace; sister Ann Ricords; bro.-in-law Charles Ricords; nephews Able Hopkins Brown and Whittington Wallace Williams; nieces Sarah Hopkins Brown and Ann Brown. Exec'r, bro.-in-law Charles Ricords. Wits., Joseph Ricords, John Brown, Nelly Brown. Prob. March 18, 1794. Arch. vol. A104, page 44. Reg. of Wills, Liber D, folio 409.

**Martin, James, Esq.** Admin. of, to Mary Martin. Granted [c. March 19, 1794]. Arch. vol. A86, page 146.

**Hopkins, Archibald.** Yeoman. Admin. of, to Robert Hunter and wife Prudence, late Prudence Hopkins. Granted [c. March 20, 1794]. Arch. vol. A77, pages 176-177.

**Watson, David.** Admin. of, to Bethuel Watson, Jr., Rachel Watson. Granted [c. April 2, 1794]. Arch. vol. A106, pages 3-4.

**Watson, Rachel.** Admin. of, to Bethuel Watson, Jr. Granted [c. April 2, 1794]. Arch. vol. A106, pages 36-37.

**Crapper, John, Jr.** Admin. of, to John Mason, D. B. N., in right of Susannah Crapper. Granted before April 22, 1794. Arch. vol. A67, pages 167-168.

**Griffith, Charles.** Admin. of, to Sarah Griffith. Granted [c. April 23, 1794]. Arch. vol. A73, pages 95-96.

**Irons, David.** Admin. of, to Lemuel Irons. Granted April 23, 1794. Arch. vol. A79, pages 193-194.

**Johnson, Peter.** Will. Made Sept. 12, 1793. Heirs: wife Sarah Johnson; sons George Passons and Peter Johnson; daus. Abigail, Hannah and Rachel Johnson. Exec'rs, wife Sarah Johnson and bro. Isaac Johnson. Wits., Elisha Evans, Abigail Dishroon, Littleton Townsend. Prob. April 23, 1794. Arch. vol. A81, pages 82-83. Reg. of Wills, Liber D, folios 411-412.

**Juley, Eleanor.** Will (copy). Made Feb. 13, 1794. Heirs: son Robert Cannon Juley; daus. Polly and Nancy Juley; bros. Thomas, John and Charles Marine; Nancy Smith (wife of Ezekiel); Sally and Betsy Smith (daus. of Ezekiel and Nancy); Sally Marine (wife of Thomas); Betsy Marine (wife of Charles); Tamzey Richards (wife of William); children of bro. Thomas Marine; children of bro. Charles Marine. Exec'r, Ezekiel Smith. Wits., Rob[er]t Clarkson, Jesse Clarkson, Robert Cannon. Prob. April 23, 1794. Arch. vol. A82, pages 19-20. Reg. of Wills, Liber D, folios 412-413.

**Short, Jonathan.** Admin. of, to Parsons Huston. Granted [c. April 23, 1794]. Arch. vol. A99, page 6.

**Hitchens, Levin Smith.** Admin. of, to Sally Cannon. Granted [c. April 29, 1794]. Arch. vol. A77, pages 28-29. [Note:— Arch. vol. A77, page 28 mentions Sally Cannon, adm'rx of Wingate Cannon, who was adm'r of Levin Smith Hitchens].

**Wails [Wales], Levin.** Admin. of, to George Vinson and wife Mary, late Mary Wails. Granted [c. April 30, 1794]. Arch. vol. A103, page 191.

**Campbell, John.** Admin. of, to Nancy Campbell. Granted [c. May, 1794]. Arch. vol. A62, page 198.

**Williams, Morgan.** Will. Made March 11, 1793. Heirs: wife Esther Williams; son Robert Williams; daus. Ann Morgan (wife of George), Elinor Short (wife of John), Betsy Holland (wife of David), and Sarah Donaho (wife of Major Donaho); grandsons, Morgan and George Frederick Williams (son of Robert), George Williams Morgan and William Morgan (sons of George Morgan); granddaus. Levina Truitt (dau. of James Truitt, dec'd) and Lottie Truitt; dau.-in-law Bridget Wallace. Exec'r, son Robert Williams. Wits., Tho[ma]s Laws, John Graham, Charles Brown. Prob. May 13, 1794. Arch. vol. A108, pages 19-21. Reg. of Wills, Liber D, folios 413-414. [Note:—Arch. vol. A108, pages 19, 20 and 21 shows the estate was settled by Sarah Hopkins Williams and Levin Richards, exec'rs of Robert Williams, dec'd, on May 2, 1799].

**Morris, Dennis.** Broadkill Hd. Will. Made March 14, 1794. Heirs: sons Joshua and Dennis Morris; daus. Judith Clendaniel (wife of Luke), Elizabeth Messick (wife of Levi), Eunice Coverdall (wife of Richard), Joanna Reed (wife of Zachariah); grandsons Jeremiah, Jacob and Noah (sons of George Morris). Exec'r, son Dennis Morris. Wits., William Riley, John Riley, James Knox. Prob. May 14, 1794. Arch. vol. A90, page 37. Reg. of Wills, Liber D, folios 415-416.

**Burton, Ann Catherine.** Will. Made April 27, 1794. Heirs: son John Burton; daus. Ann Catharine Barker and Elizabeth Carey; granddaus. Phebe, Ann Catharine and Alice Burton; grandsons Cornelius Burton, David Barker and James Burton Baily. Exec'r, son John Burton. Wits., Isaac Burton, Mary Burton, James F. Baylis. Prob. May 17, 1794. Arch. vol. A61, page 74. Reg. of Wills, Liber D, folio 415.

**Walls, Thomas.** Broadkill Hd. Will. Made April 3, 1794. Heirs: wife Mary Walls; sons Samuel, Jesse, Thomas and Burton Walls; daus. Nancy, Mary and Nelly Walls. Exec'rs, wife Mary Walls and father Samuel Walls. Wits., Eli Collins, Charity Collins, Joshua Walls. Prob. May 20, 1794. Arch. vol. A104, page 111. Reg. of Wills, Liber D, folios 414-415.

**Corbin, Stephen.** Planter. Will. Made Oct. 6, 1789. Heirs: wife Marg[ar]et Corbin; sons John and William Corbin; dau. Anna Corbin. Exec'rx, wife Marg[ar]et Corbin. Wits., Robert Clarkson, Jacob Kender, Jacob Kender, Jr. Prob. May 27, 1794. Arch. vol. A66, pages 175-176. Reg. of Wills, Liber D, folio 417.

**Crockett, Elizabeth.** Will. Made Sept. 1, 1788. Heirs: sons Richard and Winder Crockett; dau. Netty Crockett; grandsons Joseph, Newbold, Richard V[ena]bles and John Sears Crockett; granddau. Nelly Winder Crockett (dau. of Richard); Betty Turner. Exec'rs, son Winder Crockett and grandson Joseph [V.] Crockett. Wits., Levin Connaway, Jacob Adams, Joseph Boyce. Prob. May 27, 1794. Arch. vol. A67, pages 189-190. Reg. of Wills, Liber D, folios 417-418.

**Evans, John.** Will (copy). Made June 6, 1791. Heirs: wife Margaret Evans; [children] Joney, Azariah, Thomas, Edey, Charlotte and Barsheba Evans; Nancy Freeman. Exec'rs, wife Margaret Evans and Job Freeman. Wits., Thomas Gray, Sarah Dyer, Elisha Gray. Prob. May 27, 1794. Arch.

vol. A70, pages 219-221. Reg. of Wills, Liber D, folio 419. [Note:—Arch. vol. A70, page 222 mentions Sabrina and Solomon Evans].

**Hickman, Levin.** Will. Made May 3, 1794. Heirs: wife Nancy Hickman; sons Tilghman and William Hickman; daus. Rebecca and Levina Hickman, and Elinor Layton (wife of Purnel). Exec'r, friend Thomas Laws. Wits., Francis Brown, Thomas Curry, Azariah Donovan. Prob. May 27, 1794. Arch. vol. A76, page 76. Reg. of Wills, Liber D, folios 418-419.

**Simpler, Andrew.** Farmer. Broadkiln Hd. Will. Made April 19, 1794. Heirs: son Milby Simpler; daus. Nancy and Comfort Simpler; grandsons George Simpler (son of Milby), Andrew Pool; granddaus. Polly Simpler, Betsey Pool and Polly Merill Goslin. Exec'rx, daus. Nancy and Comfort Simpler. Wits., Amelia Hazzard, Sam[ue]l Paynter, Jr. Prob. May 27, 1794. Arch. vol. A99, pages 43-44. Reg. of Wills, Liber D, folios 419-420. [Note:—Arch. vol. A99, page 44 shows that Comfort Simpler later married William Simpler].

**Simpler, Nanny.** Admin. of, to Milby Simpler. Granted May 27, 1794. Arch. vol. A99, page 56.

**Windsor, Joseph.** Admin. of, to Caldwell Windsor. Granted [c. May 27, 1794. Arch. vol. A108, page 170.

**Fleetwood, John.** Yeoman. Broadkiln Hd. Will. Made May 19, 1794. Heirs: sons Joseph, Cornelius, John and Parmer Fleetwood; daus. Lydia, Mary and Nancy Fleetwood. Exec'r, son Cornelius Fleetwood. Wits., Samuel Paynter, Jr., Augusta Wiltbanks. Prob. June 9, 1794. Arch. vol. A71, pages 189-190. Reg. of Wills, Liber D, folios 420-421. [Note:— Arch. vol. A71, page 189 mentions deceased wife Mary as daughter of Joseph Parmer. Also mentions a negro man named Orange].

**Smith, Thomas.** Will. Made Nov. 13, 1789. Heirs: wife Rachel Smith; sons Henry, Clement, Thomas and Selah Smith; dau. Sally Baker (wife of Purnal Henry Baker). Exec'rs, wife Rachel Smith and son Henry Smith. Wits., John Lord, Adam Lord, Daniel Killey. Prob. July 1, 1794. Arch. vol. A100, page 9. Reg. of Wills, Liber D, folios 421-422. [Note: Arch. vol. A100, page 9 shows the estate was settled Sept. 1, 1795 by Henry Smith, surviving exec'r].

**Willin [Willing], Thomas.** Will. Made June 2, 1794. Heirs: wife Lear Willin; sons Isaac Adams, Charles and Thomas Willin; daus. Mary, Rachel and Sarah Willin. Exec'rx, wife Lear

Willin. Wits., Robert W. McCalley, Joshua Johnson, Mary Johnson. Prob. July 8, 1794. Arch. vol. A108, page 57. Reg. of Wills, Liber D, folio 423. [Note:—Arch. vol. A108, page 57 shows the estate was settled April 12, 1796 by John Day and wife Leah [Lear], late Lear Willin].

**Vaughan, William.** Will. Made Jan. 15, 1794. Heirs: nephews William and John Hammond Burton; niece Lydia Burton; friend Samuel Tingley. Exec'rx, sister Mary Burton. Wits., David Craige, Naomi Stockley, John Marsh. Prob. July 12, 1794. Arch. vol. A103, page 85. Reg. of Wills, Liber D, folios 423-424. [Note:—Arch. vol. A103, page 85 shows the estate was settled June 17, 1795 by Robert Frame, in right of his wife Mary, who was exec'rx of William Vaughan].

**Hall, Mary.** Will. Made Jan. 8, 1794. Heirs: bro. William Hall; Adam Roberts (son of Hannah Roberts). Exec'r, bro. William Hall. Wits., William Jordan Hall, Katharine Evans, Sheba Cord. Prob. July 22, 1794. Arch. vol. A73, page 231. Reg. of Wills, Liber D, folio 424.

**Lewis, Simeon.** Bricklayer. Will. Made March 23, 1787. Heirs: grandsons Simeon Lewis (son of Luke), Samuel Draper (son of Samuel), Joseph Spencer (son of Jesse); granddau. Ann Spencer (dau. of Jesse), Elizabeth Lewis (sister of Simeon Lewis); Mary Lewis (widow of Luke). Exec'r, Isaac Beauchamp. Wits., Joseph Fleming, John Clifton, Sarah Watson. Prob. July 22, 1794. Arch. vol. A84, pages 66-67. Reg. of Wills, Liber E, folio 1.

**Shankland, Samuel.** Admin. of, to David Thornton and wife [Elise], late [Elise] Shankland. Granted [c. July 22, 1794]. Arch. vol. A98, page 60.

**Tilney, Jacob Stringer.** Will. Made March 20, 1794. Heirs: bros. John and Jonathan Tilney; sister Polly Tilney. Exec'rx, mother Betty Tilney. Wits., David Thornton, Elisha Thornton, Henry Smith. Prob. July 22, 1794. Arch. vol. A101, page 189. Reg. of Wills, Liber D, folio 424.

**Wainwright, John.** Admin. of, to John [Qui]mbles and wife Temperence, late Temperence Wainwright. Granted [c. Aug. 3, 1794]. Arch. vol. A104, page 5.

**Hodgson, Gammage.** Admin. of, to Ann Hodgson. Granted [c. Aug. 5, 1794]. Arch. vol. A77, page 44.

**Cook, Mark.** Admin. of, to Levin Wright. Granted [c. Aug. 19, 1794]. Arch. vol. A66, page 157. [Note:—Arch. vol.

A66, page 157 mentions Thomas Patterson Cook, as youngest son].

**Argo, Moses.** Admin. of, to Robert Wattson. Granted [c. Sept. 2, 1794]. Arch. vol. A57, page 180. [Note:—Arch. vol. A57, page 180 mentions a grandchild Sarah Argo and dec'd wife unnamed].

**Bryan, Betsy.** Admin. of, to Sheppard Bryan. Granted [c. Sept. 2, 1794]. Arch. vol. A60, page 247.

**Murphey, Joseph.** Yeoman. Will. Made Sept. 8, 1794. Heirs: wife Priscilla Murphey; son Joseph Murphey; daus. Nancy and Polly Murphey, Sarah and Rachel Willey; dau-in-law Polly Carter. Exec'rs, son Joseph Murphey and dau. Nancy Murphey. Wits., William Carlisle, Nancy Willey, Warr[en] Burroughs. Prob. Sept. 18, 1794. Arch. vol. A90, pages 199-200. Reg. of Wills, Liber E, folio 2.

**Williams, David.** Will. Made Sept. 8, 1794. Heirs: son David Williams; bros. and sisters unnamed. Exec'r, Morgan Williams. Wits., Ephraim Pettit, Daniel Murphey, Purnel Hammond. Guardian: Morgan Williams. Prob. Sept. 23, 1794. Arch. vol. A107, pages 159-160. Reg. of Wills, Liber E, folios 2-3.

**Melson, Elijah.** Admin. of, to George Black and wife Elizabeth, late Elizabeth Melson. Granted [c. Sept. 29, 1794]. Arch. vol. A88, pages 43-44.

**Hazzard, Joseph, Esq.** Will. Made Feb. 24, 1791. Heirs: sons Cord, John, William and Joseph Hazzard; dau. Rachel Wiltbank; grandsons Cord and Simpson Hazzard (children of son William, dec'd). Exec'rs, sons Cord and John Hazzard. Wits., William Young, Mary Wiltbank, Elizabeth Lane. Prob. Sept. 30, 1794. Arch. vol. A75, pages 92-93. Reg. of Wills, Liber E, folios 3-5.

**James, Joshua.** Will (nunc.). Made Aug. 29, 1794. Heirs: bros. Elias and Noah James. [No exec'r]. Wits., Levin Connaway. Prob. Sept. 30, 1794. Arch. vol. A80, page 98. Reg. of Wills, Liber E, folio 5.

**Donovan, John.** Admin. of, to Azariah Donovan. Granted [c. Oct., 1794]. Arch. vol. A69, page 145.

**Stewart, Elizabeth.** Admin. of, to James Lank. Granted [c. Oct. 9, 1794]. Arch. vol. A100, page 182.

**Townsend, William.** Will. Made Aug. 1, 1794. Heirs: wife Betsy Townsend; dau. Nancy Townsend; and child unborn.

Exec'rx, wife Betsy Townsend. Wits., Jno. L. Bayly, Jeremiah Lee Bayly, Frederick Travers. Prob. Oct. 9, 1794. Arch. vol. A102, page 84. Reg. of Wills, Liber E, folios 5-6.

**Brown, John.** Will (nunc.). Made Oct. 17, 1794. Heir: wife Nelly Brown. [No exec'r]. Wits., John Norman, Levin Beavins, Charlotte Beavins. Prob. Oct. 18, 1794. Arch. vol. A60, pages 204-205. Reg. of Wills, Liber E, folio 6. [Note:—Arch. vol. A60, page 204 shows that Nelly Brown and Francis Wright, adm'rs C. T. A., exhibited an account on the estate April 29, 1796; page 205 shows that John Brown was the son of Israel Brown].

**Parmore, Joseph.** Admin. of, to Thomas Culver. Granted [c. Oct. 21, 1794]. Arch. vol. A92, page 86.

**Rogers, John.** Planter. Will. Made Oct. 6, 1794. Heirs: wife Comfort Rogers; sons George and John Rogers; daus. Leah, Patience and Unice Rogers, Ann Jones, Comfort Fisher, Rachel Warren, Polly Bevans, Levina Marvel and Orpha Marvel. Exec'rs, wife Comfort Rogers, son John Rogers. Wits., David Marvel, Thomas Rodney, William Rodney. Prob. Oct. 25, 1794. Arch. vol. A97, page 43. Reg. of Wills, Liber E, folio 7.

**Marvel, Thomas** (Son of Robert). Nanticoke Hd. Will. Made Oct. 30, 1793. Heirs: wife Elizabeth Marvel; bro. Philip Marvel; nephews Josiah Marvel (son of Philip), Robert Barr, Thomas Robinson (son of Joshua), James Jones (son of William); niece Betsy Robinson (dau. of Joshua); bros.-in-law Joshua Robinson and Eli McCally. Exec'rs, wife Elizabeth Marvel and bro. Philip Marvel. Wits., Simon Kollock, Mary N. Kollock, William White. Prob. Nov. 1, 1794. Arch. vol. A87, pages 25-26. Reg. of Wills, Liber E, folios 7-9.

**Pierce, William.** Yeoman. Will. Made Aug. 3, 1774. Heirs: wife Sarah Pierce; sons William, Jr., Jonathan and John Pierce; daus. Mary Couch (wife of Meshack), Sarah Hodson (wife of Jacob); granddau. Esther Hodson (dau. of Jacob and Sarah); grandsons John Hodson (son of Jacob and Sarah), Thomas Pierce (son of William, Jr.), and William Pierce (son of Jonathan). Exec'rx, wife Sarah Pierce. Wits., James Newbold, Hannah Nunez, Daniel Nunez. Prob. Nov. 4, 1794. Arch. vol. A93, pages 79-80. Reg. of Wills, Liber B, folios 528-530. [Note:—Arch. vol. A93, page 80 shows the estate was settled by Isaac Thorp and wife Sarah, late Sarah Pierce].

**Williams, Spencer.** Will. Made Aug. 29, 1787. Heirs: wife Elizabeth Williams; sons Whittington, Levin, Benjamin, Spencer, Art[hur], Stephen and Noah Williams; daus. Nancy, Sarah and Milly Williams. Exec'rx, wife Elizabeth Williams. Wits., Bart Kennedy, David Polk, Smart Hardy, James Burtell. Prob. Nov. 4, 1794. Arch. vol. A108, pages 46-47. Reg. of Wills, Liber E, folios 9-10.

**Cannon, Absalom.** Admin. of, to Frances Cannon. Granted [c. Nov. 19, 1794]. Arch. vol. A62, page 217.

**Houston, Magdalen.** Admin. of, to Robert Prettyman. Granted [c. Nov. 19, 1794]. Arch. vol. A78, page 107.

**Goddard, Francis Lane.** Planter. Little Creek Hd. Will. Made May 25, 1794. Heirs: wife Mary Goddard; sons Griffith, John and William Goddard; daus. Eunice, Sarah and Goodin Goddard; Eunice Collins (wife of William); grandson Francis Lane Goddard (son of William and Elizabeth). Exec'r, son John Goddard. Wits., Edw[ar]d Creagh, Jon[atha]n Cathell, John Bacon. Prob. Nov. 21, 1794. Arch. vol. A72, page 156. Reg. of Wills, Liber E, folios 10-11.

**Conwell, Charles.** Admin. of, to John Robinson and Sally, his wife. Granted [c. Nov. 25, 1794]. Arch. vol. A66, page 95.

**Brown, James, Sr.** Will. Made Sept. 22, 1787. Heirs: wife Priscilla Brown; sons James, Thomas and White Brown; daus. [Rebecca] Brown, Elizabeth Dawson, Priscilla Smith, Mary Twyford and Sarah Riggin; grandson James Brown; granddau. Henrietta Brown. Exec'rs, wife Priscilla Brown and son Thomas Brown. Wits., Thomas White, Charles Twyford, Humphries Brown. Prob. Nov. 27, 1794. Arch. vol. A60, pages 197-198. Reg. of Wills, Liber E, folios 12-13. [Note:—Arch. vol. A60, page 198 shows the estate was settled by [Lucretia] Brown, D. B. N., in right of Thomas W. Brown].

**Hood, Mary.** Will. Made Oct. 25, 1793. Heirs: dau. Elizabeth Black; granddaus. Elizabeth Black (wife of Benjamin), Mary Perry (wife of Aaron), Elizabeth Holland (wife of John), Magdalen Neill (wife of Robert), Peggy and Polly Hood (daus. of Robert); grandson James N. Hood (son of Robert); daus.-in-law Deborah McKnatt (wife of John) and Ann McKnatt (wife of James). Exec'rx, dau. Elizabeth Black. Wits., Charles W[arren], Joseph Black, Robert Hood. Prob. Nov. 27, 1794. Arch. vol. A77, page 163. Reg. of Wills, Liber E, folios 11-12.

**Wilson, William.** Admin. of, to John Wilson. Granted [c. Nov. 27, 1794]. Arch. vol. A108, page 136. [Note:—Arch. vol. A108, page 136 mentions Arcada, Nancy, David, Sarah, Eunice, Lovey, Margaret, Assenath Wilson; Ephraim Knowles and wife; Samuel, William and Thomas Wilson].

**Fisher, John.** Will. Made Aug. 8, 1793. Heirs: sisters [Freda], [Louisa], Sarah and Allafer Fisher; bro. Daniel Fisher. [No exec'r]. Wits., William Maloney, Daniel Fisher. Prob. Nov. 28, 1794. Arch. vol. A71, page 133. Reg. of Wills, Liber E, folio 14. [Note:—Arch. vol. A71, page 133 mentions father, mother and 3 younger bros. unnamed].

**Neal, Marg[ar]et.** Will. Made April 20, 1793. Heirs: son William Neal; unnamed daus. Exec'r, son William Neal. Wits., Robert Clarkson, Azael Ross, John Neal. Prob. Dec. 9, 1794. Arch. vol. A91, page 46. Reg. of Wills, Liber E, folios 14-15.

**Morris, John.** Admin. of, to Isaac Morris. Granted [c. Dec. 11, 1794]. Arch. vol. A90, page 76.

**Russell, Samuel.** Will. Made Nov. 17, 1794. Heirs: wife Sarah Russell; sons Thomas, Philip and John Russell; daus. Hannah Russell, Elizabeth Morgan, Sarah Taylor and Mary Frit; dau.-in-law Jean Russell (wife of son of Joseph); two children of Jean Russell. Exec'rs, wife Sarah Russell and son Thomas Russell. Wits, Hap Hazzard, Elizabeth Wright, Mary Nunam. Prob. Dec. 16, 1794. Arch. vol. A97, pages 149-150. Reg. of Wills, Liber E, folios 15-16.

**Rust, Peter.** Will. Made Sept. 19, 1794. Heirs: wife Sarah Rust; eight children unnamed. Exec'rx, wife Sarah Rust. Wits., William White, John White, Elizabeth Norman. Prob. Dec. 16, 1794. Arch. vol. A97, page 167. Reg. of Wills, Liber E, folio 15.

**Ross, Robert, Sr.** Will. Made Dec. 12, 1794. Heirs: wife Barbara Ross; son Azael Ross. Exec'rs, wife Barbara Ross and son Azael Ross. Wits., Abraham Cannon, Charles Brown. Prob. Dec. 23, 1794. Arch. vol. A97, pages 90-91. Reg. of Wills, Liber E, folios 16-17.

**Bennum [Banum], George.** Will. Made April 12, 1794. Heirs: wife Sarah Bennum; sons Henry, Joseph and George Bennum; daus. Nancy, Arcada and Eunice Bennum, and [Ann Mary] Roland. Exec'rx, wife Sarah Bennum. Wits., Abel Nottingham, Nancy Marriner, Jacob Wolfe. Prob. Dec. 25, 1794. Arch. vol. A58, pages 102 and 172. Reg. of Wills,

Liber E, folios 17-18. [Note:—Arch. vol. A58, page 102 mentions John Rowland and wife].

**Moore, William, Sr.** Farmer. Will. Made Jan. 21, 1785. Heirs: sons William, Jr., and John Moore; daus. Mary Watson and Betty Mitchell. Exec'r, son-in-law William Clayton Mitchell. Wits., Edw[ar]d Dingle, Caleb Tingle, John Darby. Prob. Dec. 30, 1794. Arch. vol. A89, page 155. Reg. of Wills, Liber E, folios 18-19.

**Bradley, Isaac.** Admin. of, to John Wilson. Granted [c. 1795]. Arch. vol. A60, page 94.

**Callaway, Eli.** Admin. of, to Peggy Callaway. Granted [c. Jan. 1, 1795]. Arch. vol. A62, page 138.

**Smith, Alexander.** Will. Made Aug. 27, 1794. Heirs: son Robert Kirkwood Smith; bro. William Smith; sister Rebecca Smith. Exec'rs, Robert Creighton, John Mitchell. Wits., Jos[eph] King, John Polk. Prob. Jan. 22, 1795. Arch. vol. A99, pages 105-106. Reg. of Wills, Liber E, folio 19. [Note:—Arch. vol. A99, page 106 shows the estate was settled by Rhoda Mitchell, exec'rx of John Mitchell].

**Dickerson, Edmond.** Will. Made Feb. 7, 1795. Heirs: wife Eunice Dickerson; sons William, Levin, Peter and Edmond Dickerson; daus. Sarah, Nancy, Comfort Dickerson, Elizabeth Cahoon and Eleanor Adams. Exec'r, son Levin Dickerson. Wits., John Scott, Elizabeth Smullen. Prob. Feb. 17, 1795. Arch. vol. A69, pages 53-54. Reg. of Wills, Liber E, folios 20-21. [Note:—Arch. vol. A69, page 53 mentions Jonathan Cahoon and also shows the estate was settled by Edmond Dickerson in lieu of Levin Dickerson, dec'd].

**Williams, Andrew.** Will. Made Oct. 4, 1794. Heirs: wife Rizear Williams; sons Andrew, Thomas, Edward, Ezekiel and Arthur Williams; dau. Rizear Godfrey; grandsons Thomas Williams (son of Andrew) and William Hudson. Exec'r, son Arthur Williams. Wits., Robert Tracy, James Tracy, Benjamin Long. Prob. Feb. 17, 1795. Arch. vol. A107, page 144. Reg. of Wiills, Liber E, folio 10.

**Murray, James.** Will. Made Dec. 27, 1793. Heirs: son John Murray; daus. Ellen, Rebecca and Esther Murray, Alice Holland. Exec'r, son John Murray. Wits., Ananias Hudson, Andrew Truitt, William Truitt. Prob. Feb. 17, 1795. Arch. vol. A91, page 11. Reg. of Wills, Liber E, folios 21-22.

**Williams, Morgan.** Will. Made Dec. 3, 1794. Heirs: wife Martha Williams; son Morgan Williams; dau. Betty Rawlins; grandsons Morgan Rawlins and George Williams. Exec'rx, wife Martha Williams. Wits., Windsor Rawlins, Benjamin Cassiday, Eunice Caassiday. Prob. Feb. 23, 1795. Arch. vol. A108, page 22. Reg. of Wills, Liber E, folios 22-23.

**Coverdale, Israel.** Yeoman. Will. Made Feb. 5, 1795. Heirs: wife Rachel Coverdale; sons Richard, Israel, William, Eli, Boaz and Purnel Coverdale; dau. Elizabeth Ratcliff. Exec'rs, wife Rachel Coverdale and sons Richard, Israel and William Coverdale. Wits., John Polk, Richard Passwaters, Mary Passwaters. Prob. March 3, 1795. Arch. vol. A67, page 76. Reg. of Wills, Liber E, folios 25-26. [Note:—Arch. vol. A67, page 76 mentions Minus Ratcliff, husband of Elizabeth Coverdale Ratcliff; also shows the estate was settled by Boaz Coverdale, D. B. N., C. T. A.].

**Hopkins, Sophia.** Admin. of, to Charles Connelly. Granted [c. March 3, 1795]. Arch. vol. A78, page 23.

**Oliver, Aaron.** Cedar Creek. Will. Made Jan. 29, 1795. Heirs: wife Abigail Oliver; daus. Esther Bennett, Abigail Hays, Elizabeth Morris and Sarah Lofland. Exec'rx, wife Abigail Oliver. Wits., John Young, Jonathan Williams, Shadrach Nickerson. Prob. March 3, 1795. Arch. vol. A91, page 148. Reg. of Wills, Liber E, folios 23-24.

**Tull, William.** Yeoman. Will. Made Feb. 14, 1795. Heirs: wife Ann Tull; son John Tull; daus. Ann, Sarah, Martha, Mary and Margaret Tull; grandson Isaac Tull; granddau. Mary Tull. Exec'rs, wife Ann Tull and dau. Ann Tull. Wits., James Elliott, Theodore Wilson, John Martin. Prob. March 3, 1795. Arch. vol. A102, page 187. Reg. of Wills, Liber E, folios 24-25. [Note:—Arch. vol. A102, page 187 shows the estate was settled April 6, 1796 by William Mitten and wife Ann, late Ann Tull, and Ann Tull, the younger].

**Polk, David.** Admin. of, to Phillip Hughes. Granted [c. March 4, 1795]. Arch. vol. A93, page 115.

**Evans, Samuel.** Admin. of, to Jacob Burton. Granted [c. March 6, 1795]. Arch. vol. A71, pages 10-12.

**Bevins, James.** Will. Made Dec. 17, 1794. Heirs: wife Nancy Bevins; son Shadrach Bevins; dau. Leah Bevins. Exec'rs, wife Nancy Bevins and Joseph Ward. Wits., John Williams, Wootten Lloyd, Mitchell Thompson. Prob. March 10, 1795. Arch. vol. A59, pages 161-162. Reg. of Wills, Liber E, folios 26-27. [Note:—Arch. vol. A59, page 162 mentions that

Nancy Bevins later married William Calhoon and that William Calhoon and Joseph Ward, surviving exec'rs settled the estate].

**Wills, Israel.** Will. Made March 5, 1795. Heirs: wife Mary Nutter Wills; sons Obediah and James Wills; daus. Elizabeth Nutter, Ele[ano]r, Ann, Mary, Abigail and Am[ethyst] Wills. Exec'rs, wife Mary Nutter Wills and James Knowles. Wits., Tho[ma]s Knowles, William Rose, Marg[ar]et Rose. Prob. March 30, 1795. Arch. vol. A108, page 61. Reg. of Wills, Liber E, folios 27-28.

**Coulter, Robert.** Admin. of, to Naomi Coulter. Granted [c. April 7, 1795]. Arch. vol. A67, page 65.

**Wiltbank, Mary.** Widow. Lewes. Will. Made March 10, 1795. Heirs: sons John, Cornelius and James Wiltbank; daus. Elizabeth Hall, Mary [or Polly] Shankland; grandsons Thomas Emery, John Hall, James Hall, Peter Hall; granddaus. Mary Hall, Mary and Ann Wiltbank (daus. of Cornelius and Nannie), Elizabeth Wiltbank (dau. of John); Maria Batson (dau. of Kendle and Margaret Batson); Margaret Batson (mother of Maria); friend Sarah Stockley (sister of Woodman Stockley, Esq.); eldest dau. of Mary Shankland. Exec'rs, sons Cornelius and James Wiltbank. Wits., Daniel Rodney, Caleb Rodney, Ruth Russell. Prob. April 10, 1795. Arch. vol. A108, pages 158-159. Reg. of Wills, Liber E, folios 28-30.

**Warren, Bennett.** Will. Made April 5, 1795. Heirs: wife Rachel Warren; sons Rickson, Spicer, Silas, Bennett and Asbury Warren; daus. Jemina Warren and Eunice Layton; cousin Purnel Warren. Exec'rs, son Rickson Warren, bro. [Alexander] Warren. Wits., John Hudson, Benjamin Hudson. Prob. April 21, 1795. Arch. vol. A105, page 98. Reg. of Wills, Liber E, folios 30-31.

**Low, William.** Will. Made March 10, 1795. Heirs: wife Nicey Low; sons John, George, Thomas Cooper and William Low; dau. Sarah Low. Exec'rx, wife Nicey Low. Wits., William Elzey, Ralph Low, Abram Cooper. Prob. April 22, 1795. Arch. vol. A85, pages 154-155. Reg. of Wills, Liber E, folios 31-32.

**Wright, Nathaniel.** Admin. of, to Rachel Wright. Granted [c. April 23, 1795]. Arch. vol. A109, page 95.

**Layton, Lowder.** Will. Made Oct. 23, 1793. Heirs: sons Tilghman, Huett and Lowder Layton; daus. Amelia Layton, Tabitha Fowler, Selah Ennals; grandsons Robert Layton and

Layton Polk; sons-in-law Joseph Polk and Joseph Gray. Exec'r, son Lowder Layton. Wits., David Nutter, Nancy Nutter, Francis Wright. Prob. April 24, 1795. Arch. vol. A83, page 184. Reg. of Wills, Liber E, folios 32-33.

**Townsend, Job.** Admin. of, to Richard Coverdill and wife Elizabeth, late Elizabeth Townsend. Granted [c. April 29, 1795]. Arch. vol. A102, page 60.

**Mosley, Absolem.** Will. Made April 25, 1795. Heirs: sons Absolem, Purnell and Curnell Mosley; other children unnamed. Exec'r, John Smith. Wits., Henry Smith, Mager Clifton, Levin Turner. Prob. April 30, 1795. Arch. vol. A90, pages 165-166. Reg. of Wills, Liber E, folios 33-34.

**Cannon, William, Sr.** Yeoman. Will. Made May 1, 1795. Heirs: nephews Matthew, Levin and Jesse Cannon; niece Milly Cannon (children of bro. Jesse); children of bro. Levin, Exec'r, William Nutter Cannon and nephew Levin Cannon. Wits., John Tennent, Jesse Cannon, William Baker. Prob. May 12, 1795. Arch. vol. A63, pages 144-146. Reg. of Wills, Liber E, folios 35-36. [Note:—Arch. vol. A63, page 145 shows the estate was settled by William N. Cannon, surviving exec'r].

**Hall, James.** Will. Made Feb. 19, 1795. Heirs: wife Judith Hall; sons William, Thomas and John Hall; daus. Nancy and Elizabeth Hall, Mary Hemons, Sarah Parmore and Miriam Clendaniel. Exec'r, son Thomas Hall. Wits., William Robins, Nancy Robins, David Robins. Prob. May 12, 1795. Arch. vol. A73, pages 211-212. Reg. of Wills, Liber E, folios 34-35.

**Marvel, Philip, Sr.** Planter. Dagsboro Hd. Will. Made May 4, 1795. Heirs: wife Comfort Marvel; sons Philip, Thomas, William, Aaron, Adam and David Marvel; daus. Mary and Cloe Marvel, and Rhoda Butcher. Exec'rx, wife Comfort Marvel. Wits., Simon Kollock, Rachel Sirman. Prob. May 12, 1795. Arch. vol. A87, pages 11-12. Reg. of Wills, Liber E, folios 36-37. [Note:—Arch. vol. A87, page 12 mentions William Butcher].

**Mariner, Gilbert.** Soldier in Delaware Regiment. Will. Made Oct. 14, 1783. Heirs: cousins Joseph, William and Anna Hoseman Russell. Exec'r, uncle John Russell (of Lewes). Wits., Phillips Russell, William Robins, Uriah Hazzard. Prob. May 16, 1795. Arch. vol. A86, page 52. Reg. of Wills, Liber E, folios 37-38.

**Culver, Aaron.** Will. Made April 14, 1795. Heirs: wife Ann Culver; sons Joshua, Samuel and James Culver; daus. Rachel, Nelly and Nancy Culver, Jane Truitt, Sarah Knowles and Mary Ryan; grandson Elijah Ryan; granddau. Elizabeth Knowles. Exec'rx, wife Ann Culver. Wits., Moses Culver, Ephraim Culver, Joseph Hardy. Prob. May 19, 1795. Arch. vol. A67, page 214. Reg. of Wills, Liber E, folios 38-39.

**Burton, William.** (Old Plantation). Will. Made March 31, 1795. Heirs: wife Rachel Burton; sons Isaac and William Burton; daus. Rachel Burton and Mary Ingram (wife of Job); grandsons Robert and Joseph Burton. Exec'rs, sons Isaac and William Burton. Wits., Benjamin Prettyman, William Prettyman, Nancy Prettyman. Prob. May 23, 1795. Arch. vol. A62, pages 24-25. Reg. of Wills, Liber E, folios 39-40. [Note:—Arch. vol. A62, page 25 shows the estate was settled Aug. 13, 1798 by William Burton, as surviving exec'r).

**Bayly, John L.** Will. Made Feb. 20, 1795. Heirs: bro. Jeremiah L. Bayly; sisters Peggy Brady, Nancy L. Travers and Elizabeth Townsend. Exec'rs, Jeremiah L. Bayly and Frederick Travers. Wits., Jacob Barney, Julius Augustus Jackson. Prob. May 26, 1795. Arch. vol. A58, page 71. Reg. of Wills, Liber E, folios 40-41.

**Truitt, John, Sr.** Admin. of, to John Truitt. Granted [c. June 9, 1795]. Arch. vol. A102, page 136.

**Young, John.** Will (copy). Made May 8, 1795. Heirs: wife Anna Young; sons Nathan, Robert, John and David Young; dau. Nancy Young. Exec'rs, wife Anna Young and son Nathan Young. Wits., Joshua Bennett, John S. Campbell, Thomas Riley. Prob. June 20, 1795. Arch. vol. A109, pages 131-132. Reg. of Wills, Liber E, folios 41-42.

**Roberts, William.** Will. Made Dec. 20, 1784. Heirs: wife Mary Roberts; sons Alexander, Adam, William and Joseph Roberts; dau. Hannah Roberts. Exec'rs, wife Mary Roberts and bro. Sanders Roberts. Wits., Levin Clark, Mary Maddux, Sanders Roberts. Prob. June 29, 1795. Arch. vol. A96, page 92. Reg. of Wills, Liber E, folio 43.

**Wildgoos, Thomas.** Will. Made Dec. 28, 1781. Heirs: wife Elizabeth Wildgoos; sons Blades, Robert and Joseph Wildgoos. Exec'rs, wife Elizabeth Wildgoos and son Joseph Wildgoos. Wits., William Rickards, Job Dirickson, William Robinson, Ezekiel Williams, William Taylor, William McCormick.

Prob. July 17, 1795. Arch. vol. A107, page 112. Reg. of Wills, Liber E, folios 43-44. [Note:—Arch. vol. A107, page 112 shows the estate was settled by Robert Wildgoos, adm'r D. B. N. of Joseph Wildgoos].

**Morris, John.** Admin. of, to Joshua Jones and wife Polly Wasdale Jones, late Polly Morris. Granted July 21, 1795. Arch. vol. A90, pages 77-78.

**Collins, Joseph.** Admin. of, to John Collins. Granted July 31, 1795. Arch. vol. A65, page 217.

**Hinds, Daniel.** Will (nunc.). Made July 29, 1795. Heirs: unnamed wife. [No exec'r]. Wits., Patience Messick, John Sharp. Prob. Aug. 11, 1795. Arch. vol. A76, page 171. Reg. of Wills, Liber E, folio 44.

**Turpin, Charles.** Admin. of, to Joshua Wright. Granted [c. Aug. 19, 1795]. Arch. vol. A103, page 28.

**Polk, Mary.** Spinster. Will (nunc.). Made Aug. 16/17, 1795. Heirs: dau. Diana Polk. [No exec'r]. Wits., Amelia Laws, Rebecca Laws. Prob. Aug. 21, 1795. Arch. vol. A93, page 143. Reg. of Wills, Liber D, folio 213.

**Truitt, Leah.** Admin. of, to Betty Truitt. Granted [c. Sept. 1, 1795]. Arch. vol. A102, page 149. [Note:—Arch. vol. A102, page 149 mentions William and Tatman Truitt].

**Phillips, John, Sr.** Planter. Dagsboro. Will. Made Aug. 29, 1795. Heirs: wife Sarah Phillips; sons Benjamin, Joseph, Shepperd, Spencer and John Phillips; daus. Mary [Polly] Phillips, Ruth Tindall (wife of Charles), Sarah Melson (wife of John) and Lavinia Truitt (wife of Josiah); mother-in-law Elinor Brothers. Exec'rs, wife Sarah Phillips, sons John and Spencer Phillips. Wits., S. Kollock, Robert Hopkins, George Hopkins. Prob. Sept. 7, 1795. Arch. vol. A93, pages 39-40. Reg. of Wills, Liber E, folios 45-48.

**Dirickson, Andries.** Admin. of, to Mary Dirickson and Robert Saunders. Granted [c. Sept. 13, 1795]. Arch. vol. A69, page 21. [Note:—Arch. vol. A69, page 21 mentions Mary Dirickson and Saunders Roberts, attorney for Luke Dirickson, adm'r of Andries Dirickson].

**Lewis, Jonathan.** Admin. of, to Adam Lewis. Granted [c. Sept. 14, 1795]. Arch. vol. A84, page 61.

**Passwaters, Richard.** Will (nunc.). Made Sept. 15, 1795. Heirs: wife and children unnamed. Exec'rs, Isaac Passwaters and William Passwaters. Wits., George Polk, Isaac Passwaters.

Prob. Sept. 18, 1795. Arch. vol. A92, page 110. [No Reg. of Wills Liber].

**Nutter, Robert.** Yeoman. Admin. of, to Thomas Nutter and wife Sarah. Granted [c. Sept. 29, 1795]. Arch. vol. A91, page 133. [Note:—Arch vol. A91, page 133 mentions a minor dau. Elizabeth Nutter].

**Nutter, John.** Admin. of, to Shadrack Shearman and wife Nancy, late Nancy Nutter. Granted [c. Oct. 6, 1795]. Arch. vol. A91, page 131.

**Evans, John.** Will. Made Feb. 15, 1791. Heirs: wife Catharine Evans; sons John and William Evans; daus. Rebecca Mumford, Elizabeth Dale and Mary Hall. Exec'r, son William Evans. Wits., Littleton Townsend, James Wharton, Samuel Cord. Prob. Oct. 13, 1795. Arch. vol. A70, pages 222-223. Reg. of Wills, Liber E, folios 48-49.

**Cary, Thomas, Jr.** Cedar Creek Hd. Will. Made Oct. 3, 1795. Heirs: grandsons Thomas and Bedwell Mur[ph]y (sons of William). Exec'r, son-in-law William Mur[ph]y. Wits., Joseph Haslet, John Haslet, Jesse Edgen. Prob. Oct. 14, 1795. Arch. vol. A64, page 107. Reg. of Wills, Liber E, folios 50-51. [Note:—Arch. vol. A64, page 107 shows a renunciation on back of will which mentions widow Mary; also shows that an account was exhibited on the estate by Mary Cary].

**Stockley, William.** Will. Made Oct. 11, 1795. Heirs: Sarah Roach; nephew Isaac Roach. Exec'r, nephew Isaac Roach. Wits., Harmon Craige, John Vessels. Prob. Oct. 17, 1795. Arch. vol. A101, page 37. Reg. of Wills, Liber E, folio 50.

**Killingsworth, John, Sr.** Will. Made June 23, 1795. Heirs: wife Rachel Killingsworth; sons Luke, John, Edward and William Killingsworth; daus. Sarah, Mary, Rachel, Hester and Leah Killingsworth. Exec'r, son William Killingsworth. Wits., Baker Abbott, Nancy Hill, John Lofland. Prob. Oct. 22, 1795. Arch. vol. A82, pages 70-71. Reg. of Wills, Liber E, folios 51-52.

**Hazzard, Hap, Esq.** Will. Made Oct. 22, 1795. Heirs: wife Mary Hazzard; David Craig Hazzard (son of William Craig Hazzard, dec'd); George Hazzard, Esq. (son of William Hazzard); Peter Hazzard (son of Jacob Hazzard); Charles King (son of wife Mary Hazzard); Eleanor Brussels (wife of Joseph Brussels); child of Betsy Hazzard (wife of William Craig Hazzard); children of bro. Jacob Hazzard, Esq.; and children of sister Sarah Morgan, dec'd. Exec'r, George

Hazzard, Esq. Wits., Joseph Hall, Sarah Russell, William King. Prob. Oct. 26, 1795. Arch. vol. A75, pages 64-67. Reg. of Wills, Liber E, folios 52-53. [Note:—Arch. vol. A75, pages 66-67 show that Thomas Bevans and wife Abigail later settled the estate in right of George Hazzard, dec'd].

**Polk, Charles.** Yeoman. Will. Made Aug. 28, 1795. Heirs: wife Mary Polk; sons Charles and John Polk; dau. Elizabeth Polk; nephew Edward Polk. Exec'rx, wife Mary Polk. Wits., Matthew Marine, Jr., Matthew Marine, Sr., W[illia]m Shankland. Prob. Oct. 29, 1795. Arch. vol. A93, page 107. Reg. of Wills, Liber E, folios 53-54. [Note:— Arch. vol. A93, page 107 mentions dec'd father, Charles Polk].

**Burton, Hester.** Will. Made June 22, 1793. Heirs: sons Daniel and Benjamin Burton; daus. Lydia Burton and Hester Hopkins; grandsons Cord, Peter, Benjamin and Woolsey Burton. Exec'r, son Benjamin Burton. Wits., Benjamin Burton, Rhoda Burton, George Green. Prob. Nov. 23, 1795. Arch. vol. A61, pages 140-141. Reg. of Wills, Liber E, folios 55-56. [Note:—Arch. vol. A61, page 141 shows Woolsey Burton exhibited an account on the estate Aug. 4, 1798 in right of Benjamin Burton, dec'd).

**Cary, Thomas, Sr.** Will. Made Jan. 25, 1787. Heirs: wife Elizabeth Cary; son Nehemiah Cary; daus. Barsheba and Charity Truitt, and Mary Watson; grandsons John and Lemuel Cary; granddau. Priscilla Cary (children of son Nehemiah); granddau. Nancy Griffith (dau. of son Bowen Cary); grandsons Benjamin Brincklee (son of William and Rhoda Brincklee) and Benjamin R[au]ghly; heirs of son Edward, dec'd. Exec'rs, wife Elizabeth and son Nehemiah Cary. Wits., Robert McGonigal, Robert Houston, John Nicholson. Prob. Nov. 24, 1795. Arch. vol. A64, page 105. Reg. of Wills, Liber E, folios 56-58.

**Patterson, Hugh.** Will. Made Nov. 28, 1795. Heir: son unnamed. Exec'r, James Fergus. Wits., Theodore Wilson, Lazarus Turner, John Franklin. Prob. Dec. 1, 1795. Arch. vol. A92, page 116. Reg. of Wills, Liber E, folio 59.

**Windsor, Jesse.** Admin. of, to William Adams and wife Peggy, late Peggy Windsor. Granted [c. Dec. 9, 1795]. Arch. vol. A108, page 169. [Note:—Arch. vol. A108, page 169 mentions Thomas Windsor].

**Hays, Thomas.** Will. Made Nov. 31, 1795. Heirs: wife Abigail Hays; son John Hays; bro. Luke Hays. Exec'rx, wife Abigail Hays. Wits., John Bennett, Thomas Riley, Philip May. Prob. Dec. 15, 1795. Arch. vol. A75, pages 31-32. Reg. of Wills, Liber E, folios 59-60.

**Fowler, John.** Admin. of, to Lydia Fowler. Granted [c. Dec. 19, 1795]. Arch. vol. A72, page 59-60.

**Lofland, Elizabeth.** Will. Made Oct. 11, 1791. Heirs: daus. Sarah Deputy, Miriam Webb, Mary Williams and Elizabeth Holleger; heirs of dec'd son Joshua Lofland. Exec'r, Jonathan Williams. Wits., John Young, Mills Rickards, John Hickman. Prob. Dec. 22, 1795. Arch. vol. A85, pages 26-27. Reg. of Wills, Liber E, folio 60. [Note:—Arch. vol. A85, page 27 shows the estate was settled April 25, 1797 by Mary Williams, exec'rx of Jonathan Williams].

**Futcher, John, Sr.** Will. [Undated]. Heirs: sons William and John Futcher; daus. Susannah Futcher and Mary Woolf. Exec'rs, sons William and John Futcher. Wits., John Marsh, Thomas Trinder, Rebecca Wyatt. Prob. Dec. 24, 1795. Arch. vol. A72, pages 92-95. Reg. of Wills, Liber E, folios 60-61. [Note:—Arch. vol. A72, page 93 contains sworn statements of above witnesses and also of Mary Harmonson, Mary Trinder, Joshua Ball, John Wilson and Richard Green; also mentions William Woolf and Woodman Stockley].

**Bacon, George.** Will. Made Sept. 24, 1795. Heirs: wife Leah Bacon; William Bacon (son of Davis Bacon); Levin Bacon (son of William Davis Bacon); George O'Neal (son of William O'Neal); bros. and sisters unnamed. Exec'rs, bro. John Bacon and William O'Neal. Wits., Isaac Cooper, William Vaughan, William Polk. Prob. Dec. 29, 1795. Arch. vol. A58, pages 33-39. Reg. of Wills, Liber E, folios 61-63. [Note:—Arch. vol. A58, pages 34-39 show that William O'Neal settled the estate as surviving exec'r].

**Barker, Zadok.** Admin. of, to Jehu Barker. Granted [c. 1796]. Arch. vol. A58, pages 193-194.

**Burroughs, William.** Admin. of, to Mary Burroughs. Granted [c. 1796]. Arch. vol. A61, pages 62-63.

**Butcher, Frances.** Admin. of, to James Stephenson, C. T. A. Granted [c. 1796]. Arch. vol. A62, page 73.

**Cary, Nelly.** Admin. of, to Elizabeth Cary. Granted [c. 1796]. Arch. vol. A64, page 83.

**Baker, Elias.** Will. Made . . . 29, 1796. Heirs: wife Naomi Baker; sons George, William and Joshua Baker; daus. Leah and Rebecca Baker. Exec'rx, wife Naomi Baker. Wits., Elizabeth Williams, George Bloxom. [No prob.]. Arch. vol. A58, pages 108-109.

**Heavelo, Hannah.** Widow. Broadkiln Hd. Will. Made May 21, 1791. Heirs: sons John, Roderick and Edward Heavelo; daus. Augusta Wiltbank, Amelia Hazzard, Hannah Cade; grandson Jonathan Naws Cade. Exec'rs, sons John and Roderick Heavelo. Wits., John Clark, Aleta Clark, Amel-[ia] Clark. Prob. Jan. 4, 1796. Arch. vol. A75, page 217. Reg. of Wills, Liber E, folio 63.

**Bloxom [Bloxsom, Blocksom], Hannah.** Widow. Will. Made June 11, 1795. Heirs: sons David, William and Fisher Bloxom; dau. Margaret Bloxom. Exec'r, son William Bloxom. Wits., Unicy Blocksom, Joseph Hall. Codicil, Nov. 11, 1795. Wits., Unicy Coulter, Joseph Hall. Prob. Jan. 5, 1796. Arch. vol. A59, pages 228-229. Reg. of Wills, Liber E, folios 63-64.

**Clarkson, Joseph.** Admin. of, to Thomas Sorden. Granted Jan. 5, 1796. Arch. vol. A64, page 211.

**Coverdale, Luke.** Yeoman. Will. Made Nov. 25, 1795. Heirs: sons Purnal, Luke and Jeremiah Coverdale; Levin Coverdale. Exec'r, William Walker. Wits., Henry Carr, Ezekiel Carr, Major Coverdale. Prob. Jan. 16, 1796. Arch. vol. A67, pages 90-91. Reg. of Wills, Liber E, folios 64-65.

**Minner, Edward.** Will. Made Dec. 29, 1795. Heirs: wife Priscilla Minner; son Richard Minner; daus. Peggy Minner, Rebecca Ross, and Elizabeth Johnson; grandsons John Kilman Shanks and Edward Shanks (sons of dau. Ann and David Shanks); John Clark (half bro. of daus. Rebecca and Elizabeth). Exec'rs, wife Priscilla Minner and son Richard Minner. Wits., Richard Foxwell, David Shanks, David Richards. Prob. Jan. 19, 1796. Arch. vol. A89, pages 20-21. Reg. of Wills, Liber E, folios 65-66. [Note:—Arch. vol. A89, page 21 shows the estate was settled Oct. 5, 1797 by Richard Minner, surviving exec'r].

**Fisher, Mary.** Admin. of, to John Fisher. Granted [c. Jan. 26, 1796]. Arch. vol. A71, page 149.

**Layton, Nehemiah.** Will. Made Dec. 26, 1795. Heirs: sons David, Robert, William and Thomas Layton; daus. Nancy, Sally and Betsy Layton, [Amelia] Bramble, Lovey Higman. Exec'r, son David Layton. Wits., Robert Williams, Andrew Dukes, Clement Rogers. Prob. Feb. 2, 1796. Arch. vol. A83, pages 194-195. Reg. of Wills, Liber E, folio 66.

**Conwell, Elias.** Farmer. Broadkiln Hd. Will. Made Jan. 23, 1796. Heirs: wife Leah Conwell; sons John, Ace and Elias Conwell; dau. Aletta Conwell; one child unnamed. Exec'rx, wife Leah Conwell. Wits., Samuel Paynter, Jr., Lydia Fleetwood. Prob. Feb. 7, 1796. Arch. vol. A66, pages 98-101. Reg. of Wills, Liber E, folios 70-71. [Note:—Arch. vol. A66, page 100 shows that Leah Conwell later married John Riley].

**Cary, Ely [Eli].** Cordwinder. Will. Made Dec. 11, 1795. Heirs: wife Elizabeth Cary; sons Joseph, Woolsey, Samuel, Ely, Cornelius, Nehemiah, Joshua, James and Lemuel Cary; daus. Phebe and Esther Russell; dau. of son John. Exec'rx, wife Elizabeth Cary. Wits., Stratton Burton, Rhoda Burton, Elizabeth Burton. Prob. Feb. 8, 1796. Arch. vol. A64, pages 34-35. Reg. of Wills, Liber E, folio 67.

**Marvel, David.** Planter. Will. Made Jan. 4, 1796. Heirs: wife Sally Marvel; sons David, Burton and Prettyman Marvel; daus. Elizabeth Marvel and Patience Knowles; dau.-in-law Polly Prettyman. Exec'rs, wife Sally Marvel and Robert Marvel. Wits., Thomas Rodney, John Rodney. Prob. Feb. 9, 1796. Arch. vol. A86, pages 193-194. Reg. of Wills, Liber E, folios 69-70. [Note:—Arch. vol. A86, page 194 shows Moses Daizy and wife Sally, late Sally Marvel, exhibited an account on the estate Sept. 13, 1797].

**Milman, Thomas.** Admin. of, to Peter Milman. Granted [c. Feb. 9, 1796]. Arch. vol. A89, page 13. [Note:—Arch. vol. A89, page 13 mentions dec'd father Peter Milman; William, Jesse and Beniah Milman].

**Warren, Wrixam.** Will. Made Nov. 14, 1795. Heirs: wife Rhoda Warren; son Alexander Warren; daus. Jemima and Mar-[gare]t Warren; grandsons Silas Warren, William Warren (son of Eli, dec'd), and Purnel Warren; dau.-in-law, widow of Eli Warren. Exec'rs, wife Rhoda Warren and son Alexander Warren. Wits., Benjamin Hudson, John Hudson, Wrixam Warren. Prob. Feb. 9, 1796. Arch. vol. A105, page 138. Reg. of Wills, Liber E, folios 67-69. [Note:—Arch. vol. A105, page 138 mentions dec'd son Bennett Warren].

**Nicolls, Nehemiah.** Will. Made Dec. 26, 1795. Heirs: wife Comfort Nicolls; sons Daniel and William Nicolls; daus. Nancy and Lydia Nicolls. Exec'rx, wife Comfort Nicolls. Wits., Curtis Morris, John M. Morris, W[illia]m Nicolls. Prob.

Feb. 16, 1796. Arch. vol. A91, pages 96-97. Reg. of Wills, Liber E, folio 70.

**Callaway, Ebenezer.** Planter. Will. Made Nov. 2, 1795. Heirs: sons Benjamin, Moses, Clement, Matthew and Job Callaway. Exec'rs, wife [Eunice] Callaway and son Benjamin Callaway. Wits., Isaac Linch, John Emerson. Prob. Feb. 17, 1796. Arch. vol. A62, pages 135-136. Reg. of Wills, Liber E, folios 71-72.

**Coulbourn [Coleburn], Michael.** Farmer. Will. Made June 9, 1792. Heirs: sons Thomas, Joseph, Elijah and Robert Coulbourn; daus. Catharine, Rebecca, Nelly, Anna and Kesiah Coulbourn, Mary Williams, Priscilla Stewart and Nancy Watts. Exec'r, son Joseph Coulbourn. Wits., Samuel Cooper, John Cannon, Sophia Smith. Prob. Feb. 25, 1796. Arch. vol. A65, pages 103-104. Reg. of Wills, Liber E, folios 72-73.

**Hitch, William.** Will. Made . . ., 1795. Heirs: bro. Gillis Hitch; Sarah Hitch; Unicy Joseph. Exec'r, bro. Gillis Hitch. Wits., John Polk, Bessie Snow, Nutter Cannon. Prob. Feb. 26, 1796. Arch. vol. A77, pages 6-7. Reg. of Wills, Liber E, folio 73.

**Evans, Walter.** Will. Made May 9, 1795. Heirs: son William Evans; daus. Rhoda and [Tabitha] Evans; grandson Lemuel Evans; granddau. Polly Evans. Exec'rs, son William Evans, sons-in-law William Freeman and Benjamin Burton. Wits., Sally Hazzard, William Howell, Thomas Hazzard. Prob. March 7, 1796. Arch. vol. A71, pages 37-38. Reg. of Wills, Liber E, folios 74-75.

**Morris, Isaac.** Will. Made Feb. 18, 1796. Heirs: wife Sarah Morris; son Joseph Morris; Seth Waples (son of Thomas). Exec'rx, wife Sarah Morris. Wits., Thomas Marvel, Richard Westley. Prob. March 7, 1796. Arch. vol. A90, pages 56-57. Reg. of Wills, Liber E, folios 73-74.

**Cade, Richardson.** Will. Made May 7, 1794. Heirs: wife Priscilla Cade; sons John and Richardson Cade; daus. Mary Johnson, Abigail Bell and Emily Read; granddaus. Comfort and Amanda Dutton (daus. of dau. Priscilla Dutton, dec'd). Exec'rx, wife Priscilla Cade. Wits., Thomas Fisher, Theodore Wilson, Elizabeth Fisher. Prob. March 15, 1796. Arch. vol. A62, pages 102-103. Reg. of Wills, Liber E, folio 75.

**Smith, Obediah.** Will. Made Oct. 30, 1794. Heirs: wife Stacey Smith; son Job Smith; daus. Sarah and Elizabeth Smith, and Margaret Clifton; grandsons Job, Benjamin, John, Judah and Smith Clifton (children of dau. M Obediah Smith (son of Job); granddaus. Priscilla ⸻, Mary Jones (wife of Matthew) and Elizabeth Nicols (wife of William); other children of son Job Smith. Exec'rx, wife Stacey Smith. Wits., Olive Jump, Priscilla Stafford, Thomas Stafford. Prob. March 15, 1796. Arch. vol. A99, pages 191-192. Reg. of Wills, Liber E, folios 76-77. [Note:—Arch. vol. A99, page 192 shows the estate was settled Nov. 14, 1797 by Joseph Kelly and wife Stacey, late Stacey Smith].

**Waples, Elihu.** Admin. of, to John Tingle. Granted [c. March 15, 1796]. Arch. vol. A105, page 13.

**Waples, Mary.** Admin. of, to John Tingle. Granted [c. March 15, 1796]. Arch. vol. A105, page 13.

**Butcher, Frances.** Will. Made June 11, 1792. Heirs: bro. Hugh Stephenson; sister Peggy Stephenson; Sally Stephenson (dau. of Hugh Stephenson); cousins Jenny Stephenson, Frances Carry, Mary and LeJay Butcher, and Elizabeth Walls. Exec'r, bro. Hugh Stephenson. Wits., John Collings, Leah Collings. Prob. March 17, 1796. Arch. vol. A62, page 72. Reg. of Wills, Liber E, folios 71-72.

**Baker, Mary.** Widow. Will (nunc.). Made March 7, 1796. Heirs: son Joshua Baker; daus. Sally and Betsy Baker. [No exec'r]. Wits., William Shockley, Betty Baker. Prob. March 18, 1796. Arch. vol. A58, pages 129-130. Reg. of Wills, Liber E, folio 78. [Note:—Arch. vol. A58, page 130 shows that Joshua Turner, adm'r C. T. A., exhibited an account on the estate June 16, 1797; also mentions Joshua Turner and Betsy Edgin as heirs].

**Dazey, Moses, Sr.** Will. Made Jan. 12, 1796. Heirs: wife Mary Dazey; sons Moses, Abraham, Jesse and Jacob Dazey; daus. Sarah Sipple, Mary Hudson, Leah Schearam; Benjamin Dazey Schearam (son of Leah). Exec'rs, wife Mary Dazey and son Jesse Dazey. Wits., Thomas Dazey, George Dazey, William Evans. Prob. March 22, 1796. Arch. vol. A68, pages 198-199. Reg. of Wills, Liber E, folios 78-79.

**Morris, Ezekiah [Hezekiah].** Planter. Will. Made Jan. 5, 1796. Heirs: wife Mary Morris; son Jacob Morris; daus. Ann and Jane Morris. Exec'rx, wife Mary Morris. Wits., John Williams, Joshua James, William J. Anderson. Prob. March 22, 1796. Arch. vol. A90, pages 50-51. Reg. of Wills, Liber E, folios 79-80.

**Crouch, John.** Admin. of, to Sarah Crouch. Granted [c. April, 1796]. Arch. vol. A67, page 202.

**Bowness, William.** Will. Made March 15, 1796. Heirs: wife Sidney Bowness; sons Edward and William Bowness; daus. Elisabeth Bowness and Polly Meads. Exec'rs, John Meads and bro.-in-law William Mason. Wits., David Owens, John B[ell] Pollock. Prob. April 6, 1796. Arch. vol. A60, pages 38-39. Reg. of Wills, Liber E, folios 80-81. [Note:—Arch. vol. A60, page 39 shows an account was exhibited on the estate by the surviving exec'r, William Mason, C. T. A., March 21, 1798].

**Bevans [Bivins], Rowland.** Will. Made Sept. 28, 1795. Heirs: wife Sarah Bevans; sons Thomas, Levin, John and Rowland Bevans; daus. Amelia and Sally Bevans. Exec'rx, wife Sarah Bevans. Wits., Nathaniel Mitchell, Watson Pepper. Prob. April 7, 1796. Arch. vol. A59, pages 167-168. Reg. of Wills, Liber E, folios 81-82. [Note:—Arch. vol. A59, page 168 shows Thomas Bivins, adm'r, D. B. N., C. T. A., settled the estate].

**Wooten, Isaac.** Planter. Will. Made March 2, 1791. Heirs: sons Peter G., John, Isaac and Billy Wooten; daus. Allefair, Nelly, Polly, Sally, Betty, Levina and Nancy Wooten. Exec'r, son Peter Gordy Wooten. Wits., John Williams, George Mitchell, John Cahoon. Prob. April 12, 1796. Arch. vol. A109, pages 56-57. Reg. of Wills, Liber E, folios 82-83. [Note:—Arch vol. A109, page 57 mentions Nancy, Littleton, Polly, Betsy, John and Jonathan Huffington].

**Virden, Marnix.** Lewes & Rehoboth Hd. Will. Made Nov. 25, 1795. Heirs: wife Lydia Virden; daus. Alice and Lydia Virden, Mary Martin (widow of James Martin); granddaus. Elizabeth and Mary Martin (children of dau. Mary Martin); grandchildren, Cornelia, Eunice, Burton, Woolsey and David Hall (children of dau. Bathsheba Hall, dec'd). Exec'rs, wife Lydia Virden, bro. William Virden. Wits., William Hopkins, Josiah Hopkins, John Mustard, Jr. Prob. April 15, 1796. Arch. vol. A103, page 180. Reg. of Wills, Liber E, folios 83-84.

**Hearn, Priscilla.** Will (copy). Made April 5, 1796. Heirs: sons Luther, Ebenezer, Thomas, Joseph and Clement Hearn; granddaus. Sally Hearn (dau. of Clement) and Priscilla Hearn. [No exec'r]. Wits., James Williams, Gammage Williams, Samuel Hearn. Prob. April 19, 1796. Arch. vol. A75, page 177. Reg. of Wills, Liber E, folios 84-85.

**Williams, Jonathan.** Will. Made March 1, 1796. Heirs: wife Mary Williams; sons Joseph, Thomas, Jonathan and David Williams; daus. Mary, Comfort, Elizabeth and Patience Williams. Exec'rx, wife Mary Williams. Wits., Joseph Haslet, John Bennett, James Townsend. Prob. April 19, 1796. Arch. vol. A108, page 9. Reg. of Wills, Liber E, folios 85-86.

**Timmons, John, Sr.** Will. Made April 20, 1792. Heirs: wife Betty Timmons; sons Robert, Eli, James and John Timmons; daus. Betty Timmons, Sarah Goddard and Mary Morgan; grandsons William Adams Timmons; Whittingham and Eli Cotman Timmons; granddaus. Peggy and Tabitha Morgan. Exec'r, son James Timmons. Wits., Jesse Saunders, Nathan Saunders, Peter Dolby. Prob. April 21, 1796. Arch. vol. A102, pages 1-2. Reg. of Wills, Liber E, folios 86-88.

**Waples, Ann.** Admin. of, to William Vaughan. Granted [c. April 21, 1796]. Arch. vol. A104, page 168. [Note:—Arch. vol. A104, page 168 mentions Thomas Waples and Betsy Vaughan].

**Waples, Peter.** Admin. of, to William Vaughan and wife Sarah, late Sarah Waples. Granted [c. April 21, 1796]. Arch. vol. A105, pages 39-40. [Note:—Arch. vol. A105, page 40 mentions Ann and Thomas Waples].

**Hosea, John.** Will. Made Sept. 18, 1792. Heirs: wife Mary Hosea; grandsons Matthew, Thomas and Jonathan Hosea, and John Hosea (son of John), John Callaway. Exec'rs, wife Mary Hosea and John Williams. Wits., James Bevins, William Cahoon, William Kirkpatrick. Prob. April 23, 1796. Arch. vol. A78, pages 66-70. Reg. of Wills, Liber E, folios 88-89. [Note:—Arch. vol. A78, page 70 mentions an heir Nelly Hosea and also shows the estate was settled by John Williams, surviving exec'r, April 25, 1798].

**Short, Isaac.** Will. Made April 23, 1796. Heirs: wife Elizabeth Short; sons Shadrach, Ned, Philip and Isaac Short; daus. Sally and Polly Short. Exec'rx, wife Elizabeth Short. Wits., Elias James, Noah James, Elzy Spicer. [No prob.]. Arch. vol. A98, pages 179-180.

**Harney, Thomas, Sr.** Will. Made Feb. 19, 1790. Heirs: sons Thomas, Selby, Mills and Joshua Harney; daus. Mary Wise, Hannah Taylor, Nancy West, Sarah Shankland. Exec'r, son Thomas Harney. Wits., Aaron Irons, Nehemiah Howard,

John Hazzard. Prob. April 26, 1796. Arch. vol. A74, page 111. Reg. of Wills, Liber E, folios 89-90.

**Tubbs, David.** Will. Made Sept. 29, 1795. Heirs: wife Elizabeth Tubbs; son Burton Tubbs. Exec'rx, wife Elizabeth Tubbs. Wits., Ezekiel Williams, Eli Rickards, Solomon Dirickson. Prob. April 26, 1796. Arch. vol. A102, pages 165-167. Reg. of Wills, Liber E, folio 90. [Note:—Arch. vol. A102, page 167 shows the estate was settled by Elizabeth Robinson and John Daizey, adm'rs of Elizabeth Tubbs].

**Hazzard, William** (son of Joseph). Admin. of, to Amelia Hazzard, who later married Bevins Morris. Granted [c. April 27, 1796].

**Auston, Isaac.** Yeoman. Admin. of, to Mary Auston. Granted [c. April 28, 1796]. Arch. vol. A57, page 227.

**Edgen, Benjamin.** Admin. of, to Lurana Edgen. Granted [c. April 28, 1796]. Arch. vol. A70, page 33.

**Rogers, Agnes.** Will. Made April 17, 1796. Heirs: son [America] Rogers; daus. Nancy Rogers, Easter Coffin, Sarah Taylor, Elizabeth Pratt; son-in-law Nathaniel Rogers. Exec'r, friend Ezekiel Williams. Wits., Isaac Duncan, Ananias Hudson, John Hamblen. Prob. April 28, 1796. Arch. vol. A97, pages 29-30. Reg. of Wills, Liber E, folio 90.

**Lingo, Samuel, Jr.** Admin. of, to Samuel Lingo. Granted [c. May 27, 1796]. Arch. vol. A84, page 142.

**Lay, Baptist.** Admin. of, to Philena Lay. Granted [c. May 30, 1796]. Arch. vol. A83, page 165.

**Walton, George.** Yeoman. Will. Made Nov. 4, 1792. Heirs: wife Jean Walton; sons George, William, Jonathan, Joseph and James Walton; daus. Esther Killen (wife of Mark Killen), Ann Murray (wife of John Murray), Eunice Chance (wife of John Chance), Betty Chance (wife of Levin Chance), Sarah Meloy (wife of Thomas Meloy), and Mary Walton. Exec'rx, wife Jean Walton. Wits., Isaac Beauchamp, William Wattson, Thomas Jones. Prob. May 31, 1796. Arch. vol. A104, page 128. Reg. of Wills, Liber E, folios 91-93.

**Williams, Robert.** Will. Made May 8, 1796. Heirs: wife Sarah Hopkins Williams; sons George Frederick and Morgan Williams; daus. Sally and Betsy Williams. Exec'rs, wife Sarah Hopkins Williams and Levin Ricords. Wits., Charles Brown, Loxley Ricards, Andrew Dukes. Prob. June 1, 1796. Arch. vol. A108, pages 35-36. Reg. of Wills, Liber E, folio 93.

[Note:—Arch. vol. A108, page 36 shows the estate was settled by Ralph Robinson and Sarah, his wife, late Sarah Rickards, who was also Sarah Hopkins Williams].

**Burton, Sarah.** Will. Made Jan. 20, 1796. Heirs: son Isaiah Burton; daus. Lydia and Leah Burton; Cornelia Burton; granddaus. Sarah Burton, Nancy Gassem, Sarah, Lydia and Mary Parker; grandsons Elisha and Matthew Parker. Exec'rx, dau. Lydia Burton. Wits., Benjamin Burton, Sarah Burton, Elizabeth Burton. Prob. June 2, 1796. Arch. vol. A62, pages 14-15. Reg. of Wills, Liber E, folios 94-95. [Note:—Arch. vol. A62, page 15 shows Lydia Burton as wife of Thomas Burton, who were adm'rs, C. T. A., and exhibited an account on the estate July 13, 1798].

**Hall, Samuel.** Admin. of, to Jean Hall. Granted [c. June 2, 1796]. Arch. vol. A74, pages 1-2.

**Rogers, Christopher.** Will. Made April 16, 1796. Heirs: wife Priscilla Rogers; son Clement Rogers; dau. Betty Rogers. Exec'rx, wife Priscilla Rogers. Wits., Isaac Cannon, John Hickman, Nehemiah Hickman. Prob. June 2, 1796. Arch. vol. A97, page 33. Reg. of Wills, Liber E, folio 95.

**Parker, Eli.** Will. Made Jan. 2, 1792. Heirs: wife Eleanor Parker; daus. Abigail, Patience, Eleanor, Peggy, Sarah and Elizabeth Parker (later married Benjamin Davis). Exec'rx, wife Eleanor Parker. Wits., Joseph Lindell, William Tatman, Jenkins Parker. Prob. June 3, 1796. Arch. vol. A92, pages 58-59. Reg. of Wills, Liber E, folios 95-96. [Note:—Arch. vol. A92, page 59 shows the estate was settled by Major Townsend, D. B. N., on May 20, 1799].

**Vent, Mary.** Admin. of, to Joseph Dodd. Adm'rs bond dated June 17, 1796. Arch. vol. A103, page 104.

**Norwood, Henry.** Admin. of, to John Willis. Granted [c. June 21, 1796]. Arch. vol. A91, page 115.

**Parmor [Parmer], Sheldon Dorman.** Will (copy). Made June 8, 1796. Heirs: wife Eusebia Parmor; wife's dau. Frances Warren. Exec'rx, wife Eusebia Parmor. Wits., Jacob Wolfe, Stephen Reddin, James Reed, Elihu McCracken. Prob. June 21, 1796. Arch. vol. A92, page 93. Reg. of Wills, Liber E, folio 96. [Note:—Arch. vol. A92, page 93 shows that Eusebia Parmer later married . . . Messick].

**Tull, Sarah.** Will. Made June 8, 1796. Heirs: sister Peggy Tull. Exec'r, John Martin. Wits., William Mitten, Isaac Mitten,

Ann Tull. Prob. June 21, 1796. Arch. vol. A102, page 183. Reg. of Wills, Liber E, folio 97.

**Truitt, Betty.** Admin. of, to Adam Short. Granted [c. June 24, 1796]. Arch. vol. A102, page 104.

**Macklin, Charles.** Will. Made June 4, 1796. Heirs: wife Elizabeth Macklin; sons Charles and Eli Macklin; daus. Katie Townsend, Polly Deputy and Basheba [Kirk]; grandsons Charles [Kirk], Charles Deputy (of John), Luke Townsend. Exec'rx, wife Elizabeth Macklin. Wits., Benjamin Hudson, Rachel Killingsworth. Prob. July 22, 1796. Arch. vol. A86, pages 6-7. Reg. of Wills, Liber E, folios 97-98.

**Beachum, Dickinson.** Admin. of, to Thomas Smith. Granted [c. Aug., 1796]. Arch. vol. A59, page 6.

**Dickerson, Levin.** Will. Made July 25, 1796. Heirs: bro. Edmund Dickerson; sisters Eleanor, Sally, Nancy and Comfort Dickerson. Exec'r, bro. Edmund Dickerson. Wits., Elizabeth James, Eunice Dickenson, James F. Baylis. Prob. Aug. 2, 1796. Arch. vol. A69, page 66. Reg. of Wills, Liber E, folio 98.

**Horsey, Halsey.** Admin. of, to William Neal. Granted [c. Aug. 2, 1796]. Arch. vol. A78, page 31.

**Clifton, Tabitha.** Widow. Will. Made May 13, 1784. Heirs: sons Daniel, Richard and Manlove Clifton; daus. Catherine Clifton, Rachel Carlile (wife of Thomas), Elizabeth Carlile (wife of John), Mary Morgan (wife of Daniel), Dorcas Killen (wife of William) and Madelin Johnston (wife of John); granddaus. Tamson Clifton and Avis Carlile. Exec'r, son-in-law John Carlile. Wits., William Hazzard, Thomas Bell, William Pride. Prob. Aug. 8, 1796. Arch. vol. A65, pages 46-47. Reg. of Wills, Liber D, folios 173-174.

**Shaver, Ann.** Will. Made Oct. 30, 1794. Heirs: son John Shaver; grandsons James and John Shaver; granddau. Ann Shaver. Exec'r, son John Shaver. Wits., Nath[anie]l Young, Esther Young, Mary McDermont. Prob. Aug. 9, 1796. Arch. vol. A98, page 100. Reg. of Wills, Liber E, folio 98.

**Richards, David.** Will. Made Jan. 15, 1796. Heirs: wife unnamed; sons John and David Richards; dau. Polly Richards. Exec'rx, unnamed wife. Wits., W[illia]m Stayton, Zebulon Wroughten, Ambrose Alford. Prob. Aug. 13, 1796. Arch. vol. A95, page 71. Reg. of Wills, Liber E, folios 99-100.

**Barr, David.** Admin. of, to Thomas Russell. Granted [c. Aug. 18, 1796]. Arch. vol. A58, page 211.

**Nottingham, Chloe.** Admin. of, to Thomas Russell and wife Polly, late Polly Barr. Granted [c. Aug. 18, 1796]. Arch. vol. A91, page 117.

**Coverdill, Richard.** Will (nunc.). Made July 20, 1796. Heirs: wife unnamed and children unnamed. Exec'rx, wife unnamed. Wits., George Polk, William Lyn[am]. Prob. Aug. 19, 1796. Arch. vol. A67, page 96. Reg. of Wills, Liber E, folio 101. [Note:—Arch. vol. A67, page 96 mentions bro. William and wife's father].

**Connaway, John** (son of Phillip). Will. Made July 25, 1796. Heirs: wife Elizabeth Connaway; sons Samuel, Jacob and Francis Connaway; daus. Tabby and Sally Connaway, Polly Shepperd, Lovey Yeats and Katie Durham. Exec'rx, wife Elizabeth Connaway. Wits., L[udwig] Connaway, William Connaway, Elisha Massey. Prob. Aug. 23, 1796. Arch. vol. A66, pages 56-57. Reg. of Wills, Liber E, folio 101.

**Warrington, William.** Admin. of, to John Lingo and wife Polly, late Polly Warrington. Granted [c. Aug. 23, 1796]. Arch. vol. A105, page 176.

**Norwood, Andrew Stewart.** Admin. of, to John Allen and wife Eunice, late Eunice Norwood. Granted [c. Aug. 30, 1796]. Arch. vol. A91, page 112.

**Brown, Humphreys.** Admin. of, to Eccleston Brown and John Langrall. Granted [c. Sept., 1796]. Arch. vol. A60, pages 190-193.

**Passwaters, William, Sr.** Will (nunc).. Made Aug. 11, 1796. Heirs: son Jonas Passwaters; dau. Nancy Passwaters; other children unnamed. [No exec'r]. Wits., John Linch, Jr., Selby Tatman. Prob. Sept. 6, 1796. Arch. vol. A92, page 112. Reg. of Wills, Liber E, folio 104.

**Waples, Burton.** Will. Made Aug. 16, 1796. Heirs: daus. Agnes Waples, Comfort King and Anne Hall; grandsons Woolsey Waples, Wallace Waples, Burton West, Jacob Bounds, William Bounds, William Vaughan; granddaus. Betty Vaughan, Neala Waples and Comfort Burton Waples; bros. William Waples, dec'd, and Peter Waples; uncle Paul Waples. Exec'rs, daus. Agnes Waples, Comfort King and Anne Hall. Wits., W[illia]m Bell, Paynter Frame, Levin [Moor] Mour. Prob. Sept. 14, 1796. Arch. vol. A104, page 171. Reg. of Wills, Liber E, folios 102-103.

**Cornwall, John, Jr.** Yeoman. Admin. of, to John Cornwall. Granted Sept. 15, 1796. Arch. vol. A66, page 229.

**Smith, William.** Will. Made Sept. 9, 1796. Heirs: dau. Elizabeth Smith. Exec'r, friend Adam Short. Wits., Curtis Cannon, Nelly Means, Esther Means. Prob. Sept. 20, 1796. Arch. vol. A100, pages 13-14. Reg. of Wills, Liber E, folio 104.

**Freeny, John.** Planter. Will. Made Sept. 4, 1786. Heirs: wife Elizabeth Freeny; sons Joshua, William, John, Elijah and Thomas Freeny; daus. Sarah, Levina, Ann, Mary and Elizabeth Freeny; Newbold Moor; Elijah Moor; Joshua Hastings. Exec'rs, wife Elizabeth Freeny and son Elijah Freeny. Wits., William Hearn, Jonathan Hearn, Elijah Hastings. Prob. Sept. 27, 1796. Arch. vol. A72, pages 82-84. Reg. of Wills, Liber E, folios 106-108. [Note:—Arch. vol. A72, page 83 mentions William Ellegood, Nehemiah Morris and Levina Moore].

**Smith, John.** Planter. Will. Made Sept. 25, 1796. Heirs: wife Sophia Smith; sons William and Holms Smith; daus. Elizabeth and Nancy Smith and Rachel Milman. Exec'rs, sons William and Holms Smith. Wits., Thomas Evans, John Tatman, Eli Shockley. Prob. Oct. 4, 1796. Arch. vol. A99, page 170. Reg. of Wills, Liber E, folios 104-105.

**Polk, Daniel, Esq.** Admin. of, to Samuel White. Granted [c. Oct. 8, 1796]. Arch. vol. A93, page 112.

**Connor, Daniel.** Admin. of, to Benjamin McIlvain. Granted [c. Oct. 11, 1796]. Arch. vol. A66, page 91.

**Hall, John** (son of James). Admin. of, to Martha Hall. Granted Oct. 11, 1796. Arch. vol. A73, pages 216-217.

**Short, Abraham.** Admin. of, to William Shelpman and wife Margaret, late Margaret Short. Granted [c. Oct. 12, 1796]. Arch. vol. A98, page 152. [Note:—Arch. vol. A98, page 152 mentions a dau. Betsy].

**Hazzard, William** (son of Jacob). Admin. of, to Elizabeth Hazzard. Granted [c. Oct. 18, 1796]. Arch. vol. A75, page 139.

**Baily, John.** Admin. of, to Betty Baily. Granted [c. Oct. 19, 1796]. Arch. vol. A58, page 72.

**Dickerson, Elisha.** Will. Made Oct. 24, 1796. Heirs: wife Elizabeth H. Dickerson; son Robert Dickerson; bro. . . . Dickerson; cousin Sally Harris. Exec'rx, wife Elizabeth H. Dickerson. Wits., Jacob Burton, William Freeman. Prob. Nov.

2, 1796. Arch. vol. A69, page 56. Reg. of Wills [No liber]. [Note:—Arch. vol. A69, page 56 shows the estate was settled by Elizabeth Holland Cullen, late Elizabeth H. Dickerson, wife of Charles M. Cullen].

**Bacon, John.** Little Creek Hd. Will. Made Oct. 1, 1796. Heirs: wife Phame Bacon; sons Henry and John Bacon; Gilbert Cannon. Exec'rs, wife Phame Bacon and James Windsor. Wits., Levi Callaway, William Vaughan, Leah Polk. Prob. Nov. 4, 1796. Arch. vol. A58, pages 41-44. Reg. of Wills, Liber E, folios 108-109. [Note:—Arch. vol. A58, pages 42-44 show that Phame Bacon later married George Armstrong].

**Virdin, Levy.** Admin. of, to Shada Virdin. Granted [c. Nov. 8, 1796]. Arch. vol. A103, page 176.

**Prider, Rachel.** Will. Made Sept. 29, 1796. Heirs: dau. Polly Smith; friend Solomon Layton. Exec'r, friend Solomon Layton. Wits., William Carlisle, John Wilson, Joseph Sedger. Prob. Nov. 10, 1796. Arch. vol. A94, page 156. Reg. of Wills, Liber E, folios 109-110.

**Short, Adam, Sr.** Will. Made Oct. 12, 1795. Heirs: wife Betty Short; sons Purnal, Adam and Tilghman Short; daus. Nancy Willis, Rebecca Waller, Katie O'Day, Lovey Johnson, Sarah McCauley and Betty Marvel. Exec'rx, wife Betty Short. Wits., William Swain, Polly Wright, Polly Rodney. Prob. Nov. 10, 1796. Arch. vol. A98, page 153. Reg. of Wills, Liber E, folios 54-56.

**Brown, Isaac.** Admin. of, to Thomas Smith. Granted [c. Nov. 15, 1796]. Arch. vol. A60, page 194.

**Vaughan, Joseph.** Admin. of, to Levin Vaughan. Granted [c. Nov. 15, 1796]. Arch. vol. A103, page 70.

**Joseph, Jacob.** Admin. of, to Levi Pullet, D. B. N., in right of Levin Walls. Granted [c. Nov. 16, 1796]. Arch. vol. A82, page 9.

**Lank, Nathaniel.** Admin. of, to John Lank. Granted [c. Nov. 16, 1796]. Arch. vol. A83, page 92.

**Walls, Levin.** Admin. of, to Levi Pullet. Granted [c. Nov. 16, 1796]. Arch. vol. A104, page 100.

**Howard, Nehemiah.** Will. Made Nov. 2, 1796. Heirs: wife Rhoda Howard; sons George, Nehemiah, William and John Howard; daus. Sally and Elizabeth Howard. Exec'rs, wife Rhoda Howard and son William Howard. Wits., Benjamin Holland, William Johnson, Leah Johnson. Prob. Nov. 17, 1796. Arch. vol. A78, pages 143-145. Reg. of Wills, Liber E, folios 110-111. [Note:—Arch. vol. A78, page 145 shows the estate was settled Nov. 16, 1798 by William Howard, as surviving exec'r].

**Parremore, Mary.** Admin. of, to Job Parremore. Granted [c. Nov. 17, 1796]. Arch. vol. A92, page 88.

**Skidmore, Henry.** Admin. of, to Job Reynolds and wife Susannah, late Susannah Skidmore. Granted [c. Nov. 17, 1796]. Arch. vol. A99, page 99.

**Wright, Ezekiel.** Farmer. Will. Made Oct. 26, 1796. Heirs: son William Wright; daus. Betsy and Polly Wright and Nancy Magee. Exec'r, son William Wright. Wits., John Dashiell, George Adams, Joshua Magee. Prob. Nov. 18, 1796. Arch. vol. A109, page 80. Reg. of Wills, Liber E, folio 111.

**Read, Job.** Admin. of, to Isaac Read. Granted [c. Nov. 22, 1796]. Arch. vol. A95, page 6.

**Nicolls, Levin.** Admin. of, to John Gullet and wife Sarah, and James Spence. Granted [c. Nov. 23, 1796]. Arch. vol. A91, page 95.

**Russel, Joseph.** Admin. of, to William Millard, in right of Jane Russel. Granted [c. Nov. 23, 1796]. Arch. vol. A97, page 143.

**Jarman [Jarmon], William.** Will (copy). Made Aug. 27, 1795. Heirs: wife Magdalena Jarman; sons James, William, Henry, George and Joshua Jarman; daus. Sally, Henrietta, Rebecca, Betty, Mary and Nelly Jarman. Exec'rx, wife Magdalena Jarman. Wits., Jesse Saunders, Eunice Downs, Polly Downs. Prob. Nov. 26, 1796. Arch. vol. A80, pages 131-132. Reg. of Wills, Liber E, folios 58-59.

**Clarkson, Margaret.** Will. Made Aug. 14, 1795. Heirs: son Thomas Clarkson; daus. Mary Hurley, Leah Cannon, Marg[ar]et Bennett and Elizabeth Clarkson. Exec'r, son Thomas Clarkson. Wits., Isaac Wright, James Wilson. Prob. Dec. 20, 1796. Arch. vol. A64, page 212. Reg. of Wills, Liber E, folio 112.

**Clarkson, Robert.** Will. Made July 2, 1796. Heirs: daus. L[eah] and Al[freda] Clarkson, Phillis Lednum and Sally Wright. Exec'rs, Zadock Lednum and Jesse Wright. Wits., Hughett Cannon, Curtis Jacobs, Hays Jacobs. Prob. Dec. 20, 1796.

Arch. vol. A64, pages 218-220. Reg. of Wills, Liber E, folios 112-113. [Note:—Arch. vol. A64, page 220 mentions Liza Jacobs and Rebecca Norman].

**Conwell, Abraham.** Admin. of, to Bevans Morris and wife Sarah. Granted [c. 1797]. Arch. vol. A66, pages 93-94.

**Culver, James.** Admin. of, to Samuel Culver. Granted [c. 1797]. Arch. vol. A67, page 219.

**Kellam, Thomas.** Will. Made Jan. 14, 1796. Heirs: wife Rhoda Kellam; bro. Jesse Kellam; William Jefferson (son of Warren). Exec'rx, wife Rhoda Kellam. Wits., S. Kollock, Jonathan Bell. Prob. Jan. 3, 1797. Arch. vol. A82, pages 42-45. Reg. of Wills, Liber E, folios 113-114. [Note:—Arch. vol. A82, pages 43-45 shows the estate was settled by Robert Houston, D. B. N., in right of Rhoda Kellam].

**Williams, Stephen.** Will (nunc.). Made Jan. 4, 1797. Heirs: bros. Noah and Ark Williams; unnamed mother; unnamed sisters. [No exec'r]. Wits., Sally Williams. [No prob.]. Arch. vol. A108, page 50.

**Wattson, Luke.** Admin. of, to Joseph Briggs and wife Elizabeth, late Elizabeth Wattson. Granted [c. Jan. 12, 1797]. Arch. vol. A106, page 30.

**Hitch, Spencer.** Will. Made Feb. 5, 1796. Heirs: wife Sophia Hitch; sons Soverign, William, Clement, Elg[in] and Spencer Hitch; daus. Anna, Lilly, Nelly, Polly Hitch, and Sarah Snellen. Exec'rx, wife Sophia Hitch. Wits., William Mason, Gillis Hitch. Prob. Jan. 21, 1797. Arch. vol. A76, pages 200-202. Reg. of Wills, Liber E, folio 119.

**Darby, Joseph.** Admin. of, to Thomas Ricords. Granted [c. Jan. 31, 1797]. Arch. vol. A68, pages 24-25.

**Willson, John.** Prime Hook Neck, Cedar Creek Hd. Will. Made Sept. 25, 1794. Heirs: wife Elizabeth Wilson; sons David and Riley Willson; daus. Polly and Eliza Willson. Exec'rx, wife Elizabeth Wilson. Wits., Nathaniel Young, John Smith, John Robinson. Prob. Feb. 9, 1797. Arch. vol. A108, pages 82-83. Reg. of Wills, Liber E, folios 114-115. [Note:—Arch. vol. A108, page 83 shows that Elizabeth Wilson later married . . . Lofland and that the estate was settled by Thomas Willson who was exec'r of Elizabeth Lofland, dec'd; also mentions heirs John Wilson and Polly Bennett].

**Johnson, John.** Planter. Will. Made July 23, 1794. Heirs: sons Bartholomew, William and Josiah Johnson; daus. Luranah James and Anna Pepper; granddau. Luranah

Johnson. [No exec'r]. Wits., Jonathan Johnson, Benjamin Melson. Prob. Feb. 11, 1797. Arch. vol. A81, page 56. Reg. of Wills, Liber E, folio 115.

**Passwaters, William.** Yeoman. Will. Made April 15, 1792. Heirs: wife Sarah Passwaters; sons Jonas, Jesse, John, Clement and Jeremiah Passwaters; dau. Nancy Passwaters. Exec'rx, wife Sarah Passwaters. Wits., Robert Shankland, Jr., Edward Polk, Jr., Charles Polk. Prob. Feb. 14, 1797. Arch. vol. A92, pages 113-114. Reg. of Wills, Liber E, folios 116-117.

**Crapper, Susannah.** Admin. of, to John Mason. Granted before Feb. 18, 1797. Arch. vol. A67, pages 180-181.

**Sturgis, Shadrach.** Admin. of, to Daniel Sturgis. Granted [c. Feb. 20, 1797]. Arch. vol. A101, page 74.

**Connaway, John.** Will. Made March 18, 1784. Heirs: wife Judith Connaway; sons Levin, Isaac, John and Jacob Connaway; daus. Sarah Beavins, Betty Short and Mary Willy. Exec'r, son John Connaway. Wits., Robert Robinson, Elisha Long, Daniel O. Long. Prob. Feb. 21, 1797. Arch. vol. A66, page 58. Reg. of Wills, Liber E, folios 118-119.

**Hopkins, George.** Will. Made Dec. 26, 1796. Heirs: wife Constant Hopkins; sons Philip and Cannon Hopkins; daus. Polly and Anne Hopkins; father Joseph Cannon. Exec'r, son Philip Hopkins. Wits., Levin Connaway, Jehu Wyatt. Prob. Feb. 21, 1797. Arch. vol. A77, page 182. Reg. of Wills, Liber E, folios 117-118.

**Kellam, William.** Admin. of, to Betsy Kellam. Granted [c. Feb. 21, 1797]. Arch. vol. A82, page 46.

**Lay, Edward.** Admin. of, to Philena Lay. Granted [c. Feb. 22, 1797]. Arch. vol. A83, page 166.

**Russel, Jane.** Admin. of, to William Millard. Granted [c. Feb. 22, 1797]. Arch. vol. A97, page 134.

**Polk, Leah.** Will. Made Aug. 19, 1796. Heirs: daus. Leah Andrews and Sally Andrews. Exec'rxs, daus. Leah and Sally Andrews. Wits., John Williams, Jane Polk, George Fletcher. Prob. Feb. 24, 1797. Arch. vol. A93, page 140. Reg. of Wills, Liber E, folios 119-120.

**King, Elizabeth.** Will. Made Feb. 19, 1796. Heirs: son Edward King; dau. Polly King. Exec'r, son Edward King. Wits., John Bloxsom, Betsy Car[diff]. Prob. Feb. 27, 1797. Arch. vol. A82, page 97. Reg. of Wills, Liber E, folio 120.

**Stockley, Jacob.** Admin. of, to Rachel Stockley and Philip Wingate. Granted [c. Feb. 28, 1797]. Arch. vol. A101, page 10.

**Waples, Burton, Jr.** Blacksmith. Admin. of, to George Rider and wife Betty, late Betty Waples. Granted [c. Feb. 28, 1797]. Arch. vol. A104, pages 172-173. [Note:—Arch. vol. A104, pages 172-173 show that William Prettyman was adm'r D. B. N.; page 173 mentions James Wakeman and wife Ruth, late Ruth West].

**Cary, Samuel.** Admin. of, to Comfort Cary. Granted [c. March, 1797]. Arch. vol. A64, pages 94-95. [Note:—Arch. vol. A64, page 95 mentions heirs: widow Comfort, Ellen, Catharine, Samuel H., Stockley, Eli, Thomas, Comfort and Nehemiah Cary].

**Rogers, Comfort.** Widow of John. Will. Made Jan. 28, 1797. Heirs: sons George and John Rogers; daus. Patience and Unice Rogers. Exec'r, son George Rogers. Wits., Thomas Marvel, Levin Stuart. Prob. March 1, 1797. Arch. vol. A97, page 34. Reg. of Wills, Liber E, folio 116. [Note:—Arch. vol. A97, page 34 mentions dec'd father, Thomas Prettyman].

**Hardy, Phillis.** Will. Made Aug. 6, 1796. Heirs: son Joseph Hardy; daus. Phillis, Rachel Jones Hardy, Sarah Wilson and Allafair Dashiell; granddaus. Peggy Hardy Dashiell, Betsy Hardy Wilson. Exec'r, son Joseph Hardy. Wits., Noble West, James Culver, Bartholomew Holloram. Prob. March 14, 1797. Arch. vol. A74, pages 69-70. Reg. of Wills, Liber E, folio 121. [Note:—Arch. vol. A74, page 70 mentions Benj[amin] Wales as one of the exec'rs who relinquished his right in favor of son Joseph Hardy].

**Vaughan, Jonathan.** Will. Made Feb. 4, 1795. Heirs: bros. Joseph and Isaac Vaughan. Exec'r, Jesse Green. Wits., Rob[er]t Green, Jesse Green, Kitty Green. Prob. March 15, 1797. Arch. vol. A103, page 68. Reg. of Wills, Liber E, folio 122.

**Donovan, Naomi.** Admin. of, to Foster Donovan. Granted [c. March 21, 1797]. Arch. vol. A69, page 150.

**Gray, Jesse.** Admin. of, to Thomas Gray. Granted [c. March 21, 1797]. Arch. vol. A73, page 10. [Note:—Arch. vol. A73, page 10 mentions James Gray].

**Robinson, William.** Admin. of, to Sarah Robinson. Granted [c. March 1797]. Arch. vol. A96, page 193.

**Laws, Saxagotha.** Admin. of, to Nathaniel Russum and wife Leah, late Leah Laws. Granted March 24, 1797. Arch. vol. A83, page 152.

**Hooper, Sarah.** Will. Made April 23, 1793. Heirs: sons Henry John and Thomas Hooper; daus. Priscilla Traverse, Nancy Dalg[reen], and Mary Tennent; grandson Henry Wallace. Exec'r, son Thomas Hooper. Wits., Elizabeth Merrill, Peter Rea. Prob. March 25, 1797. Arch. vol. A77, page 174. Reg. of Wills, Liber E, folios 122-123.

**Rogers, John.** Admin. of, to Henry Lawrence and wife Phebe. Adm'rs bond dated March 28, 1797. Arch. vol. A97, page 44.

**Chase, Sarah.** Admin. of, to Mary Chase, in right of James Chase. Granted [c. April 4, 1797]. Arch. vol. A64, page 133.

**Polk, Trusten Laws.** Admin. of, to William Polk. Granted [c. April 27, 1797]. Arch. vol. A93, page 152.

**McGee, David.** Admin. of, to George Walton. Granted [c. April 29, 1797]. Arch. vol. A87, page 166.

**Burton, Benjamin.** Will. Made April 27, 1797. Heirs: nephew Cord Burton; Benjamin Burton (son of William Burton, Jr.); and children of bros. and sisters unnamed. Exec'r, bro. Woolsey Burton. Wits., George Green, Elizabeth Robinson, James F. Baylis. ·Prob. May 5, 1797. Arch. vol. A61, pages 81-82. Reg. of Wills, Liber E, folio 124. [Note:— Arch. vol. A61, page 82 mentions heirs: Benjamin (son of William Burton); Cord Burton; children of Robert, William, John, Joseph and Woolsey Burton; David Hopkins; Jenny Paynter].

**Clifton, Matthew.** Admin. of, to John Allen and wife Elizabeth. Granted [c. May 5, 1797]. Arch. vol. A65, page 35.

**Lay, Philena.** Will. Made April 14, 1797. Heirs: dau. Elizabeth Martin; sister-in-law Ann Havilow (wife of James); friends Tabitha Woods, Susanna Wilson (dau. of Thomas Wilson), Anna Millard (dau. of William Millard), Lydia Fisher (dau. of James Fisher); negro Roads Conwell. Exec'r, friend William Millard. Wits., Thomas Wilson, Warner Mifflin, Anne Mifflin. Prob. May 5, 1797. Arch. vol. A83, page 167. Reg. of Wills, Liber E, folio 123.

**Roberts, William.** Admin. of, to Alexander Roberts. Granted [c. May 10, 1797]. Arch. vol. A96, page 93.

**Wolfe, Reece.** Will. Made April 17, 1797. Heirs: wife Mary Wolfe; sons Reece, William, Daniel, Harry, George, Benjamin and David Wolfe; children of dec'd dau. Comfort Orr; children of dau. Sarah Marriner; Jane Russell. Exec'rx, wife Mary Wolfe. Wits., James Wiltbank, William Polk, Daniel Rodney, John Parker. Prob. May 10, 1797. Arch. vol. A109, pages 37-39. Reg. of Wills, Liber E, folios 124-125.

**Stilwell, Mary.** Will. Made Oct. 23, 1796. Heirs: Nancy and Polly Merrick (daus. of Sarah Merrick). Exec'r, Waitman Gosling, Sr. Wits., William A. Hurley, Nancy Clifton, Absolam Adams. Prob. May 18, 1797. Arch. vol. A100, page 189. Reg. of Wills, Liber E, folios 125-126.

**Brown, Ezekiel.** Planter. Will. Made May 21, 1796. Heirs: wife Mary Brown; sons Clement, Jeremiah, Peter and A[u]gustus Brown; daus. Mary and Betsy Brown, and Nancy Coulbourn. Exec'rs, wife Mary Brown and son Jeremiah Brown. Wits., Henry Smith, William Davis, White B. Smith. Prob. May 20, 1797. Arch. vol. A60, page 183. Reg. of Wills, Liber E, folios 126-127.

**Cade, Thomas.** Will. Made March 1, 1797. Heirs: wife Le[titia] Cade; sons Robert and Thomas Cade. Exec'rx, wife Le-[titia] Cade. Wits., Isaac Fisher, Rebecca Cannon, Ann Coverdale. Prob. May 23, 1797. Arch. vol. A62, page 107. Reg. of Wills, Liber E, folio 127.

**Vinson, George.** Will. Made May 12, 1797. Heirs: wife Mary Vinson; sons Joseph, George and Benjamin Vinson; daus. Polly and Betsy Vinson. Exec'r, bro. Solomon Vinson. Wits., Jesse Saunders, Nathan Saunders, Benjamin Dolbee. Prob. May 23, 1797. Arch. vol. A103, pages 153-154. Reg. of Wills, Liber E, folios 127-129.

**Elliott, John.** Little Creek. Will (copy). Made May 2, 1797. Heirs: wife Ann Elliott; daus. Sarah, Joannah, Temperance, Peggy and Mary Elliott. Exec'rx, wife Ann Elliott. Wits., Nehemiah Morris, William Anderson, Sam[ue]l Hearn. Prob. June 7, 1797. Arch. vol. A70, page 76. Reg. of Wills, Liber E, folios 129-130.

**Kirkpatrick, William.** Planter. Will. Made Aug. 17, 1796. Heirs: wife Jemima Kirkpatrick; sons Hugh and Harrison Kirkpatrick. Exec'r, John Williams. Wits., Samuel Williams, Jr., Hetty Williams. Prob. June 7, 1797. Arch. vol. A82, pages 164-165. Reg. of Wills, Liber E, folio 130.

**West, John, Sr.** Will. Made Dec. 5, 1796. Heirs: sons John, Arthur, Ezekiel and Thomas West; daus. Hannah, Levinah, Nancy and Rhoda West; granddau. Jenny West (dau. of Jacob and Agnes West). Exec'rs, sons Ezekiel and John West. Wits., Major Benson, Joseph Freeman, Avery Morgan. Prob. July 3, 1797. Arch. vol. A106, pages 144-145. Reg. of Wills, Liber E, folios 130-131. [Note:— Arch. vol. A106, page 145 shows the estate was settled by Sarah West, adm'rx of Ezekeil West, dec'd, and Arthur West who was adm'r of John West, dec'd; also shows that Sarah West later married Elijah Evans].

**Rickards, John.** Will. Made April 20, 1797. Heirs: bros. William and Luke Rickards; sisters Peggy Rickards and Elizabeth Dirickson. Exec'r, Stephen Evans. Wits., Ezekiel Williams, Stephen Evans, Mary Nicholson. Prob. July 4, 1797. Arch. vol. A95, pages 125-126. Reg. of Wills, Liber E, folios 131-132. [Note:—Arch. vol. A95, page 126 mentions heirs: Mary Rickards and William Dirickson; also shows the estate was settled Aug. 21, 1799 by Ananias Evans, exec'r of Stephen Evans, dec'd].

**Wattson, Betsy.** Admin. of, to Bethuel Wattson. Granted [c. July 19, 1797]. Arch. vol. A105, page 193.

**Burton, Joseph.** Admin. of, to Thomas Burton, D. B. N. Granted ante July 28, 1797. Arch. vol. A61, pages 204-205. [Note:—Arch. vol. A61, page 204 shows the estate was formerly administered by Elizabeth Burton].

**Hand, John.** Admin. of, to Alice Hand and Nehemiah Hand. Granted [c. Aug. 15, 1797]. Arch. vol. A74, page 33.

**Dawson, Edward.** Admin. of, to Thomas Dawson. Granted [c. Aug. 31, 1797]. Arch. vol. A68, pages 143-144.

**Wattson, Bethuel, Sr.** Farmer. Cedar Creek Hd. Will. Made June 21, 1794. Heirs: sons Jesse and Bethuel Wattson; daus. Hester Metcalf, Mary Collins (widow of John Collins), Naomi Herrington; grandchildren Esther, Elizabeth, Jesse, John and Bethuel Wattson (children of dec'd son David Wattson), Luke, Nehemiah, John, Wattson, Mary, Betty and Zipporah Walton (children of dec'd dau. Elizabeth Walton). Exec'r, son Bethuel Wattson. Wits., George Cooke, Sarah Cooke, Luke Rickards. Prob. Sept. 12, 1797. Arch. vol. A105, pages 190-191. Reg. of Wills, Liber E, folios 132-134.

**Pettyjohn, Aaron.** Admin. of, to Elizabeth Steel, late Elizabeth Pettyjohn. Granted [c. Sept. 14, 1797]. Arch. vol. A92, page 194.

**McDowell, Joshua.** Will. Made Aug. 4, 1796. Heirs: wife Charity McDowell; daus. Elisabeth McDowell, Esther Knowles (wife of Richard); granddau. Rhoda Knowles (dau. of Esther and Richard). [No exec'r]. Wits., Thomas Knowles, Stephen Bennett, Robert Carter. Prob. Sept. 21, 1797. Arch. vol. A87, pages 159-160. Reg. of Wills, Liber E, folio 134.

**Evans, Catharine.** Will. Made Sept. 22, 1797. Heirs: sister Nanny Melson; Mares Wharton; Nancy Wharton; Tabitha Wharton; sister-in-law Esther Wharton; son-in-law William Evans; grandson John Cord Evans; granddaus. Elizabeth, Mary, Sarah Cord, Sarah, Ann and Martha Evans. Exec'r, son-in-law William Evans. Wits., James Tracy, Nancy Evans, Jedidiah Freeman. Prob. Oct. 3, 1797. Arch. vol. A70, pages 175-176. Reg. of Wills, Liber E, folio 135.

**Minner, Peggy.** Admin. of, to Richard Minner. Granted [c. Oct. 5, 1797]. Arch. vol. A89, page 22.

**Tully, James.** Admin. of, to Ann Tully. Granted Oct. 11, 1797. Arch. vol. A102, pages 188-189. [Note:—Arch. vol. A102, page 189 mentions Nancy, Priscilla, James, Joshua and Polly Tully].

**Steel, Samuel.** Admin. of, to Elizabeth Steel. Granted [c. Oct. 12, 1797]. Arch. vol. A100, page 145.

**Bradley, Peggy.** Admin. of, to Cannon Bradley. Granted [c. Oct. 17, 1797]. Arch. vol. A60, page 108.

**Evans, Elisha.** Will. Made Sept. 30, 1797. Heirs: wife Hannah Evans. Exec'rx, wife Hannah Evans. Wits., Major Benson, Littleton Townsend, Richard Barker. Prob. Oct. 17, 1797. Arch. vol. A70, pages 195-196. Reg. of Wills, Liber E, folios 135-136. [Note:—Arch. vol. A70, page 196 shows that McKenny Hudson and wife Hannah, late Hannah Evans, settled the estate].

**Jones, Robert.** Farmer. Broadkill Hd. Will (copy). Made July 25, 1797. Heirs: wife Ann Jones; bro. James Jones; nephews Robert and Samuel Jones (sons of James); Joseph Finnix; Margaret Barr (dau. of William). Exec'rx, wife Ann Jones. Wits., Sam[ue]l Paynter, Jr., Nelly Hardy, Joseph Finnix. Prob. Oct. 19, 1797. Arch. vol. A81, pages 184-187. Reg. of Wills, Liber E, folios 136-138. [Note:— Arch. vol. A81, pages 185-187 shows the estate was settled by Samuel Paynter, Jr., exec'r of Ann Jones].

**Ross, Matthew.** Admin. of, to Huitt Ross. Granted [c. Oct. 20, 1797]. Arch. vol. A97, page 86.

**Read, Jesse.** Admin. of, to David Wattson and wife Elizabeth, late Betsy Read. Granted [c. Nov. 13, 1797[. Arch. vol. A95, page 5.

**Meads, John.** Admin. of, to Polly Meads and Thomas Sorden. Granted [c. Nov. 14, 1797]. Arch. vol. A88, page 16.

**Stevens, Luke.** Admin. of, to Esther Stevens and Betsy Frame, late Betsy Stevens. Granted [c. Nov. 14, 1797]. Arch. vol. A100, page 168.

**Polk, Emanuel [Manuel].** Farmer. Will. Made Sept. 6, 1793. Heirs: bro. Joab Polk; sisters Polly Polk and Esther Owens; kinswoman Esther Owens, Jr.; Felix Owens; Polly Polk (dau. of Joseph); Augustus Polk (son of Joseph); male heir of Johosephat Polk. Exec'rs, bro. Joab Polk and Augustus Polk (son of Joseph). Wits., Lewis Peake, Purnal Hays, Nathaniel Hays. Prob. Nov. 16, 1797. Arch. vol. A93, page 119. Reg. of Wills, Liber E, folios 138-139.

**Magee, Benjamin.** Admin. of, to Joshua Magee. Granted [c. Nov. 17, 1797]. Arch. vol. A86, page 21.

**Oliver, Levi.** Will. Made July 12, 1797. Heirs: wife Jenny Oliver; sons Benjamin and Reuben Oliver; daus. Anna Morgan (wife of Parker Morgan), Mary Bowman (wife of Nathaniel Bowman), Je[an]nett Reed (wife of Elijah Reed); grandson Aaron Oliver (son of Benjamin). Exec'rx, wife Jenny Oliver. Wits., Daniel Rogers, Alexander Draper, Hessy Wattson. Prob. Nov. 20, 1797. Arch. vol. A91, page 153. Reg. of Wills, Liber E, folios 139-140.

**Waller, Ann.** Cedar Creek. Will. Made Nov. 16, 1795. Heirs: sons Benjamin and William Burrows; dau. Sarah Williams; granddaus. Sarah and Elizabeth Burrows (daus. of Benjamin Burrows), Susannah Mason (dau. of dau. Mary); grandsons Boaz Burrows (son of William Burrows), Alexander Manlove (son of George Manlove), James Williams (son of dau. Sarah Williams); niece Magdaline Manlove; children of George Manlove; children of Jonathan Burrows. Exec'rs, sons William and Benjamin Burrows. Wits., Warren Burro[w]s, Smith Waller, W[illia]m Adams. Prob. Nov. 21, 1797. Arch. vol. A104, page 55. Reg. of Wills, Liber E, folios 140-142.

**Downing, Jonathan.** Admin. of, to William W. Downing. Granted [c. Nov. 23, 1797]. Arch. vol. A69, page 171.

**Long, Solomon.** Admin. of, to Elinor Long. Granted [c. Nov. 24, 1797]. Arch. vol. A85, page 136.

**Rickards, John.** Admin. of, to Stayton Rickards, Zadoc Rickards. Granted [c. Nov. 24, 1797]. Arch. vol. A95, page 127.

**West, George.** Admin. of, to Hannah West. Granted [c. Nov. 24, 1797]. Arch. vol. A106, page 123.

**Wolfe, Benjamin.** Lewes & Rehoboth Hd. Will. Made Oct. 22, 1797. Heirs: mother Mary Wolfe; bros. David and Henry Wolfe; niece Mary Wolfe (dau. of bro. Reece). Exec'rx, mother Mary Wolfe. Wits., Mary Orr, Cornelius Wiltbank. Prob. Dec. 7, 1797. Arch. vol. A109, pages 16-17. Reg. of Wills, Liber E, folio 142. [Note:—Arch. vol. A109, page 17 shows the estate was settled by William Wolfe, one of the exec'rs of Mary Wolfe, dec'd].

**Robinson [Robison], Joseph.** Will. Made Oct. 21, 1795. Heirs: wife unnamed; son Joshua Robinson; daus. Naomi and Patience Robinson. Exec'r, son Joshua Robinson. Wits., Thomas Prettyman, Thomas Marvel, Wingate Jones. Prob. Dec. 11, 1797. Arch. vol. A96, page 146. Reg. of Wills, Liber E, folios 142-143.

**Evans, Isaac.** Will. Made Nov. 8, 1797. Heirs: wife Betty Evans; sons Adam, Isaac and Thomas Evans; daus. Nancy and Sally Evans. Exec'rx, wife Betty Evans. Wits., Solomon Evans, Jacob Evans, Eli Evans. Prob. Dec. 12, 1797. Arch. vol. A70, pages 207-208. Reg. of Wills, Liber E, folios 144-145.

**Stafford, Thomas.** Will. Made Nov. 12, 1797. Heirs: sons Thomas and John Stafford; daus. Alice and Nelly Stafford; grandson Joseph Stafford (son of son Thomas); Asa Stafford. Exec'r, son Thomas Stafford. Wits., Thomas Duhadway, Aden Ludenum. Prob. Dec. 12, 1797. Arch. vol. A100, page 103. Reg. of Wills, Liber E, folio 145.

**Pollock, Margaret.** Admin. of, to Manaen Bull and wife Polly Jane, late Polly Jane Pollock. Granted [c. Dec. 19, 1797]. Arch. vol. A93, pages 176-177. [Note:—Arch. vol. A93, page 177 mentions heirs: William, James and George Washington Pollock, Polly Jane Bull, Jane Bell Derickson].

**Burton, William.** Captain. Will. Made May 24, 1797. Heirs: wife Ann Burton; son Benjamin Burton; daus. Patience Caddy and Comfort Houston; granddau. Cornelia Burton. Exec'rs, son Benjamin Burton and daus. Patience Caddy and Comfort Houston. Wits., [Elisha] Dirickson, John Bagwell, James F. Baylis. Prob. Dec. 21, 1797. Arch. vol. A62, pages 26-30. Reg. of Wills, Liber E, folios 145-147. [Note:

—Arch. vol. A62, page 27 shows that Rhoda Burton, exec'rx of Benjamin Burton, and Patience Caddy and Comfort Houston settled the estate; page 28 shows that Rhoda Burton later married William Coleman and Comfort Houston later married Peter Parker].

**Collier, James.** Worcester Co., Md. Will. Made May 16, 1796. Heirs: mother Sarah Collier; sister Mary Collier; nephew John (son of Peter Collier). Exec'rs, mother Sarah Collier and sister Mary Collier. Wits., Thomas Purnell, R[oss] Fassett, John Fassett, Sr. Prob. Dec. 26, 1797. Arch. vol. A65, page 123. Reg. of Wills, Liber E, folios 148-149.

**Brown, Thomas White.** Admin. of, to Thomas Williams and wife Lucretia, late Lucretia Brown. Granted [c. 1798]. Arch. vol. A60, page 227.

**Wesley, Mary.** Lewes & Rehoboth Hd. Will. Made June 6, 1796. Heirs: dau. Bathsheba Chambers; granddau. Betsy Sutton. Exec'rs, friends Elijah Cannon, Jr., John Elliott, Richard Paynter. Wits., Caleb Rodney, Mary West, Burton West. Prob. Jan. 1, 1798. Arch. vol. A106, page 96. Reg. of Wills, Liber E, folios 147-148.

**Barker, Eley [Eli].** Will. Made Dec. 11, 1797. Heirs: wife Patience and children unnamed. Exec'rx, wife Patience Barker. Wits., Bagwell Barker, Nehemiah Coffin, Edward Hall. Guardian, Edmond Pettitt. Prob. Jan. 3, 1798. Arch. vol. A58, pages 181-183. Reg. of Wills, Liber E, folios 149-150. [Note:—Arch. vol. A58, pages 182-183 show that Patience Barker later married Isaiah Clift[on].

**Middleton, James.** Admin. of, to Dickerson Middleton. Granted [c. Jan. 10, 1798]. Arch. vol. A88, page 147.

**Vinson, Charles.** Admin. of, to William Middleton and wife Susanna, late Susanna Vinson. Granted [c. Jan. 10, 1798]. Arch. vol. A103, page 145.

**Jones, Thomas.** Will (copy). Made March 25, 1795. Heirs: sons Thomas, Miles and Ebenezer Jones; daus. Nancy Short and Elizabeth Truitt. Exec'r, son Miles Jones. Wits., Wingate Jones, Jacob Richards, J. Kollock. Prob. Jan. 12, 1798. Arch. vol. A81, pages 189-190. Reg. of Wills, Liber E, folios 150-151.

**Clifton, Major.** Admin. of, to Eunice Clifton. Granted ante Jan. 16, 1798. Arch. vol. A65, pages 24-27. [Note:—Arch. vol. A65, pages 26-27 show that Eunice Clifton later married Wrixham Warren].

**Morris, William.** Planter. Will. Made Dec. 12, 1797. Heirs: wife Betty Morris; sons Lacey, Joseph, John, Robert, Jacob and Burton Morris; dau. Betty Ennis. Exec'r, son John Morris. Wits., Sarah Hill, S. Kollock. Prob. Jan. 16, 1798. Arch. vol. A90, page 146. Reg. of Wills, Liber E, folios 151-153. [Note:—Arch. vol. A90, page 146 mentions dec'd father John Morris and dec'd grandfather W[illia]m Burton].

**Burton, Stratton.** Admin. of, to Leah Burton. Granted [c. Jan. 19, 1798]. Arch. vol. A62, pages 20-21. [Note:—Arch. vol. A62, page 21 shows that Leah Burton later married Samuel Lingo].

**Prettyman, William.** Admin. of, to Luke Burton and wife Betty, late Betty Prettyman. Granted [c. Jan. 19, 1798]. Arch. vol. A94, page 127.

**Abbott, William.** Admin. of, to Nicholas Abbott. Granted [c. Jan. 24, 1798]. Arch. vol. A57, page 26.

**Cottingham, Elisha.** Will. Made Jan. 28, 1795. Heirs: sons Elisha, Jonathan and Joshua Cottingham; dau. Rachel Cottingham; Sarah Vaughan; Elizabeth Killen; Nancy West. Exec'r, son Joshua Cottingham. Wits., John Tingle, William Solomon, James Moore. Prob. Jan. 24, 1798. Arch. vol. A67, pages 22-23. Reg. of Wills, Liber E, folios 153-154.

**Dirickson, George.** Will. Made Sept. 4, 1792. Heirs: wife Sally Dirickson; sons Benjamin, Isaiah and Solomon Dirickson; daus. Mary Dirickson, Elizabeth Tingle, Sarah Linten. Exec'r, son Benjamin Dirickson. Wits., Joseph Freeman, Leah Knox, Zachariah Freeman. Prob. Jan. 25, 1798. Arch. vol. A69, page 25. Reg. of Wills, Liber E, folios 154-155.

**Ake, Riley.** Will. Made Jan. 13, 1798. Heirs: wife Elizabeth Ake; daus. Mary and Katy Ake. Exec'r, bro.-in-law Eli Evans. Wits., Lemuel Evans, Catharine Evans, Levina West. Prob. Jan. 30, 1798. Arch. vol. A57, pages 109-112. Reg. of Wills, Liber E, folio 155.

**Knox, Thomas.** Admin. of, to Samuel Pennuel and wife Sarah, late Sarah Knox. Granted Feb. 1, 1798. Arch. vol. A82, page 200.

**Nichols [Nickels], Joseph.** Will. Made Dec. 28, 1790. Heirs: wife Sarah Nichols. Exec'rx, wife Sarah Nichols. Wits., Thomas Peachy Coates, Jonathan Arnett, Hezekiah Downs. Prob. Feb. 1, 1798. Arch. vol. A91, page 94. Reg. of Wills, Liber E, folio 156.

**Heavelo, John.** Broadkill Hd. Will. Made Jan. 26, 1798. Heirs: son John Heavelo; daus. Sally, Elizabeth, Hannah Heavelo, and Polly Johnson. Exec'r, friend Benjamin Johnson. Wits., Shepard Conwell, Edward Heavelo, John Clarke. Prob. Feb. 3, 1798. Arch. vol. A75, pages 225-229. Reg. of Wills, Liber E, folios 156-157.

**Boyce, Jonathan.** Will. Made Feb. 3, 1798. Heirs: wife Eleanor Boyce; sons Asher, Thomas and Eli[jah] Boyce; daus. Polly Boyce and Bathsheba Vickers; grandson James Moor. Exec'rs, sons Asher and Thomas Boyce, and bro. William Boyce. Wits., John Benson, William Hobbs, Peter King. Prob. Feb. 6, 1798. Arch. vol. A60, pages 49-51. Reg. of Wills, Liber E, folios 159-160. [Note:—Arch. vol. A60, page 51 mentions Polly Edger; also shows the estate was settled by William Boyce].

**Clarkson, Thomas.** Will. Made Jan. 6, 1798. Heirs: Mr. and Mrs. Hodson Cannon; Peggy Cannon; Mr. and Mrs. James Wilson; Polly and Nancy Wilson (daus. of James). Exec'r, friend James Wilson. Wits., John Rust, Hodson Cannon, [Jeremiah] R. Jackson. Prob. Feb. 6, 1798. Arch. vol. A64, page 221. Reg. of Wills, Liber E, folios 160-161.

**Fergus, James.** Merchant. Broadkill Hd. Will. Made Feb. 7, 1797. Heirs: wife Mary Fergus; daus. Eliza Fergus; bro. Francis Fergus. Exec'rs, wife Mary Fergus, James E. Wilson and John Masten. Wits., James Martin, William Dickerson, Joseph Cary. Prob. Feb. 6, 1798. Arch. vol. A71, pages 59-60. Reg. of Wills, Liber E, folios 161-162.

**Thomas, Luke.** Yeoman. Will. Made May 24, 1796. Heirs: wife Nancy Thomas; sons Abel and James Thomas; daus. Elizabeth, Milly, Hannah and Sarah Thomas, Rebecca Johnson, Anna Puckham, Susanna Smith, Mary Knox. Exec'rs, wife Nancy Thomas and son Abel Thomas. Wits., Thomas Marvel, Leah Marvel. Codicil: dated July 14, 1797. Prob. Feb. 6, 1798. Arch. vol. A101, page 146. Reg. of Wills, Liber E, folios 157-159.

**Stevens, Isaac.** Will. Made Oct. 5, 1793. Heirs: wife unnamed; sons Jesse and William Stevens; dau. Mary Hasty. Exec'rs, son Jesse Stevens and friend Mourning Wrae. Wits., John Lord, Jesse Outten. Prob. Feb. 13, 1798. Arch. vol. A100, page 167. Reg. of Wills, Liber E, folios 162-163.

**Little, Richard.** Merchant. Will. Made Dec. 4, 1796. Heirs: wife Sarah Little; adopted dau. Polly West; Richard Little West (son of Robert West). Exec'rs, wife Sarah Little and friend Robert West. Wits., Thomas Hart, Mills McIlvain, Jr., Elisabeth Stockley. Prob. Feb. 15, 1798. Arch. vol. A84, pages 167-168. Reg. of Wills, Liber E, folio 164. [Note: —Arch. vol. A84, page 168 shows the estate was settled by Robert West, surviving exec'r].

**Turner, Levin.** Admin. of, to Joshua Reed, in right of Eunice Turner. Granted Feb. 20, 1798. Arch. vol. A103, page 22.

**Tull, Levin.** Admin. of, to Elisha Cannon and wife Sally, late Sally Tull. Granted [c. Feb. 21, 1798]. Arch. vol. A102, page 176.

**Ingram, Abigail.** Will (copy). Made Feb. 2, 1797. Heirs: sons Nathan, Samuel and Isaac Ingram; daus. Rachel Ingram and Ansleo Hudson. Exec'r, son Isaac Ingram. Wits., William Robbins, John Collins, Melia Williams. Prob. Feb. 27, 1798. Arch. vol. A79, pages 136-137. Reg. of Wills, Liber E, folio 163.

**Bevans [Bivans], Mary.** Planter. Will. Made Jan. 25, 1798. Heirs: sons Zachariah, William, Hezekiah, Roland and John Bevans; daus. Elizabeth Furman and Sally Scott; grandson Jesse Bevans; granddaus. Hessy Furman, Nancy and Sally Scott. Exec'r, son Hezekiah Bevans. Wits., Thomas Rodney, John Rodney. Prob. March 7, 1798. Arch. vol. A59, pages 165-166. Reg. of Wills, Liber E, folio 165.

**Rickards, George.** Yeoman. Cedar Creek Hd. Will. Made Feb. 24, 1791. Heirs: wife unnamed; sons Thomas, George and Manlove Rickards; daus. Amelia Rickards, Elizabeth Griffith and Selah Ross. Exec'rx, wife [Elizabeth] Rickards. Wits., Elias Shockley, William Depray, [Abdel] Dawson. Prob. March 12, 1798. Arch. vol. A95, page 116. Reg. of Wills, Liber E, folios 166-167.

**Luker, William.** Admin. of, to Isaac Clowes, unadministered by Catharine Luker. Granted [c. March 13, 1798]. Arch. vol. A85, page 178. [Note:—Arch. vol. A85, page 178 mentions minor dau. Leah Luker].

**Moore, David.** Will. Made Aug. 10, 1793. Heirs: son James Moore; daus. Rachel, Zipporah and Levina Moore; grandson Isaac Moore. Exec'r, son James Moore. Wits., William Waples, Sarah Goslee, William Vaughan. Prob. March 13, 1798. Arch. vol. A89, page 97. Reg. of Wills, Liber E, folio 167.

**Hudson, Samuel.** Admin. of, to Jane Hudson. Granted [c. March 16, 1798]. Arch. vol. A79, pages 45-47. [Note:—Arch. vol.

A79, pages 46-47 shows the estate was settled by William Wyatt and wife Jane, late Jane Hudson].

**Howard, Rhoda.** Baltimore Hd. Will. Made Oct. 17, 1797. Heirs: son William Godwin; dau. Polly Godwin; Patty Holland (dau. of bro. Benjamin); Patty Lockwood (dau. of sister Betty). Exec'r, bro. Benjamin Holland and bro.-in-law Armwell Lockwood. Wits., John Howard, Job Johnson, Betsy Powell. Prob. March 21, 1798. Arch. vol. A78, pages 149-151. Reg. of Wills, Liber E, folio 168.

**Saunders, Jenny.** Widow. Will. Made April 6, 1793. Heirs: daus. Mary Downs and Betty Pusey (wife of William); grandchildren Stephen, Ephraim and Nelly Pusey (children of dau. Betty), and Betsy Layton. Exec'r, grandson Stephen Pusey. Wits., Tho[ma]s Conner, Rebecca Conner, Sally Watson. Prob. March 22, 1798. Arch. vol. A98, page 15. Reg. of Wills, Liber E, folios 168-169.

**White, Paul.** Admin. of, to Thomas Brereton and wife Mary, late Mary White. Granted [c. March 26, 1798]. Arch. vol. A107, page 82. [Note:—Arch. vol. A107, page 82 mentions Catharine, Eli, James and Nancy White].

**Smith, Mary.** Widow. Will. Made Oct. 27, 1796. Heirs: sons Jesse Williams, Ephraim Smith and George Collins; sister Elizabeth Warrington (wife of Robert); dau.-in-law Nancy Collins; grandsons John Collins and Samuel Cornell; granddaus. Polly, Betty and Rhoda Williams and Nelly Collins. Exec'r, son George Collins. Wits., Joseph Waples, Joshua Morris, Joseph Morris. Prob. March 27, 1798. Arch. vol. A99, page 189. Reg. of Wills, Liber E, folios 169-170.

**Gibbons, Joshua.** Will. Made Nov. 3, 1794. Heirs: son Joshua Gibbons; daus. Betsy and Sally Gibbons. Exec'rx, dau. Betsy Gibbons. Wits., James Gunby, William Hobbs. Prob. April 10, 1798. Arch. vol. A72, pages 125-128. Reg. of Wills, Liber E, folio 172. [Note:—Arch. vol. A72, page 126 shows that the estate was settled by Simon Kollock, Jr., and wife Elizabeth [Betsy], late Betsy Gibbons].

**Otwell, William, Sr.** Will. Made Dec. 20, 1797. Heirs: wife Grace Otwell; sons William, Parker, Francis, John, Obed and Joshua Otwell; daus. Polly and Drucilla Otwell, Hannah Beavens and Eleanor Short. Exec'rs, wife Grace Otwell and son John Otwell. Wits., Levin Connaway, John Truitt, Bathsheba Truitt. Prob. April 10, 1798. Arch. vol. A91, page 181. Reg. of Wills, Liber E, folios 170-172.

**Taylor, Tandy.** Admin. of, to Martha Taylor. Granted [c. April 24, 1798]. Arch. vol. A101, page 126.

**Massey, Absolem.** Admin. of, to Jno. Smith (merchant of Phila.). Inventory dated April 25, 1798. Arch. vol. A87, page 45.

**Holland, Israel.** Admin. of, to Mathias Aydelott and wife Elizabeth, late Elizabeth Holland. Granted [c. April 26, 1798]. Arch. vol. A77, page 82. [Note:—Arch. vol. A77, page 82 mentions Rhoda Godwin, an heir of William Holland].

**Morgan, John.** Admin. of, to Jacob Hazzard. Granted [c. April 26, 1798]. Arch. vol. A89, page 196.

**Wingate, Philip.** Will. Made Dec. 30, 1797. Heirs: sons Cannon, Philip and John Wingate; daus. Levina, Sally, Polly and Betsy Wingate. Exec'rs, son-in-law Philip Matthews, and dau. Levina Wingate. Wits., James Cannon, Jesse Saunders, Robert Timmons. Prob. April 26, 1798. Arch. vol. A109, pages 1-3. Reg. of Wills, Liber E, folios 173-174. [Note:—Arch. vol. A109, pages 2-3 show the estate was settled by Philip Matthews and Levina Short, late Levina Wingate].

**Walker, Tamer.** Will. Made April 14, 1798. Heirs: niece Comfort Russell; cousin Fanny Walker. Exec'r, Ezekiel Williams. Wits., Thomas Williams, Nancy Rogers, Andrew Truitt. Prob. April 27, 1798. Arch. vol. A104, page 36. Reg. of Wills, Liber E, folio 174.

**Dirickson, Sophia.** Admin. of, to Handy Dirickson. Granted [c. May 1, 1798]. Arch. vol. A69, page 46.

**Walter, Sally.** Admin. of, to Stephen Styer. Granted [c. May 3, 1798]. Arch. vol. A104, page 126.

**Polk, Daniel.** Admin. of, to Samuel White, in right of Margaret Nutter Polk, dec'd. Granted [c. May 4, 1798]. Arch. vol. A93, page 113.

**Smith, Job, Sr.** Yeoman. Will. Made Feb. 7, 1795. Heirs: sons David and Job Smith; daus. Sally Smith, Ann Young (wife of John), Mary Marvel (wife of Robert), Marg[ar]et Mills (wife of Richard), Jane Jones (wife of William), and Elizabeth Tindel (wife of Purnel); grandsons Jonathan Millman and Job Smith. Exec'r, son Job Smith. Wits., James Hall, William Robbins, Elizabeth Messick. Prob. May 9, 1798. Arch. vol. A99, page 159. Reg. of Wills, Liber E, folios 174-176. [Note:—Arch. vol. A99, page 159 shows the estate was settled by David Smith, exec'r of Job Smith, dec'd].

**Hitch, Isaac.** Will. Made Nov. 5, 1797. Heirs: wife Sarah Hitch; sons Robert and Severn Hitch; dau. Phyllis Hitch; other unnamed children. Exec'rs, wife Sarah Hitch and friend John Dashiell. Wits., Ezekiel Tom[ilson], Robert Hasting. Prob. May 18, 1798. Arch. vol. A76, page 185. Reg. of Wills, Liber E, folios 176-177.

**Jacobs, Albertis.** Admin. of, to Elizabeth Holland, D. B. N., in right of William Holland. Granted [c. May 22, 1798]. Arch. vol. A80, pages 44-45.

**Messick, George.** Admin. of, to Bridget and Isaac Messick. Granted [c. May 22, 1798]. Arch. vol. A88, page 94.

**Shockley, Mary.** Admin. of, to Rhoads Shockley. Granted [c. May 29, 1798]. Arch. vol. A98, page 143.

**Spencer, Nathan.** Yeoman. Will. Made Nov. 28, 1797. Heirs: wife Rachel Spencer; son Donovan Spencer; kinswoman Sarah Polk. Exec'rs, wife Rachel Spencer, son Donovan Spencer and Lewis Peake. Wits., Elisha Evans, Joshua Harp, William Moore. Prob. June 6, 1798. Arch. vol. A100, page 63. Reg. of Wills, Liber E, folio 177. [Note:—Arch. vol. A100, page 63 shows the estate was settled by Jeremiah Townsend and wife Rachel, late Rachel Spencer].

**Tatman, Delight.** Admin. of, to Sarah Tatman. Granted [c. June 7, 1798]. Arch. vol. A101, page 105.

**Polson, William.** Will. Made March 15, 1798. Heirs: bro. Edward Polson. Exec'r, bro. Edward Polson. Wits., Rob[er]t Green, Cathe[rine] Windsor, Marcellus Peets. Prob. June 12, 1798. Arch. vol. A93, page 179. Reg. of Wills, Liber E, folio 178.

**Cirwithin, John.** Admin. of, to Mark Davis, D. B. N., in right of Isaac Wattson. Granted [c. June 13, 1798]. Arch. vol. A64, page 172.

**Wattson, Betsy.** (Minor dau. of Isaac). Admin. of, to Mary Wattson and Mark Davis. Granted [c. June 13, 1798]. Arch. vol. A105, page 194.

**Robinson, Polly.** Admin. of, to Elizabeth Robinson and John Dazey. Granted [c. June 14, 1798]. Arch. vol. A96, page 170.

**Tubbs, Elizabeth.** Admin. of, to John Dazey and Elizabeth Robinson. Granted [c. June 14, 1798]. Arch. vol. A102, page 168.

**Hall, William.** Will. Made Feb. 13, 1796. Heirs: wife Zipporah Hall; son Jiddadiah Hall; dau. Polly Hall; Job Dirickson

(son of William Dirickson, dec'd). Exec'rs, wife Zipporah Hall and Thomas Hazzard. Wits., Nancy West, Reuben West, Elisha Cottingham. Prob. June 16, 1798. Arch. vol. A74, page 10. Reg. of Wills, Liber E, folios 178-179.

**Rickards, Mary.** Admin. of, to Stephen Evans. Granted [c. June 19, 1798]. Arch. vol. A95, page 135. [Note:—Arch. vol. A95, page 135 mentions Margaret Rickards].

**Vent, James.** Admin. of, to Joseph Dodd, D. B. N. Granted [c. June 19, 1798]. Arch. vol. A103, pages 101-102.

**Sharp, Job.** Will. Made May 22, 1798. Heirs: wife Naomi Sharp; son John Sharp; daus. Amelia Sharp and Betsy Dickerson. Exec'rx, wife Naomi Sharp. Wits., Windsor Rawlins, Jacob Sharp, Anzella Hudson. Prob. June 21, 1798. Arch. vol. A98, pages 77-79. Reg. of Wills, Liber E, folios 180-181. [Note:—Arch. vol. A98, page 79 shows the estate was settled by Curtis Abbott and wife Naomi, late Naomi Sharp].

**Harris, Abraham, Sr.** Will. Made May 19, 1798. Heirs: wife Director Harris; sons Abraham, Benton and Peter Parker Harris; daus. Elizabeth Mitchell, Scarb[orough] Jones; grandson Benton Marvel; children of daughter Priscilla Marvel. Exec'rx, wife Director Harris. Wits., Elizabeth Collings, Patience Harris, William Johnson, Sr. Prob. June 26, 1798. Arch. vol. A74, pages 120-121. Reg. of Wills, Liber E, folios 179-180. [Note:—Arch. vol. A74, page 121 mentions Lemuel, Edward, Stephen, Benton and Abram Harris Marvel, children of Priscilla Marvel].

**Hudson, Benjamin.** Admin. of, to Robert Owens. Granted [c. July 5, 1798]. Arch. vol. A78, page 171.

**Gray, James.** Will (nunc). Made June 18, 1798. Heirs: son Jesse Gray. Exec'r, bro.-in-law John Hamblen. Wit., Ezekiel Williams. Prob. July 7, 1798. Arch. vol. A73, page 8. Reg. of Wills, Liber E, folio 179.

**Burton, Elizabeth.** Admin. of, to Thomas Burton. Granted [c. July 13, 1798]. Arch. vol. A61, page 130.

**Linch, John.** Will. Made Jan. 20, 1797. Heirs: wife Hannah Linch; sons Abram, Eli, John, Jacobs, Bolitha and Mires Linch; daus. Peggy, Betty, Maria and Nancy Linch. Exec'r, Eli Linch. Wits., William Swain, Robert Swain, Joseph Swain. Prob. July 17, 1798. Arch. vol. A84, pages 90-91. Reg. of Wills, Liber E, folio 181.

**Brown, James.** Merchant. Admin. of, to Leah Brown. Granted ante July 19, 1798. Arch. vol. A60, pages 201-202.

**Murray, John.** Admin. of, to Ann Rogers, late Ann Murray, also known as Nancy. Granted [c. July 23, 1798]. Arch. vol. A91, page 16.

**Ross, Edward.** Admin. of, to Maud Draper and wife Anna, late Anna Ross. Granted [c. July 27, 1798]. Arch. vol. A97, pages 81-82.

**Jones, John.** Will (copy). Made April 8, 1798. Heirs: wife Peggy Jones; sons John and Giv[en] Jones; dau. Rachel Jones. Exec'rx, wife Peggy Jones. Wits., Charles Rawlins, Zadock Blades, Eleanor Middleton. Prob. July 31, 1798. Arch. vol. A81, page 169. Reg. of Wills, Liber E, folios 182-183.

**Wright, William.** Will. Made July 26, 1798. Heirs: sisters Betsy

and Polly Wright. Exec'r, friend Dr. Tho[ma]s Robertson. Wits., Jesse Jones, Joshua Megee, Ephraim Megee. Prob. July 31, 1798. Arch. vol. A109, page 104. Reg. of Wills, Liber E, folio 183.

**Maxwell, Nimrod.** Admin. of, to Henry Bennum. Granted [c. Aug. 6, 1798]. Arch. vol. A87, page 88.

**Burton, Joshua.** Admin. of, to Mary Burton. Granted [c. Aug. 16, 1798]. Arch. vol. A61, page 213. [Note:—Arch. vol. A61, page 213 shows the estate was administered by James Burton, D. B. N.].

**Long, Elisha.** Admin. of, to Daniel Horatio Long. Granted Aug. 20, 1798. Arch. vol. A85, pages 111-112. [Note:—Arch. vol. A85, page 112 mentions Elijah and Elisha Long].

**Jackson, Augustus.** Admin. of, to Sally Rust, D. B. N., in right of Peter Rust. Granted [c. Aug. 21, 1798]. Arch. vol. A80, pages 6-7.

**Cannon, Jeremiah.** Admin. of, to Lilly Cannon. Granted [c. Aug. 25, 1798]. Arch. vol. A63, page 64.

**Wiley, Ann.** Will. Made July 21, 1798. Heirs: daus. Ann and Margaret Wiley. Exec'rs, friends Robert West and Samuel Paynter. Wits., Robert Shankland, Ann Westley. Guardians: friends Robert West and Samuel Paynter. Prob. Aug. 30, 1798. Arch. vol. A107, pages 116-118. Reg. of Wills, Liber E, folio 182.

**Stockley, Ann.** Admin. of, to Robert Burton (merchant). Granted [c. Sept. 4, 1798]. Arch. vol. A100, page 191.

**Cameron, John.** Admin. of, to Daniel Miller McCallister. Granted ante Sept. 7, 1798. Arch. vol. A62, pages 189-190.

**Townsend, Isaac.** Admin. of, to Seagoe Potter and wife Jacaman, late Jacaman Townsend. Granted [c. Sept. 14, 1798]. Arch. vol. A102, page 52.

**Cade, Mary.** Admin. of, to John Cade, Jr. Granted [c. Sept. 15, 1798]. Arch. vol. A62, page 99.

**Burton, Benjamin.** Will. Made March 1, 1795. Heirs: wife Rhoda Burton; sisters Patience Caddy and Comfort Houston. Exec'rx, wife Rhoda Burton. Wits., Thomas Burton, Lydia Burton, Elizabeth Burton. Prob. Oct. 5, 1798. Arch. vol. A61, page 80. Reg. of Wills, Liber E, folios 183-184. [Note:—Arch. vol. A61, page 80 shows William Coleman and wife Rhoda, late Rhoda Burton, settled the estate].

**Hopkins, Sarah.** Admin. of, to John Gordy. Granted [c. Oct. 9, 1798]. Arch. vol. A78, page 22.

**Brown, James.** Admin. of, to White Brown, D. B. N., C. T. A., in right of Thomas W. Brown. Granted [c. Nov., 1798]. Arch. vol. A60, pages 199-200.

**Williams, Isaac.** Admin. of, to John Willis, Sr. Granted [c. Nov. 6, 1798]. Arch. vol. A107, page 175.

**Thornton, David.** Yeoman. Broadkill Hd. Will. Made April 10, 1794. Heirs: wife Eli[za] Thornton; sons William, James and Robinson Thornton. Exec'rs, sons William and James Thornton. Wits., John Ingram, Jemima Ingram, Anthony Ingram. Prob. Nov. 9, 1798. Arch. vol. A101, page 171. Reg. of Wills, Liber E, folios 184-185.

**Redden, William.** Admin. of, to John Wilson and wife Ellinor, late Ellinor Redden. Granted [c. Nov. 13, 1798]. Arch. vol. A95, page 18.

**Rust, Jonathan.** Admin. of, to Aaron Burton, William Fassitt and wife Peggy, late Peggy Rust. Granted [c. Nov. 14, 1798]. Arch. vol. A97, page 166.

**Truitt, Zadock.** Admin. of, to Sarah Truitt. Granted [c. Nov. 14, 1798]. Arch. vol. A102, page 164.

**Laverty, Thomas.** Admin. of, to Mary Laverty. Granted [c. Nov. 16, 1798]. Arch. vol. A83, page 108.

**Cannon, Levin.** Admin. of, to William White. Granted [c. Nov. 23, 1798]. Arch. vol. A63, page 103.

**Phillips, Sarah.** Widow. Will. Made Oct. 26, 1798. Heirs: sons Spencer, Joseph, John, Benjamin and Sheppard Phillips; daus. Ruth Tindell, Sarah Melson, Levina Truitt and Mary Cannon. Exec'r, son Spencer Phillips. Wits., Levin Connaway, John T. Sharp, Philip Hopkins. Prob. Nov. 23, 1798. Arch. vol. A93, page 57. Reg. of Wills, Liber E, folios 185-187.

**Ricords, Esther.** Will. Made April 19, 1794. Heirs: sons James, John, Levin and Hap Hazzard Ricords; dau. Priscilla Ricords. [No exec'r]. Wits., James P. Wilson, Anna Newcomb. Codicil: dated Oct. 30, 1795. Wits., James P. Wilson, Elizabeth Wilson. Prob. Nov. 23, 1798. Arch. vol. A95, page 164. Reg. of Wills, Liber E, folios 187-188.

**Cornwell [Conwell], Francis.** Will. Made Jan. 20, 1796. Heirs: son Avery Cornwell; daus. Betsy Connoway (wife of John) and Abigail Owens (wife of William) ; heirs of dau. Naomi Long (late wife of Solomon) ; heirs of dau. Polly Fowler (late wife of Henry). Exec'r, son Avery Cornwell. Wits., William Russell, Jacob Dickerson, Andrew Bryan. Prob. Nov. 27, 1798. Arch. vol. A67, pages 4-6. Reg. of Wills, Liber E, folios 188-189.

**Jones, Thomas.** Will (copy). Made Nov. 2, 1798. Heirs: wife Mary Jones; sons Isaac and Purnel Jones; daus. Elizabeth, Naomi, Nancy and Hannah Jones. Exec'rx, wife Mary Jones. Wits., Wingate Jones, Scarb[orough] Jones, Sarah Rodney. Prob. Dec. 4, ·1798. Arch. vol. A81, pages 191-192. Reg. of Wills, Liber E, folios 190-191. [Note:—Arch. vol. A81, page 192 shows the estate was settled by William Lacey and Mary, his wife, late Mary Jones].

**Melson, Daniel.** Farmer. Will. Made Sept. 2, 1797. Heirs: wife Love Melson; sons Elijah, Joseph, Benjamin and John Melson; daus. Tabitha, Sally, Elizabeth, Nancy and Love Melson. Exec'r, son Joseph Melson. Wits., John Williams, Thomas Records, Susannah Larrimore. Prob. Dec. 4, 1798. Arch. vol. A88, pages 40-42. Reg. of Wills, Liber E, folios 189-190. [Note:—Arch. vol. A88, page 42 mentions Sally Atkins, Elizabeth Smith, Love Hearn].

**Harris, Zachariah.** Will. Made March 27, 1792. Heirs: wife Tabitha Harris; sons Robert, William, John, Stevens and Dixon Harris; daus. Nancy Harris, Sarah Tamm, Elizabeth Holland Dickerson. Exec'rs, sons Robert and Stevens Harris. Wits., John Martin, Nancy Martin, Robert Lambden. Prob. Dec. 14, 1798. Arch. vol. A74, pages 155-159. Reg. of Wills, Liber E, folios 191-192.

**Claypoole, George.** Will. Made June 12, 1798. Heir: friend Anthony Ingram. Exec'r, friend Anthony Ingram. Wits., John Reed, John Tilney, Isaac Townsen[d]| Prob. Dec. 16, 1798. Arch. vol. A64, page 227. Reg. of Wills, Liber E, folio 193.

**Davis, Nehemiah.** Will. Made Dec. 1, 1794. Heirs: wife Sarah Davis; sons Nehemiah and John Davis; daus. Sarah Draper and Mary Cirwithen. Exec'r, son John Davis. Wits., Robert Wattson, Manlove Davis, Robert Davis. Prob. Dec. 21, 1798. Arch. vol. A68, pages 115-118. Reg. of Wills, Liber E, folios 193-194. [Note:—Arch. vol. A68, page 116 mentions Mary Hall].

**Goslen, Waitman, Sr.** Will. Made Oct. 27, 1798. Heir: son Waitman Goslen, Jr. Exec'r, son Waitman Goslen, Jr. Wits., Curtis Jacobs, Isaac Cannon. Prob. Dec. 22, 1798. Arch. vol. A72, pages 233-237. Reg. of Wills, Liber E, folio 195. [Note:—Arch. vol. A72, page 237 mentions heirs Mary Gullett, Elizabeth Townsend, Lydia Pritchard, Naomi Stafford, Tryphena Jones, Priscilla and Victor Goslin].

**Atkins, Elijah.** Admin. of, to Hannah Atkins. Granted [c., 1799]. Arch. vol. A57, page 202.

**Burcher, William.** Admin. of, to George Collins and wife Rhoda, late Rhoda Burcher. Granted [c., 1799]. Arch. vol. A61, page 26.

**Layton, John.** Will. Made Aug. 4, 1789. Heirs: wife Tabitha Layton; sons Eli and John Layton; daus. Rebecca Layton and Mary Rawlins; grandsons John and Winston Rawlins. Exec'rs, sons Eli and John Layton. Wits., Levin Connaway, Jacob Short. Prob. Jan. 5, 1799. Arch. vol. A83, pages 179-180. Reg. of Wills, Liber D, folios 204-205.

**Baker, Thomas.** Admin. of, to William Baker. Granted [c. Jan. 18, 1799]. Arch. vol. A58, page 141.

**Rickards, William, Jr.** Will. Made Jan. 8, 1799. Heirs: bro. Luke Rickards; sisters Marg[ar]et Rickards and Elizabeth Dirickson. Exec'r, bro.-in-law William Dirickson. Wits., Ezekiel Williams, William Powell, Nancy Powell. Prob. Jan. 22, 1799. Arch. vol. A95, page 151. Reg. of Wills, Liber E, folios 195-196.

**Minner, Priscilla.** Admin. of, to William Collison. Granted [c. Jan. 27, 1799]. Arch. vol. A89, page 23.

**Laverty, Mary.** Will. Made Jan. 20, 1799. Heirs: sons Samuel and William Laverty; dau. Elizabeth Morris; grandsons

Thomas, Daniel and William Morris (sons of dau. Elizabeth); granddau. Mary Laverty (dau. of Samuel); Nancy Noble. Exec'r, son William Laverty. Wits., John Davis, James Dirickson, Charles F. Merine. Prob. Jan. 29, 1799. Arch. vol. A83, pages 105-106. Reg. of Wills, Liber E, folios 196-198.

**Mifflin, Sarah.** Will. Made Aug. 3, 1775. Heirs: dau. Mary Clowes; Peter Clowes; Hannah Draper; Benjamin Draper. Exec'rx, dau. Mary Clowes. Wits., John Franklin, Isaac Clowes. Prob. Jan. 31, 1799. Arch. vol. A88, page 158. Reg. of Wills, Liber E, folio 198.

**Johnson, Isaac.** Will. Made Nov. 8, 1795. Heirs: sons Luke, Elias and Isaac Johnson; daus. Leah, Hester and Betsy Johnson. Exec'r, son Elias Johnson. Wits., Benjamin Holland, Job Johnson. Prob. Feb. 5, 1799. Arch. vol. A81, page 41. Reg. of Wills, Liber E, folio 199. [Note:—Arch. vol. A81, page 41 shows the estate was settled by Luke Johnson, D. B. N., in lieu of Elias Johnson].

**Short, Betty.** Admin. of, to John Willis, Sr. Granted [c. Feb. 7, 1799]. Arch. vol. A98, page 162.

**Smith, Ezekiel.** Will. Made Jan. 14, 1799. Heirs: wife Nancy Smith; sons Robert, Westley and Constantine Jacob Smith; daus. Sally, Betsy and Polly Smith. Exec'rs, wife Nancy Smith and son Constantine Jacob Smith. Wits., James Dirickson, Tamsey Richards, Priscilla Forkner. Prob. Feb. 12, 1799. Arch. vol. A99, page 134. Reg. of Wills, Liber E, folios 200-201. [Note:—Arch. vol. A99, page 134 shows that Betsy Smith later married Richard Cannon; also shows the estate was settled by Constantine Smith, surviving exec'r].

**Ingram, Jemima.** Will (copy). Made Nov. 22, 1796. Heirs: son John Ingram; dau. Peggy Ingram. Exec'r, son John Ingram. Wits., John Lofland, Solomon Lofland, Isaac Lofland. Prob. Feb. 19, 1799. Arch. vol. A79, pages 147-148. Reg. of Wills, Liber E, folios 201-202.

**Polk, Elizabeth.** Admin. of, to Joab Polk, D. B. N. Granted [c. March 19, 1799]. Arch. vol. A93, page 116.

**Evans, Stephen.** Will. Made March 8, 1799. Heirs: mother Hannah Evans; bros. Annanias and Kendell Evans; sister Polly Nickelson; Cathryn Nickelson. Exec'rs, bros. Annanias and Kendell Evans. Wits., William Powell, Joseph Wildgoose, William J. Hall. Prob. March 22, 1799. Arch.

vol. A71, pages 24-25. Reg. of Wills, Liber E, folios 207-208.

**Lofland, Littleton.** Will. Made March 11, 1799. Heirs: sons Luke, James, Heavelo, Elias, William and Jonathan Lofland; daus. Hannah, Grace and Comfort Lofland, and Rachel Morris; sister Marg[ar]et Lofland; mother unnamed. Exec'rs, sons Heavelo and Elias Lofland. Wits., William Veach, Benjamin Hudson. Prob. March 22, 1799. Arch. vol. A85, pages 65-66. Reg. of Wills, Liber E, folios 202-204. [Note:—Arch. vol. A85, page 66 mentions Boaz and Grace Warren].

**Phillips, Benjamin.** Will. Made Sept. 22, 1798. Heirs: wife Priscilla Phillips; sons Purnal, John and Elzy Phillips; daus. Betty Killam, Rhoda Truitt, Ann Truitt, Jean Short and Hannah Messick. Exec'r, son Purnal Phillips. Wits., William Rodney, Ephraim Wingate, Spencer Phillips. Prob. March 25, 1799. Arch. vol. A93, page 21. Reg. of Wills, Liber E, folios 206-207.

**Smith, Job.** Yeoman. Will. Made March 3, 1799. Heirs: wife Nancy Smith; bro. David Smith; sisters unnamed; nephew Jonathan Millman. Exec'rs, wife Nancy Smith and bro. David Smith. Wits., Brinkley Davis, Selby Sharp, Seagoe Potter. Prob. March 25, 1799. Arch. vol. A99, pages 160-162. Reg. of Wills, Liber E, folios 204-206. [Note:—Arch. vol. A99, page 162 shows the estate was settled by Loxley Rickards and Nancy, his wife, late Nancy Smith, and David Smith].

**Truitt, James.** Admin. of, to Major Donoho and wife Sarah, late Sarah Truitt. Adm'rs bond dated March 26, 1799. Arch. vol. A102, pages 126-127. [Note:—Arch. vol. A102, page 127 mentions a son Purnall Truitt].

**Hall, William.** Will. Made Jan. 29, 1795. Heirs: wife Mary Hall; sons David, Adam, John and William Spence Hall; daus. Elizabeth, Sarah, Nancy, Hannah and Mary Hall. Exec'rx, wife Mary Hall. Wits., Elisha Evans, William Evans, Sheba Cord. Prob. March 29, 1799. Arch. vol. A74, pages 11-12. Reg. of Wills, Liber E, folios 208-210.

**Reiley, Laurence.** Will. Made March 10, 1799. Heirs: wife Grace Reiley; sons Lawrence and John Reiley; daus. Susannah, Sarah, Grace, Elizabeth Reiley, and Marg[a]ret Kirk (wife of Barnet Kirk). Exec'rs, wife Grace Reiley and son Lawrence Reiley. Wits., William Reiley, Anthony Heavelo, Elijah Abbott. Prob. April 1, 1799. Arch. vol. A96, pages 46-47. Reg. of Wills, Liber E, folios 210-212.

**Clark, John.** Admin. of, to John S. Conwell and wife Sarah, late Sarah Clark. Granted April 2, 1799. Arch. vol. A64, pages 185-186. [Note:—Arch. vol. A64, page 186 mentions Isaac, Sally, Miers and Joshua Clark; and Margaret Jackson (granddau. of Mary Collins)].

**Fisher, George Hardy.** Will. Made April 10, 1796. Heirs: wife Rachel Fisher; sons Daniel, George and Alexander Fisher; daus. Sarah, Frances and Levina Fisher. Exec'r, son Daniel Fisher. Wits., James Harris, William Maloney, Southey Pruitt. Trustees, friends Moses Leaverton, John Pool, James Harris and William Maloney. Prob. April 8, 1799. Arch. vol. A71, pages 112-113. Reg. of Wills, Liber E, folios 212-214. [Note:—Arch. vol. A71, page 113 mentions Frances Welch and Levina Dukes].

**Stuart, Mary.** Admin. of, to Archabald Fleming. Granted [c. April 9, 1799]. Arch. vol. A101, page 61.

**Carey, Elisabeth.** Widow. Will. Made March 7, 1799. Heirs: sons Samuel, Woolsey B., Cornelius, Joseph, Eli, Nehemiah, Joshua, James and Lemuel Carey; daus. Phebe Carey and Esther Russell Carey. Exec'r, son Eli Carey. Wits., Joshua Burton, Benjamin Prettyman. Prob. April 15, 1799. Arch. vol. A64, pages 42-44. Reg. of Wills, Liber E, folios 214-215.

**Williams, Solomon.** Admin. of, to Keziah Williams and Jacob Coverdale. Granted [c. April 19, 1799]. Arch. vol. A108, page 45.

**Mitchell, George.** Will (copy). Made Sept. 13, 1798 and Feb. 3, 1799. Heirs: wife Susan Mitchell; son Fenwick Fisher Mitchell; bros. Nathaniel and William Clayton Mitchell; sister Abigail Bell; nephew John Mitchell (son of William C.); James Evans (son of Sally). Exec'rx, wife Susan Mitchell. Wits., William Hall, Risdon Bishop, Abraham Pierce. Prob. April 22, 1799. Arch. vol. A89, pages 35-42. Reg. of Wills, Liber F, folios 320-323. [Note:—Arch. vol. A89, page 36 shows the estate passed through Susan Mitchell to Nathaniel Mitchell, D. B. N.; pages 37-38 show Hannah Mitchell, adm'r of Nathaniel Mitchell; page 39 shows Col. Manaen Bull as adm'r, D. B. N., of Hannah Mitchell; and page 40-42 show the estate was settled by Manaen Bull and wife Abigail, adm'rs D. B. N.].

**Morris, Nehemiah.** Admin. of, to Sarah and Jehu Morris. Granted [c. April 23, 1799]. Arch. vol. A90, page 125.

**Knowles, Betty.** Will. Made March 11, 1799. Heirs: sons Charles and Deans Knowles; daus. Celia and Betsy Knowles; Nancy Knowles; Betsy Bennett; Scaney Vinson; Lizzy Vinson; Betsy Belling. [No exec'r]. Wits., George Bennett, Frank Clifton. Prob. April 26, 1799. Arch. vol. A82, pages 169-170. Reg. of Wills, Liber E, folios 216-217. [Note:— Arch. vol. A82, page 170 shows the estate was settled by Stephen Bennett and Newbold Vincent].

**Rickards, Elias.** Will (copy). Made Feb. 14, 1799. Heirs: sons James, Thomas, Isaac and John Rickards; daus. Betty and Polly Rickards. Exec'r, son James Rickards. Wits., Benjamin Holland, Tabitha Wharton. Prob. April 27, 1799. Arch. vol. A95, pages 111-112. Reg. of Wills, Liber E, folios 217-218.

**Furman [Firman], David.** Broadkill Hd. Will. Made April 23, 1799. Heirs: son Ebenezer Furman; daus. Holland, Sophia and Sally Furman. Exec'r, son-in-law James Wilson. Wits., William Steel,. Levin Pepper, William Russell. Codicil: wits., Milly Pepper. Prob. April 30, 1799. Arch. vol. A72, pages 85-86. Reg. of Wills, Liber E, folios 222-223.

**Hasting, Joshua.** Planter. Will. Made Oct. 13, 1794. Heirs: wife Rhoda Hasting; sons William, Job, Daniel and Ezekiah Hasting; daus. Elizabeth, Lydia, Nelly, Grace and Levinia Hasting; granddau. Leah Hasting (dau. of Ezekiah and wife Jane Hasting). Exec'r, son William Hasting. Wits., John Williams, Elijah Hearn, Samuel Hearn, Jr. Prob. April 30, 1799. Arch. vol. A74, pages 201-202. Reg. of Wills, Liber E, folios 218-219.

**Wolfe, Mary.** Lewes & Rehoboth Hd. Will. Made Oct. 1, 1798. Heirs: sons Reece, William, Daniel, Henry, David and George Wolfe, dau. Sarah Marriner (wife of Simon Marriner); grandsons George, Gilbert and Reece Marriner (sons of Sarah and Simon), David, John and William Orr (sons of dec'd dau. Comfort Orr); granddaus. Jane Russell (dau. of Sarah and Simon Marriner), Mary and Kittura Orr (daus. of dec'd dau. Comfort Orr). Exec'rs, sons William, Daniel, Henry, David and George Wolfe. Wits., Jacob Wolfe, Hannah Nunez, Sarah Burton. Prob. April 30, 1799. Arch. vol. A109, pages 32-34. Reg. of Wills, Liber E, folios 220-221.

**Carpenter, Nephtali.** Admin. of, to Samuel Paynter, Jr., and Mary Carpenter. Granted before May 1, 1799. Arch. vol. A63, pages 250-251. ,

**King, David.** Will. Made April 29, 1799. Heirs: wife Rebecca King; son George King; David King, Jr. (son of William

King, dec'd). Exec'rs, wife Rebecca King, Walter Hutson. Wits., Jno. White, Joseph Coulter, James Elliott. Prob. May 6, 1799. Arch. vol. A82, pages 94-95. Reg. of Wills, Liber E, folios 223-224. [Note:—Arch. vol. A82, page 95 shows David Stuart as an additional exec'r).

**Little, Sarah.** Widow. Will. Made Feb. 23, 1799. Heirs: nephew William Pope; friends Robert and Mary West. Exec'r, Robert West. Wits., Daniel Rodney, Winifred Harris, Mary Ewing. Prob. May 6, 1799. Arch. vol. A84, pages 169-170. Reg. of Wills, Liber E, folios 221-222.

**Walton, Mary.** Admin. of, to William Walton. Granted [c. May 10, 1799]. Arch. vol. A104, page 154.

**Lecat, Levin.** Will. Made March 29, 1795. Heirs: son James Lecat; dau. Nancy Lecat. Exec'rs, son James Lecat and dau. Nancy Lecat. Wits., George Bloxom, Elias Baker. Prob. May 15, 1799. Arch. vol. A84, pages 31-32. Reg. of Wills, Liber E, folios 224-225. [Note:—Arch. vol. A84, page 32 shows the estate was settled by James Lecat and John Holland].

**Parker, Elinor.** Admin. of, to Major Townsend. Granted [c. May 20, 1799]. Arch. vol. A92, page 60.

**Adams, George.** Admin. of, to John and William A. Adams. Granted [c. May 25, 1799]. Arch. vol. A57, pages 47-50.

**Milby, Zadock.** Admin. of, to Nanny Milby. Granted [c. June 8, 1799]. Arch. vol. A88, page 182.

**Bradley, John.** Will. Made April 8, 1799. Heir: bro. William Bradley. [No exec'r]. Wits., Gideon Bradley, Jr., Gideon Bradley, Sr., John Robertson (of James). Prob. June 11, 1799. Arch. vol. A58, page 49. Reg. of Wills, Liber E, folios 225-226.

**Bagwell, John.** Will. Made April 26, 1795. Heirs: wife Patience Bagwell; nephew William Bagwell Burton; Peter Bagwell McHam. Exec'rs, wife Patience Bagwell and Peter Bagwell McHam. Wits., Isaiah Burton, James F. Baylis, Elizabeth Rogers. Prob. June 11, 1799. Arch. vol. A58, page 52. Reg. of Wills, Liber E, folios 226-227.

**Buckhanan [Buchanan], Betsy.** Will. Made Jan. 20, 1797. Heirs: bros. James and Thomas Buckhannon; step-bro. William Washington Green. Exec'r, step-father Jesse Green. Wits., Nancy Alcock, Kitty Green. Prob. June 18, 1799. Arch. vol.

A61, pages 11-12. Reg. of Wills, Liber E, folios 228-229. [Note:—Arch. vol. A61, page 11 mentions dec'd uncle Thomas Alcock of Maryland; page 12 shows the estate was settled by Jesse Green, Esq.].

**Peery, Aaron.** Admin. of, to Joseph Black. Granted [c. June 18, 1799]. Arch. vol. A92, pages 174-176.

**Field, John.** Indian River Hd. Will. Made . . ., 1799. Heirs: sons John and Thomas Field; daus. Maggy and Polly Field, and Betsy Futcher (wife of John). Exec'rs, Nehemiah Field, John Field. Wits., John Sharp, John Hazzard. Prob. June 25, 1799. Arch. vol. A71, pages 64-66. Reg. of Wills, Liber E, folios 227-228.

**Short, Adam.** Will. Made April 29, 1799. Heirs: wife Charlotte Short; son Peter Short; dau. Patience Short. Exec'rs, wife Charlotte Short, and bro. William Short. Wits., William Truitt, Levin Coverdall. Prob. June 27, 1799. Arch. vol. A98, page 155. Reg. of Wills, Liber E, folios 229-230.

**Short, Adam.** Admin. of, to John Willis, D. B. N. Granted [c. July . . ., 1799]. Arch. vol. A98, page 154.

**Young, Robert, Jr.** Admin. of, to John Smith. Granted [c. July 3, 1799]. Arch. vol. A109, page 142. [Note:—Arch. vol. A109, page 142 mentions heirs Sarah and Christian Young].

**Verdaman, Christopher.** Admin. of, to Selby Hickman. Granted [c. July 20, 1799]. Arch. vol. A103, page 107.

**Davis, Mark.** Cedar Creek Hd. Will. Made March 5, 1799. Heirs: wife Sarah Davis; sons Manlove, Robert, Mark, Henry, Thomas, Nehemiah and John Davis; daus. Sarah Davis and Mary Manlove; granddaus. Sally Wattson (dau. of Mary Manlove), Sarah Hindes, Mary Hindes, Ann Thornton and Elizabeth Davis. Exec'rs, wife Sarah Davis and son Mark Davis. Wits., Nath[anie]l Young, James Deputy, William Truitt. Prob. Aug. 1, 1799. Arch. vol. A68, pages 91-94. Reg. of Wills, Liber E, folios 231-234. [Note:— Arch. vol. A68, page 92 shows that William Thornton was the husband of Ann].

**Smith, Nancy.** Will. Made July 23, 1799. Heirs: sons Robert and Constantine Smith; daus. Polly, Grace, Sally, Anna Smith, Betty Cannon and Rachel Spencer; mother Sarah Clarkson. Exec'rs, bro. William Jacobs and son Constantine Smith. Wits., Charles Twyford, Charlotte Twyford, Rachel Spence. Prob. Aug. 12, 1799. Arch. vol. A99, page 190. Reg. of Wills, Liber E, folios 235-236.

**Lloyd, Thomas.** Admin. of, to Isaac Fisher. Granted [c. Aug. 24, 1799]. Arch. vol. A85, page 163.

**Walter, Mitchell.** Admin. of, to Stephen Styer. Granted [c. Aug. 29, 1799]. Arch. vol. A104, page 124.

**Wyatt, John.** Admin. of, to Stephen Styer and wife Eleanor, late Eleanor Wyatt and former wife of Peleg Walter. Granted [c. Aug. 29, 1799]. Arch. vol. A109, pages 112-114. [Note:—Arch. vol. A109, page 113 mentions Sally and Ebe Walter, Polly Hellum (wife of Jacob) as heirs of Peleg Walter; Mitchell Walter also an heir of Peleg Walter and Polly Walter].

**Warren, Margaret.** Admin. of, to Major Warren. Granted [c. Sept. 5, 1799]. Arch. vol. A105, page 118.

**Laughinghoe, William.** Will. Made Aug. 23, 1783. Heirs: wife Elizabeth Laughinghoe; daus. Ann Black and Hannah Gray; grandsons Isaac Gray (son of William and Hannah Gray), John Churchill Black (son of Adam and Ann Black). Exec'rxs, daus. Ann Black and Hannah Gray. Wits., Leah Burton, Molly Burton, Benja[min] Burton. Prob. Sept. 19, 1799. Arch. vol. A83, pages 100-102. Reg. of Wills, Liber E, folios 236-237. [Note:—Arch. vol. A83, page 102 mentions Ann, John C. and Nancy Black; Hannah, Isaac, Anna, Betsy, William, Judea, Burton and Benjamin Gray. Also shows estate was settled by Isaac Gray, adm'r of William Gray, and Solomon Fountain, agent of Adam Black. William Gray and Adam Black were acting exec'rs for their wives].

**Lockwood, Armwell,** the younger. Admin. of, to Armwell Lockwood. Granted [c. Oct. 9, 1799]. Arch. vol. A84, page 182.

**Heavelow, James.** Will. Made Feb. 19, 1796. Heirs: wife Ann Heavelow; son Andrew Heavelow; dau. Rachel Eldridge; grandsons James Heavelow, John Gray; granddau. Betsy Gray; son-in-law Frazier Gray. Exec'rs, wife Ann Heavelow and son Andrew Heavelow. Wits., Peter Jackson, Jesse Heavelow, Grace Riley. Prob. Oct. 25, 1799. Arch. vol. A75, pages 220-221. Reg. of Wills, Liber E, folios 237-239.

**Evans, Sophia.** Will (copy). Made April 13, 1799. Heirs: son John M. Evans; daus. Sarah Derickson, Molly Tracy and Sophia Burton; grandsons John and Samuel Evans Tracy, Ebenezer Hazzard; granddaus. Sophia M. and Charlotte Tracy, Anna Burton. Exec'r, grandson Ebenezer Hazzard. Wits., Levin Bevans, John Buckley, Eli Evans. Prob. Nov.

5, 1799. Arch. vol. A71, pages 22-23. Reg. of Wills, Liber E, folios 239-240.

**James, Joshua.** Admin. of, to Betsy James. Granted [c. Nov. 5, 1799]. Arch. vol. A80, page 99.

**Tingle, Parthena.** Will. Made Oct. 8, 1791. Heirs: sons William, Caleb and Luke Tingle; daus. Nancy Tingle, Comfort Evans, Elizabeth Rogers and Rhoda Beau[chem]; grandsons John, Edward and Isaac Clark (children of Tabitha Clark). Exec'r, son William Tingle. Wits., Ezekiel Williams, Tandy Taylor, Martha Taylor. Prob. Nov. 13, 1799. Arch. vol. A102, page 28. Reg. of Wills, Liber E, folios 240-242.

**Cardiff, Margaret.** Admin. of, to Elizabeth (Betsy) Cardiff. Granted [c. Nov. 14, 1799]. Arch. vol. A63, page 160. [Note: —Arch. vol. A63, page 160 mentions Nancy Moore, Christopher, Rebecca and Betsy Cardiff, children of Christopher Cardiff, dec'd].

**Aydelott, John.** Bricklayer. Will. Made March 27, 1798. Heirs: sons Levin, Benjamin, Jacob, Thomas, John and Luke Aydelott. Exec'r, son Thomas Aydelott. Wits., Litteton Townsend, Major Benson, Belita Jarman. Prob. Nov. 16, 1799. Arch. vol. A58, page 1. Reg. of Wills, Liber E, folios 242-243.

**Harwood, Robert.** Admin. of, to Barbara Harwood, widow. Inventory date Nov. 18, 1799. Arch. vol. A74, page 161.

**Craig, Harmon.** Admin. of, to Mary [Polly] Craig. Granted before Nov. 20, 1799. Arch. vol. A67, pages 147-148.

**Cannon, Joseph, Sr.** Will. Made Nov. 20, 1799. Heirs: sons Robert, Elisha and Levi Cannon; daus. Margaret Cannon, Rebecca Cannon (wife of Hayward Cannon) and Betsy Collings (wife of John Collings); and granddau. Eliza Cannon (dau. of Hayward Cannon). Exec'r, son Levi Cannon. Wits., Abraham Cannon, Joseph Cannon, Jr., Isaac Wingate. Prob. Nov. 24, 1799. Arch. vol. A63, page 81. Reg. of Wills, Liber F, folios 446-448.

**Turner, Eunice.** Admin. of, to Joshua Reed. Granted [c. Nov. 26, 1799]. Arch. vol. A103, page 14.

**Hudson, Joshua.** Admin. of, to Richard Hudson and wife Polly, late Polly Hudson. Granted [c. Nov. 27, 1799]. Arch. vol. A79, page 30.

**Wright, Joshua.** Admin. of, to Clement Wright. Granted [c. Nov. 28, 1799]. Arch. vol. A109, page 90.

**Reed, Edmond.** Broadkill Hd. Will. Made Dec. 31, 1798. Heirs: wife Judah Reed; sons Parker, Charles, Joshua, Benjamin, Zadock and Elias Reed; daus. Sarah, Sinah and Peggy Reed, Polly Morris, Nicey Lofland. Exec'r, son Zadock Reed. Wits., Nathan Reed, Allen Clifton, Joshua Reed. Prob. Nov. 29, 1799. Arch. vol. A95, page 23. Reg. of Wills, Liber E, folios 243-245.

**Carlile [Carlisle], Thomas.** Will. Made Nov. 16, 1799. Heirs: sons John, Pemberton, Thomas, Daniel and William Carlile; daus. Betty Richardson (wife of Elzey), Nancy Hickman (wife of Jacob), Sally Clifton (wife of Elias), Sally Hudson (wife of Henry), Unice Warren (wife of Wrixam), Dorcas Reed (wife of Nathan), and Polly Stephens (wife of Avery). Exec'r, son Daniel Carlisle. Wits., William Reiley, John Cathell, Jemima Warren. Prob. Dec. 3, 1799. Arch. vol. A63, page 184. Reg. of Wills, Liber E, folios 246-248.

**Evans, Hannah.** Will. Made July 16, 1799. Heirs: son Kendell Evans; dau. Mary Nicholson; granddau. Katie Nicholson. Exec'r, son Kendell Evans. Wits., Ezekiel Williams, Lemuel Williams, Nancy Morris. Prob. Dec. 3, 1799. Arch. vol. A70, pages 204-206. Reg. of Wills, Liber E, folios 245-246.

**Warren, Samuel.** Will. Made May 21, 1797. Heirs: wife Mary Warren; sons Isaac, Eli and Kendle Warren; daus. Mary, Sarah, Elizabeth and Priscilla Warren; heirs of dau. Eleanor Selaven. Exec'rx, wife Mary Warren. Wits., Thomas Marvel, Abram Harris, Jr. Prob. Dec. 16, 1799. Arch. vol. A105, page 127. Reg. of Wills, Liber E, folios 248-249.

**Prettyman, John.** Will. Made Feb. 13, 1798. Heirs: wife Comfort Prettyman; sons Nehemiah and Jacob Prettyman; dau. Comfort Prettyman. [No exec'r]. Wits., Cornelius Paynter, Nehemiah Stockley, Jacob Wolfe. Prob. Dec. 17, 1799. Arch. vol. A94, page 74. Reg. of Wills, Liber E, folios 249-250.

**Ricords, Levin.** Lewes & Rehoboth Hd. Will. Made Dec. 4, 1799. Heirs: bros. Hap H., James and John Ricords; sisters Priscilla Ricords and Ann Stevenson. Exec'r, Hap Ricords. Wits., Cornelius Wiltbank, Jacob Wolfe. Prob. Dec. 17, 1799. Arch. vol. A95, page 178. Reg. of Wills, Liber E, folio 251.

# ADDENDA

As the following probate records lacked dates, it was not possible to arrange them chronologically. So that they would not be omitted from this *Calendar*, these records are presented here alphabetically and are included in the index.

Leon deValinger, Jr.
Editor

**Abbott, Temperance.** Admin. of, to Nicholas Abbott. [n. d.]. Arch. vol. A57, page 24.

**Baily, Stephen.** Admin. of, to Cornelius Lingo and wife Elizabeth, late Elizabeth Baily. [n. d.]. Arch. vol. A58, page 96.

**Cirwithin, John.** Admin. of, to John Moore and wife Nanny, late Nanny Cirwithin. [n. d.]. Arch. vol. A64, page 171.

**Coston, Matthias.** Admin. of, to Stephen Coston. Granted before 1800. Arch. vol. A67, page 13. [Note:—Arch. vol. A67, page 13 mentions heirs: Stephen Coston; Ephama Pettyjohn; and heirs of Joshua and Somerset D. Coston].

**Darby, Ephraim.** Admin. of, to Samuel Darby. [n. d.]. Arch. vol. A68, page 19.

**Falkner, Joshua.** Admin. of, to Elizabeth Falkner. [n. d.]. Arch. vol. A71, page 56.

**Halbert, Samuel, Jr.,** (son of Sarah). Admin. of, to Isaac Wattson, D. B. N. [n. d.]. Arch. vol. A73, page 175.

**Jacobs, Nathaniel.** Admin. of, to William Jacobs, D. B. N., in right of Patience Jacobs, widow. [n. d.]. Arch. vol. A80, page 70. [Note:—Arch. vol. A80, page 70 mentions a dau. Hannah Jacobs].

**Riley, Benjamin.** Yeoman. Admin. of, to John Johnson Riley. [n. d.]. Arch. vol. A96, page 34. [Note:—Arch. vol. A96, page 34, mentions Sarah Riley, widow of Laurence Riley, father of decedent].

**Riley, George.** Admin. of, to John Draper and wife Elizabeth, late Elizabeth Riley. [n. d.]. Arch. vol. A96, page 39. [Note:—Arch. vol. A96, page 39 mentions Laurence Riley, Jr., son of Benjamin Riley, dec'd].

**Rust, John.** Yeoman. Admin. of, to Samuel Hudson, Sarah Hill. [n. d.]. Arch. vol. A97, page 161.

**Till, Thomas, Esq.** Copy of Admin. account, to Mary Till, surviving adm'rx. [n. d.]. Arch. vol. A101, page 197. [Note: Arch. vol. A101, page 197 mentions William Till, the younger, dec'd, only child of Thomas].

**Warrington, Elizabeth.** Widow. Admin. of, to John Abbott Warrington. [n. d.]. Arch. vol. A105, page 148.

**Warrington, Jacob.** Yeoman. Admin. of, to John Abbott Warrington, D. B. N., in lieu of Elizabeth Warrington, dec'd. [n. d.]. Arch. vol. A105, page 150.

# INDEX

# INDEX

All names of persons appearing in the text of the probate record abstracts have been alphabetized and included in this section. The original spelling has been retained throughout, except in cases when variations of names that are phonetically the same are grouped. In these cases the names in parentheses indicate the various spellings included in the same name group.

The Arabic numbers following each name in the index indicate the pages on which these names appear. Names of places, such as villages, towns and land tracts, have been excluded from this index.

The absence of a first or given name is indicated by three dots, as . . . . An asterisk * before a name indicates that the reference refers to a will or an administration account rather than the use of the name as a witness, heir, executor or trustee.

3

John, *53
John Hancock, *239
Joseph E., 80
Sally, 298
Sarah, 73
Spencer, 178
William, 53, 73
Auston, (Austins), Isaac, *272
Mary, 272
Richard, 116
Autwell, John, 182
Nelly, 182
Avery, Mr., 9
John, Capt., *10
Aydelott, (Aydelotte), Benjamin, 307
Betsey (Bette), 122, 132, 224
Cornelius, 119, 147
Elizabeth, 293
Elizabeth Dagworthy, 158
Elon (Ellen), 119, 147
Frances, 119, *222
George, 224
Henry, 119, *122, 224
Howard, 122, 224
Isaac, 132
Jacob, 307
Jasper, 122, *147
John, 119, 122, 182, 238, *307
John, Sr., *224
Joseph, *119, 125, 145
Levin, 307
Luke, 307
Mary, 122, 147, 167, 224
Mathias, 122, 167, 224, 293
Milly, 238
Nancy, 223
Rhoda, 122, 123
Samuel, 132, 238
Thomas, 120, *125, 307
Ayres, David, 215

—B—

Bacon, . . ., 265
Betty, 156
Davis, 128, 211, 265
Dodson, *156
Elizabeth, 156
Eunice, 156
George, 156, 187, *265
Henry, 277
Jean, 211
John, 156, 202, 211, 255, 265, *277
Leah, 265
Levin, 128, *211, 265
Mary, 156
Nancy, 156

Phame, 277
Sarah, 156, 202
William, 265
William Davis, 265
Badger, John, *11
Bagnell, Frances, 27
Bagwell, Ann, 21, 80, 86, 115, 127
Catherine, 86
Elizabeth, 77, 86
Frances, 35
Francis, *29
John, 86, 287, *304
John, Sr., *77
Lydia, 86
Patience, 64, 304
Peter, 128
Sarah, 77
Thomas, 29, 35, 62, 77, 80, *86
William, 21, 77, 86, *92, *181
Bailey, (Baily, Bailley, Bayley, Baley, Bayly) . . ., 44
Ann, 52
Bethiah, 54
Betsy Lee, 228
Betty, 276
Clement Lee, *228
Comfort, 143
Davis, 179
Elias, 25, 33, 44
Elizabeth, 309
Esther, 54
George, 179
Hannah, 52
James, 44, *52
James Burton, 250
Jane, 88
Jennet, 143, 161
Jeremiah L., 261
Jeremiah Lee, 228, 254
John, 54, 72, 179, *276
John L., 254, *261
John Lee, 228
Jonathan, 20, 32, 35, 44, 52, *54, 143, *179
Jonathan, Jr., *44
Joseph, 54, 70, 84
Margery, 163, 228
Mary, 54, 77, 179
Nancy Lee, 228
Nathaniel, 70, *143
Peggy, 143
Samuel Jackson, 179
Sarah, 25, 44, 83
Stephen, 179, *309
Steward, 52
Thomas, 179
William, 111, 143
Bains, Colston, 54

4

Bainum, Bartholomew, 104
  Eleanor, *104
  Isaac, *222
  John, 104
  Levi, 104, 223
  Rachel, 104
  Sarah, 222
  William, 104
  William Beavens, 104
Baker, Betsy, 269
  Elias, *266, 304
  George, 266
  Hugh, 105, 114, *218
  Joshua, 266, 269
  Leah, 266
  Mary, 114, 148, 218, *269
  Naomi, 266
  Purnal Henry, 251
  Rebecca, 266
  Riley, 189
  Sally, 218, 251, 269
  Thomas, *299
  William, *148, 189, 260, 266, 299
Balding, Caleb, 147, 148, 213, *226
  Samuel, 226
  Sarah, 147, 148, 226
Baldrey, Mary, 27
Baley: see Bailey
Ball, Joshua, 135, 265
Bannister, Mary, 161
Banum: see Bennum
Barber, (Barbour), John, 60, 73
Barker, . . ., 288
  Ann, (Anne, Annie), 55, *181,
    *197
  Ann Catherine, 180, 250
  Bagwell, 203, 288
  Comfort, 180
  David, 250
  Eley, (Eli), *288
  Elizabeth, 18, 55
  Jean, 58
  Jehu, 180, 265
  Job, 29, 35, *55, 58, 118
  John, 9, 55
  Joseph, 203
  Leatherbury, 55, 76, 180, 181, *203
  Mary, 122
  Nancy, 203
  Patience, 78, 288
  Perry, 55, *180, 181
  Richard, 120, 285
  Sarah, 180, 203
  Temperance, 55
  William, 55
  Zadok, *265
Barnard, Bennona, 144
Barnes: see Barns

Barnet, (Barnett), Samuel, 110
  Zachariah, 229
Barney, Jacob, 261
Barns, (Barnes), Anna, 118, 203
  Annie, 215
  Betty, 215
  Daniel, *118
  George, 98, 172, *199
  Mary, 118, *203, 215
  Robert, 118, *215
  Sarah, 98
  Simeon, 118, 203, 215
  Thomas, 118, 215
Barr, Ann, 64, 165
  Betsey, 231
  Catharine, 158
  Chloe, 170
  David, *275
  Ferraby, 170
  James, 64, *170
  John, 32, *170, 192
  Margaret, 192, 285
  Pharoah, 208
  Polly, 275
  Robert, 254
  William, *158, 285
Barrey, Edward, 11
Barthelmy, Jeremiah, 16
Bartlett, Leah, 75
  Margaret, 75
  Nicholas, 75
  Solomon, 75
  Thomas, 97
  William, *75
Barton, Edward, 219
  Elizabeth, 219
  William, *219
Basnet, (Basnett, Bassnett)
  Boaz, 220
  John, 220
  Mary, 42
  Nehemiah, 204, 220
  Ralph, 42, 48
  Samuel, *204, 220
  Sarah, 204, *220
Bass, John, 70
Bassett, Richard, 156
Bassnett: see Basnet
Bate, Thomas, 27, 28
Batson, Elizabeth, 228
  Hannah, 228
  John W., 221
  John Wise, 228
  Kendle, (Kendal, Kindal), 221,
    228, 259
  Margaret, 259
  Maria, 259
  Sarah, 228
  Tabitha, 228

Butcher, Frances, 141, *265, *269
  LeJay, 269
  Mary, 141, 269
  Naomi, 141
  Rhoda, 260
  Robert, 21, 63, *75, 141, *164
  William, 21, 75, 98, *141, 164, 260
Butler, Elizabeth, 104
  Esther, 42
  William, 22, 42
Byrn, Darby, 54
Bywater, Elinor, 24
  John, 23, 26

—C—

Caddy, John, 167
  Mary, 54, 128
  Patience, 287, 288, 297
Cade, Hannah, 125, 266
  John, *147, 268
  John, Jr., 125, 297
  Jonathan Naws, 266
  Letitia, *283
  Mary, 147, *297
  Priscilla, 268
  Richardson, 105, *268
  Robert, 283
  Thomas, 26, 56, 124, 283
Cadwallader, Lambert, 158
Cahoon, (Cawhoon), David, 33
  Elizabeth, 257
  Frances, *180
  John, 242, 270
  Jonathan, 257
  Mary Ann, 140
  Sampson, *166
  William, 271
Caldwell, Susannah, 186
  Train, 186
  William, 226, 238
Calhoon, Nancy, 259
  William, 259
Callaghan, Dennis, 195
  Sarah, 195
Callaway, (Colloway)
  Abraham, 234
  Ann, 152
  Benjamin, *152, 268
  Betty, 242
  Celia, (Sealeah), 152
  Clement, 268
  Ebenezer, 146, 152, *204, *218, 229, *268
  Eli, 204, *257
  Elisha, 204, *242
  Elizabeth, *188, 192, 234
  Elsie, 104

  Eunice, 268
  Frankey, 242
  Hardy, 219
  Hetty, 242
  James, *146
  Jehu, 204
  Job, 268
  John, *142, 146, 219, 242, 271
  Joshua, *104, 229
  Leah, 204
  Levi, 277
  Levin, *161, 242
  Mary, 161
  Matthew, *219, 268
  Moses, 219, 268
  Nancy, 242
  Nehemiah, 152
  Nelly, 242
  Peggy, 229, 242, 257
  Peter, 142, 218
  Phillis, 219
  Polly, 242
  Rachel, 146
  Rebecca, 242
  Sarah, 219, 229, 236, 242
  Thomas, 234
  Tubman, 219
  William, *192, 204, 233, *242
  Winder, 242
  Wingate, 242
Cameron, John, *297
Campbell (Camble, Cambell, Cammell)
  Alexander, 39
  Ann, 67
  Dorothy, 67
  Elizabeth, 57, 63, 64, 67, 149
  Esther, 93, 96, 209
  George, *67
  James, 48
  John, *96, *249
  John S., 171, 261
  John Simpson, 96
  Joseph, 67
  Margaret, 67
  Mary, 67, 182
  Nancy, 249
  Nathan, 67, *93
  Rebeckah, 63
  Robert, 60, 67
  Samuel, *96
  Sarah, 67, 96
Cannon, . . ., 135
  Abraham, 127, 246, 256, 307
  Absalom, *237, *255
  Allen, 194
  Anne, 135
  Arcada, 194, 244

15

Selah, 242
Smith, 269
Susannah, 173, 174
Tabitha, 21, *274
Tamson, 274
Thomas, *21, 28, 40, 69, 174, 185
Ursley, 116
William, 34
Clowes, Alleta, 213
Catherine, 84, 85
David, 84, 85, 213
Gerhardus, 84
Hannah, 85
Isaac, 213, 291, 300
John, 56, 60, 61, 65, 68, 82, *84, 85,
93, 95, 105, 106, 111, 137, 142,
157, 165, 186, *213, 241
John, Jr., 74, 75, 77, 84
Lidia, 84
Mary, 84, 85, 213, 300
Peter, 62, 213, 300
Samuel, 84
Sarah, 213
Sophia, 85
William, 84
Coates, Major, 242
Thomas Peachy, 242, 289
Cobb, Elijah, 70
Oliver, 70
Sarah, 70
Stephen, 70
Cockayne, (Cokayne), Thomas, 35,
36, 39, 120, 148
Codd, Berkeley, *32
Mary, 32
St. Legar, 32
Coe, Daniel, 30
John, 23, 24, 40, 140
Mary, 30, 41
Timothy, 29, *30
Coffin (Coffan), Abner, 111
Comfort, 111, 112
Cornelius, 111
Easter, 272
John, Jr., *106, *111
Mary Chester, 111
Nehemiah, 102, 288
Thomas, 111
William, 111, 118, 171, 205, 224,
*247
Coggeshall, Isaac, *23
Preserved, 23, 25, 29, 32
Sarah, 23
Cokayne: see Cockayne
Cole, Coverdale, (Coverdill), 91, 227
Jane, 34
Jeanne, 29
John, 34

Leah, 161
Margaret, 29, 71
Matthias, *161
Patience, 34
Sarah, 34
Sophia, 91
Thomas, 29, *34
William, 34, 40
Coleburn, (Coulbourn), Anna, 268
Betsy, 189
Catharine, 156, 237, 268
Elijah, 268
Frances, 149
Jean, 139
Joseph, 229, 268
Josiah, 184
Kesiah, 268
Mary, 139
Michael, *268
Nancy, 283
Nelly, 268
Peggy, 184
Priscilla, 184, *194
Rebecca, 268
Robert, 268
Solomon, 139, 184
Solomon, Sr., *139
Stephen, 139, *184, 194
Susannah, 229
Thomas, 206, 268
William, 139, 156
Coleman, Rhoda, 288, 297
William, 241, 288, 297
Collet, . . ., 47
Betty, 47
James, *47
Collier, James, *288
John, 288
Mary, 288
Peter, 288
Sarah, 288
Collins, (Colling, Collings),
. . ., 142
Aberilla, 111
Ada, 112
Andrew, 76, *95, 112, *158, *162,
198
Ann, 200
Anna, 186
Anthony, 148
Asa, 226
Betty (Betsy), 128, 143, 158, 307
Charity, 250
Charles, 100
Darby, 209
Durustus, 226
Edy, 112
Eli, 119, 216, 250

Somerset, 117, 158, 187
Somerset Dickerson, *237
Somerset G., 309
Stephen, 117, 309
Cottingham, Elisha, *289, 295
  Jonathan, 289
  Joshua, 289
  Rachel, 289
  William, 150
Cottman, William, 184
Couch, James, 172
  Joseph, 124, *157, 165
  Percy, 157
Coudry (Cowthry), Joshua, 15
  William, *15
Coulbourn: see Coleburn
Coulter, . . ., 177
  Anna, 82
  Calvin, 79
  Charles, 63, *64, 82, 83
  Cornelius, 177, 208, 224
  David, 177, 208, 224
  Eli, 208, 224, 235
  Elizabeth, 64, 187, 223
  Esther, 99, *166, *197
  Eunice, 208, 235
  Isabel, 63, 83
  Isabel C., 64
  James, 64, 73, 83, 93, 138, 147,
    *163, 187, 205, 208, 224
  Jenet, 73
  John, *67, *73, 79, 130, 156, *177,
    *195, 208, *224
  John, Jr., 64
  Joseph, 83, 197, *223, 304
  Joseph, Jr., 180
  Josiah, 73
  Laddy, 143
  Margaret, 75, 195, *208
  Margaret, Sr., 67
  Mary, 67, 73
  Naomi, 259
  Nicey, 177
  Polly, 208, 224
  Robert, 64, 73, 83, 232, *259
  Samuel, 58, *82
  Sarah, 64, 83, 143, 232
  Thomas, 143, 163
  Unice, 156, 224
  William, 82, 143, 163, 208, 224
Coverdale, (Coverdell, Coverdill),
  . . ., 275
  Ann, 283
  Boaz, 258
  Charles, 76
  Eli, 258
  Elizabeth, 88, 260
  Eunice, 250

Hessie, 189
Isaac, 189
Israel, 88, *258
Jacob, 302
Jane, 88
Jennifer, 189
Jeremiah, 266
John, 92, *189, 231
John, Sr., *76
Levi, 189
Levin, 266, 305
Luke, *266
Major, 266
Mary, 76, 88, 146
Matthew, 88
Nathaniel, 76
Phebe, 189
Polly, 218
Purnel, 258, 266
Rachel, 258
Richard, 76, *88, 94, 106, 189, 250,
  258, 260, *275
Rosanna, 88
Samuel, 189
Sarah, 76, 88
Susannah, *92, 189
Thomas, 16, 146
William, 189, 258, 275
Covington, Esther, 116
  Jacob, 116
  Spencer, 211
Cowan, (Cowing), Alexander, *92
  Betty, 92
  Elizabeth, *122
  Esther, 92, 122
  George, 92, 122, 222
  Nanney, 92, 122
Coward, Penelope Holt, 83
Cowden, Elizabeth, 40
Coursey, John, 31
Courtman, Henry, 32
Cox, Thomas, 147
Crafford, George, 136
Craig, (Craige, Crague, Creagh)
  Alexander, 75, 103
  Betsy, 197
  Comfort, 133, 170
  David, 134, 197, 252
  Edward, 21, 24, *25, 125, 141, 165,
    183, *197, 231, 255
  Elizabeth, 25, 33
  Esther, 125, *183
  Hambleton, (Handleton), 33, 74
  Hamilton, 75, 87, 103, *125
  Hannah, 75
  Harmon, 197, 263, *307
  Jean, 37

Nehemiah, 38, 43, 44, 45, 64, 116, 152, 165. *183. 191. 201. *299. 305
Nehemiah, Jr., 133, 183
Nehemiah, Sr., 77, *201
Neomy, 55
Rachel, 94, 183
Rachel Atkinson, 165. 201
Richard, 17, 22
Robert, 17, 55, 59, 130, 299, 305
Samuel, 17, 19, 20, 33, 37, 38, 40, 70, 73, 77, 197
Samuel, Jr., 25, 29, 34, 38
Samuel, Sr., Rev., 25
Sarah, 31, 49, 64, 116, 216, 242, 299, 305
Solomon, 153
Susannah, 77, 130, 201
Thomas, 17, 34, 41, 44, 45, 49, 59, *64, 77, 94, *106, 107, 110, 201, 305
Thomas, Sr., *17, 38
William, 99, 197, 201, 283
Zerobabel, *244
Davison, Mary, 88
Dawson, Abbel, 291
  Edward, *284
  Elizabeth, 255
  Martha, 226
  Peter, 226
  Thomas, 284
Day, Abigail, 81
  George, 47, *50
  John, 38, 81, 99, 104, 185, 252
  Leah, 252
  Margaret, 81
  Mary, 32, 81, 119
  Prettyman, 47, 50, *81
  Valance, 74
  William, *47 ,65, 81, *99
Dazey: see Daizey
Deal, Campbell, 165
  Elizabeth, 165
  Thomas, 214
Dean, Charles, *187
  Ebe, 187
  Jemima, 107
  Jesse, 214, 246
  John. *246
  John W., 184, 187, 191, 196
  John Wilson, 186, 213
  Mary, 184
Debety: see Deputy
Dehart, Sarah, 158
Delaney (Dellaney): see Dulany
Depray (Depree), . . ., 9
  Andrew, 9
  Bridgett, 13

Elizabeth, 13
Jacob, 9
John, *9, *21, *78
Leah, 94
Margaret, 13
Mary, 21, 78
Thomas, 13
William, 21, 291
Deputy, (Debety), Betty, 52
  Charles, 274
  Elinor, 212
  Elizabeth, 43, 52
  Esther, 146
  James, 305
  Jesse, 241
  John, 274
  Joshua, 212, 241
  Mary, 52, 146, 170, 172
  Polly, 274
  Sarah, 52, 265
  Silvester, 43, 146
  Solomon, *146
  Steven, 53
Derickson, (Derrickson, Dirickson, Dirixson)
  Andreas, (Andries), 118, *262
  Benjamin, *118, 186, 289
  Caleb, 118
  Charles, 168
  Elisha, 287
  Elizabeth, 109, 135, 136, 238, 284, 299
  George, 118, *289
  Handy, 293
  Isaiah, 237, 289
  James, 230, 300
  Jane Bell, 287
  Job, *229, 261, 294
  Job D., 118
  Jobe, 225
  John, 118, 166
  Joseph, 118, 122, 168, 224, 229, 230
  Joseph, Sr., 238
  Leah, 186
  Levin, 150, 158, 167, *168, 230
  Luke, 262
  Margaret, 134
  Mary, 53, 102, 262, 289
  Mitchell, 147
  Polly, 166
  Sally, 289
  Samuel, 135, 136, 168, 238, 230, 242, 306
  Sarah, 132, 163, 168, *189
  Solomon, 237, 272, 289
  Sophia, 229, *293
  William, 118, 284, 295, 299
Dernie, Philip, 43

Derrickson: see Derickson
deValinger, Leon, Jr., 309
Dickason, Thomas, 50
Dickerson, . . ., 276
  Betsy, 295
  Catherine, 137
  Comfort, 257, 274
  Edmund, 186, 196, *257, 274
  Eleanor, 274
  Elisha, 203, *276
  Elizabeth H., 276, 277
  Elizabeth Holland, 298
  Eunice, 257
  Jacob, 298
  Levin, 257, *274
  Nancy, 257, 274
  Peter, *137, 186, 196, 257
  Robert, 276
  Sally, 274
  Sarah, 117, 159, 186, *196, 257
  Somerset, 117, 158, 159, *186, 196
  William, 257, 290
Dickinson (Dickenson), Alice, 170
  Annah, 55
  Eunice, 274
  Leah, 55
  Peter, 117
  Somerset, 175
  Thomas, *55
Dickson, James, 195
  Jonathan, 195
Dier: see Dyer
Dill, Abner, 143
Dinavan: see Donavan
Dingee, Catharine, 136
  Charles, 171, 172
  Daniel, 121, *171, 172
  Esther, 171, 172
  Jacob, 78
  Obadiah, 78
Dingle, Edward, 124, 207, 232, 247, 257
  Edward Carty, 182
  Richard, *124
  William, *247
Dirickson (Dirixson): see Derickson
Dishroon, Abigail, 249
Dixon, Agnes, 148
  Thomas, 30
Dobson, Elenor, *61
  Richard, 19, 21
  Sarah, 52, 76, 89
Dodd, (Dod), Aaron, 96
  Althea, 130
  Emanuel, 107
  Esther, 57
  George, 13, 27, 36, 42

  Hannah, 104
  Hepburn, *226
  Jacob, 57, 245
  Joseph, *107, 109, 113, 130, 273, 295
  Lydia, 226
  Manny, 128
  Molly, 128, 129
  Moses, *130
  Nancy, 129
  Naomy, 36
  Peggy, 245
  Rachel, 45
  Ruth, 107
  Samuel, 130, 172
  Sarah, 109, 111, 113, 172, 245
  Solomon, 77, 142
  Thomas, 36, 77
  William, 83, 143, 240, 243, *245
Dogherty: see Dougherty
Dogin, Cornelius, *41
Dogman, Levina, 187
Dolbee, Benjamin, 161, 283
  Constant, 127, 155
  Hannah, 161
  Jonathan, *155
  Leah, 155
  Peter, 115, 123, *161, 223, 271
  Polly, 155
  Sarah, 161
  Selah, 161
  Tabitha, 161
  Upsherd, 155
  Upsherd Messick, *245
Dolgren: see Dalgreen
Donaho (Donoho, Donohoe, Dunaho)
  Major, 249, 301
  Mary, 26
  Michal, 26
  Rachel, 103, 107
  Sarah, 249, 301
  Thomas, 103, *107
Donavan (Donovan, Dinaven, Dunavan)
  Abraham, 240
  Azariah, 240, 251, 253
  Foster, 240, 281
  Foster, Sr., *240
  Frances, 21
  Jacob, 240
  James, 240
  Job, 240
  John, 19, 240, *253
  Mary, 54, 55
  Naomi, 240, *281
  Randel, *54
  William, 240

Benjamin, 115
Betsey (Betty), 185, 287
Cathrine, 122, 123, 196, 263, *285, 289
Charlotte, 250
Comfort, 121, 307
Daniel, 223
Ebenezer, Sr., *242
Edey, 250
Eli, 196, 242, 287, 289, 306
Elijah, 196, 284
Elisha, 117, 249, *285, 294, 301
Elizabeth, 166, 196, 285
Enoch, 196
Hance, 117
Hannah, 67, 157, 285, 300, *308
Isaac, 109, 110, 180, *287
Jacob, 287
James, 302
Jehu, 117, 185, 195
Job, 196
John, 117, 120, 125, 150, 155, 163, 166, 188, 192, *196, 215, 223, 225, 242, 245, *250, *263
John, Sr., 236
John Cord, 285
John M., 306
Joney, 250
Joshua, 118, *166
Katharine, 252
Kendall, 300, 308
Leah, 121
Lemuel, 236, 268, 289
Lida, 125
Lurani, 66
Margaret, 166, 250
Martha, 285
Mary, 110, 196, 285
Nancy, 116, 285, 287
Owen, 66, 117
Polly, 268
Riley, 228, 236
Rhoda, 268
Robert, 223
Sabrina, 166, 251
Sally, 287, 302
Samuel, 242, *258
Sarah, 121, 165, 284, 285
Sarah Cord, 285
Solomon, 165, 251, 287
Sophia, 242, *306
Stephen, 284, 295, *300
Tabitha, 196, 268
Thomas, 75, 97, 113, *117, 149, 178, 250, 276, 287
Thomas, Jr., 95
Walter, *268

William, 53, 100, 110, 145, 153, 165, 166, 263, 268, 269, 285, 301
Everson, Mathias, 9
Ewing, Mary, 304
Eyre, Anne, 28
Daniel, *28

—F—

Fagan, Sarah, 150
Falkner (Forkner), Burton, 126
Elizabeth, 309
Joshua, *309
Priscilla, 300
Rachel, 126
Farmer, William, 19
Farquhar, Samuel, 233
Farrill, Abraham, 90
Farrington, Levin, 135
Fasit, (Fasset, Fassett, Fassitt, Fossit) . . ., 51
Charles, 15
David, 51
Elijah, 134
John, Sr., 288
Levin, 51
Naomi, 51
Peggy, 297
Rachel, 15
Ross, 288
Rous, 51
Sophia, 51
William, 51, 297
Fearies, Rhoda, 114
Fentham, William Wyatt, *246
Fenwick, (Finwick), Agnes, 205
David, 205
Gideon, 205
James, 40, *41, 205
Joseph, 205
Mary, 41
Ruth, 205
Sarah, 205
Sidney, 41, *78
Thomas, 17, *40, 41, 78
William, *205
Fergus, Eliza, 290
Francis, 290
James, 264, *290
Mary, 290
Ferguson, Catharine, 64
Dugood, *64
John, 64
Mary, 64
Field, (Fields), John, 120, 153, 174, *304, 305
Maggy, 305

Mary, 90, 153, 185, 201, 211
Nehemiah, 11, 14, 15, 17, 18, 23,
44, 90, 305
Polly, 305
Thomas, 305
Figgs, Henry, 142
Finney, Martha, 79
Samuel Latham, *79
Finnix, Joseph, 285
Finwick: see Fenwick
Firman: see Furman
Fisher, . . ., 256
Adam, 29
Adam, Jr., 29
Alexander, 302
Allafer, 256
Allis, 10
Ann, 183
Chloe, 179
Comfort, 254
Curtis, 113
Daniel, 256, 302
Derickson, 190
Dinah, 53
Edward, 48, 70
Elias, 35
Elizabeth, 23, 48, 53, 71, 113, 183,
239, 268
Esther, 53, 183
Esther Nunez, 83
Finwick, 48
Frances, 302
Freda, 256
George, *113, 302
George Handy, 113, *302
Hannah, 84
Henry, 35, 36, 38, 42, 46, *53, 83,
99, 100
Hessie, 190
Hester, 211
Hester Nunez, 100
Iabush, 29
Isaac, 113, 283, 306
Jabesh, (Jabez), Maud, 28, 41, *48
Jabez, 75, 84, 158, 167, *183
James, 10, 23, 28, 47, 50, *53, 84,
113, *179, *222, 282
John, *10, 29, 37, 61, 70, 72, *84,
113, 183, 189, 193, 227, *239,
*256, 266
Jonathan, 122
Joshua, 23, 28, 40, 46, 48, 75, 78,
84, 183
Letitia, 113, 119
Levina, 302
Louisa, 256
Lydia, 282

Margaret (Margrett), 10, 23, 48,
94, 100, 156
Margery, 23, 28
Mary, 209, *266
Miers, 172
Nancy, 167
Patience, 102, 104, 190
Penelope, 190, 211
Prudence, 158
Rachel, (Rachell), 10, 302
Rebecca, 35
Sally, 190
Samuel, 222
Samuel R., 172, 203
Samuel Rowland, 171
Sarah, 10, 48, 71, 122, 169, 222,
227, 256, 302
Thomas, 10, 20, 21, *23, 84, 183,
222, 268
Vilater, 189
William, 16, 33, *35, 37, 53, 54,
104, 106, 189, *190
Wood, 53
Fist, Andrew, 169
Betty, 169
Rachel, 169
Fleetwood, Cornelius, 251
John, 135, 144, *251
Joseph, 251
Luke, 129
Lydia, 251, 267
Mary, 135, 251
Nancy, 251
Parmer, 251
Fleming, (Flemon), Archibald, 109,
158, 192, 206, 302
Catharine, 109, 158, 192
David, 206
Elizabeth, 206
Esther, 67
George, 29
Isaac, 68
Jean, 67
John, *206
Joseph, 106, 149, 166, 252
Ruth, 104
Sarah, 19
Fletcher, George, 280
William, 200
Fling, Daniel, *32
Esther, 32
Flower, (Flowers), Ann, 160
Bartholomew, 123
Betsey, 172
Charles, 123, 168, 182
Charles McNeil, *182
Clarret, 200
Daniel, 200

28

Furbush, Polly, 189
  Sally, 189
Furcher, William, 49
Furman, (Firman), David, 58, *303
  Ebenezer, 303
  Elizabeth, 291
  Hessy, 291
  Holland, 303
  Richard, 58
  Sally, 303
  Sarah, 58
  Sophia, 303
Futcher (Footcher), Betsy, 305
  Elizabeth, 19
  John, 14, 19, 21, 22, *30, 63, 76,
    89, *265, 305
  Mary, 12, 19, 30, 63
  Richard, 14, 19
  Sarah, 195
  Susannah, 265
  William, 9, *12, 14, *19, 30, *63,
    76, 265

—G—

Gale, Levin, 30
Garner, Nathaniel, 31
Garrett, (Gerritt), Barnes, 15, 16
Garva, Elizabeth, 83
Gaskens, Robert, 181
  Sophia, 104
Gassem, Nancy, 273
Gauslin: see Goslin
Gear, Mary, 40
  Thomas, 21, 24, 29, 39, 40
Gerris, Barrents, 12
Getto, Dorothy, 11
  Henry, *11
Gibb, Anne, *24
  Betsey, 231
  Isabella, *231
  John, *24
Gibbons, (Gibbens, Gibbins)
  Betsy, 201, 292
  Elizabeth, 124
  Emory, 182
  George, *146, 182
  John, 124, 182
  John, Sr., 112
  Jonathan, 201
  Joshua, 129, 146, 182, *292
  Mary, 182
  Sally, 292
  Samuel, 129
  Sarah, 146, 182
Gibson, Robert, *151
  Sarah, 151

Giles, Mary, 233
  William, 233
Gill, Elizabeth, 174, 233
  Margaret, 174, *233
  Mary, 174
  Naomi, 174, 233
  Priscilla, 174, 233
  Richard, 9
  Robert, 57, 60
  Sarah, 174, 233
  William, 174
Givens, Dorothy, 20
Glover, Rebecca, 83
  Samuel, 151
Goddard, Elizabeth, 255
  Eunice, 255
  Francis Lane, *255
  Goodin, 255
  Griffith, 255
  John, 153, 160, 255
  Mary, 255
  Sarah, 255, 271
  William, 255
Godden, Cesar, 24
  Mary, 24
  Michael, *24
  Thomas, 24
  William, 24
Godfrey, Rizear, 257
Godsell, Peter, 11
  Robert, *11
  Sarah (Sharah), 11
Godwin, . . ., 15, 36
  Anne, 36
  Cesar, *15
  Daniel, 210
  Elizabeth, *57
  Hannah, 36
  Joseph, 36, 128, 132
  Mary, 50, *238
  Naomi, 74
  Polly, 292
  Preston, 135
  Rhoda, 105, 205, 293
  Thomas, 105, 121, 133, 134, 144,
    198, *205, 228
  William, 26, *36, 37, 81, 292
Goldsmith, Comfort, 45, 48
  Jemima, 45, 48
  Mary, 45, 48
  Neomi (Naomy), 45, 48
  Patience, 48
  Thomas, *45, *48
Gollidge, Thomas, 9
Golt, Peter, *16
Gordon, (Gordin), Ann (Anne), 99,
    192
  Anna, 72

Catharine, 72, 81, 99, 107, 180, 183
Elizabeth, 74, 85
Ephraim, 99, 185
Esther, 72
James, 58, 66, 72, 80, 83, 85, *99,
  107, 108, 192
John, 29, 34, 72, *232
Leah, 72
Marion, 29
Mary, 29
Nathaniel, 72, 81, 107, 180
Peggy, 180
Sarah, 217
Thomas, 29, *72, 74, 89, 99, 107,
  108, *180
Thomas, Sr., *29
Gordy, Elinor, 218
  Jacob, 179
  John, 218, 297
Goslee, (Gozle), Edy, 188
  Elizabeth, 186
  Hannah, 186
  Job, 186, 188
  John, 237
  Sarah, 186, 291
  Thomas, 160
  William, 175, *186
Goslin (Goslen, Gosling, Gauslin)
  Betty, 122
  Daniel, *122
  George, 122
  John, 122
  Joshua, 122
  Polly Merrill, 251
  Priscilla, 299
  Richard, 122
  Thomas, 122
  Victor, 299
  Waitman, Jr., 299
  Waitman, Sr., 283, *299
Gould, Edward, 14, 17
Gragg, Thomas, 47
Graham, John, 249
  Samuel, 239
Grande, Philip, 23
Grandy, John, 188
Granger, Abigail, 23
  Ann, 16, 23
  Frances, 32
  Hannah, 23
  Mary, 23
  Nicholas, 21, *23, *32
  Sarah, 23
Gray, Anna, 306
  Benjamin, 306
  Betsy, 306
  Bridget, *112
  Burton, 306

David, 15, *27, 33, 65, 79, *101
Elisha, 250
Elizabeth, 15, 25, 27, 33, 34, 65
Frazier, 306
Hannah, 112, 306
Hezekiah, 134
Isaac, 15, 210, 217, 306
James, 112, *183, 281, *295
Jean, 101
Jesse, *281, 295
John, 15, 306
Jonathan, 15
Joseph, 215, 221, 260
Judea, 306
Margaret, 242
Mary, 22
Miriam, 107, 229
Polly, 183
Rebeckah, 15
Samuel, 12, *15, 22, 27, 33, *65
Sarah, 15
Sophia, 111
Susannah, 15
Thomas, 15, 37, 60, 64, 67, 71, 73,
  93, 107, 109, 111, 119, *134, 176,
  *177, 185, 250, 281
William, 112, 306
Grear: see Grier
Green, Alice, 220
  Ambrose, 99, 135
  Anne, 153
  David, 153
  Elinor, 99, *127
  Ezekiel, 131
  George, 264, 282
  Jean, 99
  Jemima, 37
  Jesse, 200, 281, 304, 305
  John, 99, *117, 217, 220
  Kitty, 281, 304
  Martha, 99
  Mary, 61, 131
  Naomi, 99, *128
  Nehemiah, 217
  Nelly, 217
  Nicholas, 25, *37
  Patty, 217
  Richard, 99, 117, 127, 128, 135, 162,
    230, 265
  Robert, 281, 294
  Samuel, 220
  Sarah, 112, 200
  Stephen, *99, 111, *135
  Tabitha, 46
  Thomas, 68
  William, 73, 99, 107, *217
  William Washington, 304
Greenwood, Jonas, 20

Greer: see Grier
Grice, Betty, 140
  Easter, 200
  Esther, 217
  Polly, 200, 217
  Ruth, 168, 214, 217, *232
  Thomas, *200, *217
  William, 140, 168, 200, *214
Grier (Grear, Greer), Betty, 148
  Celia, 235
  Elizabeth, 148
  George, 49
Griffin, (Griffen), . . ., 218
  Elijah, 185
  Elizabeth, 218
Griffith, Ann, 183, 199
  Bartlett, 183
  Benjamin, 183
  Betsey, 199
  Charles, 199, *248
  Elizabeth, 183, 291
  Isaac, 177
  Jemima, 183
  Jesse, 114, 148, 177, 198
  John, *199, 218
  John, Jr., 199
  Joram, *183
  Josiah, 177
  Luke, 183
  Mary, 198
  Nancy, 264
  Oliver, *218
  Paris, 177
  Pearcy, 183
  Phebe, 112
  Rachel, 199
  Robert, 177, 192
  Samuel, *133, *177
  Sarah, 248
  Seth, 177, 228
  Sine, 193
  Unice, 199
  William, *112
Grindy, Philip, 23
Groome, Jean, 50
Groundick, Peter, 9
Grove, (Groves), Mary, 35
  Thomas, 23, 31, 142, *184
Grover, Dean, 71
Gullet, John, 278
  Mary, 299
  Sarah, 278
  William, 236
Gum, (Gumm), Abraham, 184
  Francis, 19
  Hannah, 53, 54, 184
  Jacob, 106, 119, *184
  John, 184

  Mary, 160
  Roger, 184
  Sarah, 52
  William Cottman, 184
Gumly, John, 82
Gunby, Betty, 142
  James, 292
Guttre, (Guttery), John, 105, *153

—H—

Hager, Valentine, 110
Halbert, Samuel, 130
  Samuel, Jr., *309
  Sarah, *130
Halden (Haldon), Frederick, 89
  Persis, 89
  William, 89, 91
Hall, Abigail, 222
  Adam, 123, *132, 235, 236, 301
  Agnes, 275
  Ann (Anne), 83, 275
  Anna, 25
  Bathsheba, 270
  Bersheba, 42
  Betsy (Betty), 150 207, 240,
  Burton, 270
  Cassa (Casa), 137, *223
  Cornelia, 270
  David, 42, 57, 65, 79, 85, 91, 99,
    235, 270, 301
  David, Jr., 101
  Edward, 288
  Elijah, 140, *207
  Elinor, 75
  Elizabeth, 61, 123, 235, 236, 259,
    260, 301
  Esther, 137
  Eunice, 270
  Given (Givin), 142, 207
  Hannah, 63, 301
  Henry, 28
  Hugh, 75
  Inna, 31
  Isaac. 222
  James, 65, 75, 109, 113, *172, 188,
    259, *260, 276, 293
  Jane, 31, *42, 46
  Jean, 79, 273
  Jebediah, 165
  Jiddadiah, 294
  John, 21, 25, 31, 33, 52, 57, *63,
    64, *75, 83, 109, 172, 236, 259,
    260, *276, 301
  Joseph, 100, 101, 160, 172, 192, 200,
    210, 216, 218, 228, 232, 240, 264,
    266

Harmon, Angel, 107
 Elizabeth, 107
 John, *107
 Saborah, 107
Harney, Adam, 155
 Eli, 155
 George Washington, 155
 Ginnethan, 147, *155
 Isabel, 155
 Joshua, 247, 271
 Milley, 163
 Mills, 155, 271
 Selby, 155, 271
 Thomas, 155, 233, 271
 Thomas, Jr., 155
 Thomas, Sr., *271
 William, 155
Harp, Joshua, 294
Harper, Bechamp, 75
 Elizabeth, 194
 Esther, 194
 James, *81
 John, 194
 Nelly, 194
 Priscilla, 81
 Rebeckah (Rebecca), 81, 194
 Rita, 194
 Sarah, 81, 194
 William, 81, 194
Harrington (Herington, Herring-
 ton)
 Elias, 15
 Naomi, 284
 William, 143
Harris, Abraham, 154, 295
 Abraham (Abram), Jr., 209, 308
 Abraham, Sr., 295
 Benton, 295
 Director, 186, 295
 Dixon, 298
 Hester, 72
 James, 219, 302
 John, 231, 298
 Mathias, 71, 72, 73, 79
 Nancy, 298
 Patience, 295
 Peter Parker, 295
 Robert, 298
 Sally, 276
 Stevens, 298
 Tabitha, 298
 William, 298
 Winifred, 304
 Zachariah, *298
Harrison, W., 193, 212, 221, 222
 William, 131, 160, 167, 183
Hart (Harte), Absalom, 130
 Benjamin, 130

 Hugh, 33
 Joane, *112
 John, 49, *57, *161
 Margaret, 11
 Mary, 57, 130
 Robert, *10, *11, 57, *130
 Robert, Jr., 10
 Robert, Sr., 9
 Sarah, 161
 Thomas, 161, 291
Harvey, Richard, 23
Harwood, Barbara, 307
 Robert, *307
Haslet, John, 101, 263
 Joseph, 263, 271
Hasley, John, 81
Hasting (Hastings), Aaron, 291
 Daniel, 303
 Elijah, 276
 Elizabeth, 303
 Ezekiel, 303
 Grace, 303
 Henry, 231
 Hezekiah, 248
 Jane, 303
 Job, 303
 John, *231
 Joshua, 248, 276, *303
 Leah, 303
 Levinia, 303
 Lydia, 303
 Melvin, 231
 Nelly, 303
 Rhoda, 303
 Robert, 294
 Severn, 231
 Solomon, 231
 William, 248, 303
Hasty, Mary, 290
 Prudence, 244
Hatfield, Cottingham, *151
 Delilah, 189
 Elijah, *189
 James, 118
 John, 236
 Jonathan, 106, 236
 Margaret, 236
 Piercy, 118
 Rhoda, 90
 Wheatly, 151
 Whitely, 236
 Whitlay, 90
 William, *236
Hathaway, Agnes, *154
 Burton, 154
 James, 68, 138, 154
 John, 154
 Mary, 115

Jehu, 119
John, 12, 14, 15, 17, 20, *23, 25,
  31, *35, 42, 50, *119, 134, *138,
  181, 218
John, Captain, 22
Johnson, 26
Joseph, 17
Joshua, 218
Levi, 181
Levin, 158
Margaret, 47, 89, 104, 181
Mary, 26, 181, 218
Mellicent, 25
Mitchell, 181
Molly, 119
Nancy, 237, 263
Nathan, 121, 216
Nehemiah, 119
Penelope, 116, *150
Polly, 181, 183
Richard, 18, 22, 23, *26
Robert, 18, 19, 26, 35, *116, 121,
  150, 216
Ruth, 26
Sarah, 26, 35, 36, 64, 89, 116, 121,
  181, 289, 310
Solomon, *120
Stephen, 138, 158, 233
Stephen, Dr., 138
Virden, 181
William, 116, *121
Hiller, Sarah, 104
Hilliard, Daniel, 12
  Daniel, Mrs., 12
  John, 12
Himmons, John, 54
Hindes, Mary, 305
  Sarah, 305
Hinds, Charles, *152
  Daniel, 225, *262
  Mary, 152
  Sarah, *133, *152
  Thomas, *81, 152
  William, 152, 183
Hinman, Elizabeth, 33
  John, *33, 35
  Mary, 33
  Richard, 22, 33, 41, *47
Hirons, Mary, 26
Hitch, . . ., 294
  Anna, 279
  Clement, 279
  Elgin, 279
  Gillis, 268, 279
  Isaac, *294
  Lilly, 279
  Nelly, 279
  Phyllis, 294

Polly, 279
Robert, 294
Sarah, 268, 294
Severn, 294
Sophia, 279
Soverign, 279
Spencer, *279
William, *268, 279
Hitchcock, Elinor, *222
Hitchens, . . ., 224
  Aletica, 151
  Comfort, 151
  Elizabeth, 177
  Ezekiel, *151
  Isaac, 224
  Jarred, 115, 177
  Levin Smith, *249
  Nancy, 214
  Polly, 224
  Rebecca, 224
  Sally, 224
  Sarah, 151, 162
  Tamer, *224
  Vina, 224
  William, 224
Hobbs, (Hobbe), William, 232, 290,
  292
Hodgkins (Hodgskin, Hodgkings)
  Jane, *14
  Rhoda, 195
  Thomas, 10
Hodgkinson, Hester, 220
  Peter, 220
Hodgson, Ann, 252
  Gammage, *252
  Jacob, *157
  Sarah, 120, 157
Hodson, Esther, 254
  Jacob, 254
  John, 254
  Sarah, 254
Holder, Edna, 233
  John, *233
  Joseph, 233
  Sophia, 233
  William, 233
Holland, . . ., 96
  Alice, 257
  Benjamin, 105, 277, 292, 300
  Betsy, 249
  David, 249
  Elizabeth, 42, 105, 172, 255, 293,
    294
  Esther, 42
  Hannah, 114, 142
  Isaac, 65, 79, 96
  Israel, 105, 138, *293
  James, 22, 32, *42, 65, 96, *142

Thomas, 175
Hoskins, . . ., 14
  Jane, 14
Hosman (Hoseman, Hossman)
  Daniel, 25, 47, 54, 82
  Hannah, 193
  Jane, *111
  Stokely, 139, *193
Houston, Betsy, 198
  Clement, 190
  Comfort, 56, 198, 287, 288, 297
  Elizabeth, 56
  James, 56, 115, 190
  John, *115, 167, 190
  Joseph, *56, 154, 190, 198
  Leonard, 115, 167
  Liston, 190
  Littleton, 115, *167
  Magdalen, 159, 198, *255
  Margaret, 79
  Mary, 115
  Micajah, 56, 150, *159
  Nancy, 190, 221
  Priscilla, 190, 221
  Purnel, 190
  Robert, 115, 161, 167, *190, 198,
    264, 279
  Sally Minors, 167
  Sophia, 56
  William, 56, 197, 198
How, John, 11
Howard (Haward), Comfort, 147
  Elizabeth, 109, 238, 277
  George, 109, *238, 277
  John, 277, 292
  Knights, *13
  Nehemiah, 205, 238, 271, *277
  Rhoda, 205, 277, *292
  Richard, 147
  William, 277, 278
Howell, Thomas, 71
  William, 145, 268
Hubart, John, 194
Hubbert, Peter, 135, 163, 187
  Thomas, 156
Hudson, . . ., 227
  Adylott, 111
  Amy Parker, *104
  Ananias, *91, 94, 181, 257, 272
  Anderson, 104, 200
  Anderton, 247
  Anslee, 291
  Anzella, 295
  Benjamin, 186, 227, 246, 259, 267,
    274, *295, 301
  Betty (Betsy), 114, 217, 231
  David, 140
  Eliah, 198

Elijah, 140
Elizabeth, 200, 226, 247
Ellie, 114
Ellis, 91
Gesefie, 114
Hannah, 285
Henry, 94, 114, 308
Hezekiah, *182
Jane, 291, 292
Janet, 199
Jesse, 113
John, 56, *94, 110, *114, *140, 159,
  *225, 227, 259, 267
John, Jr., 53
Joseph, 227
Joshua, 94, *146, *307
Luranah (Loranah), 91, 94, 137
Lydia, 198
Major, 94, *118
Mary, 104, 114, 182, 225, 226, 227,
  246, 269
McKenny, 285
Nancy, 140, 182, 198
Nunez, 225, 226
Parker, 140, *198
Piercy, 118
Polly, 307
Rachel, 179
Richard, 111, 114, 198, 225, 226,
  307
Ruth, 91
Sally, 228, 308
Samuel, 96, 104, 199, *291, 310
Sarah, 114, *141, 182
Shadrach, 226
Sophia, 91
Thomas, 231
Walter, 104, 222, 230
William, 91, 94, 114, *227, 257
Winifred, 198
Hufflington, Betsy, 270
  John, 270
  Jonathan, 270
  Littleton, 270
  Luke, 118, *229
  Mary, 229
  Nancy, 270
  William, 120
Huffman, Temperance, 231
Hugg, Elias, 83, *91, 99
  Mary, 91, 92, *99
Huggins, Charles, 63
  Philip, 61, 103
Hughes (Hughs), James, 11
  Mary, 166
  Phillip, 258
Huling, Elizabeth, 20
  Esther, 20

38

Martha, 20
Walton, *20
Humphrey (Humphreys,
Humphries)
James, 194
John, 242
Mary, *74
Hunt, William, 218
Hunter, Elizabeth, 89
Prudence, 248
Robert, 89, 248
Sarah, 89
Hurley, . . ., 174
Adam, 174
Caleb, 174
John, 174
Joshua, *174
Mary, 278
Nancy, 174
Pharah, 174, 181
Rachel, 199
Sarah, 181
Simon. 174
William, 174
William A., 283
Hurst, Joseph, 231
Nancy, 242
Hurt, George, 185
Sarah, 96
Huston, Parsons, 249
Sarah, 206
Hutcheson, Sarah, 226
William, 226
Hutchison, James, 69
Hutson, Mary, 229
Naoma, 164
Thomas, 109, *164
Walter, 304

—I—

Indian River Meeting House, 102
Ingram, Abigail, 222, *291
Ann, 210
Anthony, 297, 299
Betty, 61
Coane, 61
Charity, 61
Ellender, 210
Isaac, 61, 111, 210, *222, 291
Isaac, Sr., *111
Jacob, 210
Jacob, Sr., *61
Jane, 210
Jemima, 297, *300
Job, 56, 61, 117, 210, 261
John, 107, 210, 297, 300

John, Sr., 247
Margaret, 202
Mary, 220, 261
Nancy, 177, 210
Nathan, 291
Peggy, 300
Rachel, 111, 291
Robert, *210
Samuel, 291
Sarah, 210
Shilly, 61
Thomas, 210
Unice, 61
William, 117
Inkins, Comfort, *85
Esther, 60, 85
Hester, 60
Lydia, 60
Thomas, 59, *60
Inloes, (Inloss, Inlows, Inloyee)
Abharkin, 19
Abraham, 31, 32, 35
Anthony (Antony), 11, *19
Elizabeth, 19
Frances, 19
Peter, 19
Thomas, 19
Innis, Alexander, 20
Irons, . . ., 220
Aaron, 121, *144, 220, 271
David, 144, *248
Jacob, 121, 144, *191, 220
Jane, 29, 144, *220, *245
Lemuel, 144, 220, 245, 248
Naomi, 144
Rachel, 134, 144, 191
William, 29
Ironshire, William, 96
Irving, William, 215
Irwin, Esther, 186
Matthew, 186
Isaacs, Mary, 174
Ithell, Daniel, 12

—J—

Jackson, Augustus, *296
Clement, 162, 163
Elihu, 92
Elizabeth, 92, 163
James, 46, 49
Jeremiah R., 290
John, *38
Jonathan, 101
Joseph Bains, 38
Julius August, 159, 261
Lida, 87

Nancy, 298
Naomi, 107, 298
Peggy, 296
Penelope Holt, 126, *217
Phillis, 191
Polly, 191
Polly Wasdale, 262
Purnel, 298
Rachel, 296
Robert, 107, 180, 192, 235, *285
Samuel, 285
Sarah, 126, 176, 215
Scarborough, 295, 298
Susannah, 231
Tempy, 191
Thomas, 107, 133, 164, 202, *231, 272, *288, 298
Tryphena, 299
West, 191
White, 99
William, *99, 215, 254, 293
Wingate, 133, 202, 287, 288, 298
Zachariah, *133, 202
Zadock, 168
Joseph, Jacob, *277
Jeremiah, *155
Joseph, 207
Nathan, 155
Unicy, 268
Joyce, Samuel, *166
Juett (Juitt), Robert, 237
William, 131
William, Mrs., 131
Juley, Eleanor, *249
Nancy, 249
Polly, 249
Robert Cannon, 249
Julian, Elenor, 200
Jump, Leavin, 128
Olive, 201, 213, 231, 269
Sarah, 198
Justis, Robert, 18

## —K—

Kaning, Frances, 21
Kellam, (Kellum), Betsy, 280
Edward, *206
James, 206
Jesse, 243, 279
Prudence, 128, 178
Rhoda, 279
Samuel, 148, *178, 206
Thomas, *279
William, *280
Kelley (Kelly, Killey), Daniel, 251
Elizabeth, 61, 103
James, 103

Joseph, 269
Lovey, 103
Stacey, 269
Kelso (Kellso), Elizabeth, 242
Samuel, 30
Sarah, 242
Kender, (Kinder), Isaac, 221
Jacob, *221, 250
Jacob, Jr., 250
Maria, 221
Nancy, 221
Kendricks, James, *111
William, 111
Kenne, Mary, 71
Kennedy, Bart, 255
Kenney, Elijah, 148
Isaac, *148
Josiah, 148
Tabitha, 148
William, 148
Kerr, Samuel, 214
Kershaw, Mitchell, 168
Kervan, Alexander, 223
Felix, 223
Killam, Betty, 301
Killen, Dorcas, 274
Elizabeth, 289
Esther, 272
Mark, 272
William, 274
Killey: see Kelley
Killing, Abel, 189
Polly, 189
Killingsworth, Edward, 263
Hester, 263
John, 29, 83, 216, 263
John, Sr., *263
Leah, 263
Luke, 263
Mary, 263
Rachel, 263, 274
Sarah, 263
William, 216, 263
Killo, Isaac, Jr., 157
Sarah, 157
Kimmery, Aaron, 61
Jane, 61
Kimmey, (Kimmy), Aaron, 137
Abraham, 239
Jean, *137
Mary, 207, 217
Paterson, 217
Sanders, 122, 207, *217
Kinder: see Kender
King, . . ., 37
Anne, 45
Betty, 101, 106, *140, 203
Charles, 209, 263

Comfort, 209, 275
Conwell, 144
Cornelia, 99
David, 137, *303
David, Jr., 303
Edward, 187, 280
Elizabeth, 187, 203, *280
George, 303
Henry, *187
Hugh, *37, 64, 84, *137, 202, *203, 280
Isaac, 203
James, 37, 99, 137, 203
Jesse, 101
John, 137, 142, 177, *226
John Callaway, 226
Jonathan, 191
Joseph, 257
Joseph Windsor, 226
Levi, 147, 203
Margaret, 177
Mary, 87, 137, 142, 187, 201
Peggy, 226
Peter, 290
Philip, 37
Polly, 226, 227, 280
Prisilia, 37
Rebecca, 303, 304
Robert, Jr., 147
Sarah, 144
Thomas, 203
William, 31, 131, 137, 144, 191, 264, 304
Kinney, (Kinny), Annis, 219, 220
Elizabeth, 219
John, 219
Joshua, 112, *219
Mary, 219
Samuel, 219, 220
Sarah, 219
Kinneykin, Daniel, *244
Frances, 244
Matthew, 244
Sarah, 244
Waitman, 244
Kiphaven, (Kipshaven), . . ., 17
Dirrick, 17
Johannis, 15
John, 9, 10, *17
Martha, 9
Kirk, Barnet, 301
Basheba, 274
Betsey, 218
Charles, 274
Elizabeth, 42
Margaret, 301
Kirkpatrick, Harrison, 283
Hugh, 283

Jemima, 283
William, 271, *283
Kirll, Benjamin, 13
Knawood, Mary, 42
Knock, John, 221
Joseph, *221
Mary, 221, 232
Knowles, (Noles), . . ., 256
Agnes, 225
Betty, 225, *303
Celia, 303
Charles, 225, 303
Deans, 303
Edmond, 225
Elizabeth, 261
Ephraim, 225, 256
Esther, 285
Ezekiel, 243
James, 225, 259
Nancy, 303
Patience, 220, 267
Prudence, 225
Rhoda, 285
Richard, 225, 285
Richard, Sr., *225
Samuel, 20
Sarah, 261
Thomas, 225, 259, 285
William, 236
Zachariah, 225
Knox, Charles, 166, 182
Dorinda, 156
Elisha, 78
James, 250
John, *166, 232
Leah, 289
Margery, 166
Mary, *232, 290
Sarah, 289
Thomas, *289
Kollock, Alice, 68
Comfort, 57
Cornelius, (Cornelus), 29, 68, 81
Elizabeth, 68, 109, 292
George, 68, *109
Hannah, 29, 239
Hercules, 68, 109
Hester, 29, 90, 239
J., 288
Jacob, 17, 27, *29, 32, 40, 47, 48, 50, 57, 74, *90, 100, *220, 222, 239
Jacob, Jr., 27, 90
Jacob Moore, 211
John, 239
John Leech, 220
Leah, 144, 193
Magdalane, 29

Elizabeth, 93, 97, 116, 168, *265, 279
Gabriel, 180
George, 116, 180
Grace, 180, 197, 301
Hannah, 301
Heavelo, 301
Isaac, 97, 242
James, 301
Jemime, 56, 65
John, 56, 65, 93, 94, 97, 180, 184, 187, 197, 216, 233, 241, 242, 263, 300
John, Jr., 86, 94
John, Sr., *93
Jonathan, 301
Joshua, 216, *240, 265
Littleton, *301
Luke, 301
Margaret, 180, 301
Mary, 65, 93, *97, 227, 244
Nancy, 180
Nicey, 308
Nutter, 215
Phebe, 216
Priscilla, 56
Purnal, 97
Rachel, 93
Rhoda, 65
Roseanna, 65
Sarah, 56, 65, 93, 97, 258
Solomon, 300
Susannah, 93
Temperance, 226
Watson, 97
William, 56, 85, 100, 145, 152, *180, 219, 301
Zadock, 93, *226
Lofly, (Loflee), Elizabeth, 71
Gabriel, 65, *71
Grace, 49
Joshua, 71
Meriam, 71
Loncom: see Lecompt
Long, Ann, 229
Armwell, 229
Benjamin, 182, 224, 229
Betty, 175
Daniel, 191
Daniel Horatio, 296
Daniel O., 280
David, 229
David, Sr., *229.9
Elijah, 191, 296
Elinor, 286
Elisha, 121, *191, 280, *296
Horatio, 191
John, *183, 229

Mary, 183, 191
Naomi, 298
Solomon, *286, 298
Longcomb: see Lecompt
Longeon, Rachel, 107
Lord, Adam, 131, 251
Betsy, 131
Isaac, 131, 230
John, *131, 251, 290
Sarah, 131
Thomas, 131
William, 131
Wootten, 131
Lotton, James, *9
Loucom: see Lecompt
Loughten, Cornelius, 41
Dormond, 41
Elizabeth, 41
Gabriel, 41
John, *41
Persilia, 41
Rosanna, 41
William, 41
Love, James, *71
Lovine, John, 53
Lowe, (Low), Ann, 243
Elinor, 243
George, 259
James, 243
James Rencher, 243
John, 243, 259
Nicey, 259
Ralph, *243, 259
Robert, 146
Sarah, 259
Thomas Cooper, 259
William, 160, 243, *259
Lowry, Frances, 245
James, 206, *245
Lucas, Peter, *29
Sarah, 29
Ludenum, Aden, 287
Elizabeth, 213
John, *213
Lucy, 213
Margaret, 213
Mary, 213
Sarah, 213
Selah, 213
Shadrach, 213
Thomas, 233
Luke, Catherine, 137
William, 137
Luker, Catharine, 244, 291
Leah, 291
William, *244, *291
Lupecuea, John, 23

Lynch, (Linch), Abram, 295
  Betty, 295
  Bolitha, 295
  Eli, 295
  Hannah, 192, 295
  Isaac, 242, 268
  Jacob, 140, *212, 295
  John, 103, 192, *295
  John, Jr., 275
  Maria, 295
  Michael, 156
  Mires, 295
  Nancy, 170, 295
  Phebe, 212
  Sarah, 140, 241
Lynam, William, 275
Lynn, Magdelan, 147
  Moses, *147

## —Mc—

McAfee, Margaret, 59
McBride, William, 104
McCabe, Obediah, 182
McCalley: see McCauley
McCallister, Daniel Miller, 297
McCalvaine: see McIlvaine
McCarrell, Anne, 45, 50
  James, 50
  Robert, 45, *50
McCarthy, Dennis, 36
McCaskey, Alexander, 186
  Hannah, 186
McCauley, (McCalley, McColley,
  Maccally, MacCalley)
  Anthaliner, 144
  Betsey, 231
  Daniel, 209
  Eli, 144, 185, 254
  John, 209
  Robert, 185, 209
  Robert M., 142
  Robert W., 131, 144, 191, 207, 208,
    215, 252
  Robert Watson, 104, 129, 154, 209
  Sarah, 277
✓ McCay, Alexander, 91, *154
  Catharine, 154
  Naomi, 91, 154
  Phebe, 154
  Spencer, 154
  William, 154
McColley: see McCauley
McCormick, John, *226
  Sarah, 226
  William, 261
McCracken, David, Jr., *105
  Elihu, 105, 273

McCullah (Macculah, Mckollah)
  Alexander, 25, 27
  John, 33, 95, *139
McCulley, Alexander, *33
McDaniel (Macdaniel), Daniel, 34
  Elizabeth, *245
  James, 195
  Margaret, 195
  Moses, 174, 185, *195
  Sarah, 195, 196
  Zachariah, 209
McDermont, Mary, 274
McDowell, (McDowel, Macdowell)
  Andrew, 77
  Charity, 285
  Elizabeth, 285
  Isaac, 107
  Joshua, *285
McElvain (McElvaine): see
  McIlvaine
McFarling, Elizabeth, 230
  William, *230
McGee: see Magee
McGonigal, Robert, 264
McHam, Evan, 167
  Peter Bagwell, 304
McIlvaine (McIlvain, McCalvaine,
  McElvain, Muckelvaine,
  Mucklewaine)
  . . ., 36, 205
  Alexander, 36, 196, 204, 205
  Andrew, *36, 63, 76, 83, *204, 205
  Andrew, Jr., 211
  Arcada, 162
  Benjamin, 204, 276
  Comfort, 204, 205, 230
  Comfort Waples, 205
  Cornelia, 162
  David, 63, 154, 167, 245
  David Mills, 162
  Ellen, 203
  Frances, 63
  Francis, 71
  George, 36, 63
  Hessy, 203
  Jacob, 63
  James, 36, *63, 74, *154, 205, *234
  James, Jr., 64, *133
  James Mills, 204, *230
  Jane Craig, 64
  Jean, 165
  Jean J., 74
  Jenny, 203
  John, *36, 63
  Leonard, 188, 204, 205
  Lydia, 63
  Martha, 36
  Mary, 55, 63, 204, 211

Mills, 63, 83, *162
Mills, Jr., 291
Polly, 203
Prudence, 162
Robert, 63
Sarah White, 204
Shepherd, *203
Sophia, 133
Thomas Waples, 204
William, 154, *167
Winifred, 63
Wrixam, 204
McIntosh, Mary, 44
McKee, Andrew, 36
William, 36
McKelvy, William, 51
McKnatt, Ann, 255
Deborah, 255
James, 255
John, 255
McKnight, Ann, 247
James, 247
McKollah: see McCullah
McLander, Nicholas, 32
McMain, Ann, 86
McMichael, Robert, 247
McMillin, James, 38
McNaight: see McKnight
McNeal (McNeill)
James, 106, 137, *196
Jane, 196
Jannett, 106
John, 62
Margaret, 62
Neall (Neill), 49, *62
Sarah, 149
William, *149

# —M—

Maccally: see McCauley
Maccay: see McCay
Maccullah: see McCullah
Macdaniel: see McDaniel
Macdowell: see McDowell
Mackain, David, 37
Mackemy, John, 92
Mackimme, Abraham, 96
Macklain, David, 41
Macklin, (Macklen), Charles, 127,
162, *274
Eli, 274
Elizabeth, 127, 274
Hester, 170, 172
Job, 170, 172
Rachel, 61, 170, *172
Sarah, 61

Thomas, 137, *170
MacKnab, Joseph, *22
Macloh, John, 22
Maddox, (Maddux, Madock)
Joshua, 43
Lazarus, *201
Mary, 201, 261
Zephenias, 131
Magee (Megee, McGee)
Benjamin, *286
David, *282
Ephraim, 296
John, 226, 231
Joshua, 213, 226, 278, 286, 296
Mary, 226, *231
Nancy, 278
Samuel, *226
Maloney, (Melony), Manuel, 171
Richard, 73, *205
Susanna, *171
William, 171, 256, 302
Maniel, Martha, 75
Manley, Mark, 21
Thomas, 17, 21
Manlove, (Manloves), . . ., 23, 49,
286
Alexander, 286
Anne, 26
Betty, 87, 93
Boaz, 49, 89, 95, 105
David, 160
Elizabeth, 41, 43, 61, 87
Emanuel, 48
George, 87, *188, 286
John, Jr., 18
Jonathan, 49, 87, *164
Magdalene, *87, 286
Manuel, *49, 87, *93
Mark, *26
Mary, 23, 26, 41, 305
Richard, 23
Robinson, 160
Ruth, 62
Sally, 188
Sarah, 23, 41, 87, 160
Thomas, *23, 26
Mann, John, 181
Rachel, 181, 216
Manship, Henry, 208
Marine, Betsy, 249
Charles, 249
Charles F., 300
John, 150, 249
Matthew, Jr., 264
Matthew, Sr., 264
Sally, 249
Thomas, 249

Rhoda, 187
Sarah, 166, 187
Susannah, 286
William, *22, 270, 279
Massey, . . ., 130
Absolem, *293
Ann, 144
Bershaba, 209
Caty, 105
Daniel, *130
Elisha, 209, 275
Elizabeth, 209
Esther, 112
Ezekiel, 130
George, 17
Greenberry, 182
Harriet, 130
Harvey, 66
Isaac, 144, *209
Jane, 233
Job, 144, 209
John, 144
John, Jr., *233
John, Sr., 138
Joseph, 66, 130, *144
Kendal, 130
Levin, *185
Mary, 209
Milley, 185
Mitchell, 130
Moses, 144
Nancy, 209, 233
Naomi, 66, 144, 220, 233
Phillip, 209
Robert, 86
Samuel, 144, 245
Sarah, 130
Sophia, 185
Susanna, 130
Thomas, *66
Whittington, 185
William, *17, 233
Masten, (Mastin), Gilbert, 126
John, *126, 290
Rebecca, 126
Sarah, 105, 126
Mathvin: see Methvin
Matthews, (Mathews), David, 215
James, 215
Levi, 215
Mary, 184, 215
Philip, 215, 293
Priscilla, 215
Teague, 162, *215
William, 200, 214
Maull, John, 54, 78
Mary, 84

Maxwell, Elizabeth, 72
John, *72
Nanny, 129
Nimrod, 184, *296
May, Ann (Anne), *43, 94, 115, 121, *142
Anna, 30
Benjamin, 45
Betsy (Betty), 49, 115, 121, 149
Draper, 106, 107, 115, 121, 142, *196
Elizabeth, 30, 34, 47, 62
John, 24, 28, *30, 33, 34, 37, 38, 40, 42, 43, 49
Jonathan, 34, 43, 46, 49, *82, 115, 121, *142
Lucilla, 30
Margaret, (Margret), 30, 34, 112
Mary, 13, 30, 107, 115, *121, 142
Philip, 265
Rosin (Rosen), 30, 34
Sarah, 30, 34
Thomas, 13, 17, *34, 90, 94, 106, 107, *115, 121, 142
Thomas, Jr., 26, 28, *30
Meads, John, 270, *286
Polly, 270, 286
Means, Esther, 210, 276
Nelly, 276
Mears, Hannah, 129, 133
Mease, James, 203
Mecotter, William, *106
Megee: see Magee
Melony: see Maloney
Meloy, Sarah, 272
Thomas, 272
Melson, Benjamin, 280, 298
Betsey (Betty), 161, 165
Daniel, 203, *298
Daniel, Jr., 166
Elijah, *253, 298
Elizabeth, 253, 298
John, *166, 262, 298
Joseph, *132, 211, 298
Love, 298
Mary Ann, 132
Nancy, 176, 234, 285, 298
Sarah, 262, 298
Tabitha, 298
William, *234
Merrick (Merick), Nancy, 283
Polly, 283
Sarah, *134, 283
Merrill, Elizabeth, 282
Messick, . . ., 273
Ann, 127
Anna, 172
Annace, 170

Bethany, 127
Bridget, 294
Covington, 127
Elizabeth, 250, 293
Eusebia, 273
George, 103, 117, 127, *136, 190, *294
Hannah, 214, 301
Isaac, *127, 294
James, 227
Job, 136
John, 103, 127, 214
Johnson, 224
Joseph, 127
Leonard, 103
Levi, 250
Luke, 127
Mary, 135
Meley, 136
Minus, 136
Nehemiah, 127
Obediah, *192
Patience, 136, 262
Rachel, 136
Rebecca, 103
Sally, 218
Sarah, 170, 172, 192, 199, 227
Upsherd, 155
Metcalf, (Melcalfe), Betty, 90
Elizabeth, 71
Hester, 284
John, 90, 178
Richard, 52, *71
Methodist Conference, 213
Methvin, (Mathvin), James, 238
Mary, *238
Meshack, 238
Thomas, 238
Metten, James, 66
Meulah, John, 22
Mezzick, Patience, 61
Micker, Daniel, 36
Middleton, Dickerson, 288
Eleanor, 296
James, *288
Siney, 199
Susanna, 288
William, 288
Mideap, John, 112
Midghey, Thomas, 15
Miers, Ann, 56
Edward, *29
Elizabeth, 38
Hester, 61
James, 29, 38
John, 18, 22, 25, *29, 38, 56
Margery, 48, 53, *61
Mary, 28, 29, *38, 53, 61

Mary M., 22
Sarah, 29, 38
Mifflin, Anne, 282
Benjamin, *186
Edward, 28
Mary, 28
Sarah, 186, *300
Warner, 282
Milby, Ann, 133
Archady, 188
Arthur, 188
Elizabeth, *128
John, 128, 188
Joseph Hazard, 188
Levin, 128, *188
Mary, 128
Nanny, 188, 304
Nathaniel, 128, 188
Patience, 128
Polly, 128
Sarah, 128
William, 128
Zadoc, 128, 188, *304
Miles, Hudson, 130
Millard, Anna, 282
Mary, 203, 216
William, 203, 217, 278, 280, 282
Miller, . . ., 135
Anne, 41
Bathsheba, 135, *237
Burton, 136
Comfort, 136
David, 135, 237
Elizabeth, 41
James, 212, 237
John, 41, 102, 135, *183, 237
Joseph, *135, 199, 237
Lucilla, 125
Mary, 41, 136
Nancy, 135
Nanny, 102
Nathaniel, 135, 136
Peter, *125
Rachel, 183
Robert, *41
William, 41
Milles, Levin, *129
Millington, John, 11, *12
Millinor, William, 18
Mills, Agnes, 59
Bowman, 59
Edward, *59
John, 114
Littleton, 59
Luke, 59
Margaret, 142, 293
Nathan, 59
Richard, 186, 293

Mary, 82, 152, 240
Mary Horsey, 240
Nancy, 147, 240
Nanny, 309
Newbold, 276
Patty, 240
Polly, 215
Priscilla, 240
Rachel, 291
Robert, 147, *215
Samuel, 235, 240
Sarah, *224
Shiles, 147, 187, 225, 236
Temperance, 147
Thomas, 75, 78, 82, 198, 235, *240
William, *137, 143, 147, *152, 178
   213, 235, 240, 294
William, Jr., 257
William, Sr., *257
Zipporah, 291
Morain, Charles, 147
Morgan, . . ., 14, 263
  Ann, 249
  Anna, 286
  Avery, 50, 134, 284
  Daniel, 198, 274
  Edward, 14
  Elijah, 121, 148
  Elizabeth, 256
  Evan, 125
  George, 249
  George Williams, 249
  Hannah, 81
  Jacob, 81
  John, 30, 152, *293
  Joseph, 53, 55, 97
  Joshua, 107
  Levina, 107
  Mary, 15, 271, 274
  Noah, 176
  Parker, 286
  Peggy, 271
  Rebeckah, (Rebecca), 148, 191
  Robert, 81
  Sarah, 263
  Sarah Johnson, 148
  Tabitha, 271
  William, 249
Morris, Ann, 220, 269
  Antoney, Sr., 20
  Betty, 62, 289
  Bevins, (Beavins, Bevan), 53, *78,
    109, *167, 204, 272, 279
  Burton, 289
  Comfort, 145
  Curtis, 145, 199, 267
  Daniel, *145, 231, 300
  Daniel, Jr., 126

Daniel, Sr., 126
Dennis, 78, 214, *250
Elinor, 151
Elizabeth, 20, 258, 299, 300
Endless, 99
Endless, Mrs., 99
Ezekiah, 188, *269
George, *219, 250
Grace, 151
Hannah, 145, 245
Hezekiah, 126, 145, *269
Isaac, *204, 256, *268
Jacob, 78, *215, 250, 269, 289
Jane, 269
Jehu, 302
Jeremiah, *151, 250
Jerusha, 109
John, *30, 92, 145, 169, 190, *214,
   *256, *262, 289
John M., 267
John Masten, 213
Joseph, 215, 241, 268, 289, 292
Joshua, 86, 250, 292
Lacey, 289
Leah, 167
Lydia, 145
Mary, 30, 78, 219, 269
Masten, 145
Nancy, 308
Nathaniel, 145
Nehemiah, 276, 283, *302
Noah, 78, 250
Obediah, 151
Phebe, 94, 241
Polly, 262, 308
Rachel, 301
Robert, 289
Samuel, 114
Sarah, 145, 268, 279, 302
Stephen, 245
Susannah, 145
Tabitha, 220
Tamar, (Tamer), 232, *245
Thomas, 300
William, 78, 130, *232, 245, *289,
   300
Morrison, Joseph, *246
  Sarah, 167
Mosely, . . ., 260
  Absolem, *260
  Curnell, 260
  Purnell, 260
Moss, William, 164
Mouleston (Mouliston, Moulliston):
  see Molleston
Muckelvaine (Mucklewaine): see
  McIlvaine

## —O—

57

Peggy, 273
Peter, 71, 72, 152, *157, 186, *195, 232, 241, 288
Rachel, 168
Ruth, 168
Sarah, 176, 273
Susannah, 39
Thomas, 71
William, 71, 82
William Anderson, 29
Zipporah, 176
Parks, Edy, 132
William, 132
Parling, Barbara, 9
Elizabeth, 9
Simon, 9
Parmor (Parmer, Parmore, Parrmore)
Alexander 132
Eusabia, 273
James, 61
Joseph, 251, *254
Levin, 209
Lisa, 209
Mary, 132, 251
Rachel, 209
Sarah, 260
Sheldon Dorman, *273
Stephen, 209
Tabitha, 209
William, 209
Parremore (Paremore, Parimore, Parramore, Parrimore)
. . ., 207
Alexander, 61
Elizabeth, 153
Ezekiel, 153
Job, 278
John, 61, 77
Leah, 244
Martha, 207
Mary, 129, *178
Matthew, *129, *153, 162, 197
Patrick, 153, *207
Richard, 77
Solomon, Sr., 156, 177, *209
Stephen, 197
Tabitha, 156, 177
Thomas, 153, 176, 207
William, 77
Parsley, Abraham, 23, 42, 48
Frances, 43
Samuel, Jr., 251, 267, 285, 303
Comfort, 129
Isaac, 42
John, *42, 141
Neomy, 42
Sarah, 36, 42

Thomas, 42
Passwaters, . . ., 262, 275
Clement, 280
David, 88
Isaac, 262
Jesse, 280
John, 280
Jonas, 275, 280
Mary, 258
Nancy, 275, 280
Richard, 258, *262
Sarah, 280
William, 262, *280
William, Sr., *275
Patchett, Frances, 237
Patte, . . ., 14
Ann, 14
John, 14
Lidey, 14
Richard, *14
Patterson (Paterson), . . ., 264
Hugh, *264
Mary, 32
Thomas, 32
Patton, Rachel, 129
Pauling, Simon, 17
Paynter, . . ., 53
Comfort, 63
Cornelius, 308
Dogood (Doegood), 32, 53
Elizabeth, 81, 100
Hannah, 81
James, 40
Jenny, 282
John, 32, 40, 74, 81, *138, *244
John, Sr., *40
Lemuel, 244
Lemuel Coleson (Collison), 89, *146
Lida, 170
Margaret, 30, 32
Mary, 40, 53, 62, 80, 94
Priscilla, 244
Rees (Reese), 94, 138, 215
Richard, *15, 19, 20, 22, 30, *32, 40, *53, 73, 94, 138, 244, 288
Samuel, 40, 64, 71, 74, 81, 90, 94, 98, 138, 247, 296
Samuel, Jr., 51, 267, 285, 303
Samuel, Sr., *81, 114
Sarah, 15
William, 40
Peake, Lewis, 286, 294
Pearce: see Pierce
Pearson, Caty, 141
Peck, Mary, 87
Peery, Aaron, *305

William, 90, 93, 104, 108, 109, **113**, 130, 137, 138, 156, 171, 187, 199, 209, 214
Peets, Marcellus, 294
Pegg, Mary, 110
Pemberton, . . ., 42
  Joseph, *42
  Mary, 20
  Susanna, 42, 53
  Thos., 13, 17, 20
Penn, John, 84
Pennington, Benedict, *197, 213
  Deborah, 24
  Henry, *24
Pennuel, Samuel, 289
  Sarah, 289
Penoyre, Danel, 33
Penton, Esther, 130
  Philip, *130
Peplo: see Pepperlo
Pepper, Anna, 279
  Isabel, 220
  Joshua, 131
  Levin, 303
  Watson, 194, 270
  Willy, 303
Pepperlo, Joseph, 28, *38
Perkins, George, 26
  Hugh, 26
  James Dough, 185
  John, 132
  Mary, 237
  Polly, 237
  Solomon, 185
Perris, Robert, 39
Perry (Perrie), Aaron, 159, 255
  Catherine, 71
  Charles, 63, *71
  Ellinor, 71
  Ester, 19
  Mary, 149, 255
  Robert, 29
  Rowlin, *19
  William, 89
  Winifred, 71
Peterkin, David, 50, 51
  James, 14
  Thomas, 50
Peters, Abigail, 79, 151
  Elizabeth, 79
Pettion, Susanna, 22
Pettit, Edmund, 202, 288
  Edward, 229
  Ephraim, 253
  Eunice, 232
  Jacob, 90, 232
  Joanna, 90
  Laban, *90

Rachel, 202, 229
Pettyjohn, . . ., 70
  Aaron, 142, *284
  Abraham, 60
  Ann, 58
  Anzelah, 197
  Bridget, 245
  Charlotte, 128
  Comfort, 142
  Ebenezer, 177
  Elizabeth, 33, 58, 129, 131, 284
  Ephama, 309
  Hannah, 58, 60, 141, *197
  Isabell, 30, 42, 58
  Jacob, 60
  James, 42, 61, 197, 245
  James, Jr., 58, 60
  James, Sr., *60
  Jane, 142
  Job, 197
  John, 30, 36, *42, 58, 77, *141, 142, 197, *198
  John, Jr., 30, 60
  Leah, 197
  Levina, 55
  Lydia, 60
  Major, 60
  Margaret, 58
  Mary, 209
  Naomi, 60
  Patience, 197
  Richard, 30, 42, *58, 77, 197
  Ruth, 128, 129
  Samuel, 60
  Sarah, 55, 70, 142
  Sinderiah, 197
  Thomas, *30, 60, 142
  Thomas, Sr., *142
  William, 36, 42, *55, 60
  Zachariah, 131
Pey, John, 13
Phelman, Thomas, 16
Philby, Elizabeth, 177
Phillips, Benjamin, 122, 124, **126**, 135, 138, 164, 175, 211, 222, **262**, 298, *301
  Betty, 175
  Elzy, 301
  Hester, 74
  Jacob, 40, 50, 52, 56, *74
  John, 196, 211, 262, 298, 301
  John, Sr., 196, *262
  Joseph, 196, 262, 298
  Lavinia, 196
  Mary, 196, 262
  Priscilla, 301
  Purnal, 301
  Sarah, 196, 262, *298

Margaret, *287
Polly Jane, 287
Priscilla, *145
William, 287
Polson, Edward, 294
William, *294
Ponder, Daniel, 26
Elizabeth, 84, 88, 98, 187
Elsie, 88
Esther, 88
James, 26, 187
Jemima, 61
John, *26, 88, *187
Margaret, 26
Mary, 26, 39
Rosannah, 26
Sarah, 26, 88
Pool, Andrew, 247, 251
Betsey, 247, 251
John, 302
Major (Meger), 171, *247
Perry, 171, 247
Sally, 247
William, 247
Poor, Jemima, 91
Joshua, 91
Lorana, 91
Luke, 91
Major, 91
Margaret, 91
Mary, *91
Naomi, 91
Phebe, 91
Pope, Francis, 30
William, 304
Porter, David, 193
Lucretia, 193
Martha, 114
Mary, *193
Rebecca, 193
William, 193
Positt, Mary, 96
Postles, John, 100
Thomas, *100
Postly, Anne, 96
John, 96
Potter, Abraham, *48
Comfort, 149, *198
Cornelius, 74
Jacamen, 297
Jane, *19
John, 48, *149, 198
Joshua, 48
Seagoe (Seco), 100, 136, 297, 301
Powders, Mary, 120
Powell, Betsy, 292
Charles, 44
Levi, 207

Nancy, 299
Rhoda, 109, 110
William, 42, 133, 299, 300
Poynter (Pointer), . . ., 137
Castelia, 107, 122
Esther, 137
Eunice, 137
John, 137
Levin, 137
Mary, 132
Nathaniel, *132, 137
Peninah, 132
Radcliff (Ratcliff), 107, 132, 138, 197
Ruth, 137
Sally, 227
Thomas, 132
William, 91, *107, 122, 132, *137, 189
Pratt (Prat), Bridget, 47
Charles, 47, 63
Elizabeth, 272
Mary, 31
Prentice, Ruth, 68
Presbyterian Churches, Sussex County, 97
Presbyterian Meeting House, 91, 180
Preston, Samuel, 13, 15, 16, 17, 18
Prettyman, Allenar (Elinor), 96
Ann, 30, 54, 63, 98
Aseny, 225
Benjamin, 74, 98, 235, 261, 302
Betty, 50, 54, 55, 86, 289
Burton, 79, 89, 99, 190, 220
Catherine, 30
Comfort, 27, 54, 68, 74, 76, 85, *89, 92, 93, 100, 308
Elinor, 63, 96
Eleanor Craig, 64
Elizabeth, 27, 35, 52, 63, 74, 83, 85, 89, *115, 125, 183, 200, 220, 232, 234
Esther, 55
George, 165, 220
Hessy, 220
Isaac, 54, *80, *234
Jacob, 54, 308
James, 32, 235
Jean (Jeanne), 74, 98
John, 27, 30, 32, *52, 54, *63, 68, *308
John, Sr., *32
Joseph, 54, 80, 85, 98
Leah, 85
Magdalen (Magdalena, Magdelene), 79, 83, 89
Margaret, 52, 223

63

Patience, 11, 15, 41
William, 41, 83
Ricards (Ricords): see Rickards
Rich, Roddy, 243
Richards, . . ., 274
  Bathsheba, 237
  Benjamin, 102
  David, 102, 216, 266, *274
  Elizabeth, 19
  Ellenor, 9
  Elsie, 19
  Grace, 19
  Henry, 216
  Isaac, 102, *139
  Jacob, 102, 288
  James, *157
  Jean Prettyman, 102
  Jenny, 237
  John, 11, 12, *16, 34, 149, *216,
    248, 274
  John, Sr., *19
  Joseph, *248
  Joshua, 98, *102
  Levin, 250
  Margaret, 216
  Mary, 16, 19, 216
  Nancy, 216
  Patience, 102
  Polly, 274
  Robert, *9
  Sarah, 11, 216
  Tamzey, 249, 300
  Temperance, 102
  William, 16, 18, 157, 216, 249
Richardson, Betty, 308
  Elizabeth, 18
  Elzey, 245, 308
  Francis, 52
  Mary, 149
  Sarah, *244
Richie, Alexander, 35
  Hugh, 35
Rickards (Ricards, Ricords,
  Riccords)
  . . ., 138, 291
  Agnes, 245
  Amelia, 291
  Ann, 61, *79, 238, 248
  Benjamin, 68, *239
  Betty, 225, 242, 244, 303
  Charles, 170, 180, *233, 238, 248
  Comfort, 78, 79
  Dirickson, 212
  Eli, 212, 272
  Elias, 242, *303
  Elisha, 236
  Elizabeth, 79, 138, 291
  Esther, 239, *298

George, 169, *291
Hannah, 225
Hap, 239, 308
Hap H., 308
Hap Hazzard, 298
Isaac, 303
James, 82, 92, 239, 298, 303
Jehu, 138, *188
Job, 212
John, 61, 78, *107, 123, 225, 239,
  *242, *284, *287, 298, 303, 308
Jones, 157, 193, *212
Joseph, *92, 180, 248
Levin, 79, 180, 239, 272, 298, *303
Loxley, 180, 205, 272, 301
Lucy, 212
Luke, 225, 245, 284, 299
Manlove, 291
Margaret, 138, 225, 295, 299
Mary, 157, 180, 212, 225, 284, *295
Michael, *138
Mills, 245, 265
Molton, 245
Nancy, 301
Neoma, 107
Peggy, 284
Polly, 303'
Peter, 107
Priscilla, 239, 298, 308
Reece, 186
Rhoda, 212
Samuel, *61
Sarah, 61, 92, 273
Stayton, 287
Susan, 212
Susannah, 118
Thomas, 79, 279, 291, 303
William, 59, 134, 138, 153, 157, 180,
  188, 208, 215, *225, *245, 261,
  284
William, Jr., *299
Zadoc, 287
Rickets, Ann, 229
  Edward, 38
  Judith, 37, 38
  Reece, *229
Rider, . . ., 153
  Betty, *235, 281
  Charles, 153, 212, 235, 237
  Elizabeth, 153
  George, *153, 281
  John, 153, 212, 214, *237
  Susannah, 73
  Wilson, 153, *212
Riggin, Euphame, 161
  Isabella, 161
  James, 141, *161
  Joshua, *161

Nathan, 223, 271, 283
Robert, 262
Silas, *209
Savage, Nancy, 175
Peggy, 175
Robinson, *175
Say, Ann, 127
Elizabeth, 127
Mary, *127
Scarborough, Nathaniel, 21
Scheavam, Benjamin Dazey, 269
Leah, 269
Schofield (Schoolfield), . . ., 145
Angelitta, 109, 179
Ann, 145
Benjamin, 110, 118, *145
Benjamin, Sr., *109
Bridgett, 109, *110
Diligance, 109, 110
Henry, 109, 110
John, 109, 110
Joseph, 109, 110, *179
Mary, 109
Rebecca, 110
William, 109, 110, 145
Scidmer: see Skidmore
Scott, Jane, 13
John, 257
Nancy, 291
Sally, 291
Thomas, 10
Scouvemont, Ferdinand, 223
Nicholas Joseph, *223
Scroggin (Scrogin), Eunice, 202
George, 149, 187
Samuel, 187
Thomas, 187
Scudder, Chloe (Cloe), 89, 103
David, *59
Jonathan, 59, 60, *89, 103
Mary, 59, 60
Moses, 60, 82
Nancy, 158, 229
Rachel, 89
Sealtown, Baily, 25.
Elizabeth, 25
James, *25
Sedger, Joseph, 277
Selaven, Eleanor, 308
Sellers, Francis, 138
Semmons, Ann, 154
Sarah, 154
Semare, Leah, 77
Senew, May, 22
Torlah, *22
[Servant], Adam, 169
Black Will, 12
Esther, 169

Hannah, 169
Isaac, 169
Jacob, 169
Major, 169
Timothy, 48
Sethredge: see Saltredge
Seymour, . . ., 37
Ebenezer, *37
Shahan (Shehan), Daniel, 200
Daniel, Jr., 200
Jonathan, 105
Shaltham, Jacob, *10
Shand, Randle, 9
Shankland, . . ., 46, 259
Alexander, 83, 91
David, 46, 125, 141, 165, 183, 231
Edward, 141
Elijah, 165
Elise, 252
Elizabeth, 39, 141
Esther, 39, 46
Frances, 67
James, 67, 72
Joe, Jr., 78
John, 24, 39, *46, 67, 87, 125, 141
Joseph, 26, 39, 46, 67, 88, 141
Joseph, Jr., 66, 99
Mary, 46, 91, 235, 259
Naomy, 87, 88
Patience, 83
R., 39
Rhoda, 197
Rhodes (Rhoads, Roads), 82, 84,
91, 125, 126, 137, 197
Robert, 25, 39, 41, 46, 67, 72, 91,
227, 239, 296
Robert, Jr., 231, 280
Samuel, 67, 113, *252
Sarah, 39, 46, 68, 88, 91, 271
Susannah, 67
William, 21, 32, 39, 46, 51, 75, 84,
264
William W., Sr., *39
Shanks, Ann, 266
David, 266
Edward, 266
John Kilman, 266
Sharp (Sharpe), Amelia, 295
Ann, 135
Anna Maria, 43
Betsey, 172, 208
Comfort, 135
Elizabeth, 103, *135, 211
Jacob, 295
James, 135, *172
Job, *295
John, 172, 211, 236, 262, 295, 305
John T., 298

Simonton, Ann, 39
 Comfort, 59
 Elizabeth, 59
 Jean, 59
 John, *59
 Margaret, 59, *88
 Mary, 38, 59
 Sarah, 59
 Theopolus, 38
Simpler, Aaron, 139
 Anderson, 171
 Andrew, 171, 203, *251
 Comfort, 251
 George, 251
 Jacob, 139
 Leah, 86
 Margaret, 171, *203
 Milby, 200, 251
 Nanny, *251
 Paul, *171
 Philip, *136
 Polly, 251
 Susannah, 136, 139
 Thomas, 139
 William, 139, 171, 203, 251
Simpson, (Simson), Alice, 118
 E., 34
 Elizabeth, 39, 62
 James, 19, 20, 21, 28, 29, 30, 39
 Jemima, 107
 John, 243
 Margaret, 21, 25, 32, 37, 39, *62,
  243
 Peter, *243
 Samuel, 243
 William, 243
Sims, Henrietta, 71, *84
 Sarah, 71
Sipple, Sarah, 269
Sirman (Sirmane), Abigail, 126
 Anne, 153
 Betty (Betsy), 202, 211
 Elizabeth, 153, 202, *211
 George, 175
 James, 169
 Jennie, 175
 Job, *126
 John, *153, 211
 Levin, 202, 211
 Louder, 126, *202, 211
 Mary, 126
 Nancy, 126, 151, 202
 Nelly, 151, 202
 Rachel, 62, 260
 Thomas, 62
 William, 126
Skidmore, . . ., 70
 Elijah, 70

 Elizabeth, 70, 147, 158
 Henry, 29, 70, 147, *278
 Jane, 81
 Jean, 78
 Lydia, 147
 Mary, 78, 88
 Sarah, 147
 Thomas, 65, 70, 117, *147
Slantford, Emealea, 147
 Patience, 147
Small, Polly, 208
Smith, . . ., 34, 136
 Abraham, 69, 112
 Adam, 39
 Alexander, 189, 206, 237, *257
 Alice, 122
 Allen, 122, 182, 243, *244
 Ann (Anne), 31, 39, 103, 219, 230
 Anna, 305
 Archibald, 30, *38
 Bartholomew, 154, 175
 Benjamin, 79
 Benton, 101
 Bette, 70
 Betty (Betsy), 46, *70, 121, 249,
  300
 Cannon, 243
 Charity, 154, 175
 Charles, 89
 Charlotte, 122
 Charlton, 103
 Clement, 251
 Comfort, 70
 Constantine, 228, 300, 305
 Constantine Jacob, 300
 Curtis, 122, 148, 194, *228
 David, 35, 45, 46, *62, 70, 112,
  *113, 219, 293, 301
 Elizabeth, 34, 79, 80, 81, 113, 122,
  123, 135, 246, 268, 276, 298
 Ephraim, 292
 Esther, 140
 Eunice, 193
 Ezekioh, 121
 Ezekiel, 249, *300
 Feeby, 31
 George, *122, 194, *243
 Grace, 305
 Henry, 11, *13, 34, 59, 80, *107,
  122, 174, 228, 243, 245, 251, 252,
  260, 280
 Henry, Capt., 20
 Hester, 31, 193
 Holms, 276
 Hudson, 228
 Humphrey, 24
 Isaac, 79, 128, 134, *136
 Isaac, Esq., 99

Elizabeth, 94, 95, 183, 193, 227, 288
George, 10, 78, 94
Hezekiah, 50, 76, 89
James, *103, 162, 184, 218, 249, *301
James, Sr., *184
Jane, 261
Jehu, 76, 77
Jesse, 49
John, 89, 94, 95, 113, 127, *154, 184, 218, 261, 292
John, Sr., *261
Joseph, *49, 77, 89, 91, 94, 97, 100, 114, 136, *177, 183, 193, 240
Joseph, Jr., 49
Joseph, Sr., 94
Josiah, 184, 264
Lavinia, 262
Leah, 218, *262
Levina, 249, 298
Lottie, 218, 249
Lovey, 218
Margaret, 154
Mary, 67, 89, 95, 107, 117
Micajah, *107, *162
Naomi, 107, 162
Nehemiah, 227
Parker, 107
Peter, 103, 107, 162, *218
Philip, 95
Piercy, 177
Priscilla, 184
Purnal, 103, 301
Rachel, 49, 94, 113, 218
Rhoda, 301
Riley, 103
Ruth, 49, 127
Samuel, 49, *67, 95
Sarah, 107, *162, 297, 301
Solomon, *89, 92, 113
Solomon, Sr., 52
Tatman, 218, 262
Thomas, 184
William, 218, 257, 262, 305
Zadock, *297
Trusham, James, 157
Meron, 157
Trussom, Maron, 142
Trustees of Church of St. Georges, 241
Trustees of St. Peters Church, Lewes, 241
Tubbs, Burton, 272
David, 157, 212, 225, *272
Elizabeth, 157, 185, 272, *294

Tull, Agnes, 96
Ann, 224, 258, 274
Ann, Jr., 258
Elizabeth, 56, 217
Elon, 196
Esther, 217
Handy, 217
Isaac, 258
James, 160
Jesse, 217
John, 15, 56, 140, 182, 217, 258
Joshua, *217
Levi, 189
Levin, *291
Magdelan (Magdaline), 50, 56
Margaret, 258
Martha, 15, 223, 258
Milly, 217
Noble, 194, *196
Peggy, 273
Richard, 11
Sally, 189, 291
Sarah, 258, *273
Stanton, 217
Stoughton, 182
Thomas, 56
Whittington, 217
William, 50, *56, 217, 223, *258
Tully, Ann, 285
James, *285
Joshua, 285
Nancy, 285
Polly, 285
Priscilla, 285
Tunnell, Elizabeth, 109, 123
Isaac, 109
John, 109
Nehemiah, 109
Scarborough, 109, 238
Washburn, 109
William, 77, *109, 123
Turk, Andrew, 204
Robert, 41
Turlington, Sarah, *202
Turner, . . ., 58, 87, 118
Amelia, 206
Ann, 58
Betty, 118, 250
Bevins, 206
Charity, *84
Clement, 206
Cornelius, 58, 65, 74, 87, 99, 170
Edward, 118
Elizabeth, 58, 88
Ephraim, 84, 87, 88, 135, *166
Eunice, 291, *307
Hannah, 118, 222, 235, 239
Humphry, 31, 47, 58

Isaac, 239
Jehu, 79
John, 84, 88, 118, 235
Joseph, 36, 54, *58
Joshua, 269
Lazarus, *114, 264
Leticia (Letecia), 87, 91
Levi, 118
Levin, 260, 291
Lizzy, 206
Louisa, 206
Maddox, 147
Martha, 58
Mary, 62, 84, 87, 88, 89, 114, 116, 118, 239
Nathan, 84, *87
Nicey, 79
Nicholas, *118
Priscilla, 58, 170
Rachel, 118, 235
Samuel, 89
Sarah, 58
Sidney, 206, 234
Thomas, 28, 102
Turner, 118
Unice, 88
Westly, 84
William, 84, *206
William Westly, 87, *88
Turpin, Charles, 204, *262
Constant, 163, 204
Elizabeth, 105, *156, 159, 163
Francis, 156
James, *156, *202, 204
John, 135, 156, *159, 200
Joseph, 105, 160, *168
Mary, *156, 163
Nancy, 156
Peggy, 168
Priscilla, 156
Rebeckah, 105
Sarah, 163
Solomon, *105, *168, 204
Thomas Baynard, 168
White, 168
William, *204
Tuxbury, Ellenor, 14
John, 14
Twiford: see Twyford
Twilley, Patience, 38
Robert, 12
Twyford (Twiford), Brown, 139
Charles, 174, 255, 305
Charlotte, 305
John, 159
Mary, 255
Tyer, Isanna, 19
James, 18

Thomas, Jr., 19

—V—

Vanderhagen, Mathias, 10
Vankirk, (Van Kerk, Vankirks, Vankirk)
Abigail, 19, 23, 49
Art, 30, *49, 97
Art, Sr., 26
Art Johnson, 18
Barnard, *144
Dorothy, 49
John, 77, 144
Johnson, 12
Margaret, 41
Mary, 97, 144, 145
Polly, 144
William, 144
Vaughan, Ann, 197, *219
Betty, (Betsy), 68, 101, 102, 104, 106, *136, 157, 173, 271, 275
Charles, 128
Edward, 124, *141, 219
Elizabeth, 147
Ephraim, *137, 173
Eunice, 128, 137
Isaac, 157, 281
Jethro, *128
Jonathan, *197, *281
Joseph, 96, 141, 159, 205, *277, 281
Levin, 102, 157, 277
Mary, 102, 106, 128
Nathaniel, 102, 106, 140, *173
Polly, 104
Sarah, 246, 271, 289
William, *101, 102, 104, 128, 136, 137, 140, *157, 246, *252, 265, 271, 275, 277, 291
Veach, Edith, 227
Elias, 97, 168
Elizabeth, 168
Jemima, 97
Mary, 190
Purnal, 190
Sally, 226
Sarah, 190
William, 97, 180, 197, 227, 301
Veasey (Veasy, Veazey, Vezey)
. . , 165
Charles, *165
Comfort, 173
Gideon, 165
Gilbert, 165
Hezekiah, 165
John, 93

# —W—

Catharine, 36
Elizabeth, 36, 58, 292, *310
Jacob, 58, 198, *310
James Reed, 165
John, 58, 65, 74, 76, 192
John Abbott, 131, 160, 310
Joseph, 58, 65, 68, 74, *125, *167
Levi, 150
Luke, 150
Mary, 36, 58, 65, *74, 134, 163, 165
Nancy, 74
Naomi, 82
Nice, 192
Polly, 275
Purnall, 192
Rachel, 125, 202, 229
Robert, 125, 207, 209
Sally, 229
Sarah, 126, 129, 150, 167, *184
Stephen, *36, 221, 232
Tabitha, 36
Tenely, 125
Thomas, 51, 55, *58, 65, 74, 158
Tilney, 65
Vallance, 65
William, *65, 74, *150, *275
Warwick, Jeremiah, *246
　William, 246
Wastcoat, Mary, 25
Water, Nelson, 154
　William, 154
Watson (Wattson), . . ., 14, 22
　Affiance, 45, 51
　Alice, 94
　Ann, 35, 168
　Bethuel, 46, 62, 68. 80. 101, 140,
　　284
　Bethuel, Jr., 114, 248
　Bethuel, Sr., *284
　Betsy, 213, *284, *294
　David, 88, 91, 111, 118, 125, 126,
　　169, 170, 171, *248, 284, 286
　Elias, 107
　Elizabeth, 13, 24. 33. 62. 195, 279,
　　284, 286
　Elizabeth, Jr., 24
　Esther, 284
　Hessy, 286
　Hezekiah, 38
　Isaac, 20, 22, 24, 46, 62, 66, 70,
　　*94, 95, 107, 127, 130, 131, 166,
　　171, *213, 294, 309
　Israel, 140
　James, 38
　Jesse, 112, 284
　John, 20, 33, *38, *127, 140, 170,
　　*201, *216, *239
　Joseph, 94

Joshua, 66
Luke, 13, 20, *22, 33, 34, 38, 53,
　70, *131, 140, 141, 171, 201, *279
Luke, Dr., 16
Luke, Jr., 13, 14, 16, 23
Luke, Sr., 13, *20
Margery, 20
Mary, 14, 20, 33, 38, 94, 95, 107,
　168, 213, 257, 264, 294
Molly, 140
Nanny, 140, 141, 216
Naomi, 141
Purnal, *168
Rachel, 112
Rebecca, 131
Robert, 171, 213, 253, 299
Sally, 140, 170, 292, 305
Samuel, 17, 20, 22, *33, 140
Sarah, 20, 33, 38, 168, 213, 252
Selah, 94
Smothers, 210
Stephen, 38
Sukky, 140
Susanna, 33
Susannah Albound, 213
Thomas, 45, 82, 140, 168, 213, 224
William, 66, *140, 154, 168, *171,
　272
Watts, John, 219
　Nancy, 268
　Thomas, 219, 246
Way, John, 41
Weare, Robert, 43
Webb, Alice, 169, 198
　Ann, 55, 59
　Benjamin, 55, 61, 94, 97
　James, 41
　Jeremiah, 198
　John, 55, 100, *198
　John, Sr., 76
　Jonas, *55
　Liddleton, 55
　Magdalene, 61
　Miriam, 265
　Obediah, *240
　Sylvester, 149, 171, 182, 240
　William, 139, 198
Welch (Welsh), Elinor, 75
　Frances, 302
　Henry, *219
　James, 11
　John, *232
　Mary, 232
　Pennington, *235
　Rachel, 158
　Sarah, 149
　William, 158, 232
Weldredge, Leah, 163